The COMPLETE GUIDE to
Country Cooking

Editor: Mary Beth Jung
Managing Editor: Julie Schnittka
Food Editor: Coleen Martin
Associate Food Editor: Sue A. Jurack
Associate Editors: Henry de Fiebre, Kristine Krueger
Test Kitchen Home Economist: Julie Seguin
Test Kitchen Assistant: Suzanne Hampton
Art Director: Maribeth Greinke
Associate Art Directors: Linda Dzik, Stephanie Marchese, Thomas L. Hunt
Food Photography: Scott Anderson, Glenn Thiesenhusen, Mike Huibregtse
Food Photography Artist: Stephanie Marchese
Associate Food Photography Artist: Vicky Marie Moseley
Photo Studio Coordinator: Anne Schimmel
Production: Ellen Lloyd, Claudia Wardius, Ellen Jasinski
Publisher: Roy Reiman

Taste of Home Books
©1998 Reiman Publications, L.P.
5400 S. 60th St., Greendale WI 53129

International Standard Book Number: 0-89821-231-6
Library of Congress Catalog Card Number: 97-76051
Printed in U.S.A.
Seventh Printing, March 2003

TO ORDER ADDITIONAL COPIES of this book, write: *Taste of Home Books*, P.O. Box 908, Greendale WI 53129. Credit card orders call toll-free 1-800/344-2560 or visit or Web site at *www.reimanpub.com*.

The Complete Guide to
Country Cooking

CONTENTS

Introduction 6

Kitchen Basics 8

Appetizers and Beverages 16

Breads....................36

Salads and Salad Dressings 68

Soups and Sandwiches 84

Beef and Ground Beef....................102

Poultry 128

Pork 156

Seafood 178

Lamb 192

Game 202

Eggs and Cheese....................216

Grains, Beans and Pasta 234

Vegetables....................250

Condiments....................288

Desserts....................300

Cakes....................316

Pies....................332

Cookies and Candies 350

Menu Planning 374

Handy References 380

Recipe Index....................390

Reference Index 401

PICTURED ON THE COVER: Mom's Best Meat
Loaf (p. 126), Dilly Mashed Potatoes (p. 282),
Baked Carrots (p. 271) and Peach Pie (p. 336).

Finally...a _Complete_ Guide to Country Cooking

Mary Beth Jung

I HOPE you're excited to have _The Complete Guide to Country Cooking_ in your kitchen. I certainly am! It's something I always wanted but never could find.

I've been a home economist for dozens of years. During most of that time, I wondered why no one had ever put together a special kind of cookbook...the kind I needed...and, from talking with many other cooks, the kind I knew that they needed, too.

What sort of cookbook did I have in mind? A truly different one—one that focused on the reliable tried-and-true rather than the here-today gone-tomorrow trendy. It had to be a cookbook that bypassed the current fads and concentrated instead on the kind of cooking families all over enjoy most—down-home _country_.

But this book I envisioned had to be so much more.

For as long as I've been cooking—and, as a longtime food editor, telling others how to cook—I still need to consult my files when I'm roasting a 20-pound Thanksgiving turkey, canning berry jam or wondering what to substitute for buttermilk if I run out in the middle of a recipe. So this book not only had to include the _very best_ country recipes, it had to serve as a _complete_ guide by containing all the varied essential information a country cook needs.

Guess what. A few years ago, I finally got tired of waiting for "someone" to do such a book...and decided to do it myself.

Thanks to all those talented folks listed on page 4 who joined forces with me to make my dream come true, you're now holding the results in your hands. And I couldn't be happier.

So many cooks—from new graduates out on their own for the first time, to newlyweds, all the way to veterans at meal preparation—will find its hundreds of recipes and step-by-step photo-illustrated directions an invaluable tool...day after day, and year after year.

I hope you're one of them. So let me take you on a cooks' tour of this first-ever comprehensive country cooking guide...

Kitchen Basics

The Complete Guide to Country Cooking begins with the basics—recommendations for stocking your kitchen, measuring and chopping techniques to get the most out of your cooking, etc. Of course, new cooks will find this chapter indispensable.

Seasoned cooks will appreciate it, too, however—and especially benefit as they seek the best replacements for well-worn pots, pans and kitchen tools.

More Than 500 Country Recipes

This book is just what its title says—complete. It includes more than 500 family-favorite recipes from country cooks coast to coast and from the test kitchen of the most popular food magazine in North America, _Taste of Home_.

Every recipe includes a helpful preparation, serving or storage tip. Many also include step-by-step photographs that make it easy to instantly master numerous cooking techniques—the secrets to winning applause for consistently turning out tender biscuits, flaky pie pastry, lump-free gravy and more.

30-Minute and Light Recipes

Recipes that can be prepared in only about 30 minutes have been flagged with a _quick_ symbol: ○. Recipes that are lower in fat, cholesterol, sodium and calories are highlighted with a _light_ symbol: .

And More...

Refer to the Menu Planning chapter—pairing nicely complementary recipes from different chapters of this book in taste-appealing and eye-appealing complete meals—whether you need ideas for a weekday family supper or a holiday company dinner. Handy References, meanwhile, will help you set the perfect table...find the right ingredient to substitute for one you suddenly discover you've run out of...immediately come up with weight and measure equivalents...safely and efficiently store food...get familiar with herbs...and learn exactly what you need to know about key food and cooking terms.

Finally, to quickly locate anything you need between the covers of this book (_including_ tips), consult the comprehensive index.

See why I'm so excited? I've been waiting most of my life for this unique cookbook. I can't wait to get my first gravy stain on it!

Mary Beth Jung

Recipes Are Easy on the Eyes

We've purposely built some special features into each and every recipe in this book to make them as clear and helpful as possible. Here's an example:

Step-by-step photographs and captions that clearly demonstrate cooking techniques for successfully making the recipe.

Helpful hints for preparing and serving the dish.

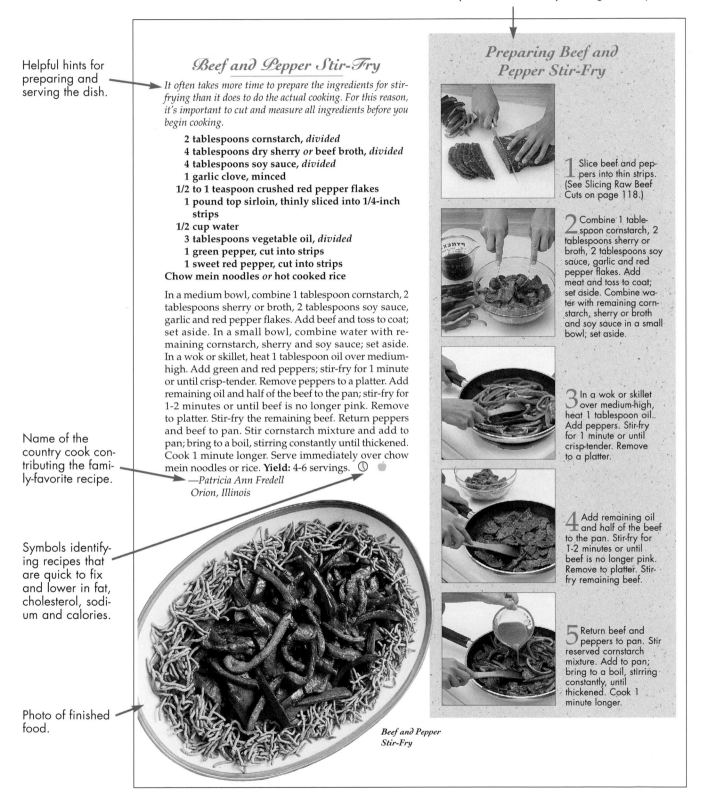

Beef and Pepper Stir-Fry

It often takes more time to prepare the ingredients for stir-frying than it does to do the actual cooking. For this reason, it's important to cut and measure all ingredients before you begin cooking.

    2 **tablespoons cornstarch,** *divided*
    4 **tablespoons dry sherry** *or* **beef broth,** *divided*
    4 **tablespoons soy sauce,** *divided*
    1 **garlic clove, minced**
 1/2 to 1 **teaspoon crushed red pepper flakes**
    1 **pound top sirloin, thinly sliced into 1/4-inch strips**
 1/2 **cup water**
    3 **tablespoons vegetable oil,** *divided*
    1 **green pepper, cut into strips**
    1 **sweet red pepper, cut into strips**
Chow mein noodles *or* **hot cooked rice**

In a medium bowl, combine 1 tablespoon cornstarch, 2 tablespoons sherry or broth, 2 tablespoons soy sauce, garlic and red pepper flakes. Add beef and toss to coat; set aside. In a small bowl, combine water with remaining cornstarch, sherry and soy sauce; set aside. In a wok or skillet, heat 1 tablespoon oil over medium-high. Add green and red peppers; stir-fry for 1 minute or until crisp-tender. Remove peppers to a platter. Add remaining oil and half of the beef to the pan; stir-fry for 1-2 minutes or until beef is no longer pink. Remove to platter. Stir-fry the remaining beef. Return peppers and beef to pan. Stir cornstarch mixture and add to pan; bring to a boil, stirring constantly until thickened. Cook 1 minute longer. Serve immediately over chow mein noodles or rice. **Yield:** 4-6 servings. ⏲ 🍎
    —Patricia Ann Fredell
    Orion, Illinois

Name of the country cook contributing the family-favorite recipe.

Symbols identifying recipes that are quick to fix and lower in fat, cholesterol, sodium and calories.

Photo of finished food.

Beef and Pepper Stir-Fry

Preparing Beef and Pepper Stir-Fry

1 Slice beef and peppers into thin strips. (See Slicing Raw Beef Cuts on page 118.)

2 Combine 1 tablespoon cornstarch, 2 tablespoons sherry or broth, 2 tablespoons soy sauce, garlic and red pepper flakes. Add meat and toss to coat; set aside. Combine water with remaining cornstarch, sherry or broth and soy sauce in a small bowl; set aside.

3 In a wok or skillet over medium-high, heat 1 tablespoon oil. Add peppers. Stir-fry for 1 minute or until crisp-tender. Remove to a platter.

4 Add remaining oil and half of the beef to the pan. Stir-fry for 1-2 minutes or until beef is no longer pink. Remove to platter. Stir-fry remaining beef.

5 Return beef and peppers to pan. Stir reserved cornstarch mixture. Add to pan; bring to a boil, stirring constantly, until thickened. Cook 1 minute longer.

Kitchen Basics

Having the right equipment and knowing how to use it is one key to cooking success. In this chapter, we'll show you the importance of owning and using the proper kitchen tools to make food preparation easy, foolproof and fun!

Measuring Tools and Techniques

Accurate measuring ensures you'll receive consistent results every time you prepare a recipe. There are specific measuring cups designed for measuring liquid and dry ingredients. They are not interchangeable.

For all liquid ingredients, including thick liquids such as honey and molasses, use clear glass measuring cups that are available in 1-, 2- and 4-cup sizes.

All dry ingredients are measured by using a set of metal or plastic cups that are available in 1/4-, 1/3-, 1/2- and 1-cup sizes.

Standard measuring spoons are used for both liquid and dry ingredients. Sets include 1/4 teaspoon, 1/2 teaspoon, 1 teaspoon and 1 tablespoon. Some also have a 1/8-teaspoon measurement.

Measuring Liquids

Pour liquids into a measuring cup on a level surface and view from eye level to be sure of accurate measurements.

Measuring Dry Ingredients

Over a canister or waxed paper, spoon fine ingredients such as flour, sugar and cornmeal into the cup until it is overflowing. Level off along the top of the cup with a metal spatula or the flat side of a knife. Spoon or pour bulky ingredients such as raisins, oatmeal and dry grains into the cup level with the rim.

Using Measuring Spoons

Over a canister or waxed paper, heap dry ingredients into the spoon and level off. Spread solid ingredients such as shortening and butter into the spoon and level off. Pour liquid ingredients into the measuring spoon over a bowl.

Measuring Brown Sugar

With its unique moist texture, brown sugar needs to be packed into the measuring cup with your hands or the back of a spoon for consistency in measuring. For this reason, recipes are written for "packed" brown sugar.

Measuring Butter

Sticks of butter often have easy tablespoon measurements right on the wrapper so you can cut off the desired amounts without the use of additional measuring tools.

Measuring Shortening

Spoon solid shortening into a dry measuring cup; pack with a spatula or spoon to be sure the cup is completely filled.

Kitchen Cutlery

A basic set of knives is essential to any well-equipped kitchen. There are a variety of knives made from many materials. The best knives, made from high-carbon steel, are resistant to corrosion (unlike carbon steel) and remain sharper longer than stainless steel.

A. Steel

This long thin rod with a handle is used to smooth out small rough spots on the edge of the blade and to reset the edge of the blade. You can also use a whetstone or electric knife sharpener to sharpen knives.

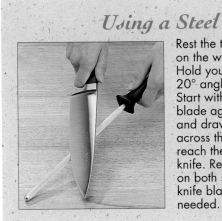

Using a Steel

Rest the tip of the steel on the work surface. Hold your knife at a 20° angle to the steel. Start with the heel of the blade against the steel and draw the blade up across the steel until you reach the tip of the knife. Repeat five times on both sides of the knife blade. Repeat as needed.

B. Chef's knife

This 8-in. to 10-in. all-purpose knife is used for mincing, chopping and dicing.

Caring for Knives

- Always wash and dry knives by hand immediately after use and never let them soak in water. Don't put knives in the dishwasher.
- Store knives in a slotted wooden block or hang them on a magnetic rack especially designed for knives. Proper storage will protect the knife edges, keep blades sharper longer and guard against injury.

C. Carving knife

This 8-in. to 10-in. knife is perfect for slicing roasts and turkey.

D. Serrated or bread knife

This knife's serrated blade is used for slicing breads, cakes and delicate foods. An 8-in. knife is most versatile, but there is a range of lengths available.

E. Utility knife

This 6-in. knife is the right size to slice small foods.

F. Boning knife

This knife's 5-in. or 6-in. tapered blade is designed to remove the meat from poultry, beef, pork or fish bones.

G. Paring knife

This 3-in. to 4-in. knife is used for peeling, mincing and slicing small foods.

H. Kitchen shears

This versatile tool is used to snip fresh herbs, disjoint chicken, trim pastry, etc.

Cutlery Techniques

Learning to use your kitchen cutlery correctly takes a little practice. However, once you've mastered the basic techniques, you'll be surprised how efficiently you and your knives will work together.

Mince and Chop

Holding the handle of a chef's knife with one hand, rest your other hand's fingers on the top of the blade near the tip. Using the handle to guide and apply pressure, move the knife in an arc across the food with a rocking motion until pieces of food are the desired size. Mincing results in pieces no larger than 1/8 in., and chopping can produce 1/4-in. to 1/2-in. pieces.

Dice and Cube

Using a chef's knife, cut foods into lengthwise sticks. Cut across sticks to make uniform squares. Dicing results in 1/8-in. to 1/4-in. uniform pieces, and cubing yields 1/2-in. to 1-in. uniform pieces.

Julienne

Using a chef's knife, cut foods into lengthwise slices, then cut a stack of slices lengthwise again to make smaller sticks.

Bias/Diagonal Cuts

Hold a chef's knife at an angle to the length of the food. Slice as thick or thin as desired. This technique is often used in stir-fry recipes.

Pare/Peel

Placing your thumbs on the fruit or vegetable, move the blade of a paring or utility knife toward you.

Chopping Onions

1 Using a chef's knife, cut onion in half lengthwise, then peel it. Place onion cut side down and make a series of cuts through the onion as shown, leaving the onion intact at the root end.

2 At right angles to the above cuts, make a series of cuts across the onion to separate pieces.

Peeling and Mincing Fresh Garlic

Using the blade of a chef's knife, crush the garlic clove. Peel away the skin. Mince as directed above left.

Snipping Fresh Herbs

Hold herbs over a small bowl and make 1/8- to 1/4-in. cuts with a kitchen shears.

Pots and Pans

The type of recipes you usually prepare—and how often you cook—can help you determine the pots and pans you should have in your kitchen. For example, if you make large quantities of soup, be sure to purchase a stockpot or soup kettle. If you like to make fried chicken, you will need a large deep skillet with a cover.

Tips for Buying Pots and Pans

- Cookware comes with several base metals. Aluminum is the most even conductor of heat and the best buy. Stainless pots and pans are very durable and stay looking like new for many years but are poor conductors of heat. However, stainless with an aluminum-clad bottom will cook evenly and is a good choice. Cast iron is also an excellent conductor of heat and will last for many years.
- Most cookware today is available with nonstick finishes for easy cleanup. If you plan to brown roasts, chops and stews and make pan gravy, you may want to purchase a Dutch oven or skillet without a nonstick finish. Meats brown better in uncoated pans and produce darker, richer gravies.
- Select pots and pans with a thick gauge (thick sides and bottom). The thicker the metal, the more even the heat will be conducted without hot-spotting, burning or warping. Pots and pans with flat bottoms are best for good heat conduction.
- The handles should feel comfortable in your hand, stay cool while cooking and be ovensafe. Covers should fit tightly.

Basic Pots and Pans

A. 1-qt. and 2-qt. saucepans with covers
B. 5-qt. to 8-qt. Dutch oven with cover
C. 10-in. to 12-in. skillet with cover
D. 8-in. omelet pan with a nonstick finish
E. Roaster with rack and cover

B

A

C

D

E

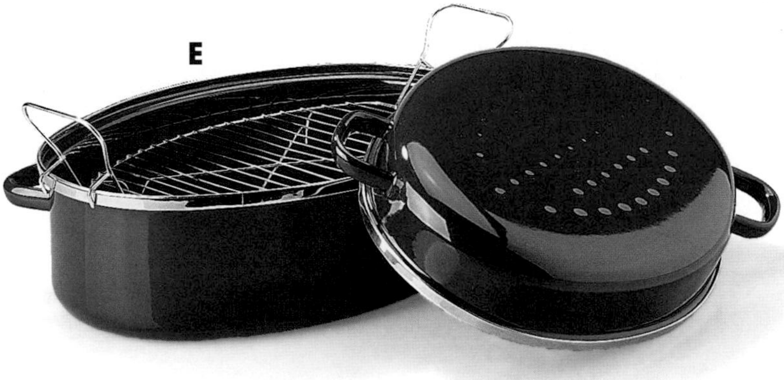

Additional Cookware

12-in. cast-iron skillet with cover
14-in. chicken fryer with cover
Stockpot or soup kettle
Griddle (square or oblong)
Additional saucepans and skillets with covers
Roasters in assorted sizes with covers
Steamer insert basket
Double boiler

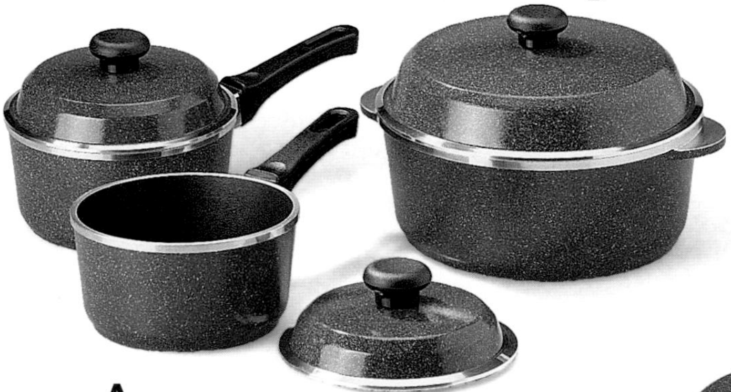

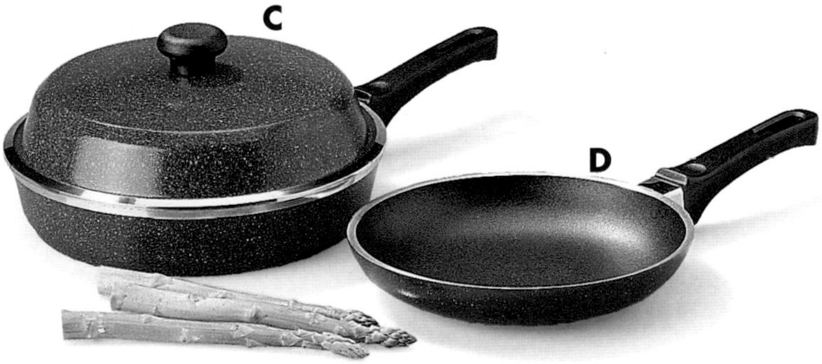

Basic Mixing Tools

Whether you're making a cake, a batch of cookies or simply beating eggs for an omelet, a few basic mixing tools are welcome and handy additions to any new kitchen.

A. Stand mixer
B. Hand mixer
C. Pastry blender
D. Rubber spatulas and scoops
E. Wooden spoons
F. Wire whisks in assorted sizes
G. Plastic spoons
H. Hand rotary beater
I. Mixing bowls (4-qt. and 1-1/2-qt.)
Blender or food processor (not shown)

Tips for Using Blenders And Food Processors

- Use a blender or food processor to make salad dressings and sauces and to puree soups.

- A food processor is best to mix and puree very thick mixtures such as cheese spreads, sandwich fillings and pesto sauces.

- Don't use a blender or food processor to mix cakes from scratch, whip cream or beat egg whites.

Choosing Bakeware

The recipes in this book call for baking pans and baking dishes. Baking dishes are made of ovensafe glass or ceramic and are most often used for casseroles, egg dishes, saucy meat dishes and yeast breads. Always use glass or ceramic baking dishes when marinating foods or making dishes with tomato sauce.

Baking pans are made of metal and are best used for baking cakes, yeast and quick breads and muffins. For best results, choose aluminum pans with dull finishes. Pans with dark finishes often cook and brown foods more quickly, and insulated pans take longer to bake and brown foods.

If you substitute a glass baking dish in a recipe calling for a metal baking pan, lower the oven temperature by 25° to avoid overbaking and overbrowning.

Basic Bakeware

8-in. x 1-1/2-in. round cake pans (two to three pans)

9-in. x 1-1/2-in. round cake pans (two to three pans)

8-in. x 8-in. x 2-in. square baking pan and dish

9-in. x 9-in. x 2-in. square baking pan and dish

11-in. x 7-in. x 2-in. baking pan and dish (2-qt.)

13-in. x 9-in. x 2-in. baking pan and dish (3-qt.)

15-in. x 10-in. x 1-in. (jelly roll) pan

9-in. x 5-in. x 3-in. loaf pans (two pans)

8-in. x 4-in. x 2-in. loaf pans (two pans)

12-cup muffin pan

10-in. tube pan

12-cup fluted tube pan

6-oz. custard cups (one set of six)

9-in. and 10-in. pie plates

Baking sheets (without sides) in assorted sizes

9-in. or 10-in. springform pan

Wire cooling racks

2-qt. and 3-qt. deep round or oval covered casserole dishes

Practical Pan Substitutions

When you don't have the right pan for a recipe, here are a few substitutions to know. (Smaller pans will require less baking time.)

One 8-in. x 4-in. x 2-in. loaf pan	= Two 5-1/2-in. x 3-1/2-in. loaf pans
One 9-in. round cake pan	= One 8-in. square pan
Two 9-in. round cake pans	= Three 8-in. round cake pans
One 12-cup fluted tube pan	= One 10-in. tube pan *or* two 9-in. x 5-in. x 3-in. loaf pans
One 13-in. x 9-in. x 2-in. pan	= Two 9-in. round cake pans

Kitchen Tools and Gadgets

When equipping a new kitchen, there are so many tools and gadgets to consider. Start with the basics listed below before expanding to the specialty ones.

- ☐ Apple corer
- ☐ Can and bottle opener, can piercer
- ☐ Canisters
- ☐ Citrus juicer
- ☐ Colander
- ☐ Cookie cutters
- ☐ Corkscrew
- ☐ Cutting boards, wood and plastic
- ☐ Egg separator
- ☐ Egg slicer
- ☐ Garlic press
- ☐ Hand grater/shredder
- ☐ Ladles, large and small
- ☐ Meat fork
- ☐ Meat mallet/tenderizer
- ☐ Metal skewers
- ☐ Metal spatulas, large and small
- ☐ Metal strainer or sieve
- ☐ Pancake turners
- ☐ Pastry brush
- ☐ Pastry wheel
- ☐ Pepper mill
- ☐ Pie server
- ☐ Pizza cutter
- ☐ Plastic storage and freezer containers
- ☐ Potato masher
- ☐ Rolling pin
- ☐ Slotted spoons, large and small
- ☐ Thermometers, instant-read, candy/deep-fat, meat, oven, refrigerator/freezer
- ☐ Timer
- ☐ Tongs
- ☐ Vegetable peeler

Kitchen Textiles

- ☐ Cheesecloth
- ☐ Dish cloth
- ☐ Dish towels
- ☐ Hand towels
- ☐ Hot pads/mitts
- ☐ Pastry cloth
- ☐ Rolling pin cover
- ☐ Twine and/or string

Appetizers and Beverages

For a great start, enjoy recipes for Spiced Lemonade (p. 35), Sweet Gingered Chicken Wings (p. 27), Festive Cheese Spread (p. 21)—and many more thirst-quenching beverages, hearty hot and cold appetizers, and satisfying snacks.

Whether you're entertaining a small group of friends or bringing a snack to the family reunion, choosing an appetizer that fits the occasion is often a challenge. For potluck suppers, it's best to select a cold appetizer that can be prepared ahead and taken in a covered container. Hot appetizers requiring last-minute preparation are best served from your own kitchen. If you plan to offer several appetizers, make it interesting for your guests and easy on yourself by preparing one cold make-ahead appetizer and one hot appetizer.

Continental Cheese Spread

Anyone watching their fat intake will be surprised that they can indulge in this spread with little guilt. Any leftovers can be spread on toasted bagels for a light lunch or snack.

    1 package (8 ounces) fat-free cream cheese,
      softened
    1 tablespoon skim milk
    3 tablespoons grated Parmesan cheese
    1 tablespoon minced fresh parsley
    1 tablespoon finely chopped green onion
    1 garlic clove, minced
    1/2 teaspoon dried thyme
    1/8 teaspoon pepper
Assorted crackers

In a mixing bowl, beat cream cheese and milk until smooth. Add Parmesan cheese, parsley, onion, garlic, thyme and pepper; mix until well blended. Cover and refrigerate for at least 1 hour. Serve with crackers.
Yield: 1 cup. ① 🍎   *—Mrs. Thomas Wigglesworth*
                              Absecon, New Jersey

Dill Dip

This classic refreshing dip is always a hit. To further enhance the flavor, prepare it the night before.

    1 cup fat-free mayonnaise
    1 cup (8 ounces) non-fat sour cream
    2 tablespoons dried parsley flakes
    1 tablespoon dried minced onion
    2 teaspoons dill weed
    1-1/2 teaspoons seasoned salt
    1 teaspoon sugar
    Fresh vegetables *or* assorted crackers

In a small bowl, combine the first seven ingredients. Chill for at least 1 hour. Serve with vegetables or crackers. **Yield:** 2 cups. ① 🍎
                              —Kathy Beldorth
                              Three Oaks, Michigan

Mustard Egg Dip

Here's a great dip that can be made the day before serving. If you have a food processor, simply chop the eggs using the pulsing button. Only one or two pulses are needed. Then add remaining ingredients, pulse one more time and it's done!

6 hard-cooked eggs, finely chopped
1/3 cup mayonnaise
1 tablespoon butter *or* margarine, softened
2 teaspoons lemon juice
1 teaspoon prepared mustard
1 teaspoon Worcestershire sauce
3/4 teaspoon liquid smoke, optional
1/2 teaspoon salt
1/4 teaspoon pepper
Hot pepper sauce to taste
Fresh vegetables

In a bowl or food processor, combine the first 10 ingredients; mix until smooth. Serve with vegetables. **Yield:** 1-3/4 cups.   —*Janie Carr, Fort Davis, Texas*

BLT Bites

Add color to your appetizer tray with these tasty snacks. Prepare them several hours ahead to allow the flavors to blend. To keep them fresh, be sure to cover loosely with plastic wrap and refrigerate.

16 to 20 cherry tomatoes
1 pound bacon, cooked and crumbled
1/2 cup mayonnaise *or* salad dressing
1/3 cup chopped green onions

3 tablespoons grated Parmesan cheese
2 tablespoons snipped fresh parsley

Cut a thin slice off of each tomato top. Scoop out and discard pulp. Invert the tomatoes on a paper towel to drain. In a small bowl, combine the remaining ingredients; mix well. Spoon into tomatoes. Refrigerate for several hours. **Yield:** 16-20 servings.

—*Kellie Remmen, Detroit Lakes, Minnesota*

BLT Bites

Stuffing Cherry Tomatoes

1 With a small sharp knife, cut the top off of each tomato. Scoop out the pulp with a small spoon, and place each tomato, cut side down, on paper towels to remove liquid. Discard pulp.

2 Combine all remaining ingredients and spoon into each tomato. Chill until ready to serve.

Shaping a Cheese Ball

To keep hands and countertop clean, spoon cheese mixture onto a piece of plastic wrap. Working from the underside of the wrap, pat the mixture into a ball. Complete recipe as directed.

Three-in-One Cheese Ball

Three-in-One Cheese Ball

For the busy cook, this recipe can be prepared through the shaping step 1 week before serving. Do not roll in nuts or parsley. Wrap and freeze. The day before serving, defrost the cheese balls in the refrigerator. Before serving, roll in pepper, parsley and nuts as directed. You may want to label each ball indicating the flavor for your guests.

    1 package (8 ounces) cream cheese, softened
    4 cups (16 ounces) shredded cheddar cheese,
        room temperature
    2 tablespoons milk
    2 tablespoons finely chopped onion
    2 tablespoons Worcestershire sauce
Coarsely cracked black pepper
    1/2 cup crumbled blue cheese
Minced fresh parsley
    1/4 teaspoon garlic powder
Finely chopped pecans
Assorted crackers

In a mixing bowl, beat cream cheese, cheddar cheese, milk, onion and Worcestershire sauce until fluffy. If a smoother spread is desired, process in a food processor until creamy. Divide into thirds (about 1 cup each). Shape first portion into a ball; roll in cracked pepper. Add the blue cheese to the second portion; mix well. Shape into a ball; roll in parsley. Add garlic powder to the remaining portion; mix well. Shape into a ball; roll in nuts. Cover and refrigerate. Remove from refrigerator and let stand 15 minutes before serving. Serve with crackers. **Yield:** 3 cheese balls.

—*Mary Anne Marston, Almonte, Ontario*

Tasty Cheese Tip

When selecting packaged shredded cheddar cheese, consider sharp cheddar for recipes that you'd like to have a bolder flavor. If you will be shredding cheese at home from bulk cheddar, you can choose from mild, medium, sharp and extra sharp.

Festive Cheese Spread

(Pictured on page 17)

Here's a cheese spread that will please a hungry crowd with its bold taste. Prepare this spread early in the day, spoon it into the wax shell and refrigerate until you are ready to serve.

> **1 gouda cheese round in red wax covering (7 ounces), room temperature**
> **1 package (2-1/2 ounces) smoked sliced beef, finely chopped**
> **1/4 cup sour cream**
> **2 tablespoons sweet pickle relish**
> **2 teaspoons prepared horseradish**

Apple slices *and/or* **assorted crackers**

Carefully slice through wax and cheese to within 1 in. of the bottom, forming eight pie-shaped wedges. Carefully fold wax back to expose cheese; remove cheese. In a mixing bowl, beat the cheese until creamy. Add the beef, sour cream, relish and horseradish; mix well. Spoon into wax shell. Chill. Serve with apples and/or crackers. **Yield:** 1-1/2 cups.　　　—*Vernie Nicolaisen*
Cherokee, Iowa

Fireside Cheese Spread

If you prefer, try a Swiss cheese spread instead of the cheddar. And, if you enjoy garlic, substitute a small clove of minced garlic for the garlic powder.

> **1 carton (16 ounces) cheddar cheese spread, softened**
> **2 packages (one 8 ounces, one 3 ounces) cream cheese, softened**
> **3 tablespoons butter** *or* **margarine, softened**
> **1 teaspoon Worcestershire sauce**
> **1/2 teaspoon garlic powder**

Paprika
Snipped fresh parsley
Assorted crackers

In a medium bowl, combine cheese spread, cream cheese, butter, Worcestershire sauce and garlic powder. Blend thoroughly. Chill for at least 3 hours or overnight. Sprinkle with paprika and parsley. Serve with crackers. **Yield:** about 3-1/2 cups.　　—*Debbie Jones*
California, Maryland

Making Tortilla Pinwheels

1 Spread one side of each tortilla with the filling mixture. Roll up tightly and wrap each roll in plastic wrap. Refrigerate.

2 Slice each roll into 1-in. pieces and arrange on a tray.

Tortilla Pinwheels

Prepare these tasty finger foods several days in advance if desired. Serve with your choice of mild or hot salsa or picante sauce.

> **1 cup (8 ounces) sour cream**
> **1 package (8 ounces) cream cheese, softened**
> **3/4 cup sliced green onions**
> **1/2 cup finely shredded cheddar cheese**
> **1 tablespoon lime juice**
> **1 tablespoon minced seeded jalapeno pepper**
> **8 to 10 flour tortillas (about 7 inches)**

Salsa *or* **picante sauce**

Combine the first six ingredients in a bowl; mix well. Spread on one side of tortillas and roll up tightly. Wrap and refrigerate for at least 1 hour. Slice into 1-in. pieces. Serve with salsa or picante sauce. **Yield:** about 5 dozen.
—*Barbara Keith*
Faucett, Missouri

Fireside Cheese Spread

Fiesta Appetizer

This favorite is best prepared within an hour of serving. You will need to plan ahead when serving this appetizer and purchase the avocados several days earlier to allow them to ripen for maximum flavor and ease in mashing.

> 1 can (15 ounces) refried beans
> 1 envelope taco seasoning
> 3 medium ripe avocados, halved, seeded
>   and peeled
> 1 tablespoon lemon juice
> 1/4 cup sour cream
> 1 can (2-1/4 ounces) sliced ripe olives, drained
> 1 can (4 ounces) chopped green chilies, drained
> 2 medium tomatoes, chopped
> 6 green onions, sliced
> 1 cup (4 ounces) shredded cheddar cheese

Tortilla chips

Combine beans and taco seasoning. Spread mixture on a round 12-in. serving platter. Mash avocados with lemon juice. Spread over beans. Spread sour cream over avocado. Sprinkle olives, chilies, tomatoes, onions and cheese over sour cream. Serve with tortilla chips. **Yield:** 8-10 servings.

—*Clarice Schweitzer*
Sun City, Arizona

Mashing Avocados

1 Cut avocado in half lengthwise. Twist to separate from the seed. With a sharp knife, strike the seed with the blade of the knife and lift out.

2 Scoop the meat from the skin with a tablespoon and place in a bowl.

3 Add lemon or lime juice; mash with a fork, leaving the mixture chunky.

Guacamole

The lemon or lime juice will keep your dip looking fresh and will prevent discoloration until serving. Or, before chilling, place the seed you removed from the avocado on top of the dip. Remove seed before serving.

> 1 medium ripe avocado, halved, seeded
>   and peeled
> 4-1/2 teaspoons lemon *or* lime juice
> 1 small tomato, seeded and finely
>   chopped
> 1/4 cup finely chopped onion
> 1 tablespoon finely chopped
>   green chilies
> 1 garlic clove, minced
> 1/4 teaspoon salt, optional

Tortilla chips

In a bowl, mash avocado with lemon juice. Stir in tomato, onion, chilies, garlic and salt if desired. Cover; chill. Serve with tortilla chips **Yield:** about 1-1/2 cups. ○

—*Anne Tipps, Duncanville, Texas*

Tomato Bread Salad

Tomato Bread Salad

For a refreshing first course, serve this fresh-from-the-garden starter all summer long. Be sure to measure the basil before mincing. For an easy way to mince basil leaves, snip into thin strips with your kitchen shears.

- 3 large tomatoes, seeded and finely chopped
- 1 medium cucumber, seeded and finely chopped
- 1/2 large sweet onion, finely chopped
- 1 cup loosely packed fresh basil, minced
- 1/4 cup olive *or* vegetable oil
- 1 tablespoon cider vinegar
- 1 garlic clove, minced
- 1/2 teaspoon salt
- 1/4 teaspoon pepper
- 1 loaf white *or* French bread (1 pound)

In a large bowl, combine tomatoes, cucumber and onion. In a small bowl, combine basil, oil, vinegar, garlic, salt and pepper. Pour over tomatoes and toss. Refrigerate for at least 1 hour. Before serving, bring to room temperature. Cut bread into thick slices; toast under broiler until lightly browned. Top with salad. Serve immediately. **Yield:** 18 servings. —Dodi Hardcastle
Harlingen, Texas

Chickaritos

This recipe is a great way to use leftover chicken. Chickaritos are easy to make and can be shaped ahead. Just bake right before serving. Enjoy them alone or serve with salsa and/or guacamole.

3 cups finely chopped cooked chicken
1-1/2 cups (6 ounces) shredded sharp cheddar cheese
1 can (4 ounces) chopped green chilies
1/2 cup finely chopped green onions
1 teaspoon hot pepper sauce
1 teaspoon garlic salt
1/4 teaspoon pepper
1/4 teaspoon ground cumin
1/4 teaspoon paprika
1 package (17-1/4 ounces) frozen puff pastry sheet, thawed *or* pie pastry for double-crust pie (10 inches)
Guacamole (recipe on page 22)
Salsa

In a bowl, combine chicken, cheese, chilies, onions and seasonings. Mix well; chill until ready to use. Remove half of the pastry from refrigerator at a time. On a lightly floured surface, roll to a 12-in. x 9-in. rectangle. Cut into nine small rectangles. Place about 2 tablespoons of filling down the center of each rectangle. Wet edges of pastry with water and roll pastry around filling. Crimp ends with a fork to seal. Repeat with remaining pastry and filling. Place seam side down on a lightly greased baking sheet. Refrigerate until ready to heat. Bake at 425° for 20-25 minutes or until golden brown. Serve warm with guacamole and salsa. **Yield:** 18 servings.

—Nancy Coates
Oro Valley, Arizona

Shaping Chickaritos

1 Prepare the filling and chill. Roll half the pastry into a 12-in. x 9-in. rectangle. Cut large rectangle into nine small rectangles. Place about 2 tablespoons filling on each rectangle.

2 Wet the edges of each rectangle with water, using a pastry brush or your finger, and roll up to form a tube.

3 With a fork, crimp the ends to seal. Repeat with remaining pastry and filling. Bake as directed.

Chickaritos

Hot Crab Dip

This dip is perfectly elegant for special occasions. Eight ounces imitation crab can be substituted for the canned crab.

- 2 cans (6 ounces *each*) crabmeat, drained and cartilage removed
- 2 packages (8 ounces *each*) cream cheese, softened
- 1/2 small onion, finely chopped
- 1 tablespoon prepared horseradish
- 2 dashes Worcestershire sauce
- 1/2 teaspoon salt
- 1/4 teaspoon pepper
- 1/3 cup slivered almonds
- Assorted crackers

In a mixing bowl, combine the first seven ingredients. Spread in a 1-qt. baking dish. Sprinkle with almonds. Bake at 350° for 10-15 minutes or until mixture bubbles. Serve with crackers. **Yield:** 6-8 servings. ◷

—Karen Buchholz, Sitka, Alaska

Asparagus Appetizer Roll-Ups

When spring is in the air and asparagus is plentiful, consider this pretty appetizer. Serve them right from the oven.

- 12 slices white bread, crusts removed
- 1 carton (8 ounces) soft cream cheese
- 2 tablespoons chopped green onions
- 8 bacon strips, cooked and crumbled
- 24 fresh asparagus spears, trimmed
- 1/4 cup butter *or* margarine, melted
- 3 tablespoons grated Parmesan cheese

Flatten bread with a rolling pin. In a small bowl, combine cream cheese, onions and bacon. Spread over bread. Place two asparagus spears on each slice; cut spears to fit bread. Roll up bread and place seam side down on a greased baking sheet. Brush with butter; sprinkle with Parmesan cheese. Bake at 400° for 10-12 minutes or until lightly browned. **Yield:** 1 dozen.

—Mrs. Howard Lansinger, Pineola, North Carolina

Chili Cheese Dip

Chili Cheese Dip

If you have a fondue pot, this is a perfect time to use it. Why not keep the ingredients for this easy dip on the pantry shelf for last-minute snacking?

- 1 pound process American cheese, cubed
- 1 can (15 ounces) chili con carne without beans
- 1 can (4 ounces) chopped green chilies
- Tortilla chips

Combine cheese, chili and chilies in a saucepan or fondue pot. Heat over medium-low, stirring frequently, until the cheese melts. Serve warm with tortilla chips. **Yield:** 12 servings. ◷

—Jerrie West
Oakhurst, California

Making Asparagus Roll-Ups

1. Remove the crusts from each slice of bread with a sharp knife. With a rolling pin, flatten each slice. Combine all filling ingredients.

2. Spread filling over bread. Place two asparagus spears on each slice; cut spears to fit bread. Roll up and gently press to seal. Place seam side down on a greased baking sheet. Brush with melted butter and sprinkle with Parmesan cheese. Bake as directed.

Orange Refresher (p. 34), Mini Hamburgers and Tater-Dipped Veggies (below)

Mini Hamburgers

These hearty snacks are perfect for Sunday afternoon football games and teen parties. The mini buns are actually store-purchased pan dinner rolls available everywhere.

    1/2 cup chopped onion
      1 tablespoon butter *or* margarine
      1 pound lean ground beef *or* ground round
      1 egg, beaten
    1/4 teaspoon seasoned salt
    1/4 teaspoon rubbed sage
    1/4 teaspoon salt
    1/8 teaspoon pepper
     40 miniature rolls, split
      8 ounces process American cheese slices, cut
         into 1-1/2-inch squares, optional
     40 dill pickle slices, optional

In a skillet, saute onion in butter. Transfer to a bowl; add meat, egg and seasonings. Spread over bottom halves of the rolls; replace tops. Place on baking sheets; cover with foil. Bake at 350° for 20 minutes. If desired, place a cheese square and pickle on each hamburger; replace tops and foil and return to the oven for 5 minutes. **Yield:** 40 appetizers.
—Judy Lewis
Sterling Heights, Michigan

Tater-Dipped Veggies

Deep-fried vegetables are terrific, but it's not always convenient to prepare them for company. Here's a recipe that produces the same deliciously crisp results in the oven. Serve with your favorite ranch-style dressing as a dip.

      1 cup instant potato flakes
    1/3 cup grated Parmesan cheese
    1/2 teaspoon celery salt
    1/4 teaspoon garlic powder
    1/4 cup butter *or* margarine, melted and cooled
      2 eggs
      4 to 5 cups fresh bite-size vegetables
         (mushrooms, peppers, broccoli, cauliflower,
         zucchini *and/or* carrots)
Ranch salad dressing *or* dip, optional

In a small bowl, combine potato flakes, Parmesan cheese, celery salt, garlic powder and butter. In another bowl, beat eggs. Dip the vegetables, one at a time, into egg, then into potato mixture; coat well. Place on an ungreased baking sheet. Bake at 400° for 20-25 minutes. Serve with dressing or dip if desired. **Yield:** 6-8 servings.
—Earleen Lillegard, Prescott, Arizona

Baked Potato Skins

Now this restaurant favorite can be prepared at home. Be sure to make enough because they will quickly disappear. You can use the leftover potato pulp to make a batch of mashed potatoes.

8 baking potatoes
1/2 cup butter *or* margarine, melted
1/2 teaspoon salt
1/2 teaspoon paprika
1/2 cup finely chopped green onions
1/2 cup crumbled cooked bacon
1/2 cup chopped cooked shrimp *or* fully cooked ham, optional
1/2 cup chopped green pepper
1 cup (4 ounces) shredded cheddar cheese
1 cup (8 ounces) sour cream

Scrub and pierce potatoes; bake at 400° for 1 hour or until tender. Cool slightly; cut in half lengthwise and scoop out pulp, leaving a 1/4-in. shell. Cut skins into strips or halves; brush skin sides with melted butter and place on a baking sheet. Sprinkle pulp sides with salt and paprika; cover with the green onions, bacon, shrimp or ham if desired, green pepper and cheese. Bake at 450° until cheese is melted and skins are crisp, about 10-15 minutes. Top each with a dollop of sour cream. Serve immediately. **Yield:** 6-10 servings.
—*Terry Hill, Hairy Hill, Alberta*

Vegetable Appetizer Pizza

This is an excellent appetizer to make when you have many mouths to feed. The recipe can be made earlier in the day and refrigerated.

3 tubes (8 ounces *each*) refrigerated crescent rolls
2 packages (8 ounces *each*) cream cheese, softened
2/3 cup mayonnaise
1 tablespoon dill weed
4 tomatoes, seeded and chopped
2 cups chopped fresh broccoli
3 green onions, thinly sliced
2 cups sliced fresh mushrooms
1/2 medium green pepper, chopped
1/2 medium sweet red pepper, chopped
1 can (2-1/4 ounces) sliced ripe olives, drained
2 cups (8 ounces) shredded cheddar cheese

Unroll crescent roll dough and place on two greased 15-in. x 10-in. x 1-in. baking pans. Flatten dough, sealing seams and perforations. Bake at 400° for 10 minutes or until light golden brown. Cool. In a small bowl, blend cream cheese, mayonnaise and dill. Spread over crusts. Top with vegetables, olives and cheese. Cut into bite-size squares. Refrigerate until ready to serve. **Yield:** about 8 dozen appetizers.
—*Marcia Tiernan Madrid, New York*

Sweet Gingered Chicken Wings

(Pictured on page 17)

Serve the wings whole or, for easier eating at a party, disjoint the wings as shown below. They make a filling appetizer or main dish.

1 cup all-purpose flour
2 teaspoons paprika
2 teaspoons salt
1/4 teaspoon pepper
24 chicken wings, whole *or* disjointed
SAUCE:
1/4 cup honey
1/4 cup orange juice concentrate
1/2 teaspoon ground ginger
Snipped fresh parsley, optional

In a bowl, combine flour, paprika, salt and pepper. Coat chicken wings in flour mixture; shake off excess. Place wings on a large greased baking sheet. Bake at 350° for 30 minutes. Remove from the oven; drain. Combine honey, orange juice concentrate and ginger; brush generously over chicken wings. Reduce heat to 325°. Bake for 30-40 minutes or until juices run clear, basting occasionally with sauce. Sprinkle with parsley if desired. **Yield:** 2 dozen.
—*Debbie Dougal Roseville, California*

Disjointing Chicken Wings

1 Place chicken wing on a cutting board. With a sharp knife, cut between the joint at the top of the tip end. Discard tips or use for preparing chicken broth.

2 Take remaining wing and cut between the joints. Proceed with recipe as directed.

Preparing Mushrooms for Stuffing

1 In one hand, hold the mushroom cap and grab the stem with the other hand. Twist to snap off the stem; place caps on a greased baking sheet. Mince or finely chop stems.

2 Spoon chopped stems onto paper towel and squeeze out any liquid. Proceed with recipe as directed.

with remaining butter. Place in a greased baking pan. Bake, uncovered, at 400° for 20 minutes, basting occasionally with pan juices. Serve hot. **Yield:** 12-15 servings.
—*Beatrice Vetrano, Landenberg, Pennsylvania*

Sausage-Stuffed Mushrooms

This classic is a little more time-consuming to prepare, but your guests will applaud your efforts and the tasty results. Prepare them with hot or mild Italian sausage to suit your tastes.

> 12 to 15 large fresh mushrooms
> 2 tablespoons butter *or* margarine, *divided*
> 2 tablespoons chopped onion
> 1 tablespoon lemon juice
> 1/4 teaspoon dried basil
Salt and pepper to taste
> 4 ounces bulk Italian sausage
> 1 tablespoon chopped fresh parsley
> 2 tablespoons dry bread crumbs
> 2 tablespoons grated Parmesan cheese

Remove stems from the mushrooms; set caps aside. Finely chop stems; place on paper towel and squeeze to remove any liquid. In a skillet, heat 4-1/2 teaspoons butter. Saute stems and onion until tender. Add lemon juice, basil, salt and pepper; cook until most of the liquid has evaporated. Cool. Add sausage and parsley. Stuff into the mushroom caps. Combine crumbs and cheese; sprinkle over stuffed mushrooms. Dot each

Creamy Hot Beef Dip

To save time, this dip may be assembled earlier in the day and refrigerated until time to bake. Allow a little extra baking time if the mixture comes directly from the refrigerator.

> 1 package (8 ounces) cream cheese, softened
> 1 cup (8 ounces) sour cream
> 3 ounces dried beef, rinsed and finely chopped
> 2 tablespoons chopped green pepper
> 1 to 2 tablespoons finely chopped onion
> 1 teaspoon dried green pepper flakes, optional
> 1/2 teaspoon garlic powder
Pepper to taste
Fresh vegetables, assorted crackers *or* snack rye bread

Combine the first eight ingredients in a 1-qt. baking dish. Bake, uncovered, at 375° for 30 minutes or until dip is hot and bubbly. Serve with vegetables, crackers or rye bread. **Yield:** about 2 cups.
—*Susan Wolfe Olathe, Kansas*

Appetizer Stromboli

Stromboli is a meal in itself, but it also makes a satisfying appetizer when sliced into strips. Using frozen bread dough makes this recipe very convenient, but feel free to use your own homemade bread dough by simply rolling as directed after the first rising.

2 loaves (1 pound *each*) frozen bread dough, thawed
1/4 pound sliced fully cooked ham
1/4 pound sliced pepperoni
1/4 cup chopped onion
1/4 cup chopped green pepper
1 jar (14 ounces) pizza sauce, *divided*
1/4 pound sliced mozzarella cheese
1/4 pound sliced bologna
1/4 pound sliced hard salami
1/4 pound sliced Swiss cheese
1 teaspoon dried basil
1 teaspoon dried oregano
1/4 teaspoon garlic powder
1/4 teaspoon pepper
2 tablespoons butter *or* margarine, melted

Let dough rise in a warm place until doubled. Punch dough down. Roll loaves together into one 15-in. x 12-in. rectangle. Layer ham and pepperoni lengthwise on half of the dough. Sprinkle with onion and green pepper. Top with 1/4 cup of pizza sauce. Layer mozzarella, bologna, salami and Swiss cheese over sauce. Sprinkle with basil, oregano, garlic powder and pepper. Spread another 1/4 cup of pizza sauce on top. Fold dough over the filling and seal edges well. Place on a greased 15-in. x 10-in. x 1-in. baking pan. Bake at 375° for 30-35 minutes or until golden brown. Brush with melted butter. Heat the remaining pizza sauce and serve with sliced stromboli. **Yield:** 8-10 servings.

—*Leigh Lauer, Hummelstown, Pennsylvania*

Making Appetizer Stromboli

1 With a rolling pin, roll dough into a 15-in. x 12-in. rectangle on a lightly floured surface. Place ingredients lengthwise down one side of the dough.

2 Fold dough over filling and crimp to seal. Bake according to directions. Slice into 1-1/4-in. pieces and arrange on platter. Serve with pizza sauce.

Appetizer Stromboli

With a sharp knife, cut off the top of each head of garlic, exposing the cloves inside. Place in a small baking dish; bake as directed.

Roasted Garlic

Roasted Garlic

When garlic is roasted, it becomes mild and soft enough to spread over bread or crackers. For additional herb flavor, place a sprig of fresh thyme over the cut surface of the garlic before roasting. Roasted garlic can also be used to flavor cream of potato soup. Simply roast as directed. When cool, squeeze the garlic from the skin into the soup and puree the entire mixture. One whole head or bulb of garlic will flavor 6 to 8 quarts of soup.

    4 whole garlic heads
1/3 cup water
1/4 cup olive *or* vegetable oil
Sliced French *or* Italian bread

Cut the top off of each garlic head (the end that comes to a closed point) so that each clove is exposed. Place with cut side up in a small ungreased baking dish; pour water around garlic. Cover and bake at 350° for 1 hour or until garlic is very soft. Cool for 5 minutes. Slowly drizzle oil into the center and over each garlic head. Remove soft garlic from skins; spread on bread or over cooked meats or vegetables. **Yield:** 4-6 servings.

Tangy Meatballs

In a hurry? Prepare these meatballs and freeze without the sauce. Defrost the meatballs in the refrigerator overnight. Before serving, prepare the sauce and bake as directed.

    2 eggs
    2 cups quick-cooking oats
    1 can (12 ounces) evaporated milk
    1 cup chopped onion
    2 teaspoons salt
1/2 teaspoon pepper
1/2 teaspoon garlic powder
    3 pounds lean ground beef
SAUCE:
    2 cups ketchup
1-1/2 cups packed brown sugar
1/2 cup chopped onion
    1 to 2 teaspoons liquid smoke, optional
1/2 teaspoon garlic powder

In a large bowl, beat eggs. Add oats, milk, onion, salt, pepper and garlic powder. Add the ground beef; mix well. Shape into 1-1/2-in. balls. Place in two greased 13-in. x 9-in. x 2-in. baking pans. Bake, uncovered, at 375° for 30 minutes; drain. Place all of the meatballs in one of the pans. In a saucepan, bring sauce ingredients to a boil. Pour over meatballs. Return to the oven and bake, uncovered, for 20 minutes or until meatballs are done. **Yield:** 4 dozen.
—*Jane Barta*
St. Thomas, North Dakota

Honey-Glazed Snack Mix

Serve up a big bowl of this sweet and crispy snack and watch it disappear. If you like, substitute peanuts, cashews or even mixed nuts for the pecans.

   8 cups Crispix cereal
   3 cups miniature pretzels
   2 cups pecan halves
   2/3 cup butter *or* margarine
   1/2 cup honey

In a large bowl, combine the cereal, pretzels and pecans; set aside. In a small saucepan, melt butter; stir in honey until well blended. Pour over cereal mixture and stir to coat. Spread into two greased 15-in. x 10-in. x 1-in. baking pans. Bake at 350° for 12-15 minutes or until mixture is lightly glazed, stirring occasionally. Cool in pan for 3 minutes; remove from pan and spread on waxed paper to cool completely. Store in an airtight container. **Yield:** about 12 cups. ○
—*Jan Olson, New Hope, Minnesota*

Three-Herb Popcorn

For a tasty twist to plain popcorn, try this specially seasoned treat. The addition of mixed nuts is optional and can be reserved for company. For fun, sprinkle a small handful of this savory popped corn on individual servings of your favorite creamed soup.

   6 quarts (24 cups) popped popcorn (about 1 cup
      kernels)
Salt to taste
   1/2 cup butter *or* margarine
   1 teaspoon dried basil
   1 teaspoon dried chervil
   1/2 teaspoon dried thyme
   1 can (12 ounces) mixed nuts, optional

Place popcorn in a large container or oven roasting pan. Add salt and set aside. Melt butter in a small saucepan. Remove from the heat; stir in basil, chervil and thyme. Drizzle over popcorn; toss lightly to coat evenly. Stir in nuts if desired. **Yield:** about 20 cups. ○
—*Flo Burtnett, Gage, Oklahoma*

Storing Popcorn

For maximum yield, store unpopped popcorn in an airtight container in a cool dry place for up to 1 year. Do not refrigerate.

Honey-Glazed Snack Mix

Buttery Onion Pretzels

Make a good snack even better by turning store-bought big pretzels into buttery onion-flavored munchies. If you like spicy flavors, add a dash or two of hot pepper sauce to the butter.

1-1/4 cups butter *or* margarine
1 envelope dry onion soup mix
1 package (16 ounces) chunky pretzels, broken into pieces

In a skillet, melt butter. Stir in soup mix. Heat and stir until well mixed. Add pretzels; toss to coat. Spread into an ungreased baking pan. Bake at 250° for 1-1/2 hours, stirring every 15 minutes. Cool. Store in an airtight container. **Yield:** 6 cups.

—Betty Claycomb
Alverton, Pennsylvania

White Chocolate Party Mix

You'll appreciate this microwave recipe when your oven is tied up with holiday baking. But don't reserve this snack just for Christmas. It's a perfect treat anytime. To color-coordinate to the season, buy red and green M & M's for Christmas, red and white for Valentine's Day, pastels for Easter and spring, or orange and black for Halloween.

5 cups Cheerios
5 cups Corn Chex
2 cups salted peanuts
1 pound M&M's
1 package (10 ounces) miniature pretzels
2 packages (12 ounces *each*) vanilla baking chips
3 tablespoons vegetable oil

In a large bowl, combine the first five ingredients; set aside. In a microwave-safe bowl, heat chips and oil on medium-high for 2 minutes, stirring once. Microwave on high for 10 seconds; stir until smooth. Pour over cereal mixture and mix well. Spread onto three waxed paper-lined baking sheets. Cool; break apart. Store in an airtight container. **Yield:** 5 quarts. **Editor's Note:** This recipe was tested in a 700-watt microwave.

—Norene Wright, Manilla, Indiana

Spiced Pecans

Spiced Pecans

Whether you prepare these for a holiday party or as a great gift from your kitchen, you'll love this easy recipe. If you're making many batches for gifts, you may want to prepare the recipe with peanuts instead of pecans. The results are just as tasty and easier on the budget.

1/2 cup sugar
1 tablespoon ground cinnamon
1/2 teaspoon salt
1 egg white
1 pound large pecan halves

Combine sugar, cinnamon and salt in a small bowl; set aside. In a large mixing bowl, lightly beat egg white. Add pecans; stir until coated. Sprinkle sugar mixture over pecans; mix well. Spread in a single layer on a baking sheet. Bake at 300° for 20 minutes. Remove nuts while warm to cool on waxed paper. **Yield:** about 6 cups.

—Brenda Schneider, Armington, Illinois

When you entertain friends and family throughout the year, welcome them into your home with a homemade beverage. Refreshing punches are perfect when feeding a crowd, while blender smoothies and freshly squeezed lemonade refresh smaller groups. Remember, beverages made in a blender need to be served immediately.

Coffee Making Tips

- To preserve maximum flavor, store fresh ground or whole bean coffee in an airtight container in the refrigerator for up to 2 weeks.

- Long-term storage is best done in the freezer for up to 1 year.

- Unopened vacuum-packed cans or packages of beans or ground coffee can be stored in the pantry for up to 1 year.

- For the best-tasting coffee, always start with a clean coffee maker that has been washed with soapy hot water, and brew coffee with fresh cold water.

Tea Making Tips

- You can store tea bags or loose tea at room temperature in an airtight container for up to 2 years. Be sure to keep each kind or flavor of tea in separate storage containers.

- To make the perfect cup of tea, pour boiling water over one tea bag or a tea infuser containing 1 teaspoon of loose tea. Allow to steep for 3-5 minutes or until the desired strength has been reached. Remove the bag or infuser.

- "Quick" iced tea can be made by pouring 4 cups boiling water over eight tea bags in a heat-resistant container. Cover and steep 3-5 minutes. Remove bags and sweeten if desired. Add 4 cups cold water or ice. Chill until ready to serve.

Orange Sherbet Party Punch

You can make the base for this punch several days ahead and chill. Before serving, add the sherbet and ginger ale.

    4 cups water, *divided*
    1 package (6 ounces) strawberry gelatin
1-1/2 cups sugar
    1 can (46 ounces) pineapple juice
    1 can (46 ounces) orange juice
    1 cup lemon juice
    1/2 gallon orange sherbet, softened
    1 liter ginger ale, chilled

Heat 2 cups water to boiling; add gelatin and sugar, stirring until dissolved. Add 2 cups cold water and fruit juices. Chill until ready to serve. Just before serving, spoon in sherbet and add ginger ale. Chill with an ice ring. **Yield:** about 36 servings (6-1/2 quarts).
—*Lannis Blunk, Mascoutah, Illinois*

Cranberry Apple Punch

The combination of brewed tea and apple and cranberry juices makes this punch perfect for fall and winter. Be sure ingredients are chilled before mixing in your punch bowl.

    2 quarts water
    2 cups sugar
    1 can (16 ounces) frozen orange juice concentrate, thawed
    1 can (12 ounces) frozen lemonade concentrate, thawed
    2 quarts cranberry juice
    1 quart apple juice
    2 cups prepared tea, cooled
Orange, lemon and lime slices

In a large saucepan, heat water and sugar until dissolved. Cool; pour into a large punch bowl. Add the next five ingredients. Garnish with orange, lemon and lime slices. Chill with an ice ring. **Yield:** about 36 serving (6-1/2 quarts).
—*Betty Hollenback*
Chesaning, Michigan

Making an Ice Ring

1 Fill a ring mold halfway with water. Freeze until solid. Top with your choice of fruit, such as peach slices, strawberries, raspberries and/or grapes. Add lemon leaves if desired. Add enough water to almost cover fruit. Freeze until solid.

2 Unmold by wrapping the bottom of the mold with a hot, damp dishcloth. Turn out onto a baking sheet; place in punch bowl fruit side up.

Liquefying Ice in a Blender

To chill and thicken beverages with ice, place all ingredients except the ice in the blender. Cover and process on high until all ingredients are blended. With the motor running, remove the feeder cap in the center of the cover and drop in one ice cube at a time. Continue until all the ice is liquefied or until the beverage is as thick as desired.

Orange Refresher

(Pictured on page 26)

For a sweet garnish, dip the rim of each glass into orange juice and then in granulated white sugar. Allow to dry 1 hour before filling glasses.

**1 can (6 ounces) frozen orange juice
  concentrate, thawed
1/3 cup sugar
1/3 cup instant nonfat dry milk powder
2 teaspoons vanilla extract**

**3/4 cup cold water
10 to 12 ice cubes
Orange slices and mint leaves, optional**

Combine the first five ingredients in a blender; cover and process on high. Add ice cubes, a few at a time, blending until slushy. Garnish with orange slices and mint if desired. Serve immediately. **Yield:** 4 servings.
                                    —Iola Egle, McCook, Nebraska

Strawberry Watermelon Slush

What could be more country and more refreshing on a hot summer day than a fresh fruit slush? Remember to use the highest speed on your blender when adding ice.

**2 cups cubed seeded watermelon
1 pint fresh strawberries, halved
1/3 cup sugar
1/3 cup lemon juice
2 cups ice cubes**

Combine the first four ingredients in a blender; cover and process until smooth. Gradually add ice, blending until slushy. Serve immediately. **Yield:** 5 cups.
                              —Patty Howse, Great Falls, Montana

Buttermilk Shake

Everyone loves a milk shake and here's one that is deliciously different. Buttermilk makes this beverage thick and rich.

**1 pint vanilla ice cream
1 cup buttermilk
1 teaspoon grated lemon peel
1/2 teaspoon vanilla extract
1 drop lemon extract**

Place all ingredients in a blender; cover and process on high until smooth. Pour into glasses. Refrigerate any leftovers. **Yield:** 2 servings.
                  *—Gloria Jarrett
Loveland, Ohio*

Holiday Wassail

12 eggs
1-1/2 cups sugar
1/2 teaspoon salt
2 quarts milk, *divided*
2 tablespoons vanilla extract
1 teaspoon ground nutmeg
2 cups whipping cream
Additional nutmeg, optional

In a heavy 4-qt. saucepan, whisk together eggs, sugar and salt. Gradually add 1 qt. of milk. Cook and stir over low heat until a thermometer reads 160°-170°, about 30-35 minutes. Pour into a large heatproof bowl; stir in vanilla, nutmeg and remaining milk. Place bowl in an ice-water bath, stirring frequently until mixture is cool. If mixture separates, process in a blender until smooth. Cover and refrigerate for at least 3 hours. When ready to serve, beat cream in a mixing bowl on high until soft peaks form; whisk gently into cooled milk mixture. Pour into a chilled 5-qt. punch bowl. Sprinkle with nutmeg if desired. **Yield:** 3-1/2 quarts.
—*Pat Waymire, Yellow Springs, Ohio*

Holiday Wassail

Prepare this beverage the day before serving if necessary and reheat on the stove or in your slow cooker. You'll love the way the spices fill your home with wonderful holiday aromas. With the "fruity" flavors of apricot and pineapple, this recipe would make a good beverage on Christmas morning.

1 can (16 ounces) apricot halves, undrained
4 cups unsweetened pineapple juice
2 cups apple cider
1 cup orange juice
18 whole cloves
6 cinnamon sticks (3-1/2 inches), broken
Additional cinnamon sticks, optional

In a blender or food processor, cover and process apricots and liquid until smooth. Pour into a large saucepan. Add pineapple juice, cider and orange juice. Place cloves and cinnamon sticks in a double thickness of cheesecloth; bring up corners of cloth and tie with a string to form a bag. Add to saucepan. (Or place loose spices in pan and strain before serving.) Bring to a boil. Reduce heat; cover and simmer for 15-20 minutes. Serve hot in mugs with cinnamon sticks if desired. **Yield:** 2 quarts. —*Ruth Seitz, Columbus Junction, Iowa*

Homemade Eggnog

Extra smooth and very rich is the only way to describe this old-fashioned holiday beverage. If desired, you may store the eggnog in the refrigerator for several days in a covered container. Whisk before serving to froth the cream.

Spiced Lemonade

(Pictured on page 16)

With its lemon/lime flavor, cinnamon and cloves, this lemonade makes a refreshing summer beverage on ice. It's also great served warm when the weather turns cooler.

6 cups water, *divided*
3/4 cup sugar
2 cinnamon sticks
6 whole cloves
1 large lime, thinly sliced
1 lemon, thinly sliced
3/4 cup fresh lemon juice
Additional cinnamon sticks, optional

In a large saucepan, bring 4 cups water, sugar, cinnamon and cloves to a boil. Reduce heat; simmer for 10 minutes. Remove from the heat; discard spices. Cool. Pour into a large pitcher. Stir in lime and lemon slices, lemon juice and remaining water. Chill for at least 1 hour. Serve cold or warm with cinnamon sticks if desired. **Yield:** about 2 quarts.
—*Kim Van Rheenen Mendota, Illinois*

Breads

Whether you're a beginning cook or a well-seasoned veteran, you can easily impress friends and family with oven-fresh breads like (clockwise from the bottom) Lemon Cheese Braid (p. 50), Raspberry Lemon Muffins (p. 57) and Wholesome Wheat Bread (p. 45).

Quick breads and yeast breads are two general categories of breads. (See page 54 for a definition of quick breads.) Yeast breads can be broken down into kneaded and batter breads. Kneaded breads are worked by hand or machine until the dough is smooth and elastic, making a dough that can be shaped into loaves or rolls. Batter breads are beaten with a mixer and then baked in a casserole or bread pan. Because of the dough's soft consistency, batter breads can't be shaped into loaves or rolls. Kneaded breads have a fine texture, while batter breads have a coarser texture.

The basic ingredients and utensils used for making all yeast breads are described here.

Yeast

Yeast leavens bread, making it rise to a light, airy texture when properly activated with warm liquid. There are several different kinds of yeast and each is handled differently. No matter which type of yeast you are using, be sure to use before the expiration date on the package.

Active Dry Yeast comes in 1/4-ounce foil packets or 4-ounce jars. With the Traditional Mixing Method (see page 40), the active yeast is dissolved in liquid that has been warmed to 110° to 115°. Temperatures lower than 110° will not activate the yeast, and temperatures higher than 115° will kill the yeast, preventing the bread from rising.

With the Quick Mixing Method (see the Country Swirl Bread recipe on page 44), the active dry yeast is added directly to the flour and dry ingredients. Then liquid that has been warmed to 120° to 130° is added.

Whichever method you use, be certain to check the temperature of the liquid with a thermometer.

Cake or Compressed Yeast is a fresh product found in your grocer's dairy case. Many old-fashioned recipes are written with a "cake of yeast". The most common size today is the 5/8-ounce cake and is equivalent to one 1/4-ounce package of active dry yeast. In recipes using the Traditional Mixing Method, the cake yeast is dissolved in liquid warmed to 80° to 90°. For Quick Mixing Method recipes, the cake yeast is crumbled and added to the dry ingredients. Then liquid that has been warmed to 120° to 130° is added.

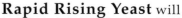

Rapid Rising Yeast will raise your bread in about half the traditional time. There are several different brands, and each has a little different way of handling mixing methods, liquid temperatures and rising time. Consult the yeast package for specific directions.

Flour

Flour gives structure and texture to your bread. As the dough is kneaded, the gluten or protein in the flour makes it elastic. All-purpose flour and bread flour have more gluten than whole wheat or rye flour. Most whole wheat or rye bread recipes contain a portion of all-purpose or bread flour so they do not become too heavy and or dense.

Liquid

Most breads are prepared with water, milk or water reserved from the cooking of potatoes. Breads prepared with water will yield a crunchy crust. The use of milk will produce a softer crust. All liquids need to be warmed to the temperature that the yeast and mixing method require.

Sugar

Sugar helps the yeast grow by producing gas that causes the bread to rise. It also browns the crust. Depending on the recipe, you may use white or brown sugar, molasses or honey to sweeten and flavor your bread.

Fat and Eggs

The addition of fat (for example, butter, margarine, shortening, olive oil, vegetable oil) and eggs not only flavors the bread and browns the crust but makes a more tender crumb.

Salt

Salt not only flavors the bread but controls the action of the yeast. For best results, use the recommended salt levels in a recipe. Never omit the salt.

Utensils

To make homemade bread, you will need a few basic utensils—a large mixing bowl, wooden spoon, wire cooling rack, loaf pans and an instant-read or yeast thermometer. Loaf pans come in many weights and materials. For golden crusts, use glass pans or heavy aluminum pans with a dull rather than shiny finish.

Country White Bread

Here's a classic white bread that is perfect for sandwiches or alongside any meal. The addition of eggs gives this bread country richness and a very tender texture.

2 packages (1/4 ounce *each*) active dry yeast
2 cups warm water (110° to 115°)
1/2 cup sugar
1 tablespoon salt
2 eggs, beaten
1/4 cup vegetable oil
6-1/2 to 7 cups all-purpose flour, *divided*

In a large mixing bowl, dissolve yeast in water. Add sugar, salt, eggs, oil and 3 cups of flour; beat until smooth. Stir in enough remaining flour to form a soft dough. Turn onto a floured surface; knead until smooth and elastic, about 6-8 minutes. Place in a greased bowl, turning once to grease top. Cover and let rise in a warm place until doubled, about 1 hour. Punch dough down. Divide in half and shape into two loaves. Place in two greased 9-in. x 5-in. x 3-in. loaf pans. Cover and let rise until doubled, about 1 hour. Bake at 375° for 25-30 minutes or until golden brown. Remove from pans; cool on wire racks. **Yield:** 2 loaves.

—*Joanne Shew Chuk, St. Benedict, Saskatchewan*

Traditional Bread Mixing and Baking Method

1 In a saucepan or microwave, heat liquid to 110° to 115°. Use a thermometer to check the temperature. Measure liquid and place in a large mixing bowl. Add yeast; stir until dissolved.

2 Add sugar, salt, fat, eggs (if required) and about half the flour. Beat with an electric mixer or by hand until smooth.

3 Gradually stir in enough of the remaining flour by hand to make a soft dough. The amount of flour will vary with the humidity in the air.

Country White Bread

4 Turn out onto a lightly floured surface; shape into a ball. Fold top of dough toward you. With palms, push with a rolling motion. Turn dough a quarter turn; repeat motion until dough is smooth and elastic. Add flour to surface only as needed.

5 Place the dough in a bowl greased with butter, margarine, oil or nonstick cooking spray; turn it over to grease the top. This prevents the dough from drying out while rising.

6 Cover with a clean cloth or plastic wrap. Place in a warm, draft-free area (80° to 85°) until dough has doubled. Or place the covered bowl on the top rack of a cold oven with a pan of steaming hot water underneath.

7 Press two fingers 1/2 in. into the dough. If the dents remain, the dough is double in size and ready to punch down.

8 To punch dough down, make a fist and push it into the center. Gather the dough to the center and shape into a ball. Place on a floured surface.

9 Divide the dough in half; shape into two balls. Roll each ball into a 12-in. x 8-in. rectangle. You will hear air bubbles "popping" as you roll the dough.

10 Dust off any loose flour that might cling to the dough. Beginning at the short end, roll up each rectangle tightly.

11 Pinch seam and each end to seal. Place seam side down in a greased pan; cover with a cloth and allow to double in size in a warm, draft-free area.

12 When breads have doubled, remove cloth; place pans, several inches apart, in the center of a preheated oven.

13 When bread is golden brown, test for doneness by carefully removing loaves from pans and tapping the bottom crusts. If it sounds hollow, the bread is done. If the bread is browning too fast and it's not done, tent with aluminum foil and continue baking.

14 Unless otherwise instructed, immediately remove yeast breads from their pans. (This prevents steam buildup that creates soggy crusts.) Cool completely on a wire rack.

Caraway Rye Bread

This old-world favorite is prepared much like the Country White Bread (page 40), except it is formed into a pheasant-shaped or round loaf.

    2 packages (1/4 ounce *each*) active dry yeast
    2 cups warm water (110° to 115°), *divided*
1/4 cup packed brown sugar
    1 tablespoon caraway seeds
    1 tablespoon vegetable oil
    2 teaspoons salt

Shaping Caraway Rye Bread

To easily shape a round loaf of bread, place ball of dough in a greased 8-in. cake pan. Flatten dough to a 6-in. diameter.

Caraway Rye Bread

2-1/2 cups rye flour
2-3/4 to 3-1/4 cups all-purpose flour, *divided*

In a large mixing bowl, dissolve yeast in 1/2 cup warm water. Add brown sugar, caraway, oil, salt and remaining water; mix well. Stir in rye flour and 1 cup all-purpose flour; beat until smooth. Add enough remaining all-purpose flour to form a soft dough. Turn onto a floured surface; knead until smooth and elastic, about 6-8 minutes. Place in a greased bowl, turning once to grease top. Cover and let rise in a warm place until doubled, about 1 hour. Punch dough down; divide in half. Shape each half into a ball; place in two greased 8-in. round cake pans. Flatten balls to a 6-in. diameter. Cover and let rise until nearly doubled, about 30 minutes. Bake at 375° for 25-30 minutes or until golden brown. **Yield:** 2 loaves.

—*Millie Feather, Baroda, Michigan*

Colonial Yeast Bread

Brown sugar adds a special sweetness and cornmeal adds a wonderful texture to this classic bread. Because of the rye and whole wheat flours, this bread's dough will be a little heavier and need a little longer rising time than breads prepared entirely with all-purpose flour.

1/2 cup cornmeal
1/2 cup packed brown sugar *or* 1/3 cup honey
    1 tablespoon salt
    2 cups boiling water
1/2 cup vegetable oil
    2 packages (1/4 ounce *each*) active dry yeast
1/2 cup warm water (110° to 115°)
3/4 cup whole wheat flour
1/2 cup rye flour
4-1/2 to 5-1/2 cups all-purpose flour

In a mixing bowl, combine cornmeal, sugar or honey, salt, boiling water and oil. Let cool to 110°. Meanwhile, dissolve yeast in warm water and let stand 5 minutes. Stir into cornmeal mixture. Add whole wheat flour, rye flour and enough all-purpose flour to form a stiff dough. Turn onto a floured surface; knead until smooth and elastic; about 6-8 minutes. Place in a greased bowl, turning once to grease top. Cover and let rise in a warm place until doubled, about 1-1/2 hours. Punch dough down. Divide into two balls. Cover and let rest 10 minutes. Shape into two loaves. Place in two greased 8-in. x 4-in. x 2-in. loaf pans. Cover and let rise until doubled, about 1-1/2 hours. Bake at 375° for 35-40 minutes. Cover loosely with foil if top browns too quickly. Remove from pans; cool on wire racks. **Yield:** 2 loaves.

—*Stella Quade, Carthage, Missouri*

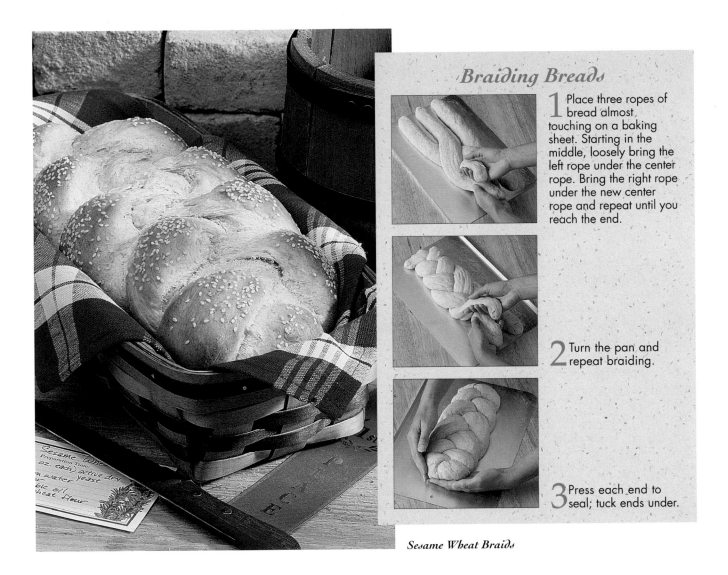

Braiding Breads

1 Place three ropes of bread almost touching on a baking sheet. Starting in the middle, loosely bring the left rope under the center rope. Bring the right rope under the new center rope and repeat until you reach the end.

2 Turn the pan and repeat braiding.

3 Press each end to seal; tuck ends under.

Sesame Wheat Braids

Sesame Wheat Braids

Nothing is prettier than a braided bread. An egg wash, which is a mixture of egg and water, is brushed on the top of the shaped bread to give the bread a golden glaze and to hold the sesame seeds.

> **2 packages (1/4 ounce *each*) active dry yeast**
> **2-1/4 cups warm water (110° to 115°)**
> **1/3 cup sugar**
> **1 tablespoon vegetable oil**
> **1 cup whole wheat flour**
> **2 eggs**
> **1 tablespoon water**
> **1 tablespoon salt**
> **5 to 6 cups all-purpose flour, *divided***
> **2 teaspoons sesame seeds**

In a large mixing bowl, dissolve yeast in warm water. Add sugar and oil; mix well. Stir in whole wheat flour; let stand until the mixture bubbles, about 5 minutes. In a small bowl, beat eggs and water. Remove 2 tablespoons to a small bowl; cover and refrigerate. Add remaining egg mixture and salt to batter; mix until smooth. Add 4 cups all-purpose flour and beat until smooth. Add enough remaining flour to form a soft dough. Turn onto a floured surface; knead until smooth and elastic, about 6-8 minutes. Place in a greased bowl, turning once to grease top. Cover and let rise in a warm place until doubled, about 1 hour. Punch dough down and divide in half. Divide each half into thirds. Shape each into a rope about 15 in. long. Place three ropes on a greased baking sheet; braid. Pinch each end firmly and tuck under. Repeat, placing second braid on another baking sheet. Let rise until doubled, about 45 minutes. Brush braids with the reserved egg mixture; sprinkle with sesame seeds. Bake at 350° for 20-25 minutes. Remove from pans; cool on wire racks. **Yield:** 2 loaves.
—*Nancy Montgomery, Hartville, Ohio*

Country Swirl Bread

After a basic white bread is mastered, this recipe is a great next step in the art of bread baking. Here you'll use the Quick Mixing Method, where the dry yeast and the dry ingredients are mixed together before the warm liquid is added. This time-saver will help in the assembly of this more complex recipe.

DARK DOUGH:
    1 tablespoon sugar
1-1/2 teaspoons salt
    2 packages (1/4 ounce *each*) active dry yeast
1-3/4 cups all-purpose flour, *divided*
    3/4 cup water
    1/4 cup dark molasses
    1 tablespoon instant coffee granules
    1 tablespoon butter *or* margarine
1-1/4 cups rye *or* pumpernickel flour, *divided*

LIGHT DOUGH:
1-1/2 teaspoons salt
    1 package (1/4 ounce) active dry yeast
1-1/4 cups whole wheat flour, *divided*
1-3/4 cups all-purpose flour, *divided*
    1 cup water
    1/4 cup honey
    2 tablespoons butter *or* margarine
    1/2 cup regular *or* quick-cooking oats

Dark Dough: In a mixing bowl, mix the sugar, salt, yeast and 1 cup all-purpose flour. Heat water, molasses, coffee and butter to 120°-130°; add to flour mixture. Beat on medium speed. Add 3/4 cup rye flour and beat 2 minutes. Stir in remaining rye flour and enough of the remaining all-purpose flour to form a soft dough. Turn onto a floured surface; knead until smooth and elastic, about 6-8 minutes. Place in a greased bowl, turning once to grease top. Cover and let rise until doubled, about 2 hours.

Light Dough: In a mixing bowl, combine salt, yeast, 1 cup whole wheat flour and 1/2 cup of all-purpose flour. Set aside. Heat water, honey and butter to 120°-130°; add to the flour mixture. Beat 2 minutes on medium speed, adding remaining whole wheat flour. Mix well. Stir in oats and enough of the remaining all-purpose flour to form a soft dough. Knead until smooth and elastic, about 6-8 minutes. Place in a greased bowl, turning once to grease top. Let rise until doubled, about 1 hour.

Punch doughs down; let rest 15 minutes. Roll light dough into a 16-in. x 9-in. rectangle. Roll dark dough into a 16-in. x 8-in. rectangle and place on top of light dough. Roll up from a long side; pinch to seal. Place seam side down on a greased baking sheet. Cover; let rise until doubled, 45-60 minutes. Bake at 350° for 40 minutes. Cool on a wire rack. **Yield:** 1 loaf.
—*Frieda Miller, Benton Harbor, Michigan*

Country Swirl Bread

Making a Swirl Bread

1 Place the dark dough rectangle over the light dough rectangle.

2 Roll up tightly and pinch seams and edges to seal.

Making a Twist-Top Bread

1 For a two-loaf recipe, divide dough into four pieces. Roll into 15-in. ropes.

2 For each loaf, twist two ropes together, pinch each end to seal and place in pans.

Wholesome Wheat Bread

Wholesome Wheat Bread

(Also pictured on page 37)

Honey, nonfat dry milk and whole wheat flour make this bread extra nutritious. Shape each bread into the traditional loaf or twist two ropes together to make a decorative loaf.

    2 packages (1/4 ounce *each*) active dry yeast
2-1/4 cups warm water (110° to 115°)
    3 tablespoons sugar
    1/3 cup butter *or* margarine, softened
    1/3 cup honey
    1/2 cup instant nonfat dry milk powder
    1 tablespoon salt
4-1/2 cups whole wheat flour
2-3/4 to 3-1/2 cups all-purpose flour

In a large mixing bowl, dissolve yeast in water. Add sugar, butter, honey, milk powder, salt and whole wheat flour; beat until smooth. Add enough all-purpose flour to form a soft dough. Turn onto a floured surface; knead until smooth and elastic, about 10 minutes. Place in a greased bowl, turning once to grease top. Cover and let rise in a warm place until doubled, about 1 hour. Punch dough down. Divide in half and shape into traditional loaves or divide into fourths and roll each portion into a 15-in. rope. Twist two ropes together. Place in greased 9-in. x 5-in. x 3-in. loaf pans. Cover and let rise until doubled, about 30 minutes. Bake at 375° for 25-30 minutes. Remove from pans to cool on wire racks. **Yield:** 2 loaves. 🍎

—*Karen Wingate, Coldwater, Kansas*

Sesame French Bread

Better than bakery bread, this is perfect alongside Italian foods. You can serve both loaves the recipe yields or freeze one for later.

    2 packages (1/4 ounce *each*) active dry yeast
2-1/2 cups warm water (110° to 115°)
    2 tablespoons sugar
    2 tablespoons vegetable oil
    2 teaspoons salt
    6 to 6-1/2 cups all-purpose flour, *divided*
Cornmeal
    1 egg white
    1 tablespoon water
    2 tablespoons sesame seeds

In a large mixing bowl, dissolve yeast in warm water. Add sugar, oil, salt and 4 cups of flour; beat until smooth. Add enough remaining flour to form a soft dough. Turn onto a floured surface; knead until smooth and elastic, about 6-8 minutes. Place in a greased bowl, turning once to grease top. Cover and let rise in a warm place until doubled, about 1 hour. Punch dough down. Divide in half. Roll each half into a 15-in. x 10-in. rectangle. Roll up from a long side; pinch to seal. Place seam side down on a greased baking sheet sprinkled with cornmeal. Beat egg white and water; brush over loaves. Sprinkle with sesame seeds. Cover with plastic wrap coated with nonstick cooking spray; let rise until nearly doubled, about 30 minutes. With a very sharp knife, make four shallow diagonal cuts across top. Bake at 400° for 25 minutes or until lightly browned. Remove from pan and cool on a wire rack. **Yield:** 2 loaves. 🍎

—*Peggy Van Arsdale*
Trenton, New Jersey

Basic bread making techniques are the same when making dough for rolls as they are for yeast breads. The difference is in the final shaping. Here are classic recipes and shapes to prepare and enjoy!

Buttery Crescents

Shaping Yeast Rolls

Crescent Rolls
Roll a portion of the dough into a 12-in. circle. Cut into wedges and roll up, beginning at the wide end. Repeat with remaining dough.

Knot-Shaped Rolls
Divide each portion into 3-in. balls. Roll each ball of dough into a rope. Tie a knot; tuck and pinch ends under. Repeat with remaining dough.

Cloverleaf Rolls
Divide a portion of the dough into 1-1/2-in. pieces. Make each piece smooth by pulling the edges under. Place three balls, smooth side up, in each greased muffin cup. Repeat with remaining dough.

Breadsticks
Divide dough into 2-1/2-in. pieces. Roll each piece back and forth with both hands until they are shaped into 10-in. x 1/2-in. ropes.

Buttery Crescents

This rich dough makes a soft and very tender roll because it is prepared with milk and eggs and brushed with butter after baking.

2 packages (1/4 ounce *each*) active dry yeast
2 cups warm milk (110° to 115°)
2 eggs, lightly beaten
1/4 cup butter *or* margarine, melted and cooled
3 tablespoons sugar
1 teaspoon salt
6-1/2 to 7 cups all-purpose flour, *divided*
Additional melted butter *or* margarine, optional

In a large mixing bowl, dissolve yeast in warm milk. Add eggs, butter, sugar, salt and 4 cups flour; beat until smooth. Add enough remaining flour to form a soft dough. Turn onto a floured surface; knead until smooth and elastic, about 6-8 minutes. Place in a greased bowl, turning once to grease top. Cover and let rise in a warm place until doubled, about 1 hour. Punch the dough down and divide in thirds. Roll each portion into a 12-in. circle; cut each circle into 12 wedges. Roll up wedges from the wide end and place with pointed end down on greased baking sheets. Cover and let rise until doubled, about 30 minutes. Bake at 400° for 12-14 minutes or until golden brown. Brush with butter if desired. **Yield:** 3 dozen.
—*Lynne Peterson*
Salt Lake City, Utah

Golden Knots

Prepare and partially bake these rolls on a day when you have plenty of time. Then freeze them for busy days ahead!

        2 packages (1/4 ounce *each*) active dry yeast
1-1/2 cups warm water (110° to 115°)
    1/2 cup plus 2 teaspoons sugar, *divided*
1-1/2 cups warm milk (110° to 115°)
    1/4 cup vegetable oil
        4 teaspoons salt
7-1/2 to 8-1/2 cups all-purpose flour
Melted butter *or* margarine

In a large mixing bowl, dissolve yeast in warm water. Add 2 teaspoons sugar; let stand for 5 minutes. Add milk, oil, salt and remaining sugar. Add enough flour to form a stiff dough. Turn onto a floured surface; knead until smooth and elastic, about 6-8 minutes. Place in a greased bowl, turning once to grease top. Cover and let rise in a warm place until doubled, about 1-1/2 hours. Punch dough down. Divide into four portions. Cover three pieces with plastic wrap. Shape one portion into 12 balls. To form knots, roll each ball into a 10-in. rope; tie into a knot. Tuck and pinch ends under. Repeat with remaining dough. Place rolls on greased baking sheets; brush with butter. Cover and let rise until doubled, about 20-30 minutes. To serve immediately, bake at 375° for 15-18 minutes. To freeze for later use, partially bake at 300° for 15 minutes. Cool and freeze. Reheat frozen rolls at 375° for 12-15 minutes or until browned. **Yield:** 4 dozen. —*Jayne Duce Raymond, Alberta*

Icebox Cloverleaf Rolls

These rolls get their name because their first rising is done overnight in the refrigerator. The next day, just shape, let rise and bake.

2-1/2 cups water, *divided*
    1 package (1/4 ounce) active dry yeast
    1/2 cup shortening
        2 eggs, beaten
1-1/2 teaspoons salt
    1/2 cup sugar
7-1/2 to 8 cups all-purpose flour
Melted butter *or* margarine

Heat 1/2 cup water to 110°-115°; add yeast and set aside to dissolve. Bring 1 cup water to a boil; place in a mixing bowl. Add shortening. Add eggs, salt, sugar, yeast mixture and remaining water. Stir in 1 cup of flour at a time, mixing well after each addition until a soft dough is formed. Turn onto a floured surface; knead until smooth and elastic, about 6-8 minutes. Place in a greased bowl, turning once to grease top. Cover and refrigerate overnight. When ready to bake, divide dough into three balls. Then divide each ball into 36 pieces. Shape into balls; place three balls in each greased muffin cup. Cover and let rise in a warm place until doubled, about 1 hour. Bake at 375° for 15-20 minutes. Remove from oven and brush with butter. **Yield:** 3 dozen. —*Jean Fox Welch, Minnesota*

Soft Breadsticks

Cornmeal on the bottom of the baking sheet gives these breadsticks added crispness. If desired, sprinkle poppy or sesame seeds on the breadsticks before baking.

    1 package (1/4 ounce) active dry yeast
    1 cup warm water (110° to 115°)
    3 tablespoons sugar
    1 teaspoon salt
    1/4 cup vegetable oil
    3 cups all-purpose flour, *divided*
Cornmeal
    1 egg white
    1 tablespoon water
Coarse salt, optional

In a mixing bowl, dissolve yeast in warm water. Add sugar, salt and oil; stir until dissolved. Add 2 cups of flour; beat until smooth. Add enough remaining flour to form a soft dough. Turn onto a floured surface; knead until smooth and elastic, about 6-8 minutes. Place in a greased bowl, turning once to grease top. Cover and let rise in a warm place until doubled, about 1 hour. Punch dough down and divide into 12 portions. Roll each portion into a 10-in. x 1/2-in. rope. Place 1 in. apart on a greased baking sheet sprinkled with cornmeal. Let rise, uncovered, until doubled, about 45-60 minutes. Beat egg white and water; brush over breadsticks. Sprinkle with coarse salt if desired. Place baking sheet on middle rack of oven; place a large shallow pan filled with boiling water on lowest rack. Bake at 400° for 10 minutes. Brush again with egg white. Bake 5 minutes longer or until golden brown. **Yield:** 1 dozen. —*Hazel Fritchie Palestine, Illinois*

Cream-Filled Coffee Cake

Preparing a Cooked Filling

1 Combine flour and milk in a heavy saucepan until smooth. Cook, stirring constantly, until thickened. Chill thoroughly, about 1 hour.

2 In a mixing bowl, beat butter, sugar and vanilla until well blended. Add flour mixture; beat until fluffy.

3 Divide filling in half and spread over the bottom half of each coffee cake; replace tops.

Cream-Filled Coffee Cake

Need to take a spectacular coffee cake to an early morning gathering? Bake this coffee cake several days ahead, slice each in half and freeze. Early the day of the event, prepare the filling and spread over the thawed cakes. Then just refrigerate filled coffee cakes until ready to serve.

CAKE:
1-1/4 cup milk
1/4 cup butter *or* margarine
1/3 cup plus 1 teaspoon sugar, *divided*
1 tablespoon salt
1 package (1/4 ounce) active dry yeast
1/4 cup warm water (110° to 115°)
5-1/2 to 6 cups all-purpose flour, *divided*
3 eggs, beaten

STREUSEL TOPPING:
1/4 cup sugar
1/4 cup packed brown sugar
2 tablespoons all-purpose flour
2 teaspoons ground cinnamon
1/4 cup butter *or* margarine

CREAM FILLING:
1/4 cup all-purpose flour
3/4 cup milk
3/4 cup butter *or* margarine
3/4 cup sugar
3/4 teaspoon vanilla extract
3 tablespoons confectioners' sugar

Heat milk, butter, 1/3 cup sugar and salt; stir until the sugar dissolves. Set aside. Mix yeast, warm water and remaining sugar; let stand 10 minutes. In a large mixing bowl, combine 3 cups flour, milk mixture, yeast mixture and eggs; beat until smooth. Add enough of the remaining flour to form a soft dough. Turn onto a floured surface; knead until smooth, about 6-8 minutes. Place in a greased bowl, turning once to grease top. Cover and let rise in a warm place until doubled, about 1 to 1-1/2 hours. Meanwhile, for topping, combine sugars, flour and cinnamon in a bowl. Cut in butter until mixture is crumbly; set aside. Punch dough down; divide in half. Pat or roll each half to fit a greased 9-in. round cake pan. With a fork, pierce entire cake top. Divide topping and sprinkle over each cake. Cover and let rise in a warm place until doubled, about 1 hour. Bake at 350° for 20-25 minutes. Remove from pans; cool on wire racks. For filling, combine flour and milk in a saucepan until smooth; cook and stir until mixture thickens. Chill about 1 hour. In a mixing bowl, cream remaining ingredients until well-mixed. Add flour mixture and beat until fluffy. Cut each cake in half horizontally; spread both bottoms with half the filling. Add the top cake layer; refrigerate. **Yield:** 2 cakes.

—*Betty Mezera, Eau Clarie, Wisconsin*

Feather-Light Doughnuts

These old-fashioned favorites make good use of leftover mashed potatoes. While warm, roll in cinnamon-sugar. Or, to make glazed doughnuts, dip in your favorite confectioners' sugar icing. Refer to the "Deep-Fat Frying Tips" on page 65 for more hints.

2 packages (1/4 ounce *each*) active dry yeast
1-1/2 cups warm milk (110° to 115°)
1 cup cold mashed potatoes
1-1/2 cups sugar, *divided*
1/2 cup vegetable oil
2 teaspoons salt
2 teaspoons vanilla extract
1/2 teaspoon baking soda
1/2 teaspoon baking powder
2 eggs
5-1/2 to 6 cups all-purpose flour
1/2 teaspoon ground cinnamon
Cooking oil for deep-fat frying

In a large mixing bowl, dissolve yeast in warm milk. Add potatoes, 1/2 cup sugar, oil, salt, vanilla, baking

Feather-Light Doughnuts

soda, baking powder and eggs; mix well. Add enough flour to form a soft dough (do not knead). Place in a greased bowl, turning once to grease top. Cover and let rise in a warm place until doubled, about 1 hour. Punch dough down; roll out on a floured surface to 1/2-in. thickness. Cut with a 3-in. doughnut cutter. Place on greased baking sheets; cover and let rise until almost doubled, about 45 minutes. Meanwhile, combine the cinnamon and remaining sugar; set aside. Heat oil in an electric skillet or deep-fat fryer to 350°; fry doughnuts until golden on both sides. Drain on paper towels; roll in cinnamon-sugar while warm. **Yield:** about 2-1/2 dozen.
—Darlene Alexander, Nekoosa, Wisconsin

Christmas Stollen

As pretty as it is tasty, this classic Christmas morning bread is a tradition in many homes. Each loaf yields about 16 slices, so you may want to serve one and freeze the second for another gathering during the holidays.

3/4 cup raisins
1/2 cup chopped mixed candied fruit
1/4 cup orange juice
1 package (1/4 ounce) active dry yeast
1/4 cup warm water (110° to 115°)
3/4 cup warm milk (110° to 115°)
1/2 cup butter *or* margarine, melted
1/4 cup sugar
2 eggs, lightly beaten
2 tablespoons grated orange peel
1 tablespoon grated lemon peel
1 teaspoon salt
5-1/4 to 5-3/4 cups all-purpose flour, *divided*
1/2 cup chopped almonds
Confectioners' sugar

Soak raisins and fruit in orange juice; set aside. In a large mixing bowl, dissolve yeast in water. Add milk, butter, sugar, eggs, orange and lemon peel, salt and 3 cups flour; beat until smooth. Add raisin mixture and almonds. Add enough remaining flour to form a soft dough. Turn onto a floured surface; knead until smooth and elastic, about 6-8 minutes. Place in a greased bowl, turning once to grease top. Cover and let rise in a warm place until doubled, about 1-1/2 hours. Punch dough down; let rest for 10 minutes. Divide in half; roll each half into a 10-in. x 7-in. oval. Fold one of the long sides over to within 1 in. of the opposite side; press edges lightly to seal. Place on greased baking sheets. Cover and let rise until nearly doubled, about 1 hour. Bake at 375° for 25-30 minutes or until golden brown. Cool on wire racks. Just before serving, dust with confectioners' sugar. **Yield:** 2 loaves.
—Sharon Hasty
New London, Missouri

Lemon Cheese Braid

(Pictured on page 36)

Don't let the fancy look keep you from preparing this special coffee cake. Use the Traditional Mixing Method on page 40, then follow the shaping directions below.

    1 package (1/4 ounce) active dry yeast
    3 tablespoons warm water (110° to 115°)
    1/4 cup sugar
    1/3 cup milk
    1/4 cup butter *or* margarine, melted
    2 eggs
    1/2 teaspoon salt
    3 to 3-1/2 cups all-purpose flour, *divided*

FILLING:

    2 packages (one 8 ounces, one 3 ounces) cream cheese, softened
    1/2 cup sugar
    1 egg
    1 teaspoon grated lemon peel

ICING:

    1/2 cup confectioners' sugar
    2 to 3 teaspoons milk
    1/4 teaspoon vanilla extract

In a mixing bowl, dissolve yeast in water; let stand for 5 minutes. Add sugar, milk, butter, eggs, salt and 2 cups flour; beat on low speed for 3 minutes. Stir in enough of the remaining flour to form a soft dough. Knead on a floured surface until smooth and elastic, about 6-8 minutes. Place in a greased bowl, turning once to grease top. Cover and let rise in a warm place until doubled, about 1 hour. Meanwhile, beat filling ingredients in a mixing bowl until fluffy; set aside. Punch dough down. On a floured surface, roll into a 14-in. x 12-in. rectangle. Place on a greased baking sheet. Spread filling down center third of rectangle. On each long side, cut 1-in.-wide strips, 3 in. into center. Starting at one end, fold alternating strips at an angle across filling. Seal end. Cover and let rise for 30 minutes. Bake at 375° for 25-30 minutes or until golden brown. Cool. Combine icing ingredients; drizzle over bread. **Yield:** 12-14 servings.   —*Grace Dickey, Vernonia, Oregon*

Braiding a Filled Coffee Cake

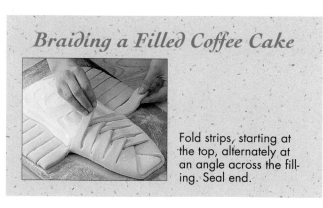

Fold strips, starting at the top, alternately at an angle across the filling. Seal end.

Hot Cross Buns

For this sweet roll recipe, shape each roll by pulling the edges under and placing the smooth side on baking sheets. Ice when cooled to room temperature. These are a must for Easter morning!

    2 packages (1/4 ounce *each*) active dry yeast
    1/2 cup warm water (110° to 115°)
    1 cup warm milk (110° to 115°)
    1/2 cup sugar
    1/4 cup butter *or* margarine, softened
    1 teaspoon vanilla extract
    1 teaspoon salt
    1/2 teaspoon ground nutmeg
    6-1/2 to 7 cups all-purpose flour, *divided*
    4 eggs
    1/2 cup dried currants
    1/2 cup raisins

GLAZE AND ICING:

    2 tablespoons water
    1 egg yolk
    1 cup confectioners' sugar
    4 teaspoons milk
    1/4 teaspoon vanilla extract

In a mixing bowl, dissolve yeast in water. Add milk, sugar, butter, vanilla, salt, nutmeg and 3 cups of flour; beat until smooth. Add eggs, one at a time, beating well after each. Stir in the currants, raisins and enough remaining flour to form a soft dough. Turn onto a floured surface; knead until smooth and elastic, about 6-8 minutes. Place in a greased bowl, turning once to grease top. Cover and let rise in a warm place until doubled, about 1 hour. Punch dough down; shape into 30 balls. Place on greased baking sheets. Cut a cross on top of each roll with a sharp knife. Cover and let rise until doubled, about 30 minutes. Beat water and egg yolk; brush over rolls. Bake at 375° for 12-15 minutes. Cool on wire racks. For icing, combine sugar, milk and vanilla until smooth; drizzle over rolls. **Yield:** 2-1/2 dozen.
  —*Dorothy Pritchett, Wills Point, Texas*

Special Cinnamon Rolls

This is a perfect recipe for the beginning bread baker to try because the dough doesn't require kneading.

    2 packages (1/4 ounce *each*) active dry yeast
    1/2 cup warm water (110° to 115°)
    8 cups all-purpose flour
    1 package (3.4 ounces) instant vanilla pudding mix
    2 cups warm milk (110° to 115°)
    2 eggs, lightly beaten
    1/2 cup sugar
    1/2 cup vegetable oil

Hot Cross Buns
Special Cinnamon Rolls

Shaping Cinnamon Rolls

1 Roll the dough into two rectangles. Brush each with butter; sprinkle with filling. Roll up, starting from the long end, and pinch the seam to seal.

2 Slice into 1-in. rolls. Place each roll cut side down in a greased pan.

3 Cover and let rise until doubled as shown. Rolls will begin to touch.

4 After baking, combine glaze ingredients; spoon in a thin stream over warm rolls.

2 teaspoons salt
1/4 cup butter *or* margarine, melted

FILLING:
1 cup packed brown sugar
2 teaspoons ground cinnamon
1 cup raisins
1 cup chopped walnuts

GLAZE:
1 cup confectioners' sugar
1 to 2 tablespoons milk
1/4 teaspoon vanilla extract

In a mixing bowl, dissolve yeast in water. Add the next seven ingredients; mix well (do not knead). Place in a greased bowl, turning once to grease top. Cover and let rise in a warm place until doubled, about 1 hour. Punch dough down. Turn onto a floured surface; divide in half. Roll each half into a 12-in. x 8-in. rectangle; brush with butter. Combine filling ingredients; sprinkle over dough. Roll up from long side; pinch seam to seal. Slice each roll into 12 rolls; place cut side down in two greased 13-in. x 9-in. x 2-in. baking pans. Cover and let rise until nearly doubled, 45 minutes. Bake at 350° for 25-30 minutes or until golden brown. Combine glaze ingredients; drizzle over rolls. Cool in pans on wire racks. **Yield:** 2 dozen.

—*Brenda Deveau*
Van Buren, Maine

Easy Cutting for Cinnamon Rolls

If you find it difficult to slice cinnamon roll dough with a knife, try this tip. Place a piece of dental floss or heavy-duty thread under the rolled dough, 1 in. from the end. Bring the sides of the thread or floss up around the dough and cross it over at the top, cutting through the dough and filling. Repeat every inch.

English Muffin Bread

This recipe is even faster than most batter breads because it has only one rising time. If you can't use both loaves right away, freeze one for later.

> 5 cups all-purpose flour, *divided*
> 2 packages (1/4 ounce *each*) active dry yeast
> 1 tablespoon sugar
> 2 teaspoons salt
> 1/4 teaspoon baking soda
> 2 cups warm milk (120° to 130°)
> 1/2 cup warm water (120° to 130°)
> Cornmeal

In a large mixing bowl, combine 2 cups flour, yeast, sugar, salt and baking soda. Add warm milk and water; beat on low speed for 30 seconds, scraping bowl occasionally. Beat on high for 3 minutes. Stir in remaining flour (batter will be stiff). Do not knead. Grease two 8-1/2-in. x 4-1/2-in. x 2-1/2-in. loaf pans. Sprinkle pans with cornmeal. Spoon batter into the pans and sprinkle cornmeal on top. Cover and let rise in a warm place until doubled, about 45 minutes. Bake at 375° for 35 minutes or until golden brown. Remove from pans immediately; cool on wire racks. **Yield:** 2 loaves.

—*Jane Zielinski, Rotterdam, New York*

Italian Parmesan Bread

When time is short but you still would like a homemade bread to serve for dinner, here's a recipe to consider. Most of the mixing is done with an electric mixer. No hand-kneading, no shaping and a quick last rising add up to big time savings for busy cooks.

> 1 package (1/4 ounce) active dry yeast
> 1 cup warm water (110° to 115°)
> 3 cups all-purpose flour, *divided*
> 1/4 cup butter *or* margarine, softened
> 1 egg, beaten
> 2 tablespoons sugar
> 1 teaspoon salt
> 1-1/2 teaspoons dried minced onion
> 1/2 teaspoon Italian seasoning
> 1/2 teaspoon garlic salt
> 1/2 cup grated Parmesan cheese, *divided*
> Melted butter *or* margarine

In a large mixing bowl, dissolve yeast in warm water. Add 2 cups flour, butter, egg, sugar, salt and seasonings. Beat on low speed until mixed, about 30 seconds; increase speed to medium and continue beating for 2 minutes. Stir in remaining flour and 1/3 cup cheese; beat until smooth. Cover and let rise in a warm place until doubled, about 1 hour. Stir batter 25 strokes. Spoon into a greased 1-1/2-qt. baking dish; brush with melted butter and sprinkle with the remaining cheese. Cover and let rise until doubled, about 30 minutes. Bake at 350° for 35 minutes or until golden brown. Cool on a wire rack for 10 minutes before removing from pan. **Yield:** 1 loaf.

—*Frances Poste, Wall, South Dakota*

English Muffin Bread

Onion Dill Bread

Buttermilk Wheat Bread

The buttermilk gives this bread a wonderfully unique taste and a pretty golden crust.

    1-1/4 cups buttermilk (70° to 80°)
    1-1/2 tablespoons butter *or* margarine
        2 tablespoons sugar
        1 teaspoon salt
        3 cups bread flour
      1/3 cup whole wheat flour
        2 teaspoons active dry yeast

In bread machine pan, place all ingredients in the order suggested by the manufacturer. Select basic bread setting. Chose crust color and loaf size if available. Bake according to bread machine directions (check dough after 5 minutes of mixing). **Yield:** 1 loaf (2 pounds). **Editor's Note:** Use of the timer feature is not recommended for this recipe.
—*Mary Jane Cantrell*
Turlock, California

Onion Dill Bread

This flavorful loaf is a nice accompaniment to a light lunch featuring chicken or tuna salad.

        2 teaspoons active dry yeast
    3-1/2 cups bread flour
        1 teaspoon salt
        1 egg
      3/4 cup cream-style cottage cheese
      3/4 cup sour cream
        3 tablespoons sugar
        3 tablespoons dried minced onion
        2 tablespoons dill seed
    1-1/2 tablespoons butter *or* margarine

In bread machine pan, place the first four ingredients in the order suggested by the manufacturer. In a saucepan, combine remaining ingredients and heat to 70° to 80°. Pour into bread pan. Select basic bread setting. Chose crust color and loaf size if available. Bake according to bread machine directions (check dough after 5 minutes of mixing). **Yield:** 1 loaf (2 pounds). **Editor's Note:** Use of the timer feature is not recommended for this recipe. 🍎

Quick breads are leavened with baking powder or baking soda instead of yeast. They require very little mixing, little or no shaping, little or no kneading and are ready to bake in minutes. The most common recipes in this category are quick bread loaves, muffins, biscuits, corn bread, scones, waffles and pancakes.

Tips for Better Quick Bread

- Be sure to mix the liquid and dry ingredients only until moistened. Overmixing causes a coarse, tough texture.

- Test loaves for doneness 10-15 minutes before end of recommended baking time. The bread is done if a toothpick inserted near the center comes out clean.

- Quick breads such as banana, zucchini and cranberry taste and slice best when served a day after baking. Wrap the cooled bread in foil or plastic wrap; leave at room temperature overnight.

Irish Soda Bread

Irish Soda Bread

This bread is prepared much like a biscuit (see page 61). Mix the dough just until moist to keep it tender.

    2 cups all-purpose flour
    2 tablespoons brown sugar
    1 teaspoon baking powder
1/2 teaspoon baking soda
1/2 teaspoon salt
    3 tablespoons butter *or* margarine
    2 eggs
3/4 cup buttermilk
1/3 cup raisins

In a bowl, combine flour, brown sugar, baking powder, baking soda and salt. Cut in butter until crumbly. Combine 1 egg and buttermilk; stir into flour mixture just until moistened. Fold in raisins. Knead on a floured surface for 1 minute. Shape into a round loaf; place on a greased baking sheet. Cut a 1/4-in.-deep cross in the top of the loaf. Beat remaining egg; brush over loaf. Bake at 375° for 30-35 minutes or until golden brown. **Yield:** 1 loaf.   —*Gloria Warczak, Cedarburg, Wisconsin*

Mom's Brown Bread

Careful and generous greasing of the baking cans is the secret to this recipe's success.

    1 cup water
1-1/4 cups raisins
    3 tablespoons butter *or* margarine
1-1/2 teaspoons baking soda

    2 eggs
    1 cup sugar
1-3/4 cups all-purpose flour
    1 teaspoon vanilla extract
1/2 teaspoon salt

In a saucepan, bring water to a boil. Add raisins, butter and baking soda; remove from the heat. In a mixing bowl, beat eggs. Add sugar, flour, vanilla and salt; stir in raisin mixture. Greased three 16-oz. vegetable or fruit cans. Divide batter between cans and place on a baking sheet. Bake at 350° for 35-40 minutes or until breads test done. Let stand 5 minutes before removing from cans. If necessary, remove bottom of cans and push breads through. Cool on a wire rack. **Yield:** 3 loaves.
  —*Patricia Woolner, Zion, Illinois*

Cranberry Orange Bread

To enjoy this moist bread year-round, keep several bags of cranberries in the freezer. Rinse to thaw and pat dry before adding to the batter.

    2 cups all-purpose flour
    1 cup sugar
1-1/2 teaspoons baking powder
    1 teaspoon baking soda
1/2 teaspoon salt
    1 egg
1/2 cup orange juice
Grated peel of 1 orange
    2 tablespoons butter *or* margarine, melted
    2 tablespoons hot water
    1 cup fresh *or* frozen cranberries
    1 cup coarsely chopped walnuts

In a large mixing bowl, combine dry ingredients. In another bowl, beat egg. Add orange juice, peel, butter and water. Add to flour mixture, stirring just until moistened. Gently fold in cranberries and walnuts. Spoon into a greased 9-in. x 5-in. x 3-in. loaf pan. Bake at 325° for 60 minutes or until a toothpick inserted near the center comes out clean. Cool for 10 minutes before removing to a wire rack. **Yield:** 1 loaf.

—*Elaine Kremenak, Grants Pass, Oregon*

Best Ever Banana Bread

For an intense banana flavor, use bananas that have speckled dark peels. For a milder flavor, use ripe bananas whose peels are still yellow.

1-3/4 cups all-purpose flour
1-1/2 cups sugar
   1 teaspoon baking soda
   1/2 teaspoon salt
   2 eggs
   1 cup mashed ripe bananas (2 to 3 medium)
   1/2 cup vegetable oil
   1/4 cup plus 1 tablespoon buttermilk
   1 teaspoon vanilla extract
   1 cup chopped walnuts

In a large bowl, stir together flour, sugar, baking soda and salt. In another bowl, combine eggs, bananas, oil, buttermilk and vanilla. Add to flour mixture, stirring just until moistened. Fold in nuts. Pour into a greased 9-in. x 5-in. x 3-in. loaf pan. Bake at 325° for 1 hour and 20 minutes or until bread tests done. Cool for 10 minutes before removing from the pan to a wire rack. **Yield:** 1 loaf.

—*Gert Kaiser, Kenosha, Wisconsin*

Pumpkin Chocolate Chip Bread

Unlike a classic quick bread, the butter in this recipe is creamed with the sugar, eggs and pumpkin, giving it a velvety texture.

   1/2 cup butter *or* margarine, softened
   1 cup sugar
   2 eggs
1-1/4 cups canned *or* cooked pumpkin
   2 cups all-purpose flour
   1 teaspoon baking soda
   1 teaspoon ground cinnamon
   1/2 teaspoon ground nutmeg
   1/2 teaspoon pumpkin pie spice
   1/4 teaspoon ground cloves
   1/4 teaspoon ground ginger
   1/4 cup semisweet chocolate chips
   1/4 cup chopped walnuts
GLAZE:
   1 tablespoon whipping cream
   1/2 cup confectioners' sugar

In a large mixing bowl, cream butter. Gradually add sugar, eggs and pumpkin. Combine dry ingredients; stir into creamed mixture and blend well. Stir in chocolate chips and nuts. Pour into a greased and floured 9-in. x 5-in. x 3-in. loaf pan. Bake at 350° for 45-50 minutes or until a toothpick inserted near the center comes out clean. Cool for 10 minutes before removing from the pan to a wire rack. Combine glaze ingredients and drizzle over cooled bread. **Yield:** 1 loaf.

—*Sheri Barber, East Aurora, New York*

Sour Cream Corn Bread

Sour cream and rosemary make this corn bread moist and extra flavorful.

   1 cup all-purpose flour
   1 cup cornmeal
   2 tablespoons sugar
   2 teaspoons baking powder
   1 teaspoon dried rosemary, crushed
   1/2 teaspoon salt
   1 egg
   1 cup (8 ounces) sour cream
   1/3 cup milk
   2 tablespoons butter *or* margarine, melted

In a medium bowl, combine dry ingredients. In another bowl, beat egg, sour cream, milk and butter; add to cornmeal mixture and mix just until moistened. Pour into a greased 8-in. square baking dish. Bake at 400° for 20-25 minutes or until a toothpick inserted near the center comes out clean. Serve warm. **Yield:** 9 servings.

—*Leonora Wilkie of Bellbrook, Ohio*

Sour Cream Corn Bread

Corn Muffins with Honey Butter

Serve these versatile muffins for breakfast, at lunch with chili or with your favorite entree at dinnertime.

2 cups all-purpose flour
2 cups cornmeal
1 cup instant nonfat dry milk powder
1/4 cup sugar
2 tablespoons baking powder
1 teaspoon salt
1/2 teaspoon baking soda
2-2/3 cups water
1/2 cup butter *or* margarine, melted
2 eggs, beaten
1 tablespoon lemon juice
HONEY BUTTER:
1/2 cup butter (no substitutes), softened
2 tablespoons honey

In a bowl, combine flour, cornmeal, milk powder, sugar, baking powder, salt and baking soda. Add water, butter, eggs and lemon juice; stir just until dry ingredients are moistened. Fill greased or paper-lined muffin cups two-thirds full. Bake at 425° for 13-15 minutes or until golden. Cool for 5 minutes before removing from pan. In a small mixing bowl, beat butter and honey. Serve with the muffins. **Yield:** 2 dozen. ⊘   —*Marilyn Platner, Marion, Iowa*

Corn Muffins with Honey Butter

Empire State Muffins

These muffins are loaded with fruit and nuts. They're perfect to serve when the autumn apple harvest is abundant.

2 cups shredded tart apples
1-1/3 cups sugar
1 cup chopped fresh *or* frozen cranberries
1 cup shredded carrots
1 cup chopped walnuts *or* pecans
2-1/2 cups all-purpose flour
1 tablespoon baking powder
2 teaspoons baking soda
1/2 teaspoon salt
2 teaspoons ground cinnamon
2 eggs, lightly beaten
1/2 cup vegetable oil

In a large mixing bowl, combine apples and sugar. Gently fold in cranberries, carrots and nuts. Combine dry ingredients; add to fruit mixture. Toss to moisten dry ingredients. Combine eggs and oil; add to fruit mixture and stir just until moistened. Fill greased or paper-lined muffin cups two-thirds full. Bake at 375° for 20-25 minutes until muffins test done. Cool for 5 minutes before removing from pan. **Yield:** 1-1/2 dozen.
          —*Beverly Collins, North Syracuse, New York*

Tips for Better Muffins

• Take care not to overmix the batter. A lumpy batter will yield more tender muffins.

• Standard muffin pans come in different sizes, which affect baking time. The muffin pans we used in this book measure 2-1/2 in. across.

• If your muffin recipe does not fill all the cups in your pan, fill the empty cups with water. The muffins will bake more evenly.

• Unless directed otherwise, muffins should go directly into the oven as soon as the batter is mixed.

• Always check muffins for doneness 5-7 minutes before the end of recommended baking time to avoid overbaking. The muffins are done if a toothpick inserted near the center comes out clean.

• Muffins are best served warm, fresh from the oven.

Preparing Perfect Muffins

1 With a pastry brush, grease all muffin cups. Or use paper liners.

2 In a large mixing bowl, combine dry ingredients with a fork.

3 Beat eggs and combine with liquid ingredients.

4 Make a well in the dry ingredients and pour egg mixture into the well all at once.

5 With a spoon or spatula, stir the ingredients together just until moistened. Fill muffin cups about two-thirds full, wiping off any spills.

6 Bake until golden or test for doneness by inserting a toothpick into the center of the muffin. If the pick comes out clean, the muffins are done. Cool in pan for 5 minutes before removing to a wire rack.

Honey Bran Muffins

When time is short and you want to serve piping-hot muffins for breakfast or brunch, keep this "do-ahead" recipe in mind.

        2 cups pineapple juice
        2 cups golden raisins
        5 eggs
        1 cup packed brown sugar
    1/2 cup vegetable oil
    1/2 cup honey
        2 cups all-purpose flour
        2 teaspoons baking
            soda
        1 teaspoon salt
        4 cups All-Bran cereal

In a small bowl, combine the pineapple juice and raisins; set aside. In a large mixing bowl, beat eggs; add brown sugar, oil and honey; mix well. Combine flour, baking soda and salt; stir in cereal. Add to sugar mixture and mix just until moistened. Fold in the raisin mixture (batter will be thin). Cover and refrigerate at least 3 hours or overnight. Stir (batter will thicken). Fill greased or paper-lined muffin cups two-thirds full. Bake at 400° for 20-25 minutes or until muffins test done. Cool for 5 minutes before removing from pan. **Yield:** about 2 dozen.   *—Pauline Rohloff*
Endeavor, Wisconsin

Raspberry Lemon Muffins

(Pictured on page 36)

When the raspberry harvest is at its peak, this is the recipe to prepare. Substitute blueberries for the raspberries if you like. The lemon flavor complements either berry.

        2 cups all-purpose flour
        1 cup sugar
        1 tablespoon baking powder
    1/2 teaspoon salt
        2 eggs, lightly beaten
        1 cup half-and-half cream
    1/2 cup vegetable oil
        1 teaspoon lemon extract
    1-1/2 cups fresh *or* frozen raspberries

In a large bowl, combine flour, sugar, baking powder and salt. Combine the eggs, cream, oil and extract; stir into dry ingredients just until moistened. Fold in raspberries. Fill greased or paper-lined muffin cups two-thirds full. Bake at 400° for 18-20 minutes or until golden brown. Cool for 5 minutes before removing from pan. **Yield:** 1-1/2 dozen. ○   *—Sharon Shine*
Bradford, Pennsylvania

Cinnamon Swirl Kuchen

Cinnamon Swirl Kuchen

Rich in cinnamon flavor, this bread is perfect with morning coffee. You'll love the magic swirl that forms when the batter is layered with the cinnamon-sugar mixture! Dust with confectioners' sugar for added sweetness if desired.

>   1/2 cup butter *or* margarine, softened
>   1/2 cup shortening
>   2-1/3 cups sugar, *divided*
>   4 eggs
>   1 cup milk
>   2 teaspoons vanilla extract
>   3 cups all-purpose flour
>   1 tablespoon baking powder
>   1 teaspoon salt
>   2 tablespoons ground cinnamon

In a large mixing bowl, cream butter and shortening. Gradually add 2 cups sugar; beat until fluffy. Add eggs, one at a time, beating well after each addition. Combine milk and vanilla; set aside. Sift together flour, baking powder and salt; add to the creamed mixture alternately with milk mixture, beating just enough after each addition to keep batter smooth. Combine cinnamon and remaining sugar; sprinkle 1-1/2 teaspoons into a greased 10-in. tube pan. Pour a third of the batter into pan. Sprinkle with half of the remaining cinnamon-sugar; top with a third of the batter. Repeat layers. Smooth with spatula. Bake at 350° for 1 hour and 15 minutes. Cool for 10 minutes; remove from pan to a wire rack to cool completely. **Yield:** 16-20 servings.

—*Nancy Brown, Janesville, Wisconsin*

Blueberry Buckle

With the moist blueberry topping, it may be hard to test this cake for doneness with a toothpick. Instead, take a look at the sides of the pan—if the cake has pulled away from the sides, it is done.

>   1/2 cup shortening
>   1 cup sugar, *divided*
>   1 egg
>   2-1/2 cups all-purpose flour, *divided*
>   2-1/2 teaspoons baking powder
>   1/2 teaspoon salt
>   1/2 cup milk
>   2 cups fresh *or* frozen blueberries
>   2 teaspoons lemon juice
>   1/2 teaspoon ground cinnamon
>   1/4 cup cold butter *or* margarine

In a mixing bowl, cream shortening and 1/2 cup sugar. Add egg and mix well. Combine 2 cups flour, baking powder and salt; add to creamed mixture alternately with the milk. Spread into a greased 9-in. square baking pan. Toss blueberries with lemon juice; sprinkle over batter. In a small bowl, combine cinnamon with remaining sugar and flour; cut in butter until mixture is crumbly. Sprinkle over berries. Bake at 350° for 60-65 minutes. **Yield:** 9-12 servings.

—*Debbie Thackrah, Latrobe, Pennsylvania*

Strawberry Rhubarb Coffee Cake

Be sure to freeze enough rhubarb and strawberries in the spring so you can enjoy this recipe all year long!

FILLING:
>   3 cups sliced fresh *or* frozen rhubarb (1-inch pieces)
>   1 quart fresh strawberries, mashed
>   2 tablespoons lemon juice
>   1 cup sugar
>   1/3 cup cornstarch

CAKE:
>   3 cups all-purpose flour
>   1 cup sugar
>   1 teaspoon baking powder
>   1 teaspoon baking soda
>   1/2 teaspoon salt
>   1 cup cold butter *or* margarine, cut into pieces
>   1-1/2 cups buttermilk
>   2 eggs
>   1 teaspoon vanilla extract

TOPPING:
>   1/4 cup butter *or* margarine
>   3/4 cup all-purpose flour
>   3/1 cup sugar

In a large saucepan, combine rhubarb, strawberries and lemon juice. Cover and cook over medium heat for 5 minutes. Combine sugar and cornstarch; stir into saucepan. Bring to a boil, stirring constantly until thickened; remove from the heat and set aside. For cake, in a large bowl, combine flour, sugar, baking powder, baking soda and salt. Cut in butter until mixture resembles coarse crumbs. Beat buttermilk, eggs and vanilla; stir into crumb mixture. Spread half of the batter evenly into a greased 13-in. x 9-in. x 2-in. baking pan. Carefully spread filling on top. Drop remaining batter by tablespoonfuls over filling. For topping, melt butter in a saucepan over low heat. Remove from the heat; stir in flour and sugar until mixture resembles coarse crumbs. Sprinkle over batter. Lay foil on lower rack of oven to catch any juicy fruit spillovers. Place coffee cake on middle rack; bake at 350° for 40-45 minutes. Cool in pan. Cut into squares. **Yield:** 16-20 servings.

—*Dorothy Morehouse, Massena, New York*

Mom's Buttermilk Biscuits

Enjoy these old-fashioned biscuits right from the oven. Or store cooled biscuits in a plastic bag at room temperature for 2-3 days, then reheat at 300° for about 10 minutes.

2 cups all-purpose flour
2 teaspoons baking powder
1/2 teaspoon baking soda
1/2 teaspoon salt
1/4 cup shortening
3/4 cup buttermilk

In a bowl, combine the flour, baking powder, baking soda and salt; cut in shortening until the mixture resembles coarse crumbs. Stir in buttermilk. On a floured surface, knead 10-12 times. Roll to 1/2-in. thickness; cut with a 2-1/2-in. biscuit cutter. Place on a lightly greased baking sheet. Bake at 450° for 10-15 minutes or until golden brown. **Yield:** 10 biscuits.

—*Vera Reid, Laramie, Wyoming*

Buttermilk Biscuit Sausage Pinwheels

Serve these delicious biscuits with scrambled eggs and fruit for a hearty breakfast or brunch. Use a lean pork sausage for best results.

1/4 cup shortening
2 cups self-rising flour
1 cup buttermilk
1 pound bulk pork sausage, room temperature

In a bowl, cut shortening into flour. Add buttermilk; mix. On a floured surface, knead five to six times, adding additional flour if necessary. Roll out on a floured surface into a 12-in. x 9-in. rectangle. Spread sausage over dough. Roll up, jelly roll-style, starting from the short side. Refrigerate. Cut into 1/2-in slices. Place cut side down on a lightly greased baking sheet. Bake at 425° for 25 minutes or until lightly browned. **Yield:** about 9 servings.

—*Gladys Ferguson Rossville, Georgia*

Mom's Buttermilk Biscuits

Tips for Better Biscuits

- For more tender biscuits, be careful not to overmix or overknead the dough.

- When reworking the trimmings, try to handle the dough as little as possible and use as little additional flour as you can to keep the dough from turning tough and dry.

- Dip biscuit cutter into flour after each cut to prevent sticking.

- If you don't have the right size biscuit cutter, roll the dough into a square or rectangle and cut into 2-1/2-in. squares, rectangles or diamonds. Cut each biscuit the same size for even baking.

- Bake biscuits until they are golden brown on the top and bottom. The sides will always be a little lighter.

Mixing and Cutting Biscuits

1 Combine all dry ingredients with a fork. With a pastry blender or fork, cut shortening into the flour until mixture resembles coarse crumbs.

2 Make a well in the center of the crumb mixture. Pour in the liquid all at once and mix with a fork just until the dry ingredients are moistened and the mixture begins to cling together.

3 Turn onto a lightly floured board and knead gently for as many times as recipe directs.

4 Roll dough evenly to 1/2-in. to 3/4-in. thickness. Cut with a floured biscuit cutter, using a straight downward motion; do not twist cutter.

5 Place biscuits on a lightly greased baking sheet. Place 1 to 1-1/2 in. apart for biscuits with crusty sides or almost touching for softer-sided biscuits.

6 Gently gather trimmings into a ball and roll out to 1/2-in. thickness. Do not knead. Cut until all of the dough is shaped into biscuits.

Nutty Sweet Potato Biscuits

Cook sweet potatoes in the microwave for real convenience and speed. Allow the potatoes to cool before peeling and do not mash with butter, milk or cream. Simply mash the plain potatoes.

2-3/4 cups all-purpose flour
4 teaspoons baking powder
1-1/4 teaspoons salt
1/2 teaspoon ground cinnamon
1/2 teaspoon ground nutmeg
3/4 cup chopped nuts
2 cups mashed sweet potatoes
3/4 cup sugar
1/2 cup butter *or* margarine, melted
1 teaspoon vanilla extract

In a large mixing bowl, combine flour, baking powder, salt, cinnamon, nutmeg and nuts. In another bowl, combine sweet potatoes, sugar, butter and vanilla; add to flour mixture and mix well. On a floured surface, knead five to six times. Roll to 1/2-in. thickness. Cut with a 2-1/2-in. biscuit cutter and place on lightly greased baking sheets. Bake at 450° for 12 minutes or until golden brown. **Yield:** 1-1/2 to 2 dozen.
—*Mrs. India Thacker, Clifford, Virginia*

Sour Cream 'n' Chive Biscuits

These flavored biscuits are tasty served with beef stew, creamed chicken, soups, salads and even scrambled eggs. Substitute freeze-dried chives for fresh when necessary.

2 cups all-purpose flour
1 tablespoon baking powder
1/2 teaspoon salt
1/4 teaspoon baking soda
1/3 cup shortening
3/4 cup sour cream
1/4 cup milk
1/4 cup snipped fresh chives

In a bowl, combine dry ingredients. Cut in shortening until mixture resembles coarse crumbs. With a fork, stir in sour cream, milk and chives until the mixture forms a ball. On a floured surface, knead five to six times. Roll to 3/4-in. thickness; cut with a 2-in. biscuit cutter. Place on an ungreased baking sheet. Bake at 350° for 12-15 minutes or until golden brown. **Yield:** 12-15 biscuits.
—*Lucile Proctor, Panguitch, Utah*

Orange Biscuits

Serve these for brunch or with a ham dinner later in the day. For any occasion, you'll love these tender biscuits with a cinnamon surprise inside!

1/2 cup orange juice
3/4 cup sugar, *divided*
1/4 cup butter *or* margarine
2 teaspoons grated orange peel
2 cups all-purpose flour
1 tablespoon baking powder
1/2 teaspoon salt
1/4 cup shortening
3/4 cup milk
Melted butter *or* margarine
1/2 teaspoon ground cinnamon

Orange Biscuits

In a saucepan, combine orange juice, 1/2 cup sugar, butter and orange peel. Cook and stir over medium heat for 2 minutes. Divide among 12 muffin cups; set aside. In a large bowl, combine flour, baking powder and salt. Cut in shortening until mixture resembles coarse crumbs. With a fork, stir in milk until mixture forms a ball. On a floured surface, knead the dough 1 minute. Roll into a 9-in. square, about 1/2 in. thick. Brush with melted butter. Combine the cinnamon and remaining sugar; sprinkle over butter. Roll up. Cut into 3/4-in. slices. Place, cut side down, over orange mixture in muffin cups. Bake at 450° for 12-16 minutes. Cool for 2-3 minutes and invert onto serving plate. **Yield:** 1 dozen.
—*Winifred Brown*
Wilmette, Illinois

Angel Biscuits

Here's a recipe that combines both yeast bread (see page 40) and quick bread techniques.

2 packages (1/4 ounce *each*) active dry yeast
1/4 cup warm water (110° to 115°)
2 cups warm buttermilk (110° to 115°)
5 cups all-purpose flour
1/3 cup sugar
2 teaspoons salt
2 teaspoons baking powder
1 teaspoon baking soda
1 cup shortening
Melted butter *or* margarine

Dissolve yeast in warm water. Let stand for 5 minutes. Stir in the buttermilk; set aside. In a large mixing bowl, combine flour, sugar, salt, baking powder and soda. Cut in shortening until mixture resembles coarse crumbs. Stir in yeast mixture; mix well. On a floured surface, knead lightly three to four times. Roll to 1/2-

Removing Biscuits from the Pan

1 Place a large serving platter over the muffin pan.

2 With hot pads, grasp both the tray and the muffin pan and carefully turn over.

in. thickness. Cut with a 2-1/2-in. biscuit cutter. Place on a lightly greased baking sheet. Cover and let rise in a warm place, about 1-1/2 hours. Bake at 450° for 8-10 minutes. Lightly brush tops with melted butter. **Yield:** about 2-1/2 dozen.
—*Faye Hintz*
Springfield, Missouri

Cherry Cream Scones

Can't find dried cherries? Substitute dried currants, raisins or cranberries and eliminate the almond extract.

      3/4 cup dried cherries
        1 cup boiling water
        3 cups all-purpose flour
        3 tablespoons sugar
        1 tablespoon baking powder
      1/2 teaspoon salt
      1/2 teaspoon cream of tartar
      1/2 cup cold butter *or* margarine
        1 egg, *separated*
      1/2 cup sour cream
      3/4 cup half-and-half cream
  1-1/2 teaspoons almond extract
Additional sugar

Soak cherries in water for 10 minutes. Drain and set aside. In a large mixing bowl, combine the flour, sugar, baking powder, salt and cream of tartar. With a pastry blender, cut in butter until mixture resembles coarse crumbs. Set aside. In a small bowl, combine egg yolk, sour cream, cream and extract. Add to flour mixture; stir until a soft dough forms. On a floured surface, knead gently six to eight times. Knead in cherries. Divide dough in half and shape into balls. Roll each ball into a 6-in. circle. Cut each into six wedges. Place on a lightly greased baking sheet. Beat the egg white until foamy; brush tops of scones and sprinkle with sugar. Bake at 400° for 15-20 minutes. Serve warm. **Yield:** 1 dozen. ⏱ —*Carrie Sherrill, Forestville, Wisconsin*

Breakfast Scones

Add a teaspoon of ground cinnamon with the flour for a tasty variation.

        2 cups all-purpose flour
        1 cup whole wheat flour
      1/2 cup packed brown sugar
        1 tablespoon baking powder
      1/2 teaspoon baking soda
      3/4 cup cold butter *or* margarine
        1 cup buttermilk

In a bowl, combine flours, brown sugar, baking powder and baking soda. Cut in butter until mixture resembles coarse crumbs. Stir in buttermilk until a soft dough forms. On a floured surface, knead gently 10-12 times or until no longer sticky. Divide dough in half; gently pat or roll each half into an 8-in. circle 1/2 in. thick. Cut each into eight wedges. Separate wedges and place on an ungreased baking sheet. Bake at 400° for 15-18 minutes. **Yield:** 16 scones. ⏱
—*Kate Carpenter, Callahan, Florida*

Cherry Cream Scones

Shaping Scones

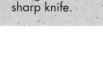

Divide dough in half and roll each portion into a circle about 1/2 in. thick. Cut into wedges with a sharp knife.

Southwestern Spoon Bread

Although this fits into the bread category, many would say it's more like a corn pudding. Serve it with a beef or pork roast or beside your favorite Tex-Mex dish. Make this as spicy as you want or your guests can handle!

- 1 can (15 ounces) cream-style corn
- 1 cup cornmeal
- 3/4 cup milk
- 1/3 cup vegetable oil
- 2 eggs, lightly beaten
- 1 teaspoon baking powder
- 1/2 teaspoon salt
- 1 can (4 ounces) chopped green chilies
- 1 cup (4 ounces) shredded cheddar cheese

In a mixing bowl, combine the first seven ingredients. Pour half of the batter into a greased 2-qt. baking dish. Sprinkle with chilies and cheese. Pour remaining batter over all. Bake at 375° for 45 minutes or just until set. Serve immediately with a spoon. **Yield:** 6-8 servings. —*Aldine Fouse, Farmington, New Mexico*

Garlic Herb Bread

Here's an enhanced version of classic garlic bread. This is a recipe that can be prepared ahead, wrapped in foil and refrigerated until you're ready to pop it into the oven.

- 6 tablespoons butter *or* margarine, softened
- 1 to 2 garlic cloves, minced
- 2 teaspoons dried parsley flakes
- 1/2 teaspoon dried oregano
- 1/2 teaspoon dill weed
- 1 teaspoon grated Parmesan cheese
- 1 loaf sourdough *or* French bread (1 pound), sliced

In a bowl, combine the first six ingredients. Spread on one side of each slice of bread; wrap loaf in foil. Bake at 350° for 20-25 minutes or until heated through. **Yield:** 6-8 servings. ◷ —*Debbie Carlson San Diego, California*

Mini Blue Cheese Rolls

Mini Blue Cheese Rolls

Keep this recipe handy when you need a special hot bread to serve in a hurry. If you have a crowd coming, simply double or triple as needed.

- 1/4 cup butter *or* margarine
- 1/2 cup blue cheese
- 1 tube (11 ounces) refrigerated breadsticks

In a saucepan, melt the butter and blue cheese over low heat. Unroll dough and cut each breadstick into six pieces; place on a foil-lined 11-in. x 7-in. x 2-in. baking pan. Pour cheese mixture over dough. Bake at 400° for 20 minutes or until butter is absorbed and rolls are lightly browned. Carefully lift foil out of pan; remove rolls from foil and place on a serving dish. Serve hot. **Yield:** 4-6 servings. ◷ —*Myrtle Albrecht Cameron Park, California*

Hush Puppies

Hush Puppies

Hush puppies are a Southern deep-fried quick bread made of cornmeal. Traditionally served at fish fries, these tasty fritter-like breads are also a great accompaniment to fried chicken or spicy Cajun foods. For those with a sweet tooth, try rolling the hush puppies in confectioners' sugar.

        2 cups cornmeal
    1/2 cup all-purpose flour
        2 tablespoons sugar
        2 teaspoons baking powder
        1 teaspoon salt
    1/2 teaspoon baking soda
        1 egg, beaten
    3/4 cup milk
    3/4 cup cream-style corn
Cooking oil for deep-fat frying
Confectioners' sugar, optional

In a bowl, combine cornmeal, flour, sugar, baking powder, salt and baking soda. Add egg, milk and corn; stir just until moistened. In a deep-fat fryer, heat oil to 375°. Drop batter by teaspoonfuls into oil. Fry until golden brown. Allow to cool slightly and roll in confectioners' sugar if desired. Serve immediately with fried chicken, ham or sausage. **Yield:** 12-15 servings.

—*Karyl Goodhart, Geraldine, Montana*

Deep-Fat Frying Tips

- If you don't have a deep-fat fryer with a thermostat, you can use a kettle or Dutch oven together with a thermometer so you can accurately regulate the temperature of the oil.

- It is important to follow the temperatures recommended in the recipes for heating oil. If oil is too hot, the foods will brown too fast and not be done in the center. If the oil is below temperature, the foods will absorb oil and taste greasy.

- Carefully place foods into the hot oil to avoid splattering.

- Do not overload your fryer. You will have better results if you fry in small batches. Keep cooked foods warm in a low oven until all the food has been fried.

- Never add water or any liquids to hot oil.

- Do not dispose of oil after deep-fat frying until it has completely cooled.

Blueberry Sour Cream Pancakes

Blueberry Sour Cream Pancakes

Serve these light pancakes as is with blueberries inside and out! Or prepare them as simple classic pancakes without the blueberries and serve with butter and warm maple syrup.

> 1/2 cup sugar
> 2 tablespoons cornstarch
> 1 cup water
> 4 cups fresh *or* frozen blueberries
> PANCAKES:
> 2 cups all-purpose flour
> 1/4 cup sugar
> 4 teaspoons baking powder
> 1/2 teaspoon salt
> 2 eggs
> 1-1/2 cups milk
> 1 cup (8 ounces) sour cream
> 1/3 cup butter *or* margarine, melted
> 1 cup fresh *or* frozen blueberries

In a medium saucepan, combine sugar and cornstarch. Gradually stir in water. Add blueberries; bring to a boil over medium heat. Boil for 2 minutes, stirring constantly. Remove from the heat; cover and keep warm. For pancakes, combine dry ingredients in a bowl. In another bowl, beat the eggs. Add milk, sour cream and butter; mix well. Stir into dry ingredients just until moistened. Fold in the blueberries. Pour batter by 1/4 cupfuls onto a greased hot griddle; turn when bubbles form on top of pancakes. Cook until the second side is golden brown. Serve with blueberry topping. **Yield:** about 20 pancakes (3-1/2 cups topping). ⏱
—*Paula Hadley, Forest Hill, Louisiana*

Preparing Pancakes

1 Using a 1/4-cup measure, pour batter onto a hot griddle or skillet, 5-6 in. apart, making sure you leave enough room between pancakes for expansion.

2 Turn pancakes over when edges become dry and bubbles that appear on top begin to pop.

Freezer French Toast

For a fast breakfast for family or guests, try this do-ahead recipe. As the French toast bakes to a golden brown, you can assemble the rest of the meal.

     4 eggs
     1 cup milk
     2 tablespoons sugar
     1 teaspoon vanilla extract
     1/4 teaspoon ground nutmeg
     10 slices day-old French bread (3/4 inch thick)
     1 to 2 tablespoons butter *or* margarine, melted

In a large bowl, beat eggs, milk, sugar, vanilla and nutmeg. Place bread in a well-greased 13-in. x 9-in. x 2-in. baking dish. Pour egg mixture over bread. Let soak for several minutes, turning bread once to coat. Freeze until firm. Store in an airtight container. To bake, place frozen bread on a well-greased baking sheet. Dot with butter. Bake at 450° for 7 minutes; turn and bake 10-12 minutes longer or until golden brown. **Yield:** 4-5 servings. ○ *—Diane Perry, Castro Valley, California*

Buttermilk Waffles

These waffles are extra-light because they have beaten egg whites folded into them. Be careful to lightly fold the egg whites into the batter, leaving a few lumps of white.

     2 cups all-purpose flour
     2 teaspoons baking powder
     1 teaspoon baking soda
     1 teaspoon salt
     3 eggs, *separated*
     2 cups buttermilk
     2/3 cup sour cream
     1/2 cup vegetable oil
Fresh apricot slices and mint,
     optional

In a mixing bowl, combine dry ingredients. In another bowl, beat egg yolks. Add buttermilk, sour cream and oil; stir into dry ingredients just until moistened. Beat egg whites until stiff peaks form; fold into batter. Bake in a preheated waffle iron according to manufacturer's directions until golden brown. Garnish with apricots and mint if desired. **Yield:** 14-16 waffles (4 inches). ○ *—Darla Reynolds Willmar, Minnesota*

Cranberry Doughnuts

These drop doughnuts are a quick version of the classic doughnut. When fresh cranberries are out of season, substitute dried cranberries.

     1 egg
     1/2 cup sugar
     1 tablespoon butter *or* margarine, melted
     1-1/2 cups all-purpose flour
     2 teaspoons baking powder
     1/2 teaspoon ground cinnamon
     1/2 teaspoon ground nutmeg
     1/4 teaspoon salt
     1/2 cup milk
     1/2 cup chopped fresh *or* frozen cranberries
Cooking oil for deep-fat frying
Additional sugar

In a bowl, beat egg; add sugar and butter. Combine flour, baking powder, cinnamon, nutmeg and salt; add to sugar mixture alternately with milk. Stir in cranberries. Heat oil in an electric skillet or deep-fat fryer to 375°. Drop batter by tablespoonfuls into hot oil. Fry doughnuts a few at a time, turning with a slotted spoon until golden, about 2 minutes per side. Drain on paper towels; roll in sugar while still warm. **Yield:** 1-1/2 dozen. *—Roberta Archer, Passadumkeag, Maine*

Buttermilk Waffles

Freezing Homemade Waffles

For fast homemade freezer waffles, bake and cool on a wire rack; freeze in a single layer on a baking sheet. When frozen, store in heavy-duty freezer bags. When ready to use, pop into the toaster or toaster oven to defrost and reheat.

Salads and Salad Dressings

For easy eating, you can toss together side-dish and main-dish recipes like Cherry Tomato Salad (p. 81), Grilled Chicken Salad (p. 76) and Strawberry Spinach Salad (p. 71). Don't forget to top off any of your creations with homemade dressings!

A salad can be a simple mixture of tossed greens served with a light dressing or a heartier combination of creative ingredients served as a side dish or whole meal. There are salads that need last-minute attention and salads that can be prepared and held overnight. When planning a meal, select the entree first, then take a look at the many delicious choices that await you in this chapter.

Creamy Sliced Tomatoes

Tips for Great Salads

- Select greens that are crisp and free of discoloration. Iceberg lettuce and cabbage should be firm and solid.

- Wash greens thoroughly in cool water. Pat them dry with a clean towel or paper towel to remove water. Store in a covered container or plastic bag, and refrigerate at least 1 hour before serving to crisp the greens. Place a piece of paper towel in the bottom of the container or bag to absorb excess moisture.

- For iceberg lettuce, cut out the core with a paring knife. Or grasp the head in your hand and hit the core area against the countertop; lift out the core. Rinse the head under running water and drain core side down.

- Just before serving, tear—don't cut—the greens into bite-size pieces. Cutting greens with a knife will turn the edges brown with time.

- Allow greens to stand at room temperature no longer than 15 minutes before serving.

- Toss greens with the dressing and serve immediately or place greens in a salad bowl and pass the dressing at the table. Adding too much dressing will make a salad soggy.

- Pasta, rice and vegetable salads should chill for a few hours to allow flavors to blend.

Creamy Sliced Tomatoes

When tomatoes are abundant, serve this pleasing salad. Nothing beats the combination of fresh basil and garden tomatoes.

> 1/2 cup mayonnaise
> 1/4 cup half-and-half cream
> 1-1/2 teaspoons chopped fresh basil *or* 1/2 teaspoon dried basil, *divided*
> Lettuce leaves
> 3 medium tomatoes, sliced
> 1 small red onion, thinly sliced into rings

In a small bowl, combine mayonnaise, cream and half of the basil; mix well. Refrigerate. Just before serving, arrange lettuce, tomatoes and onion on individual salad plates. Drizzle with dressing. Sprinkle with remaining basil. **Yield:** 6 servings.
—*Doris Smith*
Woodbury, New Jersey

Bibb

Green Leaf

Red Leaf

Watercress

Romaine

Escarole

Iceberg

Curly Endive

Spinach

Strawberry Spinach Salad

(Pictured on page 68)

Enjoy this pretty salad in the spring when fresh berries are abundant. Be sure to wash the spinach several times to remove all the sand that may be clinging to the leaves. To save time, wash the spinach early in the day and refrigerate until serving.

            2 bunches fresh spinach, washed and dried
            1 pint fresh strawberries, hulled and sliced
        1/2 cup sugar
            2 tablespoons sesame seeds
            1 tablespoon poppy seeds
    1-1/2 teaspoons finely chopped onion
        1/4 teaspoon Worcestershire sauce
        1/4 teaspoon paprika
        1/2 cup vegetable oil
        1/4 cup cider vinegar

Arrange spinach and strawberries on individual salad plates or in a large salad bowl. Place the next six ingredients in a blender or food processor. With unit running, add oil and vinegar in a steady stream. Blend until thickened. Drizzle over salad; serve immediately. **Yield:** 6-8 servings.   —*Jamie Stoneman*
                              Winston-Salem, North Carolina

Wilted Lettuce

Orange and Red Onion Salad

This colorful and tasty salad is nice to serve in the winter when oranges are in season and at their peak. Serve in a large bowl for a buffet or make individual salads for a sit-down dinner.

        1 tablespoon butter *or* margarine
        1 cup sliced almonds
        2 tablespoons lemon juice
        1 teaspoon Dijon mustard
    1/2 teaspoon sugar
    1/2 teaspoon salt
    1/4 teaspoon white pepper
    1/2 cup vegetable oil
        1 bunch romaine, torn
        2 medium oranges, peeled and sectioned
        1 small red onion, thinly sliced

In a skillet, melt butter over medium heat. Saute the almonds until golden brown. Remove almonds to paper towels to drain. In a small bowl, combine the next five ingredients; whisk in oil. In a large bowl, combine lettuce, oranges, onion and almonds; add dressing and toss. Serve immediately. **Yield:** 6 servings.
                      —*Nancy Schmidt, Gustine, California*

Wilted Lettuce

This old-fashioned recipe is a wonderful way to use fresh-from-the-garden leaf lettuce. It is important to serve this salad as soon as you add the dressing and toss.

        4 cups torn leaf lettuce
        1 small onion, sliced
        3 radishes, sliced
        6 bacon strips, diced
        2 tablespoons vinegar
        1 teaspoon brown sugar
    1/4 teaspoon ground mustard
    1/4 to 1/2 teaspoon salt
    1/8 teaspoon pepper

In a large salad bowl, toss lettuce, onion and radishes; set aside. In a skillet, cook bacon until crisp; remove with a slotted spoon to drain on paper towels. To the drippings, add vinegar, brown sugar, mustard, salt and pepper; bring to a boil. Pour over lettuce and toss; sprinkle with bacon. Serve immediately. **Yield:** 4-6 servings.   —*Rosemary Falls, Austin, Texas*

Homemade Dressing Tips

- If you plan on serving a vinegar and oil dressing right away, you can combine all ingredients in a jar with a tight-fitting lid and shake well. (The mixture will separate upon standing; simply shake before serving.) To mix a vinegar and oil dressing that will stand for an hour or two without separating, follow the "Whisking Vinegar and Oil Dressings" instructions at right. (Also use this method for dressings made with mayonnaise or prepared mustard.)
- Sturdy greens such as iceberg, romaine and cabbage taste best with mayonnaise- and sour cream-based dressings. Delicate greens such as Bibb or Boston lettuce are best served with vinegar and oil dressings.
- Experiment with homemade salad dressings by adding your favorite herbs and flavored vinegars or oils to the recipe.

Banana Poppy Seed Dressing

This dressing really complements any fruit salad or orange and grapefruit sections. This dressing is best used the same day it is prepared.

1 ripe banana
1 cup (8 ounces) sour cream
1/4 cup sugar
1 tablespoon poppy seeds
1 tablespoon lemon juice
1 teaspoon ground mustard
3/4 teaspoon salt

In a small bowl, finely mash banana. Add sour cream, sugar, poppy seeds, lemon juice, mustard and salt. Refrigerate. **Yield:** 1-3/4 cups.

—Gloria Kirchman, Eden Prairie, Minnesota

Banana Poppy Seed Dressing

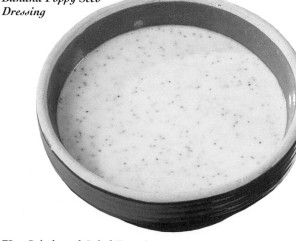

Whisking Vinegar and Oil Dressings

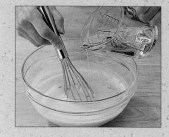

Combine all ingredients except oil in a small bowl. Slowly add oil while mixing vigorously with a wire whisk.

Honey Mustard Salad Dressing

Serve this dressing over mixed greens or a fresh spinach salad. For more zest, use spicy brown mustard.

1 cup mayonnaise
1/2 cup vinegar
1 teaspoon prepared mustard
1/2 cup honey
1 teaspoon sugar
1 teaspoon finely chopped onion
1 teaspoon minced fresh parsley
1/4 teaspoon salt
1/4 teaspoon pepper
1/2 cup vegetable oil

In a small bowl, combine the mayonnaise, vinegar and mustard. Add honey, sugar, onion, parsley, salt and pepper. Slowly add oil while mixing briskly with a wire whisk. Refrigerate. **Yield:** 2 cups.

—Shirley Sybesma, Ontario, California

Buttermilk Salad Dressing

Why buy salad dressing when it's so easy to make your own? This favorite is great for folks watching their diet.

1 garlic clove, minced
3/4 cup light *or* fat-free mayonnaise
1 teaspoon dried parsley flakes
1/2 teaspoon dried minced onion
1/4 to 1/2 teaspoon salt
1/8 teaspoon pepper
1/2 cup buttermilk

In a small bowl, combine the first six ingredients; slowly add buttermilk while mixing briskly with a wire whisk. Or combine all ingredients in a jar with a tight-fitting lid and shake until smooth. Refrigerate. **Yield:** 1-1/4 cups.

—Mary Gehl, Victor, Montana

Favorite French Dressing

Here's a classic that is bound to please everyone! Prepare it a day ahead to allow the flavors to blend.

1 cup vinegar
3/4 cup sugar
1/4 cup grated onion
1-1/2 teaspoons salt
1-1/2 teaspoons ground mustard
1-1/2 teaspoons paprika
1 bottle (12 ounces) chili sauce
1 cup vegetable oil

In a bowl or a jar with tight-fitting lid, mix vinegar, sugar and onion. Combine salt, mustard, paprika and 2 tablespoons chili sauce to form a paste. Add remaining chili sauce and mix well. Pour into vinegar mixture; whisk in oil, or add oil and shake well. Refrigerate. **Yield:** 3-1/2 cups. ○ 🍎

—*Linda Nilsen*
Anoka, Minnesota

Favorite French Dressing

Herb Vinegar

Flavored vinegars can be used in a variety of recipes, including the Herbed Salad Dressing below. Why not prepare a few extra bottles to give as gifts?

1 garlic clove, optional
1 sprig of fresh oregano, basil *or* tarragon (12 to 18 inches)
1-1/4 cups white vinegar *or* white wine vinegar

If desired, cut garlic in half and skewer with a toothpick. Place in a glass jar or bottle. Add herb sprig; set aside. In a saucepan, bring vinegar to a simmer (do not boil). Carefully pour into container. Let cool to room temperature. Remove garlic after 24 hours. Cover and store in a cool dry place for up to a year. **Yield:** 1-1/4 cups. 🍎

Herbed Salad Dressing

This recipe is easy to assemble and simply needs a brisk shaking before serving over your choice of greens.

1 to 1-1/3 cups tarragon vinegar
1 cup vegetable oil
2/3 cup olive oil
4 teaspoons mayonnaise
3 garlic cloves, minced
1 tablespoon minced fresh thyme *or* 1 teaspoon dried thyme
2 teaspoons Dijon mustard
1-1/2 teaspoons minced fresh tarragon *or* 1/2 teaspoon dried tarragon
1 teaspoon brown sugar
1 teaspoon salt

In a jar with tight-fitting lid, combine all ingredients; shake well. Refrigerate. **Yield:** 3 cups. ○

—*Marge Clark, West Lebanon, Indiana*

Blue Cheese Dressing

This dressing makes enough for 2 to 3 quarts of greens and vegetables and serves about 8 people.

2 ounces blue cheese, crumbled
1/3 cup vegetable oil
2 tablespoons lemon juice
1/2 teaspoon sugar
1/4 teaspoon salt
3 tablespoons chopped green onion
2 tablespoons chopped fresh parsley

Combine all ingredients in a small bowl or jar with tight-fitting lid. Refrigerate. **Yield:** about 3/4 cup. ○

—*Peggy Hughes, Albany, Kentucky*

Patriotic Gelatin Salad

Although this impressive-looking salad takes time to prepare, you'll agree it was worth the work when your guests feast their eyes on it. Be careful to leave enough time for each layer to almost set before adding a new layer.

> **2 packages (3 ounces *each*) berry blue gelatin**
> **2 packages (3 ounces *each*) strawberry gelatin**
> **4 cups boiling water, *divided***
> **2-1/2 cups cold water, *divided***
> **2 envelopes unflavored gelatin**
> **2 cups milk**
> **1 cup sugar**
> **2 cups (16 ounces) sour cream**
> **2 teaspoons vanilla extract**

In four separate bowls, dissolve each package of gelatin in 1 cup of boiling water. Add 1/2 cup of cold water to each and stir. Pour one bowl of blue gelatin into an oiled 10-in. fluted tube pan; chill until almost set, about 30 minutes. Set other three bowls of gelatin aside at room temperature. Soften unflavored gelatin in remaining cold water; let stand 5 minutes. Heat milk in a saucepan over medium heat just below boiling. Stir in sugar and softened gelatin until sugar is dissolved. Remove from heat; stir in sour cream and vanilla until smooth. When blue gelatin in pan is almost set, carefully spoon 1-1/2 cups sour cream mixture over it. Chill until almost set, about 30 minutes. Carefully spoon one bowl of strawberry gelatin over cream layer. Chill until almost set. Carefully spoon 1-1/2 cups cream mixture over strawberry layer. Chill until almost set. Repeat, adding layers of blue gelatin, cream mixture and strawberry gelatin, chilling in between each. Chill until firm, several hours or overnight. **Yield:** 16 servings.
— *Sue Gronholz, Columbus, Wisconsin*

Patriotic Gelatin Salad

Tips for Better Gelatin Salads

- Always use canned or cooked pineapple in gelatin salads. Fresh pineapple and kiwifruit will prevent the salad from setting.

- For easy removal of gelatin salads from the mold, moisten the interior of the mold with cold water, rub vegetable oil inside or coat with nonstick cooking spray before filling.

- When unmolding a large gelatin salad, rinse the serving platter with cold water before turning the gelatin out. The moisture will allow the salad to be easily centered on the platter.

- If your gelatin mixture sets too fast and you've passed the partially set step, place the bowl of gelatin in a pan of warm water and stir until the gelatin has softened. Chill again until the mixture is the consistency of unbeaten raw egg whites.

Autumn Apple Salad

This salad is refreshing and very pretty when cut into squares and served on a lettuce-lined plate. It's best if prepared the day before to allow enough time to set properly.

> **1 can (20 ounces) crushed pineapple, undrained**
> **2/3 cup sugar**
> **1 package (3 ounces) lemon gelatin**
> **1 package (8 ounces) cream cheese, softened**
> **1 cup diced unpeeled apples**
> **1 cup chopped celery**
> **1 cup whipped topping**
> **1/2 to 1 cup chopped nuts**

Lettuce leaves

In a saucepan, combine pineapple and sugar; bring to a boil and boil for 3 minutes. Add gelatin; stir until dissolved. Add cream cheese; stir until the mixture is thoroughly blended. Cool. Fold in the apples, celery, whipped topping and nuts. Pour into a 9-in. square pan. Chill until firm, several hours or overnight. Cut into squares and serve on individual lettuce-lined plates. **Yield:** 9-12 servings.
— *Melissa Bowers
Sidney, Ohio*

Rosy Rhubarb Salad

You can serve this delightful recipe anytime of the year if you have frozen rhubarb in your freezer. Just defrost and blot excess moisture before cooking.

3 cups sliced fresh *or* frozen rhubarb (1-inch pieces)
1 tablespoon sugar
1 package (3 ounces) raspberry gelatin
1 cup unsweetened pineapple juice
1 teaspoon lemon juice
1 cup diced peeled apples
1 cup diced celery
1/4 cup chopped pecans

In a medium saucepan, cook and stir rhubarb and sugar over medium-low heat until rhubarb is soft and tender. Remove from the heat; add gelatin and stir until dissolved. Stir in pineapple and lemon juices. Chill until partially set. Fold in apples, celery and pecans. Pour into an oiled 4-1/2-cup mold or glass bowl. Chill until firm, several hours or overnight. **Yield:** 8 servings. —*Wanda Rader Greeneville, Tennessee*

Golden Glow Salad

To keep fruit from rising to the top of your molded salad, allow the gelatin to partially set to a consistency that resembles unbeaten raw egg whites.

1 package (3 ounces) orange gelatin
1 cup boiling water
1 can (8 ounces) crushed pineapple
1 tablespoon lemon juice
Cold water
1/4 teaspoon salt
3/4 cup finely shredded carrots

In a bowl, dissolve gelatin in boiling water. Drain pineapple, reserving juice. Add lemon juice and enough cold water to pineapple juice to measure 1 cup; add salt. Stir into gelatin. Chill until partially set. Stir in pineapple and carrots. Pour into an oiled 4-cup mold; chill until firm, several hours or overnight. **Yield:** 6 servings. —*Thelma Waggoner, Hopkinsville, Kentucky*

Golden Glow Salad

Unmolding Gelatin Salads

1 Dip firm gelatin salad in a sink or large pan of warm water for just a few seconds or until the edges begin to release from the side of the mold.

2 Place a plate over the mold and invert. Carefully lift the mold from the salad.

Spicy Beef Salad

Spicy Beef Salad

Because it cooks in no time, you'll want to cut and measure all ingredients before stir-frying the beef.

1/2 pound boneless lean sirloin steak
1/3 cup lime juice
  1 tablespoon brown sugar
  1 tablespoon soy sauce
  1 tablespoon minced fresh basil *or* 1 teaspoon dried basil
  2 teaspoons minced fresh mint *or* 3/4 teaspoon dried mint
  1 jalapeno pepper, seeded and minced
  2 to 3 garlic cloves, minced

  1 teaspoon grated fresh gingerroot *or* 1/4 to 1/2 teaspoon ground ginger
  1 large sweet red pepper, julienned
1/2 medium cucumber, chopped
  6 cups torn mixed salad greens

Place beef in the freezer for 15 minutes. Slice across the grain into thin strips; set aside. For dressing, combine lime juice, brown sugar, soy sauce, basil and mint; set aside. In a medium skillet that has been coated with nonstick cooking spray, saute jalapeno, garlic and ginger for 30 seconds. Add beef; stir-fry until cooked as desired. Remove beef from pan; gently toss with red pepper and cucumber. Place greens in a large bowl or divide among individual bowls or plates; top with beef mixture. Add dressing to pan and bring to a boil; remove from the heat and drizzle over salad. Serve immediately. **Yield:** 4 servings. 🕐 🍎   *—Peggy Allen Pasadena, California*

Grilled Chicken Salad

(Pictured on page 69)

As pretty as it is delicious, this spectacular salad is almost a complete meal. Simply add freshly baked rolls and dessert.

  6 boneless skinless chicken breast halves
  2 tablespoons lemon juice
  1 pound macaroni, ziti *or* corkscrew pasta, cooked and drained
  1 medium sweet red pepper, chopped
2-1/2 cups sliced celery
  1 medium red onion, chopped
1/4 cup minced fresh dill *or* 5 teaspoons dill weed
  3 tablespoons white wine vinegar
  2 tablespoons mayonnaise
  2 tablespoons Dijon mustard
1/2 teaspoon salt
1/4 teaspoon pepper
2/3 cup olive *or* vegetable oil
Lettuce leaves

Grill the chicken breasts over medium-hot heat for 15-18 minutes or until tender and juices run clear, turning once. Remove from the grill and place in a single layer on a platter; sprinkle with lemon juice and set aside. In a large bowl, toss pasta, red pepper, celery, onion and dill. Remove chicken from platter; pour juices into a bowl. Slice chicken crosswise into thin strips; add to pasta mixture. To the juices, add vinegar, mayonnaise, mustard, salt and pepper; whisk well. Add oil slowly while mixing briskly with wire whisk. Pour over salad and toss. Serve in a lettuce-lined bowl or on individual lettuce-lined plates. **Yield:** 6 servings.   *—Juli Stewart, Coppell, Texas*

Ham Pasta Salad

THOUSAND ISLAND DRESSING:
    1 cup mayonnaise *or* salad dressing
    1/2 cup *each* ketchup, sweet pickle relish and
       chopped onion
Dash garlic salt

In a large salad bowl, combine lettuce, beans if desired, onion, radishes, cucumber and tomato. Arrange ham and cheese on top. Cover and refrigerate until serving. In a small bowl, combine all dressing ingredients; stir until well blended. Chill for 1 hour. Serve with the salad. **Yield:** 6 servings.
—Eleanore Hill
Fresno, California

Ham Pasta Salad

Ham is the star of this tasty salad. It's perfect for every day but can be easily doubled for a potluck supper. To speed the chilling process, rinse cooked pasta in cold water.

    1 package (7 ounces) shell macaroni, cooked
      and drained
    2 cups cubed fully cooked ham
    1 cup chopped green pepper
    1 cup chopped tomato
    1/4 cup chopped onion
DRESSING:
    1/2 cup mayonnaise *or* salad dressing
    1/4 cup grated Parmesan cheese
    2 tablespoons milk
    1/4 teaspoon salt
Additional Parmesan cheese

In a large bowl, toss macaroni with ham, green pepper, tomato and onion. In a small bowl, combine mayonnaise, Parmesan cheese, milk and salt. Pour over pasta mixture and stir to coat. Cover and chill. Sprinkle with additional Parmesan before serving. **Yield:** 4-6 servings.
—Deanna Mitchell, Independence, Kansas

Chef's Salad

When the garden is in full swing and a light meal is just what you want for a summer's day, try this favorite. The accompanying dressing is a classic.

    1/2 head iceberg lettuce, torn
    1 can (15 ounces) garbanzo beans, rinsed and
      drained, optional
    1 small red onion, chopped
    1/2 cup sliced radishes
    1 small cucumber, chopped
    1 small tomato, chopped
    1 cup julienned fully cooked ham
    1 cup julienned Swiss *or* cheddar cheese

Crunchy Pork and Rice Salad

Here's a tasty salad that uses both leftover pork and rice. You'll enjoy the down-home flavor and wonderful texture of this hearty salad. It's best prepared a few hours before serving.

    1 head Chinese or green cabbage, shredded
      (about 6 cups)
    2 cups cubed cooked pork roast
1-1/2 cups cold cooked rice
    1 package (10 ounces) frozen peas, thawed
    1 can (8 ounces) sliced water chestnuts, drained
DRESSING:
    1/2 cup sour cream
    1/2 cup mayonnaise
    1 teaspoon celery seed
    1/2 teaspoon salt

In a large bowl, toss cabbage, pork, rice, peas and water chestnuts. In a small bowl, combine dressing ingredients; mix well. Pour over the salad and stir gently to mix. Chill for several hours. **Yield:** 8-10 servings.
—Susan Kemmerer, Telford, Pennsylvania

Crunchy Pork and Rice Salad

Tips for Potato Salads

- To cook potatoes for salads, scrub and wash potatoes; remove any eyes or sprouts. Place whole unpeeled potatoes in a large kettle. Cover with cold water; add 1-2 teaspoons salt for each quart of water. Cover and boil until fork-tender yet firm. (Cooking times vary greatly with size and variety—small potatoes may cook in 15 minutes while larger ones may need 30 minutes.) Drain potatoes; allow to cool. Use a paring knife to peel if desired. Slice or cut potatoes into chunks.

- Red potatoes are especially good for salads because they don't absorb excess dressing or break apart as easily as other varieties. And because of their thin edible skin, they don't need to be peeled.

Red, White and Green Salad

Unlike some potato salads, this version is prepared with oil and vinegar instead of mayonnaise. So it doesn't need to be refrigerated in hot weather, making it great for picnics.

> 1 pound small red potatoes, cooked and cubed
> 2 large tomatoes, diced
> 1 pound fresh green beans, cut into 2-inch pieces and cooked
> 7 tablespoons olive *or* vegetable oil
> 5 tablespoons white wine vinegar
> 3/4 teaspoon salt
> 1/2 teaspoon pepper

In a large bowl, combine potatoes, tomatoes and beans. In a small bowl, combine oil, vinegar, salt and pepper. Pour over vegetables; toss to coat. Refrigerate for several hours before serving. **Yield:** 8-10 servings.
—Jodie McCoy
Tulsa, Oklahoma

Sweet Potato Salad

You can serve this hearty potato salad all year-round. It's a wonderful accompaniment to ham or pork and makes an easy-to-serve addition to a buffet table.

> 3 pounds sweet potatoes, cooked, peeled and cubed
> 1 cup chopped sweet red pepper
> 1/2 cup chopped onion
> 1-1/4 cups mayonnaise
> 1-1/2 teaspoons salt
> 1/2 teaspoon pepper
> 1/4 teaspoon hot pepper sauce

In a large bowl, toss sweet potatoes, red pepper and onion. In a small bowl, blend remaining ingredients; add to potato mixture and toss to coat. Chill. **Yield:** 10-12 servings.
—Mrs. Willard Wilson
Woodsfield, Ohio

German Potato Salad

Red potatoes remain firm—even when cooked—so they won't break apart when tossed. This potato salad tastes best served warm.

> 12 to 14 medium red potatoes (about 4 pounds), cooked and peeled
> 2 hard-cooked eggs, sliced
> 4 bacon strips, diced
> 1 medium onion, chopped
> 2 cups water
> 1/2 cup vinegar
> 1/2 cup sugar
> 2 tablespoons cornstarch
> 4 teaspoons salt
> 1-1/2 teaspoons prepared mustard
> 1 teaspoon celery seed
> 1/4 teaspoon pepper

Slice potatoes into a large bowl. Add eggs; set aside. In a skillet, cook bacon and onion. Drain, reserving 3 tablespoons drippings. Add bacon and onion to potato mixture. Add remaining ingredients to the drippings; cook and stir until slightly thickened. Pour over potato mixture and toss to coat. Serve warm. **Yield:** 8-10 servings.　　—Mary Fritch, Jasper, Indiana

German Potato Salad
Sweet Potato Salad
Red, White and Green Salad

Fresh Corn Salad

You'll especially love the taste of fresh corn in this salad. But you can prepare it anytime of the year by substituting 4 cups frozen or canned kernel corn.

8 ears fresh corn, husked
1/2 cup vegetable oil
1/4 cup cider vinegar
1-1/2 teaspoons lemon juice
1/4 cup minced fresh parsley
2 teaspoons sugar
1 teaspoon salt
1/2 teaspoon dried basil
1/8 to 1/4 teaspoon cayenne pepper
2 large tomatoes, seeded and coarsely chopped
1/2 cup chopped onion
1/3 cup chopped green pepper
1/3 cup chopped sweet red pepper

Place corn in a large saucepan and cover with water. Bring to a boil; cook for 5-7 minutes or until tender. Drain, cool and set aside. In a large bowl, mix the oil, vinegar, lemon juice, parsley, sugar, salt, basil and cayenne. Cut cooled corn off the cob (should measure 4 cups). Add corn, tomatoes, onion and peppers to the oil mixture. Mix well. Cover and chill for several hours or overnight. **Yield:** 10 servings.

—*Carol Shaffer, Cape Girardeau, Missouri*

Marinated Zucchini Salad

When you have lots of zucchini, reach for this do-ahead salad. A food processor makes easy work of slicing the zucchini.

6 small zucchini (about 1-1/4 pounds), thinly sliced
1/2 cup chopped green pepper
1/2 cup diced celery
1/2 cup diced onion
1 jar (2 ounces) diced pimientos, drained
2/3 cup vinegar
1/3 cup vegetable oil
1/2 cup sugar
3 tablespoons white wine vinegar
1/2 teaspoon salt
1/2 teaspoon pepper

Combine zucchini, green pepper, celery, onion and pimientos in a medium bowl; set aside. Combine remaining ingredients in a jar with tight-fitting lid; shake well. Pour over vegetables; toss gently. Cover and chill 8 hours or overnight. Serve with a slotted spoon. **Yield:** 8 servings.

—*Billie Blanton, Kingsport, Tennessee*

Fresh Corn Salad

Cutting Kernels From Corncobs

Stand one end of the cob on a cutting board. Starting at the top, run a sharp knife down the cob, cutting deeply to remove whole kernels. One medium cob yields about 1/2 cup of kernels.

Dilly Asparagus

Cherry Tomato Salad

(Pictured on page 68)

Keep this recipe handy when the garden is producing cherry tomatoes faster than you can pick them! For the best flavor, prepare and serve this salad the same day.

> 1 quart cherry tomatoes, halved
> 1/4 cup vegetable oil
> 3 tablespoons vinegar
> 1/4 cup minced fresh parsley
> 1 to 2 teaspoons minced fresh basil
> 1 to 2 teaspoons minced fresh oregano
> 1/2 teaspoon salt
> 1/2 teaspoon sugar

Place tomatoes in a shallow bowl. In a jar with a tight-fitting lid, combine the oil, vinegar, parsley, basil, oregano, salt and sugar; shake well. Pour over tomatoes. Cover and refrigerate. **Yield:** 6-8 servings.
—*Sally Sibley, St. Augustine, Florida*

Dilly Asparagus

You'll appreciate the fact that there's no last-minute preparation with this salad. Use a large skillet to cook the asparagus so you can keep it whole for a pretty presentation.

> 1 pound fresh asparagus, trimmed
> 1 jar (2 ounces) diced pimientos, drained
> 1/2 cup vinegar
> 1/4 cup olive *or* vegetable oil
> 1 tablespoon sugar
> 1 tablespoon chopped fresh parsley
> 2 teaspoons dried minced onion
> 1 teaspoon dill weed
> 1/2 teaspoon salt
> 1/4 teaspoon coarse ground black pepper

Cook the asparagus in a small amount of water until crisp-tender; drain. In a jar with a tight-fitting lid, combine remaining ingredients; shake well. Place asparagus in a shallow dish; pour marinade over asparagus. Cover and refrigerate for 8 hours. To serve, remove asparagus and arrange on a platter. With a slotted spoon, remove pimientos and onion from marinade and sprinkle over asparagus. **Yield:** 4 servings.
—*Margot Foster, Hubbard, Texas*

Sour Cream Cucumbers

For best flavor, chill these cucumbers at least 1 hour before serving. And for added interest, add a little fresh or dried dill.

> 2 large cucumbers, peeled and sliced
> 1 large onion, sliced into rings
> 3/4 cup light *or* nonfat sour cream
> 3 tablespoons cider vinegar
> 2 tablespoons sugar
> Salt and pepper to taste

In a bowl, combine the cucumbers and onion. Combine remaining ingredients and pour over cucumbers; mix well. Chill. **Yield:** 6-8 servings.
—*Karen Holt Redding, California*

Easy Sauerkraut Salad

Keep a can of sauerkraut and a jar of pimientos on the pantry shelf so you can make this recipe whenever you need a salad for the next day.

> 1 can (27 ounces) sauerkraut, rinsed and drained
> 1 cup finely chopped celery
> 1 cup finely chopped onion
> 1 jar (2 ounces) diced pimientos, drained
> 1 cup sugar

In a large bowl, combine the first four ingredients. Add sugar and mix well. Cover and refrigerate overnight. Serve chilled. **Yield:** 8-10 servings.
—*Diane Hays, Morris, Minnesota*

Creamy Coleslaw

Shredding Cabbage

To shred cabbage by hand, cut cabbage into wedges. Place cut side down on a cutting board. With a large sharp knife, cut into thin slices.

Norwegian Coleslaw

If you're having a busy week and need a salad ready when you are, consider this crunchy slaw. You prepare it a week before serving and can keep it in the refrigerator for 4 to 6 weeks!

> 1 medium head cabbage
> 1 tablespoon salt
> 1-1/2 cups sugar
> 1 cup vinegar
> 1 teaspoon mustard seed
> 1 teaspoon celery seed
> 2 cups chopped celery
> 1 small green pepper, chopped
> 1 small sweet red pepper, chopped
> 2 carrots, shredded

Shred cabbage and toss with salt. Cover and refrigerate at least 2 hours. In a saucepan, heat sugar, vinegar, mustard and celery seeds. Cook until the sugar dissolves, about 10 minutes. Cool completely. Add to the cabbage along with remaining vegetables; toss. Cover and refrigerate at least 1 week before serving. **Yield:** 12-16 servings. 🍎

—*Gerry Beveridge*
Beaufort, North Carolina

Creamy Coleslaw

For maximum flavor, coleslaw needs to be prepared several hours before serving to allow the cabbage to blend with the dressing.

> 3 to 4 cups shredded cabbage
> 1 cup shredded carrots
> 1 cup thinly sliced green pepper
> 1/2 cup mayonnaise *or* salad dressing
> 1/4 cup lemon juice
> 1 to 2 tablespoons sugar
> 1 tablespoon prepared mustard
> 1 teaspoon celery seed
> 1 teaspoon salt

In a large salad bowl, toss cabbage, carrots and green pepper. In a small bowl, combine the remaining ingredients. Pour over the cabbage mixture and toss to coat. Chill for at least 2-3 hours. **Yield:** 6-8 servings.

—*Dianne Esposite, New Middletown, Ohio*

cream cheese mixture. Spread in a 13-in. x 9-in. x 2-in. glass dish or three foil-lined 8-in. x 4-in. x 2-in. loaf pans. Cover and freeze. Remove from freezer 10-15 minutes before serving. Cut into squares or slices and serve on lettuce-lined plates. **Yield:** 24 servings.
—*Beverly Mix, Missoula, Montana*

Frozen Cranberry Salad

Are you busy entertaining around the holidays? Prepare this refreshing salad weeks before, cover with heavy-duty foil and freeze. Remove from the freezer 10 to 15 minutes before cutting and serving.

>   4 packages (3 ounces *each*) cream cheese,
>   softened
> 1/4 cup mayonnaise *or* salad dressing
>   2 tablespoons sugar
>   1 carton (16 ounces) frozen whipped topping,
>   thawed
>   2 cans (20 ounces *each*) crushed pineapple,
>   drained
>   2 cups chopped walnuts
>   2 cups flaked coconut
>   2 cans (16 ounces *each*) whole-berry cranberry
>   sauce
>   1 cup fresh *or* frozen cranberries, chopped,
>   optional
> Lettuce leaves

In a mixing bowl, blend cream cheese, mayonnaise and sugar. Fold in the whipped topping; set aside. In a large bowl, combine pineapple, nuts, coconut and cranberry sauce. Add cranberries if desired. Gently fold in

Three-Bean Salad

You'll prepare this classic dish for years to come. If you like zesty flavors, purchase a variety of dressing that has more zip.

>   1 pound fresh green beans
>   1 pound fresh wax beans
>   1 can (15-1/2 ounces) kidney beans, rinsed and
>   drained
>   1 cup fat-free Italian salad dressing
> 1/4 cup finely chopped onion
>   2 garlic cloves, minced
>   1 tablespoon dried parsley flakes

Cut green and wax beans into 1-1/4-in. pieces; place in a saucepan. Cover with water and cook for 8-10 minutes or until crisp-tender. Drain; place in a large bowl. Add remaining ingredients; mix gently. Cover and refrigerate for several hours. **Yield:** 12-16 servings. 🍎
—*Katie Koziolek, Hartland, Minnesota*

Layered Fresh Fruit Salad

Whether you serve this for your next brunch, as a salad for the ladies or as a dessert with cookies, it's bound to be a hit.

> **CITRUS SAUCE:**
> 2/3 cup orange juice
> 1/3 cup lemon juice
> 1/3 cup packed brown sugar
>   1 cinnamon stick
> 1/2 teaspoon grated orange peel
> 1/2 teaspoon grated lemon peel
> **FRUIT SALAD:**
>   2 cups cubed fresh pineapple
>   1 pint fresh strawberries, hulled and sliced
>   2 kiwifruit, peeled and sliced
>   3 medium bananas, sliced
>   2 oranges, peeled and sectioned
>   1 red grapefruit, peeled and sectioned
>   1 cup seedless red grapes

In a saucepan, bring sauce ingredients to a boil; simmer for 5 minutes. Cool. Meanwhile, in a large clear glass salad bowl, arrange fruit in layers in order listed. Remove cinnamon stick from the sauce and pour over fruit. Cover and refrigerate for several hours. **Yield:** 10-12 servings.   —*Page Alexander, Baldwin City, Kansas*

Sectioning Citrus Fruits

1 Cut a thin slice off the bottom and top of the fruit. Rest fruit cut side down on a cutting board. With a sharp paring knife, remove peel and white rind from fruit.

2 Holding fruit over a bowl, slice between the membrane of a section and the fruit until the knife reaches the center. Turn the knife and follow the membrane so the fruit is released. Repeat until all sections are removed.

Soups and Sandwiches

Cooks can depend on savory soups and filling sandwiches to satisfy their hungry families. After a few basic instructions, you, too, can create flavorful combinations like Peasant Bean Soup (p. 92) and Bacon-Stuffed Burgers (p. 98)!

There are as many kinds of soups as there are occasions to serve them. From nutritious broth-based varieties like chicken noodle and vegetable beef to the richer creamed soups and chowders, everyone has their favorites. Soup can be served as the first course to a large meal, as a perfect accompaniment to a sandwich or salad or as a meal in itself.

Basic Broth

Many recipes call for beef, chicken or turkey broth. You can make your own for just pennies and keep it on hand in the freezer.

> 2-1/2 pounds chicken pieces (wings, backs, necks and giblets) *or* a turkey carcass with some meat on the bones *or* 3 to 4 pounds meaty beef soup bones
> 2 to 3 celery ribs with leaves
> 2 carrots, cut into chunks
> 1 large onion
> 2 to 3 sprigs fresh parsley
> 2 bay leaves
> 1/2 teaspoon dried basil *or* thyme, optional
> 8 to 10 whole peppercorns, optional
> 1 garlic clove, optional
> 6 to 8 cups water

Place chicken pieces, turkey carcass or soup bones in a soup kettle or Dutch oven. Add celery, carrots, onion, parsley, bay leaves and seasonings if desired. For chicken broth, add 6 cups water. For turkey or beef broth, add 8 cups water. Cover and simmer 2 hours for chicken or turkey broth and 3-4 hours for beef broth. Remove meat and bones. Discard bones; save meat for another use. Strain broth, discarding vegetables and seasonings. Refrigerate broth for up to 3 days or freeze in ice cube trays or serving-size freezer containers. **Yield:** 6-7 cups.

Straining Broth

Remove meat and bones from broth. Line a colander with a double thickness of cheesecloth; place in a large heat-resistant bowl. Pour broth into colander. Discard vegetables, seasonings and cheesecloth.

Tips for Making Soup

- Because everyone likes different levels of salt in their dishes, you may want to add only a portion of the salt called for in a soup recipe at the beginning of the cooking process. When the soup is just about ready to be served, taste it and adjust the salt as needed.

- For golden homemade chicken and turkey broths, add a pinch of turmeric or simmer an unpeeled whole onion in the cooking liquid.

- Many broth-based soups and chili freeze well. It's best not to freeze soups that are prepared with sour cream, large chunks of potatoes, natural cheese or fruit.

- If you're watching your fat intake, you may want to skim the fat from the broth before adding the ingredients to complete the soup. See Step 3 under Making Chicken Noodle Soup (page 87).

Turkey Vegetable Soup

This is a great soup to prepare after the Thanksgiving turkey is almost gone. Canned turkey broth is not available, but you can easily make your own by using the Basic Broth recipe at left.

> 6 cups turkey *or* chicken broth
> 3 medium potatoes, peeled and chopped
> 2 carrots, chopped
> 2 celery ribs, chopped
> 2 medium onions, chopped
> 2 cans (15 ounces *each*) cream-style corn
> 2 cans (8-1/2 ounces *each*) lima beans, drained
> 1 to 2 cups chopped cooked turkey
> 1/2 to 1 teaspoon chili powder
> Salt and pepper to taste

In a large soup kettle or Dutch oven, combine broth, potatoes, carrots, celery and onions. Bring to a boil. Reduce heat; cover and simmer for 30 minutes or until the vegetables are tender. Add remaining ingredients. Cover and simmer for 10 minutes or until heated through. **Yield:** 12-14 servings (about 3-1/2 quarts). 🍎

—*Bonnie Smith, Clifton, Virginia*

Chicken Noodle Soup

Making Chicken Noodle Soup

1 Remove the giblets and excess fat from cavity of chicken. In a kettle or Dutch oven, combine chicken, giblets if desired, vegetables, water and seasonings.

2 Bring to a boil. Skim foam as it rises to the top of the water. Reduce heat; cover and simmer until the chicken is tender, 1 to 1-1/2 hours.

3 Remove chicken to a bowl; cool. Chill broth several hours or overnight; lift fat from surface of broth and discard.

4 Remove chicken from bones; discard skin and bones. Dice chicken; set aside. Bring soup to a boil; add noodles. Cook until tender. Stir in chicken; heat through.

Chicken Noodle Soup

You can prepare this comforting soup to the point of adding the noodles, then stir in the diced chicken and freeze. When ready to serve, simply defrost the soup, bring to a boil, add the noodles and cook as directed.

    1 broiler/fryer chicken (3 to 3-1/2 pounds)
2-1/2 quarts water
    1 cup diced carrots
    1 cup diced celery
    1 tablespoon salt
    2 chicken bouillon cubes
  1/4 cup chopped onion
  1/4 teapoon dried marjoram
  1/4 teaspoon dried thyme
  1/8 teaspoon pepper
    1 bay leaf
1-1/2 cups uncooked fine noodles

In a large saucepan, place all ingredients except noodles. Bring to a boil; skim foam from broth. Reduce heat; cover and simmer for 1 to 1-1/2 hours or until chicken is tender. Remove chicken from broth; allow to cool. Debone chicken; dice. Skim fat from broth; bring to a boil. Add noodles; cook until tender. Return chicken to pan; adjust salt to taste. Remove bay leaf before serving. **Yield:** 8-10 servings (2-1/2 quarts).

—*Diane Edgecomb, Humboldt, South Dakota*

Steak Soup

It can be difficult to brown more than 1 pound of meat at a time. Brown half the meat in half the butter and oil. Remove browned meat and repeat with the remaining butter, oil and meat. Return all meat to the kettle and continue with the recipe.

2 tablespoons butter *or* margarine
2 tablespoons vegetable oil
1-1/2 to 2 pounds lean round steak, cut into 1/2-inch cubes
1/4 cup chopped onion
3 tablespoons all-purpose flour
1 tablespoon paprika
1 teaspoon salt
1/4 teaspoon pepper
4 cups beef stock *or* broth
2 cups water
1 bay leaf
4 sprigs fresh parsley, chopped
2 sprigs celery leaves, chopped
1/2 teaspoon dried marjoram
1-1/2 cups cubed peeled potatoes
1-1/2 cups sliced carrots
1-1/2 cups chopped celery
1 can (6 ounces) tomato paste

In a large saucepan, melt butter over medium heat; add oil. Brown beef and onion. Combine flour, paprika, salt and pepper; sprinkle over beef and mix well. Stir in stock and water. Add bay leaf, parsley, celery leaves and marjoram; bring to a boil. Reduce heat; cover and simmer for 1 hour or until tender. Add potatoes, carrots and celery. Cover and simmer for 30-45 minutes or until vegetables are tender and soup begins to thicken. Stir in tomato paste; simmer, uncovered, for 15 minutes. Remove bay leaf before serving. **Yield:** 6 servings (2 quarts).
—*Mary Dice*
Chemainus, British Columbia

Steak Soup

Garden Vegetable Soup

When you don't have time to simmer a soup all day, adding sausage is a wonderful way to flavor soup quickly. This recipe makes a large batch, but don't worry about leftovers—it reheats beautifully!

1-1/2 cups chopped onion
1 cup chopped leeks
1 garlic clove, minced
1 tablespoon vegetable oil
8 cups chicken broth
8 cups cubed peeled potatoes
4 carrots, sliced
2 cups diced turnips
2 cups sliced fresh mushrooms
1 pound smoked sausage, thinly sliced and browned
6 ounces spinach, cut into thin strips
1 package (8 ounces) pasta wheels, cooked and drained
1/2 teaspoon salt
1/4 teaspoon pepper
Grated Parmesan cheese, optional

In a large soup kettle or Dutch oven, saute onion, leeks and garlic in oil until tender, about 5 minutes. Add broth, potatoes, carrots, turnips and mushrooms. Cover and cook over low heat until vegetables are tender, about 30-40 minutes. Add sausage and spinach; cook for 10 minutes. Add pasta, salt and pepper; heat through. Garnish with Parmesan cheese if desired. **Yield:** 16 servings (4 quarts).

—Kelly Rettiger, Emporia, Kansas

Beef and Barley Soup

Beef and Barley Soup

This is a soup that can be a filling whole meal with the addition of bread and a salad. Like many soups, this one is even better when reheated the next day.

1 tablespoon vegetable oil
2 pounds boneless short ribs
2 medium onions, coarsely chopped
3 large carrots, sliced
3 celery ribs, sliced
1 can (28 ounces) diced tomatoes, undrained
2 quarts water
4 chicken bouillon cubes
1/3 cup medium pearl barley

In a large soup kettle or Dutch oven, heat oil over medium-high; brown beef. Add onions, carrots, celery, tomatoes, water and bouillon; bring to a boil. Cover and simmer for 2 hours. Add barley; simmer 50-60 minutes longer or until beef and barley are tender. **Yield:** 10-12 servings (3-1/2 quarts). *—Phyllis Utterback Glendale, California*

Making Cream Soups

1 Melt butter in a saucepan over low heat; stir in the flour until well mixed. Cook and stir until the mixture is thick and bubbly.

2 Remove from the heat and gradually stir in broth. Return to the heat; cook and stir until mixture comes to a boil. Cook, stirring constantly, 1 minute longer. Finish recipe as directed.

Cheesy Vegetable Soup

Once the egg yolk and cream mixture and cheese are added, do not allow the soup to come to a boil. Otherwise, the soup will curdle.

        3 tablespoons butter *or* margarine
        3 tablespoons all-purpose flour
        2 cans (14-1/2 ounces *each*) chicken broth
        2 cups coarsely chopped broccoli
    3/4 cup chopped carrots
    1/2 cup chopped celery
        1 small onion, chopped
    1/2 teaspoon salt
    1/4 teaspoon garlic powder
    1/4 teaspoon dried thyme
        1 egg yolk
        1 cup whipping cream
    1-1/2 cups (6 ounces) shredded Swiss cheese

Melt butter in a large heavy saucepan over low heat; add flour. Cook and stir until thick and bubbly; remove from the heat. Gradually blend in broth. Return to the heat. Cook and stir until mixture comes to a boil. Cook and stir 1 minute longer. Add the next seven ingredients. Reduce heat; cover and simmer for 20 minutes or until vegetables are tender. In a small bowl, beat egg yolk and cream. Gradually stir in several tablespoonfuls of hot soup; return all to pan, stirring until slightly thickened. Simmer 15-20 minutes longer. Stir in cheese and heat over medium just until melted. Do not boil. **Yield:** 8-10 servings (2-1/2 quarts).

—*Amy Sibra, Big Sandy, Montana*

Wisconsin Potato Cheese Soup

Another way to make a thick creamy soup is to puree it in a blender. The soup ingredients should be cool before blending.

    1/3 cup chopped celery
    1/3 cup chopped onion
        2 tablespoons butter *or* margarine
        4 cups diced peeled potatoes
        3 cups chicken broth
        2 cups milk
    1-1/2 teaspoons salt
    1/4 teaspoon pepper
Dash paprika
        2 cups (8 ounces) shredded cheddar cheese
Croutons
Chopped fresh parsley

In a large saucepan, saute celery and onion in butter until tender. Add potatoes and broth. Cover and simmer until potatoes are tender, 12-15 minutes. Allow mixture to cool. In batches, puree potato mixture in a blender or food processor. Return to pan. Stir in milk and seasonings. Add the cheese and heat just until melted. Garnish with croutons and parsley. **Yield:** 8 servings (2 quarts).

—*Darlene Alexander Nekoosa, Wisconsin*

Garden-Fresh Tomato Soup

Here's a soup that can be prepared year-round. Use garden tomatoes in season and canned tomatoes all winter long.

  1/2 cup butter *or* margarine
  2 tablespoons olive *or* vegetable oil
  1 large onion, sliced
  2 sprigs fresh thyme *or* 1/2 teaspoon dried thyme
  4 fresh basil leaves *or* 1/2 teaspoon dried basil
  1 teaspoon salt
  1/4 teaspoon freshly ground black pepper
2-1/2 pounds diced fresh ripe tomatoes *or* 2 cans (16 ounces *each*) Italian tomatoes, undrained
  3 tablespoons tomato paste
  1/4 cup all-purpose flour
3-3/4 cups chicken broth, *divided*
  1 teaspoon sugar
  1 cup whipping cream
CROUTONS:
  1 large garlic clove, sliced lengthwise
  8 slices day-old French *or* Italian bread
  2 tablespoons olive *or* vegetable oil

In a large saucepan, heat butter and oil over medium-high. Add onion and seasonings. Cook, stirring occasionally, until the onion is soft. Add tomatoes and tomato paste; stir to blend. Simmer for 10 minutes. In a small bowl, combine flour and and 1/4 cup chicken broth until smooth. Stir into the tomato mixture. Add remaining broth. Simmer for 30 minutes, stirring frequently. Allow mixture to cool. In batches, puree tomato mixture in a blender or food processor. Return mixture to the pan. Add sugar and cream. Heat through, stirring occasionally. For croutons, rub garlic clove over both sides of the bread. Brush with oil and place on a baking sheet. Bake at 350° for 10-12 minutes or until toasted. Turn and toast other side for 2-3 minutes. Just before serving, top each bowl with one or two croutons. **Yield:** 8 servings (2 quarts).   —*Charlotte Goldbery Honey Grove, Pennsylvania*

New England Clam Chowder

The secret to this soup is to add the clams as the last step so that they only heat through. Extended heating or boiling will make the clams tough.

  4 medium potatoes, peeled and cubed
  2 medium onions, chopped
1/2 cup butter *or* margarine
3/4 cup all-purpose flour
  2 quarts milk
  3 cans (6-1/2 ounces *each*) chopped clams, undrained
  2 to 3 teaspoons salt
  1 teaspoon rubbed sage
  1 teaspoon ground thyme
1/2 teaspoon celery salt
1/2 teaspoon pepper
Minced fresh parsley

Place potatoes in a saucepan and cover with water; bring to a boil. Cover and cook until tender, 12-15 minutes. Meanwhile, in a soup kettle or Dutch oven, saute onions in butter until tender. Add flour; mix until smooth. Stir in milk. Cook over medium heat, stirring constantly, until thickened and bubbly. Drain potatoes; add to kettle. Add clams and remaining ingredients; heat through. **Yield:** 10-12 servings (3 quarts).

—*Rachel Nydam, Uxbridge, Massachusetts*

New England Clam Chowder

Peasant Bean Soup

Black-Eyed Pea Chowder

For a filling yet speedy soup, try this country favorite. You can substitute canned black beans for the black-eyed peas.

> **1 pound sliced bacon**
> **1 cup chopped celery**
> **1 cup chopped onion**
> **1 cup chopped green pepper**
> **2 cans (16 ounces *each*) black-eyed peas, rinsed and drained**
> **1 can (10-1/2 ounces) beef consomme**
> **2 cans (14-1/2 ounces *each*) stewed tomatoes, cut up**

In a large saucepan, cook bacon until crisp. Remove bacon; crumble and set aside. Drain, reserving 2 tablespoons of drippings; saute celery, onion and green pepper in drippings until tender. Add bacon and remaining ingredients; heat through. **Yield:** 8 servings (2-1/4 quarts). 🕐
—*Brenda Bates, Mesquite, Texas*

Peasant Bean Soup

(Also pictured on page 84)

This is a classic vegetable-bean soup. If desired, you could add several cups of cubed fully cooked ham to this recipe along with the vegetables.

> **1 pound dry great northern beans, washed and sorted**
> **3 carrots, sliced**
> **3 celery ribs, sliced**
> **2 medium onions, chopped**
> **1 garlic clove, minced**
> **1 to 2 bay leaves**
> **2 quarts water**
> **1 can (14-1/2 ounces) stewed tomatoes, cut up**
> **2 tablespoons olive *or* vegetable oil**
> **Salt and pepper to taste**

Place beans in a large saucepan; add water to cover by 2 in. Bring to a boil; boil for 2 minutes. Remove from the heat; cover and let stand 1 hour. Drain and discard liquid. In the same pan, combine beans, carrots, celery, onion, garlic, bay leaves and 2 qts. water; bring to a boil. Reduce heat; cover and simmer for 1 to 1-1/2 hours or until beans are tender. Add tomatoes, oil, salt and pepper. Simmer until heated through, about 15 minutes. Remove bay leaves before serving. **Yield:** 8 servings (2-1/2 quarts). 🍎
—*Bertha McClung Summersville, West Virginia*

Making a Spice Bag

To keep spices together so they can be removed from a saucepan or kettle, place them on several thicknesses of cotton cheesecloth that has been cut into 3-in. squares. Tie with kitchen string to form a bag.

Split Pea Vegetable Soup

Beef Lentil Soup

Lentils don't need to be soaked before cooking, so you can make this meal-in-one soup in just a few hours.

- 1 pound lean ground beef
- 1 quart water
- 1 can (48 ounces) tomato juice
- 2 cups chopped cabbage
- 1 cup dry lentils, rinsed
- 1 cup sliced carrots
- 1 cup sliced celery
- 1 cup chopped onion
- 1/2 cup chopped green pepper
- 1 teaspoon salt
- 1/2 teaspoon pepper
- 1/2 teaspoon dried thyme
- 1 bay leaf
- 2 beef bouillon cubes
- 1 package (10 ounces) frozen chopped spinach, thawed

In a large saucepan or Dutch oven, brown beef; drain. Add the next 13 ingredients; bring to a boil. Reduce heat and simmer, uncovered, for 1 to 1-1/2 hours or until the lentils and vegetables are tender. Add spinach and heat through. Remove bay leaf before serving. **Yield:** 8 servings (2-1/2 quarts).
—*Constance Turnbull, Arlington, Massachusetts*

Split Pea Vegetable Soup

Like lentils, split peas do not need to be soaked before cooking. The allspice adds a very full flavor to this pea soup.

- 1-1/2 cups dry split peas, rinsed
- 2-1/2 quarts water
- 7 to 8 whole allspice, tied in a cheesecloth bag
- 2 teaspoons salt
- 1/2 teaspoon pepper
- 6 large potatoes, peeled and cut into 1/2-inch cubes
- 6 carrots, chopped
- 2 medium onions, chopped
- 2 cups cubed fully cooked ham
- 1/2 medium head cabbage, shredded

In a soup kettle or Dutch oven, combine peas, water, allspice, salt and pepper; bring to a boil. Reduce heat; cover and simmer for 1 hour. Stir in potatoes, carrots, onions, ham and cabbage; return to a boil. Reduce heat; cover and simmer for 30 minutes or until vegetables are tender, stirring occasionally. Discard allspice before serving. **Yield:** 16-20 servings (about 5 quarts).
—*Maureen Ylitalo, Wahnapitae, Ontario*

Gazpacho

On a hot summer's day, this chilled soup will refresh your guests. This soup is best prepared the day before serving—making it convenient for the cook.

1 can (28 ounces) diced tomatoes, undrained
2 cups V-8 juice
2 tablespoons red wine vinegar
1 garlic clove, minced
1 teaspoon salt
1/2 teaspoon pepper
8 to 10 drops hot pepper sauce
1 package (6 ounces) seasoned croutons
1 medium cucumber, peeled and diced
1 medium green pepper, diced
1 bunch green onions with tops, sliced

In a large bowl, combine the first seven ingredients. Cover and refrigerate overnight. Stir well; ladle into soup bowls and garnish with croutons, cucumber, pepper and onions. **Yield:** 6-8 servings (2 quarts). 🍎
—*Sharon Balzer, Phoenix, Arizona*

Gazpacho

Taco Soup

If you like tacos, you'll love this soup. It's easy to assemble and needs to simmer a mere 30 minutes. Tortilla chips or warmed flour tortillas make a great accompaniment.

2 pounds lean ground beef
1 small onion, chopped
1-1/2 cups water
3 cans (14-1/2 ounces *each*) stewed tomatoes
1 can (16 ounces) lima beans, rinsed and drained
1 can (16 ounces) kidney beans, rinsed and drained
1 can (15 to 16 ounces) pinto beans, rinsed and drained
1 can (15-1/2 ounces) hominy, drained
3 cans (4 ounces *each*) chopped green chilies
1 teaspoon salt
1 teaspoon pepper
1 envelope taco seasoning mix
1 envelope ranch dressing mix
Shredded cheddar cheese, optional

In a large saucepan, brown beef and onion; drain. Add the next 11 ingredients; bring to a boil. Reduce heat; cover and simmer for 30 minutes. Top with cheese if desired. **Yield:** 10 servings (2-1/2 quarts). 🕐
—*Tonya Jones, Sundown, Texas*

Pronto Beef Vegetable Soup

Here's a budget and time stretcher! Leftover roast beef combined with vegetables and herbs can make a meal in 30 minutes. Serve with generous slices of French bread for a satisfying supper.

4 cans (8 ounces *each*) tomato sauce
3 cups cubed cooked roast beef
1 cup diced carrots
1 cup diced peeled potatoes
1 cup corn
1 cup cut green beans
1/2 cup chopped onion
1/2 teaspoon salt
1 teaspoon dried basil
1 teaspoon dried oregano
1 tablespoon chopped fresh parsley

In a large saucepan, combine all ingredients. Bring to a boil; reduce heat and simmer, uncovered, for 30 minutes or until vegetables are tender. If desired, add 1/2 to 1 cup water to thin the soup. **Yield:** 6-8 servings (2 quarts). 🕐 🍎
—*Dottie Casale, Ilion, New York*

Classic Chili

This basic chili recipe tastes great as is. But feel free to add more of your favorite spices or other ingredients.

2 medium onions, chopped
1 medium green pepper, chopped
1/2 cup chopped celery
1 tablespoon vegetable oil
2 pounds lean ground beef
2 cans (28 ounces *each*) diced tomatoes, undrained
1 can (8 ounces) tomato sauce
1 cup water
2 tablespoons Worcestershire sauce
1 to 2 tablespoons chili powder
1 teaspoon garlic powder
1 teaspoon dried oregano
1 teaspoon salt
1/2 teaspoon pepper
2 cans (16 ounces *each*) kidney beans, rinsed and drained

In a soup kettle or Dutch oven, saute onions, green pepper and celery in oil until tender, about 5 minutes. Add beef and cook until browned; drain. Stir in tomatoes, tomato sauce, water, Worcestershire sauce and seasonings. Bring to a boil; reduce heat. Cover and simmer for 1-1/2 hours, stirring occasionally. Add kidney beans. Simmer, uncovered, 10 minutes longer. **Yield:** 10-12 servings (3 quarts). —*Marjorie Carey Belfry, Montana*

Classic Chili

Santa Fe Chicken Chili

Looking for a change of pace from basic ground beef chili? Chili with nuggets of chicken is the answer. Make this recipe as spicy as you like by varying the chili powder, cayenne pepper and the heat level of the salsa.

2 pounds boneless skinless chicken breasts, cut into 1/2-inch cubes
4 medium sweet red peppers, chopped
2 large onions, chopped
4 garlic cloves, minced
1/4 cup olive *or* vegetable oil
3 tablespoons chili powder
2 teaspoons ground cumin
1/4 teaspoon cayenne pepper
1 can (28 ounces) diced tomatoes, undrained
2 cans (14-1/2 ounces *each*) chicken broth
2 cans (16 ounces *each*) kidney beans, rinsed and drained
1 jar (12 ounces) salsa
1 package (10 ounces) frozen corn
1/2 teaspoon salt
1/2 teaspoon pepper

In a soup kettle or Dutch oven over medium heat, saute chicken, peppers, onions and garlic in oil until the chicken is no longer pink and vegetables are tender, about 5 minutes. Add chili powder, cumin and cayenne pepper; cook and stir for 1 minute. Add the tomatoes and broth; bring to a boil. Reduce heat; simmer, uncovered, for 15 minutes. Stir in remaining ingredients; bring to a boil. Reduce heat; cover and simmer for 10-15 minutes or until the chicken is tender. **Yield:** 14-16 servings (4 quarts). —*Sonia Gallant St. Thomas, Ontario*

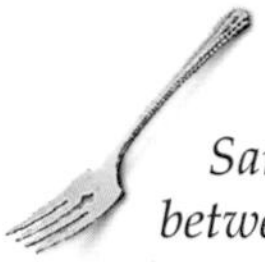

Sandwiches are often defined as a portable meal between two pieces of bread, perfect for taking to picnics, school or work. Sandwiches come in a variety of sizes and shapes. Many are hand-held, while some need to be eaten with a knife and fork. Sandwiches can be served hot or cold, presented open-faced, stacked high or enclosed in a tortilla wrapper.

Grilled Ham and Egg Salad Sandwiches

When plain egg salad just won't do, try this hefty sandwich. Like French toast, this sandwich needs to be served hot, right from the skillet or griddle, to be at its best.

6 hard-cooked eggs, chopped
1 cup diced fully cooked ham
1/2 cup diced celery
1/2 cup mayonnaise
1 tablespoon diced onion
2 teaspoons prepared mustard
1/2 teaspoon salt
1/4 teaspoon pepper
12 slices whole wheat *or* white bread
Vegetable oil
BATTER:
1/2 cup cornmeal
1/2 cup all-purpose flour
1 teaspoon baking powder
1 teaspoon salt
2 cups milk
2 eggs, lightly beaten

Combine eggs, ham, celery, mayonnaise, onion, mustard, salt and pepper; spread on six slices of bread. Top with remaining bread and set aside. In a bowl, whisk batter ingredients until well blended. Heat about 1/2 in. of oil in a large deep skillet. Dip sandwiches into the batter. Fry in hot oil for 3 minutes on each side or until golden brown. Drain on paper towels. **Yield:** 6 servings.

—Beverly Stiger
Wolf Creek, Montana

Tips for Tasty Sandwiches

- If you enjoy grilled sandwiches, you may want to invest in an electric or stovetop griddle, which will allow you to grill four to six sandwiches at a time.
- Mayonnaise is a favorite spread for sandwiches. But if you want to add extra flavor to a basic roast beef, turkey or chicken sandwich, stir in any one of these ingredients to 1 cup mayonnaise: 1 to 2 tablespoons Dijon mustard and 1 teaspoon dill weed; 2 tablespoons *each* chopped green onions and prepared horseradish; 1 tablespoon tomato paste and 1/2 teaspoon dried basil; 1 to 2 tablespoons seeded chopped jalapenos.
- When assembling sandwiches ahead, spread them with butter or margarine to seal the bread and keep the meat's moisture from being absorbed into the bread.
- Enhance a plain cooked hamburger with toppings such as guacamole, salsa, cheese spreads, mayonnaise, Swiss cheese, blue cheese, sauteed mushrooms or strips of crisp bacon.

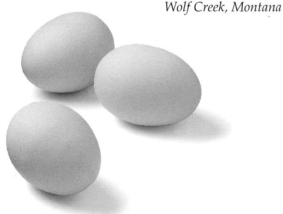

Preparing Batter-Dipped Sandwiches

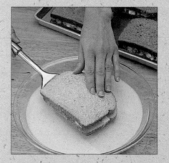

1 Combine filling ingredients and spread over half of the bread slices. Top with remaining bread; set aside. In a shallow bowl, whisk batter ingredients together. Dip both sides of the sandwich into the batter.

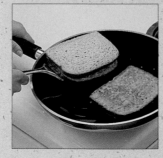

2 Fry over medium-high heat for 3 minutes on each side or until golden brown. Drain on paper towels; serve immediately.

Big Sandwich

Big Sandwich

Perfect for casual entertaining, this sandwich is impressive and easy to prepare. Assemble the recipe earlier in the day and wrap in foil. Refrigerate until it's time to pop it in the oven. Serve it with coleslaw or potato salad and you have a complete meal!

> 1 unsliced round loaf of bread (8 inches)
> 2 tablespoons prepared horseradish
> 1/2 pound thinly sliced cooked roast beef
> 2 tablespoons prepared mustard
> 1/2 pound thinly sliced fully cooked ham *or* turkey
> 4 slices Swiss cheese
> 2 tablespoons mayonnaise
> 1 small tomato, thinly sliced
> 6 bacon strips, cooked
> 4 slices American cheese
> 1 small onion, thinly sliced
> 1/4 cup butter *or* margarine, melted
> 1 tablespoon sesame seeds
> 1/2 teaspoon onion salt

Slice bread horizontally into five equal layers. Spread bottom layer with horseradish; top with roast beef. Place the next slice of bread over beef; spread with mustard and top with ham or turkey and Swiss cheese. Add the next slice of bread; spread with mayonnaise and top with tomato and bacon. Add the next slice of bread; top with American cheese and onion. Cover with remaining bread. Combine butter, sesame seeds and onion salt; brush over top and sides of loaf. Place on a baking sheet; loosely tent with heavy-duty foil. Bake at 400° for 15-20 minutes or until heated through. Carefully slice into wedges. **Yield:** 8 servings.

—*Margaret Yost, Tipp City, Ohio*

Chicken Salad Sandwiches

When you roast a chicken or turkey, plan to reserve 2 cups of cooked meat for this favorite filling that can be served on white or wheat bread or in pita pockets.

> 2 cups diced cooked chicken
> 2 hard-cooked eggs, chopped
> 1 small cucumber, diced
> 1 celery rib, diced
> 1/3 cup mayonnaise *or* salad dressing
> 1/4 teaspoon salt
> 1/8 teaspoon ground mustard
> 1/8 teaspoon white pepper

Bread *or* pita bread

In a bowl, combine the first eight ingredients. Serve on bread or in pita bread. **Yield:** 4-6 servings. ○

—*Anna Mowan, Spencerville, Indiana*

Ham Buns

Serve these do-ahead sandwiches in mini buns when you need a substantial appetizer that serves many. Or for an easy meal on a busy day, serve with full-size buns and soup. To save preparation time, chop the ham in a food processor or meat grinder.

1/2 cup butter *or* margarine, softened
1 small onion, grated
1 tablespoon poppy seeds
2 teaspoons Worcestershire sauce
2 teaspoons prepared mustard
1-1/4 cups finely chopped fully cooked ham (about 8 ounces)
1 cup (4 ounces) shredded Swiss cheese
6 to 8 hamburger buns *or* 16 to 20 mini buns, split

In a bowl, mix butter, onion, poppy seeds, Worcestershire sauce and mustard until well blended. Add ham and cheese; mix well. Divide evenly among buns. Place in a shallow baking pan and cover with foil. Bake at 350° for 15-20 minutes or until hot. **Yield:** 6-8 main-dish or 16-20 appetizer servings.
—Esther Shank
Harrisonburg, Virginia

Ham Buns

Preparing Stuffed Burgers

1 Shape ground beef mixture into 16 patties and divide bacon-mushroom mixture over half of the patties.

2 Top with remaining plain patties and press edges together to seal. Cook as directed.

Bacon-Stuffed Burgers

(Pictured on page 85)

When forming ground beef into patties, lightly form them rather than compacting with force. Gentle shaping will result in more tender burgers.

4 bacon strips
1/4 cup chopped onion
1 can (4 ounces) mushroom stems and pieces, drained and finely chopped
1 pound ground beef
1 pound bulk pork sausage
1/4 cup grated Parmesan cheese
1/2 teaspoon pepper
1/4 teaspoon garlic powder
2 tablespoons steak sauce
8 hamburger buns, split and toasted
Lettuce leaves, optional

Cook bacon until crisp. Remove bacon to paper towels; drain, reserving 2 tablespoons drippings. Saute onion in drippings until tender. Crumble bacon; add with mushrooms to skillet and set aside. In a large bowl, combine beef, pork, cheese, pepper, garlic powder and steak sauce. Shape into 16 patties. Divide bacon mixture over half of the patties. Place remaining patties on top and press edges tightly to seal. Grill over medium heat until *well-done* (pork sausage in burgers requires thorough cooking). Serve on buns with lettuce if desired. **Yield:** 8 servings.
—Sandy McKenzie
Braham, Minnesota

Reuben Sandwiches

Whether you use leftover corned beef or buy it sliced from the deli, this sandwich is guaranteed to please. To easily slice homemade corned beef, chill the cooked meat overnight and use a sharp carving knife.

> 12 ounces thinly sliced canned *or* fully cooked
>   corned beef
> 8 slices light *or* dark rye bread
> 1 can (8 ounces) sauerkraut, drained
> 1/2 cup Thousand Island dressing
> 4 slices Swiss cheese

Butter *or* margarine

Arrange corned beef on four slices of bread. Top each with a quarter of the sauerkraut, 2 tablespoons of dressing and a slice of cheese. Top with remaining bread. In a skillet over medium heat, melt 2-3 tablespoons butter. Toast sandwiches until bread is lightly browned on one side. Turn sandwiches and brown other side, adding butter if necessary. Cook until cheese is melted and meat is heated through. **Yield:** 4 servings.

—*Kathy Jo Scott, Hemingford, Nebraska*

Pronto Pizza Burgers

Served with salad or soup, these pizza-style sandwiches make a great meal. Adding 1 to 2 teaspoons fennel seeds to the beef mixture will make the sandwiches taste even more like real pizza!

> 1 pound ground beef
> 1/3 cup grated Parmesan cheese
> 1 tablespoon chopped onion
> 1 tablespoon tomato paste
> 1 teaspoon dried oregano
> 1/2 teaspoon salt
> 1/4 teaspoon pepper
> 4 English muffins, split
> 8 slices tomato
> 8 slices mozzarella cheese

Additional oregano, optional

In a bowl, mix beef, Parmesan cheese, onion, tomato paste, oregano, salt and pepper just until combined. Toast muffins in the broiler until lightly browned. Divide meat mixture among muffins. Broil 4 in. from the heat for 8-10 minutes or until meat is cooked. Top with tomato and mozzarella cheese. Return to broiler until cheese is melted. Sprinkle with oregano if desired. **Yield:** 4 servings. —*Karen Kruse, Gahanna, Ohio*

Pounding Chicken Breasts

Place boneless chicken breast between two pieces of waxed paper. Starting in center and working out to edges, pound lightly with a meat mallet's flat side until the chicken is even in thickness.

Spicy Chicken Heroes

When you can't grill outdoors, use your broiler to cook the chicken. Broil 4 to 5 inches from the heat.

> 6 boneless skinless chicken breast halves
> 1 tablespoon vegetable oil
> 1/4 to 1/2 teaspoon pepper
> 1/4 to 1/2 teaspoon crushed red pepper flakes
> 1/4 to 1/2 teaspoon chili powder
> 6 slices Monterey Jack cheese
> 6 French *or* Italian rolls, split
> 2 tablespoons butter *or* margarine, melted

Lettuce leaves and tomato slices
Salsa *or* picante sauce, optional

Pound chicken breasts slightly to flatten evenly. Brush both sides with oil. Combine seasonings; sprinkle on both sides of chicken. Grill over medium-hot heat for 6-8 minutes; turn and grill 4-6 minutes more or until chicken is no longer pink. Top with cheese; allow to melt, about 2 minutes. Meanwhile, brush rolls with butter; grill just until toasted. Place lettuce, tomato and chicken on rolls; top with salsa or picante sauce if desired. **Yield:** 6 servings.

—*Bonnie Link*
Goose Creek, South Carolina

Spicy Chicken Heroes

French Dip Sandwiches

Shredding Meat For Sandwiches

Remove meat from broth and place in a shallow pan. With two forks or a pastry blender, pull meat into thin shreds.

French Dip Sandwiches

Make this in your slow cooker one day…reheat and serve it the next. What could be easier?

> 1 lean beef roast (3 to 4 pounds)
> 1/2 cup light soy sauce
> 1 low-sodium beef bouillon cube
> 1 bay leaf
> 3 to 4 whole peppercorns
> 1 teaspoon dried rosemary, crushed
> 1 teaspoon dried thyme
> 1 teaspoon garlic powder
> Hard rolls *or* sliced French bread

Trim and discard all visible fat from roast. Place in a slow cooker. Combine soy sauce, bouillon and spices; pour over roast. Add water to almost cover. Cover and cook on low for 10-12 hours or until meat is very tender. Remove meat; strain and reserve broth. Shred meat with two forks. Serve on rolls or bread with broth for dipping. **Yield:** 12 servings. 🍎

—*Dianne Joy Richardson, Colorado Springs, Colorado*

Curried Egg Salad Sandwiches

For a different twist to egg salad, try this curried version. If you prefer a stronger curry flavor, first taste the mixture before adding more curry.

> 1/2 cup mayonnaise
> 1/2 teaspoon honey
> 1/2 teaspoon curry powder
> Dash ground ginger
> 6 hard-cooked eggs, coarsely chopped
> 3 green onions, sliced
> 6 slices whole wheat bread
> Tomato slices, optional

In a bowl, blend mayonnaise, honey, curry and ginger. Stir in eggs and onions. Spread on three slices of bread; top with a tomato slice if desired and remaining bread. **Yield:** 3 servings. ○

—*Joyce McDowell Winchester, Ohio*

Sloppy Joes

Everyone loves sloppy joes. This recipe serves 6, but if you need to feed more, double or triple as needed.

1 tablespoon butter *or* margarine
1 pound ground beef
1/2 cup chopped onion
1 medium green pepper, chopped
3/4 cup ketchup
1/4 cup water
1 tablespoon sugar
2 tablespoons prepared mustard
1 tablespoon vinegar
Salt and pepper to taste
6 hamburger buns, split

In a skillet, melt butter over medium-high heat. Cook the beef, onion and green pepper until meat is browned and vegetables are tender; drain. Add all remaining ingredients except buns. Simmer, uncovered for 15 minutes. Serve on buns. **Yield:** 6 servings. —*Alpha Wilson Roswell, New Mexico*

Italian Sausage Sandwiches

When shopping for Italian sausages, you may have a choice of mild (sometimes called sweet) or hot and spicy. Select the one that suits your tastes and that of your guests.

10 sweet *or* hot Italian link sausages
2 large green peppers, thinly sliced
1/4 cup chopped onion
1 can (8 ounces) tomato sauce
1 can (6 ounces) tomato paste
1/2 cup water
1-1/2 teaspoons sugar
2 garlic cloves, minced
1 teaspoon dried basil
1/2 teaspoon dried oregano
1/2 teaspoon salt
10 sandwich buns, split
Shredded mozzarella cheese, optional

In a large Dutch oven, brown sausages; drain, reserving 1 tablespoon drippings. Saute peppers and onion in drippings until crisp-tender; drain. Return sausages to pan along with tomato sauce and paste, water, sugar, garlic, basil, oregano and salt; bring to a boil. Reduce heat; cover and simmer for 30 minutes. Serve on buns. Top with cheese if desired. **Yield:** 10 servings.
—*Mike Yaeger, Brookings, South Dakota*

Barbecued Pork Sandwiches

To easily remove excess fat, refrigerate mixture until it is cold; skim and discard fat.

1 pork shoulder roast (about 5 pounds), trimmed and cut into 1-inch cubes
2 medium onions, coarsely chopped
2 tablespoons chili powder
1/2 teaspoon salt
1-1/2 cups water
1 cup ketchup
1/4 cup vinegar
16 hamburger buns, split

In a Dutch oven, combine meat, onions, chili powder, salt, water, ketchup and vinegar. Cover and simmer for 4 hours or until the meat falls apart easily. Skim off excess fat. Remove meat with a slotted spoon, reserving cooking liquid. Shred the meat with two forks or a pastry blender. Return to the cooking liquid and heat through. Serve on buns. **Yield:** 16 servings.
—*Thelma Waggoner, Hopkinsville, Kentucky*

Barbecued Pork Sandwiches

Beef and Ground Beef

Whether you prepare classic Summer Stuffed Peppers (p. 123), old-fashioned Perfect Pot Roast (p. 107) or any of the other hearty dishes in this chapter, beef and ground beef make favorite staples in today's country kitchens.

From tenderloin, T-bones and rib eyes to round steak, briskets and ground chuck, there are beef cuts to fit every budget and every occasion. Plus, beef lends itself to a wide variety of cooking methods. It's no wonder cooks of every generation have come to depend on beef's versatility and great flavor.

Tips for Buying and Cooking Cuts of Beef

- Select beef with a bright cherry-red color, without any gray or brown patches.

- Make sure the package is cold and has no holes or tears.

- For best quality, purchase beef before the "sell by" date on the packaging.

- The amount of beef you need to buy varies with the cut selected. Follow these guidelines: 2-1/2 servings per 1 pound of bone-in roasts and steaks; 2-1/2 to 3-1/2 servings per 1 pound of boneless cuts that will be trimmed of fat; 3 to 4 servings per 1 pound of lean boneless cuts without waste, such as eye of round, flank and tenderloin.

- Less tender cuts of beef can be marinated to tenderize and add flavor. A tenderizing marinade must contain an acidic ingredient such as lemon juice, vinegar, yogurt or wine. Marinades without an acid can be used to flavor tender cuts.

- Always marinate meat in the refrigerator, turning or stirring several times to evenly coat. Less tender cuts need 6 to 24 hours to tenderize. Marinating longer than 24 hours will result in a mushy surface texture.

- If a marinade is to be used later for basting or serving sauce, reserve a portion of it before adding the beef. A marinade that has been in contact with the raw beef must be brought to a full rolling boil before it can be used as a sauce.

- Allow 1/4 to 1/2 cup marinade for each 1 to 2 pounds of beef.

- A "rub" is a blend of seasonings, such as fresh or dried herbs and spices, applied to the surface of uncooked cuts, such as roasts or steaks. Rubs add a burst of flavor to the meat but do not tenderize.

- Choose an appropriate cooking method for the cut you've selected. Tender cuts can be cooked quickly using dry-heat methods (broiling, grilling, pan-broiling, pan-frying, roasting and stir-frying); less tender cuts need to be cooked slowly using moist-heat methods (braising and cooking in liquid).

Basic Cooking Methods for Beef

Braising

Recommended for less tender cuts such as chuck roasts, round steak and short ribs. Brown beef on all sides in a small amount of butter, margarine or oil. Add a small amount of liquid (1/2 to 2 cups) to the pan. Cover tightly; simmer gently over low heat for 1-2 hours or bake at 325° for 2-3 hours or until tender. When the meat has finished cooking, the pan juices can be reduced or thickened for gravy. (See Reducing Pan Juices for Gravy on page 105 or Thickening Pan Juices from Braised Beef on page 106.)

Broiling

Recommended for tender cuts such as sirloin, T-bones, porterhouse steaks, rib and rib eye steaks, marinated flank steak, marinated top round or chuck shoulder steaks and ground beef patties. Place meat on a broiler pan (3 to 4 in. from the heat for cuts 3/4 in. thick; 4 to 6 in. from the heat for cuts 1 to 1-1/2 in. thick). Broil, turning once, until meat is browned and cooked to desired doneness.

Cooking in Liquid

Recommended for less tender cuts such as beef stew meat, brisket or beef shanks. Coat beef with a seasoned flour mixture; brown on all sides in a small amount of butter, margarine or oil. Cover beef with liquid; bring to a boil. Reduce heat to low; cover and simmer 1-2 hours or until beef is tender. When the meat has finished cooking, the cooking liquid can be thickened for gravy. (See Thickening Pan Juices from Braised Beef on page 106.)

Grilling

Recommended for the same tender cuts as for broiling. Preheat the grill to medium heat. Season beef according to recipe; place on cooking grate directly over heat. Grill to desired doneness, turning once. Cuts thicker than 1 in. should be covered during cooking. (See Grilling Guidelines on page 120.)

Pan-Broiling

Recommended for tender cuts such as steak, tenderloin and ground beef patties. Preheat a heavy nonstick skillet over medium for 3 minutes. Season the beef as desired. (No fat is required.) Pan-broil, uncovered, until browned and cooked to desired doneness, turning once.

Pan-Frying

Recommended for thin, tender beef cuts such as liver and cubed steaks. In

a heavy skillet over medium, heat a small amount of butter, margarine or oil. Season the beef as desired. (Do not add liquid.) Pan-fry, uncovered, until browned and cooked to desired doneness, turning occasionally.

Roasting

Recommended for tender cuts such as rib roasts, rib eye roasts and whole tenderloin. For this dry-heat method, the roast is cooked without water or liquid in an open roaster. (See the Roasting Beef chart on page 114 for specific information.)

Reducing Pan Juices for Gravy

To thicken pan juices without flour, remove the meat to a warm serving platter. Bring the pan juices or cooking liquid to a boil; cook, uncovered, until the liquid evaporates enough that it thickens to a gravy consistency.

Stir-Frying

Recommended for tender cuts or cuts that have been marinated or cut into thin strips. In a wok or heavy skillet over medium-high heat, stir-fry meat in a small amount of oil, stirring constantly to ensure even cooking. (See the stir-frying basics on page 116.)

Southwestern Beef Brisket

Serve this dish with mashed potatoes, cooked noodles or on a bun as a sandwich. It's perfect for buffet suppers.

      1 fresh beef brisket (3 pounds)
      1 teaspoon salt
  1/4 to 1/2 teaspoon pepper
      2 tablespoons vegetable oil
1-1/2 cups water
      1 can (8 ounces) tomato sauce
      1 small onion, chopped
      2 tablespoons red wine vinegar
      1 tablespoon chili powder
      1 teaspoon dried oregano
  3/4 teaspoon ground cumin
  1/2 teaspoon garlic powder
  1/4 teaspoon salt
  1/8 to 1/4 teaspoon cayenne pepper
      3 medium sweet red peppers, cut into strips
1-1/2 cups sliced carrots (1-inch chunks)

Season beef with salt and pepper. In a Dutch oven, heat oil over medium-high; brown beef on both sides. Drain. Combine the next 10 ingredients; pour over meat. Cover and bake at 325° for 2 hours. Add red peppers and carrots; bake 1 hour longer or until meat is tender. Remove meat and vegetables to a warm serving platter. Skim fat. Reduce pan juices for gravy (see tip above). Slice meat thinly across the grain; serve with vegetables and gravy. **Yield:** 8-10 servings.
                                    —Lois McAtee, Oceanside, California

Southwestern Beef Brisket

Mom's Roast Beef

Coffee is the secret ingredient in this recipe—it gives the pan juices rich color and flavor.

  1 tablespoon vegetable oil
  1 eye of round beef roast (about 2-1/2 pounds)

  1 medium onion, chopped
  1 cup brewed coffee
3/4 cup water
  1 beef bouillon cube
  2 teaspoons dried basil
  1 teaspoon dried rosemary, crushed
  1 garlic clove, minced
  1 teaspoon salt
1/2 teaspoon pepper

Mom's Roast Beef

Heat oil in a Dutch oven over medium-high. Brown roast on all sides. Add onion and cook until transparent. Add coffee, water, bouillon, basil, rosemary, garlic, salt and pepper. Cover and simmer for 2-1/2 hours or until meat is tender. Remove to a warm serving platter. Skim fat. Thicken pan juices for gravy (see tip below); serve with sliced meat. **Yield:** 8-10 servings.
                              —Linda Gaido
                    New Brighton, Pennsylvania

Midget Pot Roast

Beef shanks are traditionally used for making homemade beef broth and soup. Here, they make individual pot roasts complete with potatoes, vegetable and gravy. Double or triple the recipe as necessary.

  2 beef shanks (about 1-1/2 pounds)
  1 tablespoon all-purpose flour
  1 cup water
1/2 cup beef broth
  1 tablespoon onion soup mix
  1 garlic clove, minced
  1 teaspoon Worcestershire sauce
1/4 teaspoon dried thyme
  1 large potato, peeled and cut into eighths
  2 medium carrots, cut into 2-inch lengths
  6 pearl onions

Sprinkle meat with flour; place in a shallow 2-qt. baking dish. Mix water, broth, soup mix, garlic, Worcestershire sauce and thyme; pour over meat. Cover and bake at 325° for 1-1/2 hours. Turn meat; add potato, carrots and onions. Cover and bake 30-45 minutes longer or until the meat and vegetables are tender. Remove meat and vegetables to a warm serving platter. Skim fat. Thicken pan juices for gravy (see tip at left); serve with meat and vegetables. **Yield:** 2 servings.

—*Marian Platt, Sequim, Washington*

Thickening Pan Juices from Braised Beef

Remove meat to a warm serving platter; skim fat from pan juices. (See Step 1 of Making Pan Gravy from Roasted Meats on page 145.) Measure juices and return to pan. For each cup of juices, combine 3 tablespoons all-purpose flour and 1/3 cup cold water; mix until smooth. Stir flour mixture into pan; bring to a boil, stirring constantly. Cook until thickened, adding additional water if necessary. Season with salt and pepper.

Old-World Sauerbraten

Perfect Pot Roast

(Pictured on page 102)

This classic pot roast is full of flavor because of the garlic and thyme added to the braising liquid. Leftovers can be frozen in individual portions for quick meals at a moment's notice.

   1 teaspoon seasoned salt
   1/2 teaspoon onion powder
   1/4 teaspoon pepper
   1/8 teaspoon garlic powder
   1 beef chuck roast (3 to 4 pounds)
   1 tablespoon olive *or* vegetable oil
   3/4 cup water
   1 large onion, chopped
   1/4 cup chopped green pepper
   2 garlic cloves, minced
   2 bay leaves
   2 teaspoons dried parsley flakes
   1/4 teaspoon dried thyme
Hot cooked potatoes and carrots

Combine the first four ingredients; rub over roast. In a Dutch oven, heat oil over medium-high. Brown roast on all sides; drain. Add water, onion, green pepper and seasonings. Cover and bake at 325° for 2-1/2 to 3 hours or until tender. Remove roast to a warm serving platter. Discard bay leaves. Skim fat. Thicken pan juices for gravy (refer to page 106); serve with roast, potatoes and carrots. **Yield:** 8-10 servings.
—*Melody Sroufe*
Wichita, Kansas

Old-World Sauerbraten

In most sauerbraten recipes, the meat marinates in a brine to tenderize and flavor for several days before being cooked. This recipe saves you time by simmering the meat in the brine for just a few hours. The gingersnaps complete the traditional sweet-and-sour flavor and thicken the gravy.

   2 tablespoons vegetable oil
   1 boneless beef rump roast (5 to 6 pounds)
   2 large onions, sliced
   2 cups water
   1 cup vinegar
   1/4 cup lemon juice
   4 to 5 tablespoons ketchup
   3 bay leaves
   6 whole cloves
   2 teaspoons salt
   1/2 teaspoon pepper
   12 gingersnaps, crushed

In a Dutch oven, heat oil over medium-high. Brown beef on all sides; drain. Add the next nine ingredients; bring to a boil. Reduce heat; cover and simmer for 3 hours or until the meat is tender. During the last 30 minutes, stir in gingersnaps. Remove meat to a warm serving platter; discard bay leaves and cloves. Reduce pan juices for gravy (refer to page 105); serve over sliced meat. **Yield:** 15-18 servings.
—*Phyllis Berenson, Cincinnati, Ohio*

Caraway Pot Roast

Braising Beef

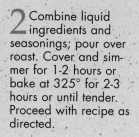

1 Heat oil in a Dutch oven over medium-high. Brown roast on all sides, turning with a sturdy meat fork.

2 Combine liquid ingredients and seasonings; pour over roast. Cover and simmer for 1-2 hours or bake at 325° for 2-3 hours or until tender. Proceed with recipe as directed.

Caraway Pot Roast

Caraway seeds and Worcestershire sauce add a rich robust flavor to the roast and gravy. Prepare this recipe with either a chuck or rump roast using the braising method.

> 3 tablespoons vegetable oil
> 1 beef chuck roast *or* boneless rump roast
>   (3 pounds)

> 1 cup hot water
> 1-1/2 teaspoons beef bouillon granules
> 1/4 cup ketchup
> 1 tablespoon Worcestershire sauce
> 1 tablespoon dried minced onion
> 2 teaspoons caraway seeds
> 1 teaspoon salt
> 1/2 teaspoon pepper
> 2 bay leaves

Hot cooked potatoes and carrots

In a Dutch oven, heat oil over medium-high. Brown roast on all sides; drain. Combine water, bouillon, ketchup, Worcestershire sauce, onion, caraway, salt and pepper; pour over roast. Add bay leaves. Cover and bake at 325° for 3 hours or until tender. Remove roast to a warm serving platter. Discard bay leaves. Skim fat. Thicken pan juices for gravy (refer to page 106); serve with roast, potatoes and carrots. **Yield:** 8-10 servings.

—*Beverly Swanson, Red Oak, Iowa*

Old-Fashioned Swiss Steak

If you'd like to remove some of the fat from the pan juices, take a piece of paper towel and drag it across the surface of the juices. Repeat if necessary.

> 1/2 cup plus 2 tablespoons all-purpose flour, *divided*
> 2 teaspoons salt, *divided*
> 3/4 teaspoon pepper, *divided*
> 1/2 teaspoon garlic salt
> 2 pounds boneless beef round steak (3/4 to 1 inch thick), cut into serving-size pieces
> 3 tablespoons vegetable oil
> 2 cups chopped green pepper
> 1 cup chopped celery
> 1 cup chopped onion
> 1 garlic clove, minced
> 2 cans (14-1/2 ounces *each*) diced tomatoes, undrained
> 1 cup beef broth
> 1 tablespoon soy sauce
> 1/4 cup cold water

In a large resealable plastic bag, combine 1/2 cup flour, 1 teaspoon salt, 1/2 teaspoon pepper and garlic salt. Add beef, a few pieces at a time, and shake to coat. Remove meat from bag and pound with a mallet to tenderize. Heat oil in a Dutch oven over medium-high. Brown the meat on both sides. Add green pepper, celery, onion and garlic; cook and stir for 10 minutes. Add tomatoes, broth, soy sauce and remaining salt and pepper. Cover and bake at 325° for 2 hours or until ten-der. Remove from the oven and return to stovetop. Skim fat. In a small bowl, combine cold water and remaining flour; stir into pan juices. Bring to a boil over medium heat, stirring constantly until thickened. **Yield:** 6-8 servings. —*Eleanore Hill, Fresno, California*

Osso Buco

These braised veal shanks can be assembled a day ahead if desired (except for the topping) and refrigerated. Then bake as directed and add the topping just before serving.

> 1/3 cup all-purpose flour
> 1 teaspoon salt
> 1/2 teaspoon pepper
> 4 to 6 veal shanks (2 inches thick)
> 5 tablespoons olive *or* vegetable oil
> 1 teaspoon Italian seasoning
> 1/2 teaspoon rubbed sage
> 1 medium onion, chopped
> 2 medium carrots, sliced
> 1 celery rib, cut into 1/2-inch slices
> 1 garlic clove, minced
> 1-1/2 cups dry white wine *or* chicken broth
> 1 can (14-1/2 ounces) chicken broth
> 2 tablespoons tomato paste
> **LEMON HERB TOPPING:**
> 2 garlic cloves, minced
> 1-1/2 tablespoons minced fresh parsley
> 1 tablespoon grated lemon peel

In a large resealable plastic bag, combine flour, salt and pepper; coat the meat. In a large skillet, heat oil over high. Brown meat on all sides. Lay shanks flat in an ungreased Dutch oven or 13-in. x 9-in. x 2-in. baking pan. Sprinkle with Italian seasoning and sage. Combine onion, carrots, celery and garlic; sprinkle over meat. In a small bowl, whisk wine, broth and tomato paste; pour over vegetables. Cover and bake at 325° for 3 hours or until the meat easily falls away from the bone. Just before serving, combine topping ingredients; sprinkle over each shank. **Yield:** 4-6 servings.

—*Karen Jaffe, Short Hills, New Jersey*

Old-Fashioned Swiss Steak

Coating Meat with Flour

Combine flour and any other dry seasonings in a large resealable plastic bag. Add meat, a few pieces at a time; shake until meat is completely coated with the flour mixture.

Hungarian Short Ribs

Make these ribs spicy if you like, with the addition of Hungarian paprika.

    2 to 3 tablespoons vegetable oil
    4 pounds bone-in beef short ribs
    2 medium onions, sliced
    1 can (15 ounces) tomato sauce
    1 cup water
    1/4 cup packed brown sugar
    1/4 cup vinegar
 1-1/2 teaspoons salt
 1-1/2 teaspoons ground mustard
 1-1/2 teaspoons Worcestershire sauce
    1/4 teaspoon paprika
Hot cooked noodles

In a Dutch oven, heat oil over medium-high; brown ribs on all sides. Add onions; cook until tender. Combine the next eight ingredients; pour over ribs. Reduce heat; cover and simmer for 3 hours or until the meat is tender. Skim fat. Reduce or thicken pan juices for gravy (refer to pages 105 and 106). Serve meat and gravy over noodles. **Yield:** 6-8 servings.

—*Joanne ShewChuk, St. Benedict, Saskatchewan*

Hungarian Short Ribs

Round Steak Stroganoff

The thinner you slice the round steak, the quicker the meat will cook and become tender. After the sour cream is added, do not boil the mixture or it will curdle.

    1/2 cup all-purpose flour
      1 teaspoon paprika
      1 teaspoon salt
    1/2 teaspoon pepper
 1-1/2 to 2 pounds beef round steak, trimmed and
          cut into thin strips
      3 tablespoons butter *or* margarine
      1 cup chopped onion
      1 garlic clove, minced
      1 can (14-1/2 ounces) beef broth
      3 tablespoons chili sauce
    1/2 teaspoon ground mustard
      1 pound fresh mushrooms, sliced
      2 cups (16 ounces) sour cream
Hot cooked noodles
Minced fresh parsley, optional

Combine flour, paprika, salt and pepper in a large resealable plastic bag. Add beef, a few pieces at a time, and shake to coat. In a large skillet, melt butter over medium heat. Brown half the beef at a time; remove. Add onion and garlic; saute until tender. Return beef to the pan. Add broth, chili sauce, mustard and mushrooms; cover and simmer for 1 hour or until the beef is tender. Stir in sour cream; heat gently but do not boil. Serve immediately over noodles. Garnish with parsley if desired. **Yield:** 6-8 servings.

—*Brenda Read*
Burns Lake, British Columbia

Slow-Cooked Pepper Steak

Slow-Cooked Pepper Steak

A slow cooker is perfect to use for less tender meats such as round steak. Because the meat is cooked in liquid for hours, it turns out tender and juicy.

    2 tablespoons vegetable oil
1-1/2 to 2 pounds beef round steak, trimmed and
        cut into 3-inch x 1-inch strips
    1 cup chopped onion
1/4 cup soy sauce
    1 garlic clove, minced
    1 teaspoon sugar
1/2 teaspoon salt
1/4 teaspoon pepper
1/4 teaspoon ground ginger
    4 tomatoes, cut into eighths *or* 1 can (14-1/2
        ounces) diced tomatoes, undrained
    2 large green peppers, cut into strips
1/2 cup cold water
    1 tablespoon cornstarch
Hot cooked noodles

In a skillet, heat oil over medium-high. Brown beef; drain. Transfer beef to a slow cooker. Combine the next seven ingredients; pour over beef. Cover and cook on high for 1 hour. Reduce heat to low; cook for 3-4 hours or until meat is tender. Add tomatoes and green peppers; cook on low 1 hour longer. Combine the cold water and cornstarch until smooth; stir into liquid in slow cooker. Cook on high until thickened. Serve over noodles. **Yield:** 6-8 servings.

—Sue Gronholz
Columbus, Wisconsin

Slow Cooker Tips

- Trim as much visible fat from meat before placing in the slow cooker to avoid greasy gravy.
- For more flavorful gravy, first brown the meat in a skillet. Then scrape all browned bits from the bottom of the skillet and add to the slow cooker along with the meat.

Corned Beef and Cabbage

Corned Beef and Cabbage

Corned beef is a cured product that is made from either a fresh beef brisket or beef round. The meat comes packed in a brine and often has additional spices to add to the cooking liquid. Corned beef is naturally salty and has a deep red color from the curing process.

>   1 corned beef brisket (4 to 6 pounds)
>   2 tablespoons brown sugar
>   2 to 3 bay leaves
>   16 to 24 small potatoes, peeled
>   8 to 12 medium carrots, halved
>   1 large head cabbage, cut into wedges

HORSERADISH SAUCE:
>   3 tablespoons butter *or* margarine
>   2 tablespoons all-purpose flour
>   1 to 1-1/2 cups cooking liquid (from brisket)
>   1/4 cup prepared horseradish
>   1 tablespoon vinegar
>   1 tablespoon sugar

SOUR CREAM AND MUSTARD SAUCE:
>   1 cup (8 ounces) sour cream
>   2 tablespoons Dijon mustard
>   1/4 teaspoon sugar

Place brisket in a large Dutch oven; cover with water. Add brown sugar and bay leaves. (If a spice packet is enclosed with the brisket, add it also.) Bring to a boil. Reduce heat; cover and simmer for 2 hours. Add potatoes and carrots. Return to a boil. Reduce heat; cover and simmer for 30-40 minutes or until meat and vegetables are just tender. If your Dutch oven is not large enough for cabbage to fit, remove potatoes and carrots and keep warm (they can be returned to cooking liquid and heated through before serving). Add cabbage; cover and cook for 15 minutes or until tender. Discard bay leaves. Remove cabbage and meat. If making Horseradish Sauce, strain and remove about 1-1/2 cups cooking liquid. Let meat stand a few minutes; slice across the grain. Serve with vegetables and Horseradish Sauce or Sour Cream and Mustard Sauce. **Yield:** 10-15 servings.

Horseradish Sauce: In a small saucepan, melt butter. Stir in flour until smooth. Gradually add 1 cup of cooking liquid. Add horseradish, vinegar and sugar; cook and stir over medium heat until thickened and bubbly. Adjust seasoning with additional vinegar, sugar or horseradish if needed. Thin sauce if necessary with the remaining cooking liquid. **Yield:** about 1-1/2 cups.

Sour Cream and Mustard Sauce: Combine all ingredients in a small bowl; mix until blended. **Yield:** 1 cup.
—Evelyn Kenney, Trenton, New Jersey

Beef Stew with Cheddar Dumplings

Baked Beef Stew

This recipe is one of the few that does not require you to brown the beef before combining it with the other ingredients. To save on your budget, purchase a beef chuck roast and cut it into cubes at home.

2 pounds lean beef stew meat, cut into 1-inch cubes
6 medium carrots, cut into strips
3 medium potatoes, peeled and quartered
1 medium onion, sliced into rings
1/2 cup thickly sliced celery
1 cup diced canned tomatoes
1 cup water
3 tablespoons quick-cooking tapioca
1/2 cup soft bread crumbs

In large bowl, combine all ingredients. Spoon into a 3-qt. baking dish that has been coated with nonstick cooking spray. Cover and bake at 325° for 3-1/2 hours or until the meat is tender. **Yield:** 6 servings.

—*Sue Hecht, Roselle Park, New Jersey*

Beef Stew with Cheddar Dumplings

The secret to making dumplings is to resist the urge to lift the cover and peek. After 12 minutes, test a dumpling by inserting a toothpick in the center. If it comes out clean, the dumpling is cooked through.

1/2 cup all-purpose flour
1/2 teaspoon salt
1/2 teaspoon pepper
2 pounds beef stew meat, cut into 1-inch cubes
2 tablespoons vegetable oil
5 cups water
5 beef bouillon cubes
1/2 teaspoon onion salt
1/2 teaspoon garlic salt
1 tablespoon browning sauce, optional
4 carrots, sliced
1 medium onion, cut into wedges
1 can (14-1/2 ounces) green beans, drained
DUMPLINGS:
2 cups biscuit/baking mix
1 cup (4 ounces) shredded cheddar cheese
2/3 cup milk

In a large resealable plastic bag, combine flour, salt and pepper. Add beef, a few pieces at a time, and shake to coat. In a Dutch oven, heat oil over medium-high. Brown meat on all sides; drain. Add water, bouillon, onion salt, garlic salt and browning sauce if desired; bring to a boil. Reduce heat; cover and simmer for 1 hour. Add carrots and onion. Cover and simmer until the vegetables are tender. Stir in green beans. For dumplings, combine biscuit mix and cheese. Stir in enough milk to form a soft dough. Drop by tablespoonsful onto simmering stew. Cover and simmer for 12 minutes (do not lift cover) or until dumplings test done. Serve immediately. **Yield:** 6 servings.

—*Jackie Riley, Garrettsville, Ohio*

Baked Beef Stew

Roasting Beef

Place meat on a rack in a shallow roasting pan with the fat side up. Insert an oven-safe meat thermometer (or use an instant-read thermometer toward the end of the roasting time). Roast without liquid, uncovered, at 325° unless otherwise noted in the recipe. Because roasts will continue to cook after being removed from the oven, remove the meat when the internal temperature is 5-10° below desired doneness. Cover with foil and allow to stand for 10-15 minutes before carving.

Savory Beef Rub

Prepare this seasoning and keep it in a spice jar. Then when you are preparing an ordinary roast, simply rub it over the meat and roast as directed. This homemade seasoning mix also makes a wonderful gift!

1 tablespoon dried marjoram
1 tablespoon dried basil
2 teaspoons garlic powder
2 teaspoons dried thyme
1 teaspoon dried rosemary, crushed
3/4 teaspoon dried oregano

Combine all ingredients; store in a covered container. Rub over meat before roasting. Will season one 3- to 4-pound roast. **Yield:** 1/4 cup.
—*Donna Brockett*
Kingfisher, Oklahoma

Cut	Weight in Pounds	Doneness	Approximate Roasting Time
Rib Eye Roast—small end (350°)	3 to 4	145° (medium-rare)	1-1/2 to 1-3/4 hours
		160° (medium)	1-3/4 to 2 hours
		170° (well-done)	2 to 2-1/2 hours
	4 to 6	145° (medium-rare)	1-3/4 to 2 hours
		160° (medium)	2 to 2-1/2 hours
		170° (well-done)	2-1/2 to 3 hours
Rib Roast (350°)	4 to 6 (2 ribs)	145° (medium-rare)	1-3/4 to 2-1/4 hours
		160° (medium)	2-1/4 to 2-3/4 hours
		170° (well-done)	2-3/4 to 3-1/4 hours
	6 to 8 (2 to 4 ribs)	145° (medium-rare)	2-1/4 to 2-1/2 hours
		160° (medium)	2-3/4 to 3 hours
		170° (well-done)	3-1/4 to 4-1/2 hours
Round Tip Roast	3 to 4	145° (medium-rare)	1-3/4 to 2 hours
		160° (medium)	2-1/4 to 2-1/2 hours
		170° (well-done)	2-1/2 to 3 hours
	4 to 6	145° (medium-rare)	2 to 2-1/2 hours
		160° (medium)	2-1/2 to 3 hours
		170° (well-done)	3 to 3-1/2 hours
Boneless Rolled Rump Roast	4 to 6	160° (medium)	1-3/4 to 2-3/4 hours
		170° (well-done)	2 to 3 hours
Eye of Round Roast	2 to 3	145° (medium-rare)	1-1/2 to 1-3/4 hours
Tenderloin (425°)	4 to 5 (whole)	145° (medium-rare)	50 to 60 minutes
		160° (medium)	60 to 70 minutes
		170° (well-done)	70 to 80 minutes

Stuffed Beef Tenderloin

Instead of using toothpicks to secure the tenderloin after stuffing, you may substitute metal skewers usually used for trussing a turkey.

   1/4 cup butter *or* margarine
   1 medium onion, chopped
   1/2 cup diced celery
   1 can (4 ounces) mushroom stems and pieces, drained
   2 cups soft bread crumbs (about 3 slices)
   1 teaspoon minced fresh basil *or* 1/4 teaspoon dried basil
   1 teaspoon minced fresh parsley *or* 1/4 teaspoon dried parsley flakes
   1/2 to 1 teaspoon salt
   1/8 teaspoon pepper
   1 beef tenderloin (about 3 pounds), trimmed
   4 bacon strips

In a small skillet, melt butter over low heat. Saute onion, celery and mushrooms until onion is tender. Meanwhile, in a bowl, combine bread crumbs, basil, parsley, salt and pepper. Add onion mixture and mix well. Make a lengthwise cut three-quarters of the way through the tenderloin. Lightly place stuffing in the pocket; close with toothpicks. Place bacon strips diagonally across the top, covering the toothpicks and the pocket. Place meat, bacon side up, in a shallow roasting pan. Insert meat thermometer into meat, not stuffing. Bake, uncovered, at 350° until meat reaches desired doneness: 145° for medium-rare, 160° for medium and 170° for well-done (meat will need to bake about 1 hour for medium). Remove from the oven; let stand for 10-15 minutes. Remove toothpicks and slice. **Yield:** 10-12 servings.

—Norma Blank
Shawano, Wisconsin

Standing Rib Roast

Often a standing rib roast is simply roasted with salt and pepper. This festive version has a lemon and rosemary coating that flavors the meat and the pan juices as well.

   1 tablespoon lemon-pepper seasoning
   1 tablespoon paprika
   1-1/2 teaspoons garlic salt
   1 teaspoon dried rosemary, crushed
   1/2 teaspoon cayenne pepper
   1 standing beef rib roast (6 to 8 pounds)
   2 cups boiling water
   1 teaspoon beef bouillon granules

Combine lemon pepper, paprika, garlic salt, rosemary and cayenne; rub over roast. Place roast with fat side up in a large roasting pan. Bake, uncovered, at 350° until roast reaches desired doneness (see chart). Remove to a warm serving platter. Let stand 10-15 minutes before carving. Pour pan juices into a glass measuring cup; skim fat. Add boiling water and bouillon to pan and stir to remove browned bits. Stir in reserved juices. Serve with the roast. **Yield:** 10-12 servings.

—Lucy Meyring
Walden, Colorado

Stuffed Beef Tenderloin

Beef and Pepper Stir-Fry

It often takes more time to prepare the ingredients for stir-frying than it does to do the actual cooking. For this reason, it's important to cut and measure all ingredients before you begin cooking.

> 2 tablespoons cornstarch, *divided*
> 4 tablespoons dry sherry *or* beef broth, *divided*
> 4 tablespoons soy sauce, *divided*
> 1 garlic clove, minced
> 1/2 to 1 teaspoon crushed red pepper flakes
> 1 pound top sirloin, thinly sliced into 1/4-inch strips
> 1/2 cup water
> 3 tablespoons vegetable oil, *divided*
> 1 green pepper, cut into strips
> 1 sweet red pepper, cut into strips
> Chow mein noodles *or* hot cooked rice

In a medium bowl, combine 1 tablespoon cornstarch, 2 tablespoons sherry or broth, 2 tablespoons soy sauce, garlic and red pepper flakes. Add beef and toss to coat; set aside. In a small bowl, combine water with remaining cornstarch, sherry and soy sauce; set aside. In a wok or skillet, heat 1 tablespoon oil over medium-high. Add green and red peppers; stir-fry for 1 minute or until crisp-tender. Remove peppers to a platter. Add remaining oil and half of the beef to the pan; stir-fry for 1-2 minutes or until beef is no longer pink. Remove to platter. Stir-fry the remaining beef. Return peppers and beef to pan. Stir cornstarch mixture and add to pan; bring to a boil, stirring constantly until thickened. Cook 1 minute longer. Serve immediately over chow mein noodles or rice. **Yield:** 4-6 servings. ① 🍎

—Patricia Ann Fredell
Orion, Illinois

Beef and Pepper Stir-Fry

Preparing Beef and Pepper Stir-Fry

1 Slice beef and peppers into thin strips. (See Slicing Raw Beef Cuts on page 118.)

2 Combine 1 tablespoon cornstarch, 2 tablespoons sherry or broth, 2 tablespoons soy sauce, garlic and red pepper flakes. Add meat and toss to coat; set aside. Combine water with remaining cornstarch, sherry or broth and soy sauce in a small bowl; set aside.

3 In a wok or skillet over medium-high, heat 1 tablespoon oil. Add peppers. Stir-fry for 1 minute or until crisp-tender. Remove to a platter.

4 Add remaining oil and half of the beef to the pan. Stir-fry for 1-2 minutes or until beef is no longer pink. Remove to platter. Stir-fry remaining beef.

5 Return beef and peppers to pan. Stir reserved cornstarch mixture. Add to pan; bring to a boil, stirring constantly, until thickened. Cook 1 minute longer.

Country-Fried Steaks

in a large resealable plastic bag. Add steaks and shake until meat is completely coated. Beat egg white and water; dip steaks in egg mixture, then coat with cornmeal mixture. In a skillet, heat 1 tablespoon oil over medium-high. Cook two steaks for 5-7 minutes on each side or until crisp, lightly browned and cooked as desired. Remove steaks and keep warm. Repeat with the remaining oil and steaks. Meanwhile, for gravy, melt butter in a saucepan; stir in flour until smooth. Gradually add milk; bring to a boil over medium heat. Boil for 2 minutes, stirring constantly; reduce heat. Add bouillon, marjoram, thyme and pepper; simmer, uncovered, for 4-5 minutes, stirring occasionally. Serve over steaks. **Yield:** 4 servings. 🕐
—*Bonnie Malloy, Norwood, Pennsylvania*

Country-Fried Steaks

Store-bought cube steaks have already been tenderized by the butcher, making this beef cut great for pan-frying. Use a heavy skillet—like cast iron—to brown the breading quickly and to produce a wonderful rich gravy.

    5 tablespoons all-purpose flour, *divided*
1/4 cup cornmeal
1/2 teaspoon salt
1/4 teaspoon pepper
    4 beef cube steaks (about 1 pound)
    1 egg white
    1 teaspoon water
    2 tablespoons vegetable oil, *divided*
GRAVY:
    1 tablespoon butter *or* margarine
    2 tablespoons all-purpose flour
1-1/2 cups milk
    1 teaspoon beef bouillon granules
1/2 teaspoon dried marjoram
1/4 teaspoon dried thyme
1/8 teaspoon pepper

In a shallow bowl, combine 3 tablespoons flour, cornmeal, salt and pepper; set aside. Place remaining flour

Italian-Style Beef Liver

No one will turn up their noses at this liver dish. Cook the liver until it is slightly pink in the center. That way, the meat won't become tough and overcooked when it's reheated in the sauce.

1/3 cup all-purpose flour
1/4 teaspoon salt
    1 pound beef liver, cut into bite-size pieces
    4 teaspoons vegetable oil, *divided*
    1 cup thinly sliced onion
1/2 cup chopped celery
    2 cans (14-1/2 ounces *each*) diced tomatoes, undrained
    1 bay leaf
    2 tablespoons minced fresh parsley *or* 2 teaspoons dried parsley flakes
    1 tablespoon minced fresh basil *or* 1 teaspoon dried basil
    1 teaspoon salt
1/4 teaspoon pepper
Hot cooked spaghetti
Grated Parmesan cheese

Combine flour and salt in a large resealable plastic bag. Add liver, a few pieces at a time; shake until completely coated. Heat 2 teaspoons oil in a skillet; cook liver to desired doneness. Remove and set aside. In the same skillet, heat remaining oil. Saute onion and celery until tender, about 5 minutes. Stir in tomatoes, bay leaf, parsley, basil, salt and pepper. Cover and simmer for 20 minutes, stirring occasionally. Add liver; cover and cook 5 minutes longer or until heated through. Discard bay leaf. Serve over spaghetti; sprinkle with cheese. **Yield:** 4 servings. —*Mina Dyck, Boissevain, Manitoba*

Fantastic Beef Fajitas

Fantastic Beef Fajitas

For an authentic bold flavor, add 1 teaspoon ground cumin to the marinade. Cook the beef as you like it and keep the vegetables crisp-tender.

- **1 pound beef top sirloin** *or* **flank steak, trimmed and cut into 1/4-inch strips**
- **5 tablespoons vegetable oil,** *divided*
- **2 tablespoons lemon juice**
- **1 teaspoon dried oregano**
- **1 garlic clove, minced**
- **1/4 teaspoon salt**
- **1/4 teaspoon pepper**
- **1 medium sweet red pepper, cut into thin strips**
- **1/2 medium onion, sliced**
- **8 flour tortillas, warmed**
- **2 ripe avocados, peeled and sliced**

Salsa

Sour cream

In a large resealable plastic bag, combine 3 tablespoons oil, lemon juice, oregano, garlic, salt and pepper; add beef and toss to coat. Refrigerate for 3 hours or overnight, turning occasionally. Remove meat and discard marinade. In a skillet, heat 1 tablespoon of oil. Saute red pepper and onion until crisp-tender; remove and set aside. Heat remaining oil; cook meat for 2-4 minutes or until it reaches desired doneness. Return vegetables to pan; heat through. Place a spoonful of meat and vegetables on each tortilla. Top with avocado, salsa and sour cream; roll up. **Yield:** 4-6 servings.

—*Marla Brenneman, Goshen, Indiana*

Slicing Raw Beef Cuts

To easily slice raw beef, first place the meat in the freezer for about 30 minutes or until it is firm but not solidly frozen. Slice to desired thinness.

Peppery London Broil

Serve this well-seasoned flank steak anytime of year using either your broiler or outdoor grill. Rub the beef with the garlic mixture early in the day and refrigerate until serving time. The longer it marinates, the better the flavor!

> 1 beef flank steak (about 3/4 pound)
> 1 garlic clove, minced
> 1/2 teaspoon seasoned salt
> 1/8 teaspoon crushed red pepper flakes
> 1/4 cup Worcestershire sauce

With a meat fork, pierce holes in both sides of meat. Make a paste with garlic, seasoned salt and red pepper flakes; rub over both sides of meat. Place in a large resealable plastic bag; add Worcestershire sauce. Seal bag. Refrigerate for at least 4 hours, turning once. Remove meat; discard marinade. Broil or grill over hot heat until meat reaches desired doneness, 4-5 minutes on each side. To serve, thinly slice across the grain. **Yield:** 2 servings. *—Dan Wright, San Jose, California*

Crisp Hash for Two

Next time you have leftover roast beef and cooked potatoes, make this country favorite. A metal spatula will keep this patty together when flipping.

> 2 tablespoons butter *or* margarine
> 1 cup diced cooked beef chuck
> 1 cup diced cooked potato
> 1 medium onion, diced
> 1 tablespoon minced fresh parsley
> 1/2 cup milk
> **Salt and pepper to taste**

In a heavy skillet, melt butter over medium-high heat. Add remaining ingredients; mix well. Flatten mixture with a metal spatula. Cover and cook until crisp on the bottom. Turn and brown the other side. **Yield:** 2 servings. ⏱ *—Flo Burtnett, Gage, Oklahoma*

Peppery London Broil

Grilling Guidelines

The following times assume the grill is at medium heat and uncovered unless otherwise noted. Keep in mind that these grilling times are only approximate because outdoor weather conditions greatly impact how hot your grill gets and how fast your meat will cook.

Cut	Thickness/Weight	Approximate Grilling Time
Rib Eye Steak	1 inch	11 to 14 minutes
	1-1/2 inches	17 to 22 minutes (covered)
T-bone or Porterhouse Steak	3/4 inch	10 to 12 minutes
	1 inch	14 to 16 minutes
Tenderloin Steak	1 inch	13 to 15 minutes
	1-1/2 inches	14 to 16 minutes (covered)
Top Sirloin Steak—boneless	1 inch	17 to 21 minutes
Flank Steak (marinated)	1-1/2 to 2 pounds	17 to 21 minutes
Top Round Steak (marinated)	1 inch	16 to 18 minutes
Chuck Shoulder Steak (marinated)	1 inch	16 to 20 minutes
Ground Beef Patties	1/4 pound each	11 to 13 minutes (160° or until no longer pink)

Grilled Beef Kabobs

When threading skewers, if you leave a little space between the meat and vegetables, they'll cook more quickly.

- **1 pound boneless beef sirloin steak, cut into 1-1/2-inch cubes**
- **1 bottle (8 ounces) French *or* Russian salad dressing**
- **2 tablespoons Worcestershire sauce**
- **2 tablespoons lemon juice**
- **1/8 teaspoon pepper**
- **1/8 teaspoon garlic powder**
- **8 to 10 bacon strips, halved**
- **1 medium sweet red pepper, cut into chunks**
- **1 medium green pepper, cut into chunks**
- **2 small zucchini, cut into chunks**
- **8 medium fresh mushrooms**
- **1 large onion, quartered, optional**

Place beef in a shallow glass container. Combine salad dressing, Worcestershire sauce, lemon juice, pepper and garlic powder; reserve 1/4 cup and refrigerate. Pour remaining marinade over beef. Cover and refrigerate for 8 hours or overnight. Remove beef; discard marinade. Wrap bacon around beef cubes. On metal or soaked wooden skewers, alternately thread beef and vegetables. Grill over hot heat for 10-15 minutes or until the beef reaches desired doneness, basting frequently with reserved marinade. **Yield:** 4 servings.
—*Dolores Lueken, Ferdinand, Indiana*

Grilled Beef Kabobs

Marinated Sirloin Steak

Marinated Sirloin Steak

If you like the taste of black pepper on a steak, use freshly ground or cracked pepper instead of commercially ground pepper in the marinade.

    2 to 2-1/2 pounds beef sirloin steak (about 1
      inch thick)
  1-1/2 cups water
    1 medium onion, chopped
    3/4 cup soy sauce
    1/4 cup Worcestershire sauce
    2 tablespoons white wine vinegar
    2 tablespoons lemon juice
    2 tablespoons Dijon mustard
    2 garlic cloves, minced
    2 teaspoons dried parsley flakes
    1 teaspoon dried thyme
    1 teaspoon Italian seasoning
    1 teaspoon pepper

Place steak in a shallow glass container or large resealable plastic bag. Combine remaining ingredients; pour over the meat. Cover and refrigerate overnight. Remove meat; discard marinade. Grill, uncovered, over medium heat until meat is cooked to desired doneness (see chart). **Yield:** 6 servings.

—*Karen Mattern, Spokane, Washington*

Peppered Rib Eye Steaks

You can use this herb rub on other tender cuts of beef such as sirloin, T-bone and tenderloin steaks.

    4 beef rib eye steaks (1-1/2 inches thick)
    1 tablespoon olive *or* vegetable oil
    1 tablespoon garlic powder
    1 tablespoon paprika
    2 teaspoons dried thyme
    2 teaspoons dried oregano
  1-1/2 teaspoons pepper
    1 teaspoon salt
    1 teaspoon lemon-pepper seasoning
    1 teaspoon cayenne pepper

Brush steaks lightly with oil. In a small bowl, combine the seasonings. Sprinkle over steaks and press into both sides. Cover and refrigerate for at least 1 hour. Grill steaks, turning once, over medium-high heat until meat is cooked to desired doneness (see chart). Cut across the grain into thick slices. **Yield:** 8 servings.

—*Sharon Bickett, Chester, South Carolina*

Tips for Buying and Cooking Ground Beef

- Ground beef is often labeled using the cut of meat that it is ground from, such as ground chuck or ground round. (Ground beef comes from a combination of beef cuts.) Ground beef can also be labeled according to the fat content of the ground mixture or the percentage of lean meat to fat, such as 85% or 90% lean. The higher the percentage, the leaner the meat.

- When buying ground beef, select meat that is bright red in color in a package that is tightly sealed. Purchase all ground beef before the "sell by" date.

- One pound of ground beef serves 3 to 4.

- When shaping hamburgers, meat loaves or meatballs, handle the mixture as little as possible to keep the final product light in texture.

- Ground beef needs to be cooked until it is well-done and no longer pink. For patties and loaves, where it is difficult to judge color, make sure the internal temperature reaches 160° before serving.

Shepherd's Pie

If your family loves meat and potatoes, try this economical one-pot casserole. It's full of flavor and just what a hungry crowd needs. Add a green salad to complete the meal.

> 2-1/2 pounds potatoes, peeled and cooked
> 1 to 1-1/2 cups (8 to 12 ounces) sour cream
> Salt and pepper to taste
> 2 pounds ground beef
> 1 medium sweet red pepper, chopped
> 1/2 cup chopped onion
> 1 can (15-1/4 ounces) whole kernel corn, drained
> 1 can (10-3/4 ounces) condensed cream of mushroom soup, undiluted
> 1/2 cup milk
> 1 teaspoon garlic salt
> 2 tablespoons butter *or* margarine, melted
> Minced fresh parsley

Mash potatoes with sour cream. Add salt and pepper; set aside. In a skillet, cook beef, red pepper and onion until meat is browned and vegetables are tender; drain. Add corn, soup, milk and garlic salt; mix well. Spread meat mixture in an ungreased 3-qt. baking dish. Top with mashed potatoes; drizzle with butter. Bake, uncovered, at 350° for 30-35 minutes or until heated through. For additional browning, place under broiler for a few minutes. Sprinkle with parsley. **Yield:** 8-10 servings.

—*Valerie Merrill, Topeka, Kansas*

Shepherd's Pie

Salisbury Steak Deluxe

Bring water to a boil in a Dutch oven or soup kettle. Cook seeded peppers until crisp-tender, about 2-3 minutes depending on the size of the pepper. Remove from the water with a tongs and invert on paper towels to drain before stuffing.

Summer Stuffed Peppers

(Pictured on page 103)

To cut even more fat from this recipe, you may want to rinse the ground beef with warm water and drain after browning. Then return to the skillet and continue with the recipe.

> 8 medium sweet red, yellow *or* green peppers
> 1-1/2 pounds lean ground beef
> 1 medium onion, finely chopped
> 1 medium carrot, shredded
> 1/2 cup finely chopped cabbage
> 1/2 cup shredded zucchini
> 1 garlic clove, minced
> 1 can (28 ounces) diced tomatoes, undrained
> 1/2 cup uncooked long grain rice
> 1 tablespoon brown sugar
> 1/4 teaspoon dried basil

Pepper to taste

Cut the tops off each pepper and set aside. Remove seeds and membranes. Cook whole peppers in boiling water for 2-3 minutes or until crisp-tender. Remove and invert on paper towels to drain. Remove stems from pepper tops and chop enough of the tops to make 1/3 cup. In a skillet, brown beef over medium heat. Add onion, carrot, cabbage, zucchini, garlic and chopped peppers; saute until tender. Add tomatoes, rice, brown sugar, basil and pepper. Reduce heat; cover and simmer for 20 minutes or until the rice is tender. Stuff hot meat mixture into peppers. **Yield:** 8 servings.

—*Pat Whitaker, Lebanon, Oregon*

Salisbury Steak Deluxe

Serve the meat patties and gravy over a bed of cooked noodles or mashed potatoes for a hearty meal. If desired, the patties and gravy can be prepared ahead and reheated when it's time to eat.

> 1 can (10-3/4 ounces) condensed cream of mushroom soup, undiluted
> 1 tablespoon prepared mustard
> 2 teaspoons Worcestershire sauce
> 1 teaspoon prepared horseradish
> 1 egg
> 1/4 cup dry bread crumbs
> 1/4 cup finely chopped onion
> 1/2 teaspoon salt

Dash pepper
> 1-1/2 pounds ground beef
> 1 to 2 tablespoons vegetable oil
> 1/2 cup water

In a bowl, combine the soup, mustard, Worcestershire sauce and horseradish; blend well. Set aside. In another bowl, lightly beat the egg. Add bread crumbs, onion, salt, pepper and 1/4 cup of the soup mixture. Add beef and mix well. Shape into six patties. In a large skillet, heat oil over medium-high. Brown the patties on both sides; drain. Combine remaining soup mixture with water; pour over patties. Cover and cook over low heat for 10-15 minutes or until meat is no longer pink. Remove patties to a serving platter; top with sauce. **Yield:** 6 servings. ①

—*Denise Barteet
Shreveport, Louisiana*

Chili Skillet

This meal in a pan goes from start to finish in about 40 minutes. If you like spicy flavors, add a dash of cayenne pepper or a couple drops of hot pepper sauce along with the other seasonings.

    1 pound ground beef
    1 cup chopped onion
  1/2 cup chopped green pepper
    1 garlic clove, minced
    1 cup tomato juice
    1 can (16 ounces) kidney beans, undrained
  1/2 cup uncooked long grain rice
    4 teaspoons chili powder
    1 teaspoon dried oregano
    1 teaspoon salt
    1 cup canned *or* frozen corn
  1/2 cup sliced ripe olives
    1 cup (4 ounces) shredded cheddar *or* Monterey Jack cheese

In a large skillet over medium heat, cook beef, onion, green pepper and garlic until meat is browned and vegetables are tender; drain. Add tomato juice, beans, rice, chili powder, oregano and salt; cover and simmer for 25 minutes or until the rice is tender. Stir in corn and olives; cover and cook for 5 minutes. Sprinkle with cheese; cover and cook until the cheese is melted, about 5 minutes. **Yield:** 4 servings.

—Katherine Brown, Fredericktown, Ohio

Chili Skillet

All-Purpose Meat Sauce

Everyone needs a basic meat sauce that can be used in a variety of recipes. This sauce can be served over rice or pasta or can be used as the meat sauce for lasagna, tacos, pizza, chili dogs or sloppy joes. It's handy to have on hand in the freezer.

    1 pound ground beef
    1 to 2 garlic cloves, minced
    1 can (15 ounces) tomato sauce
    1 can (10-3/4 ounces) condensed tomato soup, undiluted
  1/4 cup grated Parmesan cheese
    1 tablespoon Worcestershire sauce
1-1/2 teaspoons dried oregano
    1 teaspoon dried basil
  1/2 teaspoon sugar
  1/2 teaspoon salt
  1/2 teaspoon dried parsley flakes
  1/4 teaspoon crushed red pepper flakes
Pinch *each* **dried thyme, tarragon and ground cinnamon**
Hot pepper sauce and cayenne pepper to taste

In a large skillet or Dutch oven, cook the beef and garlic until beef is browned; drain. Stir in remaining ingredients. Simmer, uncovered, for 30 minutes or until sauce is as thick as desired, stirring occasionally. **Yield:** 4 cups.   *—Sonja Fontaine, Winnipeg, Manitoba*

Tater Tot Bake

Keep a pound of ground beef and a package of tater tots in the freezer, a can of soup in the pantry, a little cheese in the refrigerator and you'll be ready to make this satisfying casserole without going to the market.

  3/4 to 1 pound ground beef
    1 small onion, chopped
Salt and pepper to taste
    1 package (16 ounces) frozen tater tot potatoes
    1 can (10-3/4 ounces) condensed cream of mushroom soup, undiluted
  2/3 cup milk *or* water
    1 cup (4 ounces) shredded cheddar cheese

In a skillet, cook beef and onion until beef is browned and onion is tender; drain. Season with salt and pepper. Transfer to a greased 1-1/2- to 2-qt. baking dish. Top with potatoes. Combine soup and milk or water; pour over potatoes. Sprinkle with cheese. Bake, uncovered, at 350° for 30-40 minutes. **Yield:** 2-3 servings.

—Jean Ferguson, Elverta, California

Shaping Cabbage Rolls

1 Place whole head of cabbage in boiling water until the outer leaves begin to loosen. Remove cabbage from water and remove as many leaves as will come off easily. Place cabbage back in water if more leaves are needed. Cut out the thick vein from each leaf for easier rolling.

2 Place 2-3 tablespoons of the ground beef mixture on each leaf; fold up sides and roll up to completely enclose meat mixture in cabbage leaf. Fasten with a toothpick if desired.

Stuffed Cabbage Rolls

Stuffed Cabbage Rolls

Because there is no way to drain off any excess fat as the cabbage rolls cook, it's best to use lean ground beef in this recipe.

- 1 large head cabbage
- 1 pound lean ground beef
- 1 cup instant rice, cooked and cooled
- 1 medium onion, chopped
- 2 tablespoons Worcestershire sauce
- 1/2 teaspoon salt
- 1/4 teaspoon pepper
- 1 can (10-3/4 ounces) condensed tomato soup, undiluted, *divided*
- 1/2 cup water

Cook cabbage in boiling water only until outer leaves fall off head. Reserve 14-16 large leaves for rolls and set remaining cabbage aside. In a bowl, combine beef, rice, onion, Worcestershire sauce, salt, pepper and 1/4 cup soup; mix well. Place 2-3 tablespoons meat mixture on each cabbage leaf. Fold in sides, starting at an unfolded edge, and roll up leaf completely to enclose meat. Cut reserved cabbage into wedges and place in a Dutch oven. Combine water and remaining soup; pour over cabbage wedges. Stack cabbage rolls on top of sauce. Cover and bring to a boil. Reduce heat and simmer for 1 to 1-1/2 hours or until meat is done and rolls are tender. Remove rolls and cabbage. If desired, reduce pan juices for gravy. Spoon sauce over rolls and cabbage. **Yield:** 4-6 servings.

—Jean Parsons
Sarver, Pennsylvania

Meat Loaf and Meatball Tips

- In a bowl, combine all ingredients except the ground beef. Crumble the meat over the mixture. With a sturdy spoon or by hand, gently combine ingredients.

- Insert an instant-read thermometer in the center of the meat loaf near the end of the baking time. When it reads 160°, the meat loaf is done.

- After baking, drain any fat. Let the meat loaf stand for 10 minutes before slicing.

Mom's Best Meat Loaf

(Also pictured on cover)

Here's a classic meat loaf that has real personality with the addition of horseradish, allspice and dill. Instead of bread crumbs, you can use quick-cooking oats for added nutrition.

    1 cup milk
    1 egg, lightly beaten
  3/4 cup soft bread crumbs
    1 medium onion, chopped
    1 tablespoon finely chopped green pepper
    1 tablespoon ketchup
1-1/2 teaspoons salt
    1 teaspoon prepared horseradish
    1 teaspoon sugar
    1 teaspoon ground allspice
    1 teaspoon dill weed
1-1/2 pounds ground beef *or* a combination of
      ground beef, pork and veal
Additional ketchup

In a large bowl, combine the first 11 ingredients. Crumble meat over mixture and mix well. Press into an ungreased 8-in. x 4-in. x 2-in. loaf pan. Bake at 350° for 1 hour. Drizzle top of loaf with ketchup; bake 15 minutes longer or until no pink remains and a meat thermometer reads 160°. **Yield:** 6-8 servings.

—Linda Nilsen, Anoka, Minnesota

Mom 's Best Meat Loaf

Cranberry Meatballs

Baking these meatballs instead of browning in a skillet makes this a speedy recipe. While the meatballs bake, you can prepare the rest of the meal. These meatballs also make a great appetizer served with toothpicks.

      1 egg, lightly beaten
  1/2 cup crushed saltines (about 15 crackers)
  1/4 cup diced onion
      1 teaspoon salt
  1/2 teaspoon pepper
      1 pound ground beef
      1 can (16 ounces) whole-berry cranberry sauce
      1 can (10-3/4 ounces) condensed tomato soup,
        undiluted
Hot cooked rice *or* noodles

In a bowl, combine the first five ingredients. Crumble meat over mixture and mix well. Shape into 1-1/2-in. balls. Place on a rack in a baking pan. Bake, uncovered, at 400° for 20 minutes or until no longer pink. Meanwhile, combine cranberry sauce and soup in a large saucepan; heat through. Add meatballs; simmer for 10 minutes. Serve over rice or noodles. **Yield:** 4 servings. —*Helen Wiegmink, Tucson, Arizona*

Baking Meatballs

Place shaped meatballs on a rack in a shallow baking pan. Bake at 400° until no longer pink, about 20 minutes for 1-1/2-in. meatballs.

Spaghetti and Meatballs for Two

When you're cooking for two, sometimes you just don't want leftovers. Purchase a spaghetti sauce that suits your taste. Some are plain, while others are spicy or enhanced with herbs, mushrooms or olives.

      1 egg
      3 tablespoons Italian-seasoned bread crumbs
      2 tablespoons chopped onion
      1 tablespoon grated Parmesan cheese
  1/8 teaspoon pepper
  1/4 pound ground beef
  1/4 pound bulk Italian sausage
      1 jar (14 ounces) spaghetti sauce *or* 1-1/2 cups
        homemade spaghetti sauce

Spaghetti and Meatballs for Two

Hot cooked spaghetti
Additional Parmesan cheese, optional

In a bowl, combine the first five ingredients. Crumble meat over mixture and mix well. Shape into 2-in. balls; brown in a skillet over medium heat. Drain. Stir in spaghetti sauce. Simmer, uncovered, for 20-30 minutes or until meatballs are no longer pink. Serve over spaghetti; sprinkle with Parmesan cheese if desired. **Yield:** 2 servings. —*David Stierheim*
Pittsburgh, Pennsylvania

Poultry

When fantastic fowl is the featured fare on your menu, the meal is certain to be a hit. Roasted Chicken with Rosemary (p. 140), your favorite turkey served with Country Ham Stuffing (p. 144) and a host of other mouth-watering ideas await you in this chapter.

Besides being versatile and tasty, poultry is economical, making it the right choice for casual weekday meals as well as festive Sunday suppers or holidays. Cooks will appreciate the assortment of classic recipes and helpful tips this chapter has to offer.

Basic Cooking Methods for Poultry

Broiling
Recommended for broiler-fryer halves, boneless chicken breast halves, bone-in breasts, thighs, drumsticks, boneless breast cubes threaded onto skewers, Cornish game hen halves, turkey breast tenderloin steaks and ground turkey patties. Preheat boiler for 5-10 minutes and brush poultry with vegetable oil. Place meat 4-6 in. from the heat on a broiler pan. Cook until juices run clear.

Frying
Recommended for chicken parts that have been disjointed and coated with a batter, a seasoned flour mixture or breading. The chicken can be fried in oil for the entire cooking time or browned in oil and then roasted in the oven to complete cooking. Cook until juices run clear.

Grilling
Recommended for the same cuts as for broiling. Preheat the grill to medium. Season the meat as recipe directs and place on cooking grate directly over the heat. Grill, turning once, until juices run clear.

Purchasing Poultry
Select poultry well within the "sell by" date on the packaging. Packages should be well-sealed and free of tears. Frozen poultry should be solidly frozen. The amount of poultry you need to buy varies with the type and cut. Follow the guidelines below.

Type of Poultry	Servings Per Pound
Chicken, boneless cuts	3 to 4
Chicken, whole and bone-in parts	1 to 2
Cornish game hens	1/2 to 1 hen per person or serving
Duckling	1
Goose	3/4 to 1
Turkey, boneless breasts	3 to 4
Turkey, thighs and bone-in breasts	2 to 3
Turkey, whole (under 12 pounds)	1
Turkey, whole (over 12 pounds)	2

Poaching

Recommended for bone-in or boneless chicken breasts. Use this method for recipes calling for cubed cooked chicken. Place chicken in a Dutch oven. Add enough water to cover and bring to a boil. Reduce heat; cover and simmer until chicken is tender and juices run clear (18-20 minutes for bone-in breasts and 12-14 minutes for boneless breasts). Drain and allow to cool; bone if necessary and cut into cubes.

Roasting

Recommended for whole birds, halves and pieces. The poultry is cooked without liquid in an open roaster. See Roasting Poultry on page 138 for specific information.

Sauteing

Recommended for boneless chicken breasts or turkey breast (tenderloin), whole or cut into cubes or strips. In a skillet, melt a small amount of butter, margarine or oil. Brown meat until juices run clear. A sauce can be added to complete the dish.

Stir-Frying

Recommended for boneless chicken breasts or turkey breast (tenderloin), whole or cut into cubes or strips. In a skillet or wok, heat a small amount of oil over medium-high. Stir-fry meat until juices run clear, stirring constantly. See page 116 for stir-frying basics.

Oven-Fried Chicken

There's no better way to welcome family and friends to the table than with this country favorite. In the summer, prepare this chicken ahead of time and serve chilled at picnics.

> 1 broiler-fryer chicken (3 to 4 pounds), cut up
> 1/4 cup butter *or* margarine, melted
> 1/2 cup grated Parmesan cheese
> 1/2 cup dry bread crumbs
> 2 tablespoons sesame seeds
> 1 teaspoon paprika
> 1/2 teaspoon dried thyme

Dip chicken pieces in butter. Combine remaining ingredients; dip chicken into crumb mixture. Place on a greased 15-in. x 10-in. x 1-in. baking pan. Drizzle any remaining butter over chicken. Bake at 375° for 45-55 minutes or until juices run clear. **Yield:** 4-6 servings.
—*Marie Lully, Boulder, Colorado*

Testing Poultry for Doneness

- The internal temperature is the best test for doneness. All whole birds need to be cooked to an internal temperature of 180° (see Step 5 of Stuffing and Roasting a Turkey on page 142). If it is stuffed, the internal temperature of the stuffing should be 165°. White meat turkey or chicken pieces must reach 170° and dark meat 180°.

- Pierce poultry with a fork in several places. The juices of thoroughly cooked poultry should run clear.

- Whole birds are done when the drumsticks move easily at the joint. To test, use several thicknesses of paper towel to hold on to the end of the drumsticks. Lift or twist to check for ease of movement.

- Browned skin is not always an indication of doneness. Browning may mean that the temperature of your oven is running higher than it should or the heat circulation in the oven cavity is poor.

- Do not rely solely on a roasting chicken's or turkey's "pop-up" temperature indicator for doneness. Use a conventional thermometer to read the exact temperature.

Oven-Fried Chicken

Oven-Barbecued Chicken

The homemade barbecue sauce is a perfect balance of sweet and sour with the tang of onion and mustard. Serve this saucy chicken anytime of year.

Vegetable oil
  1 broiler-fryer chicken (3 to 4 pounds), cut up
  3 tablespoons butter *or* margarine
  1/3 cup chopped onion
  3/4 cup ketchup
  1/2 cup water
  1/3 cup vinegar
  3 tablespoons brown sugar
  1 tablespoon Worcestershire sauce
  2 teaspoons prepared mustard
  1/4 teaspoon salt
  1/8 teaspoon pepper

Heat 1/4 in. of oil in a large skillet; brown chicken on all sides. Drain; transfer chicken to a greased 13-in. x 9-in. x 2-in. baking dish. In a saucepan, melt butter; saute onion until tender. Stir in remaining ingredients. Simmer, uncovered, for 15 minutes. Pour over chicken. Bake at 350° for 1 hour or until juices run clear, basting occasionally. **Yield:** 6 servings.

—*Esther Shank, Harrisonburg, Virginia*

Oven-Barbecued Chicken

Cutting Up a Whole Chicken

1 Pull the leg and thigh away from the body. With a small sharp knife, cut through the skin to expose the joint.

2 Cut through the joint, then cut the skin around the drumstick to free the leg. Repeat with the other leg.

3 To separate the drumstick from the thigh, cut the skin at the joint. Bend the drumstick to expose the joint; cut through the joint and skin.

4 Pull the wing away from the body. Cut through the skin to expose the joint. Cut through the joint and skin to separate the wing from the body. Repeat with the other wing.

5 With a kitchen or poultry shears, snip along each side of the backbone between rib joints.

6 Hold chicken breast in both hands (skin side down) and bend it back to snap breastbone. Turn over. With a knife, cut in half along the breastbone. The breastbone will remain attached to one of the halves. (See Boning Chicken Breasts on page 136.)

Sunday Fried Chicken

Like most fried chicken recipes, the chicken parts are coated with a seasoned flour mixture and browned in oil. This recipe, however, adds the convenient step of finishing the cooking in the oven. This gives the cook time to prepare the rest of the meal.

        2 cups all-purpose flour
    1/2 cup cornmeal
        2 tablespoons salt
        2 tablespoons ground mustard
        2 tablespoons paprika
        2 tablespoons garlic salt
        1 tablespoon celery salt
        1 tablespoon pepper
        1 teaspoon ground ginger
    1/2 teaspoon dried thyme
    1/2 teaspoon dried oregano
        1 broiler-fryer chicken (3 to 4 pounds), cut up
Vegetable oil

Combine the first 11 ingredients. Place about 1 cup flour mixture in a large resealable plastic bag. Add a few chicken pieces to the bag at a time; shake to coat. Heat 1/4 in. of oil in large skillet on medium-high. Brown chicken on all sides; transfer to an ungreased 13-in. x 9-in. x 2-in. baking pan. Bake, uncovered, at 350° for 45-55 minutes or until juices run clear. Recipe makes enough coating for three chickens. Store unused mixture in an airtight container. **Yield:** 4-6 servings.

—*Audrey Read, Fraser Lake, British Columbia*

Spicy Breaded Chicken

Mild chili powder will add just a little zip to this classic breaded chicken.

    1/2 cup dry bread crumbs
        1 tablespoon nonfat dry milk powder
1-1/2 teaspoons chili powder
    1/4 teaspoon garlic powder
    1/4 teaspoon ground mustard
    1/4 cup skim milk
        1 broiler-fryer chicken (3 to 4 pounds), cut up
        and skin removed

In a large resealable plastic bag, combine bread crumbs, milk powder, chili powder, garlic powder and mustard; set aside. Place milk in a shallow pan. Dip chicken pieces in milk, then add to bag and shake to coat. Place chicken, bone side down, in a 13-in. x 9-in. x 2-in. baking pan coated with nonstick cooking spray. Bake, uncovered, at 350° for 50-60 minutes or until juices run clear. **Yield:** 6 servings. 🍎

—*Polly Coumos
Mogadore, Ohio*

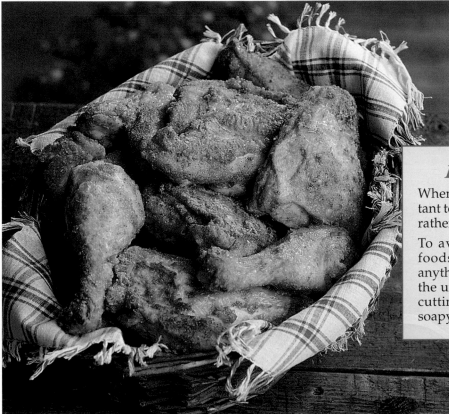

Sunday Fried Chicken

Handling Raw Poultry

When cutting raw poultry, it's important to place it on a plastic cutting board rather than wood for easier cleaning.

To avoid contamination with other foods, always wash your hands and anything that has come in contact with the uncooked poultry (such as knives, cutting boards, countertops) with hot soapy water.

Squash-Stuffed Chicken

The skin of the chicken makes a natural pocket to hold a flavorful stuffing and keeps the naturally lean chicken breasts moist during roasting.

> 3 tablespoons butter *or* margarine
> 1/4 cup chopped onion
> 1 tablespoon minced fresh parsley
> 1/2 teaspoon dried basil
> 2 medium zucchini, shredded (about
>   2-1/2 cups)
> 3 slices bread, torn into coarse crumbs
> 1 egg, beaten
> 3/4 cup shredded Swiss cheese
> 1/2 teaspoon salt
> 1/8 teaspoon pepper
> 4 bone-in chicken breast halves (with skin)

In a skillet, melt butter over medium-high heat. Saute onion, parsley and basil until the onion is tender. Add zucchini and cook 2 minutes longer. Remove from the heat; stir in bread crumbs, egg, cheese, salt and pepper. Carefully loosen the skin of the chicken on one side to form a pocket. Stuff each breast with the zucchini mixture and place in a greased 13-in. x 9-in. x 2-in. baking pan. Bake at 375° for 50-60 minutes or until juices run clear. **Yield:** 4 servings.   —*Bernadette Romano*
Shaftsbury, Vermont

Honey-Mustard Baked Chicken

This recipe easily doubles for company, but make sure you use a second baking dish instead of crowding the chicken into one pan.

> 1 broiler-fryer chicken (3 to 4 pounds), cut up
> 1/4 cup butter *or* margarine
> 1/4 cup honey
> 2 tablespoons Dijon mustard
> 1/2 teaspoon curry powder
> 1/4 teaspoon salt

Place chicken in a greased 13-in. x 9-in. x 2-in. baking pan. In saucepan, melt butter; stir in remaining ingredients and heat through. Brush glaze over chicken. Bake at 350° for 1-1/4 hours or until juices run clear. **Yield:** 4-6 servings.   —*Kate Peterson, Cincinnati, Ohio*

Squash-Stuffed Chicken

Stuffing Chicken Breasts

1 Work fingers under the skin to loosen and form a pocket.

2 Lightly fill each pocket with the stuffing mixture. Proceed with recipe.

Cranberry Chicken

barbecue sauces; mix well. Pour over chicken. Bake, uncovered, at 350° for 1-1/2 hours or until juices run clear, basting every 15 minutes. **Yield:** 4-6 servings.
—*Kay Simpson, Hull, Quebec*

Chicken and Dumplings

This recipe can be prepared in stages if desired. The day before serving, cook, bone and cube the chicken; refrigerate in the cooking liquid. The next day, add the vegetables to the cooking liquid and cook until tender. Proceed with the recipe as directed.

 1 broiler-fryer chicken (3 to 4 pounds), cut up
 3 cups water
 1 cup chopped onion
 4 celery ribs, sliced
 3 medium carrots, sliced
 1 teaspoon celery seed
 2 teaspoons rubbed sage, *divided*
 1 teaspoon salt
1/4 teaspoon pepper
 3 cups biscuit/baking mix
3/4 cup plus 2 tablespoons milk
 1 tablespoon minced fresh parsley

Place chicken and water in a Dutch oven. Cover and bring to a boil. Reduce heat; simmer until chicken is tender, about 30-45 minutes. Remove chicken from pan; bone and cube. Return chicken to pan along with onion, celery, carrots, celery seed, 1 teaspoon sage, salt and pepper. Cover and simmer for 45-60 minutes or until the vegetables are tender. For dumplings, combine biscuit mix, milk, parsley and remaining sage to form a stiff batter. Drop by tablespoonfuls onto the simmering mixture. Cover and simmer for 15 minutes (do not lift the cover). Serve immediately. **Yield:** 6-8 servings.
—*Patricia Collins, Imbler, Oregon*

Cranberry Chicken

Pretty enough for company but easy enough for a weekday family meal, this recipe will put anyone in the holiday spirit.

 1 broiler-fryer chicken (3 to 4 pounds), cut up
1/2 teaspoon salt
1/4 teaspoon pepper
 2 tablespoons butter *or* margarine
1/2 cup chopped onion
1/2 cup chopped celery
 1 can (16 ounces) whole-berry cranberry sauce
 1 cup barbecue sauce

Sprinkle chicken with salt and pepper. In a skillet, melt butter; brown chicken on all sides. Transfer to a greased 13-in. x 9-in. x 2-in. baking pan. Saute onion and celery in the drippings until tender. Add cranberry and

Skillet Chicken Stew

Unlike a beef stew that simmers for hours, this meat-and-potatoes one-pot meal is ready in 30 minutes!

    1/3 cup all-purpose flour
    1/2 teaspoon salt
Dash pepper
 1-1/2 pounds boneless skinless chicken breasts,
        cut into 1-inch pieces
      3 tablespoons butter *or* margarine
      1 medium onion, sliced
      3 celery ribs, sliced

      2 medium potatoes, peeled and cut into 3/4-
        inch cubes
      3 medium carrots, sliced 1/4 inch thick
      1 cup chicken broth
      1 tablespoon ketchup
      1 tablespoon cornstarch
    1/2 teaspoon dried thyme

Combine flour, salt and pepper in a shallow bowl; coat chicken. In a large skillet, melt butter; brown chicken on all sides. Add onion and celery; cook for 3 minutes. Stir in potatoes and carrots. Combine broth, ketchup, cornstarch and thyme until smooth; stir into skillet. Bring to a boil. Reduce heat; cover and simmer for 15-20 minutes or until vegetables are tender. **Yield:** 4-6 servings. ○
—*Valerie Jordan*
Kingmont, West Virginia

Skillet Chicken Stew

Chicken Stir-Fry

The cornstarch coats the chicken to keep it moist and also acts as the thickening agent at the end of the recipe. (Refer to the stir-frying basics on page 116.)

      4 boneless skinless chicken breast halves (1
        pound), cut into 1/2-inch strips
      3 tablespoons cornstarch
      2 tablespoons soy sauce
    1/2 teaspoon ground ginger
    1/4 teaspoon garlic powder
      3 tablespoons vegetable oil, *divided*
      2 cups broccoli florets
      1 cup sliced celery (1/2-inch pieces)
      1 cup thinly sliced carrots
      1 small onion, cut into wedges
      1 cup water
      1 teaspoon chicken bouillon granules

Place chicken in a large resealable plastic bag. Add cornstarch and toss to coat. Combine soy sauce, ginger and garlic powder; add to bag and shake well. Refrigerate for 30 minutes. In a large skillet or wok, heat 2 tablespoons of oil; stir-fry chicken until no longer pink, about 3-5 minutes. Remove and keep warm. Add remaining oil; stir-fry broccoli, celery, carrots and onion for 4-5 minutes or until crisp-tender. Add water and bouillon. Return chicken to pan. Cook and stir until thickened and bubbly. **Yield:** 4 servings. ○ 🍎
—*Lori Schlecht, Wimbledon, North Dakota*

Boning Chicken Breasts

Insert a small boning or paring knife between the ribs and breast meat. Pressing knife along bones, cut to remove meat. If desired, remove skin by pulling from breast meat.

Chicken Italiano

If time is short, this sauce can be made the day before and refrigerated. Reheat the sauce at the same time you boil the water for the pasta.

    1 tablespoon olive *or* vegetable oil
    1 medium onion, chopped
    1 medium green *or* sweet red pepper,
        chopped
    6 large fresh mushrooms, thinly sliced
  1/3 cup chicken broth
    2 tablespoons red wine vinegar
    1 can (29 ounces) tomato sauce
    2 garlic cloves, minced
    1 teaspoon sugar
  1/4 teaspoon salt
  1/4 teaspoon pepper
    1 pound boneless skinless chicken breasts,
        cut into 1-inch cubes
    2 tablespoons minced fresh basil *or* 2
        teaspoons dried basil
    1 tablespoon minced fresh sage *or* 1
        teaspoon dried sage
    1 pound linguini, cooked and drained
    2 to 3 tablespoons grated Parmesan cheese
    2 tablespoons minced fresh parsley

In a skillet, heat oil over medium-high. Saute onion, pepper and mushrooms until tender. Add broth and vinegar; bring to a boil. Boil for 2 minutes. Add tomato sauce, garlic, sugar, salt and pepper. Bring to a boil. Reduce heat; cover and simmer for 25 minutes. Add chicken, basil and sage. Cook, uncovered, 15 minutes longer or until chicken juices run clear and sauce is slightly thickened. Serve chicken and sauce over linguini. Sprinkle with cheese and parsley. **Yield:** 4 servings.   —*Marshall Simon, Grand Rapids, Michigan*

Chicken Italiano

Artichoke Chicken

This is an elegant but very easy dish to serve when entertaining. Just before company arrives, assemble the dish and put it in the oven. While the dish bakes for 1 hour, enjoy appetizers with your guests.

    2 tablespoons butter *or* margarine
    8 boneless skinless chicken breast halves
    2 jars (6 ounces *each*) marinated artichoke
        hearts, drained
    1 jar (4-1/2 ounces) whole mushrooms, drained
  1/2 cup chopped onion
  1/3 cup all-purpose flour
1-1/2 teaspoons dried rosemary, crushed
    1 teaspoon salt
  1/4 teaspoon pepper
    2 cups chicken broth *or* 1 cup broth and 1 cup
        dry white wine
Hot cooked noodles
Minced fresh parsley

In a skillet, melt butter; brown chicken on both sides. Transfer to an ungreased 13-in. x 9-in. x 2-in. baking dish (do not drain pan drippings). Cut the artichokes into quarters. Arrange artichokes and mushrooms on top of chicken; set aside. Saute onion in pan drippings; blend in flour, rosemary, salt and pepper until smooth. Gradually add broth; cook until thickened and bubbly. Remove from the heat and spoon over chicken. Cover and bake at 350° for 50-60 minutes or until chicken juices run clear. Place noodles on a serving platter; top with chicken and sauce. Sprinkle with parsley. **Yield:** 8 servings.

—*Ruth Stenson*
Santa Ana, California

Roasting Poultry

Prepare poultry for roasting as directed on page 139. Place with breast side up on a rack in a shallow roasting pan. For chicken, turkey or Cornish game hens, brush the skin with oil or melted butter or margarine. For ducklings and geese, prick the skin. Insert an oven-safe meat thermometer into the thigh area of large birds without touching the bone (or use an instant-read thermometer toward the end of roasting time). For smaller birds, take the temperature periodically by placing and holding the thermometer in the inner thigh area. Roast without liquid, uncovered, at 350° unless otherwise noted on the chart or in the recipe. Baste chicken and turkey frequently with pan drippings. Roast until the internal temperature of the meat reaches 180° for whole birds and 170° for turkey breasts. Cover with foil and allow to stand for 10-20 minutes before removing any stuffing and carving. (See Carving Basics on page 140.)

Type of Poultry (unstuffed)*	Weight	Approximate Cooking Times
Broiler-fryer chicken	3 to 4 pounds	1-1/4 to 1-1/2 hours
Roasting chicken, whole	5 to 7 pounds	2 to 2-1/4 hours
Capon, whole	4 to 8 pounds	2 to 3 hours
Cornish game hens	1-1/4 to 1-1/2 pounds	50 to 60 minutes
Duckling, whole (domestic)	4 to 6 pounds	2 to 3 hours
Goose, whole (domestic)	8 to 12 pounds	2-1/2 to 3 hours
Turkey, whole (325°)	8 to 12 pounds	2-3/4 to 3 hours
	12 to 14 pounds	3 to 3-3/4 hours
	14 to 18 pounds	3-3/4 to 4-1/4 hours
	18 to 20 pounds	4-1/4 to 4-1/2 hours
	20 to 24 pounds	4-1/2 to 5 hours
Turkey breast, whole (325°)	4 to 6 pounds	1-1/2 to 2-1/4 hours
*For stuffed birds, add 15-45 minutes to the roasting time.		

Roasted Chicken and Potatoes

When the weather starts turning cooler in your area, warm the house with the delicious aroma of a stuffed chicken baking in the oven. This recipe has both stuffing and roasted potatoes to serve with the chicken and gravy.

1/2 cup butter *or* margarine
1 cup chopped celery
1 medium onion, chopped
2 tablespoons poultry seasoning
1/2 teaspoon rubbed sage
8 cups cubed day-old bread
1/2 cup chicken broth
1 roasting chicken (5 to 7 pounds)
1/2 teaspoon paprika

Roasted Chicken and Potatoes

1/4 teaspoon salt
Pinch pepper
   6 medium baking potatoes, peeled and
     quartered
   1 teaspoon minced fresh parsley

In a skillet, melt butter. Saute celery and onion until tender, about 5 minutes. Add the poultry seasoning and sage. Place bread cubes in a large bowl. Stir in celery mixture and broth; mix lightly. Just before baking, stuff the chicken. Place with breast side up on a rack in a roasting pan; tie the drumsticks together. Combine paprika, salt and pepper; rub over chicken. Bake, uncovered, at 350° for 1-1/2 hours, basting every 30 minutes. Arrange the potatoes around chicken; cover and bake 1 hour longer or until potatoes are tender and a meat thermometer reads 180°. Sprinkle with parsley. Cover and let stand for 10 minutes before removing stuffing and carving. To make gravy from pan drippings, see Basic Pan Gravy from Roasted Meats on page 145. **Yield:** 4-6 servings.
                        —*Sandra Melnychenko*
                            Grandview, Manitoba

Preparing Poultry for Roasting

- It is recommended to thaw frozen poultry in the refrigerator. Plan on 24 hours for every 5 pounds. For example, a 20-pound turkey will need to thaw in the refrigerator for 4 days.

- Cold-water thawing is an option that takes less time but more attention. The poultry must be in a leakproof bag such as its original tightly sealed wrapper or a plastic bag. Immerse the wrapped poultry in cold tap water. Check the water frequently to be sure it stays cold. Change the water every 30 minutes until the bird is thawed. For this method, allow 30 minutes for every pound.

- Make sure whole birds are completely thawed before stuffing and/or roasting, or the roasting times will need to be increased and internal temperature checked often.

- Remove giblets (heart, gizzard and liver) that are usually stored in a packet in the neck area of the bird. Use for the preparation of broth if desired. Remove and discard any large pockets of fat that may be present in the neck area.

- Rinse the bird inside and out with cold water. Pat dry with paper towels. Place on a non-wood surface.

- Rub the inside cavity and neck area with salt.

Carving Basics

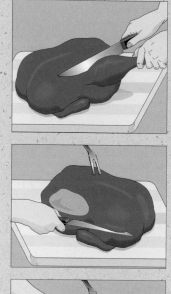

1 Pull the leg away from the body and cut between the thigh joint and the body to remove the entire leg. Repeat with the other leg. Disjoint the drumstick and thigh. Hold each part by the bone and cut off 1/4-in. slices.

2 Hold the bird with a meat fork and make a deep cut into the breast meat just above the wing area.

3 Slice down from the top of the breast into the cut made in Step 2. Slice meat 1/4 in. thick.

Greek Roasted Chicken and Potatoes

Oregano and lemon are wonderful complements to chicken. Although fresh lemon juice is preferred, bottled can also be used.

  1 whole roasting chicken (5 to 7 pounds)
Salt and pepper to taste
  2 to 3 teaspoons dried oregano, *divided*
  4 to 6 baking potatoes, peeled and quartered
  1/4 cup butter *or* **margarine, melted**
  3 tablespoons lemon juice
  3/4 cup chicken broth

Place chicken with breast side up on a rack in a roasting pan. Sprinkle with salt, pepper and half of the oregano. Arrange potatoes around the chicken; sprinkle with salt, pepper and remaining oregano. Pour butter and lemon juice over chicken and potatoes. Add broth to pan. Bake, uncovered, at 350° until juices run clear and a meat thermometer reads 180°, basting frequently (see chart for roasting time). Cover and let stand 10 minutes before carving. To make gravy from pan drippings, see Basic Pan Gravy from Roasted Meats on page 145. **Yield:** 8-10 servings.
—*Pella Visnick, Dallas, Texas*

Roasted Chicken with Rosemary

(Pictured on page 128)

Because rosemary is a strong-flavored herb, try just half the amount called for in the recipe until you know how much suits your taste.

  1/2 cup butter *or* **margarine**
    2 tablespoons dried rosemary, crushed
    2 tablespoons minced fresh parsley
    3 garlic cloves, minced
    1 teaspoon salt
  1/2 teaspoon pepper
    1 whole roasting chicken (5 to 7 pounds)
    8 small red potatoes, halved
    6 medium carrots, cut into 2-inch pieces and halved lengthwise
    2 medium onions, quartered

In a small saucepan, melt butter. Add rosemary, parsley, garlic, salt and pepper. Place chicken with breast side up on a rack in a roasting pan; tie drumsticks together. Spoon half of the butter mixture over chicken. Arrange potatoes, carrots and onions around chicken. Drizzle remaining butter mixture over vegetables. Cover and bake at 350° for 1-1/4 hours, basting every 30 minutes. Uncover; bake 1 hour longer or until juices run clear and a meat thermometer reads 180°, basting occasionally. Cover and let stand 10 minutes before carving. To make gravy from pan drippings, see Basic Pan Gravy from Roasted Meats on page 145. **Yield:** 6 servings.
—*Isabel Zienkosky, Salt Lake City, Utah*

Greek Roasted Chicken and Potatoes

Apple-Stuffed Chicken

Apple-Stuffed Chicken

The dressing and glaze make this recipe festive enough to serve for a small gathering at Thanksgiving or Christmas. If desired, golden raisins or dried cranberries or currants can be substituted for the raisins.

    1 package (6 ounces) chicken-flavored stuffing mix
    1 broiler-fryer chicken (3 to 4 pounds)
1/2 teaspoon salt
1/4 teaspoon pepper
    1 tablespoon vegetable oil
    1 cup chopped peeled tart apple
1/4 cup chopped celery
1/4 cup chopped walnuts
1/4 cup raisins
1/2 teaspoon grated lemon peel
GLAZE:
1/2 cup apple jelly
    1 tablespoon lemon juice
1/2 teaspoon ground cinnamon

Prepare stuffing according to package directions. Meanwhile, sprinkle inside of chicken with salt and pepper; rub outside with oil. In a large bowl, mix stuffing with apple, celery, nuts, raisins and lemon peel. Stuff chicken. Place with breast side up on a rack in a roasting pan. Bake, uncovered, at 350° for 1 hour. In a saucepan, combine glaze ingredients; simmer for 3 minutes. Brush over chicken. Bake 30-45 minutes longer or until juices run clear and a meat thermometer reads 180° for the chicken and 165° for the stuffing, brushing occasionally with glaze. Cover and let stand 10 minutes before removing stuffing and carving. To make gravy from pan drippings, see Basic Pan Gravy from Roasted Meat on page 145. **Yield:** 4-6 servings.
—*Joan Wrigley, Lynden, Washington*

Savory Roasted Chicken

When a simple roasted chicken dinner is in order, prepare this lemony favorite. To save time in preparation and roasting, don't tie the legs together. The heat circulates faster around the thigh area when the legs are free.

    1 broiler-fryer chicken (3 to 4 pounds)
    2 tablespoons butter *or* margarine, melted
    3 tablespoons lemon juice
    1 tablespoon minced fresh savory *or* 1 teaspoon dried savory

Place chicken with breast side up on a rack in a shallow roasting pan. Combine butter, lemon juice and savory; brush over chicken. Bake, uncovered, at 350° until a meat thermometer reads 180° and juices run clear, basting occasionally (see chart for roasting time). Cover and let stand 10 minutes before carving. To make gravy from pan drippings, see Basic Pan Gravy from Roasted Meats on page 145. **Yield:** 4 servings.
—*Connie Moore, Medway, Ohio*

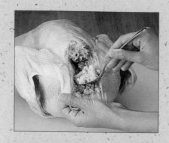

1 Combine stuffing ingredients according to recipe directions. Do not stuff turkey until you are ready to place it in the oven. Spoon the stuffing loosely into the neck cavity.

2 Place the neck skin over the stuffing to the back of the turkey and secure with a skewer. Tuck the wing tips under the body to avoid overbrowning while roasting.

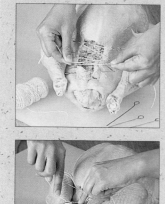

3 Loosely spoon the stuffing into the body cavity. Position skewers and lace shut, using kitchen string.

4 Tie drumsticks together with kitchen string.

5 Place turkey with breast side up on a rack in a shallow roasting pan. Brush with oil or melted butter or margarine. Insert an oven-safe meat thermometer into the thick portion of the inner thigh area. Do not touch bone. Or use an instant-read thermometer toward the end of the roasting time.

6 Roast turkey at 325°, basting with pan juices every half hour to keep meat moist. (See Roasting Poultry on page 138 for roasting times.)

7 When the breast area has browned, loosely cover with foil to avoid excess browning. Continue roasting until the thermometer reads 180° and the internal temperature in the center of the stuffing is 165°.

Turkey with Corn Bread Stuffing

Prepare your favorite basic corn bread recipe—or even a corn bread mix—the day before making this stuffing.

- 1/2 cup butter *or* margarine
- 2 cups chopped celery
- 1 cup chopped onion
- 6 cups cubed day-old corn bread
- 2 cups fresh bread crumbs
- 1 tablespoon rubbed sage
- 1 tablespoon poultry seasoning
- 2 eggs, lightly beaten
- 1 cup chicken broth
- 1 turkey (10 to 12 pounds)

Melted butter *or* **margarine**

In a skillet, melt butter. Saute celery and onion until tender. Place in a large bowl with corn bread, crumbs, sage and poultry seasoning. Combine eggs and chicken broth; add to bread mixture, stirring gently to mix. Just before baking, stuff turkey. Skewer or fasten openings. Tie drumsticks together. Place with breast side up on a rack in a roasting pan. Brush with melted butter. Bake at 325° until a meat thermometer reads 180° for the turkey and 165° for the stuffing (see chart for roasting time). When turkey begins to brown, cover lightly with a tent of aluminum foil. Cover and let stand 20 minutes before removing stuffing and carving. To make gravy from pan drippings, see Basic Pan Gravy from Roasted Meats on page 145. **Yield:** 10-12 servings. **Editor's Note:** Stuffing may also be baked in a greased 2-qt. casserole dish. Cover and bake at 325° for 60 minutes. Uncover and bake 10 minutes longer or until lightly browned. —*Norma Poole, Auburndale, Florida*

Most folks agree that stuffing and gravy really complete a chicken or turkey dinner. The Basic Pan Gravy recipe on page 145 can be used for roasted chicken or turkey as well as beef and pork. The stuffing recipes can be used for any roasted chicken or turkey.

Herbed Rice Stuffing

For a change of pace, try a rice stuffing for your holiday turkey. If you're entertaining a crowd, prepare two different stuffing recipes, one in the bird and one baked in a casserole, to add interest to your meal.

- **1/2 pound bulk pork sausage**
- **1/2 pound ground beef**
- **1/2 cup chopped onion**
- **2 eggs, lightly beaten**
- **1 tablespoon poultry seasoning**
- **2 tablespoons minced fresh parsley**
- **2 tablespoons minced celery leaves**
- **1 teaspoon salt**
- **1 teaspoon pepper**
- **1/2 teaspoon garlic powder**
- **4 cups cooked white rice, cooled**

In a large skillet, brown sausage, beef and onion; drain. In a large bowl, combine eggs, poultry seasoning, parsley, celery leaves, salt, pepper and garlic powder; mix well. Add meat mixture and rice. Transfer to a greased 2-1/2-qt. baking dish. Cover and bake at 325° for 60 minutes. Uncover and bake 10 minutes longer or until lightly browned. **Yield:** 8 cups (enough for one 10- to 12-pound turkey).

—*Melanie Habener, Lompoc, California*

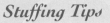

Stuffing Tips

- How much stuffing will fit into a bird? Prepare about 3/4 cup stuffing for every 1 pound of poultry.

- You can prepare stuffing ahead of time and refrigerate it. But never stuff the poultry until you are ready to bake. Loosely spoon stuffing into the neck and body cavities to allow for expansion as the poultry roasts.

- Stuffed poultry requires more roasting—add 15-45 minutes to the time unstuffed poultry takes.

- The internal temperature of the stuffing must reach 165° in order to be fully cooked.

- Cover the whole bird and let it stand for 10-20 minutes before removing the stuffing. Remove all stuffing and store any leftovers in separate containers in the refrigerator.

- Stuffing can also be baked in a casserole dish as the poultry bakes. See specific recipes for baking directions.

Herbed Rice Stuffing

Country Ham Stuffing

(Pictured on page 129)

This traditional bread stuffing is enhanced with ham to add flavor and moisture. For a tasty variation, substitute rye bread for the whole wheat bread.

 3 cups cubed crustless day-old white bread
 3 cups cubed crustless day-old whole wheat bread
 1/2 cup butter *or* margarine
 1-1/2 cups cubed fully cooked ham
 3 cups chopped onion
 2 cups chopped celery
 1-1/2 teaspoons rubbed sage
 1-1/2 teaspoons dried thyme
 1/2 teaspoon pepper
 1 to 1-1/2 cups chicken broth

Place bread cubes in a single layer in an ungreased 13-in. x 9-in. x 2-in. baking pan. Bake, uncovered, at 325° for 20-25 minutes or until golden, stirring occasionally. Place in a large bowl; set aside. In a large skillet, melt butter. Cook ham for 5-10 minutes or until edges are crisp. Remove with a slotted spoon and place over bread cubes. In the same skillet, saute onion, celery, sage, thyme and pepper until the vegetables are tender; toss with bread and ham. Stir in enough broth to moisten. Transfer to a greased 3-qt. baking dish. Cover and bake at 325° for 60 minutes. Uncover and bake 10 minutes longer or until lightly browned. **Yield:** 10 cups (enough for one 12- to 14-pound turkey).

—*Bobbie Love, Kapaa, Hawaii*

Dutch Potato Poultry Stuffing

If you like potatoes and celery, you'll enjoy this old-world stuffing that has its roots in Pennsylvania Dutch country. This is also a good casserole to make and serve with oven-fried chicken.

 5 cups mashed potatoes (without added milk, butter *or* seasoning)
 6 cups cubed crustless day-old white bread
 2-1/2 cups chopped onion
 1 cup minced celery leaves
 1 cup minced fresh parsley
 3 tablespoons butter *or* margarine, melted
 1 teaspoon salt
 3/4 teaspoon pepper
 3 eggs
 1 tablespoon all-purpose flour
 1 cup milk

In a large bowl, combine potatoes, bread cubes, onion, celery leaves, parsley, butter, salt and pepper. In a small

bowl, beat eggs and flour until smooth; gradually stir in milk. Pour into the potato mixture and mix well. Add more milk if stuffing seems dry. Transfer to a greased 3-qt. baking dish. Cover and bake at 325° for 60 minutes. Uncover and bake 10 minutes longer or until lightly browned. **Yield:** about 10 cups (enough for one 12- to 14-pound turkey).

—*Sarah Krout*
Warrington, Pennsylvania

Creole Stuffing

This unique stuffing uses both corn bread and wheat bread to produce a wonderful texture. Creole seasoning is available in the spice section of grocery stores.

 4 cups cubed corn bread
 2 cups cubed crustless day-old whole wheat bread
 1 cup chopped fully cooked ham
 3/4 cup chopped smoked kielbasa
 1/2 cup finely chopped sweet red pepper
 1/2 cup finely chopped green pepper

Dutch Potato Poultry Stuffing

1/4 cup finely chopped celery
3 tablespoons finely chopped onion
2-1/2 teaspoons Creole seasoning
2 eggs, lightly beaten
1 to 1-1/2 cups chicken broth

In a large bowl, combine the first 10 ingredients; add enough chicken broth to moisten. Transfer to a greased 2-qt. baking dish. Cover and bake at 325° for 60 minutes. Uncover and bake 10 minutes longer or until lightly browned. **Yield:** about 6 cups (enough for one 8- to 10-pound turkey).

—*Sandy Szwarc*
Albuquerque, New Mexico

Making Pan Gravy from Roasted Meats

1 Pour pan drippings into a heat-resistant measuring cup along with any browned bits that can be scraped from the roasting pan. Skim fat.

2 Reserve 1/4 cup fat and place in a saucepan. Whisk in flour until smooth.

3 Add enough broth or water to the reserved pan drippings to equal 2 cups. Add all at once to flour mixture. Cook and stir over medium high until thickened; cook and stir 1 minute longer. Season with salt and pepper if desired.

Basic Pan Gravy from Roasted Meats

For maximum flavor and rich color, stir to loosen as much of the browned bits from the roasting pan as possible. If the color is still light, add 1/4 to 1/2 teaspoon bottled browning sauce or soy sauce to the gravy.

Pan drippings
1/4 cup all-purpose flour
Broth *or* water
Salt and pepper to taste

Transfer meat to a warm platter. Pour pan drippings into a measuring cup. Loosen browned bits from the roaster and add to the cup. Skim off all fat that rises to the top of the cup. Reserve 1/4 cup fat and pour into a saucepan; whisk in flour. Add enough broth or water to pan drippings to measure 2 cups. Stir into flour mixture. Cook and stir constantly over medium-high heat, until thickened and bubbly; cook 1 minute longer. Season with salt and pepper if desired. **Yield:** 2 cups.

Mushroom Gravy

Keep this recipe handy for the times when you are serving leftovers and you're out of gravy. This version is nice, too, for folks who can't have traditional gravy. If serving more than eight or 10, or if you like leftover gravy, double the recipe.

1/2 cup finely chopped onion
1/2 cup finely chopped fresh mushrooms
2 tablespoons minced fresh parsley
2 cups low-sodium beef *or* chicken broth, *divided*
2 tablespoons cornstarch
Pinch pepper

In a saucepan, cook onion, mushrooms and parsley in 1/4 cup broth until vegetables are tender. Combine cornstarch, pepper and 1/2 cup of broth; stir until smooth. Add to pan with the remaining broth. Bring to a boil, stirring occasionally; boil for 2 minutes. **Yield:** 2 cups. ⏱ 🍎   —*Mary Fry, Cedar Rapids, Iowa*

Turkey Drumstick Dinner

onion. Cover and bake at 325° for 2 hours, basting once or twice. Add potatoes and zucchini. Cover and bake 20 minutes longer. Transfer turkey and vegetables to a serving dish and keep warm. Combine the cornstarch and water until smooth; stir into tomato mixture. Bake, uncovered, for 10-15 minutes or until slightly thickened. Pour over turkey and vegetables. Sprinkle with parsley. **Yield:** 4 servings.
—*Alice Balliet
Kane, Pennsylvania*

Teriyaki Turkey

Turkey pieces are budget-savers and make hearty meals when there isn't time to roast a whole turkey.

    1/2 cup soy sauce
    1/2 cup vegetable oil
      2 tablespoons honey
      2 teaspoons Worcestershire sauce
      1 teaspoon ground ginger
      1 teaspoon ground mustard
      1 teaspoon lemon juice
      2 garlic cloves, minced
      6 to 7 pounds turkey pieces
    1/4 cup all-purpose flour, optional
Salt and pepper, optional

In a small bowl, combine the soy sauce, oil, honey, Worcestershire sauce, ginger, mustard, lemon juice and garlic. Place turkey pieces in a large resealable plastic bag; add marinade. Seal bag; refrigerate overnight, turning bag occasionally. Arrange turkey in a single layer in a large shallow roasting pan. Pour marinade over turkey. Bake, uncovered, at 325° for 1-1/2 to 2 hours or until tender. Baste occasionally if desired. Remove turkey to serving platter and keep warm. To make gravy from pan drippings, see Basic Pan Gravy from Roasted Meats on page 145. **Yield:** 8-10 servings.
—*Wilma Lovejoy, Hastings, Nebraska*

Turkey Drumstick Dinner

Kids will love being served their own drumstick. You'll love that this easy whole meal requires just one pot.

      2 tablespoons vegetable oil
      1 tablespoon butter *or* margarine
      4 turkey drumsticks (about 3 pounds)
      1 medium onion, sliced
      1 can (14-1/2 ounces) stewed tomatoes
      3 chicken bouillon cubes
      1 teaspoon garlic salt
    1/2 teaspoon dried oregano
    1/2 teaspoon dried basil
      4 large potatoes, peeled, cooked and quartered
      2 medium zucchini, cut into 3/4-inch slices
      2 tablespoons cornstarch
      2 tablespoons water
Minced fresh parsley

In a large skillet, heat oil and butter; brown drumsticks. Transfer to a 3-qt. Dutch oven. Top with onion. In the same skillet, heat tomatoes, bouillon and seasonings until bouillon is dissolved. Pour over the turkey and

Turkey Minute Steaks

Here's a deliciously different way to prepare turkey. Serve these seasoned steaks on bread or over a bed of buttered noodles.

　　3/4 cup seasoned dry bread crumbs
　　1/4 cup grated Parmesan cheese
　　1/2 teaspoon dried basil
Salt and pepper to taste
　1 1/2 pounds uncooked sliced turkey breast
　　　1 egg, beaten
　　　3 tablespoons butter *or* margarine

In a shallow bowl, combine the bread crumbs, Parmesan cheese, basil, salt and pepper; mix well. Dip turkey in egg, then in crumbs, coating all sides. Melt butter in a skillet over medium-high heat. Cook turkey for 2-3 minutes on each side or until golden brown and juices run clear. **Yield:** 6-8 servings. ○
　　　　　　　　　　　　—Barbara Powell, Laramie, Wyoming

Turkey in a Hurry

Turkey tenderloins are boneless breast meat available in the meat case. Use them as you would boneless skinless chicken breasts.

　　2 turkey tenderloins (1-1/2 pounds)
　　1/4 cup butter *or* margarine
　　3/4 teaspoon dried thyme
　　1/2 teaspoon dried rosemary, crushed
　　1/4 teaspoon paprika
　　1/8 teaspoon garlic powder

Cut tenderloins in half lengthwise, then into serving-size pieces. Place on the rack of a broiler pan. In a small saucepan, heat remaining ingredients until butter is melted. Broil turkey until lightly browned on one side. Brush with the herb butter; turn and brown the other side. Brush with butter. Broil 6-8 minutes longer or until juices run clear, brushing frequently with butter. **Yield:** 6 servings. ○
　　　　　　　　　　　　　　—Denise Goedeken
　　　　　　　　　　　　　Platte Center, Nebraska

Turkey with Mushroom Gravy

These turkey legs become extra tender when braised in mushroom gravy. Serve with gravy over egg noodles or mashed potatoes

　　4 turkey drumsticks (about 3 pounds)
　　1/4 cup lemon juice
　　2 tablespoons vegetable oil
　　1 teaspoon dried oregano
　　1 teaspoon dried basil
　　1 teaspoon garlic powder
　　1/4 teaspoon salt
　　1/4 teaspoon pepper
MUSHROOM GRAVY:
　　1 tablespoon cornstarch
　　1 cup water
　　1 can (10-1/2 ounces) mushroom gravy
　　1 can (4 ounces) mushroom stems and
　　　pieces, drained
　　1 teaspoon dried minced onion
　　1 teaspoon minced fresh parsley
　　1 teaspoon garlic powder

Place drumsticks in a roasting pan. Combine lemon juice, oil and seasonings; pour over turkey. Bake, uncovered, at 325° for 45 minutes or until lightly browned. Turn turkey twice and baste occasionally. Meanwhile, for gravy, combine cornstarch and water in a saucepan until smooth. Stir in remaining ingredients and bring to a boil over medium heat. Spoon over turkey. Cover loosely with foil. Bake, basting frequently, for 1 hour or until turkey is tender. **Yield:** 4 servings.
　　　　　　　　　　—Wanda Swenson, Lady Lake, Florida

Turkey with Mushroom Gravy

Grilled Tarragon Chicken

These chicken breasts can also be served on rolls as sandwiches with lettuce and tomato.

2 teaspoons Dijon mustard
4 boneless skinless chicken breast halves (1 pound)
1/4 teaspoon pepper
1/3 cup butter *or* margarine, melted
2 teaspoons lemon juice
2 teaspoons minced fresh tarragon *or* 1/2 teaspoon dried tarragon
1/2 teaspoon garlic salt

Spread mustard on all sides of chicken; sprinkle with pepper. Cover and refrigerate for at least 2 hours. Combine butter, lemon juice, tarragon and garlic salt. Grill chicken, uncovered, over hot heat until juices run clear, basting with butter mixture during the last 3-5 minutes. **Yield:** 4 servings. 🍎
— *Janie Thorpe*
Tullahoma, Tennessee

Dilly Grilled Turkey

This recipe calls for half of a fresh or frozen turkey breast. If your market carries only whole turkey breasts, ask the butcher to cut one in half for you.

1 bone-in turkey breast half (2-1/2 to 3 pounds)
1 cup plain nonfat yogurt
1/4 cup lemon juice
3 tablespoons vegetable oil

Barbecued Chicken

1/4 cup minced fresh parsley
1/4 cup chopped green onions
2 garlic cloves, minced
2 tablespoons fresh minced dill *or* 2 teaspoons dill weed
1/2 teaspoon dried rosemary, crushed
1/2 teaspoon salt
1/4 teaspoon pepper

Place turkey in a glass container. In a small bowl, combine remaining ingredients; spread over turkey. Cover and refrigerate for 6-8 hours or overnight. Remove turkey; discard marinade. Cover and grill over medium-hot heat for 1 to 1-1/4 hours or until juices run clear and a meat thermometer reads 170°. **Yield:** 6 servings. 🍎
— *Sue Walker, Greentown, Indiana*

Barbecued Chicken

With both a dry rub and a basting sauce, this recipe has lots of flavor. Brush on the sauce during the last 10 minutes to keep the skin from burning.

2 broiler-fryer chickens (3 to 4 pounds *each*), cut up
SEASONING MIX:
3 tablespoons salt
2 tablespoons onion powder
1 tablespoon paprika
2 teaspoons garlic powder
1-1/2 teaspoons chili powder
1-1/2 teaspoons pepper
1/4 teaspoon ground turmeric
Pinch cayenne pepper
SAUCE:
2 cups ketchup
3 tablespoons brown sugar
2 tablespoons dried minced onion
2 tablespoons orange juice concentrate
1/2 teaspoon liquid smoke, optional

Pat chicken dry with paper towels; set aside. Combine seasoning mix ingredients; reserve 1 tablespoon for sauce. Sprinkle mix generously over all sides of the chicken (store leftovers in a covered container). Grill chicken, skin side down, uncovered, over medium heat for 20 minutes. Turn; grill 20-30 minutes longer or until juices run clear. Meanwhile, combine sauce ingredients and 1 tablespoon seasoning mix; brush over chicken frequently during the last 10 minutes of grilling. **Yield:** 12 servings.
— *Linda Scott*
Hahira, Georgia

Marinated Thanksgiving Turkey

Marinated Thanksgiving Turkey

For a real change of pace, why not grill your Thanksgiving turkey on the outdoor barbecue? You'll love the smoked flavor of the meat, which makes excellent sandwiches later.

       2 cups water
   1-1/2 cups chicken broth
       1 cup soy sauce
       2/3 cup lemon juice
       2 garlic cloves, minced
   1-1/2 teaspoons ground ginger
       1 teaspoon pepper
       1 turkey (12 to 14 pounds)

Combine the first seven ingredients; reserve 1 cup for basting. Pour remaining marinade into a 2-gal. resealable plastic bag. Add the turkey and seal bag; turn to coat. Refrigerate overnight, turning several times. Discard marinade. Heat grill according to manufacturer's directions for indirect cooking. Tuck wings under turkey and place with breast side down on cooking grate. Cover and grill for 1 hour. For charcoal grills, add 10 briquettes to coals; turn the turkey breast side up. Brush with reserved marinade. Cover and cook for 2 hours, adding 10 briquettes to maintain heat and brushing with marinade every 30 minutes until a meat thermometer reads 180°. Cover and let stand 20 minutes before carving. **Yield:** 8 servings. **Editor's Note:** To roast in a conventional oven, place turkey on a rack in a large roasting pan. Bake, uncovered, at 325° for 3 to 3-1/2 hours or until a meat thermometer reads 180°, basting frequently with reserved marinade.

—*Ken Churches, San Andreas, California*

Turkey Biscuit Stew

After a multi-course holiday meal, here's a one-pot supper using leftover turkey that's easy on the cook. If you have leftover peas and/or carrots, use them in this dish.

    1/4 cup butter *or* margarine
    1/3 cup chopped onion
    1/3 cup all-purpose flour
    1/2 teaspoon salt
    1/8 teaspoon pepper
      1 can (10-1/2 ounces) chicken broth
    3/4 cup milk
      2 cups cubed cooked turkey
      1 cup cooked peas
      1 cup cooked whole baby carrots
      1 tube (10 ounces) refrigerated buttermilk
        biscuits

In a 10-in. ovenproof skillet, melt butter. Saute onion until tender. Stir in flour, salt and pepper until smooth. Gradually add broth and milk; cook, stirring constantly, until thickened and bubbly. Add the turkey, peas and carrots; heat through. Separate biscuits and arrange over the stew. Bake, uncovered, at 375° for 20-25 minutes or until biscuits are golden brown. **Yield:** 6-8 servings. —*Lori Schlecht, Wimbledon, North Dakota*

Hot Chicken Salad

A good choice for your next potluck supper or a light luncheon, this casserole can be assembled and refrigerated 24 hours in advance.

 2-1/2 cups diced cooked chicken
    2 cups cooked rice
    1 can (8 ounces) sliced water chestnuts, drained
    1 cup diced celery
    1 cup sliced fresh mushrooms
    1 tablespoon finely chopped onion
    1 teaspoon lemon juice
  1/2 teaspoon dried rosemary, crushed
  1/4 teaspoon pepper
    1 can (10-3/4 ounces) condensed cream of
      chicken soup, undiluted
  3/4 cup mayonnaise
TOPPING:
    3 tablespoons butter *or* margarine
  1/2 cup cornflake crumbs
  1/2 cup slivered almonds

In a 2-1/2-qt. casserole, combine the first nine ingredients. Blend soup and mayonnaise; toss with chicken mixture. Spoon into a greased 2-qt. baking dish. Melt butter; toss with crumbs and almonds. Sprinkle over casserole. Bake, uncovered, at 350° for 30 minutes. **Yield:** 6 servings.
—*Michelle Wise*
Spring Mills, Pennsylvania

Hot Chicken Salad

Turkey Dressing Pie

Cheddar Chicken Potpie

With its rich cheddar-flavored sauce and homemade pastry crust, this is a real old-fashioned potpie. It is important to cut slits in the crust to allow the steam to escape. If desired, use small cookie cutters to make decorative steam vents.

CRUST:
    1 cup all-purpose flour
    1/2 teaspoon salt
    5 tablespoons cold butter *or* margarine, cut into
        pieces
    3 tablespoons cold water
FILLING:
 1-1/2 cups chicken broth
    2 cups cubed peeled potatoes
    1 cup sliced carrots
    1/2 cup sliced celery
    1/2 cup chopped onion
    1/4 cup all-purpose flour
 1-1/2 cups milk
    2 cups (8 ounces) shredded sharp cheddar
        cheese
    4 cups diced cooked chicken
    1/4 teaspoon poultry seasoning
Salt and pepper to taste

Combine flour and salt in a mixing bowl. Cut in butter until crumbly. Gradually add water, tossing with a fork until dough forms a ball. Cover with plastic wrap and refrigerate for at least 30 minutes. For filling, bring broth to a boil in a Dutch oven or large saucepan. Add vegetables; simmer for 10-15 minutes or until tender. Blend flour with milk until smooth; stir into broth mixture. Cook and stir over medium heat until slightly thickened and bubbly. Stir in cheese, chicken, poultry seasoning, salt and pepper; heat until cheese is melted. Spoon into a 2-1/2- to 3-qt. baking dish; set aside. On a floured board, roll crust 1 inch larger than dish. Ease crust over filling; seal edges to side of dish. Make several slits in center of crust. Bake, uncovered, at 425° for 40 minutes or until golden. **Yield:** 6 servings.

—Sandra Cothran, Ridgeland, South Carolina

Turkey Dressing Pie

After Thanksgiving, this recipe is a must! It gives leftover turkey, dressing and gravy new life.

 3-1/2 to 4 cups cooked turkey dressing
    1/2 cup turkey *or* chicken broth
    2 tablespoons butter *or* margarine, melted
    1 egg, beaten
    1 tablespoon vegetable oil
    1/2 cup chopped onion
    3 cups diced cooked turkey
    1 cup turkey gravy
    1 cup frozen peas, optional
    2 tablespoons dried parsley flakes
    2 tablespoons diced pimientos
    1 teaspoon Worcestershire sauce
    1/2 teaspoon dried thyme
    4 slices process American cheese, optional

In a large bowl, combine dressing, broth, butter and egg; mix well. Press onto the bottom and up the sides of an ungreased 10-in. pie plate; set aside. In a large skillet, heat oil. Saute onion until tender. Stir in turkey, gravy, peas if desired, parsley, pimientos, Worcestershire sauce and thyme; heat through. Pour over crust. Bake, uncovered, at 375° for 20 minutes or until golden. If desired, arrange cheese slices on top of pie and return to the oven for 5 minutes or until cheese is melted. **Yield:** 6 servings.

—De De Boekelheide
Northville, South Dakota

Mexican Turkey Roll-Ups

Mexican Turkey Roll-Ups

If you have cooked turkey in the freezer, make this Southwestern favorite. Serve it with Spanish rice and canned refried beans for a dinner the kids are sure to enjoy.

2-1/2 cups cubed cooked turkey
1-1/2 cups (12 ounces) sour cream, *divided*
    1 can (10-3/4 ounces) condensed cream of
      mushroom soup, undiluted, *divided*
    3 teaspoons taco seasoning, *divided*
1-1/2 cups (6 ounces) shredded cheddar cheese,
    divided
    1 small onion, chopped
    1/2 cup salsa
    1/4 cup sliced ripe olives
    10 flour tortillas (7 inches)
Shredded lettuce
Chopped tomatoes
Additional olives and salsa, optional

Tips for Freezing Leftover Poultry

To freeze leftover cooked poultry, slice or cube the meat. Freeze in serving- or recipe-size portions in airtight containers, heavy-duty freezer bags or heavy-duty foil. For maximum flavor and moistness, use within 2 to 3 months.

In a bowl, combine turkey, 1/2 cup sour cream, half of the soup, 1-1/2 teaspoons taco seasoning, 1 cup of cheese, onion, salsa and olives. Spoon 1/3 cup onto each tortilla. Roll up and place seam side down in a greased 13-in. x 9-in. x 2-in. baking dish. Combine remaining sour cream, soup and taco seasoning; pour over tortillas. Cover and bake at 350° for 30 minutes or until heated through. Sprinkle with remaining cheese. Garnish with lettuce, tomatoes and olives if desired. Serve with salsa if desired. **Yield:** about 5 servings.
        —Marlene Muckenhirn, Delano, Minnesota

Chicken and Hash Brown Bake

Serve this versatile casserole with a fruit salad for a late-morning brunch or with a tossed green or spinach salad for dinner.

    1 package (32 ounces) frozen Southern-style
      hash brown potatoes, thawed
    1 teaspoon salt
  1/4 teaspoon pepper
    4 cups diced cooked chicken
    1 can (4 ounces) mushroom stems and pieces,
      drained
    2 cups chicken broth *or* stock
    1 can (10-3/4 ounces) condensed cream of
      chicken soup, undiluted
    1 cup (8 ounces) sour cream
    2 teaspoons chicken bouillon granules
    2 tablespoons finely chopped onion
    2 tablespoons finely chopped sweet red pepper
    1 garlic clove, minced
Paprika
  1/4 cup sliced almonds

Layer hash browns in an ungreased 13-in. x 9-in. x 2-in. baking dish. Sprinkle with salt and pepper. Place chicken and mushrooms over the hash browns. Stir together broth, soup, sour cream, bouillon, onion, red pepper and garlic; pour over all. Sprinkle with paprika and almonds. Bake, uncovered, at 350° for 50-60 minutes or until heated through. **Yield:** 8-10 servings.
—Ruth Andrewson, Leavenworth, Washington

Chicken Broccoli Casserole

For added convenience, substitute two 10-ounce packages of frozen chopped broccoli for the fresh. Simply defrost, drain and place in the baking pan. You don't need to cook the broccoli before assembling this casserole.

    3 cups broccoli florets (about 1-1/4
      pounds)
    2 cups cubed cooked chicken *or* turkey
    1 can (10-3/4 ounces)
      condensed cream of chick-
      en soup, undiluted
  1/2 cup mayonnaise *or* salad
      dressing
  1/2 cup grated Parmesan
      cheese
  1/2 teaspoon curry powder
    1 cup soft bread cubes
    2 tablespoons butter *or* margarine,
      melted

Place broccoli in a saucepan; cover with 1 in. of water. Bring to a boil. Reduce heat; cover

and simmer for 5-8 minutes or until crisp-tender. Drain. Place in a greased 11-in. x 7-in. x 2-in. baking dish; set aside. Combine chicken, soup, mayonnaise, Parmesan cheese and curry powder; spoon over broccoli. Top with bread cubes and butter. Bake, uncovered, at 350° for 25-30 minutes or until heated through. **Yield:** 6 servings. *—Colleen Lewis, Cottonwood, Arizona*

Chicken a la King

This speedy entree is even easier to prepare if you have left-over cooked cubed chicken or turkey in the freezer. Defrost in the microwave for last-minute meals.

  1/4 cup butter *or* margarine
  1/3 cup all-purpose flour
  1/2 teaspoon salt
    1 cup chicken broth
    1 cup milk
    2 cups diced cooked chicken
    1 can (4 ounces) mushroom stems and pieces,
      drained
    1 jar (2 ounces) diced pimientos, drained
Toast points, biscuits, rice, noodles *or* puff pastry
    shells

In a saucepan, melt butter; stir in flour and salt until smooth. Add the broth and milk; bring to a boil over medium heat. Cook and stir for 2 minutes or until thickened. Stir in the chicken, mushrooms and pimientos; heat through. Serve over toast points, biscuits, rice, noodles or puff pastry shells. **Yield:** 4 servings. 🕐
—Polly Hurst, Flemingsburg, Kentucky

Chicken Broccoli Casserole

for sauce, heat jelly, lemon juice and butter in a small saucepan until jelly and butter are melted. Combine vinegar, cornstarch, salt and cloves; add to pan. Bring to a boil; boil for 2 minutes. After hens have baked for 30 minutes, baste and bake 30 minutes longer or until meat is tender and juices run clear and a meat thermometer inserted into the stuffing reads 165°. Bake extra stuffing in a greased 1-qt. covered baking dish at 350° for 30 minutes. **Yield:** 4 servings. —*Lori Bluml Carroll, Iowa*

Currant-Glazed Cornish Hens

Currant-Glazed Cornish Hens

The use of a store-bought wild rice mix makes this festive entree easy to assemble.

        1 package (6 ounces) long grain and wild rice mix
        2 tablespoons vegetable oil
        1 medium onion, chopped
    1/2 pound fresh mushrooms, sliced
    1/4 cup chopped celery
    1/2 cup chopped pecans, toasted
        2 tablespoons minced fresh parsley
    1/4 teaspoon dried thyme
    1/4 teaspoon dried marjoram
        4 Cornish game hens
        2 tablespoons butter *or* margarine, softened
CURRANT SAUCE:
    1/2 cup currant jelly
        2 tablespoons lemon juice
        1 tablespoon butter *or* margarine
    1/4 cup cider vinegar
        1 tablespoon cornstarch
        1 teaspoon salt
        3 whole cloves

Prepare rice according to package directions. In a large skillet, heat oil. Saute onion, mushrooms and celery until tender. Remove from the heat; add rice, pecans, parsley, thyme and marjoram. Loosely stuff hens; rub skin with butter. Place on a rack in a shallow baking pan. Bake, uncovered, at 350° for 30 minutes. Meanwhile,

Roasted Duck with Apple-Raisin Dressing

If a recipe calls for soft bread rather than croutons, use bread that is 1 to 2 days old. Fresh bread is too soft and will create a mushy final result.

        2 domestic ducklings (4 to 6 pounds *each*)
Salt
DRESSING:
    12 ounces bulk pork sausage
    1/2 cup chopped onion
    1/2 cup chopped celery
        1 cup chopped peeled apple
    1/2 cup water
        1 cup raisins
        2 tablespoons minced fresh parsley
1-1/2 teaspoons salt
        1 teaspoon rubbed sage
    1/4 teaspoon pepper
        8 cups cubed crustless day-old white bread
        3 eggs, lightly beaten
    1/2 cup chicken broth

Sprinkle the inside of ducklings with salt; prick skin well and set aside. In a large skillet, cook sausage

Plumping Raisins

Place 1 cup raisins in a bowl and add 1/2 cup boiling water. Cover with plastic wrap and allow to stand for 10 minutes. Follow specific recipe as to whether the liquid should be drained.

with onion and celery until sausage is no longer pink and vegetables are tender. Add apple and simmer for 3 minutes, stirring occasionally; drain. Meanwhile, heat water to boiling; pour over raisins. Let stand for 10 minutes; do not drain. In a large bowl, combine sausage mixture, parsley, raisins, salt, sage and pepper; mix well. Add the bread cubes, eggs and broth; mix lightly. Divide and spoon into ducklings. Place with breast side up on a rack in a large shallow roasting pan. Bake, uncovered, at 350° until juices run clear and a meat thermometer reads 180° for the duck and 165° for the stuffing (see chart for roasting time). Drain fat from pan as it accumulates. Cover and let stand 20 minutes before removing stuffing and carving. **Yield:** 4 servings.   —Fran Kirchhoff, Harvard, Illinois

Tips for Roasting Ducklings and Geese

- Ducklings and geese have more fat than other poultry. To remove the fat, prick the skin with a sharp tined fork before roasting to allow the fat to drain.

- With a baster, remove and discard fat from the bottom of the roaster as it accumulates during the roasting time.

- Because the drippings are very rich with fat, gravy is not usually prepared from roasted duck or goose.

Goose with Apple-Prune Stuffing

The sweet yet savory flavors of the glaze is a bold complement to the dark meat of goose. Remember to wait to glaze meats and poultry until the last 20-30 minutes of roasting. Otherwise, the glaze will darken and burn.

　　1 domestic goose (8 to 12 pounds)
Salt
STUFFING:
　　3 tablespoons butter *or* margarine
　　2 cups chopped celery
　　1 cup chopped onion
　　1 garlic clove, minced
　　6 cups chopped peeled tart apples
　　1 package (12 ounces) pitted prunes, cut up
　　1 cup apple juice
　　1 egg, lightly beaten
　1/3 cup minced fresh parsley
　　1 tablespoon rubbed sage
　1/2 teaspoon salt
　1/4 teaspoon pepper
　1/4 teaspoon ground thyme
　　1 bay leaf, crumbled
　　3 to 4 cups coarse bread crumbs
GLAZE (optional):
　　1 cup orange juice
　1/2 cup chili sauce
　　1 tablespoon brown sugar
　　2 tablespoons cornstarch
　　1 tablespoon soy sauce
　　1 teaspoon prepared mustard
　1/4 teaspoon garlic powder

Sprinkle the inside of goose with salt. Prick skin well; set aside. In a skillet, melt butter. Saute celery, onion and garlic until tender; transfer to a large bowl. Add the next 10 ingredients. Add bread crumbs until stuffing has the desired consistency. Loosely stuff the goose. Place with breast side up on a rack in a large shallow roasting pan. Bake, uncovered, at 350° until juices run clear and a meat thermometer reads 180° for the goose and 165° for the stuffing (see chart for roasting time). Drain fat from pan as it accumulates. If desired, combine glaze ingredients in a saucepan. Cook and stir until bubbly; cook and stir 2 minutes longer. Brush over the goose during the last 20 minutes of baking. Cover and let stand 20 minutes before removing stuffing and carving. **Yield:** 8-10 servings.   —Violet Klause Onoway, Alberta

Goose with Apple-Prune Stuffing

Pork

From chops, roasts and tenderloin to ham, ribs and sausage, pork is the answer to any everyday or special-occasion dinner dilemma. With versatility, great taste and preparation ease, pork dishes like Cherry Almond Glazed Ham (p. 172) and Pork Chops with Apple Stuffing (p. 159) will be mainstays at your table.

Today's pork is easier than ever to cook because it's lean and tender. No longer is it necessary to overcook any cut of pork. Follow the techniques and guidelines below for cooking your favorite cuts of pork, and you'll have perfect results every time!

Basic Cooking Methods for Fresh Pork

Braising
Recommended for 1/2-in.-thick to 1-1/2-in.-thick chops, cubes of pork or steaks when a more tender texture is desired. Season the meat as desired. In a heavy skillet, brown pork in a small amount of oil on both sides. Drain; add a small amount of water or other liquid. Cover; simmer over low heat on the stovetop or bake at 325° to 350° until fork-tender.

Broiling and Grilling
Recommended for chops (at least 1 in. thick), steaks (1/2 to 3/4 in. thick), ground pork patties (1/2 in. thick) and tenderloin. Place pork on a preheated broiler pan or grill rack that is positioned 3-5 in. from the heat. Thin cuts should be closer to the heat, thick cuts further away from the heat. Broil or grill until browned on both sides and juices run clear.

Pan-Broiling
Recommended for small cuts such as chops, steaks and ground pork patties that are no more than 1 in. thick when a firmer texture is desired. Preheat a heavy skillet over medium-high. If the cut is very lean, brush with a little oil. Pan-broil, uncovered, until browned on both sides and juices run clear.

Tips for Buying and Cooking Pork

- The amount of pork you need varies with the cut selected. Follow these guidelines: 2 to 2-1/2 servings per 1 pound of bone-in chops and roasts; 3 to 4 servings per 1 pound of boneless chops and roasts; 1-1/4 servings per 1 pound of spareribs.

- Fresh pork cooks quickly and needs only to be cooked to an internal temperature of 160° to 170°. At 160°, the internal color of boneless roasts may be faint pink and bone-in roasts may be slightly pink near the bone. But if the juices run clear, the meat is properly cooked.

- Unlike beef, cuts of pork vary little in tenderness. Use dry-heat cooking methods (broiling, grilling, pan-broiling, roasting and stir-frying) when a firm texture is desired. The moist-heat method of braising is used when a fork-tender texture is desired.

Roasting
Recommended for larger cuts of pork such as loin roasts, leg/ham, shoulder (picnic), crown roast and tenderloin when a juicy, firm texture is desired. Trim excess fat from roast, leaving a thin cover of fat. If the roast doesn't have a fat cover, brush with oil. Season roast as desired. See the Roasting Fresh Pork chart on page 162 for details.

Stir-Frying
Recommended for tender cuts such as boneless loin and tenderloin that have been sliced into thin strips. In a heavy skillet or wok over medium-high, heat a small amount of oil. Stir-fry pork for 5-10 minutes or until lightly browned and no longer pink, stirring constantly. See page 116 for stir-frying basics.

Breaded Pork Chops

When planning a side dish for this entree, consider a creamy scalloped potato casserole for a delicious contrast to the crisp breading of the pork chops.

  1 egg
  1/2 cup milk
  6 loin *or* rib pork chops (1 inch thick)
  1-1/2 cups crushed saltines (about 45
    crackers)
  1/4 cup vegetable oil

In a shallow pan, beat egg and milk. Dip each pork chop in the mixture, then coat with cracker crumbs, patting to make a thick coating. Heat oil in a large skillet. Cook pork chops, uncovered, for about 8-10 minutes per side or until browned and juices run clear. **Yield:** 3-6 servings.
　　　　　　　　　　　　　　　—Deborah Amrine
　　　　　　　　　　　　　　　Grand Haven, Michigan

Pork Chops with Apple Stuffing

(Also pictured on page 156)

A serving of this recipe is like having an individual roast on your plate. The stuffing is "sandwiched" between two pork chops for a pretty presentation and hearty flavor.

  1-1/3 cups soft bread crumbs
  1/4 cup butter *or* margarine
    1 tablespoon vegetable oil
    1 medium onion, finely chopped
    1 celery rib, finely chopped
    2 garlic cloves, minced
    1 medium tart apple, chopped
    1 egg, beaten
    1 teaspoon dried basil
  1/2 teaspoon salt
  1/2 teaspoon dried oregano
  1/4 teaspoon pepper
    8 loin *or* rib pork chops (1/2 inch thick)
Chicken broth

Pork Chops with Apple Stuffing

In a skillet, brown crumbs in butter until golden; remove and set aside. In the same skillet, heat oil over medium-high. Saute onion, celery and garlic until tender. Remove from the heat. Add crumbs, apple, egg and seasonings; mix well. Lay one pork chop flat; spoon a fourth of the stuffing on top. Top with another chop and secure with string. Repeat with remaining chops and stuffing. Stand chops vertically, but not touching, in a deep roasting pan. Pour chicken broth around chops to a depth of 1/4 in. Cover and bake at 350° for 1-1/4 hours. Uncover and bake 15 minutes longer or until chops are browned and juices run clear. **Yield:** 4 servings.
　　　　　　　　　　　　　　—Laura Enrico
　　　　　　　　　　　　　　Westford, Massachusetts

Chops and Chilies Casserole

This is a convenient casserole for busy days. A salad or vegetable completes the meal.

> 1 tablespoon vegetable oil
> 4 rib pork chops (3/4 to 1 inch thick)
> 1 medium onion, chopped
> 1 can (4 ounces) chopped green chilies
> 1/2 cup chopped celery
> 1-1/2 cups uncooked instant rice
> 1 can (10-3/4 ounces) condensed cream of
>   mushroom soup, undiluted
> 1-1/3 cups water
> 3 tablespoons soy sauce

In a skillet, heat oil over medium-high. Brown pork chops on both sides. Remove and set aside. In the same skillet, saute onion, chilies and celery until vegetables are tender. Stir in rice; saute until lightly browned. Add remaining ingredients; blend well. Transfer to a greased 2-qt. casserole. Top with pork chops. Bake, uncovered, at 350° for about 30 minutes or until rice is tender and the juices run clear. **Yield:** 2-4 servings. —*Mickey O'Neal Chula Vista, California*

Chops and Chilies Casserole

Sauerkraut Pork Chops

Sauerkraut, apples and caraway add a German twist to these chops. If you prefer a more mild flavor, rinse and drain the sauerkraut before adding it to the skillet.

> 2 tablespoons vegetable oil
> 4 loin pork chops (3/4 inch thick)
> 1 cup chopped onion
> 1 can (14-1/2 ounces) chicken broth
> 1/2 teaspoon caraway seed
> 1/4 teaspoon celery seed
> 1/4 teaspoon pepper
> 1 can (16 ounces) sauerkraut, drained
> 1 tart apple, cored and chopped
> 4 bacon strips, cooked and crumbled, optional

In a skillet, heat oil over medium-high. Brown pork chops on both sides; drain. Stir in onion, broth, caraway seed, celery seed and pepper. Cover and simmer for 45-50 minutes. Add sauerkraut and apple. Cover and simmer 10-15 minutes longer or until heated through. Sprinkle with bacon if desired. **Yield:** 2-4 servings. —*Erika Taylor Hopedale, Massachusetts*

Oven-Barbecued Pork Chops

A large cast-iron skillet can also be used for this recipe. Because cast iron is a great conductor of heat, the chops will cook quickly and the sauce will thicken a little faster than in an aluminum or glass pan.

   6 loin *or* rib pork chops (3/4 inch thick)
3/4 cup ketchup
1/3 cup water
   2 tablespoons vinegar
   1 tablespoon Worcestershire sauce
   2 teaspoons brown sugar
1/2 teaspoon pepper
1/2 teaspoon chili powder
1/2 teaspoon paprika

Place chops in an ungreased 13-in. x 9-in. x 2-in. baking pan. Combine remaining ingredients; pour over chops. Bake, uncovered, at 375° for 1 hour. **Yield:** 3-6 servings.   —*Teresa King, Whittier, California*

Zesty Grilled Chops

These chops are very thick, so it's easy to test for doneness with a meat thermometer toward the end of the cooking time.

   6 loin *or* rib pork chops (about 1-1/2 inches thick)
3/4 cup soy sauce
1/4 cup lemon juice
   1 tablespoon chili sauce
   1 tablespoon brown sugar
   1 garlic clove, minced

Place chops in a resealable plastic bag or shallow glass container. Combine remaining ingredients; reserve 1/3 cup for basting. Cover and refrigerate. Pour remaining marinade over chops. Seal bag or cover container; refrigerate overnight. Drain and discard marinade. Grill chops, covered, or broil 4 in. from the heat for 12-16 minutes or until a meat thermometer reads 160° and juices run clear, turning once. Brush occasionally with reserved marinade. **Yield:** 6 servings.

   —*Blanche Babinski, Minto, North Dakota*

Zesty Grilled Chops

Roasting Fresh Pork

Place meat in a shallow roasting pan on a rack with the fat side up. Insert an oven-safe thermometer (or use an instant-read thermometer toward the end of the roasting time). Roast without liquid, uncovered, at 350° unless otherwise noted in the recipe. Because roasts will continue to cook after being removed from the oven, remove the meat when the internal temperature is 5-10° below the desired doneness and juices run clear. Cover with foil and allow to stand 10-15 minutes before carving.

Cut	Weight in Pounds	Doneness	Approximate Roasting Time
Loin Roast— with bone	3 to 5	160°	1 to 1-3/4 hours
Loin Roast— boneless	2 to 4	160°	40 to 80 minutes
Crown Roast	6 to 8	160°	2 to 3 hours
Shoulder or Boston Butt	3 to 6	160°-170°	2-1/4 to 4-3/4 hours
Leg—half (fresh ham or picnic)	3-1/2	160-170°	2-1/2 hours
Tenderloin (450°)	1/2 to 1	160°	20 to 30 minutes

Spiced Apple Pork Roast

Spiced Apple Pork Roast

This deluxe pork roast is seasoned three times, making it extra moist and flavorful. Country Potato Pancakes (page 280) make a nice accompaniment.

   1 cup applesauce
   1/3 cup packed brown sugar
   2 teaspoons vinegar
   1/8 to 1/4 teaspoon ground cloves
   1 rolled boneless pork loin roast (3 to 4 pounds), trimmed
   1 garlic clove, cut into lengthwise strips
   2 tablespoons all-purpose flour
   1 teaspoon salt
   1/2 teaspoon sugar
   1/8 teaspoon pepper
   1 teaspoon prepared mustard

In a small bowl, combine applesauce, brown sugar, vinegar and cloves; set aside. Cut slits in top of roast; insert garlic strips. Combine flour, salt, sugar, pepper and mustard; rub over roast. Place roast on a rack in a shallow roasting pan. Bake, uncovered, at 350° until a meat thermometer reads 160° (see chart for roasting time). Brush applesauce mixture over roast during the last half hour of baking. Remove roast to a warm serving platter. To make gravy from pan drippings, see Basic Pan Gravy from Roasted Meats on page 145. Slice roast and serve with gravy if desired. **Yield:** 8-12 servings.
   —*Lydia Robotewskyj, Franklin, Wisconsin*

Using an Herb Rub

Crush any large herbs. Combine all herbs. Sprinkle mixture over entire roast and rub into the surface of the meat. Roast as directed.

Herbed Pork Roast

Herb rubs are a quick way to season meat without marinating for hours. The meat will develop a delicious crusty herb layer as it roasts and the gravy will be seasoned to perfection.

- 1/4 cup packed brown sugar
- 1 tablespoon dried thyme
- 1 teaspoon *each* garlic salt, pepper, dried sage and rosemary, crushed
- 1 rolled boneless pork loin roast (3 to 4 pounds)

Combine brown sugar, herbs and seasonings; rub over entire roast. Place roast, fat side up, on a rack in a shallow roasting pan. Place in a 500° oven; immediately reduce heat to 350°. Bake, uncovered, until a meat thermometer reads 160° (see chart for roasting time). Remove to a warm serving platter. To make gravy from pan drippings, see Basic Pan Gravy from Roasted Meats on page 145. Slice roast and serve with gravy if desired. **Yield:** 8-12 servings.

—*Jean Harris*
Central Point, Oregon

Stuffed Crown Roast of Pork

A crown roast of pork is generally not available in the meat case, except perhaps at holiday time. Call your butcher to order the size you need. Ask to have the roast tied into the traditional "crown" shape.

- 1 crown roast of pork (about 8 pounds *or* about 16 ribs)
- 1 pound ground pork
- 1/2 pound bulk pork sausage
- 3/4 cup finely chopped onion
- 3 tablespoons butter *or* margarine
- 1/2 cup diced peeled tart apple
- 1/4 cup finely chopped celery
- 1-1/2 cups soft bread crumbs
- 1/2 cup minced fresh parsley
- 1-1/2 teaspoons salt
- 1/2 teaspoon pepper
- 1/2 teaspoon rubbed sage

Spiced crab apples, optional

Place roast on a rack in a large roasting pan. Cover rib ends with foil. Bake, uncovered, at 350° for 2 hours. Meanwhile, in a large skillet, brown the ground pork and sausage; drain and set aside. In the same skillet, saute onion in butter until tender. Add apple and celery; cook for 5 minutes. Remove from the heat. Add the sausage mixture, crumbs, parsley, salt, pepper and sage; mix well. Carefully spoon stuffing into center of roast. Return to oven and bake 1 hour longer or until a meat thermometer reads 160° and juices run clear. Transfer to serving platter. Remove foil. Garnish with spiced crab apples if desired. Cut between ribs to serve. **Yield:** 12-16 servings.

—*Marianne Severson*
West Allis, Wisconsin

Stuffed Crown Roast of Pork

Harvest Stew

Harvest Stew

Savory pieces of pork plus vegetables and herbs season this fall favorite. And homemade easy-to-cut biscuits make it extra eye-appealing.

HERBED BISCUITS:
 1-3/4 cups all-purpose flour
   1 tablespoon sugar
   2 teaspoons baking powder
   2 teaspoons minced fresh basil *or* 3/4 teaspoon dried basil
   1 teaspoon minced fresh rosemary *or* 1/4 teaspoon dried rosemary, crushed
   1/2 teaspoon baking soda
   1/2 teaspoon salt
   6 tablespoons cold butter *or* margarine
   2/3 cup buttermilk
STEW:
   2 tablespoons vegetable oil
 1-1/2 pounds boneless pork, cut into 1-inch cubes
   2 cups chicken broth
 1-1/2 cups chopped onion
   2 garlic cloves, minced
   2 teaspoons *each* minced fresh basil and rosemary *or* 3/4 teaspoon *each* dried basil and rosemary, crushed
   1/2 teaspoon salt
   1/4 teaspoon pepper
   1 medium rutabaga (1-1/4 pounds), peeled and cut into 1/2-inch cubes

   2 large carrots, cut into 1/2-inch slices
 3/4 pound fresh green beans, cut into 1-1/2-inch pieces
   3 tablespoons cornstarch
   3 tablespoons cold water

In a medium bowl, combine the first seven ingredients. Cut in butter until mixture resembles coarse crumbs. Stir in buttermilk to form a soft dough (dough will be slightly sticky). Turn onto a floured surface; knead gently 3-4 times. Roll dough to 1/4-in. thickness; cut with a 2-1/2-in. maple leaf or round cutter. Cover and refrigerate. In a 5-qt. Dutch oven, heat oil over medium-high. Brown pork. Add broth, onion, garlic, basil, rosemary, salt and pepper; cover and simmer for 1 hour. Add rutabaga and carrots; cover and simmer for 30 minutes or until vegetables are crisp-tender. Add beans; cook for 20 minutes. Combine cornstarch and water; stir into stew. Bring to a boil; boil for 2 minutes. Pour into an ungreased shallow 2-1/2- to 3-qt. baking dish. Immediately top with 12 biscuits. Bake, uncovered, at 400° for 15 minutes or until biscuits are golden brown. Bake remaining biscuits on an ungreased baking sheet for 10-12 minutes. **Yield:** 6-8 servings.

Chalupa

Chalupa is a thick Mexican stew prepared with beans and pork. After the meat is cooked, shred it into bite-size pieces with two forks. See Shredding Meat for Sandwiches on page 100.

  1 pound dry pinto beans, sorted and rinsed
  1 bone-in pork loin roast (3 pounds), trimmed
  4 to 5 garlic cloves, minced
  2 tablespoons chili powder
  1 to 1-1/2 teaspoons ground cumin
  1 teaspoon dried oregano
  2 cans (4 ounces *each*) chopped green chilies
  6 cups water
  5 carrots, sliced
  4 celery ribs, sliced
  1 can (14-1/2 ounces) diced tomatoes, undrained
  3 small zucchini, sliced
Pepper to taste
Warm flour tortillas

Place beans in a soup kettle or Dutch oven; add water to cover by 2 in. Bring to a boil; boil for 2 minutes. Remove from the heat; cover and let stand 1 hour. Drain and discard liquid. In the same pot, combine beans, pork, garlic, chili powder, cumin, oregano, chilies and water; bring to a boil. Reduce heat; cover and simmer for 3 to 4 hours or until meat and beans are tender (add an additional 1-2 cups of water if necessary). Cool slightly; remove meat from bones. Shred meat and return to kettle. Add carrots, celery and tomatoes; cover and simmer until vegetables are tender, about 20 minutes. Add zucchini; simmer 10 minutes longer. Season with pepper. Serve with tortillas. **Yield:** about 12 servings. 🍎
— *Anne Fatout, Phoenix, Arizona*

Pork and Winter Squash Stew

For this recipe, you can purchase boneless pork that has been cubed for stewing or cut your own from a pork shoulder or blade roast.

  2 tablespoons vegetable oil, *divided*
  2 pounds lean boneless pork, cut into
    1-inch cubes
  2 cups chopped onion
  2 garlic cloves, minced
  3 cups sliced fresh mushrooms
2-1/2 cups diagonally sliced carrots
  2 cans (14-1/2 ounces *each*) Italian
    stewed tomatoes
  2 teaspoons dried thyme
1-1/2 teaspoons salt
  1/2 teaspoon pepper
  4 cups cubed peeled butternut squash
Hot cooked noodles, optional

In a 4-qt. Dutch oven, heat 1 tablespoon oil over medium-high. Brown pork; remove from pan. Drain and set aside. Heat remaining oil in the same pan over medium; saute onion and garlic for 3 minutes. Return pork to pan. Add mushrooms, carrots, tomatoes and seasonings; bring to a boil. Reduce heat; cover and simmer for 1 hour. Add squash; simmer, uncovered, for 30 minutes or until tender. Serve over noodles if desired. **Yield:** 8 servings. 🍎
— *Evelyn Plyler*
Apple Valley, California

Pork and Winter Squash Stew

Pork Tenderloin Diane

When company is coming, here's a quick but very special dish to prepare. Serve this pork and its delicious gravy with egg noodles or rice.

1 pork tenderloin (about 1 pound)
1 tablespoon lemon-pepper seasoning
2 tablespoons butter *or* margarine
2 tablespoons lemon juice
1 tablespoon Worcestershire sauce
1 teaspoon Dijon mustard
1 tablespoon minced fresh parsley

Cut tenderloin into eight pieces. Place each piece between two pieces of plastic wrap or waxed paper and flatten to 1/2-in. thickness. Sprinkle with lemon pepper. Melt butter in a large skillet over medium heat; cook pork for 3-4 minutes on each side or until no longer pink and juices run clear. Remove to a serving platter and keep warm. To the pan juices, add lemon juice, Worcestershire sauce and mustard; heat through, stirring occasionally. Pour over the pork and sprinkle with parsley. **Yield:** 4 servings. — *Janie Thorpe*
Tullahoma, Tennessee

Pork Tenderloin Diane

Grilled Pork Tenderloin

This is a great recipe to keep in mind when you can't decide what to make for dinner. With only two ingredients, it's a snap to get ready for the grill.

2 pork tenderloins (about 1 pound *each*)
1 bottle (8 ounces) light Italian dressing

Place tenderloins in a bowl. Pour dressing over. Cover and refrigerate for 6-8 hours or overnight. Drain, discarding marinade. Grill over hot heat for 15-20 minutes or until a meat thermometer reads 160° and juices run clear. **Yield:** 6-8 servings. — *Lillian Owens*
New Castle, Kentucky

Tenderloin Tips

- Because pork tenderloin defrosts and cooks quickly, it is a good cut to keep in the freezer for last-minute meals. Thaw tenderloin using the "defrost" cycle of your microwave according to the manufacturer's directions.

- For quick, hearty sandwiches, cut a tenderloin into 3-ounce portions, pound into patties and pan-fry for 2 to 3 minutes on each side or until juices run clear. Serve on rolls.

- Cut pork tenderloin while partially frozen into thin, even slices and use in place of beef or chicken in your favorite stir-fry or fajita recipes.

Cranberry Sweet-and-Sour Pork

Try making this popular restaurant favorite at home for a special treat. It's foolproof and goes from stovetop to tabletop in about 20 minutes.

1 tablespoon vegetable oil
1-1/2 pounds pork tenderloin, cut into 1/2-inch cubes
1/2 teaspoon salt
1/4 teaspoon pepper
1 can (8-3/4 ounces) pineapple tidbits, undrained
1 medium green pepper, cut into strips
1 tablespoon cornstarch
1 cup whole-berry cranberry sauce
1/2 cup barbecue sauce
Hot cooked rice

In a large skillet over high, heat oil. Add pork, salt and pepper; stir-fry for about 3 minutes or until meat is no longer pink. Drain pineapple, reserving juice. Add pineapple and green pepper to the skillet; stir-fry for 2 minutes. Combine pineapple juice and cornstarch; add to skillet with cranberry sauce and barbecue sauce. Cook over medium-high heat, stirring constantly, until thickened. Serve over rice. **Yield:** 6 servings.
—*Gert Snyder, West Montrose, Ontario*

Cranberry Sweet-and-Sour Pork

Creamy Pork Tenderloin

Breaded pork tenderloin is a wonderful treat, but with this sour cream sauce, it's paradise! Serve with cooked rice or noodles garnished with chopped fresh parsley.

2 pork tenderloins (about 1 pound *each*)
1 egg
1 tablespoon water
1/2 teaspoon dried rosemary, crushed
1/4 teaspoon pepper
Dash garlic powder
1 cup Italian-seasoned dry bread crumbs
3 tablespoons vegetable oil
1/2 pound fresh mushrooms, sliced
2 tablespoons butter *or* margarine
1 can (10-3/4 ounces) condensed cream of chicken soup, undiluted
1 cup (8 ounces) sour cream
1/4 cup chicken broth

Cut each tenderloin into eight pieces. Place each piece between two pieces of plastic wrap or waxed paper and flatten to 3/4-in. thickness. In a shallow dish, combine the next five ingredients. Dip pork into egg mixture, then into bread crumbs. In a large skillet, heat oil over medium. Brown pork for 5 minutes on each side. Remove to an ungreased 13-in. x 9-in. x 2-in. baking dish. In the same skillet, saute mushrooms in butter until tender. Stir in soup, sour cream and broth; pour over pork. Cover and bake at 325° for 1 hour. **Yield:** 6-8 servings.
—*Janice Christofferson, Eagle River, Wisconsin*

Honey Spareribs

Honey Spareribs

If you prefer barbecued ribs, precook these in the oven for 1 hour, then grill them over medium heat for about 20 minutes, basting often and turning once.

3 pounds pork spareribs *or* pork loin back ribs, cut into serving-size pieces
3 tablespoons lemon juice
2 tablespoons honey
2 tablespoons vegetable oil
1 tablespoon soy sauce
1 tablespoon dried minced onion
1 teaspoon paprika
1 teaspoon salt
1/2 teaspoon dried oregano
1/8 teaspoon garlic powder

Place ribs, bone side down, on a rack in a shallow roasting pan. Cover and bake at 350° for 1 hour; drain. Combine all remaining ingredients in a bowl; brush some of the glaze on ribs. Bake, uncovered, 30-45 minutes longer or until meat is tender, brushing occasionally with remaining glaze. **Yield:** 4 servings.   —*Belle Kemmerer*
Stanfordville, New York

Barbecued Spareribs

Everyone enjoys their ribs seasoned differently. If you like garlic, add an additional clove to this sauce. If you prefer zesty ribs, use a generous dash of cayenne pepper.

    4 pounds pork spareribs, cut into serving-size
      pieces
    1 medium onion, quartered
    2 teaspoons salt
    1/4 teaspoon pepper
SAUCE:
    1/2 cup cider vinegar
    1/2 cup packed brown sugar
    1/2 cup ketchup
    1/4 cup chili sauce
    1/4 cup Worcestershire sauce
    2 tablespoons chopped onion
    1 tablespoon lemon juice
    1/2 teaspoon ground mustard
    1 garlic clove, minced
Dash cayenne pepper

In a large kettle or Dutch oven, place ribs and onion; sprinkle with salt and pepper. Add enough water to cover; bring to a boil. Reduce heat; cover and simmer for 1-1/2 hours or until tender. Meanwhile, combine sauce ingredients in a saucepan. Simmer, uncovered, for 1 hour or until slightly thickened, stirring occasionally. Drain ribs; place on a rack in a broiler pan. Brush with sauce. Broil 5 in. from the heat for 5 minutes on each side, brushing frequently with sauce. **Yield:** 4 servings. —*Bette Brotzel, Billings, Montana*

Tips for Great Ribs

- If time does not permit tenderizing and cooking ribs on the same day, precook and refrigerate one day, then bake the next.
- To hold ribs until serving time or to transport hot cooked ribs to a party, place ribs in heavy-duty foil and then in a brown paper bag. The ribs can stand this way for up to 1 hour.

Hearty Ribs and Beans

Meaty country-style pork ribs can be substituted for regular pork spareribs in any recipe.

    3 to 3-1/2 pounds country-style pork ribs
    1/4 cup water
    1 can (15 ounces) tomato sauce
    1 envelope onion soup mix
    1/3 cup packed brown sugar
    2 tablespoons prepared mustard
    1/8 teaspoon hot pepper sauce
    2 cans (16 ounces *each*) kidney beans, rinsed
      and drained
    2 cans (15-1/2 ounces *each*) great northern
      beans, rinsed and drained
1-1/2 cups thinly sliced celery
    1 sweet red pepper, thinly sliced

Place ribs in an ungreased 13-in. x 9-in. x 2-in. baking pan; add water. Cover and bake at 350° for 1-1/2 hours. Drain, reserving liquid; skim fat. Set ribs aside. Add enough water to liquid to measure 1 cup; place in a saucepan. Add tomato sauce, soup mix, sugar, mustard and hot pepper sauce. Simmer for 10 minutes; reserve 1/2 cup. To the remaining sauce, add beans, celery and red pepper. Pour into the baking pan; add ribs. Pour reserved sauce over ribs. Cover and bake for 45 minutes or until meat is tender. **Yield:** 6-8 servings. —*Marlene Muckenhirn Delano, Minnesota*

Barbecued Spareribs

Breakfast Sausage

1/2 teaspoon garlic salt
1/2 teaspoon pepper
  3 cups whole kernel corn
  2 medium green peppers, sliced into 1-inch pieces
1/4 cup cornstarch
1/4 cup water
Shredded mozzarella cheese

In a 4-qt. Dutch oven, brown sausage. Add celery and cook for 15 minutes; drain. Add tomatoes, tomato juice, zucchini and seasonings; bring to a boil. Reduce heat; cover and simmer for 20 minutes. Add corn and green peppers; cover and simmer for 15 minutes. Combine cornstarch and water until smooth; stir into stew. Bring to a boil; cook and stir until thickened. Sprinkle with cheese. **Yield:** 6-8 servings.
—*Helen Miller*
Hickory Hills, Illinois

Breakfast Sausage

Making your own fresh pork sausage is easy and fun. Buy a pork shoulder roast, cut it into pieces and grind in a food grinder. For best results, the pork should have at least 15% fat. Freeze whatever you can't use in 2 days.

  2 tablespoons brown sugar
  1 tablespoon rubbed sage
  4 teaspoons salt
  2 teaspoons ground savory
  1 teaspoon pepper
  1 teaspoon crushed red pepper flakes
1/2 teaspoon ground nutmeg
2-1/2 pounds fresh ground pork

In a large bowl, combine the first seven ingredients. Mix thoroughly. Add pork; mix well. Cover and refrigerate 6 hours or overnight. Shape into 12 patties. Cook patties in a skillet over medium-low heat for 10-12 minutes or until no longer pink, turning once. Drain. **Yield:** 12 patties. —*Gloria Jarrett, Loveland, Ohio*

Tomato Zucchini Stew

If your garden has long given up on fresh tomatoes, substitute three 14-1/2-ounce cans of diced tomatoes (undrained) for the tomatoes and tomato juice.

1-1/4 pounds bulk Italian sausage
1-1/2 cups sliced celery (3/4-inch pieces)
  8 medium fresh tomatoes (about 3 pounds), peeled and cut into wedges
1-1/2 cups tomato juice
  4 small zucchini, sliced into 1/4-inch pieces
2-1/2 teaspoons Italian seasoning
1-1/2 to 2 teaspoons salt
  1 teaspoon sugar

Tomato Zucchini Stew

Cranberry Stuffing Balls

Sausage Tips

- Before you use cooked pork sausage in a recipe, drain, rinse and pat dry with paper towels to cut calories and fat.
- Combine equal amounts of ground pork and ground beef for flavorful and juicy burgers. Cook the burgers until well-done (160°).

Sausage and Wild Rice Casserole

You can assemble this casserole and refrigerate until ready to bake. Remove from the refrigerator 30 minutes before baking.

>   1 package (6 ounces) long grain and wild rice mix
>   1 pound bulk pork sausage
>   1 can (10-3/4 ounces) condensed cream of mushroom soup, undiluted
>   1 cup sliced fresh mushrooms
>   1/2 cup chopped onion
>   1/2 cup chopped green pepper
>   1/2 cup shredded sharp cheddar cheese
>   1/2 cup chicken broth
>   1/4 cup chopped celery
>   1 teaspoon dried parsley flakes
>   1/2 teaspoon pepper

Cook rice according to package directions. Meanwhile, brown sausage in a skillet; drain. Add rice and remaining ingredients. Transfer to a greased 2-qt. baking dish. Bake, uncovered, at 350° for 1 hour. **Yield:** 6-8 servings.
—Elsie Pritschau, Ravenna, Nebraska

Cranberry Stuffing Balls

When you're looking for a different way to prepare stuffing, you'll find these balls tasty and easy to make. They're great served with pork roast and gravy.

>   1 pound bulk pork sausage
>   1/2 cup chopped celery
>   1/4 cup chopped onion
>   2 tablespoons minced fresh parsley
>   1 package (7 ounces) herb-seasoned stuffing croutons
>   3/4 cup fresh *or* frozen cranberries, halved
>   2 eggs, beaten
>   1 to 1-1/2 cups chicken broth

In a skillet, cook sausage, celery and onion until sausage is no longer pink and vegetables are tender; drain. Place in a large bowl; add parsley, croutons, cranberries, eggs and enough broth to hold mixture together. Shape into 8-10 balls. Place in a greased shallow baking dish. Bake, uncovered, at 325° for 30 minutes. **Yield:** 8-10 servings.
—Bernadine Dirmeyer
Harpster, Ohio

Roasting Fully Cooked Ham

Place ham on a rack in shallow roasting pan. Insert an oven-safe thermometer (or use an instant-read thermometer toward the end of the roasting time). Roast without liquid, uncovered, at 325° for the recommended time or until the thermometer reads 140° and ham is heated through. Remove ham from the oven; cover with foil and let stand 10-15 minutes before carving.

Cut	Weight in Pounds	Approximate Roasting Time
Bone-in, whole	10 to 14	2-1/2 to 3-1/2 hours
Bone-in, half	5 to 7	1-1/2 to 2 hours
Semi-boneless, half	4 to 6	1-3/4 to 2-1/2 hours
Boneless	4 to 6	1-1/4 to 2 hours

Cherry Almond Glazed Ham

(Pictured on page 156)

Turn a plain ham dinner into a festive occasion when you prepare this ham and its fruity glaze.

    1 jar (12 ounces) cherry preserves
    1/4 cup vinegar
    2 tablespoons corn syrup
    1/4 teaspoon ground cinnamon
    1/4 teaspoon ground cloves
    1/4 teaspoon ground nutmeg
    1/3 cup slivered almonds
    1 boneless fully cooked ham (3 to 4 pounds)
    3 tablespoons water

In a saucepan, combine the first six ingredients; bring to a boil. Reduce heat and simmer for 2 minutes, stirring frequently. Stir in almonds; set aside. Place ham, cut side down, on a rack in a shallow roasting pan. Bake at 325° for 1 to 1-1/2 hours or until a meat thermometer reads 140° and ham is heated through. About 15 minutes before the ham is done, spoon 1/4 to 1/3 cup glaze over ham. Stir water into remaining glaze; heat through and serve with sliced ham. **Yield:** about 12 servings (1-1/2 cups glaze).

—Julie Sterchi
Fairfield, Illinois

Carving a Half Ham with Bone

1 Place ham cut side down on a carving board. Using a meat fork to anchor the meat, cut down and remove the large meaty area of the roast from the bone.

2 Place the chunk of meat on its cut surface and slice 1/4 to 1/2 in. thick. Cut remaining meat from around the bone.

Tips for Buying and Cooking Ham

- Most hams in grocery stores have been cured, smoked and fully cooked and can be served warm (internal temperature 140°) or cold.

- Country hams have been salt-cured, smoked and aged; they're usually labeled "cook before eating". Follow the cooking directions attached to the country ham.

- There are several kinds of fully cooked hams to choose from. A bone-in ham can be purchased whole or cut in half. Rump portions are more expensive because they have more meat and less bone than the shank cuts. Semi-boneless and boneless hams are also available.

- Buy ham with a rosy pink color. The meat should be firm to the touch when pressed.

- When buying ham, allow about 3 servings per 1 pound of a bone-in ham and 4 servings per 1 pound of boneless ham.

Baked Ham with Cumberland Sauce

Baked Ham with Cumberland Sauce

Use this recipe when you want a basic brown sugar-mustard glazed ham. The cumberland sauce is an extra bonus that is easy to prepare and fun to serve.

1/2 fully cooked bone-in ham (4 to 5 pounds)
1/2 cup packed brown sugar
1 teaspoon ground mustard
Whole cloves
CUMBERLAND SAUCE:
1 cup red currant *or* apple jelly
1/4 cup orange juice
1/4 cup lemon juice
1/4 cup red wine *or* apple juice
2 tablespoons honey
1 tablespoon cornstarch

Remove skin from ham; score the surface with shallow diagonal cuts, making diamond shapes. Combine brown sugar and mustard; rub into fat of ham. Insert a

Scoring and Studding Ham

With a sharp knife, make diagonal cuts in a diamond pattern about 1/2 in. deep in the surface of the ham. Push a whole clove into the points of each diamond.

whole clove in center of each diamond. Place ham on a rack in a shallow roasting pan. Bake, uncovered, at 325° for 1-1/4 to 1-1/2 hours or until a meat thermometer reads 140° and ham is heated through. Combine sauce ingredients in a saucepan. Cook over medium heat until thickened, stirring often. Serve over the sliced ham. (Sauce recipe can be doubled if desired.) **Yield:** about 16 servings (1-3/4 cups sauce). —*Eunice Stoen*
Decorah, Iowa

Sunday Boiled Dinner

Dilly Ham Balls

If you're using leftovers from a baked ham, grind the ham in a food grinder or a food processor. If you don't have leftovers, ask the butcher to grind a pound of ham for you.

> 1/2 cup dry bread crumbs
> 1/4 cup finely chopped green onions
>   3 tablespoons finely chopped fresh dill *or*
>   3 teaspoons dill weed, *divided*
> 1/4 cup milk
>   1 egg, lightly beaten
>   1 teaspoon Dijon mustard
> 1/2 teaspoon pepper, *divided*
>   1 pound ground fully cooked ham
>   1 to 2 tablespoons butter *or* margarine
>   1 to 2 tablespoons vegetable oil
>   2 tablespoons all-purpose flour
>   1 cup water
>   1 cup (8 ounces) sour cream

Hot cooked noodles

In a bowl, combine bread crumbs, onions, 1 tablespoon fresh dill (or 1 teaspoon dried), milk, egg, mustard and 1/4 teaspoon pepper. Add ham; mix well. Shape into 1-in. balls. In a large skillet, heat 1 tablespoon butter and 1 tablespoon oil. Brown ham balls, adding remaining butter and oil as needed. Remove to a serving dish; cover and keep warm. Drain drippings into a saucepan; blend in flour until smooth. Gradually add water. Cook over low heat, stirring constantly until mixture thickens. Add sour cream and remaining dill and pepper; heat through (do not boil). Pour over the ham balls. Serve over noodles. **Yield:** 6 servings.

         —Dixie Terry, Marion, Illinois

Sunday Boiled Dinner

Test the cabbage with a fork to determine when it's done. If a fork can easily be pushed into the core of the cabbage, it is ready to serve.

>   1 fully cooked boneless ham *or* smoked pork
>   shoulder (about 2 pounds)
>   2 pounds carrots, halved
>   2 pounds red potatoes, quartered
>   2 pounds rutabaga, peeled and cut into
>   1-1/2-inch cubes
>   1 medium onion, quartered
>   1 teaspoon salt
> 1/2 teaspoon pepper
>   1 medium cabbage, halved

Prepared horseradish, optional

In a large Dutch oven or soup kettle, place ham, carrots, potatoes, rutabaga, onion, salt and pepper. Add water just to cover; bring to a boil. Place cabbage on top of vegetables. Reduce heat; cover and simmer for 1 hour or until the vegetables are tender. Drain. Cut cabbage into wedges; remove core. Serve meat and vegetables with horseradish if desired. **Yield:** 8 servings.

         —Arlene Oliver, Bothell, Washington

Dilly Ham Balls

Peachy Ham Slice

Peachy Ham Slice

Before cooking a ham slice, trim fat and slash edges at 1-inch intervals to prevent it from curling as it heats.

> 1 can (16 ounces) sliced peaches
> 1 tablespoon butter *or* margarine
> 1 fully cooked ham slice (about 1-1/2 pounds and 1 inch thick)
> 1 tablespoon sugar
> 2 teaspoons cornstarch
> 1/8 teaspoon ground nutmeg
> 1/2 cup orange juice
> 1 tablespoon lemon juice

Drain peaches, reserving 1/2 cup syrup; set aside. In a large skillet, melt butter over medium heat. Brown ham slice on both sides. Remove ham to a platter and keep warm, reserving drippings in skillet. In a small bowl, combine sugar, cornstarch and nutmeg. Add orange juice, lemon juice and reserved peach syrup; stir until smooth. Add to drippings. Cook over medium heat until thick, stirring constantly. Stir in peaches and heat through. Add ham slice; heat for 2-3 minutes. Cut into serving-size pieces. **Yield:** 4-6 servings.
—*Erika Klop, Agassiz, British Columbia*

Grilled Ham Steak

When buying a large half of a ham, ask the butcher to cut off the center slice so you can have another meal.

> 1 cup packed brown sugar
> 1/3 cup prepared horseradish
> 1/4 cup lemon juice
> 1 fully cooked ham slice (about 1-1/2 pounds and 1 inch thick)

In a small saucepan, bring brown sugar, horseradish and lemon juice to a boil. Brush over both sides of ham. Grill over medium-hot heat, turning once, until heated through and well-glazed, about 20-25 minutes. **Yield:** 4-6 servings.
—*Mary Ann Lien, Tyler, Texas*

Church Supper Ham Loaf

To easily shape this loaf, press into a greased loaf pan. Turn out into a shallow baking pan; bake as directed.

  2 cups soft bread crumbs
  2 eggs, beaten
  1 cup (8 ounces) sour cream
1/3 cup chopped onion
  2 tablespoons lemon juice
  1 teaspoon curry powder
  1 teaspoon ground mustard
  1 teaspoon ground ginger
1/8 teaspoon ground nutmeg
1/8 teaspoon paprika
  1 pound ground fully cooked ham
  1 pound bulk pork sausage
BASTING SAUCE:
1/2 cup packed brown sugar
1/4 cup water
1/4 cup cider vinegar
1/8 teaspoon pepper

In large mixing bowl, combine the first 10 ingredients. Add ham and sausage; mix well. Form into a loaf; place in an ungreased shallow baking pan. Bake, uncovered, at 350° for 1 hour. In a small saucepan, combine sauce ingredients; bring to a boil. Drain any drippings from ham loaf; pour sauce over loaf. Continue baking, basting occasionally with pan juices, for 15-30 minutes longer or until lightly browned and a meat thermometer reads 160°. **Yield:** 8-10 servings. —*Pat Habiger, Spearville, Kansas*

Church Supper Ham Loaf

Broccoli-Ham Hot Dish

Serve this casserole for brunch or for dinner; it's a convenient one-dish meal that uses leftover ham.

  2 packages (10 ounces *each*) frozen chopped
    broccoli
  2 cups cooked rice
  6 tablespoons butter *or* margarine, *divided*
  1 medium onion, chopped
  3 tablespoons all-purpose flour
  1 teaspoon salt
1/4 teaspoon pepper
  3 cups milk
1-1/2 pounds fully cooked ham, cubed
  2 cups fresh bread crumbs (about 2-1/2 slices)
Shredded cheddar *or* Swiss cheese

Cook broccoli according to package directions; drain. Spoon rice into a greased 13-in. x 9-in. x 2-in. baking dish. Place broccoli over rice. In a large skillet, melt 4 tablespoons butter; saute onion until tender. Stir in

flour, salt and pepper until smooth. Gradually add milk, stirring constantly. Bring to a boil. Cook and stir for 1 minute or until thickened. Add ham; heat through. Pour over rice and broccoli. Melt remaining butter; stir in bread crumbs. Sprinkle over top. Bake, uncovered, at 350° for 30 minutes or until heated through. Sprinkle with cheese; let stand 5 minutes before serving. **Yield:** 8 servings. —*Margaret Wagner Allen*
Abingdon, Virginia

Ham a la King

Here's a comforting dish that is easy to prepare. Just remember to cook and stir the white sauce for an extra minute once the milk is added to thoroughly cook the flour. If you like, serve the creamed ham over warm biscuits instead of in puff pastry shells.

      2 tablespoons butter *or* margarine
  1/4 cup diced green pepper
      3 tablespoons sliced green onions
      1 cup sliced fresh mushrooms
      1 package (10 ounces) frozen peas, cooked and
         drained
      2 cups cubed fully cooked ham
  3/4 teaspoon ground mustard
  1/2 teaspoon salt
      3 hard-cooked eggs, coarsely chopped
      1 package (10 ounces) frozen puff pastry shells,
         baked

WHITE SAUCE:
  1/4 cup butter *or* margarine
  1/4 cup all-purpose flour
  1/4 teaspoon salt
Dash white pepper
      2 cups milk

In a skillet, melt butter over medium heat. Saute green pepper, onions and mushrooms until tender. Stir in peas, ham, mustard and salt; heat through. Gently stir in the eggs; set aside. For sauce, melt the butter in a saucepan. Stir in flour, salt and pepper until smooth. Gradually add milk. Bring to a boil; cook and stir until thickened and bubbly. Cook and stir 1 minute longer. Add ham mixture and heat through. Serve in pastry shells. **Yield:** 6 servings.

—Doris Christman
Middletown, Pennsylvania

Ham a la King

Seafood

Reel in rave reviews from dinner guests with North Carolina Shrimp Saute (p. 189) and Golden Catfish Fillets (p. 186). With such easy preparation, you're sure to fall for these delectable dishes—hook, line and sinker!

Whether you're using fresh or frozen fish, shellfish or canned seafood products, it's important to avoid overcooking. Follow basic cooking directions and specific recipes closely but test for doneness often to preserve the seafood's delicate, moist texture.

Basic Cooking Methods for Fish

Baking

Recommended for large whole fish, steaks and fillets. Place the fish in a greased baking pan; brush with butter, margarine or oil to keep moist. Bake, uncovered, in a preheated oven (350° for pan-dressed whole fish; 450° for fillets and steaks) about 10 minutes for every inch of thickness or until fish tests done. You don't need to turn the fish halfway through baking.

Broiling

Recommended for fillets or steaks. Place fillets with skin side down and steaks cut side down on a greased rack of a broiler pan. Brush with melted butter or margarine and place under a preheated broiler 4 to 6 in. from the heat. Broil 10 minutes for each inch of thickness. Test for doneness often.

Pan-Frying

Recommended for fillets and pan-dressed fish. Bread fish as desired, then fry in 1/4 in. of oil or shortening over medium-high heat until golden. Turn fish; cook until fish is brown and tests done.

Sauteing

Recommend for smaller cuts such as fillets or steaks. Season all-purpose flour with salt, pepper and paprika; coat fish. Heat several tablespoons of butter, margarine or oil in a skillet over medium-high heat. Saute fish until lightly brown. Turn fish; saute until fish is brown and tests done. Allow 3-4 minutes per side for each 1/2 in. of thickness.

Poaching

Recommended for fillets, steaks or pan-dressed fish. "Poaching" means to cook in a flavorful liquid, such as water, that has been lightly salted and seasoned with bay leaf, onion, celery and white wine if desired. Bring

the liquid and seasonings to a boil. Carefully add fish; reduce heat. Cover and simmer 10 minutes for every inch of thickness or until fish tests done. Do not boil.

Steaming

Recommended for fillets, steaks or pan-dressed fish. Bring a small amount of water to a boil in a skillet or Dutch oven. Place fish on a rack or in a steaming basket; set above boiling water. Cover and cook for about 10 minutes for every inch of thickness or until fish tests done.

Grilling

Recommended for fillets, steaks and pan-dressed fish. Brush fish with butter, margarine, oil or marinade; place on a greased grill grate or in a wire grill basket. Turn thick pieces of fish halfway through cooking time. Cooking times vary greatly due to the temperature of the coals and weather conditions.
Test for doneness often.

Tips for Buying and Storing Fish

- When buying fresh fish fillets or steaks, look for firm flesh that has a moist look. Don't purchase fish that looks dried out. Whole fish should have bright clear eyes that are not sunken and a firm body that is springy to the touch. Fresh fish should have a mild smell, not a strong odor.

- When buying frozen fish, look for packages that are solidly frozen, tightly sealed and free of freezer burn and odor.

- Follow these guidelines for how much fish to purchase per person: about 1 pound whole, 1/2 pound pan-dressed or steaks and 1/4 to 1/3 pound fillets.

- Fresh fish is highly perishable and should be prepared within a day or two after it is caught or purchased. Freshly caught fish should be pan-dressed, washed in cold water, blotted dry with paper towels, placed in an airtight container or heavy-duty plastic bag and refrigerated.

- For long-term storage, wrap fish in freezer paper, heavy-duty foil or heavy-duty plastic bags and freeze no longer than 3 months for fatty or oily fish (such as salmon, whitefish, mackerel) or 6 months for lean fish (such as sole, catfish, cod, orange roughy).

Foil-Steamed Salmon

You'll love this fast, foolproof recipe. And because the fish is prepared and cooked in a foil packet, cleanup couldn't be easier. Serve this fish with plenty of fresh lemon wedges.

- 1 salmon *or* halibut fillet (about 2 pounds)
- 2 tablespoons minced fresh basil *or* 2 teaspoons dried basil
- 1 tablespoon minced fresh rosemary *or* 1 teaspoon dried rosemary, crushed
- 1 teaspoon minced fresh parsley
- 3 tablespoons butter *or* margarine
- 3 to 4 tablespoons lemon juice

Salt and pepper to taste

Place fish on a large double sheet of heavy-duty foil. Sprinkle with basil, rosemary and parsley. Dot with butter. Season with lemon juice, salt and pepper. Seal foil tightly to retain juices. Bake at 375° for 25-30 minutes or until the fish flakes easily with a fork. **Yield:** 4-6 servings. ○

—*Jutta Doening*
Kelowna, British Columbia

Testing for Doneness

For fish fillets, check for doneness by inserting a fork at an angle into the thickest portion of the fish and gently parting the meat. When it flakes into sections, it is cooked completely. Whole fish or steaks are done when the flesh is easily removed from the bones. Cooked fish is opaque in color and the juices are milky white.

Barbecued Trout

If you plan to cook fish on the outdoor grill often, you may want to invest in a grill basket. It makes turning and removing fish easy.

- 6 pan-dressed trout (about 8 ounces *each*)
- 2/3 cup soy sauce
- 1/2 cup ketchup
- 2 tablespoons lemon juice
- 2 tablespoons vegetable oil
- 1 teaspoon dried rosemary, crushed

Lemon wedges, optional

Place trout in a single layer in a glass baking dish. Combine the soy sauce, ketchup, lemon juice, oil and rosemary. Reserve 1/4 cup; set aside. Pour remaining marinade over fish. Cover and let stand for 1 hour, turning once. Place fish in a single layer in a well-greased hinged wire grill basket or directly on grill grate. Grill, covered, over medium heat for 8-10 minutes or until fish is browned on the bottom. Turn and baste with reserved marinade; grill 5-7 minutes longer or until the flesh is easily removed from the bones. Serve with lemon if desired. **Yield:** 6 servings.

—*Vivian Wolfram*
Mountain Home, Arkansas

Barbecued Trout

Stuffed Sole

For an elegant dinner with little preparation, try this speedy recipe. To assemble the recipe before your company arrives, stuff the fish and place in the baking dish; cover. Combine sauce ingredients; refrigerate sauce and fish separately. Pour sauce over fish just before baking.

- 1 cup chopped onion
- 2 cans (4-1/4 ounces *each*) shrimp, rinsed and drained
- 1 jar (4-1/2 ounces) sliced mushrooms, drained
- 2 tablespoons butter *or* margarine
- 1/2 pound cooked *or* canned crabmeat, drained and cartilage removed
- 8 sole or flounder fillets (2 to 2-1/2 pounds)
- 1/2 teaspoon salt
- 1/4 teaspoon pepper
- 1/4 teaspoon paprika
- 2 cans (10-3/4 ounces *each*) condensed cream of mushroom soup, undiluted
- 1/3 cup chicken broth
- 2 tablespoons water
- 2/3 cup shredded cheddar cheese
- 2 tablespoons minced fresh parsley
- Cooked wild, brown *or* white rice *or* a mixture, optional

In a saucepan, saute onion, shrimp and mushrooms in butter until onion is tender. Add crabmeat; heat through. Sprinkle fillets with salt, pepper and paprika. Spoon crab mixture onto fillets; roll up and fasten with a toothpick. Place in a greased 13-in. x 9-in. x 2-in. baking dish. Combine the soup, broth and water; blend until smooth. Pour over fillets. Sprinkle with cheese. Cover and bake at 400° for 30 minutes. Sprinkle with parsley. Bake, uncovered, 5 minutes longer or until fish flakes easily with a fork. Remove toothpicks. Serve over rice if desired. **Yield:** 8 servings.

—*Winnie Higgins, Salisbury, Maryland*

Stuffing Fish Fillets

Spoon stuffing equally over fish fillets. Roll up tightly and fasten with a toothpick.

Stuffed Sole

Sole in Herbed Butter

1/4 teaspoon paprika
1/8 teaspoon garlic powder
4 orange roughy, red snapper, catfish *or* trout fillets (6 ounces *each*)

Combine the first seven ingredients; dip fillets into mixture to coat both sides. Grill, covered, over hot heat for 10 minutes or until fish flakes easily with a fork. **Yield:** 4 servings. ○
—*Sue Kroening*
Mattoon, Illinois

Golden Baked Whitefish

You'll come to depend on this classic recipe time and again. Using light or fat-free mayonnaise helps reduce fat grams.

  2 pounds whitefish fillets
1/8 teaspoon pepper
  1 egg white
1/2 teaspoon salt
1/4 cup light *or* fat-free mayonnaise
1/4 teaspoon dill weed
1/2 teaspoon onion juice *or* 1 teaspoon grated onion
Fresh dill and lemon wedges, optional

Place fish in a greased 13-in. x 9-in. x 2-in. baking dish; sprinkle with pepper. Beat egg white with salt until stiff peaks form. Fold in mayonnaise, dill and onion juice; spoon over fish. Bake, uncovered, at 425° for 15-20 minutes or until topping is puffed and fish flakes easily with a fork. Garnish with dill and lemon if desired. **Yield:** 8 servings. ○ 🍎
—*Polly Habel*
Monson, Massachusetts

Sole in Herbed Butter

Just a few minutes of sauteing is all that's needed to cook this fish to perfection. If you have fresh dill on hand, mince 1 tablespoon and substitute it for the dill weed.

1/4 cup butter *or* margarine, softened
  1 teaspoon dill weed
1/2 teaspoon onion powder
1/2 teaspoon garlic powder
1/2 teaspoon salt
1/4 teaspoon white pepper
  2 pounds sole *or* flounder fillets
Fresh dill and lemon wedges, optional

In a bowl, combine butter, dill, onion powder, garlic powder, salt and pepper. Transfer to a skillet; heat on medium until melted. Add the fish and saute for several minutes on each side or until it flakes easily with a fork. Garnish with dill and lemon if desired. **Yield:** 6 servings. ○ 🍎 —*Marilyn Paradis, Woodburn, Oregon*

Herbed Orange Roughy

Everyone enjoys orange roughy's mild flavor. Because of its delicate texture, don't turn this fish over on the grill grate unless you have it in a grill basket. Orange roughy can also be broiled, baked and sauteed.

  2 tablespoons lemon juice
  1 tablespoon butter *or* margarine, melted
1/2 teaspoon dried thyme
1/2 teaspoon grated lemon peel
1/4 teaspoon salt

Golden Baked Whitefish

Grilled Salmon

Salmon has a firm texture, making it one of the best kinds of fish to cook directly on the barbecue grill without foil or a basket. Outdoor barbecuing enhances its bold flavor.

- 2 salmon fillets (about 1 pound *each*)
- 1/2 cup vegetable oil
- 1/2 cup lemon juice
- 4 green onions, thinly sliced
- 3 tablespoons minced fresh parsley
- 1-1/2 teaspoons minced fresh rosemary *or* 1/2 teaspoon dried rosemary, crushed
- 1/2 teaspoon salt
- 1/8 teaspoon pepper

Place salmon in a shallow dish. Combine remaining ingredients and mix well. Set aside 1/4 cup for basting; pour the rest over the salmon. Cover and refrigerate for 30 minutes. Drain, discarding marinade. Cover and grill salmon, skin side down, over medium heat for 5 minutes. Brush with the basting sauce. Continue grilling for 10-15 minutes or until fish flakes easily with a fork. Baste occasionally with reserved marinade. **Yield:** 4 servings. ⏱ 🍎
—Monell Nuckols
Carpinteria, California

Salmon Pasta Salad

This recipe is great prepared with canned salmon. But for a real treat, season 1 pound fresh salmon with salt, pepper and lemon juice. Poach, grill, bake or broil. Allow to cool; bone, skin and flake.

- 1 package (8 ounces) spiral pasta, cooked and drained
- 2 cups fully cooked salmon chunks *or* 1 can (14-3/4 ounces) pink salmon, drained, bones and skin removed
- 1-1/2 cups quartered cherry tomatoes
- 1 medium cucumber, quartered and sliced
- 1 small red onion, sliced
- 1/2 cup vegetable oil
- 1/3 cup lemon *or* lime juice
- 1-1/2 teaspoons dill weed
- 1 garlic clove, minced
- 3/4 teaspoon salt
- 1/4 teaspoon pepper

In a large bowl, toss the pasta, salmon, tomatoes, cucumber and onion. For dressing, combine remaining ingredients; mix well. Pour over pasta. Cover and chill. **Yield:** 6-8 servings.
—Mary Dennis, Bryan, Ohio

Lemony Salmon Patties

For every day or special occasions, this recipe is packed with great taste and eye appeal. Serve two patties per person and top each patty with lemon sauce and fresh parsley for added flavor. Substitute canned tuna for the salmon if you like.

- 1 can (14-3/4 ounces) pink salmon, drained, bones and skin removed
- 3/4 cup milk
- 1 cup soft bread crumbs
- 1 egg, beaten
- 1 tablespoon minced fresh parsley
- 1 teaspoon diced onion
- 1/2 teaspoon Worcestershire sauce
- 1/4 teaspoon salt
- 1/8 teaspoon pepper

LEMON SAUCE:
- 2 tablespoons butter *or* margarine
- 4 teaspoons all-purpose flour
- 3/4 cup milk
- 2 tablespoons lemon juice
- 1/4 teaspoon salt
- 1/8 to 1/4 teaspoon cayenne pepper

Combine the first nine ingredients; mix well. Spoon into eight greased muffin cups, using 1/4 cup in each. Bake at 350° for 45 minutes or until browned. Meanwhile, melt butter in a saucepan; stir in the flour to form a smooth paste. Gradually stir in milk; bring to a boil over medium heat, stirring constantly. Cook for 2 minutes or until thickened. Remove from the heat; stir in lemon juice, salt and cayenne. Serve over patties. **Yield:** 4 servings. *—Lorice Britt, Severn, North Carolina*

Lemony Salmon Patties

Crumb-Topped Salmon

Crumb-Topped Salmon

Crumb-Topped Salmon

The crumb mixture gives a crunchy light texture, and the herbs and Parmesan cheese add the perfect flavor complement to fish. You can also use this topping on catfish, cod and orange roughy.

2-1/2 cups fresh bread crumbs
4 garlic cloves, minced
1/2 cup chopped fresh parsley
6 tablespoons grated Parmesan cheese
1/4 cup chopped fresh thyme _or_ 1 tablespoon dried thyme
2 teaspoons grated lemon peel
1/2 teaspoon salt
6 tablespoons butter _or_ margarine, melted, _divided_
1 salmon fillet (3 to 4 pounds)

Making Fresh Bread Crumbs

Tear several slices of fresh white, French or whole wheat bread into 1-in. pieces. Place in a food processor or blender; cover and push pulse button several times to make coarse crumbs. One slice of bread yields 1/2 cup of crumbs.

In a bowl, combine bread crumbs, garlic, parsley, cheese, thyme, lemon peel and salt; mix well. Add 4 tablespoons butter and toss lightly to coat; set aside. Pat salmon dry. Place skin side down in a greased baking dish. Brush with remaining butter; cover with crumb mixture. Bake at 350° for 20-25 minutes or until fish flakes easily with a fork. **Yield:** 8 servings.

—_Perlene Hoekema, Lynden, Washington_

Lime Broiled Catfish

to a warm serving dish; spoon pan juices over each fillet. Garnish with lime and parsley if desired. **Yield:** 2 servings. ① ●

—Nick Nicholson
Clarksdale, Mississippi

Golden Catfish Fillets

(Also pictured on page 179)

Most folks love catfish with a crispy breaded coating. This breading is especially nice because the cayenne balances the bold flavor of catfish.

    1 **egg white**
    1 **cup milk**
    1 **cup cornmeal**
  3/4 **teaspoon salt**
  1/4 **teaspoon garlic powder**
  1/4 **to 1/2 teaspoon cayenne pepper**
  1/8 **teaspoon pepper**
    4 **catfish fillets (8 ounces** *each***)**
Vegetable oil
Lemon *or* **lime wedges, optional**

In a shallow bowl, beat the egg white until foamy; add milk and mix well. In another shallow bowl, combine the cornmeal, salt, garlic powder, cayenne and pepper. Dip fillets in milk mixture, then coat with cornmeal mixture. Heat 1/4 in. of oil in a large skillet; fry fish over medium-high heat for 3-4 minutes on each side or until it flakes easily with a fork. Garnish with lemon or lime if desired. **Yield:** 4 servings. ①

—Tammy Moore-Worthington, Artesia, New Mexico

Lime Broiled Catfish

Lime gives fish a wonderful citrus flavor. Try it as a change of pace from lemon.

    1 **tablespoon butter** *or* **margarine**
    2 **tablespoons lime juice**
  1/2 **teaspoon salt**
  1/4 **teaspoon pepper**
  1/4 **teaspoon garlic powder**
    2 **catfish fillets (6 ounces** *each***)**
Lime slices *or* **wedges, optional**
Fresh parsley, optional

Melt butter in a saucepan. Stir in lime juice, salt, pepper and garlic powder; mix well. Remove from the heat and set aside. Place fillets on greased broiler pan. Brush each fillet generously with butter sauce. Broil for 5-8 minutes or until fish flakes easily with a fork. Remove

Golden Catfish Fillets

Pan-Fried Trout

The smoky flavor from the crackers makes you think you've cooked this fish out on an open campfire.

4 pan-dressed lake trout (about 8 ounces *each*)
1/2 cup grated Parmesan cheese
1/2 cup bacon-flavored crackers, crushed
1/2 cup cornmeal
1/4 to 1/2 teaspoon garlic salt
Pinch pepper
2 eggs
1/2 cup milk
1/2 cup vegetable oil
Lemon wedges *and/or* snipped fresh chives or
parsley, optional

Rinse fish in cold water; pat dry. In a shallow bowl, combine the cheese, cracker crumbs, cornmeal, garlic salt and pepper. In another bowl, beat eggs and milk. Dip fish in the egg mixture, then gently roll in the crumb mixture. In a skillet, fry fish in oil for 5-7 minutes or until the flesh is easily removed from the bones, turning once. If desired, garnish with lemon, chives and/or parsley. **Yield:** 4 servings. ◐
—*Felicia Cummings, Raymond, Maine*

Tuna Mushroom Casserole

Tuna Mushroom Casserole

Green beans, garlic, dill and Swiss cheese make this recipe a dressed-up version of the classic casserole Mom used to make.

1/2 cup water
1 teaspoon chicken bouillon granules
1 package (10 ounces) frozen cut green beans
1 cup chopped onion
1 cup sliced fresh mushrooms
1/4 cup chopped celery
1 garlic clove, minced
1/2 teaspoon dill weed
1/2 teaspoon salt
1/8 teaspoon pepper
4 teaspoons cornstarch
1-1/2 cups milk
1/2 cup shredded Swiss cheese
1/4 cup mayonnaise
2-1/2 cups medium noodles, cooked and drained
1 can (12-1/4 ounces) tuna, drained and flaked
1/3 cup dry bread crumbs
1 tablespoon butter *or* margarine

In a large saucepan, bring water and bouillon to a boil, stirring to dissolve. Add the next eight ingredients; bring to a boil. Reduce heat; cover and simmer 5 minutes or until vegetables are tender. Combine cornstarch and milk until smooth; add to vegetable mixture, stirring constantly. Bring to a boil; boil 2 minutes or until thickened. Remove from the heat; stir in cheese and mayonnaise until cheese is melted. Fold in noodles and tuna. Pour into a greased 2-1/2-qt. baking dish. Brown bread crumbs in butter; sprinkle over casserole. Bake, uncovered, at 350° for 25-30 minutes or until heated through. **Yield:** 4-6 servings.
—*Jone Furlong*
Santa Rosa, California

Breading Fish

Combine dry ingredients in a pie plate or shallow bowl. In another pie plate or bowl, whisk egg, milk and/or other liquid ingredients. Dip fish into egg mixture, then roll gently in dry ingredients. Fry as directed.

Jambalaya

Buying and Cooking Shrimp

- Shrimp are available fresh or frozen (raw or cooked, peeled or in the shell) or canned. Shrimp in the shell (fresh or frozen) are available in different varieties and sizes (medium, large, extra large, jumbo). Uncooked shrimp will have shells that range in color from gray or brown to pink or red. Fresh shrimp should have a firm texture with a mild odor.

- To cook raw shrimp in water, add 1 pound shrimp (with or without shells) and 1 teaspoon salt to 3 quarts boiling water. Reduce heat and simmer, uncovered, for 1-3 minutes or until the shrimp turns pink and curls. Watch closely to avoid overcooking—the meat of uncooked shrimp will turn from translucent when raw to pink and opaque when cooked. Drain immediately. Serve warm or chilled.

Jambalaya

You can use any size shrimp in this recipe. Buy the most economical size your grocer has to offer.

    3/4 cup chopped onion
    1/2 cup chopped celery
    1/4 cup chopped green pepper
      2 garlic cloves, minced
      2 tablespoons butter *or* margarine
      2 cups cubed fully cooked ham
      1 can (28 ounces) diced tomatoes, undrained
      1 can (10-1/2 ounces) beef broth
      1 cup uncooked long grain rice
      1 cup water
      1 teaspoon sugar
      1 teaspoon dried thyme
    1/2 teaspoon chili powder
    1/4 teaspoon pepper
  1-1/2 pounds fresh *or* frozen uncooked shrimp, peeled and deveined
      1 tablespoon chopped fresh parsley

In a Dutch oven, saute onion, celery, green pepper and garlic in butter until tender. Add the next nine ingredients; bring to a boil. Reduce heat; cover and simmer until rice is tender, about 25 minutes. Add shrimp and parsley; simmer, uncovered, until shrimp are cooked, 7-10 minutes. **Yield:** 8 servings. 🍎

—*Ruby Williams, Bogalusa, Louisiana*

North Carolina Shrimp Saute

(Pictured on page 178)

Remember, it takes longer to cook the pasta than it does the shrimp. Cook the shrimp only until they turn pink and immediately remove the pan from the heat.

        8 ounces linguini *or* spaghetti
    1/4 cup butter *or* margarine
        1 pound raw shrimp, peeled and deveined
    1/2 pound fresh mushrooms, sliced
        1 small green pepper, chopped
        3 garlic cloves, minced
    1/2 cup grated Romano cheese
    1/2 teaspoon salt
    1/4 teaspoon pepper
Chopped fresh parsley
Lemon slices

Cook pasta according to package directions. Meanwhile, in a skillet, melt butter over medium heat. Add shrimp, mushrooms, green pepper and garlic. Saute until shrimp turn pink, about 3-5 minutes. Drain pasta; place in a serving dish. Top with shrimp mixture. Sprinkle with cheese, salt, pepper and parsley; toss. Garnish with lemon. **Yield:** 4 servings. 🕐

—*Teresa Hildreth, Stoneville, North Carolina*

Crab Quiche

Peeling and Deveining Shrimp

1 Remove the shell from raw or cooked shrimp by opening the shell at the underside or leg area and peeling it back. A gentle pull may be necessary to release the shell from tail area.

2 To remove the black vein running down the back of the shrimp, make a slit with a paring knife along the back from the head area to the tail.

3 Rinse shrimp under cold water to remove the exposed vein.

Crab Quiche

Before combining canned crab with other ingredients, first pick through the drained crab with your fingers to remove any pieces of cartilage.

        2 eggs
    1/2 cup mayonnaise
        2 tablespoons all-purpose flour
    1/2 cup milk
        2 cans (6 ounces *each*) crabmeat, drained and
            cartilage removed
    1/3 cup chopped green onions
        1 tablespoon minced fresh parsley
        2 cups (8 ounces) shredded Swiss cheese
        1 unbaked pastry shell (9 inches)

In a bowl, beat eggs; add mayonnaise, flour and milk. Stir in crab, onions, parsley and cheese. Spoon into pie shell. Bake at 350° for 1 hour. **Yield:** 6-8 servings.

—*Michele Field, Burtonsville, Maryland*

Florida Seafood Casserole

Corn Bread Dressing with Oysters

Prepare your favorite basic corn bread recipe and allow it to cool to room temperature. You can even freeze it weeks before preparing the dressing to save time.

> 8 to 10 cups coarsely crumbled corn bread
> 2 slices white bread, toasted and torn into small pieces
> 2 hard-cooked eggs, chopped
> 2 cups chopped celery
> 1 cup chopped onion
> 1 pint shucked oysters, drained and chopped *or* 2 cans (8 ounces *each*) whole oysters, drained and chopped
> 2 eggs, beaten
> 1 teaspoon poultry seasoning
> 5 to 6 cups turkey *or* chicken broth

Combine the first eight ingredients in a large bowl. Stir in enough broth until the mixture is very wet. Pour into a greased 13-in. x 9-in. x 2-in. or shallow 3-qt. baking dish. Bake, uncovered, at 400° for 45 minutes or until lightly browned. **Yield:** 12-15 servings.

—*Nell Bass, Macon, Georgia*

Florida Seafood Casserole

To flake cooked crab, simply shred or break any large chunks into smaller pieces for better distribution throughout the dish.

> 1/3 cup chopped onion
> 1/4 cup butter *or* margarine
> 1/4 cup all-purpose flour
> 1 cup milk
> 1 cup half-and-half cream
> 1/2 teaspoon salt
> 1/2 teaspoon pepper
> 1 tablespoon chopped pimientos
> 1 can (8 ounces) sliced water chestnuts, drained
> 2 tablespoons lemon juice
> 1 tablespoon chopped fresh parsley
> 1 cup cooked *or* canned crabmeat, drained and cartilage removed
> 1 cup peeled cooked shrimp
> 3 cups cooked rice
> 1 cup (4 ounces) shredded cheddar cheese, *divided*

In a saucepan, saute onion in butter; blend in flour. Add milk and cream; cook and stir until thickened and bubbly. Remove from the heat; stir in salt, pepper, pimientos, water chestnuts, lemon juice, parsley, crab, shrimp, rice and half of the cheese. Spoon into a greased 2-1/2-qt. baking dish. Bake, uncovered, at 350° for 25 minutes or until heated through. Sprinkle with remaining cheese just before serving. **Yield:** 6 servings.   —*Lucille Pennington, Ormond Beach, Florida*

Corn Bread Dressing with Oysters

Linguini with Clam Sauce

When you're cooking for two, this dish is just right. Keep a can of clams and a package of linguini on the pantry shelf so you can make this whenever you need a quick meal.

- **2 to 3 garlic cloves, minced**
- **3 tablespoons olive *or* vegetable oil**
- **1/4 cup minced fresh parsley**
- **1 can (6-1/2 ounces) minced clams**
- **4 ounces linguini *or* spaghetti**
- **1/4 teaspoon salt**
- **Pinch pepper**

In a skillet, saute garlic in oil over medium heat for 1 minute. Stir in parsley; saute 2 minutes. Drain clams, reserving juice; set clams aside. Add juice to skillet; cook, uncovered, for 10-15 minutes or until liquid is reduced by half. Meanwhile, cook pasta according to package directions. Add clams, salt and pepper to skillet; heat through. Drain pasta; toss with clam sauce. **Yield:** 2 servings. ⏱

New Year's Oyster Stew

If you plan to serve this for company, you may prepare the stew to the point of cooling the potato mixture. Refrigerate until the next day and complete the recipe.

- **1/4 cup butter *or* margarine**
- **3 leeks (white part only), chopped**
- **2 potatoes, peeled and diced**
- **2 cups water**
- **3 chicken bouillon cubes**
- **2 cups milk**
- **2 cups half-and-half cream**
- **1/4 teaspoon cayenne pepper**
- **4 cans (16 ounces *each*) whole oysters, drained**
- **Salt and pepper to taste**
- **Chopped fresh parsley**

In a large soup kettle or Dutch oven, melt butter; saute leeks until tender, about 10 minutes. Add potatoes, water and bouillon; cover and simmer for 20 minutes or until potatoes are tender. Allow mixture to cool, then puree in a blender or food mill. Return to kettle; add remaining ingredients. Heat slowly to serving temperature (do not boil). **Yield:** 12 servings.

—Christa Scott
Santa Fe, New Mexico

New Year's Oyster Stew

Lamb

When you want to add variety to everyday meals or elegance to special-occasion suppers, consider serving Barbecued Lamb Kabobs (p. 195), Southwestern Grilled Lamb (p. 194) or Old-Fashioned Lamb Stew (p. 199).

Lamb is a wonderfully tender and moist meat that lends itself to a variety of cooking styles and an assortment of flavor possibilities. From savory herb rubs to sweet glazes, here's a host of exciting grilled, stovetop and oven recipes that will make anyone a lamb lover.

Tips for Cooking and Serving Lamb

- Don't be afraid to use generous amounts of fresh garlic and herbs when cooking lamb. These bold flavors will enhance any cut.

- Lamb chops and the loin are very tender and can be pan-fried, broiled or grilled. Serve rare to well-done.

- Lamb shoulder, neck and shanks are less tender cuts and need to be simmered, covered, in a small amount of liquid until fork-tender. Trim all visible fat before cooking.

- Cuts such as a leg of lamb, rack of lamb and shoulder roast can be "dry-roasted" or cooked without liquid in an open roaster.

- When roasting lamb, it's best to use a meat thermometer to ensure the meat is cooked just the way you like it. For best flavor and tenderness, serve roasted lamb rare to medium-well. (See chart on page 196.)

- Lamb is best served piping hot. Warming the platter and dinner plates in the oven just before serving will keep your entree hot during the meal. Make sure your dishes are oven-safe and be careful to use hot pads when handling the warmed plates.

Grilled Lamb Chops

This recipe's flavorful marinade will help to keep the chops moist as they cook on the grill. Remember, the longer the chops marinate, the more flavor they will absorb.

    1/2 cup vegetable oil
    1/4 cup finely chopped onion
      2 tablespoons lemon juice
      1 teaspoon ground mustard
    1/2 teaspoon garlic salt
    1/2 teaspoon dried tarragon
    1/8 teaspoon pepper
      6 loin lamb chops (1-1/2 to 1-3/4 pounds)

In a resealable plastic bag or shallow glass container, combine the first seven ingredients; mix well. Add lamb chops and turn to coat. Seal bag or cover container; refrigerate several hours or overnight, turning occasionally. Drain and discard marinade. Grill chops, covered, over medium-hot heat for 14 minutes, turning once, or until a meat thermometer reads 140° for rare, 160° for medium-well or 170° for well-done. **Yield:** 4-6 servings.
—*DeLea Lonadier*
Montgomery, Louisiana

Southwestern Grilled Lamb

(Pictured on page 193)

If you like spicy dishes and want a change from traditional herb flavors for lamb, give this recipe a try. Use as much jalapeno as you like—remember to seed the peppers unless you like it really hot!

      1 cup salsa
    1/2 cup chopped onion
    1/4 cup molasses
    1/4 cup lime juice
    1/4 cup chicken broth
      2 garlic cloves, minced
      1 to 3 tablespoons chopped seeded jalapeno
        peppers
      2 teaspoons sugar
      4 loin lamb chops (1 inch thick)
Sour cream

In a saucepan, combine the first eight ingredients. Simmer, uncovered, for 15-20 minutes. Meanwhile, grill lamb chops, turning once, over medium-hot heat for 14 minutes, turning once, or until a meat thermometer reads 140° for rare, 160° for medium-well or 170° for well-done. Brush with sauce during the last few minutes of grilling. Serve with sour cream. **Yield:** 2 servings.
—*Margaret Pache, Mesa, Arizona*

Barbecued Lamb Kabobs

(Also pictured on page 193)

In this recipe, you can use any cut of lamb you wish. Shoulder chops or boneless lamb marked for stew would be good choices.

   2-1/2 pounds boneless lamb, cut into 1-inch cubes
MARINADE:
   1/2 cup lemon juice
   1/2 cup white wine *or* broth of choice
   2 tablespoons soy sauce
   2 tablespoons dried parsley flakes
   2 tablespoons dried minced onion
   1 teaspoon salt
   1/2 teaspoon black pepper
DIPPING SAUCE:
   1/2 cup vegetable oil
   1/2 cup lemon juice
   1 large onion
   2 garlic cloves, minced
Salt and pepper to taste
Chopped hot peppers to taste
Pita bread *or* French bread, warmed

In a resealable plastic bag or shallow glass container, combine marinade ingredients; add lamb. Seal bag or cover container; refrigerate at least 5 hours or overnight, turning occasionally. Drain and discard marinade. Thread meat on skewers; broil or grill, turning at intervals until meat is brown and cooked (about 15 minutes on medium-hot grill). Combine first six dipping sauce ingredients in a blender. Cover and process on high until smooth. Heat sauce; serve with meat and warm bread. **Yield:** 8-10 servings. —*Gloria Jarrett Loveland, Ohio*

Greek Burgers

Whether you grill these burgers or cook them indoors, you won't believe the burst of flavor you'll get with each bite. Serving with cucumbers, tomatoes and ranch salad dressing is a fun twist.

   1 pound ground lamb
   1 tablespoon Dijon mustard
   1 tablespoon lemon juice
   1 tablespoon finely chopped onion
   1 garlic clove, minced
   1/2 teaspoon dried rosemary, crushed
   1/2 teaspoon salt
   1/4 teaspoon pepper
   4 hamburger buns *or* hard rolls, split
Sliced cucumbers and tomatoes, optional
Ranch salad dressing, optional

In a medium bowl, combine the first eight ingredients; mix well. Shape into four patties. Pan-fry, grill or broil until no longer pink. Serve on buns with cucumbers, tomatoes and ranch dressing if desired. **Yield:** 4 servings. —*Michelle Curtis, Baker City, Oregon*

Barbecued Lamb Kabobs

Roasting Lamb

Place meat in a shallow roasting pan on a rack with the fat side up. Insert an oven-safe meat thermometer (or use an instant-read thermometer toward the end of the roasting time). Roast without liquid, uncovered, at 325° unless otherwise noted in the recipe. Because roasts will continue to cook after being removed from the oven, remove meat from the oven when the internal temperature is 5-10° below desired doneness. Cover and allow to stand for 10-15 minutes before carving.

Cut	Weight in Pounds	Doneness	Approximate Roasting Time
Leg—Whole	5 to 7	140° (rare) 160° (medium-well) 170° (well-done)	1-1/2 to 2 hours 2 to 3 hours 2-1/2 to 3-1/2 hours
Leg—Shank Half	3 to 4	140° (rare) 160° (medium-well) 170° (well-done)	1-1/4 to 1-3/4 hours 1-1/2 to 2 hours 1-3/4 to 2-1/4 hours
Leg—Sirloin Half	3 to 4	140° (rare) 160° (medium-well) 170° (well-done)	1 to 1-1/4 hours 1-1/4 to 1-3/4 hours 1-1/2 to 2 hours
Rib Roast (Rack)	1-3/4 to 2-1/2	140° (rare) 160° (medium-well)	3/4 to 1 hour 1 to 1-1/2 hours
Shoulder Roast—Boneless	3-1/2 to 5	160° (medium-well) 170° (well-done)	2 to 3 hours 2-1/2 to 3-1/2 hours

Carving a Leg of Lamb

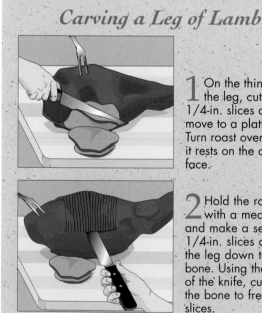

1 On the thin side of the leg, cut a few 1/4-in. slices and remove to a platter. Turn roast over so that it rests on the cut surface.

2 Hold the roast with a meat fork and make a series of 1/4-in. slices along the leg down to the bone. Using the blade of the knife, cut along the bone to free slices.

Roast Lamb with Plum Sauce

The sweet yet spiced plum sauce is used as a delightful glaze and sauce to pass. To avoid burning, only baste the roast during the last hour of baking.

> 1 leg of lamb (5 to 7 pounds)
> 3 garlic cloves
> 1/2 cup thinly sliced green onions
> 1/4 cup butter *or* margarine
> 1 jar (12 ounces) plum jam
> 1/2 cup chili sauce
> 1/4 cup white grape juice
> 1 tablespoon lemon juice
> 1/2 teaspoon ground allspice
> 1 tablespoon dried parsley flakes

Remove thin fat layer from the roast. Make three deep cuts in the meat; insert a garlic clove in each. Place on a rack in a large roasting pan. Bake, uncovered, at 325° for 1-1/2 hours. Meanwhile, in a medium saucepan, saute onions in butter until soft but not brown. Add jam, chili sauce, juices and allspice; bring to a boil, stirring occasionally. Simmer, uncovered, for 10 minutes. Baste roast with sauce. Bake 1 hour longer or until meat reaches desired doneness (see chart), basting occasionally. Bring the remaining sauce to a boil; stir in parsley. Serve with the roast. **Yield:** 10-12 servings.
—*Dorothy Pritchett, Wills Point, Texas*

California Roast Lamb

This is a great dish to serve when artichokes are plentiful in the market. If fresh artichokes are not available in your area, use two packages of frozen artichokes or two cans of water-packed artichokes that have been drained; add to the pan juices 30 minutes before serving.

    1 leg of lamb (5 to 7 pounds)
    2 to 3 garlic cloves, halved
    1 teaspoon seasoned salt
    1 teaspoon pepper
    1 teaspoon dried oregano
    2 cans (8 ounces *each*) tomato sauce
    1 cup water
Juice of 1 lemon
    3 to 5 large fresh artichokes, quartered
Lemon slices, optional

Cut two to three slits in the meat; insert garlic. Rub meat with salt, pepper and oregano. Place on a rack in a large roasting pan; bake, uncovered, at 400° for 30 minutes. Reduce heat to 350°; bake 1 hour longer. Skim off any fat in pan; pour tomato sauce, water and lemon juice over lamb. Place artichokes around meat. Bake 1 hour longer or until meat reaches desired doneness (see chart), basting occasionally with pan juices. Garnish with lemon if desired. **Yield:** 10-12 servings.

—*Ann Eastman, Greenville, California*

California Roast Lamb

Herbed Leg of Lamb

In many recipes, you will notice that the garlic is inserted into slits cut in the roast. To do this, use a sharp paring knife to make 1-in.-deep cuts in the roast. With your fingers, push each garlic clove into a slit. Large garlic cloves may need to be halved lengthwise to fit into the slits.

    1/2 leg of lamb (3 to 4 pounds)
    5 garlic cloves
    1 teaspoon salt
    1 teaspoon pepper
    1/4 teaspoon ground thyme
    1/4 teaspoon garlic powder
    1/4 cup all-purpose flour

Cut five slits in the meat; insert garlic. Combine salt, pepper, thyme and garlic powder; rub over meat. Place on a rack in a roasting pan. Broil 5-6 in. from the heat until browned; turn and brown the other side. Turn oven to 350°. Add 1/2 cup water to pan. Cover and bake for 1-1/2 to 2 hours or until meat reaches desired doneness (see chart). Remove to carving board and keep warm. Pour pan drippings into a large mea-

Preparing Fresh Artichokes

1 Rinse each artichoke well to remove any sand. Trim stem. Cut 1 in. off the top of the artichoke. Snip the tip end of each leaf with a kitchen shears.

2 Cut each artichoke into quarters and rub cut sides with lemon juice. With a spoon, remove and discard the center fuzzy "choke". Use artichoke quarters as directed in recipe.

suring cup, scraping browned bits. Skim fat. Add water to drippings to measure 2 cups. In a saucepan, whisk flour and drippings together until smooth. Bring to a boil; cook and stir 1-2 minutes longer. Slice lamb and serve with the gravy. **Yield:** 6-8 servings.

—*Barbara Tierney, Farmington, Connecticut*

Creamy Lamb Stew

der. Combine cream and remaining flour; stir into stew. Bring to a boil. Cook and stir for 1-2 minutes. Serve over biscuits. **Yield:** 6 servings.

—*Jeanne Dahling, Elgin, Minnesota*

Mushroom Lamb Chops

Because this recipe calls for using the blade chop—a more economically priced cut of lamb—you'll be able to serve it often for a hearty weeknight meal.

>   6 shoulder blade lamb chops (about 3 pounds)
>   1 tablespoon olive *or* vegetable oil
> 1/2 teaspoon dried thyme
> 1/2 teaspoon salt
> 1/4 teaspoon pepper
> 1/2 cup chopped celery
> 1/2 cup chopped green onions
>   1 can (10-1/2 ounces) beef consomme, undiluted
>   3 tablespoons all-purpose flour
> 1/4 cup water
>   1 jar (4-1/2 ounces) whole mushrooms, drained
>   1 tablespoon minced fresh parsley
> Hot cooked noodles

In a large skillet, brown the chops in oil; drain. Sprinkle with thyme, salt and pepper. Add celery, onions and consomme; cover and simmer for 40-45 minutes or until meat is tender. Remove chops and keep warm. Combine flour and water until smooth; gradually stir into skillet and bring to a boil. Cook and stir for 2 minutes. Add mushrooms and parsley; heat through. Serve over chops and noodles. **Yield:** 6 servings.

—*Ruth Andrewson, Leavenworth, Washington*

Creamy Lamb Stew

Here's a good recipe for busy schedules. Prepare this stew on the weekend and enjoy the leftovers during the week. The addition of dill and cream makes this stew extra special.

>   6 tablespoons all-purpose flour, *divided*
>   1 teaspoon salt
> 1/8 teaspoon pepper
> 1-1/2 pounds boneless lamb stew meat, cut into
>   1-inch cubes
>   2 tablespoons vegetable oil
>   3 cups water
> 1/2 teaspoon dill weed
>   8 pearl onions
>   3 medium carrots, cut into 1-inch pieces
>   2 large potatoes, peeled and cubed
> 1/2 cup half-and-half cream
> Hot biscuits

Combine 4 tablespoons flour, salt and pepper in a resealable plastic bag. Add lamb; shake to coat. In a 4-qt. Dutch oven, heat oil; brown lamb on all sides. Add water and dill; bring to a boil; Reduce heat; cover and simmer for 1-1/2 hours or until meat is almost tender. Add onions, carrots and potatoes. Cover and simmer for 30 minutes or until the meat and vegetables are ten-

Braised Lamb Shanks

For lamb enthusiasts, there is nothing quite like lamb shanks cooked long and slow until the meat begins falling off the bones. Plan time to cook them until the meat is fork-tender. If it's more convenient, you may cook the shanks earlier in the day and reheat before serving.

>   2 lamb shanks (about 2 pounds)
>   2 tablespoons vegetable oil
>   1 medium onion, diced
>   2 garlic cloves, minced
>   1 tablespoon all-purpose flour
>   2 beef bouillon cubes
> 1/4 cup boiling water
>   1 can (14-1/2 ounces) diced tomatoes, undrained
> 1/2 cup chopped celery
> 1/2 cup chopped carrot
> 1/2 teaspoon dried marjoram
> 1/4 teaspoon salt

In a large skillet, brown shanks in oil; remove and set aside. Add the onion and garlic; saute until tender. Stir in flour; cook and stir for 1 minute. Add bouillon and water; stir to dissolve. Return lamb to pan. Add remaining ingredients; bring to a boil. Reduce heat; cover and simmer for 1-1/2 to 2 hours or until meat is tender. **Yield:** 2 servings.
—Billie Moss
El Sobrante, California

Old-Fashioned Lamb Stew

(Also pictured on page 193)

Everyone is sure to enjoy the taste of a traditional stew. Be sure to add the peas and mushrooms just before serving to avoid overcooking.

    1/4 cup all-purpose flour
      1 teaspoon salt
    1/2 teaspoon pepper
      3 pounds boneless lamb stew meat, cut into
          1-inch cubes
      2 tablespoons vegetable oil
      1 can (28 ounces) diced tomatoes, undrained
      1 medium onion, cut into eighths
      1 tablespoon dried parsley flakes
      2 teaspoons dried rosemary, crushed
    1/4 teaspoon garlic powder
      4 large carrots, cut into 1/2-inch pieces
      4 medium potatoes, peeled and cut into 1-inch
          cubes
      1 package (10 ounces) frozen peas
      1 can (4 ounces) mushroom stems and pieces,
          drained

In a resealable plastic bag, combine flour, salt and pepper; add lamb and toss to coat. In a Dutch oven, brown the lamb in several batches in oil; drain. Add tomatoes, onion, parsley, rosemary and garlic powder. Cover and simmer for 2 hours. Add carrots and potatoes; cover and cook 1 hour longer or until the meat is tender. Add peas and mushrooms; heat through. Thicken if desired. **Yield:** 10-12 servings.
—Michelle Wise, Spring Mills, Pennsylvania

Braised Lamb Shanks
Old-Fashioned Lamb Stew
Mushroom Lamb Chops

Thicker Stews

If your stew needs just a little extra thickening, stir in a few tablespoons of fresh white, whole wheat or rye bread crumbs.

Lamb Chops with Mint Stuffing

Mint is a classic companion to lamb, served traditionally in the form of jelly. This unique recipe makes good use of your garden-fresh mint by flavoring the stuffing that tops the lamb chops.

1/4 cup chopped onion
1/4 cup chopped celery
1/2 cup butter *or* margarine
2/3 cup fresh mint leaves, chopped
4 cups white *or* whole wheat bread, torn into 3/4-inch pieces
Salt and pepper to taste
1 egg, beaten
8 shoulder blade lamb chops

Saute onion and celery in butter; remove from the heat. Toss with mint and bread. Season with salt and pepper. Add egg; mix lightly. Place lamb chops in a greased 13-in. x 9-in. x 2-in. baking dish. Top with bread mixture. Bake at 350° for 1 hour. **Yield:** 8 servings.

—*Ione Banks, Jefferson, Oregon*

Lamb Chops with Mint Stuffing

New England Lamb Bake

You'll love the aroma almost as much as the dish itself! This meaty stew is flavored with robust herbs and topped generously with oven-browned potatoes.

2 pounds boneless lamb stew meat, cut into 1/2-inch pieces
1 large onion, chopped
1 tablespoon vegetable oil
1/4 cup all-purpose flour
5 cups chicken broth
2 large carrots, sliced
2 large leeks, cut into 2-inch pieces
2 tablespoons minced fresh parsley, *divided*
1 bay leaf
1/2 teaspoon dried rosemary, crushed
1/4 teaspoon dried thyme
1/2 teaspoon salt
1/4 teaspoon pepper
3 large potatoes, peeled and sliced
1/4 cup butter *or* margarine

In a Dutch oven, brown lamb and onion in oil. Stir in flour; mix well. Gradually add broth. Bring to a boil, stirring to remove browned bits from pan. Add carrots, leeks, 1 tablespoon parsley, bay leaf, rosemary, thyme, salt and pepper. Spoon into a greased 3-qt. baking dish. Cover with potatoes and dot with butter. Bake, uncovered, at 375° for 1-1/2 to 2 hours or until the meat and potatoes are tender. Remove bay leaf. Garnish with remaining parsley. **Yield:** 6-8 servings. —*Frank Grady Fort Kent, Maine*

Curried Lamb and Barley

If you like the taste of lamb but you're on a budget, give this economical recipe a try. The cucumber salsa cools the spicy curry flavor for a perfect balance.

> 1 pound ground lamb
> 1 large onion, chopped
> 1 cup pearl barley
> 1/2 cup sliced celery
> 1 tablespoon vegetable oil
> 3 cups chicken broth
> 1 to 2 tablespoons curry powder

CUCUMBER SALSA:
> 1-1/2 cups coarsely chopped seeded cucumber
> 1/2 cup plain yogurt
> 1/4 cup snipped fresh parsley
> 1 tablespoon chopped green onion
> 1 tablespoon snipped fresh mint
> 2 teaspoons lemon juice
> 2 teaspoons olive *or* vegetable oil
> 1 garlic clove, minced

In a skillet, saute lamb, onion, barley and celery in oil until meat is browned and barley is golden; drain. Add broth and curry powder; bring to a boil. Pour into a greased 2-qt. baking dish. Bake, uncovered, at 350° for 1-1/4 to 1-1/2 hours or until barley is tender. Meanwhile, combine the salsa ingredients in a small bowl. Cover and refrigerate for 1 hour. Serve with the casserole. **Yield:** 4-6 servings.

Lamb Noodle Stroganoff

Rich and comforting is the only way to describe this dish. Serve with a tossed green salad for a complete meal. You can also try it with ground beef for variety.

> 2 pounds ground lamb
> 2 garlic cloves, minced
> 1 can (15 ounces) tomato sauce
> 1 teaspoon salt
> 1/4 teaspoon pepper
> 1 package (12 ounces) medium noodles, cooked and drained
> 1 package (8 ounces) cream cheese, softened
> 2 cups (16 ounces) sour cream
> 6 green onions, sliced
> 1-1/2 cups (6 ounces) shredded cheddar cheese

Paprika

In a skillet, saute the lamb and garlic until meat is browned; drain. Stir in tomato sauce, salt and pepper. Simmer, uncovered, for 10 minutes. Place noodles in a greased 13-in. x 9-in. x 2-in. baking dish. Top with meat mixture. In a small mixing bowl, beat cream cheese and sour cream until smooth; stir in onions. Spread over meat mixture. Bake, uncovered, at 350° for 30 minutes or until heated through. Sprinkle with cheese and paprika; let stand for 5 minutes. **Yield:** 8-10 servings.

—*Margery Bryan, Royal City, Washington*

Lamb Noodle Stroganoff

Game

When you want to get a little "wild" with your cooking, nothing can compare to the distinctive, delectable flavor of game. Pheasant and Wild Rice (p. 211) and Hasenpfeffer (p. 208) are just a few of this chapter's savory selections.

Wild game cooking is a delicious adventure that begs the cook to be creative with herbs, marinades and sauces. Whether you're cooking game birds, small game or large game, this hearty fare deserves careful attention because it is lean and tends to dry out if overcooked.

Tips for Cooking Wild Game

- Use marinades to tenderize and sweeten wild game that is traditionally strong flavored. You can use any of your favorite chicken marinades with game birds and beef marinades for large game.
- Before cooking, trim as much fat as possible from all wild game.
- If dry-roasting small young game birds, lay strips of bacon over the breast area to keep meat moist. Older birds will need to be tenderized by cooking over low heat with liquid in a covered container.
- Oven cooking bags are a good way to keep wild game moist and tender while roasting.
- Always check game for doneness and tenderness before recommended cooking times to ensure perfect results.

Grilled Venison and Vegetables

Grilled Venison and Vegetables

The marinade in this recipe is guaranteed to season venison to perfection. Cooked out of doors as directed or broiled indoors, this dish is wonderful for entertaining. And to make sure your meat and vegetables are cooked "just right", be sure to cut them into uniform pieces.

> 1/2 cup red wine vinegar
> 1/4 cup honey
> 1/4 cup soy sauce
> 2 tablespoons ketchup
Dash pepper
Dash garlic powder
> 1-1/2 pounds boneless venison steak, cut into 1-1/4-inch cubes
> 8 to 12 cherry tomatoes
> 8 to 12 fresh mushrooms, optional
> 1/2 medium green *or* sweet red pepper, cut into 1-1/2-inch pieces
> 1 to 2 small zucchini, cut into 1-inch chunks
> 1 large onion, cut into wedges
> 8 to 12 small red potatoes, parboiled

In a glass bowl or large resealable plastic bag, combine vinegar, honey, soy sauce, ketchup, pepper and garlic powder; set aside 1/4 cup. Add meat to bowl or bag; stir or shake to coat. Cover (or seal bag) and refrigerate for 4 hours. One hour before grilling, toss vegetables with reserved marinade. Drain meat, discarding marinade. Drain vegetables, reserving marinade. Thread meat and vegetables alternately on skewers. Brush with reserved vegetable marinade. Grill over medium-hot coals, turning and basting often, for 15-20 minutes or until meat and vegetables reach desired doneness. Remove from skewers and serve. **Yield:** 4-6 servings.

—*Eva Miller-Videtich*
Cedar Springs, Michigan

Venison Meat Loaf

You'd never know this meat loaf was prepared from venison. Leftovers make a great sandwich. Put chilled meat loaf slices on Italian bread, then top with a slice of Provolone or mozzarella cheese and broil until the cheese is melted.

    2 eggs
    1 can (8 ounces) tomato sauce
    1 medium onion, finely chopped
    1 cup dry bread crumbs
 1-1/2 teaspoons salt
    1/8 teaspoon pepper
 1-1/2 pounds ground venison
    2 tablespoons brown sugar
    2 tablespoons spicy brown mustard
    2 tablespoons cider vinegar

In a large bowl, lightly beat eggs; add tomato sauce, onion, crumbs, salt and pepper. Add venison and mix well. Press into an ungreased 9-in. x 5-in. x 3-in. loaf pan. Combine brown sugar, mustard and vinegar; pour over meat loaf. Bake, uncovered, at 350° for 70 minutes. **Yield:** 6-8 servings.   —*Liz Gilchrist, Bolton, Ontario*

Venison Pot Roast

Here's a perfect Sunday supper idea that cooks while the family goes to church. You'll love the way the garlic, soy sauce and ginger flavor the venison and gravy.

    1 boneless shoulder venison roast (3 to 4
      pounds)
    3 tablespoons vegetable oil
    1 can (14-1/2 ounces) chicken broth
    1/3 cup soy sauce
    1 large onion, sliced
    4 garlic cloves, minced
    1/2 teaspoon ground ginger
SPAETZLE:
    2 eggs
    1/2 teaspoon salt
 2-1/4 cups all-purpose flour
    2/3 cup milk
    2 quarts beef broth
    1/4 cup butter *or* margarine, melted
    1/8 teaspoon pepper
GRAVY:
    1/3 cup water
    1/3 cup all-purpose flour

In a Dutch oven, brown roast in oil; add the next five ingredients. Cover and simmer for 4 hours or until meat is tender. For spaetzle, beat eggs and salt in a medium bowl. With a wooden spoon, gradually stir in flour and milk. In a large saucepan, bring broth to a boil. Spoon dough into a colander or spaetzle maker; place over boiling broth. Press dough with a wooden spoon until bits drop into broth. Cook for 5 minutes or until tender. Drain; toss spaetzle with butter. Sprinkle with pepper and keep warm. Remove roast to a serving platter and keep warm. For gravy, measure 3 cups pan juices; return to pan. Combine water and flour; stir into pan juices. Cook and stir until thickened and bubbly. Cook and stir 1 minute more. Slice roast; serve with spaetzle and gravy. **Yield:** 6-8 servings.
—*Helen Featherly, Hamburg, Michigan*

Making Spaetzle

1 Beat eggs and salt in a mixing bowl. Gradually stir in flour and milk. Bring broth or water to a boil in a large saucepan. Spoon dough into a metal colander with large holes or into a spaetzle maker.

2 Place colander over boiling broth or water; press dough with a wooden spoon until dough is forced through bottom of colander and falls into broth. Cook until tender, about 5 minutes.

Venison Pot Roast

Swiss Elk Steak

2 pounds elk steak
All-purpose flour
    2 tablespoons butter *or* margarine
    1 can (15 ounces) tomato sauce
    1/2 cup red wine *or* beef broth
    2 tablespoons Worcestershire sauce
    1/2 cup diced onion
    1/2 cup diced green pepper
    1 can (2-1/4 ounces) sliced ripe olives, drained
    1 cup sliced fresh mushrooms
    1/2 teaspoon salt
    1/2 teaspoon pepper
    4 slices Swiss cheese, optional
Hot cooked noodles

Coat elk steak lightly in flour; shake off excess. Melt butter in a large skillet; brown steak on both sides. Place in an ungreased 13-in. x 9-in. x 2-in. baking pan. Combine the next nine ingredients; pour over steak. Cover and bake at 350° for 1-1/2 hours or until meat is tender. If desired, place cheese over steak before serving. Serve over noodles. **Yield:** 4 servings.

—*Carma Ochse, Bremerton, Washington*

Venison Tenderloin Sandwiches

The secret to keeping the venison tender for this sandwich is careful cooking. It is important to flatten each steak to 1/2 inch as directed and to not overcook them.

    2 large onions, sliced
    2 cans (4 ounces *each*) sliced mushrooms, drained
    1/4 cup butter *or* margarine
    1/4 cup Worcestershire sauce
    8 venison tenderloin steaks (12 ounces), about 3/4 inch thick
    1/2 teaspoon garlic powder
    1/4 teaspoon pepper
    1/2 teaspoon salt
    4 hard rolls, split

In a skillet, saute the onions and mushrooms in butter and Worcestershire sauce until onions are tender. Flatten steaks to 1/2 in. thick; add to the skillet. Cook over medium heat until meat is cooked to desired doneness, about 3 minutes on each side. Sprinkle with garlic powder, pepper and salt. Place two steaks on each roll; top with onions and mushrooms. **Yield:** 4 servings.

—*Patricia El-Zoghbi*
Wells, New York

Swiss Elk Steak

Elegant enough for company yet hearty for the family, this pretty dish is easy to prepare. If time is short, you may prepare this recipe the day before serving to the point of adding the cheese. To reheat, cover and bake at 350° for 45 minutes. If desired, place cheese over steak before serving.

Moose Meatballs

Moose Meatballs

This recipe is also a good way to use ground venison, elk or buffalo. And if you're looking for a hearty appetizer, prepare the dish without the peppers and noodles and serve with toothpicks.

> **1 pound ground moose meat**
> **1 egg, lightly beaten**
> **4 tablespoons cornstarch,** *divided*
> **1 teaspoon salt**
> **1/4 teaspoon pepper**
> **2 tablespoons chopped onion**
> **1 tablespoon vegetable oil**
> **3 tablespoons vinegar**
> **1 can (8 ounces) pineapple chunks**
> **1/2 cup sugar**
> **1 tablespoon soy sauce**
> **1 medium green pepper, cut into strips**
> **Hot cooked wide egg noodles**

In a bowl, combine meat, egg, 1 tablespoon cornstarch, salt, pepper and onion. Shape into 1-1/2-in. balls. In a large skillet, brown meatballs in oil. Cover and cook over low heat until the meatballs are no longer pink, about 10 minutes. In a saucepan, stir vinegar and re-

Making Meatballs of Equal Size

1 Lightly pat meat mixture into a 1-in.-thick rectangle. Cut the rectangle into the same number of squares as meatballs in the recipe.

2 Gently roll each square into a ball.

maining cornstarch until smooth. Drain pineapple, reserving juice. Set pineapple aside. Add enough water to juice to equal 1-1/2 cups; stir into vinegar mixture. Add sugar and soy sauce; cook and stir over medium heat until thickened. Add the meatballs, pineapple and green pepper; cook until heated through and the green pepper is tender. Serve over noodles. **Yield:** 3-4 servings.

—Janis Plourde
Smooth Rock Falls, Ontario

Buffalo Chili Con Carne

Buffalo Chili Con Carne

Prepare this favorite in large quantities and freeze in serving-size portions to save time months from now. You can also substitute cubed or ground venison or elk for the buffalo.

> 1 pound cubed *or* coarsely ground buffalo meat
> 2 tablespoons vegetable oil
> 1 to 2 cups diced onion
> 1 to 2 cups diced green pepper
> 2 cans (16 ounces *each*) diced tomatoes, undrained
> 1-1/2 to 2 cups tomato juice
> 1 can (4 ounces) chopped green chilies
> 2 teaspoons chili powder
> 1 teaspoon salt
> 1/2 teaspoon pepper
> 1 can (16 ounces) kidney beans, rinsed and drained
> 1 can (15 ounces) pinto beans, rinsed and drained

In a large kettle or Dutch oven, brown meat in oil; drain. Add onion and green pepper; saute for 5 minutes. Stir in the next six ingredients and bring to a boil. Reduce heat; cover and simmer 1 to 1-1/2 hours. Stir in beans. Cover and simmer 30 minutes longer or until meat is tender and beans are heated through. **Yield:** 6 servings (1-1/2 quarts). 🍎 *—Donna Smith, Victor, New York*

Hasenpfeffer

(Pictured on page 203)

Here's a traditional German dish that is known for its "pickled" flavor. This particular recipe has a wonderfully different twist with the addition of sour cream to the pan juices. To avoid curdling the sour cream, gently heat it in the pan juices; do not boil.

> 1 large onion, sliced
> 3 cups vinegar
> 3 cups water
> 1 tablespoon pickling spice
> 2 teaspoons salt
> 1/2 teaspoon pepper
> 2 bay leaves
> 8 whole cloves
> 1 dressed rabbit (2-1/2 pounds), cut into pieces
> 1/4 cup all-purpose flour
> 2 to 3 tablespoons butter *or* margarine
> 1 cup (8 ounces) sour cream

In a large non-metallic bowl, combine onion, vinegar, water and seasonings. Add rabbit pieces; cover and refrigerate for 48 hours, turning occasionally. Remove meat; strain and reserve marinade. Dry meat well; coat lightly with flour. In a skillet, melt butter; brown meat. Gradually add 2 to 2-1/2 cups of reserved mari-

nade. Cover and bring to a boil. Reduce heat and simmer until tender, about 30 minutes. Remove meat to a warm platter. Add sour cream to pan juices; stir just until heated through. Spoon over the meat and serve immediately. **Yield:** 6 servings. —*Mary Calendine*
Hiddenite, North Carolina

Rabbit Dijon

The sauce in this recipe is made by "deglazing" the pan or adding a liquid to the pan juices after the meat is removed. This technique loosens the pan drippings to make a rich flavorful sauce or gravy. This recipe can also be made with a 2- to 3-pound broiler/fryer chicken.

> **2 dressed rabbits, cut into pieces**
> **Salt and pepper to taste**
> **1 cup all-purpose flour**
> **8 tablespoons butter** *or* **margarine,** *divided*
> **1/4 cup brandy** *or* **chicken broth**
> **1 cup chopped green onion**
> **1/2 cup chopped parsley**
> **1 pound fresh mushrooms, sliced**
> **2 cups (16 ounces) sour cream**
> **2 tablespoons Dijon mustard**

Season rabbit with salt and pepper; coat with flour. Heat 4 tablespoons butter in a large skillet; brown meat. Remove to a roasting pan. Add brandy or broth to pan juices. Scrape browned bits from bottom and sides of skillet; pour over meat. Saute onion, parsley and mushrooms in remaining butter; pour over meat. Cover and bake at 350° for 1 hour. Remove meat to a warm platter. Stir sour cream and mustard into liquid in roaster; heat through. Pour over meat. **Yield:** 8 servings.
—*Kathryn Wolter, Sturgeon Bay, Wisconsin*

Rabbit with Tarragon Sauce

If you haven't cooked with tarragon, this is a great way to try it. It provides subtle flavor that goes well with rabbit. If you happen to have garden-fresh tarragon available, you will need to chop 2 tablespoons of it for this recipe.

> **1/2 cup all-purpose flour**
> **2 teaspoons dried tarragon**
> **1-1/2 teaspoons salt**
> **1 teaspoon pepper**
> **2 dressed rabbits (2 to 2-1/2 pounds** *each***), cut into pieces**
> **1/4 cup butter** *or* **margarine**
> **1/4 cup vegetable oil**
> **2 cups chicken broth**

In a large resealable plastic bag, combine flour, tarragon, salt and pepper. Add the rabbit pieces, one at a time, and shake well. In a large skillet, melt butter; add oil. Brown meat, a few pieces at a time. Add broth; cover and simmer for 50-60 minutes or until tender. Thicken the pan juices if desired. **Yield:** 8 servings.
—*Yvonne Kessler, Pangman, Saskatchewan*

Rabbit with Tarragon Sauce

Pheasant Potpie

If desired, you may prepare this recipe to the step of straining the broth. Then cool, refrigerate and finish the recipe the next day. For fun, cut decorative shapes from pastry leftovers with small cookie cutters and place on top of crust.

- 2 dressed pheasants (2-1/2 pounds *each*)
- 4 cups water
- 1 medium onion, quartered
- 1 celery rib, quartered
- 1 garlic clove, minced
- 2 tablespoons lemon juice
- 1-1/4 teaspoons salt
- 1/2 teaspoon pepper
- 1/4 teaspoon Worcestershire sauce
- 1/8 teaspoon ground nutmeg
- 3/4 cup all-purpose flour
- 1 jar (16 ounces) whole onions, drained
- 1 package (10 ounces) frozen peas
- 1-1/2 cups sliced carrots
- 1 jar (2 ounces) sliced pimientos, drained
- 1/4 cup minced fresh parsley

Pastry for single-crust pie

In a large saucepan or Dutch oven, place pheasants, water, quartered onion, celery and garlic; bring to a boil. Reduce heat; cover and simmer for 1 hour or until meat is tender. Remove pheasants; cool. Debone and cut into pieces; set aside. Strain broth, discarding veg-

etables. Measure 3-1/2 cups of broth and place in a saucepan. Add lemon juice, salt, pepper, Worcestershire sauce and nutmeg. Remove 1/2 cup and stir in flour. Bring broth in saucepan to a boil. Add flour mixture; boil 1 minute or until thickened and bubbly. Add the whole onions, peas, carrots, pimientos, parsley and pheasant; mix well. Spoon into a 2-1/2-qt. baking dish. Roll pastry to fit dish; place over meat mixture and seal edges to dish. Cut small steam vents in crust. Bake at 425° for 35-40 minutes or until filling is bubbly and pastry is golden. **Yield:** 6 servings.

—*Tawnya Coyne, Harrisburg, Pennsylvania*

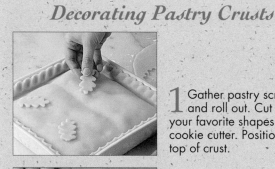

Decorating Pastry Crusts

1 Gather pastry scraps and roll out. Cut into your favorite shapes with a cookie cutter. Position on top of crust.

2 With a small sharp knife, cut slits in the crust to allow steam to escape. Bake as directed.

Pheasant Potpie

Pheasant in Mustard Sauce

Pheasant and Wild Rice

(Pictured on page 202)

This savory dish cooks the rice and makes its own gravy right in the oven cooking bag. Cleanup couldn't be easier! Substitute wild turkey parts, grouse or even chicken breasts for the pheasant if you prefer.

    1 tablespoon all purpose flour
    1 oven cooking bag
    6 bacon strips, diced
    2 cups uncooked wild rice
1/2 pound fresh mushrooms, sliced
    1 large dressed pheasant, halved *or* 2 small dressed pheasants (about 4 pounds)
    1 can (10-3/4 ounces) condensed cream of mushroom soup, undiluted
2-2/3 cups water
3/4 cup chopped onion
2-1/2 teaspoons dried parsley flakes
    2 teaspoons dried oregano
    2 teaspoons garlic powder
1-1/2 teaspoons paprika
    2 teaspoons salt
    1 teaspoon pepper

Shake flour in cooking bag; place in baking pan. Add bacon; top with rice, mushrooms and pheasant. Combine remaining ingredients; pour into bag. Tie and slit bag according to package directions. Bake at 325° for 2 to 2-1/2 hours. **Yield:** 6-8 servings. —*Debbie McCoic Hillsboro, Wisconsin*

Pheasant in Mustard Sauce

This recipe is just right for two, but it can easily be doubled or tripled for company.

    2 boneless skinless pheasant breast halves
1/4 teaspoon salt
1/8 teaspoon pepper
    1 tablespoon vegetable oil
    1 tablespoon butter *or* margarine
1/4 cup chopped onion
    1 garlic clove, minced
1/2 cup chicken broth
    2 tablespoons lemon juice
    3 tablespoons Dijon mustard
3/4 teaspoon dried marjoram
Hot cooked rice

Sprinkle pheasant with salt and pepper. In a skillet over medium heat, brown pheasant in oil and butter on both sides, about 6-8 minutes. Combine onion, garlic, broth, lemon juice, mustard and marjoram; add to skillet. Bring to a boil. Reduce heat; cover and simmer for 15-20 minutes or until meat juices run clear. Serve over rice. **Yield:** 2 servings.
—*Joan Mihalko, Elkton, South Dakota*

Creamed Grouse on Toast

You'll love the tangy lemon cream sauce that tames the strong flavor of grouse in this dish. It's perfect served as a brunch entree or a light supper.

>   2 quarts water
>   1 bay leaf
>   4 dressed grouse *or* squab (3/4 to 1 pound *each*)
>   1/2 cup chopped onion
>   1/2 cup sliced fresh mushrooms
>   2 tablespoons butter *or* margarine
>   2 tablespoons all-purpose flour
>   1 cup chicken broth
>   2 tablespoons lemon juice
>   1/2 teaspoon salt
>   1/8 teaspoon pepper
>   1/4 cup whipping cream
>   2 tablespoons minced fresh parsley
> Toast or hot cooked rice
> Additional parsley, optional

In a Dutch oven, bring water, bay leaf and grouse to a boil. Reduce heat; cover and simmer until meat is tender. Remove grouse; cool. Debone and cut into pieces. Strain broth; set aside.In a skillet over medium heat, saute onion and mushrooms in butter until tender. Add flour. Stir in broth, lemon juice, salt and pepper; bring to a boil. Cook and stir for 2 minutes. Add grouse and heat through. Add cream and parsley; mix well. Heat through. Serve over toast or rice; sprinkle with parsley if desired. **Yield:** 4 servings. —*Philan Welsh Spencer, Wisconsin*

Turtle Soup

This soup has a real "snappy" flavor from the cayenne pepper and lemon juice. You may want to start with just a pinch of cayenne and work your way up to a level that fits your personal spice preference.

> 1-1/3 pounds turtle meat
> 4-1/2 cups water
>   2 medium onions
>   1 bay leaf
>   1/4 teaspoon cayenne pepper
> 1-1/4 teaspoons salt
>   5 tablespoons butter *or* margarine
>   1/3 cup all-purpose flour
>   3 tablespoons tomato puree
>   3 tablespoons Worcestershire sauce
>   1/3 cup chicken broth
>   2 hard-cooked eggs, chopped
>   1/4 cup lemon juice
> Chopped fresh parsley, optional

In a heavy 4-qt. saucepan, bring turtle meat and water to a boil. Skim off foam. Chop 1 onion and set aside. Quarter the other onion; add to saucepan along with bay leaf, cayenne pepper and salt. Cover and simmer for 2 hours or until the meat is tender. Remove meat with a slotted spoon and cut into 1/2-in. cubes; set aside. Strain broth and set aside. Rinse and dry saucepan; melt butter over medium-high heat. Saute chopped onion until tender. Add flour; cook and stir until bubbly and lightly browned. Whisk in reserved broth; cook and stir until thickened. Reduce heat; stir in tomato puree and Worcestershire sauce. Simmer, uncovered, for 10 minutes. Add chicken broth, eggs, lemon juice and meat. Simmer for 5 minutes or until heated through. Sprinkle with parsley if desired. **Yield:** 4-6 servings.

—*Dave Wood Elmwood Park, New Jersey*

Creamed Grouse on Toast

Wild Duck Gumbo

Wild Duck Gumbo

Gumbo is a meal in itself. All you need to serve with it is a generous spoonful of hot rice and a basket of rolls. The recipe yields a generous 4 quarts, but any leftovers can be frozen for several meals later.

2 dressed wild ducks, cut up
1/2 cup vegetable oil
2/3 cup all-purpose flour
1 pound smoked sausage, sliced
2 cups chopped onion
1-1/2 cups chopped green pepper
1-1/2 cups sliced celery
2 tablespoons minced fresh parsley
1 tablespoon minced garlic
1 can (14-1/2 ounces) stewed tomatoes
2 bay leaves
2 tablespoons Worcestershire sauce
1-1/2 teaspoons pepper
1 teaspoon salt
1 teaspoon dried thyme
1/4 teaspoon cayenne pepper
2 quarts water
Hot cooked rice

In a Dutch oven over medium heat, brown duck in batches in oil. Remove and set aside. To prepare roux,

Browning a Roux

A roux is a mixture of fat and flour used to thicken gravy and soup. In a traditional gumbo, flour is added to the fat and heated until it reaches a reddish-brown color. It is important to stir while the mixture is browning.

reserve 2/3 cup drippings in pan. Add flour; cook and stir constantly over medium heat until reddish brown, about 12-14 minutes. Add sausage, onion, green pepper, celery, parsley and garlic. Cook for 10 minutes, stirring occasionally. Add the next eight ingredients; mix well. Add duck; bring to a boil. Reduce heat; cover and simmer for 60-75 minutes or until meat is tender. Remove meat; cool. Debone and cut into pieces; return to pan. Simmer for 5-10 minutes or until heated through. Remove bay leaves. Serve with rice. **Yield:** 16 servings (4 quarts). —*Doris Heath*
Bryson City, North Carolina

Wild Goose with Giblet Stuffing

Wild Goose with Giblet Stuffing

Wild goose is very lean and needs the addition of butter to keep the breast meat from drying out. You may also want to baste the bird with pan juices several times while roasting to keep it moist.

    1 dressed wild goose (6 to 8 pounds)
Lemon wedges
Salt
STUFFING:
Goose giblets
    2 cups water
    10 cups crumbled corn bread
    2 large tart apples, chopped
    1 large onion, chopped
    1/3 cup minced fresh parsley
    1 to 2 tablespoons rubbed sage
    1 teaspoon salt
    1/4 teaspoon pepper
    1/4 teaspoon garlic powder
Butter *or* margarine, softened

Rub inside goose cavity with lemon and salt; set aside. In a saucepan, cook the giblets in water until tender, about 20-30 minutes. Remove giblets with a slotted spoon and reserve liquid. Chop giblets and place in a large bowl; add corn bread, apples, onion, parsley, sage, salt, pepper and garlic powder. Add enough of the reserved cooking liquid to make a moist stuffing; toss gently. Stuff the body and neck cavity; truss openings. Place goose, breast side up, on a rack in a shallow roasting pan. Spread with butter. Bake, uncovered, at 325° for 2-1/2 to 3 hours or until fully cooked and tender. If goose is an older bird, add 1 cup of water to pan and cover for the last hour of baking. **Yield:** 6-8 servings. *—Louise Laginess, East Jordan, Michigan*

Roast Wild Duck

For basic preparation of a wild duck, follow this recipe. Tenderness may vary with the age of the duck. Younger birds are best for roasting. Older birds may need to be roasted longer or cooked in liquid to tenderize.

    1 dressed wild duck (about 2 pounds)
Salt
    1 large onion, quartered
    1 large tart apple, quartered
    4 bacon strips

Rub the inside of the duck with salt. Stuff the body and neck cavity with onion and apple pieces; truss openings. Place duck, breast side up, on a rack in a shallow roasting pan. Lay bacon strips over breast area. Bake, uncovered, at 400° for 1-1/2 hours or until tender. Cover loosely with foil if necessary to prevent excess browning. Discard onion and apple before serving. **Yield:** about 2 servings.

Quail in Mushroom Gravy

Quail are small, averaging 4 to 6 ounces apiece. Plan on serving one or two quail per person.

    3/4 cup all-purpose flour, *divided*
    1 teaspoon salt
    1/2 teaspoon pepper
    6 dressed quail (4 to 6 ounces *each*)
    1/2 cup butter *or* margarine
    1/2 pound fresh mushrooms, sliced
    2 cups chicken broth
    2 teaspoons minced fresh thyme *or* 3/4
        teaspoon dried thyme
Hot cooked noodles, optional

Combine 1/2 cup flour, salt and pepper; coat each quail. Melt butter in a skillet; brown the quail. Transfer to an ungreased 2-1/2-qt. baking dish. In the pan drippings, saute the mushrooms until tender. Add remaining flour and stir to make a smooth paste. Add broth and thyme, stirring constantly. Bring to a boil; boil for 1 minute or until thickened. Pour over the quail. Cover and bake at 350° for 40-50 minutes or until tender and juices run clear. Serve over noodles if desired. **Yield:** 3-6 servings. *—Jean Williams, Hurtsboro, Alabama*

Eggs and Cheese

As staples in every kitchen, eggs and cheese are certain to liven up menus morning, noon and night. Chili Cheese Strata (p. 229), Sheepherder's Breakfast (p. 223) and the other delicious dishes in this chapter are perfect for breakfast, brunch or even a light supper.

No two ingredients are quite as versatile and compatible in country recipes as eggs and cheese. Whether starring in a basic breakfast omelet or in an elegant dinner quiche, they are practical ingredients you'll want to keep on hand in your kitchen.

Tips for Buying, Storing and Cooking Eggs

- Buy eggs with clean, unbroken shells from refrigerated cases; refrigerate them as soon as possible after purchase.
- Store eggs in their carton or in the egg compartment of your refrigerator and use by the expiration date on the carton.
- Generally, plan on one to two eggs per serving.
- Eggs should always be cooked over low to medium heat.
- Never use recipes where the eggs will not be thoroughly cooked.
- Quiches and custard are thoroughly baked when a knife inserted near the center comes out clean. See Testing Baked Egg Dishes for Doneness on page 225.
- The dark green ring that forms around the yolk of a hard-cooked egg is caused by cooking the eggs too long at too high a temperature and not chilling the cooked eggs fast enough. See the Hard-Cooked Eggs recipe at right.

Fried Eggs

If you're watching calories, fry eggs in a nonstick pan coated with nonstick cooking spray.

1 to 2 tablespoons butter *or* margarine
1 to 2 eggs

In a 7- or 8-in. skillet or omelet pan, melt butter over medium heat. Break eggs, one at a time, into a custard cup or saucer, then gently slide into the pan. Immediately reduce heat to low. Cook slowly until the whites are completely set and the yolks begin to thicken. For sunny-side up eggs, cover the pan and cook until the yolk thickens to desired doneness, from soft to hard. For basted eggs, spoon butter in pan over eggs while cooking. For over-easy eggs, carefully turn the eggs to cook both sides. **Yield:** 1-2 servings.

Hard-Cooked Eggs

You may want to purchase eggs several days before hard-cooking them because they will be easier to peel.

4 eggs
Water

Place unshelled eggs in a single layer in a saucepan; add enough cold water to cover by 1 in. Cover and bring to a boil. Remove from the heat. Let eggs stand, covered, in the hot water for 15 minutes for large eggs. (Add or subtract 3 minutes for each size larger or smaller.) Rinse in cold water and place eggs in ice water until completely cooled. Store in the refrigerator up to 1 week. To peel eggs, gently tap and roll egg on countertop to break shell. Peel, beginning at the large end of the egg. **Yield:** 2-4 servings.

Soft-Cooked Eggs

Everyone likes their soft-cooked eggs cooked to a specific doneness. Experiment with different times—when you find the perfect doneness for you, note the cooking time.

4 eggs
Water

Place unshelled eggs in a single layer in a saucepan; add enough cold water to cover by 1 in. Cover and bring to a boil. Remove from the heat. Let eggs stand, covered, for 4-5 minutes in the hot water. Immediately run cold water over the eggs until they are cool enough to handle but still warm. To serve, break the shell in half with a knife. With a teaspoon, scoop the egg out of the shell into a serving dish or eat out of the shell. **Yield:** 2-4 servings.

Scrambling Eggs

1 Pour beaten egg mixture into prepared skillet. As eggs begin to set, gently move a spatula across the bottom and sides of pan, allowing the uncooked egg to flow underneath.

2 Continue to cook the eggs, stirring occasionally, until the eggs are set and no visible liquid remains.

Basic Scrambled Eggs

This is the standard "recipe" for scrambled eggs. You can easily adjust the number of servings to suit your needs.

> **2 eggs**
> **2 tablespoons milk, cream *or* water**
> **Salt and pepper to taste**
> **2 teaspoons butter *or* margarine**

In a small bowl, beat eggs, milk, salt and pepper until combined. In a 7- or 8-in. skillet, melt butter over medium heat. Pour in egg mixture. As eggs begin to set, gently move a spatula across the bottom and sides of the pan, allowing the uncooked egg to flow underneath. Continue cooking and stirring the eggs until the eggs are set and no liquid remains. **Yield:** 1-2 servings. ○

Scrambled Egg Casserole

When you're planning a brunch, consider this do-ahead recipe. The recipe calls for ham, but substitute 1 cup cooked crumbled sausage if you like.

1/2 cup butter *or* margarine, *divided*
2 tablespoons all-purpose flour
1/2 teaspoon salt
1/8 teaspoon pepper
2 cups milk
1 cup (4 ounces) shredded process American cheese
1 cup cubed fully cooked ham
1/4 cup sliced green onions
12 eggs, beaten
1 can (4 ounces) mushroom stems and pieces, drained
1-1/2 cups soft bread crumbs
Additional sliced green onions, optional

In a medium saucepan, melt 2 tablespoons butter. Add flour, salt and pepper; cook and stir until mixture begins to bubble. Gradually stir in milk; cook until thickened and bubbly, stirring constantly. Remove from the heat. Add cheese; mix well and set aside. In a large skillet, saute ham and onions in 3 tablespoons butter until onions are tender. Add eggs. Cook over medium heat, stirring occasionally, until eggs begin to set. Add the mushrooms and cheese sauce; mix well. Pour into a greased 11-in. x 7-in. x 2-in. baking dish. Melt remaining butter; toss with bread crumbs. Sprinkle over top of casserole. Cover

Scrambled Egg Casserole

and refrigerate for 2-3 hours or overnight. Remove from the refrigerator 30 minutes before baking. Bake, uncovered, at 350° for 25-30 minutes or until top is golden brown. Sprinkle with onions if desired. **Yield:** 6-8 servings. —*Mary Anne McWhirter, Pearland, Texas*

Breakfast Burritos

Breakfast Burritos

If desired, the burritos can be filled, folded and refrigerated several hours before serving—but be sure to add another 10 to 15 minutes to the baking time.

    1 package (16 ounces) frozen Southern-style hash brown potatoes
  12 eggs
    1 large onion, chopped
    1 medium green pepper, chopped
 1/2 pound bulk pork sausage, browned and drained
  12 flour tortillas (10 inches)
    3 cups (12 ounces) shredded cheddar cheese
Salsa, optional

In a large skillet, fry hash browns according to package directions; remove and set aside. In a large bowl, beat eggs; add onion and green pepper. Pour into the same skillet; cook over medium heat, stirring occasionally, until eggs are set. Remove from the heat. Add hash browns and sausage; mix gently. Place about 3/4 cup of filling on each tortilla; top with 1/4 cup cheese. Roll up and place on a greased baking sheet. Bake, uncovered, at 350° for 15-20 minutes or until heated through. Serve with salsa if desired. **Yield:** 12 servings.
—*Catherine Allan, Twin Falls, Idaho*

Deluxe Ham Omelet

Omelets are especially fun because you can enjoy them plain or add your favorite ingredients. The only rule to follow when making an omelet is to avoid overcooking.

    3 eggs
    2 tablespoons half-and-half cream
    2 tablespoons snipped chives
 1/2 teaspoon garlic salt
 1/4 teaspoon pepper
    1 tablespoon vegetable oil, butter *or* margarine
 1/2 cup finely chopped fully cooked ham
    2 tablespoons chopped green pepper
    2 tablespoons chopped tomato
    2 fresh mushrooms, sliced
    2 tablespoons shredded cheddar cheese
    2 tablespoons shredded mozzarella cheese

In a small bowl, beat the eggs, cream, chives, garlic salt and pepper. Heat oil in a 10-in. nonstick skillet over medium heat; add egg mixture. As the eggs set, lift edges, letting uncooked portion flow underneath. Sprinkle with ham, green pepper, tomato and mushrooms. When eggs are set, remove from the heat; fold omelet in half. Sprinkle with cheeses; cover for 1-2 minutes or until melted. **Yield:** 1-2 servings. ○
—*Iola Egle, McCook, Nebraska*

Making an Omelet

1 Beat eggs, milk or cream and any seasonings. Heat oil, butter or margarine in a 10-in. nonstick skillet over medium heat. Add eggs; cook until partially set. Lift the edges, letting the uncooked egg flow underneath.

2 Sprinkle your favorite filling ingredients (such as ham, chopped green pepper, chopped tomato, shredded cheese or mushrooms) over half of the omelet.

3 When eggs are set but still moist, remove from the heat, fold omelet in half and slip onto a serving plate.

Hearty Egg Scramble

Next time you prepare baked potatoes for dinner, make a couple extra to use in this country breakfast the next morning.

1/4 cup butter *or* margarine
1/4 cup chopped green pepper
1/3 cup chopped onion
2 medium potatoes, peeled, cooked and cubed
1-1/2 cups julienned fully cooked ham
6 eggs
2 tablespoons water
Dash pepper

In a large skillet, melt butter. Saute green pepper and onion until crisp-tender. Add potatoes and ham; cook and stir for 5 minutes. In a bowl, beat the eggs, water and pepper; pour over ham mixture. Cook over medium heat, stirring occasionally, until eggs are set. **Yield:** 6 servings. ◔ *—Marsha Ransom, South Haven, Michigan*

Ham and Potato Frittata

Ham and Potato Frittata

A frittata is an unfolded omelet that begins cooking on the stovetop and finishes under the broiler.

3 tablespoons butter *or* margarine, *divided*
1 pound red potatoes, cooked and sliced
1-1/2 cups thinly sliced fresh mushrooms
1 cup thinly sliced onion
1 sweet red pepper, julienned
2 cups diced fully cooked ham
2 garlic cloves, minced
1 tablespoon olive *or* vegetable oil
1/2 cup minced fresh parsley *or* basil
8 eggs
Salt and pepper to taste
1-1/2 cups (6 ounces) shredded cheddar *or* Swiss cheese

In a 10-in. cast-iron or other ovenproof skillet, melt 2 tablespoons butter over medium-high heat. Brown potatoes; remove and set aside. In the same skillet, melt the remaining butter; saute mushrooms, onion, red pepper, ham and garlic over medium-high heat until vegetables are tender. Remove and set aside. Wipe skillet clean. Heat oil over medium-low heat. Add potatoes, ham/vegetable mixture and parsley. In a bowl, beat eggs, salt and pepper. Pour into skillet; cover and cook for 10-15 minutes or until eggs are nearly set. Preheat broiler; place uncovered skillet 6 in. from the heat for 2 minutes or until eggs are set. Sprinkle with the cheese and broil until melted. Cut into wedges to serve. **Yield:** 6 servings.
—Katie Dreibelbis, State College, Pennsylvania

Basic Poached Eggs

Poached eggs are cooked out of the shell in liquid such as hot water, milk or broth.

4 cold eggs
Water, milk *or* broth

In a skillet, saucepan or omelet pan with high sides, bring 1 to 3 in. liquid to a boil. Reduce heat; simmer gently. Break cold eggs, one at a time, into a custard cup or saucer. Holding the dish close to the simmering liquid's surface, slip the eggs, one at a time, into the liquid. Cook, uncovered, until the whites are completely set and the yolks begin to thicken, about 3-5 minutes. With a slotted spoon, lift each egg out of the liquid. Gently tilt the spoon to allow any liquid to drain from under the egg. **Yield:** 2-4 servings. ◷

Zesty Poached Eggs

For a very pretty presentation and change of pace, place these poached eggs on toasted English muffins instead of plain toast.

4 poached eggs
2 slices whole wheat bread, toasted
1/4 cup process cheese spread, melted
1/4 cup salsa

Place two eggs on each slice of toast. Top with cheese and salsa. **Yield:** 2 servings. ◷   —*Kathy Scott*
Hemingford, Nebraska

Poaching Eggs

Break cold eggs, one at a time, into a custard cup or saucer. Holding the dish close to the simmering liquid's surface, slip the eggs, one at a time, into the liquid. Cook, uncovered, until the whites are completely set and the yolks begin to thicken, about 3-5 minutes.

Zesty Poached Eggs

Bacon and Cheese Breakfast Pizza

Sheepherder's Breakfast

(Also pictured on page 216)

The eggs in this dish are steamed over the hash browns. You will have to watch the eggs carefully to make sure they are cooked to your liking.

> 1 pound sliced bacon, diced
> 1 medium onion, chopped
> 2 packages (16 ounces *each*) frozen shredded
>   hash brown potatoes, thawed
> 7 to 10 eggs
> Salt and pepper to taste
> 2 cups (8 ounces) shredded cheddar cheese,
>   optional
> Minced fresh parsley

In a 12- or 14-in. skillet, cook bacon and onion until bacon is crisp. Remove mixture and set aside. Reserve 1/2 cup of drippings. Add hash browns to drippings; mix well. Cook over medium heat for 10 minutes, turning when browned. Stir in reserved bacon mixture. Using a spoon, make 7-10 "wells" evenly spaced in the hash browns. Break an egg into each well. Sprinkle with salt, pepper and cheese if desired. Cover and cook over low heat for about 10 minutes or until eggs are set. Garnish with parsley; serve immediately. **Yield:** 7-10 servings.
—*Pauletta Bushnell, Albany, Oregon*

Bacon and Cheese Breakfast Pizza

Everyone will love this pizza for breakfast or brunch. To save time, roll out the crust the night before and cover tightly with plastic wrap. The bacon can also be cooked, drained and refrigerated. Then just assemble and bake the next morning.

> Pastry for single-crust pie (9 inches)
> 1/2 pound sliced bacon, cooked and crumbled
> 2 cups (8 ounces) shredded Swiss cheese
> 4 eggs
> 1-1/2 cups (12 ounces) sour cream
> 2 tablespoons chopped fresh parsley

Roll pastry to fit a 12-in. pizza pan. Bake at 425° for 5 minutes. Sprinkle bacon and cheese evenly over crust. In a bowl, beat eggs, sour cream and parsley until smooth; pour over crust. Bake, uncovered, for 20-25 minutes or until puffy and lightly browned. **Yield:** 6 main-dish or 18 appetizer servings.
—*Dina Davis*
Madison, Florida

Sheepherder's Breakfast

Hash Brown Quiche

Bake, uncovered, at 425° for 25 minutes. Combine the ham, cheese and green pepper; spoon into crust. In a small bowl, beat eggs, milk, salt and pepper. Pour over all. Reduce heat to 350°; bake, uncovered, for 25-30 minutes or until a knife inserted near the center comes out clean. Let stand for 10 minutes before cutting. **Yield:** 6 servings.   —*Jan Peters, Chandler, Minnesota*

Breakfast Custard

If you like custard, you must try this savory version. With a side of warmed ham and whole wheat toast, it makes for a satisfying breakfast.

> 4 eggs
> 1 cup milk
> 2 tablespoons butter *or* margarine, melted
> 1 teaspoon cornstarch
> 1/8 teaspoon baking powder
> 1/4 teaspoon salt
> Dash pepper
> 1/2 cup shredded cheddar cheese

In a bowl, beat eggs. Add the next six ingredients. Stir in cheese. Pour into four buttered 4-oz. custard cups. Place cups in a baking pan. Fill pan with hot water to a depth of 1 in. Bake, uncovered, at 425° for 15-20 minutes or until a knife inserted near the center comes out clean. **Yield:** 4 servings.   —*Arlene Bender Martin, North Dakota*

Broccoli Pie

Your family won't miss the meat in this hearty egg dish. A dash of nutmeg adds the right accent.

> 3 tablespoons vegetable oil
> 1 large onion, chopped
> 4 eggs, lightly beaten
> 4 cups chopped fresh broccoli, cooked
> 2 cups (8 ounces) shredded mozzarella cheese
> 1 carton (15 ounces) ricotta cheese
> 1/3 cup grated Parmesan cheese
> 1/4 teaspoon salt
> Dash ground nutmeg
> 1 unbaked pastry shell (9 inches)

In a skillet, heat oil. Saute onion until tender, about 5 minutes. Transfer to a large bowl; add eggs, broccoli, cheeses, salt and nutmeg. Pour into pie shell. Bake at 350° for 50-55 minutes or until a knife inserted near the center comes out clean. Let stand 10 minutes before cutting. **Yield:** 6-8 servings.

Hash Brown Quiche

If you love quiche but want to avoid having to make a pie crust, try this recipe. The convenient crust is made from hash brown potatoes. Serve with a fruit salad for a pretty, no-fuss meal.

> 3 cups frozen shredded hash browns, thawed
> 1/3 cup butter *or* margarine, melted
> 1 cup diced fully cooked ham
> 1 cup (4 ounces) shredded cheddar cheese
> 1/4 cup diced green pepper
> 2 eggs
> 1/2 cup milk
> 1/2 teaspoon salt
> 1/4 teaspoon pepper

Press hash browns between paper towel to remove excess moisture. Press onto the bottom and up the sides of an ungreased 9-in. pie plate. Drizzle with butter.

Tomato Quiche

When garden tomatoes are plentiful, plan to prepare this dazzling egg dish. The secret to the recipe's success is cooking the tomatoes until almost all of the water is evaporated. Serve for a brunch, ladies' luncheon or light supper.

2 tablespoons butter *or* margarine
1 cup chopped onion
4 large tomatoes, peeled, seeded, chopped and drained
1 teaspoon salt
1/4 teaspoon pepper
1/4 teaspoon dried thyme
2 cups (8 ounces) shredded Monterey Jack cheese, *divided*
1 unbaked pastry shell (10 inches)
4 eggs
1-1/2 cups half-and-half cream

In a skillet, melt butter. Saute onion until tender. Add tomatoes, salt, pepper and thyme. Cook over medium-high heat until liquid is almost evaporated, about 10-15 minutes. Remove from the heat. Sprinkle 1 cup cheese into bottom of pastry shell. Cover with tomato mixture; sprinkle with remaining cheese. In a mixing bowl, beat eggs. Stir in cream; mix well. Pour into pie shell. Bake, uncovered, at 425° for 10 minutes. Reduce heat to 325°; bake 40 minutes more or until top begins to brown and a knife inserted near the center comes out clean. Let stand 10 minutes before cutting. **Yield:** 6-8 servings.

—*Heidi Anne Quinn, West Kingston, Rhode Island*

Testing Baked Egg Dishes For Doneness

Egg dishes containing beaten eggs—like quiche, strata or custard—are tested for doneness by inserting a knife near the center of the dish. If the knife comes out clean, the eggs are cooked.

Tomato Quiche

Tips for Beating Egg Whites

After you separate eggs, allow the egg whites to stand at room temperature for 30 minutes before beating to obtain maximum volume.

Three-Cheese Souffles

This recipe can be can be made ahead and frozen. Cover each dish with foil and freeze. To bake, remove the foil and place frozen souffles in a shallow pan. Fill pan with hot water to a depth of 1 inch. Bake, uncovered, at 325° for 60-65 minutes or until golden brown.

1/3 cup butter *or* margarine
1/3 cup all-purpose flour
2 cups milk
1 teaspoon Dijon mustard
1/4 teaspoon salt
Dash hot pepper sauce
1-1/2 cups (6 ounces) shredded Swiss cheese
1 cup (4 ounces) shredded cheddar cheese
1/4 cup shredded Parmesan cheese
6 eggs, *separated*
1/2 teaspoon cream of tartar

Melt butter in a medium saucepan. Stir in flour; cook for 1 minute or until bubbly. Gradually add milk, mustard, salt and hot pepper sauce; cook and stir until thickened and bubbly. Add cheeses; stir until melted. Remove from the heat and set aside. In a small mixing bowl, beat egg yolks until thick and lemon-colored, about 3-4 minutes. Add 1/3 cup cheese mixture and mix well. Return all to the saucepan; return to the heat and cook for 1-2 minutes. Cool completely, about 30-40 minutes. In another mixing bowl, beat egg whites until soft peaks form. Add cream of tartar; beat until stiff peaks form. Gently fold into cheese mixture. Pour into ungreased 1-cup souffle dishes or custard cups. Place in a shallow pan. Pour hot water into pan to a depth of 1 in. Bake, uncovered, at 325° for 40-45 minutes or until tops are golden browned. Serve immediately. **Yield:** 8 servings. *—Jean Ference*
Sherwood Park, Alberta

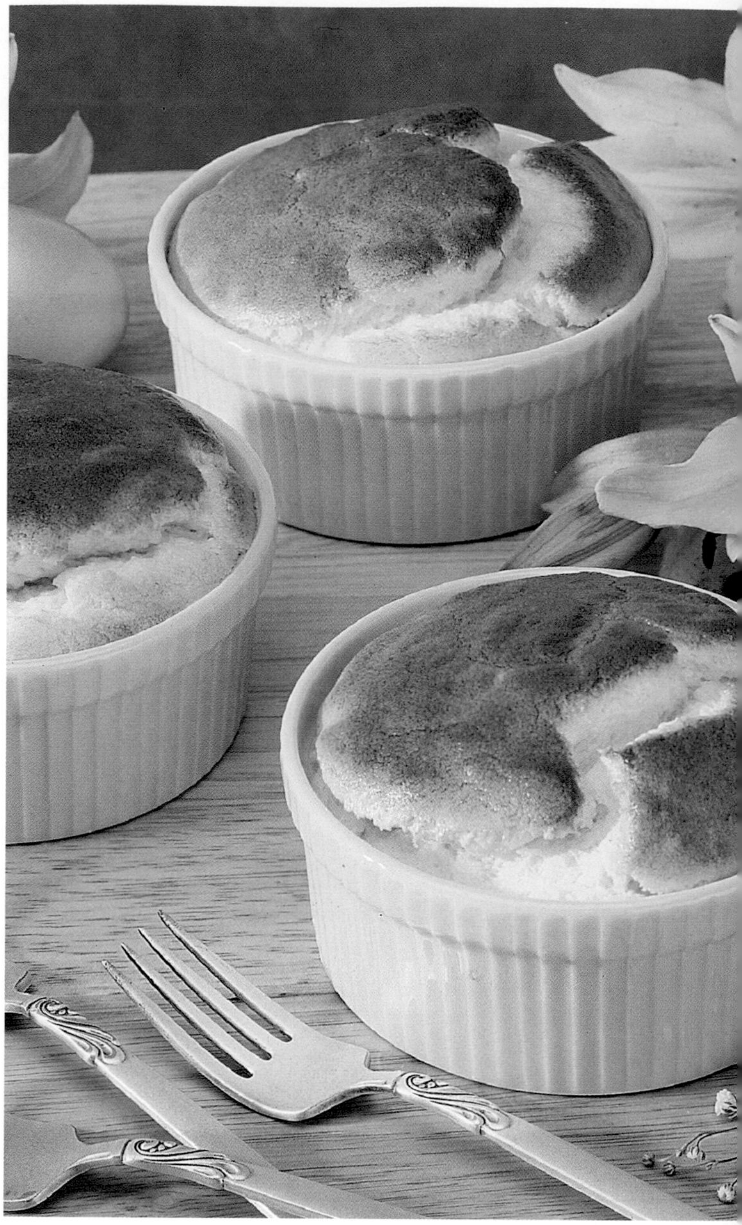

Three-Cheese Souffles

Separating Eggs

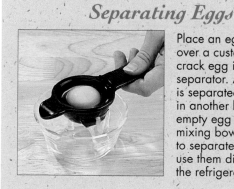

Place an egg separator over a custard cup; crack egg into the separator. As each egg is separated, place yolk in another bowl and empty egg whites into a mixing bowl. It's easier to separate eggs if you use them directly from the refrigerator.

Old-World Puff Pancake

This recipe looks difficult, but it's really not. All the ingredients for the pancake are placed in a blender for quick mixing. Be sure the oven is preheated to 425° before putting the skillet into the oven. A cast-iron skillet is a helpful tool because it heats up more quickly than other metals and makes a better puff.

    2 tablespoons butter *or* margarine
    3 eggs
    3/4 cup milk
    3/4 cup all-purpose flour
    2 teaspoons sugar
    1 teaspoon ground nutmeg
Confectioners' sugar
Lemon wedges
Syrup, optional

Place butter in a 10-in. ovenproof skillet; place in a 425° oven for 2-3 minutes or until melted. Place the eggs, milk, flour, sugar and nutmeg in a blender; cover and process until smooth. Pour into prepared skillet. Bake, uncovered, at 425° for 16-18 minutes or until puffed and browned. Dust with sugar. Serve with lemon and syrup if desired. **Yield:** 4-6 servings.

—Auton Miller, Piney Flats, Tennessee

Old-World Puff Pancake

Egg-Filled Buns

Egg-Filled Buns

Here's a hearty, tasty hand-held morning dish that is very easy to eat for those on the go. Add a little fruit on the side and breakfast is soon served!

    2 tablespoons butter *or* margarine
    4 eggs, beaten
    2 packages (2-1/2 ounces *each*) sliced fully
      cooked smoked beef, chopped
    1/3 cup mayonnaise
    1/4 teaspoon salt
    1/4 teaspoon pepper
    1 package (16 ounces) hot roll mix
    1 tablespoon milk

In a medium skillet, melt butter over medium heat. Add the eggs; cook and stir gently until set. Remove from the heat. Add beef, mayonnaise, salt and pepper; mix well. Chill. Prepare roll mix according to package directions. Divide dough into six portions; roll each portion into an 8-in. x 3-in. rectangle. Spoon 1/3 cup of egg mixture on half of each rectangle. Fold over and seal edges. Place on a greased baking sheet. Cover and let rise in a warm place until doubled, about 30 minutes. Brush tops with milk. Bake, uncovered, at 350° for 20-25 minutes or until golden brown. Serve warm. **Yield:** 6 servings.

—Kathy Wells
Brodhead, Wisconsin

Asparagus Strata

If fresh asparagus is not available, frozen is the next best choice. Just allow it to defrost and blot any excess moisture before adding to the casserole.

12 slices white bread
12 ounces process American cheese, diced
1-1/2 pounds fresh asparagus, trimmed and cut into
    1-1/4-inch pieces
2 cups diced fully cooked ham
6 eggs
3 cups milk
2 tablespoons finely chopped onion
1/2 teaspoon salt
1/4 teaspoon ground mustard

Using a doughnut cutter, cut 12 circles and holes from bread; set aside. Tear remaining bread in pieces and place in a greased 13-in. x 9-in. x 2-in. baking pan. Layer cheese, asparagus and ham over torn bread; arrange bread circles and holes on top. Lightly beat eggs with milk. Add onion, salt and mustard; mix well. Pour egg mixture over bread circles and holes. Cover and refrigerate at least 6 hours or overnight. Remove from the refrigerator 30 minutes before baking. Bake, uncovered, at 325° for 55 minutes or until a knife inserted near the center comes out clean. Let stand 10 minutes before serving. **Yield:** 6-8 servings.

—*Ethel Pressel, New Oxford, Pennsylvania*

Chili Cheese Strata

(Pictured on page 217)

This do-ahead casserole has a south-of-the-border flavor. Adjust the chilies and salsa to suit your tastes.

- 1 loaf (12 ounces) French bread, cut into 1-inch cubes
- 2 cups shredded cheddar *or* Monterey Jack cheese, *divided*
- 1 jar (8 ounces) mild green chili salsa *or* 4 ounces chopped green chilies and 4 ounces salsa, combined
- 4 eggs
- 1 can (10-3/4 ounces) condensed cheddar cheese soup, undiluted
- 2 cups milk *or* half-and-half cream
- 2 tablespoons finely chopped onion
- 1 teaspoon Worcestershire sauce

Place bread cubes evenly in a greased 2-qt. shallow baking dish. Sprinkle with 1 cup cheese. Pour salsa over cheese; set aside. In blender, combine eggs, soup, milk, onion and Worcestershire sauce; pour over bread mixture. Sprinkle with remaining cheese. Cover and refrigerate 6 hours or overnight. Remove from the refrigerator 30 minutes before baking. Bake, uncovered, at 350° for 30 minutes or until a knife inserted near the center comes out clean. Let stand 10 minutes before serving. **Yield:** 8 servings.

—*Shirley Smith*
Anaheim, California

Herbed Baked Eggs

If you're in a rut when it comes to preparing eggs, try this easy but unique recipe. Serve these in individual souffle dishes or custard cups.

- 2 tablespoons butter *or* margarine, softened
- 1/2 teaspoon *each* dried chives, tarragon and parsley flakes
- 4 eggs
- 1/4 teaspoon pepper
- 4 tablespoons half-and-half cream
- 4 tablespoons grated Parmesan cheese

Combine the butter and herbs; divide among four 4-oz. baking dishes. Place dishes in a large baking pan. Place in a 350° oven for 2-4 minutes or until butter has melted. Break one egg into each dish. Sprinkle with pepper. Top with cream and Parmesan cheese. Bake, uncovered, for 12-15 minutes or until eggs reach desired doneness. Serve immediately. **Yield:** 2-4 servings.

—*Sandy Szwarc, Albuquerque, New Mexico*

Egg Pizzas

This may be the one egg dish picky youngsters will try. The individual pizzas are sure to appeal to kids of all ages.

- 4 eggs
- 3 tablespoons milk
- 3 tablespoons finely chopped green pepper
- 1/2 teaspoon dried oregano
- Dash salt and pepper
- 1 tablespoon butter *or* margarine
- 4 English muffins
- 4 to 6 tablespoons pizza sauce
- 1/2 pound bulk pork sausage, cooked and drained
- 2 tablespoons sliced ripe olives
- 2 tablespoons grated Parmesan cheese

In a bowl, beat eggs; add milk, green pepper, oregano, salt and pepper. Melt butter in a skillet; add egg mixture. Cook and stir over medium heat until eggs are set. Remove from the heat. Split and toast English muffins; spread with pizza sauce. Top with eggs. Sprinkle with sausage, olives and cheese. Place under broiler for a few minutes to heat through. **Yield:** 4 servings.

—*Olive Ranck, Williamsburg, Indiana*

Egg Pizzas

Baked Stuffed Eggs
Puffy Apple Omelet

Stuffing Eggs Using a Pastry Bag

Mash yolks with a fork. Add remaining filling ingredients; mix well. Spoon filling into a pastry bag fitted with a #20 decorating tip. Pipe filling into egg white halves.

Best Deviled Eggs

It's best to let hard-cooked eggs chill several hours before using them for deviled eggs. So be sure to allow enough time when you plan on preparing them.

   12 hard-cooked eggs
   1/2 cup mayonnaise
   2 tablespoons milk
   1 teaspoon dried parsley flakes
   1/2 teaspoon dried chives
   1/2 teaspoon ground mustard
   1/2 teaspoon dill weed
   1/4 teaspoon salt
   1/4 teaspoon paprika
   1/8 teaspoon pepper
   1/8 teaspoon garlic powder
Fresh parsley and additional paprika

Slice eggs in half lengthwise; remove yolks and set whites aside. In a small bowl, mash yolks with a fork. Add the next 10 ingredients; mix well. Evenly fill the whites. Garnish with parsley and paprika. **Yield:** 24 servings. —*Anne Foust, Bluefield, West Virginia*

Baked Stuffed Eggs

Here's a great recipe to utilize all those leftover hard-cooked eggs from Easter. Serve with fresh asparagus for a real springtime meal.

STUFFED EGGS:
   6 hard-cooked eggs
   3 to 4 tablespoons sour cream
   2 teaspoons prepared mustard
   1/2 teaspoon salt
SAUCE:
   1/2 cup chopped onion
   2 tablespoons butter *or* margarine
   1 can (10-3/4 ounces) condensed cream of
      mushroom soup, undiluted
   1 cup (8 ounces) sour cream
   1/2 cup shredded cheddar cheese
   1/2 teaspoon paprika

Slice eggs in half lengthwise; remove yolks and set whites aside. In a bowl, mash yolks with a fork. Add sour cream, mustard and salt; mix well. Evenly fill the egg whites; set aside. In a saucepan, saute onion in butter until tender. Add soup and sour cream; mix well. Pour half into an ungreased 11-in. x 7-in. x 2-in. baking pan. Arrange stuffed eggs over the sauce. Spoon remaining sauce on top. Sprinkle with cheese and paprika. Cover and refrigerate overnight. Remove from the refrigerator 30 minutes before baking. Bake, uncovered, at 350° for 25-30 minutes or until heated through. Serve immediately. **Yield:** 6 servings.
—*Lorraine Bylsma, Eustis, Florida*

Puffy Apple Omelet

When autumn is in the air, it's time to prepare this comforting breakfast or brunch dish. Take it right to the table from the oven. Like a souffle, it will fall as it cools.

   3 tablespoons all-purpose flour
   1/4 teaspoon baking powder
   1/8 teaspoon salt
   2 eggs, *separated*
   3 tablespoons milk
   3 tablespoons sugar
   1 tablespoon lemon juice
TOPPING:
   1 large tart apple, thinly sliced
   1 teaspoon sugar
   1/4 teaspoon ground cinnamon

In a small bowl, combine flour, baking powder and salt; mix well. Add egg yolks and milk; mix well and set aside. In a small mixing bowl, beat egg whites until foamy. Gradually add sugar, beating until stiff peaks form. Fold into yolk mixture; add lemon juice. Pour into a greased 1-1/2-qt. shallow baking dish. Arrange apple slices on top. Combine sugar and cinnamon; sprinkle over all. Bake, uncovered, at 375° for 18-20 minutes or until a knife inserted near the center comes out clean. Serve immediately. **Yield:** 2 servings.
—*Melissa Davenport, Campbell, Minnesota*

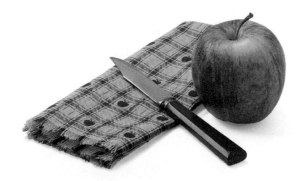

Herbed Macaroni and Cheese

This is an extraordinary departure from the classic dish. Herbs, spices and sour cream add wonderful flavor.

    1 package (7 ounces) elbow macaroni
    2 tablespoons butter *or* margarine
    2 tablespoons all-purpose flour
    1/2 teaspoon Italian seasoning
    1/4 teaspoon onion powder
Salt and pepper to taste
    1 cup milk
    1/4 cup sour cream
    1/2 cup cubed Havarti *or* Muenster cheese
    3/4 cup shredded cheddar cheese, *divided*
    2 tablespoons grated Parmesan cheese
    2 tablespoons Italian-seasoned bread crumbs

Cook macaroni according to package directions. Meanwhile, in a saucepan, melt butter over medium heat. Stir in the flour and seasonings; gradually add milk. Cook and stir until thickened. Remove from the heat; add sour cream, Havarti cheese and 1/2 cup cheddar cheese. Stir until melted. Drain macaroni; place in an ungreased 1-1/2-qt. baking dish. Add cheese sauce and mix well. Combine Parmesan cheese, bread crumbs and remaining cheddar cheese; sprinkle over casserole. Bake, uncovered, at 350° for 15-20 minutes. **Yield: 4** servings. —*Nancy Raymond, Waldoboro, Maine*

Cheese Tips

- When buying bulk cheese, 4 ounces equals 1 cup shredded.
- Store cheese in airtight containers, plastic bags or plastic wrap in the refrigerator (about 4 months for soft cheeses and 6 months for hard cheeses).
- Cheese can be frozen for longer storage time. Because the freezing process changes the cheese's texture slightly, it is best to use it in cooking or baking.
- When cooking with natural unprocessed cheese, melt at low temperatures to keep the cheese from turning tough and stringy.
- When adding cheese to a soup or sauce, stir in the cheese at the end of cooking to avoid overheating. Shredding the cheese allows it to melt faster with a minimum of heating.

Stovetop Macaroni and Cheese

There's no need to wait for this dish to bake...it's ready in almost the time it takes to cook the macaroni.

    1 package (7 ounces) elbow macaroni
    1/4 cup butter *or* margarine
    1/4 cup all-purpose flour
    1/2 teaspoon salt
Pinch pepper
    2 cups milk
    2 cups (8 ounces) shredded cheddar cheese
Paprika, optional

Cook macaroni according to package directions. Meanwhile, in a medium saucepan, melt butter over medium heat. Stir in flour, salt and pepper; cook until bubbly. Gradually add milk; cook and stir until thickened. Stir in cheese until melted. Drain macaroni; add to cheese sauce and stir to coat. Sprinkle with paprika if desired. **Yield: 4** servings. ○ —*Imogene Hutton Norton, Texas*

Old-World Pizza

This recipe's dough is soft, so butter your fingers before patting it into the baking pan.

> 1 package (1/4 ounce) active dry yeast
> 1 cup warm water (110° to 115°)
> 2-1/2 cups all-purpose flour
> 2 tablespoons vegetable oil
> 1 teaspoon sugar
> 1 teaspoon salt
> 1 can (8 ounces) pizza sauce
> 1 pound ground beef, browned and drained
> 2 cups sliced pepperoni
> 1-1/2 cups (6 ounces) shredded mozzarella cheese
> 1-1/2 cups (6 ounces) shredded cheddar cheese
> 1/3 cup grated Parmesan cheese

In a mixing bowl, dissolve yeast in warm water. Add flour, oil, sugar and salt. Beat vigorously 20 strokes. Cover and let rest about 15 minutes. With buttered fingers, pat crust into a greased 15-in. x 10-in. x 1-in. baking pan. Cover with pizza sauce. Sprinkle with toppings. Bake at 425° for 15-20 minutes or until crust and cheese are lightly browned. **Yield:** 8-12 servings.

—*Linda Hovey, Mondovi, Wisconsin*

Three-Cheese Enchiladas

For a change of pace, prepare this dish with warmed corn tortillas. Follow package directions for softening the tortillas before filling.

> 1-1/2 cups (6 ounces) shredded Monterey Jack
>   cheese, *divided*
> 1-1/2 cups (6 ounces) shredded cheddar cheese,
>   *divided*
> 1 package (3 ounces) cream cheese, softened
> 1 cup picante sauce, *divided*
> 1 medium green *or* sweet red pepper, diced
> 1/2 cup sliced green onions
> 1/2 to 1 teaspoon ground cumin
> 8 flour tortillas (7 to 8 inches)

Shredded lettuce
Chopped tomato
Sliced ripe olives
Additional picante sauce, optional

Combine 1 cup Monterey Jack cheese, 1 cup cheddar cheese, cream cheese, 1/4 cup picante sauce, green or red pepper, onions and cumin; mix well. Spoon 1/4 cup down the center of each tortilla. Roll up and place seam side down in a greased 13-in. x 9-in. x 2-in. baking dish. Spoon remaining picante sauce evenly over

Old-World Pizza

enchiladas; sprinkle with remaining cheeses. Bake, uncovered, at 350° for 20 minutes or until heated through. Top with lettuce, tomato and olives; serve with additional picante sauce if desired. **Yield:** 4 servings.

—*Gretchen Mellberg, Hawarden, Iowa*

Grains, Beans and Pasta

Add palate-pleasing possibilities to your menu with Country Cassoulet (p. 240) packed with beans, chicken and sausage. Or for side dishes to round out a variety of entrees, reach for zesty Texas-Style Spanish Rice (p. 237) or easy Homemade Noodles (p. 244).

Common grains, which include rice, barley, wild rice, oats and hominy grits, can be found in the most classic of country recipes. Team grains with vegetables, beans, meat or fish for hearty, nutritious and budget-conscious side-dish or main-dish fare.

Tips for Storing and Cooking Grains

- You can store white and wild rice in an airtight container indefinitely. Brown rice has an oily bran layer that can turn rancid at room temperature. Store in the refrigerator for up to 6 months.

- Always rinse wild rice before cooking. It is not necessary to rinse other grains.

- When cooking rice, do not stir or lift the cover unless instructed in the recipe.

- Wild rice and barley may become tender without absorbing all the cooking liquid. If necessary, drain before serving or combining with other recipe ingredients.

- For fluffier rice, remove the saucepan from the heat after the cooking time is complete and let stand for 5 to 10 minutes. Fluff with a fork and serve.

- Leftover cooked white or brown rice, wild rice and barley freeze well; defrost and reheat in the microwave oven for use in recipes calling for cooked rice or for a quick side dish.

- Allow 1/2 to 3/4 cup cooked rice, wild rice or barley for each side-dish serving.

Baked Mushroom Rice

This side dish pairs nicely with roast beef, pork or poultry. It is extremely easy to assemble and can be put into the oven 45 minutes before the meat is done.

1-1/3 cups chicken broth
1 cup sliced fresh mushrooms
1 medium onion, chopped
1/2 cup uncooked long grain rice
1/4 teaspoon dried basil
1/4 teaspoon dried oregano
1/8 teaspoon lemon-pepper seasoning

Combine all ingredients in a 1-1/2-qt. baking dish coated with nonstick cooking spray. Cover and bake at 350° for 45 minutes or until rice is tender. **Yield:** 4 servings.
—*Alcy Thorne, Los Molinos, California*

Cooking Grains

Follow these guidelines to cook grains to serve as a simple side dish or to use as an ingredient in a recipe. Bring water,

1/4 teaspoon salt and 1 tablespoon butter to a boil in a 2-qt. saucepan. Stir in grain; return to a boil. Cover and reduce heat to simmer. Cook for the specified time or until tender.

Grain Type	Water	Grain Amount	Cooking Time	Yield
Rice, white—long grain	2 cups	1 cup	12 to 15 minutes	3 cups
Rice, white—instant	1 cup	1 cup	5 minutes	2 cups
Rice, white—converted	2-1/4 cups	1 cup	20 minutes	4 cups
Rice, brown	2-1/3 cups	1 cup	40 to 45 minutes	3 cups
Rice, wild	3 cups	1 cup	45 to 50 minutes	3 cups
Barley, quick-cooking	2 cups	1-1/4 cups	10 to 12 minutes	3 cups
Barley, regular pearl	3 cups	3/4 cup	35 to 45 minutes	3 cups

Wild Rice and Barley Pilaf

Texas-Style Spanish Rice

(Pictured on page 235)

Here's a perfect accompaniment to grilled meats or your favorite Mexican entree. Use canned tomatoes with either mild or hot chilies based on your preference.

   2 tablespoons vegetable oil
1/4 cup chopped onion
1/4 cup chopped green pepper
   1 cup uncooked long grain rice
   2 cups water
1/2 cup tomatoes with green chilies
   1 teaspoon ground cumin
1/2 teaspoon salt
1/4 teaspoon garlic powder
1/4 teaspoon ground turmeric
   2 to 3 tablespoons chopped fresh cilantro *or* parsley, optional

In a skillet, heat oil over medium. Saute onion and green pepper for about 2 minutes. Add rice and stir until coated with oil. Add water, tomatoes, cumin, salt, garlic powder and turmeric; bring to a boil. Reduce heat; cover and simmer for 15 minutes or until liquid is absorbed and rice is tender. Add cilantro if desired. **Yield:** 6 servings.   —*Melissa Pride Plano, Texas*

Wild Rice and Barley Pilaf

Wild rice and barley combine with the fruitiness of currants and dried cranberries to make this a good complement to poultry and wild game.

3/4 cup uncooked wild rice
   3 cups chicken broth
1/2 cup pearl barley
1/4 cup dried cranberries
1/4 cup dried currants
   1 tablespoon butter *or* margarine
1/3 cup sliced almonds, toasted

Rinse and drain rice; place in a saucepan. Add broth and bring to a boil. Reduce heat; cover and simmer for 10 minutes. Remove from the heat; stir in barley, cranberries, currants and butter. Transfer to a greased 1-1/2-qt. baking dish. Cover and bake at 325° for 55 minutes or until liquid is absorbed and rice is tender. Add almonds and fluff with a fork. **Yield:** 6-8 servings.
—*Pat Gardetta, Osage Beach, Missouri*

Three-Rice Pilaf

Special enough for a holiday feast, this skillet dish is as pretty as it is flavorful. Rice lovers will truly enjoy this recipe!

 2 tablespoons vegetable oil
1/2 cup uncooked brown rice
1/2 cup finely chopped carrots
1/2 cup chopped onion
1/2 cup sliced fresh mushrooms
 3 cups chicken broth
1/2 cup uncooked wild rice
1/4 teaspoon dried thyme
1/4 teaspoon dried rosemary, crushed
1/2 cup uncooked long grain rice
1/3 cup chopped dried apricots
 2 tablespoons minced green onions
1/4 teaspoon salt
1/8 teaspoon pepper
1/2 cup chopped pecans, toasted

In a large saucepan, heat oil over medium. Saute brown rice, carrots, onion and mushrooms for 10 minutes or until rice is golden. Add broth, wild rice, thyme and rosemary; bring to a boil. Reduce heat; cover and simmer for 25 minutes. Stir in long grain rice; cover and simmer 25 minutes longer or until liquid is absorbed and wild rice is tender. Remove from the heat; stir in apricots, green onions, salt and pepper. Cover and let stand for 5 minutes. Sprinkle with pecans just before serving. **Yield:** 8-10 servings.

—Ricki Bingham
Ogden, Utah

Beefy Spanish Rice

To add extra zest to this classic dish, stir in 1 teaspoon prepared mustard to the mixture before cooking.

 1 pound ground beef
1 medium onion, chopped
1 medium green pepper, chopped
1 garlic clove, minced
1 can (14-1/2 ounces) stewed tomatoes
1-1/2 cups water
 1 cup uncooked long grain rice
1 teaspoon salt
1/2 to 1 teaspoon chili powder
1/2 teaspoon dried thyme
1/4 teaspoon dried basil
1/4 teaspoon pepper
 2 tablespoons tomato paste

In a large skillet, cook beef, onion, green pepper and garlic until the meat is browned; drain. Stir in the next eight ingredients; bring to a boil. Reduce heat; cover and simmer for 20 minutes or until liquid is absorbed and rice is tender. Stir in tomato paste; heat through. **Yield:** 4 servings.

—Laurie Smith Murphy
Foster, Rhode Island

Three-Rice Pilaf

Chili-Cheese Bake

When a recipe calls for cooked rice, you can conveniently prepare it earlier in the day—or even the day before—and refrigerate until ready to use. Plus, you'll find it's easier to mix well-chilled cooked rice with other ingredients.

- 3 cups cooked white *or* brown rice
- 1 can (16 ounces) kidney beans, rinsed and drained
- 1 medium onion, chopped
- 1 can (4 ounces) chopped green chilies
- 2 garlic cloves, minced
- 2 teaspoons chili powder
- 2 teaspoons ground cumin
- 1 teaspoon dried oregano
- 1 teaspoon Creole seasoning
- 1/2 teaspoon salt
- 2 cups (8 ounces) shredded sharp cheddar cheese, *divided*

In a greased 2-qt. baking dish, combine all ingredients except cheese. Top with 1-1/2 cups of cheese. Cover and bake at 350° for 25 minutes. Sprinkle with remaining cheese. Bake, uncovered, 10 minutes longer. **Yield:** 6 servings.   —*Rosemary West, Topsham, Maine*

Chili-Cheese Bake

Carrot Pilaf

Colorful and tasty, this side dish recipe is basic enough to serve with meat, poultry or fish.

- 1 tablespoon butter *or* margarine
- 1 cup shredded carrots
- 1/2 cup chopped onion
- 1 cup uncooked long grain rice
- 1 can (14-1/2 ounces) chicken broth
- 1 teaspoon lemon-pepper seasoning

In a saucepan, melt butter over medium heat. Saute carrots and onion until tender. Add rice and stir to coat. Stir in broth and lemon pepper; bring to a boil. Reduce heat; cover and simmer for 20 minutes or until liquid is absorbed and rice is tender. **Yield:** 6 servings.
🕐 🍎   —*Grace Yaskovic, Branchville, New Jersey*

Cheesy Grits Casserole

To help the eggs cook evenly, stir a little of the hot grits into the eggs to gently warm them before they are added to the ingredients in the saucepan.

- 4 cups water
- 1 teaspoon salt
- 1 cup quick-cooking grits
- 4 eggs, lightly beaten
- 1 pound pork sausage, browned and drained
- 1-1/2 cups (6 ounces) shredded sharp cheddar cheese, *divided*
- 1/2 cup milk
- 1/4 cup butter *or* margarine, softened

In a saucepan, bring water and salt to a boil. Slowly stir in grits. Reduce heat and cook for 4-5 minutes, stirring occasionally. Remove grits from the heat; add a small amount of hot grits to the eggs. Return all to pan. Stir in sausage, 1 cup cheese, milk and butter; stir until the butter is melted. Pour into a greased 13-in. x 9-in. x 2-in. baking dish. Sprinkle with remaining cheese. Bake, uncovered, at 350° for 50-55 minutes or until the top begins to brown. **Yield:** 10-12 servings.
—*Georgia Johnston, Auburndale, Florida*

Beans are a member of the legume family, a tasty source of protein and fiber in the diet. Years back, country cooks depended on dry beans to make economical and filling meals for their families. With today's quicker preparation methods for dry beans and a variety of canned bean products, it's easy to make delicious bean recipes no matter how busy your schedule is.

Country Cassoulet

(Pictured on page 234)

A cassoulet is a classic hearty French country meal that is a mixture of beans, meat and sausage. Always a favorite, this dish is a good choice for a fall harvest celebration.

      3 cups water
   3/4 pound dry navy beans, sorted and rinsed
      1 bay leaf
   1/4 teaspoon pepper
      1 can (14-1/2 ounces) chicken broth
   1/4 pound sliced bacon, diced
      4 chicken legs *or* thighs
      2 carrots, quartered
      2 medium onions, quartered
   1/4 cup coarsely chopped celery with leaves
      2 garlic cloves, minced
   1/2 teaspoon dried marjoram
   1/2 teaspoon rubbed sage
      1 teaspoon whole cloves
   1/2 pound smoked sausage, cut into 2-inch pieces
      1 can (14-1/2 ounces) diced tomatoes, undrained
      1 teaspoon salt
Chopped fresh parsley

In a soup kettle or Dutch oven, combine water, beans, bay leaf and pepper. Bring to a boil; boil for 2 minutes. Remove from the heat. Cover and let stand for 1 hour. Do not drain. Add chicken broth; bring to a boil. Reduce heat; cover and simmer for 1 hour. Meanwhile, cook bacon until crisp. Remove bacon and reserve 2 tablespoons of the drippings. Brown chicken in drippings; set aside. In a 3-qt. baking dish, combine beans with cooking liquid, bacon, carrots, onion, celery, garlic, marjoram and sage. Sprinkle with cloves; top with chicken. Cover and bake at 350° for 1 hour. Add sausage. Bake, uncovered, about 30 minutes longer or until beans are tender. Discard bay leaf and cloves. Stir in tomatoes and salt; heat through. Garnish with parsley. **Yield:** 4 servings.

—*Roberta Strohmaier*
Lebanon, New Jersey

Soaking Methods for Dry Beans

One-Hour Soak
Sort and rinse beans. Place in a soup kettle or Dutch oven; add enough water to cover beans by 2 inches. Bring to a boil; boil for 2 minutes. Remove from the heat; cover and let stand for 1 hour. Drain and rinse beans; discard liquid unless recipe directs otherwise. Proceed with recipe as directed.

Overnight Soak
Sort and rinse beans. Place in a soup kettle or Dutch oven; add enough water to cover beans by 2 inches. Cover and let stand for 6-8 hours or overnight. Drain and rinse beans; discard liquid unless recipe directs otherwise. Proceed with recipe as directed.

Maple Baked Beans

In this recipe, you're instructed to reserve the cooking liquid just in case the beans have absorbed all the sauce but still need additional cooking.

> 1 pound dry navy beans, sorted and rinsed
> 2 quarts water
> 6 bacon strips, diced *or* 1 cup cubed fully cooked ham
> 1 medium onion, chopped
> 1 cup maple *or* maple-flavored syrup
> 1/2 cup ketchup
> 1/4 cup barbecue sauce
> 5 teaspoons cider vinegar
> 1 teaspoon prepared mustard
> 1 teaspoon salt
> 1/2 teaspoon pepper

Place beans in a soup kettle or Dutch oven; add water to cover by 2 in. Bring to a boil; boil for 2 minutes. Remove from the heat; cover and let stand for 1 hour. Drain and rinse beans, discarding liquid. Return beans to Dutch oven; cover with 2 qts. water. Bring to a boil; reduce heat and simmer for 30-40 minutes or until almost tender. Drain and reserve liquid. In a 2-1/2-qt. baking dish, combine beans with remaining ingredients. Cover and bake at 300° for 2-1/2 hours or until tender, stirring occasionally. Add reserved bean liquid if necessary. **Yield:** 10-12 servings.

—*Cindy Huitema, Dunnville, Ontario*

Maple Baked Beans

Black-Eyed Peas with Bacon

Black-Eyed Peas with Bacon

This is a favorite Southern side dish that is traditionally served on New Year's Day to bring good luck.

> 1 pound dry black-eyed peas, sorted and rinsed
> 1/2 pound bacon, cooked and crumbled
> 1 tablespoon butter *or* margarine
> 1 large onion, chopped
> 1 garlic clove, minced
> 1/2 teaspoon dried thyme
> Salt to taste
> Additional crumbled bacon, optional

Place peas and bacon in a soup kettle or Dutch oven; add water to cover by 2 in. Bring to a boil; boil for 2 minutes. Remove from the heat; cover and let stand for 1 hour. Do not drain. In a skillet, melt butter over medium heat. Saute onion and garlic until tender. Add to pea mixture with thyme. Return to the heat; cover and simmer for 30 minutes or until peas are soft. Add salt. Top with bacon if desired. **Yield:** 6-8 servings.

—*Ruby Williams, Bogalusa, Louisiana*

Succotash

Corn and lima beans are the standard ingredients in succotash. You'll find many different recipes that add a variety of other ingredients.

    1 smoked ham hock (about 1-1/2 pounds)
    4 cups water
    1 can (28 ounces) diced tomatoes, undrained
    1 package (10 ounces) frozen lima beans,
      thawed
    1 package (10 ounces) frozen crowder peas,
      thawed *or* 1 can (15-1/2 ounces) black-eyed
      peas, drained
    1 package (10 ounces) frozen corn, thawed
    1 medium green pepper, chopped

    1 medium onion, chopped
    1/3 cup ketchup
    1-1/2 teaspoons salt
    1-1/2 teaspoons dried basil
    1 teaspoon rubbed sage
    1 teaspoon paprika
    1/2 teaspoon pepper
    1 bay leaf
    1 cup sliced fresh *or* frozen okra

In a Dutch oven or large saucepan, simmer ham hock in water for 1-1/2 hours or until tender. Cool; remove meat from the bone and return to pan. (Discard bone and broth or save for another use.) Add the tomatoes, beans, peas, corn, green pepper, onion, ketchup and seasonings. Simmer, uncovered, for 45 minutes. Add okra; simmer, uncovered, 15 minutes longer. Discard bay leaf before serving. **Yield:** 12-16 servings.

—*Rosa Boone, Mobile, Alabama*

Succotash

Ham, Red Beans and Rice

For this recipe, be sure to use red beans packed in liquid, not gravy. If your market doesn't carry red beans, simply substitute kidney beans.

    3 cans (15 ounces *each*) red beans, rinsed and
      drained
    1 can (14-1/2 ounces) Cajun stewed tomatoes
    2 cups cubed fully cooked ham
    1/2 cup water
    1/2 teaspoon garlic powder
    1/2 teaspoon ground cumin
    1/2 teaspoon dried oregano
    1/2 teaspoon dried thyme
    1/2 teaspoon salt
    1/4 teaspoon pepper
    2 to 5 dashes hot pepper sauce
Hot cooked rice

In a large saucepan, combine all ingredients except rice. Bring to a boil. Reduce heat; cover and simmer for 30 minutes. Serve over rice. **Yield:** 6-8 servings.

—*Vanita Davis, Camden, Arkansas*

Bean Substitutions

- 1 pound packaged dry beans (uncooked) equals 2 cups dry or 6 to 7 cups cooked (drained).

- 1 cup packaged dry beans (uncooked) equals about two 15-1/2-ounce cans of beans (drained).

- One 15-1/2-ounce can of beans equals about 1-2/3 cups cooked beans (drained).

Calico Beans

Calico Beans

This recipe can be doubled for a large group. Place ingredients in one 4-quart or two 2-quart baking dishes and bake for an additional 30 minutes.

    6 bacon strips, diced
    1 pound ground beef
    1/2 cup chopped onion
    1 can (21 ounces) pork and beans, undrained
    1 can (16 ounces) kidney beans, rinsed and
       drained
    1 can (15 ounces) butter *or* lima beans, rinsed
       and drained
    1/2 cup ketchup
    1/2 cup packed brown sugar
    1 tablespoon vinegar
    1 teaspoon prepared mustard
    1 teaspoon salt

In a skillet, cook bacon until crisp. Remove to paper towels to drain. Discard drippings. In the same skillet, cook beef and onion until the beef is browned and the onion is tender. Drain. Combine beef and bacon with remaining ingredients. Spoon into a greased 2-qt. baking dish. Bake, uncovered, at 300° for 1 hour or until the beans reach desired thickness. **Yield:** 8-10 servings.
    —*Betty Claycomb, Alverton, Pennsylvania*

Black Beans and Sausage

Instant brown rice and canned black beans certainly make quick work of this dish. Substitute a spicy sausage for the pork sausage links if desired.

    1 tablespoon vegetable oil
    1 medium onion, chopped
    1 can (15 ounces) black beans, undrained
    1 can (14-1/2 ounces) stewed tomatoes
    1 teaspoon dried oregano
    1/2 teaspoon garlic powder
Salt to taste
 1-1/2 cups uncooked instant brown rice
    1 pound pork sausage links, cooked and sliced

In a skillet, heat oil over medium. Saute onion until tender. Add the beans, tomatoes and seasonings; bring to a boil. Stir in rice. Reduce heat; simmer, uncovered, for 5 minutes. Add sausage; remove from the heat and let stand for 5 minutes. **Yield:** 6-8 servings. ○
    —*Sharon Hunt, Spring Hill, Florida*

Quick Baked Beans

Keep this recipe handy for those last-minute potlucks when you don't have time to prepare a recipe using dry beans.

    1 pound sliced bacon, diced
    1 large onion, chopped
    3 cans (28 ounces *each*) pork and beans,
       undrained
    1 cup barbecue sauce
    1/2 cup packed brown sugar
    1/3 cup prepared mustard

In a large saucepan, cook bacon and onion until bacon is crisp and onion is tender; drain. Add remaining ingredients; simmer, uncovered, for 10 minutes. **Yield:** 10-12 servings. ○ —*Connie Tiesenausen, Demmitt, Alberta*

Cooking with pasta gives you so many creative choices. You can prepare homemade pasta with a few simple ingredients, choose from the many shapes available in packaged dry pasta or purchase freshly made pasta in your grocer's refrigerator or freezer case.

Homemade Noodles

(Pictured on page 234)

There's nothing like homemade noodles in soups or as a side dish with meat and gravy. If desired, serving-size portions of uncooked homemade noodles can be frozen in airtight containers for up to 1 month. Defrost, then cook as directed in the recipe.

2 to 2-1/2 cups all-purpose flour, divided
1/2 teaspoon salt
3 eggs
1 tablespoon cold water

Place 2 cups flour and salt in a mixing bowl. Make a well in the center of the flour; add eggs and water. Gradually mix with hands or a wooden spoon until well blended. Gather into a ball and knead on a floured surface until smooth, about 10 minutes. If necessary, add remaining flour to keep dough from sticking to kneading surface or hands. Divide the dough into thirds. On a lightly floured surface, roll each portion into a paper-thin rectangle. Dust top of dough with flour to prevent sticking while rolling. Trim the edges. Roll up jelly-roll style. Using a sharp knife, cut into 1/4-in. slices. Unroll noodles and allow to dry on paper towels at least 1 hour before cooking. To cook, bring salted water to a rapid boil. Add 1 tablespoon oil to the water; drop noodles into water and cook for 2 minutes or until tender but not soft. Drain. **Yield:** 10-12 servings.
—Helen Heiland, Joliet, Illinois

Making Homemade Noodles

1 Place flour and salt in a mixing bowl or on a floured surface. Make a well in the center; add eggs and water.

2 Mix until well blended; gather mixture into a ball. Turn onto a floured surface. Knead for about 10 minutes. Divide into thirds.

3 Roll out each portion of dough into a paper-thin rectangle. Lightly dust both sides with flour; roll up jelly-roll style. Cut into 1/4-in. slices.

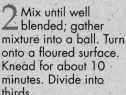

4 Unroll noodles on paper towels to dry for at least 1 hour. Proceed with recipe as directed.

Spinach Noodles

You'll love the pretty green color and delicate spinach flavor of these noodles. Use them in any recipe calling for egg noodles.

1 package (10 ounces) frozen chopped spinach, thawed and well drained
2 eggs
1 teaspoon salt
2 cups all-purpose flour

In a blender or food processor, combine spinach, eggs and salt; cover and process until smooth. Pour into a bowl. Gradually add enough flour to make a firm, but not sticky, dough. On a floured surface, knead about 20 times. Wrap in plastic wrap and let rest 30 minutes. Divide dough in half. On a floured surface, roll each portion to 1/16-in. thickness. Roll up jelly-roll style and cut into 1/4-in. slices. Unroll noodles and allow to dry on paper towels at least 1 hour before cooking. To cook, bring salted water to a rapid boil. Add 1 tablespoon oil to the water; drop noodles into water and cook for 2 minutes or until tender but not soft. Drain. **Yield:** 4-6 servings.
—Bernice Smith
Sturgeon Lake, Minnesota

Pasta with Asparagus

Although this pasta tastes great with a roast, it also makes a hearty main dish. Shredded Parmesan cheese lends a robust flavor to every bite.

1/4 cup olive *or* vegetable oil
1 tablespoon butter *or* margarine
5 garlic cloves, minced
1 teaspoon crushed red pepper flakes
2 to 3 dashes hot pepper sauce
1 pound fresh asparagus, trimmed and cut into 1-1/2-inch pieces
Salt to taste
1/4 teaspoon pepper
1/4 cup shredded Parmesan cheese
8 ounces mostaccioli *or* rotini, cooked and drained

In a skillet, heat oil and butter over medium-high. Cook garlic, red pepper flakes and hot pepper sauce for 2-3 minutes. Add asparagus, salt and pepper; saute until asparagus is crisp-tender, about 8-10 minutes. Add Parmesan cheese; mix well. Pour over hot pasta and toss to coat. Serve immediately. **Yield:** 4-6 servings. ◔

—*Jean Fisher, Redlands, California*

Pasta with Asparagus

Parmesan Noodles

Puzzled about what to serve with grilled or broiled chicken or fish? Try this speedy recipe that is ready in about 15 minutes!

8 ounces uncooked wide noodles
2 tablespoons butter *or* margarine
1/4 teaspoon garlic powder
1/4 cup grated Parmesan cheese
2 tablespoons minced fresh parsley

Cook noodles according to package directions; drain. Place in a bowl. Immediately add remaining ingredients and toss well. **Yield:** 4 servings. ◔

—*Jean Brenneman, Cedar Rapids, Iowa*

Tips for Cooking Pasta

- To cook pasta more evenly, prevent it from sticking together and avoid boil-overs, always cook pasta in a large kettle or Dutch oven. Unless you have a very large kettle, don't cook more than 2 pounds of pasta at a time.

- For 8 ounces of pasta, bring 3 quarts water to a full rolling boil. To flavor, add 1 tablespoon salt if desired. To prevent pasta from sticking, add 1 tablespoon olive or vegetable oil if desired. Stir in the pasta all at once. Return to a boil; boil, uncovered, stirring occasionally.

- Cooking times vary with the size and variety of pasta. Dried pasta can take from 5 to 15 minutes to cook; fresh pasta can cook in as little as 2 to 3 minutes. Follow the recommended cooking directions on packaged pasta.

- To test for doneness, use a fork to remove a single piece of pasta from the boiling water. Rinse in cold water and taste. Pasta should be cooked until "al dente", or firm yet tender. Test often while cooking to avoid overcooking, which can result in a soft or mushy texture. If pasta will be used in a recipe that requires further cooking, such as a casserole, undercook by one-third the recommended time.

- As soon as the pasta tests done, pour into a large colander to drain, being careful of the steam as you pour. If using the pasta in a salad or at a later time, rinse it with cold water to stop cooking and to remove excess starch.

- Allow 2 to 4 ounces of pasta per person for a main-dish serving.

Spaghetti Pie

Spaghetti Pie

beef, onion and green pepper until beef is browned and vegetables are tender; drain. Stir in tomatoes, tomato paste, sugar, oregano and garlic salt; heat through. Pour over cottage cheese layer. Bake, uncovered, at 350° for 20 minutes or until set. Sprinkle with mozzarella cheese. Bake 5 minutes longer or until cheese is melted. **Yield:** 6 servings.

—Mary Miller, Hopewell, Pennsylvania

Spaghetti Pie

Kids will love this recipe because of its spaghetti "crust". You'll love it because it's easy to make and pretty to serve.

CRUST:
    7 ounces uncooked spaghetti
    2 tablespoons butter *or* margarine
    1/3 cup grated Parmesan cheese
    2 eggs, beaten
FILLING:
    1 cup (8 ounces) cottage cheese
    1 pound ground beef
    1/2 cup chopped onion
    1/4 cup chopped green pepper
    1 can (14-1/2 ounces) diced tomatoes, undrained
    1 can (6 ounces) tomato paste
    1 teaspoon sugar
    1 teaspoon dried oregano
    1/2 teaspoon garlic salt
    1/2 cup shredded mozzarella cheese

Cook spaghetti according to package directions; drain. Combine hot spaghetti, butter, Parmesan cheese and eggs in a large bowl. Transfer to a greased 10-in. pie plate. Using your fingers, form a crust. Spoon cottage cheese evenly over crust; set aside. In a skillet, cook

Cooking Spaghetti

Carefully hold spaghetti in boiling water and ease it down into the water as it softens, pushing it around the edge of the pan. When it's fully immersed in the water, stir the spaghetti to separate strands.

Four-Cheese Lasagna

Lasagna takes time to assemble. To avoid last-minute preparation, make this casserole early in the day or the night before and refrigerate. Remove from the refrigerator 30 minutes before baking.

    1 pound ground beef
    1 medium onion, chopped
    2 garlic cloves, minced
    1 can (28 ounces) crushed tomatoes
    2 cans (4 ounces *each*) mushroom stems and pieces, drained
    1 can (6 ounces) tomato paste
    1 teaspoon salt
    1 teaspoon dried oregano
    1 teaspoon dried basil
    1/2 teaspoon pepper
    1/2 teaspoon fennel seed
    1 carton (16 ounces) cottage cheese
    2/3 cup grated Parmesan cheese
    1/4 cup shredded cheddar cheese
1-1/2 cups (6 ounces) shredded mozzarella cheese, *divided*
    2 eggs, beaten
    1 package (12 ounces) lasagna noodles, cooked and drained

In a skillet, cook beef, onion and garlic until beef is browned and onion is tender; drain. In a blender, cover and process the tomatoes until smooth. Stir into beef mixture along with mushrooms, tomato paste and seasonings; simmer for 15 minutes. In a bowl, combine cottage cheese, Parmesan, cheddar, 1/2 cup of mozzarella and eggs. Spread 2 cups meat sauce in the bottom of an ungreased 13-in. x 9-in. x 2-in. baking dish. Arrange half the noodles over sauce. Spread cheese mixture over noodles. Top with remaining noodles and meat sauce. Cover and bake at 350° for 45 minutes. Uncover; sprinkle with remaining mozzarella. Bake 15 minutes longer or until cheese melts. Let stand 15 minutes before cutting. **Yield:** 12 servings. *—Janet Myers Napanee, Ontario*

Chicken Cheese Lasagna

Next time you're planning a buffet supper for a large gathering, prepare one traditional red-sauce lasagna and this version, which features chicken and a white sauce. Everyone can have a serving of both along with salad and garlic bread.

1/2 cup butter *or* margarine
1 medium onion, chopped
1 garlic clove, minced
1/2 cup all-purpose flour
1 teaspoon salt
2 cups chicken broth
1-1/2 cups milk
4 cups (16 ounces) shredded mozzarella cheese, *divided*
1 cup grated Parmesan cheese, *divided*
1 teaspoon dried basil
1 teaspoon dried oregano
1/2 teaspoon white pepper
1 carton (15 ounces) ricotta cheese
1 tablespoon minced fresh parsley
9 lasagna noodles (8 ounces), cooked and drained
2 packages (10 ounces *each*) frozen spinach, thawed and well drained
2 cups cubed cooked chicken

In a saucepan, melt butter over medium heat. Saute onion and garlic until tender. Stir in flour and salt; cook until bubbly. Gradually stir in broth and milk. Bring to a boil, stirring constantly. Boil 1 minute. Stir in 2 cups mozzarella, 1/2 cup Parmesan cheese, basil, oregano and pepper; set aside. In a bowl, combine the ricotta cheese, parsley and remaining mozzarella; set aside. Spread one-quarter of the cheese sauce into a greased 13-in. x 9-in. x 2-in. baking dish; cover with one-third of the noodles. Top with half of the ricotta mixture, half of the spinach and half of the chicken. Cover with one-quarter of cheese sauce and one-third of noodles. Repeat layers of ricotta mixture, spinach, chicken and one-quarter cheese sauce. Cover with remaining noodles and cheese sauce. Sprinkle with remaining Parmesan cheese. Bake, uncovered, at 350° for 35-40 minutes. Let stand 15 minutes before cutting. **Yield:** 12 servings.
—*Mary Ann Kosmas, Minneapolis, Minnesota*

Italian Stuffed Shells

Instead of pouring these shells into a colander to drain, carefully lift the cooked shells out of the water with a tongs. Pour out any water from inside the shells. Place on lightly greased waxed paper until you're ready to stuff them.

    1 pound ground beef
    1 cup chopped onion
    1 garlic clove, minced
    2 cups hot water
    1 can (12 ounces) tomato paste
    1 tablespoon beef bouillon granules
1-1/2 teaspoons dried oregano
    1 carton (16 ounces) cottage cheese
    2 cups (8 ounces) shredded mozzarella cheese,
       divided
 1/2 cup grated Parmesan cheese
    1 egg, beaten
   24 jumbo pasta shells, cooked and drained

In a large skillet, brown beef, onion and garlic; drain well. Stir in water, tomato paste, bouillon and oregano; simmer, uncovered, for 30 minutes. Meanwhile, in a medium bowl, combine cottage cheese, 1 cup mozzarella, Parmesan cheese and egg; mix well. Stuff shells with cheese mixture; arrange in a greased 13-in. x 9-in. x 2-in. baking dish. Pour meat sauce over shells.

Cover and bake at 350° for 30 minutes. Uncover; sprinkle with remaining mozzarella cheese. Bake 5 minutes longer or until the cheese is melted. **Yield:** 6-8 servings.
—*Beverly Austin, Fulton, Missouri*

Tomato Basil Pasta

During the winter months, use a 14-1/2-ounce can of drained diced tomatoes instead of fresh.

    2 large tomatoes, chopped
    2 tablespoons snipped fresh basil *or* 2
       teaspoons dried basil
    1 garlic clove, minced
 1/2 teaspoon salt
 1/4 teaspoon pepper
    4 ounces bow tie pasta *or* spaghetti, cooked and
       drained
Fresh basil and grated Parmesan cheese, optional

Combine the tomatoes, basil, garlic, salt and pepper. Set aside at room temperature for several hours. Serve over hot pasta. If desired, garnish with basil and sprinkle with Parmesan cheese. **Yield:** 2 servings.
—*Earlene Ertelt, Woodburn, Oregon*

Italian Stuffed Shells

Chicken Tetrazzini

After roasting a chicken or a turkey, reserve 3 cups cubed cooked meat for this delicious casserole. Serve with a tossed green salad for an easy but elegant dinner.

  1/4 cup butter *or* margarine
    2 cups sliced fresh mushrooms
  1/4 cup all-purpose flour
    2 cups chicken broth
  1/4 cup half-and-half cream
    1 tablespoon minced fresh parsley
    1 teaspoon salt
  1/8 to 1/4 teaspoon ground nutmeg
  1/4 teaspoon pepper
    3 tablespoons dry white wine, optional
    3 cups cubed cooked chicken
    8 ounces spaghetti, cooked and drained
  3/4 cup shredded Parmesan cheese
Additional parsley

In a skillet, melt butter over medium heat. Cook mushrooms until tender. Stir in flour; gradually add the broth. Cook, stirring constantly, until sauce comes to a boil. Remove from the heat; stir in cream, parsley, salt, nutmeg, pepper and wine if desired. Fold in the chicken and spaghetti. Transfer to a greased 13-in. x 9-in. x 2-in. baking dish; sprinkle with Parmesan cheese. Bake, uncovered, at 350° for 30 minutes or until heated through. Garnish with parsley. **Yield:** 8 servings.
—*Kelly Heusmann, Cincinnati, Ohio*

Chicken Tetrazzini

350° for 40 minutes. Top with Romano cheese; bake 5 minutes longer or until heated through. **Yield:** 6-8 servings.
—*Nancy Mundhenke, Kinsley, Kansas*

Mostaccioli Bake

If you can't find bulk Italian sausage in the meat case, buy link sausage and remove the casings.

1-1/2 pounds bulk Italian sausage
    4 cups meatless spaghetti sauce
    1 pound mostaccioli, cooked and drained
    1 egg, beaten
    1 carton (15 ounces) ricotta cheese
    2 cups (8 ounces) shredded mozzarella cheese
  1/2 cup grated Romano cheese

In a Dutch oven, brown sausage; drain. Stir in spaghetti sauce and mostaccioli; set aside. In a bowl, combine egg, ricotta and mozzarella. In a greased 13-in. x 9-in. x 2-in. or 2-1/2- to 3-qt. baking dish, spread half of the mostaccioli mixture. Top with cheese mixture and the remaining mostaccioli mixture. Cover and bake at

Turkey Pasta Supreme

This rich and flavorful dish is well-suited for busy everyday dining or casual company fare. Fresh basil makes this recipe extra special.

    2 tablespoons butter *or* margarine
  3/4 pound uncooked turkey breast, cut into
        2-inch x 1/4-inch pieces
    2 garlic cloves, minced
1-1/4 cups whipping cream
    2 tablespoons minced fresh basil *or* 2
        teaspoons dried basil
  1/4 cup grated Parmesan cheese
Dash pepper
    8 ounces mostaccioli *or* rigatoni, cooked and
        drained

In a skillet, melt butter over medium heat. Saute turkey and garlic until turkey is browned and no longer pink, about 6 minutes. Add cream, basil, Parmesan and pepper; bring to a boil. Reduce heat; simmer for 3 minutes, stirring frequently. Stir in pasta and toss to coat. **Yield:** 4 servings. ◷
—*Cassie Dion*
South Burlington, Vermont

Vegetables

Side dishes featuring the season's finest produce are sure to steal the show at all of your gatherings. Get ready to harvest a bushel of compliments when you treat family and friends to a bowful of Peas and Carrots with Mint (p. 279) or a platter stacked high with freshly cooked corn on the cob dripping with Spicy Corn Spread (p. 272)!

When you're looking for creative ways to vary the family menu, vegetables certainly are the place to start. Pretty, tasty and nutritious, vegetables can be prepared in minutes using the basic methods of boiling or steaming, or they can be teamed with other ingredients to make unique flavor combinations as they stew or bake. However you prepare them, avoid overcooking vegetables. Cook them until they are crisp-tender or just tender as recipes direct. Keep in mind that cooking times will vary due to the size, freshness and ripeness of the vegetable.

ASPARAGUS

Asparagus have a slender light green stalk with a tightly closed bud at the top. They are most often served cooked as a side dish but can be enjoyed raw on vegetable platters.

Buying tips:
Available mainly from February until late June. Peak months are April and May. Buy small straight stalks with tightly closed, compact tips. The spears should be smooth and round. Stalks should have a bright green color, while the tips may have a slight lavender tint.

Storage tips:
Keep unwashed asparagus in a sealed plastic bag in the refrigerator crisper drawer for up to 4 days.

Preparation tips:
Soak asparagus stalks in cold water to clean. Snap off the stalk ends as far down as they will easily break when gently bent, or cut off the tough white portion. (See photo at left.)

If stalks are large, use a vegetable peeler to gently peel the tough area of the stalk from the end to just below the tip. If tips are large, scrape off scales with a knife.

Cooking tips:
To boil: Place whole asparagus in a skillet or cut asparagus in a saucepan. Add 1/2 in. of water and bring to a boil. Reduce heat; cover and simmer for 3-5 minutes or until crisp-tender. Drain. *To steam:* Place asparagus in a basket over 1 in. of boiling water in a saucepan. Cover; steam for about 5 minutes or until crisp-tender.

Yields: 1 pound of asparagus (about 14 spears) equals 2 cups cut
1 pound of asparagus serves 4

BEANS

Green and wax beans, also know as string beans, are members of the legume family. Green and wax beans may be used interchangeably in recipes and are known for their mild flavor and general appeal.

Buying tips:
Available year-round. Peak months are from July to October. Buy brightly colored, straight, smooth pods that are unblemished. Beans should be crisp and have a firm, velvety feel. Seeds inside the bean should be small.

Storage tips:
Store unwashed beans in a sealed plastic bag or covered container in the refrigerator crisper drawer for up to 3 days.

Preparation tips:
Snap off the stem end of the bean and the other end if desired. Leave whole or cut into 1-in. pieces.

Cooking tips: *To boil:* Place beans in a saucepan and cover with water; bring to a boil. Cook, uncovered, for 8-10 minutes or until crisp-tender. Drain. *To steam:* Place beans in a basket over 1 in. of boiling water in a saucepan. Cover; steam for 8-10 minutes or until crisp-tender.

Yields: 1 pound of beans equals about 4 cups cut
1 pound of beans serves 4 to 6

Green beans

Wax beans

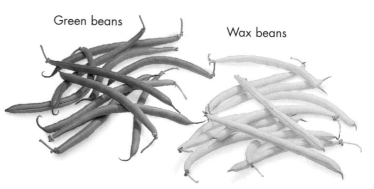

BEETS

This is a very deep red bulb-shaped root vegetable with edible dark green leaves. Beets and their greens are hearty in flavor. Beet greens can be served raw in salads or cooked. Beets are always cooked before serving and can be enjoyed (hot or cold) whole, sliced, shredded or diced.

Buying tips:
Available mainly from June to October. Peak months are June through August. Buy firm, deep red, round beets with unwilted green tops. The skin should be smooth, unblemished and unbroken. Small and medium-sized beets are usually the most tender (maximum size should be about 2 in.). Beet greens should have a reddish tint.

Storage tips:
Remove greens 2 in. from beets. If you plan on using the greens, store separately in a sealed plastic bag in the refrigerator for up to 3 days. Fresh uncooked beets will keep for about 3 weeks in open plastic bags in the refrigerator crisper drawer.

Preparation tips:
Wash beets gently. If you haven't already done so, remove greens. So that beets will maintain their flavor and color after cooking, do not peel or trim. You may find that when you cook beets in hard water, their brilliant color fades. To prevent this, try adding a small amount of vinegar to the cooking water.

Cooking tips:
To boil: Place whole unpeeled beets in a saucepan; cover with water. Bring to a boil; cover and simmer until fork-tender (about 30 minutes for large beets or 20 minutes for small beets). Drain; cool slightly and peel. *To bake:* Brush whole unpeeled beets with oil; place in a shallow pan. Bake, uncovered, at 350° for 1 hour or until tender. Cool slightly and peel. *To cook greens:* Place in a saucepan with a small amount of water; boil for 9-12 minutes or until tender. Drain.

Yields: 1 pound of beets equals 2-1/2 cups sliced or cubed (cooked)
1 pound of beets serves 4 to 5

BROCCOLI

A member of the cauliflower family, broccoli has pale green thick stalks with tightly packed dark green heads (florets) with a slight purple tint. Stalks and florets are eaten raw or cooked.

Buying tips:
Available year-round. Select firm but tender stalks with compact, dark green or slightly purplish florets.

Storage tips:
Keep unwashed broccoli in an open plastic bag in the refrigerator crisper drawer up to 4 days.

Preparation tips:
Remove larger leaves and tough ends of lower stalks. Wash broccoli. If using whole spears, cut lengthwise into 1-in.-wide pieces; stalks may also be peeled for more even cooking. If using florets, cut 1/4 in. to 1/2 in. below heads; discard stalks.

Cooking tips:
To boil: Place broccoli in a saucepan; add 1 in. of water. Bring to a boil. Reduce heat; cover and simmer for 5-8 minutes or until crisp-tender. Drain. *To steam:* Place broccoli in a basket over 1 in. of boiling water in a saucepan. Cover; steam for 5-8 minutes or until crisp-tender and bright green in color.

Yields: 1 pound of broccoli equals 3-1/2 cups florets
1 pound of broccoli serves 3 to 4

BRUSSELS SPROUTS

A delicately flavored member of the cabbage family, this tiny green vegetable averages 1 in. in diameter. The name originates from Brussels, Belgium, where

Brussels Sprouts (continued)

brussels sprouts were first grown centuries ago.

Buying tips:
Available primarily from September through May. Peak months are October to February. Buy small, firm, tightly closed heads that have a bright green color.

Storage tips:
Keep unwashed brussels sprouts in an open plastic bag in the refrigerator crisper drawer for up to 2 days.

Preparation tips:
Remove any loose or yellowed outer leaves; trim stem end. Rinse sprouts. When cooking brussels sprouts whole, cut an "X" in the core end with a sharp knife. (See photo at left.)

Cooking tips:
To boil: Place brussels sprouts in a saucepan; add 1 in. of water. Bring to a boil. Reduce heat; cover and simmer for 10-12 minutes or until crisp-tender. Drain. *To steam:* Place sprouts in a basket over 1 in. of boiling water in a saucepan. Cover; steam for 10-15 minutes or until crisp-tender.

Yields: 1 pound of brussels sprouts equals 24 to 28 medium sprouts or 4 cups trimmed
4 cups of brussels sprouts serves 4 to 6

CABBAGE

Cabbage is a fleshy-leafed member of the mustard family that ranges in color from white to green to deep reddish-purple. Heads are dense and heavy. Serve raw in salads or use cooked in entrees and side dishes. Cabbage is often shredded for slaw (see the index for instructions) and sliced or cut into wedges for cooking.

Buying tips:
Available year-round. For green cabbage, buy round, compact, solid heads that seem heavy for their size. Cabbage heads will vary in size, but the leaves should be tight, smooth and unblemished. Red cabbage heads are not as compact as green cabbage heads. The color should be a reddish-purple.

Storage tips:
Place unwashed cabbage in a sealed plastic bag in the refrigerator crisper drawer for up to 7 days.

Preparation tips:
Wash head. Trim center core to within 1/4 in. of leaves; remove any discolored, damaged or tough outer leaves from head.

Cooking tips:
To boil: Place cabbage wedges or slices in a saucepan; add 1 in. of water. Bring to a boil. Reduce heat; cover and simmer until crisp-tender (3-5 minutes for slices or 6-8 minutes for wedges). Drain. *To steam:* Place cabbage wedges or slices in a basket over 1 in. of boiling water in a saucepan. Cover; steam until crisp-tender (6-8 minutes for slices or 15 minutes for wedges).

Yields: 3 pounds of cabbage (1 large head) equals 14 to 16 cups shredded (uncooked)
3-1/2 cups of raw cabbage equals 2-1/2 cups cooked slices
1 pound of cabbage serves 3

Green cabbage

Red cabbage

CARROTS

Carrots are a long slender root vegetable related to the parsnip that have a distinctive orange color. Smaller varieties, called baby carrots, are also available.

Buying tips:
Available year-round. Buy crisp firm, smooth, well-shaped carrots with deep orange color. Smaller carrots are tender and sweet. Carrots sold in bunches with fern-like green tops are fresher but not always available in the market.

Storage tips:
Trim tops and roots when present. Store unwashed unpeeled carrots in a sealed plastic bag in the refrigerator crisper drawer for 1 to 2 weeks.

Preparation tips:
Young carrots may be used unpeeled if they are well scrubbed. Larger carrots should be thinly peeled with a vegetable peeler.

Cooking tips:
To boil: Place sliced or whole baby carrots in a saucepan; add 1 in. of water. Bring to a boil. Reduce heat; cover and simmer until crisp-tender (7-9 minutes for slices or 10-15 minutes for baby carrots). Drain. *To steam:* Place whole or sliced carrots in a basket over 1 in. of boiling water in a saucepan. Cover; steam until crisp-tender (12-15 minutes for whole carrots or 8-10 minutes for cut carrots).

Yields: 1 pound of carrots (6 to 7 medium) equals 3 to 3-1/2 cups sliced (uncooked)
2 medium carrots equals 1 cup sliced or shredded
1 pound of carrots serves 4

CAULIFLOWER

This snowy-white vegetable has a flower-like appearance and a mild cabbage-like flavor. Cauliflower can be eaten raw or cooked.

Buying tips:
Available year-round. Peak months are October through March. Buy firm, solid white or creamy-colored heads that feel heavy for their size. The florets should be clean and tightly packed and the surrounding jacket leaves should be fresh and green.

Storage tips:
Place unwashed cauliflower in an open plastic bag in the refrigerator crisper drawer for up to 4 days.

Preparation tips:
Trim off leaves. Remove base stem at an angle so the core comes out in a cone and the head remains intact. Separate into florets if desired.

Cooking tips:

To boil: Place cauliflower florets in a saucepan; add 1 in. of water. Bring to a boil. Reduce heat; cover and simmer 5-10 minutes or until crisp-tender. Drain. *To steam:* Place cauliflower in a basket over 1 in. of boiling water in a saucepan. Cover; steam until crisp-tender (15-20 minutes for whole head or 5-12 minutes for florets). (See photo above.)

Yields: 1-1/2 pounds of cauliflower (about 1 head), trimmed, equals 3 cups florets
1-1/2 pounds of cauliflower serves 4

CORN ON THE COB

Also known as sweet corn, this vegetable is available with bright yellow or white kernels or a mix of both. Corn on the cob is served cooked with silk and husks removed. Cooked kernels can be cut from the cob and used in recipes in place of canned or frozen corn. (See Cutting Kernels from Corncobs on page 80.)

Buying tips:
Available May through August. Peak months are July and August. Select corn that has fresh green, tightly closed husks with dark brown, dry (but not brittle) silk. The stem should be moist, but not chalky, yellow or discolored. Ears should have plump, tender, small kernels in tight rows up to the tip. Kernels should be firm enough to resist slight pressure. A fresh kernel will spurt "milk" if punctured.

Storage tips:
Keep unshucked ears in opened plastic bags in the refrigerator crisper drawer and use within 1 day.

Preparation tips:
If boiling or steaming, remove husk by pulling the husks down the ear; break off the undeveloped tip. Trim ➡

Corn on the Cob (continued)

stem. Pull out silk between kernel rows or remove with a dry vegetable brush; rinse in cold water.

Cooking tips:
To boil: Drop shucked ears into a large kettle of rapidly boiling unsalted water. Cover; return to a boil and cook for 3-5 minutes or until tender. Drain. *To roast:* Pull back husk but don't remove; remove silk. Replace husk and tie with string at the top. Soak corn for at least 1 hour in cold water. Remove from water; grill over high heat for 20-25 minutes, turning frequently. To roast corn in foil, see page 273.

Yields: 6 ears of corn equals about 3 cups kernels
1 ear of corn (1/2 cup kernels) serves 1

EGGPLANT

Eggplant are pear-shaped and most commonly deep purple in color, although some white varieties are available. The interior flesh is creamy white with small edible seeds. Eggplant is served cooked as a side dish or combined with cheese and/or meat as a main dish.

Buying tips:
Available year-round. Peak season is mainly July through September. Select firm, round or pear-shaped heavy eggplant with a uniformly smooth color and glossy taut skin. The eggplant should be free from blemishes and rust spots with intact green caps and mold-free stems.

Storage tips:
Keep unwashed egg-plant in an open plastic bag in the refrigerator crisper drawer for up to 3 days.

Preparation tips:
Wash eggplant; cut off stem and peel if desired. Cut eggplant discolors quickly, so cut into slices, strips or cubes just before salting. Salt eggplant at least 30 minutes before cooking. See Salting Eggplant on page 275.

Cooking tips:
To boil: Add eggplant slices, strips or cubes to boiling water. Boil for 5-8 minutes or until tender. Drain. *To steam:* Place eggplant slices, strips or cubes in a basket over 1 in. of boiling water in a saucepan. Cover; steam for 5-7 minutes or until tender. *To saute:* Heat 3-4 tablespoons of oil in a skillet. Saute eggplant slices, strips or cubes for 5-10 minutes or until tender.

Yields: 1 medium eggplant (1 pound) equals 5 cups cubed
1 medium eggplant serves 3 to 4

KOHLRABI

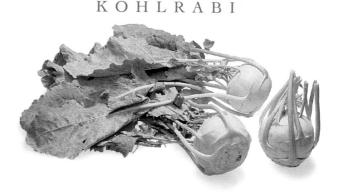

Kohlrabi is a pale green bulb-shaped vegetable with white flesh and dark green leaves. Less common varieties of kohlrabi have bulbs with purple skin. Kohlrabi bulbs have a mild turnip-like flavor. Bulbs and their leaves can be enjoyed raw or cooked.

Buying tips:
Available mainly from May to December. Peak months are June and July. Buy small (no larger than 3 in.), firm pale green bulbs. The bulbs should have tender skins and the leaves should appear fresh and crisp.

Storage tips:
Trim leaves and root ends. Store unwashed kohlrabi in an open plastic bag in the refrigerator crisper drawer for up to 5 days. If you plan on using the greens, store separately in a sealed plastic bag in the refrigerator for up to 3 days.

Preparation tips:
Cut off leaves and stems. Thinly peel bulbs. Cut into slices, strips or cubes.

Cooking tips:
To boil: Place kohlrabi in a saucepan; add 1 in. of water. Bring to a boil. Reduce heat, cover and simmer for 6-8 minutes or until tender. Drain. *To steam:* Place kohlrabi in a basket over 1 in. of boiling water in a saucepan. Cover; steam for 8-10 minutes or until tender. *To cook greens:* Saute in several tablespoons of butter or oil over medium-high heat for 3-4 minutes or until wilted.

Yields: 1 pound kohlrabi (without leaves) equals 3 to 4 medium bulbs
1 pound peeled kohlrabi bulbs serves 3 to 4

Yields: 2 pounds leeks equals 1 pound trimmed
1 pound trimmed leeks equals 4 cups chopped leeks (2 cups cooked)
2 cups cooked leeks serves 4

LEEKS

Leeks are part of the onion family and are tasty additions to soups, casseroles or egg dishes.

Buying tips:
Available mainly from October to March. Buy young, straight, cylindrical stalks with moist, pliable green upper leaves. The white bulbs should extend 2 to 3 in. above the roots, and the diameter should not exceed 1-1/2 in.

Storage tips:
Place unwashed, untrimmed leeks loosely wrapped in an open plastic bag in the refrigerator crisper drawer for up to 2 weeks.

Preparation tips:
Remove any withered outer leaves. Trim root end. Cut off and discard the green upper leaves at the point where the pale green becomes dark green. Leeks often contain sand between their many layers. If using the leek whole, cut an "X" 1/4 to 1/2 in. deep in the root end and soak for 30 minutes in water containing a splash of vinegar. Rinse under cold running water, gently opening the slit area as it is rinsed. If leeks are to be sliced or chopped, cut the leek open lengthwise down one side and rinse under cold running water, separating the leaves. (See photo above.)

Cooking tips:
To boil: Add whole leeks to boiling water. Boil for 12-15 minutes or until just tender. Drain. *To steam:* Place whole leeks in a basket over 1 in. of boiling water in a saucepan. Cover; steam for 13-15 minutes or until just tender.

MUSHROOMS

White (button) mushrooms have a mild flavor and range in color from pure white to creamy white. The caps of the mushrooms can range in size from 1/2 to 3 in. and can be eaten raw or cooked.

Buying tips:
Available year-round. Buy firm, dry mushrooms with a cap that is tightly closed around the stem. The color of the mushroom cap should be solid white while the stem should be beige. If the cap is open, the gills should be light pink or tan.

Storage tips:
Place unwashed mushrooms in a paper bag or in an open container loosely covered with a lightly moistened paper towel, so that air circulates around them. Refrigerate for up to 2 days.

Preparation tips:
If mushrooms aren't too dirty, remove any sand or dirt by rubbing with a mushroom brush or a moist paper towel. (See photo at right.) If it's necessary to wash mushrooms, quickly rinse but do not soak. Pat dry immediate-

Mushrooms (continued)

ly with paper towel. Trim stems, but do not peel mushrooms. Use whole, sliced, quartered or diced. Slice lengthwise across the cap and stem.

Cooking tips:

To saute: In a skillet, heat 1/4 cup of butter or oil over high heat. Add 1 pound cleaned whole or sliced mushrooms and saute for 2 minutes, stirring constantly.

Yield: 1 pound of mushrooms serves 3 to 4

OKRA

Okra is a slender ribbed
edible pod with small white seeds. This mild vegetable tastes a little like asparagus and is known for its thickening power when cooked in gumbo, soups or stews.

Buying tips:

Available year-round in the Southern states, but only from April to November in the North. Peak months are June through November. Buy young tender, unblemished, bright green pods less than 4 in. long. The pods may be smooth or ridged and should snap easily and not have any hard seeds. The tips should bend under slight pressure.

Storage tips:

Place unwashed okra in a sealed plastic bag in the refrigerator crisper drawer for up to 2 days.

Preparation tips:

Wash and remove stem ends. Leave small pods whole; cut larger pods into 1/2-in. slices.

Cooking tips:

To boil: Place whole or cut okra in a saucepan; add 1 in. of water. Bring to a boil. Reduce heat; cover and simmer for 8-10 minutes or until tender. Drain. Overcooked okra will have a gummy consistency.

Yields: 1 pound of okra equals 3 to 4 cups sliced
1 pound of okra serves 3 to 4

ONIONS

White onion

Green onions

Yellow onion

Red onion

A member of the lily family, onions can be green, white, yellow or red with flavor ranging from sharp when eaten raw to mild and sweet when cooked.

Buying tips:

Available year-round. Green onions (also known as scallions) should have bright green tops with white bulbs and short roots. All other onions should have a dry, smooth papery skin. They should be unblemished, hard and globe-shaped with small necks. Avoid moist, blemished or sprouting onions. White onions have the mildest flavor. Yellow onions are the most common.

Storage tips:

Place unwashed green onions in a sealed plastic bag in the refrigerator crisper drawer for up to 5 days. All other onions should be stored in a net bag or open basket in a dry, dark, cool place for up to 4 weeks.

Preparation tips:

For green onions, wash and cut root end. Cut off green tops, leaving about 3 in. For all other onions, peel loose layers of skin and cut onions just prior to cooking. Red or purple onions are used uncooked because the color fades as it cooks.

Cooking tips:

To saute: Heat 2 tablespoons of butter or oil in a skillet over medium-high heat. Saute sliced or chopped onion until translucent. *To bake:* Place a large onion in an ungreased baking dish; add 1/4 in. of water. Cover and bake at 350° for 40-50 minutes or until tender.

Yields: 1 green onion equals 2 tablespoons sliced
1 small onion equals 1/3 cup chopped
1 medium onion equals 1/2 cup chopped
1 large onion equals 1 cup chopped

PEAS AND PEA PODS

Fresh green peas, sugar snap peas and snow peas are members of the legume family. All three have a soft green color and a mild flavor. Sugar snap and snow peas have tender edible pods and can be served raw or cooked.

Buying tips:
Available year-round. Peak months are January to August. Buy firm, bright green unblemished pods that are well filled with plump peas. Snow peas are flat and limp, while sugar snap peas are round and very crisp.

Storage tips:
Keep unwashed unshelled green peas or pea pods in an open plastic bag in the refrigerator crisper drawer for up to 2 days.

Preparation tips:
Shell and wash fresh green peas. For snow peas and sugar snap peas, rinse and trim the stem end. Remove string from pod if desired. (See photo at left.) Do not shell snow or sugar snap peas.

Cooking tips:
To boil: Place shelled fresh peas or pea pods in a saucepan; add 1 in. of water. Bring to a boil. Reduce heat; cover and simmer until tender and bright green (5-8 minutes for fresh peas or 2-3 minutes for pea pods). Drain. *To saute:* Add snow peas to several tablespoons of hot oil; stir-fry for 2-3 minutes. Sugar snap peas may be stir-fried if they are blanched first for 1 minute.

Yields: 2 pounds unshelled peas equals 3 cups shelled and serves 6

1 pound snow peas equals 4 cups and serves 4 to 6

1 pound sugar snap peas equals 4 cups and serves 4 to 6

PEPPERS

Sweet bell peppers

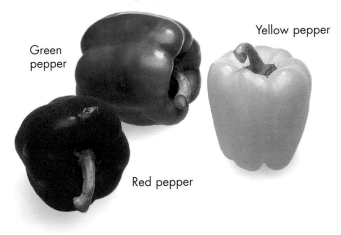

Green pepper

Yellow pepper

Red pepper

Classified as a fruit, sweet bell peppers are enjoyed as a vegetable. They can range in color from dark green and dark purple to bright yellow and vibrant red. Sweet peppers are mild in flavor and enhance hot and cold dishes alike.

Chili (hot) peppers come in endless varieties and heat levels. Fresh chili peppers can be yellow, red, orange or green. Dried chili peppers most often are a black-red color.

Buying tips:
Both sweet bell and chili peppers are available year-round. Peak months are March through October. Buy firm, glossy, bright-colored peppers that are unblemished and have smooth skins. Bell peppers should be relatively heavy in weight.

Storage tips:
Keep unwashed bell peppers in the refrigerator crisper drawer for up to 1 week. Store unwashed fresh chili peppers in a paper bag or wrapped in paper towels in the refrigerator crisper drawer for up to 2 weeks.

Preparation tips:
Bell peppers may be left whole, chopped or cut into slices or rings. Wash; remove stems, seeds and membranes (ribs).

Snow peas

Sugar snap peas

Fresh green peas

Peppers (continued)

Chili peppers

Habanero
Jalapeno
Anaheim
Banana
Pequin
Serrano

When handling chili peppers, wear rubber gloves or cover your hands with plastic sandwich bags to prevent burning your skin and eyes. (See the photo at left.) Wash hands and cutting surfaces thoroughly with hot soapy water when finished. To reduce the heat of chili peppers, remove the seeds and membranes.

Cooking tips:

To steam: Place whole seeded bell peppers in a basket over 1 in. of boiling water in a saucepan. Cover; steam for 8-10 minutes or until crisp-tender. Use this technique to prepare peppers for stuffing. Whole peppers may also be parboiled (see Parboiling Peppers on page 123). *To saute:* Heat 1-2 tablespoons of oil in a skillet. Saute bell pepper strips or pieces for 3-5 minutes or until crisp-tender.

Follow individual recipe directions for cooking the many varieties of chili peppers.

Yields: 1 pound of bell peppers (3 medium) equals 4 cups thinly sliced
1/2 pound chili peppers equals about 20 small

POTATOES

Known as a tuberous vegetable, potatoes are round or elongated with smooth edible skins that range in color from brown or red to white or yellow-gold. Small potatoes that are fresh from the garden and have never been placed in storage are called new potatoes.

Buying tips:
White and red potatoes are available year-round.

Peak months are spring and early summer for new potatoes and August to February for other varieties. Buy well-shaped, firm potatoes that are free from cuts, decay, blemishes or green discoloration under the skin. Avoid sprouted or shriveled potatoes.

Sweet potatoes (sometimes called yams) are available year-round. The peak month is November. Look for well-shaped potatoes, free of blemishes and large knots. Skins that are darker tend to be sweeter and moister.

Storage tips:
Store potatoes in a basket, net bag or paper bag in a dry, dark, cool well-ventilated area for up to 2 weeks; do not refrigerate.

Preparation tips:
Scrub with a vegetable brush. Remove eyes or sprouts. When working with large quantities of potatoes, peel and place in cold water to prevent browning.

Cooking tips for white or red potatoes:
To boil: Use red, white, yellow-gold or new potatoes. Cut large potatoes into quarters or chunks. Place in a saucepan; cover with water. Cover and bring to a boil. Cook until tender, 15-30 minutes; drain well. *To steam:* Place potato chunks in a basket over 1 in. of boiling water in a saucepan. Cover and steam until tender, 15-30 minutes. *To bake:* Use a russet potato. Pierce potato skins several times with a fork. (See photo at left.) Bake directly on oven rack at 375° for 1 hour or until potato feels soft when it's gently squeezed. If you prefer a soft-skinned baked potato, wrap in foil or rub with oil before baking.

Sweet potato
Round potato
Russet potato
Red potato
White potato
New potato

Cooking tips for sweet potatoes:
To boil: Place whole scrubbed potatoes in a large kettle and cover with water. Cover and boil gently until potatoes can easily be pierced with the tip of a sharp knife, about 30-45 minutes. Drain and peel as soon as they are cool enough to handle. *To bake:* Pierce potatoes several times with a fork. Bake directly on oven rack at 400° for about 45 minutes or until soft when gently squeezed. Place a piece of foil under potatoes to catch drips.

Yields: 1 pound russet potatoes equals about 3 medium
1 pound small new potatoes equals 8 to 10 (about 3 servings)
1 pound potatoes equals 2-1/4 cups diced or sliced
1 medium white, red or sweet potato serves 1
1 pound sweet potatoes (3 medium) equals about 2 cups mashed

PUMPKIN

A member of the gourd family, pumpkins can be cooked as you would any winter squash. Varieties known as pie pumpkins are smaller than the "jack-o'-lantern" type and make flavorful puree for use in pies and cakes.

Buying tips:
Available only in autumn and winter months. Buy pumpkins with firm, blemish-free rinds that are bright orange in color.

Storage tips:
Store in a cool, dry place for up to 1 month. A cut pumpkin may be stored in an open plastic bag in the refrigerator for up to 1 week.

Preparation tips:
Cut off top stem section. Remove seeds and scrape out stringy fibers.

Cooking tips:
To boil: Cut pumpkin into 2-in. pieces; peel. Place in a large saucepan and cover with water. Cover and boil for 25-30 minutes or until tender; drain. *To steam:* Cut pumpkin into 2-in. pieces; peel. Place in a basket over 1 in. of boiling water in a saucepan. Cover; steam for 50 minutes or until tender. *To bake:* Cut pumpkin into 4- to 5-in. pieces. Place with skin side up in a large baking pan. Cover pan with foil. Bake at 375° until tender, about 1 hour. Cool and scoop out pulp.

Yield: 1 pie pumpkin (3 pounds) equals about 2 cups cooked pureed

SPINACH

Dark green in color and tender in texture, spinach leaves can be eaten raw in salads or lightly cooked and used in soups, side dishes and main dishes.

Buying tips:
Available year-round. Peak seasons are late spring and early summer. Buy crisp, dark green, tender leaves. Avoid yellowed or wilted spinach.

Storage tips:
Keep unwashed spinach in a sealed plastic bag in the refrigerator crisper drawer for up to 3 days.

Preparation tips:
Cut off the tough stems. Wash several times in cold water to remove sand; drain well and pat dry.

Cooking tips:
To steam: Place spinach in a basket over 1 in. of boiling water in a saucepan. Cover; steam for 3-4 minutes or until wilted. *To saute:* Heat several tablespoons of butter or oil in a skillet over medium-high heat. Add spinach and cook, stirring occasionally, until wilted and tender, about 3-4 minutes.

Yields: 1 to 1-1/2 pounds fresh spinach equals 1 cup cooked
1 cup cooked spinach serves 2

SQUASH

Summer squash, a member of the gourd family, are soft-skinned, tender and quick-cooking. Varieties include pattypan, sunburst, yellow crookneck and zucchini. All contain small soft edible seeds and edible skins. Summer squash can be eaten raw or cooked.

Winter squash, also a member of the gourd family, are dense vegetables with a hard shell and large seeds. Va-

Squash (continued)

Summer Squash

Zucchini

Yellow crookneck

Sunburst

Pattypan

Winter Squash

Butternut

Spaghetti

Acorn

Turban

Keep unwashed winter squash in a dry, cool, well-ventilated place for up to 4 weeks.

Preparation tips:
Wash summer squash, but do not peel. Remove stem and blossom ends. Serve pattypan squash whole if young (1 to 2 in.). Slice zucchini and yellow squash into 1/2-in. circles.

Wash winter squash. Trim stem; cut into halves or individual portions. Remove seeds and stringy portions. Acorn squash can be cut into decorative rings and steamed or baked. (See photo at right.)

Cooking tips for summer squash:
To steam: Place squash in a basket over 1 in. of boiling water in a saucepan. Cover; steam for 5 minutes or until crisp-tender. *To saute:* Heat several tablespoons of butter or oil in a skillet. Saute squash over medium-high heat for 5 minutes or until crisp-tender.

Cooking tips for winter squash:
To steam: Peel and dice squash. Place in a basket over 1 in. of boiling water in a saucepan. Cover; steam for 15-20 minutes or until tender. *To bake:* Cut squash in half or quarters if large; place cut side down in a greased baking dish. Bake, uncovered, at 350° for 45-60 minutes or until tender.

Yields for summer squash:
    1 pound of squash equals 4 cups grated or
      3-1/2 cups sliced
    1 pound of squash serves 3 to 4

Yields for winter squash:
    1 pound of squash equals 2 cups cooked mashed
    1 pound of squash serves 2

rieties include acorn, butternut, spaghetti and turban. Winter squash is always cooked before serving.

Buying tips:
Summer squash are available year-round. Peak months are May through August. Buy squash that have glossy, smooth and firm but tender skins. Small squash are more tender and flavorful.

Winter squash are available year-round. Peak months are October through December. Buy squash that have a coarse, hard rind. The squash should feel heavy for its size.

Storage tips:
Keep unwashed summer squash in a sealed plastic bag in the refrigerator crisper drawer for up to 4 days.

TOMATOES

Classified as a fruit, but used as a vegetable, tomatoes are smooth-skinned, round or pear-shaped and bright red or yellow when ripe. They are eaten raw or cooked.

Buying tips:
Available year-round. Peak months are June through October for local vine-ripened tomatoes. Buy nicely ripe, rich-colored, well-shaped tomatoes that are slightly soft. Tomatoes should be free of blemishes.

Common red tomato

Plum tomatoes

Pear-shaped tomatoes

Cherry tomatoes

Storage tips:
Keep unwashed tomatoes at room temperature for 1 to 2 days. Keep out of direct sunlight.

Preparation tips:
Wash and core tomatoes. To remove peel, place tomato in boiling water for 30 seconds. Immediately dip in ice water. Remove skin with a sharp paring knife. (See photos at right.)

To seed a tomato, cut in half and gently squeeze the tomato over a bowl. Use a small spoon to remove any seeds still remaining.

Cooking tips:
To broil: Place tomato halves 3-4 in. from the heat. Broil just until heated through or when the skin begins to split. *To bake:* Place tomato halves cut side up in a greased baking dish. Season as desired. Bake at 400° for 8-15 minutes or until just heated through and skin begins to wrinkle.

Yield: 1 pound of tomatoes (about 3 medium) equals 1-1/2 cups peeled seeded pulp

TURNIPS, RUTABAGAS AND PARSNIPS

These are root vegetables that are commonly used in soups, stews and vegetable dishes. Both young parsnips and turnips have a mild sweet flavor. Rutabagas are mild-flavored when young but naturally stronger in flavor than turnips and parsnips.

Buying tips:
Available year-round. Peak seasons for these root vegetables are fall and winter. Buy firm, smooth vegetables that feel heavy for their size and have unblemished skins. Look for turnips no larger than 2 in. in diameter.

Storage tips:
Keep unwashed root vegetables in a plastic bag in the refrigerator crisper drawer for up to 1 week.

Rutabagas

Preparation tips:
Wash turnips; slice off top and root ends. Young small turnips only need to be scrubbed, but larger turnips should be peeled. Rutabagas and parsnips must be washed and peeled. Cut all into 1/2-in. cubes for cooking.

Cooking tips:
To boil: Place in a large saucepan and cover with water. Cover and boil for 15 minutes or until tender; drain. *To steam:* Place in a basket over 1 in. of boiling water in a saucepan. Cover; steam for 10-15 minutes or until tender.

Yield: 1 pound of trimmed turnips, rutabagas or parsnips equals about 3 cups cubed

Parsnips

Turnip

Sugared Asparagus

Here's a different twist to cooking fresh asparagus that is sure to please. The brown sugar brings out the delicate flavor of the asparagus. It's a real winner with ham!

- 3 tablespoons butter *or* margarine
- 2 tablespoons brown sugar
- 2 pounds fresh asparagus, trimmed and cut into 2-inch pieces (about 4 cups)
- 1 cup chicken broth

In a skillet over medium-high, heat butter and brown sugar until sugar is dissolved. Add asparagus; saute for 2 minutes. Stir in chicken broth; bring to a boil. Reduce heat; cover and simmer for 8-10 minutes or until asparagus is crisp-tender. Remove asparagus to a serving dish and keep warm. Cook sauce, uncovered, until reduced by half. Pour over asparagus and serve immediately. **Yield:** 8 servings. ⏱ —*Billie Moss El Sobrante, California*

Dill Butter for Asparagus

It doesn't matter what method you use to cook the asparagus for this recipe. But the presentation is prettier if the spears are left whole, so be sure to use a large skillet to accommodate their length.

- 1/2 cup butter *or* margarine, softened
- 1/4 cup snipped fresh dill
- 1-1/2 teaspoons lemon juice
- Fresh asparagus, trimmed

In a small bowl, combine butter, dill and lemon juice; mix until well blended. Place on a piece of plastic wrap and shape into a log. (If necessary, refrigerate butter until firm enough to shape.) Refrigerate until firm, at least 1 hour or up to several weeks. Steam or boil desired amount of asparagus until crisp-tender. Drain; place on a platter. Slice butter 1/4 in. thick and place on asparagus. **Yield:** Recipe will season about 4 pounds of asparagus. —*Mildred Sherrer, Bay City, Texas*

Dill Butter for Asparagus

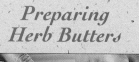

Preparing Herb Butters

Combine butter and seasonings. If butter is very soft, refrigerate until firm enough to shape easily. Place butter on a piece of plastic wrap. Shape into a log and wrap. Refrigerate until ready to serve. Slice butter 1/4 in. thick and use as directed.

Oven-Baked Asparagus

For real convenience, you can bake this asparagus in a foil packet while roasting your favorite cut of meat. Simply place the foil packet in the oven about 25 minutes before the end of the meat's recommended baking time.

   1 pound fresh asparagus, trimmed
   2 tablespoons butter *or* margarine
Salt and pepper to taste

Place the asparagus on a large piece of heavy-duty aluminum foil. Dot with butter. Bring long edges of foil together and fold over to seal. Crimp ends tightly; place foil packet on a baking sheet. Bake at 350° for 25-30 minutes or until asparagus is crisp-tender. Carefully open foil to allow steam to escape. Season with salt and pepper. **Yield:** 4 servings. 🕐   —*Bob Foust*
Indianapolis, Indiana

Sesame Asparagus

Add a little crunch and a lot of flavor to tender asparagus spears with this sesame sauce.

   2 pounds fresh asparagus, trimmed
   1 cup boiling water
   1 tablespoon cornstarch
   1/4 cup cold water
   1/4 cup butter *or* margarine
   3 tablespoons sesame seeds, toasted

Place asparagus spears in a large skillet; add 1/2 in. of water and bring to a boil. Reduce heat; cover and simmer until crisp-tender, 3-5 minutes. Remove asparagus and keep warm. Drain, reserving 1/2 cup cooking liquid in a small saucepan. Combine cornstarch and cold water; stir into liquid. Cook and stir over medium heat until thickened and bubbly; cook and stir 1 minute longer. Stir in butter until melted. Spoon over asparagus; sprinkle with sesame seeds and serve immediately. **Yield:** 6-8 servings. 🕐
—*Eunice Stoen, Decorah, Iowa*

Country Green Beans

Country Green Beans

Here's a tasty way to make good use of a little leftover ham. And the garlic and onion blend so well with the beans.

   1 pound fresh green beans, cut into 1-1/2-inch
      pieces
   1/4 cup chopped onion
   1/4 cup chopped fully cooked ham
   1/4 cup butter *or* margarine
   1/4 cup water
   1 garlic clove, minced
   1/2 teaspoon salt
   1/4 teaspoon pepper

In a saucepan, combine all ingredients. Cover and simmer for 8-10 minutes or until beans are crisp-tender. **Yield:** 4 servings. 🕐   —*Linda Gaido*
New Brighton, Pennsylvania

Tangy Green Bean Casserole

To make last-minute meal preparation a breeze, cook the green beans until crisp-tender earlier in the day; drain and rinse with cold water. Cover and refrigerate until you're ready to assemble and bake the casserole.

> 2 pounds fresh green beans, cut into 1-1/2-inch pieces
> 2 tablespoons finely chopped onion
> 2 tablespoons olive *or* vegetable oil
> 1 tablespoon vinegar
> 1 garlic clove, minced
> 1/2 teaspoon salt
> 1/4 teaspoon pepper
> 2 tablespoons dry bread crumbs
> 2 tablespoons grated Parmesan cheese
> 1 tablespoon butter *or* margarine, melted

In a saucepan, cover beans with water; bring to a boil. Cook, uncovered, for 8-10 minutes or until crisp-tender; drain. Add onion, oil, vinegar, garlic, salt and pepper; toss to coat. Transfer to an ungreased 2-qt. baking dish. Toss crumbs, cheese and butter; sprinkle over bean mixture. Bake, uncovered, at 350° for 20-25 minutes or until golden brown. **Yield:** 6-8 servings.

—*Judy Rush, Newport, Rhode Island*

Basil Buttered Beans

Basil and green beans make a wonderful flavor combination. Be sure to try this when your herb and vegetable gardens are at their peak.

> 2 pounds fresh green beans, cut into 1-1/2-inch pieces
> 2 tablespoons chopped onion
> 2 tablespoons chopped celery
> 1/4 cup water
> 2 tablespoons butter *or* margarine, melted
> 1-1/2 teaspoons minced fresh basil *or* 1/2 teaspoon dried basil
> 1/4 teaspoon salt
> 1/8 teaspoon pepper

In a saucepan, combine beans, onion, celery and water. Bring to a boil; cook, uncovered, for 8-10 minutes or until beans are crisp-tender. Drain. Add the butter, basil, salt and pepper; stir to coat. **Yield:** 10 servings. ⏱

—*Laura Porter, Sheridan, Oregon*

Easy Pickled Beets

Everyone enjoys pickled beets at family reunions or other occasions. This recipe allows you to make even larger quantities by doubling or tripling as needed.

> 1 tablespoon mixed pickling spices
> 2 cups vinegar
> 2 cups sugar
> 1 teaspoon ground cinnamon
> 1 teaspoon salt
> 4 cans (16 ounces *each*) sliced beets

Place pickling spices in a cheesecloth bag (refer to page 93). In a large saucepan, combine vinegar, sugar, cinnamon and salt; add the spice bag. Bring to a boil. Drain the beets, reserving 3/4 cup juice. Stir beets and reserved juice into saucepan. Pour into a 1-1/2-qt. glass container. Cover and refrigerate overnight. Remove spice bag before serving. **Yield:** 18-20 servings.

—*Cordie Cash, Silsbee, Texas*

Spiced Baked Beets

When your garden is overflowing with beets, prepare this hearty dish loaded with root vegetables. It will make delicious use of your abundant harvest.

> **4 cups shredded peeled raw beets (4 to 5 medium)**
> **1 medium onion, shredded**
> **1 medium potato, peeled and shredded**
> **3 tablespoons brown sugar**
> **3 tablespoons vegetable oil**
> **2 tablespoons water**
> **1 tablespoon vinegar**
> **1/2 teaspoon salt**
> **1/4 teaspoon pepper**
> **1/4 teaspoon celery seed**
> **1/8 to 1/4 teaspoon ground cloves**

In a large bowl, combine beets, onion and potato; set aside. In a small bowl, combine brown sugar, oil, water, vinegar and seasonings. Pour over vegetables; toss to coat. Pour into a greased 1-1/2-qt. baking dish. Cover and bake at 350° for 45 minutes, stirring occasionally. Uncover and bake 15-25 minutes longer or until vegetables are tender. **Yield:** 8-10 servings. 🍎
—*Margery Richmond*
Lacombe, Alberta

Harvard Beets

You'll certainly appreciate this quick-to-fix and pretty side dish. Be sure to bring the sauce to a boil to make a thick and shiny glaze.

> **1 can (16 ounces) sliced beets**
> **1/4 cup sugar**
> **1-1/2 teaspoons cornstarch**
> **2 tablespoons vinegar**
> **2 tablespoons orange juice**
> **1 tablespoon grated orange peel**

Drain beets, reserving 2 tablespoons juice; set beets and juice aside. In a saucepan, combine sugar and cornstarch. Add vinegar, orange juice and reserved beet juice; bring to a boil. Reduce heat and simmer for 3-4 minutes or until thickened. Add beets and orange peel; heat through. **Yield:** 4-6 servings. ⏱
—*Jean Ann Perkins, Newburyport, Maryland*

Spiced Baked Beets

Salting Vegetables

When cooking vegetables in boiling or simmering water, you can sprinkle a little salt into the cooking water before adding the vegetables if desired. However, if the vegetables are to be served in a sauce containing salt or salty ingredients, omit the salt in the cooking water.

Broccoli Mushroom Medley

1/2 cup chopped onion
1 can (10-3/4 ounces) condensed cream of
  mushroom soup, undiluted
1/2 teaspoon ground mustard
1/2 teaspoon salt
4 hard-cooked eggs, chopped
1-1/2 cups (6 ounces) shredded cheddar cheese
1 can (2.8 ounces) french-fried onions

Cook broccoli according to package directions; drain and set aside. In a skillet or saucepan, melt butter. Saute onion until tender. Stir in soup, mustard and salt; heat until bubbly. Place half of the broccoli in a greased 1-1/2-qt. baking dish; top with half of the eggs, cheese and mushroom sauce. Repeat layers. Bake, uncovered, at 350° for 20 minutes. Sprinkle onions on top and bake 5 minutes longer. **Yield:** 6 servings. —*Carolyn Griffin, Macon, Georgia*

Broccoli Mushroom Medley

When a speedy side dish's in order, turn to this simple stir-fry.

1-1/2 pounds fresh broccoli, cut into florets
1 teaspoon lemon juice
1 teaspoon salt
1 teaspoon sugar
1 teaspoon cornstarch
1/4 teaspoon ground nutmeg
3 tablespoons vegetable oil
1 cup sliced fresh mushrooms
1 medium onion, sliced into rings
1 to 2 garlic cloves, minced

Place broccoli in a basket over 1 in. of boiling water in a saucepan. Cover; steam for 5-8 minutes or until crisp-tender. Rinse in cold water; drain and set aside. In a bowl, combine lemon juice, salt, sugar, cornstarch and nutmeg; set aside. In a large skillet or wok, heat oil over high. Stir-fry mushrooms, onion and garlic for 3 minutes. Add broccoli and lemon juice mixture; stir-fry for 1-2 minutes or until broccoli is crisp-tender. Serve immediately. **Yield:** 6 servings. ⏲ 🍎
—*Cherie Sechrist, Red Lion, Pennsylvania*

Broccoli Bake

For showers, parties or any other family event, this casserole is sure to be a hit. After Easter, it's a great way to use leftover hard-cooked eggs.

2 packages (10 ounces *each*) frozen cut broccoli
1 tablespoon butter *or* margarine

Broccoli Bake

Herbed Broccoli

This zesty recipe really adds personality to plain broccoli and is bound to please the picky eaters at your table!

>   1 pound fresh broccoli, cut into spears
>   2 tablespoons butter *or* margarine
> 1-1/2 teaspoons lemon juice
> 1-1/2 teaspoons finely chopped onion
>   1/4 teaspoon salt
>   1/8 teaspoon *each* dried thyme, marjoram and
>   savory

Place broccoli in a saucepan; add 1 in. of water. Bring to a boil. Reduce heat; cover and simmer for 5-8 minutes or until crisp-tender. Drain broccoli and place in a serving dish; keep warm. Melt butter; add lemon juice, onion, salt and herbs. Pour over broccoli; stir to coat. **Yield:** 4 servings. ○ 🍎
—Norma Apel
Dubuque, Iowa

Fancy Brussels Sprouts

Here's a perfect side dish to serve alongside your Thanksgiving or Christmas turkey. For added holiday color, toss in 2 tablespoons chopped pimientos with the butter and water chestnuts.

>   1 cup water
>   1/4 cup minced fresh parsley
>   1 teaspoon sugar
>   1/2 teaspoon salt
>   2 pints fresh brussels sprouts, halved *or* 2
>   packages (10 ounces *each*) frozen brussels
>   sprouts, thawed

>   1 can (8 ounces) water chestnuts, drained and
>   diced
>   1 tablespoon butter *or* margarine

In a saucepan over medium heat, bring water, parsley, sugar and salt to a boil. Add brussels sprouts. Cover and simmer for 6-8 minutes or until crisp-tender; drain. Add water chestnuts and butter; heat through. **Yield:** 6 servings. ○ 🍎
—Dorothy Anderson
Ottawa, Kansas

Company Brussels Sprouts

The preparation of this dish is made even faster by cutting the brussels sprouts in half before cooking.

>   4 bacon strips, diced
>   12 brussels sprouts, trimmed and halved
>   1 medium onion, chopped
>   1 carrot, thinly sliced
>   10 stuffed olives, sliced
>   1/3 cup chicken broth *or* dry white wine
>   2 tablespoons snipped fresh chives
>   1 teaspoon olive *or* vegetable oil
>   1/2 teaspoon dried basil
>   1/2 teaspoon pepper
> Pinch salt

In a skillet, fry bacon just until cooked. Drain, reserving 2 tablespoons drippings. Add remaining ingredients; cook and stir over medium-high heat for 10-15 minutes or until brussels sprouts are crisp-tender. **Yield:** 4 servings. ○
—Donald Roberts
Amherst, New Hampshire

Fancy Brussels Sprouts

Sweet-and-Sour Red Cabbage

Bring a taste of Germany to your table with this traditional recipe. Leftovers freeze well.

    2 tablespoons bacon drippings *or* vegetable oil
    1/4 cup packed brown sugar
    3 tablespoons vinegar
    1 cup water
    1/4 teaspoon salt
Dash pepper
    4 cups shredded *or* thinly sliced red cabbage
    2 apples, peeled and sliced

In a large skillet, combine drippings, brown sugar, vinegar, water, salt and pepper. Cook for 2-3 minutes or until hot, stirring occasionally. Add cabbage; cover and cook over medium-low heat for 10 minutes, stirring occasionally. Add apples; cook, uncovered, about 10 minutes longer or until tender, stirring occasionally. **Yield:** 6-8 servings.
                                    —Barbara White
                                    Cross Plains, Wisconsin

Sweet-and-Sour Red Cabbage

Cabbage Casserole

This is just the right side dish to serve with your favorite pork roast. Put it in the oven 20 to 30 minutes before the roast is done.

    1 large head cabbage, thinly sliced (about 12
      cups)
    6 tablespoons butter *or* margarine, *divided*
    1 large onion, chopped
    1 can (10-3/4 ounces) condensed cream of
      mushroom soup, undiluted
    8 ounces process American cheese, cubed
Salt and pepper to taste
    1/4 cup dry bread crumbs

Place cabbage in a saucepan; add 1 in. of water. Bring to a boil. Reduce heat; cover and simmer for 3-5 minutes or until crisp-tender. Drain and set aside. In a large skillet, melt 5 tablespoons butter. Saute onion until tender. Add soup and mix well. Add cheese; heat and stir until melted. Remove from the heat. Stir in cabbage, salt and pepper. Transfer to an ungreased 2-qt. baking dish. In a small skillet, melt remaining butter. Add crumbs; cook and stir until lightly browned. Sprinkle over casserole. Bake, uncovered, at 350° for 20-30 minutes or until heated through. **Yield:** 6-8 servings.
                —Ruby Williams, Bogalusa, Louisiana

Dilled Carrots

If fresh gingerroot is available at your local grocer's, try grating 1/2 teaspoon of it and substituting it for the ground ginger.

    2 to 3 cups sliced carrots
    1/4 cup diced green pepper
    2 tablespoons minced fresh dill
    1 tablespoon honey
    1 tablespoon butter *or* margarine
    2 teaspoons lemon juice
    1/2 teaspoon salt
    1/4 teaspoon ground ginger

Place carrots in a saucepan; add 1 in. of water. Bring to a boil. Reduce heat; cover and simmer for 7-9 minutes or until crisp-tender. Drain. Add remaining ingredients. Cook over low heat for 1-2 minutes or until heated through. **Yield:** 3-4 servings.
                                    —Verona Koehlmoos
                                    Pilger, Nebraska

Glazed Carrots

Glazed Carrots

Brown sugar and lemon enhance the natural sweetness of carrots. This recipe is unique because the carrots are left whole lengthwise. If desired, the carrots can be cut diagonally or on the bias for easier eating at buffets.

9 to 12 medium carrots (about 1-1/2 pounds)
1/4 cup butter *or* margarine
1 to 2 tablespoons lemon juice
2 tablespoons brown sugar

Place carrots in a skillet; add 1 in. of water. Bring to a boil. Reduce heat, cover and simmer for 15-20 minutes or until crisp-tender. Drain. Melt butter in a heavy skillet; add lemon juice and brown sugar and stir until thickened. Add carrots; stir until well glazed and heated through. **Yield:** 6 servings. *—Iona Redemer Calumet, Oklahoma*

Baked Carrots

(Pictured on cover)

These carrots are compatible with most any meal. Green onions and chicken broth give great flavor.

1 pound whole baby carrots
1 bunch green onions with tops, chopped
1 cup chicken broth

Place the carrots and onions in an ungreased 1-qt. baking dish; pour chicken broth over all. Cover and bake at 325° for 1 hour or until carrots are tender. **Yield:** 4 servings. *—Eleanore Hill, Fresno, California*

Cauliflower Au Gratin

This pretty, rich and tasty casserole is perfect with just about any roast or variety of poultry. For added interest, substitute broccoli for half of the cauliflower.

        6 tablespoons butter *or* margarine
        4 ounces fully cooked ham, chopped
        1 to 2 garlic cloves, minced
        1 head cauliflower (3 pounds), broken into
            florets
        2 tablespoons all-purpose flour
    1-1/2 cups whipping cream
        1/4 teaspoon salt
    Pepper to taste
    Pinch cayenne pepper
    1-1/2 cups (6 ounces) shredded Swiss cheese
        2 to 3 tablespoons chopped fresh parsley

In a large skillet, melt butter. Saute ham and garlic for 2 minutes. Add cauliflower and cook just until crisp-tender, about 10 minutes. Combine flour and cream; stir into skillet and blend well. Add salt, pepper and cayenne. Cook and stir until thickened and bubbly; cook and stir 1 minute more. Transfer to a 2-qt. baking dish. Sprinkle with cheese. Place under a preheated broiler until lightly browned, about 2-4 minutes. Sprinkle with parsley. Serve immediately. **Yield:** 6-8 servings.
—*Jacki Ricci, Ely, Nevada*

Cauliflower Au Gratin

Cauliflower with Mushroom Almond Sauce

This recipe is a hit at special meals, yet it is easy enough for everyday dining. If you plan on serving a whole head of cauliflower at the table, it's best to cook the cauliflower until tender, rather than crisp-tender, for easier cutting.

        1 large head cauliflower (about 2-1/2 pounds)
        1/2 cup butter *or* margarine
        1/4 pound fresh mushrooms, thinly sliced
        1/2 cup sliced almonds
        1/3 cup sliced green onions with tops
        2 teaspoons chicken bouillon granules
        3/4 cup hot water
        1 tablespoon cornstarch
        1/4 cup cold water

In a saucepan containing 1 in. of water, steam whole cauliflower until tender, about 20 minutes. Meanwhile, in a skillet, melt butter; saute mushrooms, almonds and onions until mushrooms are tender. Dissolve bouillon in hot water; add to skillet. Dissolve cornstarch in cold water; add to skillet. Bring to a boil over medium heat, stirring constantly. Cook and stir for 2 minutes. Place cauliflower in a large bowl; pour sauce over it and serve immediately. **Yield:** 6-8 servings.
—*Elinor Levine, West Palm Beach, Florida*

Spicy Corn Spread

(*Pictured on page 250*)

Chili powder is available in different heat levels, from mild to hot. Be sure to purchase the one that suits your taste.

        1/4 cup butter *or* margarine, softened
        1/2 teaspoon dried parsley flakes
        1/4 teaspoon chili powder
        1/4 teaspoon salt
        6 to 8 ears hot cooked corn on the cob

In a small bowl, combine the butter, parsley, chili powder and salt until smooth. Spread on ears of corn. Refrigerate any leftovers. **Yield:** 1/4 cup.

Corn Balls

Freezer Sweet Corn

If the end of summer finds you with lots of sweet corn, why not take a little time and freeze it to enjoy all winter long? (See Cutting Kernels from Corncobs on page 80.)

- **4 quarts fresh-cut sweet corn kernels (32 ears)**
- **1 quart hot water**
- **2/3 cup sugar**
- **1/2 cup butter *or* margarine**
- **2 teaspoons salt**

Combine all ingredients in a large kettle; simmer for 5-7 minutes, stirring occasionally. Pour into large shallow containers to cool; stir occasionally. Spoon into freezer bags or containers; freeze. To serve, reheat as you would any commercially frozen kernel corn. **Yield:** 3 quarts. —*Judi Oudekerk St. Michael, Minnesota*

Roast Corn on the Cob

Preparing corn in foil packets on the grill is quick and easy. The ice cube adds just the right amount of water to create the steam to cook the corn.

- **6 ears fresh corn on the cob**
- **6 tablespoons butter *or* margarine**
- **6 ice cubes**
- **Salt and pepper to taste**
- **Additional butter *or* margarine, optional**

Place each ear of husked corn on a piece of heavy-duty aluminum foil. Add 1 tablespoon butter and 1 ice cube. Wrap securely, twisting ends to make handles for turning. Grill over hot heat for 25 minutes, turning three times. Season with salt and pepper and additional butter if desired. **Yield:** 6 servings.

—*Johnnie McLeod, Bastrop, Louisiana*

Corn Balls

Place these stuffing balls in the oven along with your roast 15 to 20 minutes before it's done. While the Corn Balls continue to bake, make the gravy and slice the roast.

- **1/2 cup butter *or* margarine**
- **1 cup chopped celery**
- **1/2 cup chopped onion**
- **3-1/2 cups herb-seasoned stuffing croutons**
- **3 cups fresh, frozen *or* canned whole kernel corn**
- **3 eggs, beaten**
- **1/2 cup water**
- **1/2 teaspoon salt**
- **1/4 teaspoon pepper**

In a saucepan, melt butter. Saute celery and onion until tender; set aside to cool. In a bowl, combine croutons, corn, eggs, water, salt, pepper and onion mixture; mix well. Shape into eight to 10 balls. Place in an ungreased shallow baking dish. Bake, uncovered, at 375° for 25-30 minutes. **Yield:** 8-10 servings.

—*Sharon Knicely, Harrisonburg, Virginia*

Roasting Corn in Foil

Place each ear of husked corn on a 12-in. square piece of heavy-duty foil. Top with a pat of butter and a standard-size ice cube. Wrap each ear tightly and grill as directed.

Hominy Casserole

The cumin and canned chilies add a Southwestern taste to this comforting dish. Canned chilies are packed with a little liquid. Unless otherwise noted, use the liquid along with the chilies in your recipes.

    1 tablespoon vegetable oil
    1 medium onion, chopped
    1 garlic clove, minced
    1 cup (8 ounces) sour cream
    3/4 cup shredded cheddar cheese, *divided*
    1/4 cup milk
    1 can (4 ounces) chopped green chilies
    1/4 teaspoon ground cumin
    3 cans (15 ounces *each*) golden hominy, drained

In a small skillet, heat oil. Saute onion and garlic until tender. Place in a bowl; add sour cream, half of the cheese, milk, chilies and cumin. Add hominy; mix well. Pour into a greased 2-qt. baking dish. Bake, uncovered, at 350° for 30 minutes or until heated through. Sprinkle with remaining cheese. Serve immediately. **Yield:** 8-10 servings.   —*Marion Thurman, Crossett, Arkansas*

Hominy Casserole

Cream-Style Corn

Once you sample this homemade creamed corn, you'll never rely on store-bought varieties again. Freeze in serving-size portions; when you need a fast side dish, simply thaw and reheat. Or use in any recipe calling for cream-style corn.

    18 cups fresh-cut sweet corn kernels (36 ears)
    2 cups milk
    1/2 cup butter *or* margarine
    1/3 cup sugar
    1 tablespoon salt

Place half of the corn in a food processor; cover and process until creamy. Pour into a large baking pan; add milk, butter, sugar, salt and remaining corn. Cover and bake at 325° for 1 hour and 30 minutes, stirring frequently. **Yield:** 2 quarts.   —*Vivian Gouliquer Vanderhoof, British Columbia*

Corn Pudding Supreme

Nothing is more country than a ham dinner with corn pudding. This version is especially easy because it uses a corn bread mix.

    1 package (8 ounces) cream cheese, softened
    2 eggs, beaten
    1/3 cup sugar
    1 package (8-1/2 ounces) corn bread/muffin mix

    1 can (14-3/4 ounces) cream-style corn (1-3/4 cups)
  2-1/3 cups fresh, frozen *or* canned whole kernel corn
    1 cup milk
    2 tablespoons butter *or* margarine, melted
    1 teaspoon salt
  1/2 teaspoon ground nutmeg

In a mixing bowl, blend cream cheese, eggs and sugar. Add all of the remaining ingredients and mix well. Transfer to a greased 13-in. x 9-in. x 2-in. baking pan. Bake, uncovered, at 350° for 45-50 minutes or until set. **Yield:** 12-16 servings.
—*Martha Fehl Brookville, Indiana*

Eggplant with Tomato Sauce

There's no need to peel the eggplant in this recipe—by the time the eggplant has browned on both sides, the skin will become soft and tender. To make an even heartier meal, serve this dish with cooked Italian sausage.

2 pounds unpeeled eggplant
1 teaspoon salt
1 tablespoon olive *or* vegetable oil
1 can (28 ounces) crushed tomatoes
2 garlic cloves, minced
1 teaspoon dried basil
1 to 2 teaspoons sugar
Salt and pepper to taste
Additional oil for frying
1/4 cup shredded Parmesan cheese

Cut eggplant into 1/2-in.-thick slices. Sprinkle with salt. Place in a colander over a plate; let stand for 30 minutes. Pat dry on paper towels. In a 2-qt. saucepan, heat oil over medium. Add tomatoes, garlic, basil and sugar; bring to a boil. Reduce heat and simmer, uncovered, about 45 minutes or until thickened, stirring occasionally. Season with salt and pepper. Keep warm while preparing eggplant. In a large skillet, heat about 1/4 cup oil; brown eggplant, a quarter at a time, adding more oil as needed. Layer on a serving platter. Cover with sauce and sprinkle with cheese. Serve warm.
Yield: 8 servings.

—Theresa Grassi
St. Louis, Missouri

Salting Eggplant

To remove excess moisture from eggplant, slice, cube or cut into strips. Sprinkle with salt and place in a colander over a plate. Allow to stand for 30 minutes. Blot moisture that beads on eggplant with a paper towel and continue with recipe.

Eggplant with Tomato Sauce

Creamed Kohlrabi

The flavor of this recipe's creamed sauce is robust and delightful. Watch this dish quickly disappear!

**1-1/2 pounds kohlrabi, peeled and cut into 1/2-inch
       cubes**
1 tablespoon butter *or* margarine
1 tablespoon all-purpose flour
1/8 teaspoon salt
Pinch ground nutmeg
Pinch sugar
3/4 cup milk
1/2 cup shredded process Swiss cheese

Place kohlrabi in a saucepan; add 1 in. of water. Bring to a boil. Reduce heat; cover and cook over medium heat until tender, 6-8 minutes. Meanwhile, melt butter in a saucepan. Stir in flour, salt, nutmeg and sugar until smooth. Stir in milk. Bring to a boil over medium heat, stirring constantly. Boil 2 minutes. Remove from the heat; stir in cheese until smooth. Drain kohlrabi; stir into cheese sauce. Heat through. **Yield:** 6 servings.

Grilled Mushrooms

Basting the mushrooms frequently while grilling will keep them moist and flavorful. These will become a standby anytime you make a steak.

1/2 pound medium whole fresh mushrooms
1/4 cup butter *or* margarine, melted

1/2 teaspoon dill weed
1/2 teaspoon garlic salt

Thread mushrooms on skewers. Combine butter, dill and garlic salt; brush over the mushrooms. Grill over high heat for 10-15 minutes, basting and turning every 5 minutes. **Yield:** 4 servings. ⏱ —*Melanie Knoll
Marshalltown, Iowa*

Corn Okra Creole

Prepare this recipe using garden-fresh produce in season and canned or frozen the rest of the year.

3 tablespoons vegetable oil
1 cup chopped green pepper
1/2 cup chopped onion
**2 cups fresh *or* frozen corn *or* 1 can (17 ounces)
       whole kernel corn**
**1-1/2 cups sliced fresh okra *or* 1 package
       (16 ounces) frozen okra**
**3 medium tomatoes, peeled and chopped (1-1/2
       cups)**
1 tablespoon tomato paste
1/4 teaspoon dried thyme
Salt to taste
1/4 teaspoon coarsely ground black pepper
1/2 teaspoon hot pepper sauce, optional

In a saucepan, heat oil. Saute green pepper and onion for 5 minutes. Add corn and okra; cook over medium heat for 6-8 minutes, stirring occasionally. Add tomatoes, tomato paste, thyme, salt, pepper and hot pepper sauce if desired; mix thoroughly. Cover and simmer for 3-5 minutes, stirring occasionally. **Yield:** 4-6 servings. ⏱ —*Ruth Aubey, San Antonio, Texas*

Grilled Mushrooms

Southern Okra

Fried Onion Rings

The addition of cayenne pepper in this recipe makes these onion rings a little spicier than traditional ones. If you don't like spicy foods, eliminate the cayenne.

        2 large sweet onions
        1 egg
    2/3 cup water
        1 tablespoon vegetable oil
        1 teaspoon lemon juice
        1 cup all-purpose flour
    1-1/2 teaspoons baking powder
        1 to 1-1/4 teaspoons salt
    1/8 to 1/4 teaspoon cayenne pepper
Oil for deep-fat frying

Cut onions into 1/2-in. slices; separate into rings. Place in a bowl; cover with ice water and soak for 30 minutes. Meanwhile, in a bowl, beat egg, water, oil and lemon juice. Combine flour, baking powder, salt and cayenne; stir into egg mixture until smooth. Drain onion rings; dip into batter. In an electric skillet or deep-fat fryer, heat 1 in. of oil to 375°. Fry onion rings, a few at a time, for 1 to 1-1/2 minutes on each side or until golden brown. Drain on paper towels. **Yield:** 4-6 servings.
—*Marsha Moore, Poplar Bluff, Missouri*

Southern Okra

Once okra is cooked, it becomes very delicate. So carefully fold it into the tomato mixture.

        2 cups sliced fresh okra (1/2 inch thick)
        1 tablespoon sugar
        1 teaspoon all-purpose flour
    1/2 teaspoon salt
    1/2 teaspoon pepper
        2 tablespoons vegetable oil
        1 medium onion, chopped
        1 medium green pepper, chopped
        3 medium tomatoes, peeled and chopped
Hot cooked rice, optional

Place okra in a saucepan; add 1 in. of water. Bring to a boil. Reduce heat; cover and simmer for 8-10 minutes or until tender. Drain and set aside. Combine the next four ingredients; set aside. In a skillet, heat oil over medium. Saute onion and green pepper until tender. Stir in sugar mixture and tomatoes; cook for 5 minutes. Add okra and simmer until heated through, stirring as little as possible. Serve with rice if desired. **Yield:** 6 servings. ○ 🍎 —*Bobbie Jo Yokley, Franklin, Kentucky*

Fried Onion Rings

Cheesy Onion Casserole

If you like French onion soup, you'll love this dish. It's perfect to serve with a Sunday roast beef dinner.

- 2 tablespoons butter *or* margarine
- 3 large sweet onions, sliced
- 2 cups (8 ounces) shredded Swiss cheese, *divided*

Pepper to taste

- 1 can (10-3/4 ounces) condensed cream of chicken soup, undiluted
- 2/3 cup milk
- 1 teaspoon soy sauce
- 8 slices French bread, buttered on both sides

In a large skillet, melt butter. Saute onions until translucent and slightly brown. Layer onions and two-thirds of the cheese in a 2-qt. baking dish, sprinkling pepper between layers. In a saucepan, heat soup, milk and soy sauce; stir to blend. Pour over onions and stir gently. Top with bread. Bake, uncovered, at 350° for 15 minutes. Push bread under sauce; sprinkle with remaining cheese. Bake 15 minutes longer. **Yield:** 8 servings.

—*Beth Perry, Jacksonville, Florida*

Peas and Potatoes

Cheesy Onion Casserole

Peas and Potatoes

No fresh dill on hand? You can substitute 2 teaspoons dill weed without sacrificing any of the flavor.

- 4 medium red potatoes, cubed
- 1 package (10 ounces) frozen peas
- 1 teaspoon sugar
- 2 tablespoons butter *or* margarine
- 2 tablespoons all-purpose flour
- 1/2 teaspoon salt
- 1/4 teaspoon white pepper
- 1-1/2 cups milk
- 2 tablespoons minced fresh dill

Place potatoes in a saucepan; cover with water. Cover and bring to a boil; cook until tender, about 15 minutes. Drain well. Cook peas according to package directions, adding the sugar. Meanwhile, melt butter in a saucepan; Stir in flour, salt and pepper until smooth. Gradually stir in milk. Bring to a boil; boil for 1 minute. Add dill; cook until thickened and bubbly. Drain potatoes and peas; place in a serving bowl. Pour sauce over and stir to coat. Serve immediately. **Yield:** 6-8 servings.

—*Linda Nilsen, Anoka, Minnesota*

Peas and Carrots with Mint

(Pictured on page 251)

Fresh mint is often used to flavor iced tea and to garnish a variety of foods. Here it takes center stage as a special seasoning for cooked carrots and sugar snap peas.

    4 large carrots, julienned
    1/2 pound sugar snap peas
    3 tablespoons butter *or* margarine
    1 to 2 tablespoons finely
        chopped fresh mint
    1/4 teaspoon salt
    1/8 teaspoon pepper

Place carrots in a saucepan; add 1 in. of water. Bring to a boil. Reduce heat; cook, uncovered, for 4-6 minutes or until crisp-tender. Drain.

Add remaining ingredients. Cook and stir for 3-4 minutes or until the peas are crisp-tender. **Yield:** 6-8 servings. —*Margie Snodgrass*
Gig Harbor, Washington

Oven-Roasted Potatoes

This recipe saves time by calling for unpeeled potatoes. Simply cut them into wedges, toss with remaining ingredients and pop into the oven.

    2 pounds small unpeeled red potatoes, cut into
        wedges
    2 to 3 tablespoons olive *or* vegetable oil
    2 garlic cloves, minced
    1 tablespoon chopped fresh rosemary *or* 1
        teaspoon dried rosemary, crushed
    1/2 teaspoon salt
    1/4 teaspoon pepper

Place potatoes in an ungreased 13-in. x 9-in. x 2-in. baking pan. Drizzle with oil. Sprinkle with garlic, rosemary, salt and pepper; toss gently to coat. Bake, uncovered, at 450° for 20-30 minutes or until potatoes are golden brown and tender when pierced with a fork. **Yield:** 6-8 servings. —*Margie Wampler*
Butler, Pennsylvania

Creamed Potatoes

Using an old-fashioned potato masher is the best way to mash potatoes and keep them light and fluffy.

    3-1/2 to 4 pounds russet potatoes, peeled and
        quartered
    1/4 cup butter *or* margarine
    1 ounce cream cheese, softened
    1/3 to 2/3 cup evaporated milk *or* whipping
        cream, *divided*
Salt and pepper to taste

Place potatoes in a saucepan; cover with water. Cover and bring to a boil; cook for 20-25 minutes or until very tender. Drain well. Add butter, cream cheese and 1/3 cup milk or cream. Whip with electric mixer on low speed or mash with a potato masher, adding remaining milk or cream as needed to make potatoes light and fluffy. Season with salt and pepper. **Yield:** 8-10 servings. —*Mary Lewis, Memphis, Tennessee*

Creamed Potatoes

Cheddar Parmesan Potatoes

Country Potato Pancakes

Shredding the potatoes for this recipe is a snap with a food processor. If you use a fine shredder, the pancakes will cook a little quicker and have crisp lacy edges.

   3 large potatoes (about 2 pounds), peeled
   2 eggs, lightly beaten
   1 tablespoon finely chopped onion
   2 tablespoons all-purpose flour
   1 teaspoon salt
   1/2 teaspoon baking powder
Oil for deep-fat frying

Finely shred potatoes; drain any liquid. Place in a bowl; add eggs, onion, flour, salt and baking powder. In an

Keeping Fried Foods Warm

When foods need to be cooked in stages, such as potato pancakes and fried onion rings, you'll want to keep each batch warm until the entire recipe is cooked. Drain fried foods on paper towels, then place on an ovenproof platter. Cover loosely with foil and place in a 200° oven until the entire recipe is completed.

electric fry pan, heat 1/8 in. of oil to 375°. Drop batter by heaping tablespoonfuls into hot oil. Flatten to form patties. Fry until golden brown; turn and cook the other side. Drain on paper towels. **Yield:** about 24 pancakes.
　　　　　　　　　—*Lydia Robotewskyj, Franklin, Wisconsin*

Cheddar Parmesan Potatoes

This recipe is a deluxe version of scalloped potatoes. Parmesan and cheddar cheeses and a buttery crumb topping make it extraordinary.

   5 tablespoons butter *or* margarine, *divided*
   1/4 cup all-purpose flour
   2 cups milk
   1/2 teaspoon salt
   1 cup (4 ounces) shredded cheddar cheese
   1/2 cup grated Parmesan cheese
   5 cups sliced cooked peeled potatoes (about 5 medium)
   1/4 cup dry bread crumbs

In a saucepan, melt 4 tablespoons butter over low heat. Stir in flour until smooth. Gradually add milk; cook and stir over medium heat until thickened. Remove from the heat. Stir in salt and cheeses until melted. Add potatoes; stir gently to mix. Place in a greased 2-qt. baking dish. Melt the remaining butter; toss with bread crumbs. Sprinkle over potatoes. Bake, uncovered, at 350° for 30-35 minutes. **Yield:** 6-8 servings.
　　　　　　　　　—*Nellie Webb, Athens, Tennessee*

Twice-Baked Potatoes

You can assemble these potatoes up to 24 hours ahead of time, then cover and refrigerate. When you're ready to bake, remove them from the refrigerator while the oven preheats. Bake as directed.

6 large russet potatoes
1/2 cup butter *or* margarine, softened
3/4 to 1 cup milk *or* half-and-half cream
3 tablespoons crumbled cooked bacon
3 tablespoons finely chopped onion
1 tablespoon snipped chives
1/2 teaspoon salt
Dash pepper
1-1/2 cups (6 ounces) shredded cheddar cheese,
    divided
Paprika

Bake potatoes at 375° for 1 hour or until soft. Allow to cool. Cut a thin slice off the top of each potato. Scoop out the pulp and place in a bowl; add butter and mash the pulp. Blend in milk, bacon, onion, chives, salt, pepper and 1 cup of cheese. Spoon into potato shells. Top with remaining cheese and sprinkle with paprika. Place on a baking sheet. Bake, uncovered, at 375° for 25-30 minutes or until heated through. **Yield:** 6 servings.
—*Debbie Jones, California, Maryland*

Twice-Baked Potatoes

Making Stuffed Potatoes

Cut a lengthwise slice from the top of each potato. With a spoon, scoop potato pulp from the slice and the inside of the potato, leaving a 1/4-in. shell. Discard skin from slice. Mash the pulp and spoon into shells. Bake as directed.

Apricot-Glazed Sweet Potatoes

greased 2-qt. baking dish; sprinkle with nuts and marshmallows. Bake, uncovered, at 350° for 30 minutes or until heated through and marshmallows begin to brown. **Yield:** 8-10 servings.
—*Nell Bass*
Macon, Georgia

Apricot-Glazed Sweet Potatoes

To save time in the kitchen around the holidays, cook, peel and refrigerate the sweet potatoes a day in advance. The next day, complete the recipe as directed.

> 3 pounds sweet potatoes, cooked, peeled and cut up
> 1 cup packed brown sugar
> 5 teaspoons cornstarch
> 1/4 teaspoon salt
> 1/8 teaspoon ground cinnamon
> 1 cup apricot nectar
> 1/2 cup hot water
> 2 teaspoons grated orange peel
> 2 teaspoons butter *or* margarine
> 1/2 cup chopped pecans

Place sweet potatoes in a greased 13-in. x 9-in. x 2-in. baking dish and set aside. In a saucepan, combine brown sugar, cornstarch, salt and cinnamon; stir in apricot nectar, water and orange peel. Bring to a boil, stirring constantly. Cook and stir for 2 minutes more. Remove from the heat; stir in butter and pecans. Pour over sweet potatoes. Bake, uncovered, at 350° for 20-25 minutes or until heated through. **Yield:** 8-10 servings.
—*Joan Huggins, Waynesboro, Mississippi*

Sweet Potato Bake

For a new twist to this classic recipe, add 1 teaspoon grated orange peel while mashing the sweet potatoes.

> 2 to 2-1/2 pounds sweet potatoes
> 1/4 cup butter *or* margarine, melted
> 1/4 to 1/2 cup sugar
> 1/4 cup raisins
> 1/3 cup chopped nuts
> 1/3 cup miniature marshmallows

Place sweet potatoes in a large saucepan or Dutch oven; cover with water. Cover; bring to a boil. Boil for 30-45 minutes or just until tender. Drain; cool slightly and peel. In a large bowl, mash potatoes. Stir in butter, sugar and raisins. Place in a

Dilly Mashed Potatoes

(Pictured on cover)

For light, fluffy mashed potatoes, rely on Idaho or russet potatoes.

> 6 medium russet potatoes, peeled and cubed
> 1/2 cup milk
> 1 cup (8 ounces) sour cream
> 2 tablespoons minced fresh dill *or* 2 teaspoons dill weed
> 1 tablespoon dried minced onion
> 3/4 teaspoon seasoned salt

In a saucepan, cover potatoes with water. Cover and bring to a boil; cook for 20-25 minutes or until very tender. Drain well; mash with milk. Stir in remaining ingredients. **Yield:** 6-8 servings.
—*Annie Tompkins, Deltona, Florida*

Herbed Spinach Bake

When using cooked spinach in a recipe, remove as much liquid as possible by pressing or squeezing it dry with your hands. This will prevent the dish from becoming watery.

- 2 packages (10 ounces *each*) frozen chopped spinach
- 2 cups cooked rice
- 2 cups (8 ounces) shredded cheddar cheese
- 4 eggs, beaten
- 2/3 cup milk
- 1/4 cup butter *or* margarine, softened
- 1/4 cup chopped onion
- 2 teaspoons salt
- 1 teaspoon Worcestershire sauce
- 1 teaspoon ground thyme

Cook spinach according to package directions; drain well, squeezing out excess liquid. Place in a large bowl; add remaining ingredients. Transfer to a greased 13-in. x 9-in. x 2-in. baking dish. Cover and bake at 350° for 20 minutes. Uncover and bake 5 minutes longer or until set. **Yield:** 16 servings.

—Nancy Frank
Lake Ariel, Pennsylvania

Herbed Spinach Bake

Summer Squash Saute

If you don't have sunburst or pattypan squash available, substitute zucchini that has been cut into 1/2-inch chunks.

- 2 tablespoons vegetable oil
- 1 large red onion, sliced
- 2 cups halved small sunburst *or* pattypan squash
- 2 small yellow summer squash, cut into 1/2-inch slices
- 1 medium sweet red pepper, julienned
- 1 medium green pepper, julienned
- 2 teaspoons minced fresh basil *or* 1/2 teaspoon dried basil
- 2 tablespoons red wine vinegar
- 4 bacon strips, cooked and crumbled
- 1/4 cup grated Parmesan cheese

In a large skillet, heat oil. Saute onion until tender. Stir in the squash, peppers and basil. Cover and cook until vegetables are crisp-tender, about 5 minutes. Remove from the heat; stir in vinegar and bacon. Sprinkle with Parmesan cheese. **Yield:** 8-10 servings.

—Jane Chartrand, *Shelbyville, Tennessee*

Cider Baked Squash

This recipe requires the uncooked squash to be cut into 1-inch rings. To do this, you'll need a large sharp knife to cut through the hard shell of the squash. The squash circles are pretty enough to garnish your meat platter.

- 2 medium acorn squash, cut into 1-inch rings and seeds removed
- 1/2 cup apple cider
- 1/4 cup packed brown sugar
- 1/2 teaspoon salt
- 1/8 teaspoon ground cinnamon
- 1/8 teaspoon ground mace

Place squash in an ungreased 15-in. x 10-in. x 1-in. baking pan. Pour cider over squash. Combine remaining ingredients; sprinkle on top. Cover and bake at 325° for 45 minutes or until squash is tender. **Yield:** 6 servings.

—Christine Gibson, *Fontana, Wisconsin*

Cooking Spaghetti Squash

Cut the squash in half length-wise and remove seeds. Place cut side down in a greased baking dish; bake at 350° for 45-60 minutes or until you can pierce the shell easily with a fork. Allow to cool slightly; using a fork, separate squash into strands that resemble spaghetti.

Spaghetti Squash Casserole

If you've never prepared spaghetti squash before, you're in for a treat! For a quick, low-calorie entree, cook the squash as directed, separate it into strands and serve with your favorite tomato pasta sauce.

1 medium spaghetti squash (about 8 inches)
1 cup water
1 tablespoon butter *or* margarine
1 cup chopped onion
2 garlic cloves, minced
1/2 pound fresh mushrooms, sliced
1 teaspoon dried basil
1/2 teaspoon dried oregano
1/4 teaspoon dried thyme
1/2 teaspoon salt
1/4 teaspoon pepper
2 medium tomatoes, diced
1 cup (8 ounces) ricotta *or* cottage cheese
1 cup (4 ounces) shredded mozzarella cheese
1/4 cup minced fresh parsley
1 cup dry bread crumbs
1/4 cup grated Parmesan cheese

Slice the squash in half lengthwise; remove and discard the seeds. Place squash cut side down in a baking dish. Bake at 350° for 45-60 minutes or until easily pierced with a fork. Meanwhile, melt butter in a skillet. Saute onion, garlic, mushrooms, herbs and seasonings until onion is translucent. Add the tomatoes; cook until most of the liquid has evaporated. Set aside. When squash is cool enough to handle, use a fork to separate into strands. Combine squash, tomato mixture, ricotta, mozzarella, parsley and crumbs. Pour into a greased 2-qt. casserole. Sprinkle with Parmesan cheese. Bake, uncovered, at 375° for 40 minutes or until heated through and top is golden brown. **Yield:** 6 servings.

—*Glenafa Vrchota, Mason City, Iowa*

Pumpkin Vegetable Stew

Use a pumpkin or any winter squash to make this harvest stew. Serve it with a beef pot roast for a hearty meal on a brisk autumn day.

4 cups cubed peeled pumpkin *or* winter squash
1 can (14-1/2 ounces) diced tomatoes,
  undrained
2 cups fresh cut green beans (1-inch pieces)
1 cup fresh *or* frozen corn
1/2 cup sliced onion
1/2 cup chopped green pepper
1/2 cup chicken broth
1 garlic clove, minced
1/2 teaspoon chili powder
1/4 teaspoon pepper

In a large saucepan, combine all the ingredients. Bring to a boil. Reduce heat; cover and simmer for 40-45 minutes or until the vegetables are tender. **Yield:** 6 servings (2 quarts).

—*Gerald Knudsen*
Quincy, Massachusetts

Fried Green Tomatoes

This recipe is a good way to use those garden tomatoes that never ripened. Seasoned bread crumbs make these fried tomatoes especially flavorful.

1 cup all-purpose flour
1 tablespoon brown sugar
1 egg, beaten
1/4 cup milk
4 to 6 medium green tomatoes, sliced
  1/2 inch thick
1 cup seasoned dry bread crumbs
3 tablespoons butter *or* margarine
1 tablespoon vegetable oil

Combine flour and brown sugar; place on a shallow plate. In a bowl, combine egg and milk. Coat both sides of each tomato with the flour mixture. Dip in the milk mixture, then dredge in the bread crumbs. In a skillet, heat butter and oil over medium-high. Fry tomatoes until brown on both sides but firm enough to hold their shape. **Yield:** about 6 servings.

—*Helen Bridges*
Washington, Virginia

Pumpkin Vegetable Stew

Meatless Spaghetti Sauce

When garden tomatoes are plentiful, it's a good time to make this classic recipe. Freeze in serving-size portions to enjoy all winter long. If desired, add cooked meatballs or Italian sausage to the sauce before serving.

> 1/2 cup vegetable *or* olive oil
> 4 medium onions, chopped
> 1-1/4 teaspoons pepper
> 4 garlic cloves, minced
> 12 cups chopped peeled fresh tomatoes (about 24 medium)
> 3 bay leaves
> 4 teaspoons salt
> 2 teaspoons dried oregano
> 1/2 teaspoon dried basil
> 2 cans (6 ounces *each*) tomato paste
> 1/3 cup packed brown sugar
> Hot cooked pasta

In a large Dutch oven, heat oil. Saute the onions and pepper until onions are tender. Add garlic, tomatoes, bay leaves, salt, oregano and basil. Simmer for 2 hours, stirring occasionally, Add tomato paste and brown sugar; simmer 1 hour longer. Remove bay leaves. Serve over pasta. **Yield:** 2 quarts.

—*Sondra Bergy*
Lowell, Michigan

Spinach-Topped Tomatoes

Spinach-Topped Tomatoes

It's best to use large tomatoes for this recipe. If desired, seed the tomatoes first by cutting in half and gently squeezing the tomato over a bowl. Use a spoon to remove any remaining seeds.

> 1 package (10 ounces) frozen chopped spinach
> 2 chicken bouillon cubes
> Salt
> 3 large tomatoes, halved
> 1 cup soft bread crumbs
> 1/2 cup grated Parmesan cheese
> 1/2 cup chopped onion
> 1/2 cup butter *or* margarine, melted
> 1 egg, beaten
> 1 garlic clove, minced
> 1/4 teaspoon pepper
> 1/8 teaspoon cayenne pepper
> Shredded Parmesan cheese, optional

Cook spinach according to package directions, adding the bouillon; drain well. Press out excess liquid. Lightly salt tomato halves; place cut side down on a paper towel for 15 minutes to absorb excess moisture. Meanwhile, in a small bowl, combine spinach, bread crumbs, grated Parmesan cheese, onion, butter, egg, garlic, pepper and cayenne; mix well. Place tomato halves cut side up in a shallow baking dish. Divide the spinach mixture over tomatoes. Sprinkle with shredded Parmesan cheese if desired. Bake, uncovered, at 350° for about 15 minutes or until heated through. **Yield:** 6 servings.

—*Ila Alderman, Galax, Virginia*

Root Vegetable Medley

Root Vegetable Medley

Looking for a delicious way to serve nutritious root vegetables? Try this idea! To avoid overcooking, test the vegetables for tenderness often with a fork.

> 6 small red potatoes, quartered
> 1 medium rutabaga, peeled and cut into 1-inch cubes
> 3 medium carrots, cut into 1/2-inch slices
> 1 medium turnip, peeled and cut into 1-inch cubes
> 1 to 2 medium parsnips, peeled and cut into 1/2-inch slices
> 2 large leeks (white portion only), cut into 1-inch slices

GLAZE:

> 1 tablespoon butter *or* margarine
> 3 tablespoons brown sugar
> 1 teaspoon cornstarch
> 1/4 cup water
> 3 tablespoons lemon juice
> 1/2 teaspoon dill weed
> 1/2 teaspoon salt
> 1/8 teaspoon pepper

Place potatoes and rutabaga in a large saucepan; cover with water. Bring to a boil. Reduce heat; cover and simmer for 8 minutes. Add remaining vegetables; return to a boil. Reduce heat; cover and simmer for 10 minutes or until vegetables are tender. Drain. For glaze, melt butter in a saucepan; stir in brown sugar and cornstarch. Stir in water, lemon juice, dill, salt and pepper; bring to a boil. Cook and stir for 2 minutes. Pour over vegetables and toss to coat. **Yield:** 8 servings.
—*Marilyn Smudzinski, Peru, Illinois*

Parsnip Saute

Peel parsnips as you would peel a carrot and boil just until crisp-tender. They'll become tender when cooked with the other vegetables.

> 3 large parsnips, peeled and diced
> 2 tablespoons butter *or* margarine
> 1/2 cup diced carrot
> 1/2 cup sliced celery
> 1/2 cup diced onion
> 3/4 teaspoon salt
> 1/8 teaspoon pepper

Place parsnips in a saucepan and cover with water. Cover and bring to a boil; boil for 15 minutes or until crisp-tender. Drain. In a skillet over medium heat, melt butter. Saute carrot, celery and onion until crisp-tender, about 6 minutes. Add the parsnips, salt and pepper; cook and stir for 4 minutes or until all vegetables are tender. **Yield:** 6 servings.
—*Janice Van Wassehnova, South Rockwood, Michigan*

Condiments

As a treat for family and friends, why not prepare such homemade sensations as Cranberry Salsa (p. 291), Lemon Curd (p. 291) and Tri-Berry Jam (p. 296)? They'll tastefully top off a variety of your favorite foods.

Condiments add flavor and enhance other foods, either as a cooking ingredient or as a topping at the table. They can be as simple as salt or pepper or a little more elaborate like mustards, jams, jellies, salsas, relishes and pickled vegetables.

Northwest Cherry Salsa

Serve this zesty salsa with leftover chicken or turkey to add interest the second time around!

 1 cup fresh *or* frozen pitted dark sweet cherries, chopped
 2 tablespoons chopped fresh basil *or* 2 teaspoons dried basil
 1 tablespoon finely chopped green pepper
 1 teaspoon lemon juice
 1/4 teaspoon Worcestershire sauce
 1/4 teaspoon grated lemon peel
 1/8 teaspoon salt
Dash hot pepper sauce

Combine all ingredients; cover and refrigerate at least 1 hour before serving. Store in the refrigerator. **Yield:** 3/4 cup. 🍎
—*Margaret Slocum*
Ridgefield, Washington

Fresh Tomato Salsa

A jar of this homemade salsa and a bag of tortilla chips make a nice gift for an informal get-together. Also try this as a topping for grilled chicken breasts.

 4 cups chopped peeled fresh tomatoes (about 2-1/2 pounds)
 1/4 cup finely chopped onion
 1 to 4 jalapeno peppers, seeded and finely chopped
 1 tablespoon olive *or* vegetable oil
 1 tablespoon vinegar
 1 teaspoon ground cumin
 1 teaspoon salt
 1 garlic clove, minced

In a bowl, combine all ingredients; mix well. Let stand for about 1 hour. Serve at room temperature. Cover and store in the refrigerator for up to 1 week. **Yield:** 3-1/2 cups. 🍎
—*Myra Innes, Auburn, Kansas*

Spicy Garden Salsa

If you have tomatoes, peppers and onions in your garden, why not "put up" a batch of salsa for the long winter ahead? (See the canning information on page 294.)

 10 cups chopped peeled fresh tomatoes (about 6 pounds)
 5 cups chopped green peppers (about 2 pounds)
 5 cups chopped onions (about 1-1/2 pounds)
 2-1/2 cups chopped seeded chili peppers (about 1 pound)
 1-1/4 cups cider vinegar
 3 garlic cloves, minced
 2 tablespoons minced fresh cilantro *or* parsley
 1 tablespoon salt

In a large kettle, combine all ingredients; bring to a boil. Reduce heat; simmer, uncovered, for 10 minutes. Ladle hot mixture into hot jars, leaving 1/4-in. headspace. Adjust caps. Process for 15 minutes in a boiling-water bath. **Yield:** about 8 pints. 🍎

Northwest Cherry Salsa

Sweet-and-Sour Mustard

When heating this homemade mustard, be careful to stir the ingredients constantly—doing so evenly distributes the eggs. Enjoy this as a dipping sauce for pretzels or spread it on sandwiches.

>   1 cup packed brown sugar
>   1/2 cup cider *or* raspberry vinegar
>   1/3 cup ground mustard
>   2 tablespoons water
>   2 eggs, lightly beaten

In a saucepan, whisk together all ingredients. Cook over low heat, stirring constantly, until mixture thickens and reaches 160°. Pour into small jars. Cover and store in the refrigerator for up to 1 week. **Yield:** 1-1/2 cups.
—*Cheri White, Richland, Michigan*

Sweet-and-Sour Mustard

Cranberry Salsa

(Pictured on page 288)

Fruit salsas make wonderful meat relishes. This cranberry salsa is especially festive served with Cornish game hens, turkey or pork.

>   2 cups fresh *or* frozen cranberries
>   2 cups water
>   1/2 cup sugar
>   1/4 to 1/2 cup minced fresh cilantro *or* parsley
>   2 to 4 tablespoons chopped seeded jalapeno peppers
>   1/4 cup finely chopped onion
>   2 tablespoons grated orange peel
>   1/2 teaspoon salt
>   1/4 teaspoon pepper

In a saucepan, bring cranberries and water to a boil; boil for 2 minutes. Drain. Stir in sugar until dissolved. Add cilantro, peppers, onion, orange peel, salt and pepper; mix well. Cool. Cover and store in the refrigerator. **Yield:** 2 cups.
—*Arline Roggenbuck Shawano, Wisconsin*

Easy Applesauce

Homemade applesauce can be pureed in a food processor or food mill until smooth for a fine texture. If you like chunky applesauce, use a potato masher to break up the apples to the desired consistency.

>   8 cups chopped peeled tart apples (about 3-1/2 pounds)
>   1/2 cup packed brown sugar
>   2 teaspoons vanilla extract
>   1 teaspoon ground cinnamon

Place all ingredients in a large saucepan or Dutch oven. Cover and cook over medium-low heat for 30-40 minutes or until apples are tender. Remove from the heat; mash until sauce has reached the desired consistency. Serve warm or cold. Cover and store in the refrigerator. **Yield:** 6 servings (about 3-1/2 cups).
—*Deborah Amrine, Grand Haven, Michigan*

Lemon Curd

(Pictured on page 289)

Curd is a thick and tangy spread for toast, biscuits or scones. It can also be used as a filling for small tart shells.

>   3 eggs
>   1 cup sugar
>   1/2 cup fresh lemon juice (about 2 lemons)
>   1/4 cup butter *or* margarine, melted
>   1 tablespoon grated lemon peel

In the top of a double boiler, beat eggs and sugar. Stir in lemon juice, butter and lemon peel. Cook over simmering water for 15 minutes or until mixture thickens and reaches 160°. Chill before serving. Cover and store in the refrigerator for up to 1 week. **Yield:** 1-2/3 cups.
—*Margaret Balakowski, Kingsville, Ontario*

Beet Relish

Prepare this recipe with either freshly cooked beets or two 15-ounce cans of beets, drained and shredded.

2 cups coarsely shredded cooked beets
3 tablespoons vegetable oil
2 tablespoons chopped red onion
2 tablespoons red wine vinegar
2 tablespoons Dijon mustard
1 teaspoon sugar
Salt and pepper to taste

Combine all ingredients in a small bowl and blend well. Cover and chill for at least 4 hours before serving. Store in the refrigerator for up to 1 week. **Yield:** about 2 cups. *—Evelyn Kenney, Trenton, New Jersey*

Easy Berry Relish

For holiday meal preparation, here's a do-ahead relish that will make a perfect complement to a turkey dinner. Substitute cranberry gelatin for the raspberry if you like.

1 package (12 ounces) fresh *or* frozen cranberries
2-1/2 cups sugar
1-2/3 cups ginger ale
1/3 cup lemon juice
1 package (3 ounces) raspberry gelatin

In a saucepan, combine the first four ingredients. Cook over medium heat until the berries pop, about 15 minutes. Remove from the heat; stir in gelatin until dissolved. Pour into a serving bowl. Cover and chill for 8 hours or overnight before serving. Store in the refrigerator. **Yield:** 5 cups.
—Dorothy Anderson
Ottawa, Kansas

Cranberry Apple Relish

This tart and tangy relish is made with uncooked cranberries. When using frozen cranberries, don't thaw them before chopping for best results.

1 navel orange
4 cups fresh *or* frozen cranberries
4 large red apples, peeled and shredded
2 cups sugar

Finely grate orange rind and set aside. Peel off and discard white membrane. Slice the orange into eight pieces. Place a fourth of the cranberries and orange slices in a food processor or blender; cover and process until evenly chopped. Transfer to a large bowl; repeat until all cranberries and oranges have been chopped.

Beet Relish

Stir in the rind, apples and sugar. Cover and chill for 4 hours or overnight before serving. Store in the refrigerator. **Yield:** 6 cups.
—Bonnie Lee Morris
Chase, British Columbia

Dilled Onions

Served as a relish or on sandwiches, these onions are especially tasty when the sweet Vidalia onions are in season. But don't hesitate to make them anytime of year.

2 large sweet onions, cut into 1/4-inch slices
1 teaspoon dill seed
1/2 cup sugar
1/2 cup vinegar
1/4 cup water
1 teaspoon salt

Sprinkle onions with dill seed. Layer in a wide-mouth pint jar. In saucepan, combine remaining ingredients; cook and stir over medium heat until sugar is dissolved. Pour over onions. Cover and chill 36 hours before serving. Store in the refrigerator. **Yield:** 2 cups.
—Donna Torres, Grand Rapids, Minnesota

Pickled Mushrooms

Make relish trays more interesting with the addition of home-made pickled vegetables like these mushrooms. To make your own tarragon vinegar for this recipe, see the Herb Vinegar recipe on page 73.

    2/3 cup tarragon vinegar
    1/2 cup vegetable oil
    2 tablespoons water
    1 tablespoon sugar
    1-1/2 teaspoons salt
    1 garlic clove, minced
    Dash hot pepper sauce
    1 pound fresh mushrooms
    1 medium onion, thinly sliced into rings
    Finely diced sweet red pepper

In a glass bowl, combine the first seven ingredients.

Pickled Mushrooms

Add mushrooms and onion; toss to coat. Cover and chill for 8 hours or overnight. Sprinkle with red pepper before serving. Store in the refrigerator. **Yield:** 4 cups.
—*Sandra Johnson, Tioga, Pennsylvania*

Homemade Steak Sauce

There's no need to buy steak sauce when you can prepare your own. Add more garlic if you like and a dash of hot pepper sauce if you want more zest.

    2 cups ketchup
    2/3 cup chopped onion
    1/2 cup *each* lemon juice, water, Worcestershire
        sauce and vinegar
    1/4 cup soy sauce
    1/4 cup packed dark brown sugar
    2 tablespoons prepared mustard
    2 garlic cloves, minced

Combine all of the ingredients in a 3-qt. saucepan; bring to a boil over medium heat. Reduce heat and simmer, uncovered, for 30 minutes. Cool. Strain if desired. Cover and store in the refrigerator. **Yield:** about 3 cups. —*Patricia Yurcisin, Barnesboro, Pennsylvania*

Pesto

Toss a few tablespoons of pesto with hot or chilled cooked pasta. Or for fun and added flavor, stir 1 to 2 tablespoons into individual servings of your favorite vegetable soup.

    1 cup tightly packed fresh basil *or* cilantro
        leaves
    1 cup tightly packed fresh parsley leaves
    1 to 2 garlic cloves, peeled
    1/2 cup olive *or* vegetable oil
    1/2 cup grated Parmesan cheese
    1/4 teaspoon salt

Place all ingredients in a food processor. Cover and process on high until pureed. Refrigerate for several weeks or freeze in a tightly covered container for up to 6 months. **Yield:** 3/4 cup.

If you've ever sampled home-canned goods, you'll agree that no store-bought varieties can beat their delicious, wholesome flavor. Most jams, jellies, relishes and pickles are preserved by processing in a boiling-water bath, a technique that you, too, can master with a little practice!

Canning Tips

- Select fruits and vegetables that are free of blemishes. Wash thoroughly and prepare according to recipe directions.

- Measure all ingredients and lay out all equipment before beginning.

- Only use canning or mason jars that are recommended for home canning. They come in a wide variety of sizes and styles. Check all jars to make sure they are in good condition. Don't use jars with any chips or cracks.

- The jar is sealed with a two-piece cap consisting of a flat lid and screw band. The lid is not reusable, but the band can be reused if it isn't warped or rusty.

- Your boiling-water-bath canner should have a base deep enough to hold the jars with 1 to 2 inches of water to cover the two-piece cap. It will also contain a rack to hold jars upright and a lid to keep water boiling during processing.

- A jar lifter, which is a rubber-coated grip for moving the hot jars in and out of the canner, is also an important tool.

- Use a canning funnel when pouring the product into jars to keep the rim area of the canning jar clean. Wipe the threads and rim of each jar to remove any food that may have spilled.

- Follow directions for each recipe exactly without substituting ingredients or changing processing times. Prepare only one recipe at a time—do not double recipes.

- Store home-canned foods in a cool location (50° to 70°) for up to 1 year for maximum flavor, color and nutritional value.

- When canning pickles, use canning salt to keep the brine from turning cloudy and the pickles from turning dark.

Boiling-Water-Bath Basics

1 Wash jars and two-piece caps in hot soapy water; rinse thoroughly. Dry bands on a towel. Put jars in a large kettle with enough water to cover; simmer to 180°. Remove from the heat. Place lids in a small saucepan and cover with water; simmer to 180°. Remove from the heat.

2 Place rack in canner. Add several inches of water; bring to a simmer. Meanwhile, prepare recipe. Ladle or pour hot mixture into hot jars, leaving the recommended amount of headspace for expansion during processing.

3 Wipe threads and rim of jar with a clean damp cloth. Place a warm lid on each jar with the sealing compound next to the glass. Screw a band onto the jar just until a point of resistance is met.

4 Immediately after filling each jar, use a jar lifter to place the jar onto the rack in the canner, making sure the jars are not touching. Lower the rack when filled. If necessary, add enough boiling water to canner to cover jar lids by 1 to 2 in. Cover the canner with its lid. Adjust heat to hold a steady rolling boil. Start counting the processing time when the water returns to a boil. If the water level decreases while processing, add additional boiling water.

5 When the processing time has ended, remove jars from the canner with jar lifter. Stand upright on a towel, out of drafts. After 12 to 24 hours, test each of the lids to determine if they have sealed by pressing the center of the lid. If it is concave (indented), remove the band and try to lift the lid. If the lid is secure, the jar is vacuum-sealed. Wipe the jars to remove any food. Label and date the jars.

Reprocessing Unsealed Jars

If a lid does not seal within 24 hours, the product must either be stored in the refrigerator and used within several days or reprocessed. To reprocess:

- Remove and discard the lid. The band may be reused if in good condition. Don't reuse a jar with chips or cracks.

- Reheat the product. Ladle or pour hot mixture into a hot clean jar, leaving the recommended amount of headspace. Adjust cap.

- Process in a boiling-water bath as recipe directs.

Heavenly Jam

Heavenly Jam

This recipe uses the natural pectin from the fruit and does not require commercially made pectin.

2 medium oranges
1 lemon
Pinch baking soda
6 medium pears
6 medium peaches
6 medium apples
Sugar

Grind unpeeled oranges and lemon in a food processor or grinder; transfer to a large kettle. Add baking soda; simmer for 10 minutes. Peel and core the remaining fruit; grind or process until finely chopped. Add to orange mixture; measure and return to kettle. Add sugar equal to the amount of fruit. Boil until thick, about 30 minutes. Pour hot mixture into hot jars, leaving 1/4-in. headspace. Adjust caps. Process for 20 minutes in a boiling-water bath. **Yield:** about 7 pints.

—*Kathleen Bailey, Penetanguishene, Ontario*

Strawberry Rhubarb Jam

If the rhubarb and strawberry harvests are at different times, freeze the fruit in recipe-size portions until you have enough to prepare this recipe.

2-1/2 cups fresh *or* frozen strawberries, crushed
1-1/2 cups finely diced fresh *or* frozen rhubarb
2-1/2 cups sugar
1 can (8 ounces) crushed pineapple, undrained
1 package (3 ounces) strawberry gelatin

In a large kettle, combine strawberries, rhubarb, sugar and pineapple. Bring to a boil; reduce heat and simmer for 20 minutes. Remove from the heat; stir in gelatin until dissolved. Pour into jars or freezer containers, leaving 1/2-in. headspace. Cool. Top with lids. Refrigerate or freeze. **Yield:** 5-1/2 cups. ○

—*Deb Kooistra, Kitchener, Ontario*

Tri-Berry Jam

(Also pictured on page 289)

Freeze the berries as they come in season until you have enough of each to make this recipe.

4 cups fresh *or* frozen blueberries
2-1/2 cups fresh *or* frozen red raspberries
2-1/2 cups fresh *or* frozen strawberries
1/4 cup lemon juice
2 packages (1-3/4 ounces *each*) powdered fruit pectin
11 cups sugar

Combine the berries and lemon juice in a large kettle; crush fruit lightly. Stir in pectin. Bring to a full rolling boil over high heat, stirring constantly. Stir in sugar; return to a full rolling boil. Boil 1 minute, stirring constantly. Remove from the heat; skim off foam. Pour hot mixture into hot jars, leaving 1/4-in. headspace. Adjust caps. Process for 15 minutes in a boiling-water bath. **Yield:** about 6 pints.
—*Karen Maerkle*
Baltic, Connecticut

Rhubarb Jelly

A jelly bag is used in this recipe to strain the juice from the pulp of the rhubarb. If you don't have a jelly bag, line a colander with several thicknesses of cheesecloth. The jelly bag or the cheesecloth must be dampened with water before using.

4-1/2 to 5 pounds rhubarb (4-1/2 to 5 quarts), cut into 1-inch pieces
7 cups sugar
1 to 2 drops red food coloring, optional
2 pouches (3 ounces *each*) liquid fruit pectin

Grind the rhubarb in a food processor or grinder. Strain through a jelly bag, reserving 3-1/2 cups of juice. Pour juice into a large kettle; add sugar and food coloring if desired. Bring to a boil over high heat, stirring constantly. Add pectin; bring to a full rolling boil. Boil for 1 minute, stirring constantly. Remove from the heat; let stand a few minutes. Skim off foam. Pour hot liquid into hot jars, leaving 1/4-in. headspace. Adjust caps. Process for 10 minutes in a boiling-water bath. **Yield:** 8 half-pints.
—*Jean Coleman*
Ottawa, Ontario

Making Berry Jams

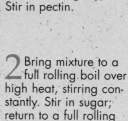

1 In a large kettle, combine berries and lemon juice (if required). Crush lightly with a potato masher or the back of a large spoon. Stir in pectin.

2 Bring mixture to a full rolling boil over high heat, stirring constantly. Stir in sugar; return to a full rolling boil. Boil for 1 minute, stirring constantly.

3 Remove from the heat and skim off foam with a large spoon. Proceed with recipe.

Oven Apple Butter

This apple butter needs less stirring than those prepared on top of the stove. It is important to tightly cover the roaster for the first 3 hours of baking to avoid excess evaporation.

40 large tart apples (about 13 pounds), quartered and cored
1/4 cup water
8 cups sugar
1 cup cider vinegar
4 teaspoons ground cinnamon
1 cinnamon stick (3 inches)

In a large kettle, cover and simmer the apples and water until tender. Press through a sieve or food mill. Measure 1 gallon of pulp; place in a large heavy roaster. Add sugar, vinegar, cinnamon and cinnamon stick. Cover and bake at 400° for 3 hours, stirring often.
Uncover and bake 1 hour longer or until very thick, stirring occasionally. Remove cinnamon stick. Pour hot mixture into hot jars, leaving 1/4-in. headspace. Adjust caps. Process for 10 minutes in a boiling-water bath. **Yield:** 8 pints.
—*Virginia McNeese*
Greenville, Illinois

Using a Sieve to Puree

Position the sieve over a large bowl. Place cooked fruit, a few at a time, in sieve; press fruit through the sieve with the back of a large spoon. Repeat with remaining fruit. Proceed with recipe as directed.

Rhubarb Jelly
Tri-Berry Jam
Oven Apple Butter

Red Corn Relish

Use a food processor to chop the onions, peppers and cucumbers and shred the cabbage. Tomatoes are best chopped by hand.

4-1/2 cups fresh-cut sweet corn kernels (about 9 ears)
4 pounds tomatoes, peeled and chopped
3 cups shredded cabbage
3 large cucumbers, seeded and chopped
3 large onions, chopped
1 large sweet red pepper, chopped
1 large green pepper, chopped
2 cups sugar
1-1/2 cups vinegar
1/4 cup salt
1 tablespoon celery seed
1 tablespoon mustard seed
1-1/2 teaspoons ground turmeric

Combine all ingredients in a large Dutch oven. Bring to a boil over medium heat, stirring occasionally. Reduce heat; simmer, uncovered, for 40 minutes or until vegetables are tender and mixture has thickened. Pack hot mixture into hot jars, leaving 1/4-in. headspace. Adjust caps. Process for 15 minutes in a boiling-water bath. **Yield:** about 10 pints. —*Belva Parker*
Viroqua, Wisconsin

Red Corn Relish

Seeding Cucumbers

Cut the cucumbers in half lengthwise. With a teaspoon, scrape out the seeds; discard.

Tomato Chutney

This spicy relish is wonderful served with ham or poultry. Chutney also makes a great appetizer spread. Simply spread one 8-ounce package of cream cheese on a serving plate; top with 1 cup of chutney and serve with crackers.

2 pounds tomatoes, peeled and coarsely chopped
1 pound tart apples, peeled, cored and chopped
2 medium onions, chopped
1 cup cider vinegar
1 tablespoon salt
1 cup packed brown sugar
1 cup golden raisins
1 garlic clove, minced
1/2 teaspoon ground cinnamon
1/2 teaspoon ground mustard
1/4 teaspoon cayenne pepper
1/8 teaspoon ground allspice
1/8 teaspoon ground ginger
1/8 teaspoon ground cloves

Combine all the ingredients in a large saucepan; bring to a boil. Reduce heat and simmer, uncovered, for 1-1/2 to 2 hours or until mixture thickens, stirring frequently. Pack hot mixture into hot jars, leaving 1/4-in. headspace. Adjust caps. Process for 10 minutes in a boiling-water bath. **Yield:** 3 pints. —*Mrs. W.C. Tucker*
San Antonio, Texas

Freezer Cucumber Pickles

If time is short and the garden has given you lots of pickling cucumbers, make these sweet and crunchy pickles. They're a real hit at picnics and potluck suppers.

- 4 pounds pickling cucumbers, sliced
- 8 cups thinly sliced onions
- 1/4 cup canning salt
- 3/4 cup water
- 4 cups sugar
- 2 cups cider vinegar

Combine cucumbers, onions, salt and water in two large bowls. Let stand at room temperature for 2 hours. Do not drain. Add sugar and vinegar; stir until sugar dissolves. Pack into 1-pint freezer containers, leaving 1-in. headspace. Cover and freeze for up to 6 weeks. Thaw at room temperature for 4 hours before serving. **Yield:** 10 pints.

—Connie Goense
Pembroke Pines, Florida

Dill Pickle Spears

Using a cheesecloth bag to hold the pickling spices makes it easy to remove after the brine has boiled. (See Making a Spice Bag on page 93.)

- 1 quart vinegar
- 1 quart water
- 3/4 cup sugar
- 3/4 cup canning salt
- 3 tablespoons mixed pickling spices
- 25 to 30 medium pickling cucumbers, cut lengthwise into quarters
- 8 fresh dill heads
- 8 garlic cloves, peeled

In a saucepan, combine vinegar, water, sugar and salt; bring to a boil. Tie pickling spices in a cheesecloth bag. Place in the hot liquid; bring to a boil. Boil for 10 minutes. Remove cheesecloth bag and discard. Place dill heads in the bottom of eight pint jars. Pack cucumbers into jars to within 1/2 in. of jar top. Place 1 garlic clove in each jar. Ladle boiling liquid over cucumbers, leaving 1/4-in. headspace. Adjust caps. Process for 10 minutes in a boiling-water bath. **Yield:** 8 pints.

—Polly Coumos, Mogadore, Ohio

Bread 'n' Butter Pickles

When the garden has produced more cucumbers, onions and green peppers than you can use in salads, it's time to make pickles! Canning salt keeps the brine clear and sparkling.

- 8 pounds large cucumbers (about 12), cut into 1/4-inch slices
- 8 large onions, cut into 1/8-inch slices
- 4 large green peppers, sliced
- 2/3 cup canning salt
- 6 cups vinegar
- 6 cups sugar
- 2 teaspoons celery seed
- 2 teaspoons mustard seed
- 1 teaspoon ground turmeric

In a large container, combine cucumbers, onions, green peppers and salt. Add enough cold water to cover. Chill for 2 hours. Drain and rinse. In a large kettle, combine remaining ingredients; bring to a boil. Add cucumber mixture; return to a boil. Ladle hot mixture into hot jars, leaving 1/4-in. headspace. Adjust caps. Process for 10 minutes in a boiling-water bath. **Yield:** 10 pints.

—Muriel Looney, Eugene, Oregon

Bread 'n' Butter Pickles

Desserts

You'll taste sweet success with dessert delights like Strawberry Cheesecake (p. 302) and Milky Way Ice Cream (p. 313). Family and friends will savor every mouth-watering morsel of the cheesecakes, custards, puddings, shortcake, ice cream and more in this chapter.

Desserts are an excellent way to display your creativity to dinner guests. In this chapter, you will find desserts for many occasions and for cooks of any skill level. And for the final touch that is sure to impress, don't forget to garnish your creations—whether with a simple sprinkle of nutmeg or a sprig of fresh mint.

Tips for Making Cheesecake

- For best results, it's recommended that you not use light, low-fat or fat-free cream cheese and sour cream.

- Always soften cream cheese at room temperature before mixing. Or to soften in the microwave, place an unwrapped 8-ounce package of cream cheese on a microwave-safe plate; microwave on medium for 1 to 1-1/2 minutes or until softened.

- Add the eggs one at a time, beating on low speed after each addition just until blended. Avoid overbeating.

- Open the oven door as little as possible while baking the cheesecake.

- A cheesecake is done when the edges are slightly puffed and the center (about the size of a walnut) is still soft and moist. The center will firm upon cooling. A crack in the cheesecake may be an indicator of overbaking.

- As soon as you remove a cheesecake from the oven, run a sharp knife around the edge to loosen the crust from the springform pan. Don't remove the sides of the pan.

- Cool the cheesecake on a wire rack in a draft-free location for 1 hour; refrigerate, uncovered, for at least 3-4 hours. When the cheesecake is cold, cover it with a piece of foil or plastic wrap across the top of the pan and refrigerate over-night before serving.

- When ready to serve, loosen the latch of the springform and carefully lift the rim of the pan straight up. Slice the cheesecake chilled, but for maximum flavor, allow slices to stand at room temperature for 15-30 minutes before serving.

Strawberry Cheesecake

(Pictured on page 300)

This is a classic sour cream-topped cheesecake that can be prepared with the strawberry glaze and fresh berries for a summertime delight or served plain anytime of year.

CRUST:
   3/4 cup ground pecans
   3/4 cup graham cracker crumbs
   3 tablespoons butter *or* margarine, melted
FILLING:
   4 packages (8 ounces *each*) cream cheese, softened
 1-1/4 cups sugar
   1 tablespoon lemon juice
   2 teaspoons vanilla extract
   4 eggs
TOPPING:
   2 cups (16 ounces) sour cream
   1/4 cup sugar
   1 teaspoon vanilla extract
STRAWBERRY GLAZE:
   2 tablespoons cornstarch
   1/4 cup water
   1 jar (12 ounces) strawberry jelly
   3 tablespoons orange-flavored liqueur *or* lemon juice
Red food coloring, optional
   1 quart whole fresh strawberries, hulled

Combine pecans, crumbs and butter. Press onto the bottom of a 10-in. springform pan; set aside. For filling, beat cream cheese in a mixing bowl until smooth. Add sugar, lemon juice and vanilla; mix just until combined. Add eggs one at a time, beating on low after each addition. Spoon over crust. Bake at 350° for 50 minutes or until filling is almost set. Remove from the oven and let stand for 15 minutes, but leave oven on. Meanwhile, combine sour cream, sugar and vanilla; spread over cheesecake. Return to the hot oven for 5 minutes. Cool on a wire rack for 1 hour; refrigerate 3-4 hours uncovered. Cover and refrigerate 24 hours. Several hours before serving, prepare glaze: In a saucepan, combine cornstarch and water until smooth. Add jelly and cook over medium-high heat, stirring constantly, until jelly melts and the mixture thickens. Remove from the heat; stir in liqueur or lemon juice and food coloring if desired. Cool to room temperature. Just before serving, loosen and remove sides of springform pan. Arrange strawberries on top of cake with pointed ends up. Spoon glaze over berries, allowing some to drip down sides of cake. Refrigerate leftovers. **Yield:** 12 servings.—*L.C. Herschap, Luling, Texas*

Making Meringue Cups

1 In a large mixing bowl, beat egg whites, vinegar, vanilla and salt until the egg whites begin to increase in volume and soft peaks form. (Stop the mixer and pull the beaters out of the mixture. The peaks should fall over.)

2 While beating, add 1 cup sugar 1 tablespoon at a time. Beat until stiff peaks form. (Stop the mixer and pull the beaters out of the mixture. The peaks should stand up straight.)

3 Cover a baking sheet with plain brown wrapping paper, parchment paper or foil. Divide meringue equally into eight mounds. Using the back of a spoon, make an indentation in the center of each mound to form a 3-in. cup.

4 Bake as directed. After 1 hour, remove meringues from oven and cool completely on baking sheet. Carefully remove meringues from paper and store in an airtight container at room temperature for up to 2 days.

Lemon Custard in Meringue Cups

You may want to watch the weather before making this dessert. Preparing meringues on a day that is high in humidity may cause them to weep or bead with tiny droplets of water.

    3 **eggs,** *separated*
    1/2 **teaspoon vinegar**
    1/4 **teaspoon vanilla extract**
    1/4 **teaspoon salt,** *divided*
    2 **cups sugar,** *divided*
    1/3 **cup cornstarch**
1-1/2 **cups water**
    6 **tablespoons lemon juice**
    2 **tablespoons butter** *or* **margarine**
    1 **tablespoon grated lemon peel**
Sweetened whipped cream (See Tips for Whipping Cream on page 322)

In a mixing bowl, combine egg whites, vinegar, vanilla and 1/8 teaspoon salt. Beat until soft peaks form. Gradually add 1 cup sugar; continue beating until stiff peaks form. Cover baking sheet with plain brown wrapping paper, parchment paper or foil. Spoon meringue into eight mounds on paper. Using the back of a spoon, shape into 3-in. cups. Bake at 300° for 35 minutes. Turn oven off and do not open door; let dry in oven 1 hour. Remove from the oven and cool on baking sheet. When cooled completely, remove meringues from paper and store in an airtight container at room temperature. For custard, combine cornstarch and remaining salt and sugar in a saucepan. Add water; stir until smooth. Cook and stir until thick and bubbly, about 2 minutes. Beat egg yolks; add a small amount of hot mixture. Return all to pan. Cook and stir 2 minutes longer. Remove from the heat; blend in lemon juice, butter and lemon peel. Chill. Just before serving, fill meringue shells with custard and top with whipped cream. **Yield:** 8 servings. —*Marie Frangipane Eugene, Oregon*

Strawberry Cream Puffs

This is a classic dessert shell that can be filled with whipped cream, ice cream, custard or fruit.

        1 cup water
    1/2 cup butter *or* margarine
        1 teaspoon sugar
    1/4 teaspoon salt
        1 cup all-purpose flour
        4 eggs
FILLING:
        2 pints fresh strawberries, sliced
    1/2 cup sugar, *divided*
        2 cups whipping cream
Confectioners' sugar
Additional sliced strawberries
Fresh mint

In a large saucepan, bring water, butter, sugar and salt to a boil. Add flour all at once and stir until a smooth ball forms. Remove from the heat; let stand for 5 minutes. Add eggs one at a time, beating well after each addition. Continue beating until mixture is smooth and shiny. Drop by 12 rounded tablespoonfuls 3 in. apart onto a greased baking sheet. Bake at 400° for 30-35 minutes or until golden brown. Transfer to a wire rack. Immediately cut a slit in each puff to allow steam to escape; cool. Split puffs and set tops aside; remove soft dough from inside with a fork. Cool puffs. For filling, combine berries and 1/4 cup sugar; chill for 30 minutes. Beat cream and remaining sugar until stiff. Fold in berries. Fill cream puffs and replace tops. Dust with confectioners' sugar; garnish with additional berries and mint. Serve immediately. **Yield:** 12 servings. 　　　　　*—Sherry Adams, Mt. Ayr, Iowa*

Making Cream Puffs

1 Bring water, butter, sugar and salt to a boil in a saucepan. Add flour all at once; stir briskly until the mixture leaves the sides of the pan and forms a smooth ball.

2 Remove from the heat and let stand for 5 minutes. Add eggs one at a time, beating well after each addition. Continue beating until mixture is smooth and shiny.

3 Drop by rounded tablespoonfuls 3 in. apart onto a greased baking sheet. Bake as directed in recipe.

4 Remove baked puffs to a wire rack. Immediately cut a slit in each puff to allow steam to escape; cool. Split puffs and set tops aside; remove soft dough from inside with a fork and discard. Cool puffs; fill as directed.

Strawberry Cream Puffs

Raspberry Trifle

Raspberry Trifle

A trifle is an English dessert containing layers of cake, pudding or custard and fruit or jam that is topped with whipped cream and sprinkled with nuts.

   1/4 cup sugar
     3 tablespoons cornstarch
     3 cups milk
     4 egg yolks, beaten
     2 teaspoons vanilla extract
     1 loaf (1 pound) frozen pound cake, thawed
   3/4 cup raspberry jam
     3 cups fresh *or* frozen unsweetened raspberries, thawed and drained
     1 cup whipping cream
     2 tablespoons confectioners' sugar
     2 tablespoons sliced almonds, toasted
Fresh raspberries, optional

In a heavy 2-qt. saucepan, combine sugar and cornstarch; gradually stir in milk. Bring to a boil over medium heat, stirring constantly. Boil for 2 minutes; remove from the heat. Gradually stir 1/2 cup into egg yolks; return all to pan and mix well. Cook and stir over medium-low heat for 15 minutes or until mixture thickens slightly (do not boil). Stir in vanilla. Pour into a bowl; press a piece of waxed paper or plastic wrap on top of the pudding. Chill for 20 minutes. Meanwhile, cut cake into 3/4-in. slices; spread with jam. Cut each slice into thirds; place with jam side up in a 3-qt. trifle dish or a deep salad bowl. Cover with berries. Top with pudding. Cover and chill overnight. Just before serving, whip cream and sugar until stiff; spread over pudding. Garnish with almonds and berries if desired. **Yield:** 10-12 servings.   —*Betty Howlett, Elmira, Ontario*

Old-Fashioned Rice Pudding

This recipe relies on the starch from rice to thicken the pudding. For those watching their fat intake, this is a good dessert to consider.

   3-1/2 cups skim milk
     1/2 cup uncooked long grain rice
     1/3 cup sugar
     1/2 teaspoon salt
     1/2 cup raisins
       1 teaspoon vanilla extract
Ground cinnamon, optional

In a saucepan, combine milk, rice, sugar and salt; bring to a boil over medium heat, stirring constantly. Pour into a greased 1-1/2-qt. baking dish. Cover and bake at 325° for 45 minutes, stirring every 15 minutes. Add raisins and vanilla; cover and bake 15 minutes longer. Sprinkle with cinnamon if desired. Serve warm or chilled. Store in the refrigerator. **Yield:** 4-6 servings.
    —*Sandra Melnychenko, Grandview, Manitoba*

Berry Rhubarb Fool

Berry Rhubarb Fool

A "fool" is a cold dessert that has sweetened cooked fruit folded into whipped cream and that is layered with fresh fruit.

> 3 cups sliced fresh *or* frozen rhubarb
>   (1-inch pieces)
> 1/3 cup sugar
> 1/4 cup orange juice
> Pinch salt
> 1 cup whipping cream
> 1 pint fresh strawberries, halved
> Additional sliced strawberries
> Fresh mint

In a saucepan, combine rhubarb, sugar, orange juice and salt; bring to a boil. Reduce heat; cover and simmer for 6-8 minutes or until rhubarb is tender. Cool slightly. Pour into a blender; cover and process until smooth. Chill. Just before serving, whip cream until stiff peaks form. Fold cream into rhubarb mixture until lightly streaked. In chilled parfait glasses, alternate layers of the cream mixture and strawberries. Garnish with strawberries and mint. **Yield:** 6 servings.   —*Cheryl Miller, Fort Collins, Colorado*

Chocolate Pudding

There's nothing like homemade pudding for a quick dessert. Be sure to add the vanilla after the pudding is cooked and removed from the heat to retain the maximum flavor.

> 1 cup sugar
> 1/2 cup baking cocoa
> 1/4 cup all-purpose flour
> 2 cups water
> 3/4 cup evaporated milk
> 1 tablespoon vanilla extract
> Pinch salt

In a saucepan, combine sugar, cocoa and flour. Add water and milk; stir until smooth. Cook over medium heat, stirring constantly, until mixture comes to a boil. Cook until thick, about 1 minute. Remove from the heat; stir in vanilla and salt. Cool to room temperature, stirring several times. Pour into a serving bowl or individual dishes. **Yield:** 4-6 servings.
          —*Donna Hughes, Rochester, New Hampshire*

Testing and Cooling Stirred Custards

1 To test a stirred custard for doneness, dip a metal spoon into the hot mixture. If the custard coats the back of the spoon (as shown at left), it is sufficiently cooked. If too thin, continue to cook.

2 Chill stirred custard quickly by placing the pan in a large bowl or sink of ice water. Stir for several minutes or until no longer hot. Proceed with recipe as directed.

Cherry Cheesecake Tarts

When you don't have time to bake a cherry cheesecake, here's the next best thing! Keep all the ingredients on hand to make this easy dessert on short notice.

1 package (10 ounces) frozen puff pastry shells
2 packages (3 ounces *each*) cream cheese, softened
1/4 cup confectioners' sugar
1/2 teaspoon almond extract
1 can (21 ounces) cherry pie filling
Additional confectioners' sugar

Bake pastry shells according to package directions. Meanwhile, in a mixing bowl, beat cream cheese, sugar and extract. With a fork, carefully remove the circular top of each baked shell and set aside. Remove any soft layers of pastry inside shells and discard. Divide the cheese filling between the shells; place on a baking sheet. Return to the oven for 5 minutes. Cool. Just before serving, fill each shell with pie filling. Top with reserved pastry circles. Dust with confectioners' sugar. **Yield:** 6 servings.
—*Mary Lindell Sanford, Michigan*

Stirred Lemon Rice Custard

Stirred custards, or those cooked on top of the stove, require long slow cooking with constant stirring until the mixture is thick enough to coat a spoon. It is then cooled quickly in ice water to stop the cooking.

1-1/2 quarts milk
2 cups cooked long grain rice, chilled
9 eggs, well beaten
1-1/2 cups sugar
1/2 teaspoon salt
2 teaspoons lemon extract
1/2 teaspoon grated lemon peel

In a Dutch oven over low heat, cook milk and rice for 1 hour. Combine eggs, sugar and salt. Slowly pour into hot rice mixture, stirring constantly. Cook over medium-low heat, stirring constantly, just until the mixture coats a metal spoon. Remove from the heat; stir in lemon extract and peel. Place pan in a large bowl or sink filled with ice for 1-2 minutes or until no longer hot, stirring constantly. Transfer custard to a bowl; press a piece of waxed paper or plastic wrap on top of the custard (see Preventing Film from Forming on Pudding on page 305). Refrigerate for several hours or overnight before serving. **Yield:** 14-16 servings.
—*Shirley Pewtress, Kaysville, Utah*

Cherry Cheesecake Tarts

Creamy Caramel Flan

A caramel flan is a custard baked over caramelized sugar. When the cooked and cooled flan is inverted onto a platter, the delicious caramel sauce runs over the flan. This dessert needs to be prepared the day before serving.

3/4 cup sugar
1 package (8 ounces) cream cheese, softened
5 eggs
1 can (14 ounces) sweetened condensed milk
1 can (12 ounces) evaporated milk
1 teaspoon vanilla extract

In a heavy saucepan over medium-low, heat sugar until melted, about 10 minutes. Do not stir. When sugar is melted, reduce heat to low and continue to cook, stirring occasionally, until syrup is golden, about 5 minutes. Quickly pour into an ungreased 2-qt. round baking or souffle dish, tilting to coat the bottom; let stand for 10 minutes. In a mixing bowl, beat cream cheese until smooth. Add eggs one at a time, beating well after each addition. Add milk and vanilla; mix well. Pour over caramelized sugar. Place the dish in a larger baking pan. Pour boiling water into larger pan to a depth of 1 in. Bake at 350° for 50-60 minutes or until center is just set (mixture will jiggle). Remove dish from larger pan to a wire rack; cool for 1 hour. Refrigerate overnight. To unmold, run a knife around edge and invert onto a large rimmed serving platter. Cut into wedges or spoon onto dessert plates; spoon sauce over each serving. **Yield:** 8-10 servings. *—Pat Forte Miami, Florida*

Creamy Caramel Flan

Making a Caramel Custard

1 Place sugar in a heavy saucepan over medium-low; heat the sugar until melted, about 10 minutes. Do not stir. When sugar is melted, reduce heat to low. Cook, stirring constantly, with a metal spoon, until syrup is golden, about 5 minutes.

2 Immediately pour into an ungreased 2-qt. round baking dish, tilting pan to evenly distribute caramelized sugar over the bottom of the pan. Let stand for 10 minutes.

3 Prepare custard as directed in recipe. Pour over caramelized sugar. Place dish in a baking pan and add boiling water to pan to a depth of 1 in. Bake and unmold as recipe directs.

Crunchy Baked Apples

When the autumn winds begin to blow, this is a wonderfully easy recipe to prepare. Make it earlier in the day and reheat in the microwave just until warm.

- 1/2 cup chopped walnuts
- 1/4 cup sugar
- 1/2 teaspoon ground cinnamon
- 1/4 cup packed brown sugar
- 1/4 cup raisins
- 6 tablespoons butter *or* margarine, melted, *divided*
- 4 medium tart apples
- 1 lemon, halved
- 4 cinnamon sticks (3 inches)
- 3/4 cup apple juice

In a blender or food processor, grind walnuts and sugar. Add cinnamon and set aside. Combine the brown sugar, raisins and 2 tablespoons of butter; set aside. Core apples and peel the top two-thirds of each. Rub tops and sides with lemon; squeeze juice into centers. Brush apples with 2 tablespoons butter; press nut mixture evenly over peeled portion. Place in an ungreased 9-in. baking dish. Fill apples with raisin mixture. Insert a cinnamon stick into each apple; drizzle with remaining butter. Pour apple juice around apples. Bake, uncovered, at 375° for 40-50 minutes or until tender. Cool for 15 minutes before serving. **Yield:** 4 servings.   —*Jayne King, Liberty, South Carolina*

Crunchy Baked Apples

Patriotic Dessert

The buttery pecan crust can be baked the day before the rest of this melt-in-your-mouth dessert is assembled.

- 1 cup all-purpose flour
- 1 cup finely chopped pecans

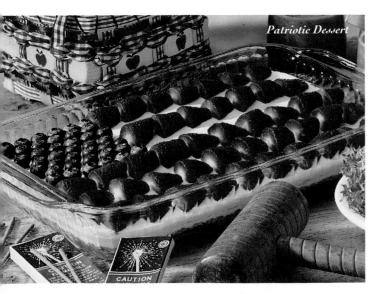

Patriotic Dessert

- 1/2 cup butter *or* margarine, softened
- 1 package (8 ounces) cream cheese, softened
- 1 cup confectioners' sugar
- 1 carton (16 ounces) frozen whipped topping, thawed, *divided*
- 1 package (5.1 ounces) instant vanilla pudding mix
- 1-1/2 cups cold milk
- 1/2 cup fresh blueberries
- 3 cups fresh strawberries, halved

Combine flour, pecans and butter. Press onto the bottom of an ungreased 13-in. x 9-in. x 2-in. baking pan. Bake at 350° for 20 minutes. Cool. In a mixing bowl, beat cream cheese and sugar. Fold in half of the whipped topping; mix until smooth. Spread over crust. In another mixing bowl, beat pudding and milk until smooth. Spread over cream cheese layer. Cover with remaining whipped topping. Decorate with blueberries and strawberries to resemble a flag, using blueberries as stars and strawberries as stripes. Refrigerate for at least 1 hour before serving. **Yield:** 12-15 servings.
—*Flo Burtnett, Gage, Oklahoma*

Fruit and Nut Bread Pudding

This is a pretty, tasty way to use stale bread. If you have some slices of leftover bread at the end of each week, place them in freezer bags and freeze until you have accumulated enough for this recipe.

16 slices day-old bread, torn into 1-inch pieces
2 cups sugar
4 eggs
3 cups milk
2 teaspoons ground cinnamon
1/2 teaspoon salt
2 tablespoons vanilla extract
1 can (21 ounces) apple pie filling
2 cups coarsely chopped pecans
1 cup golden raisins
3/4 cup butter *or* margarine, melted
Whipped cream, optional

In a large bowl, combine bread and sugar; set aside. In another bowl, beat eggs, milk, cinnamon, salt and vanilla until foamy. Pour over bread mixture; mix well. Cover and refrigerate for 2 hours. Cut apples from pie filling in half; add apples and filling to bread mixture. Stir in pecans, raisins and butter. Pour into a greased 13-in. x 9-in. x 2-in. baking pan. Bake at 350° for 45-50 minutes or until firm. Cut into squares. Serve warm or cold with whipped cream if desired. **Yield:** 12-15 servings. —*Alice Mathews, Alexandria, Louisiana*

Blueberry and Peach Cobbler

Cobbler is best served warm about 45-60 minutes after removing from the oven. If desired, pour a little half-and-half cream over each serving.

1/2 cup water
2 tablespoons sugar
2 tablespoons brown sugar
1 tablespoon cornstarch
1 tablespoon lemon juice
2 cups sliced peeled fresh peaches
1 cup blueberries
TOPPING:
1 cup all-purpose flour
1/4 cup sugar
1-1/2 teaspoons baking powder
1/2 teaspoon salt
1/2 cup milk
1/4 cup butter *or* margarine, melted

In a saucepan, combine the first five ingredients. Bring to a boil, stirring until thick. Add fruit. Pour into a greased 2-qt. baking dish. For topping, combine flour, sugar, baking powder and salt in a mixing bowl. Stir in milk and butter. Spread over fruit mixture. Bake at 375° for 50 minutes or until topping is golden brown and tests done. Serve warm. **Yield:** about 6 servings.
—*Laura Jansen, Battle Creek, Michigan*

Fruit and Nut Bread Pudding

Apple Crisp

To prevent lumps from developing in the sauce, thoroughly combine the sugar and cornstarch before adding the water.

1 cup all-purpose flour
1 cup packed brown sugar
3/4 cup old-fashioned *or* quick-cooking oats
1 teaspoon ground cinnamon
1/2 cup cold butter *or* margarine
4 cups coarsely chopped peeled apples
1 cup sugar
2 tablespoons cornstarch
1 cup water
1 teaspoon vanilla extract
Vanilla ice cream, optional

In a mixing bowl, combine the first four ingredients. Cut in butter until crumbly. Press half into a greased 2-1/2-qt. baking dish or 9-in. square baking pan. Top with apples. In a saucepan, combine sugar, cornstarch, water and vanilla; cook and stir until thick and clear. Pour over apples. Sprinkle with remaining crumb mixture. Bake at 350° for 1 hour or until the apples are tender. Serve warm with ice cream if desired. **Yield:** 8 servings. —*Gertrude Bartnick, Portage, Wisconsin*

Christmas Special Fruitcake

Removing fruitcakes from their pans can be difficult unless the pan is lined with waxed paper. See Lining a Baking Pan with Waxed Paper on page 320.

> 3 cups coarsely chopped Brazil nuts, walnuts, pecans *or* hazelnuts
> 1 pound pitted dates, coarsely chopped
> 1 cup halved maraschino cherries
> 3/4 cup all-purpose flour
> 3/4 cup sugar
> 1/2 teaspoon baking powder
> 1/2 teaspoon salt
> 3 eggs
> 1 teaspoon vanilla extract

In a mixing bowl, combine nuts, dates and cherries. In another bowl, combine flour, sugar, baking powder and salt; stir into nut mixture until nuts and fruit are well-coated. Beat eggs until foamy; stir in vanilla. Fold into nut mixture and mix well. Pour into a greased and waxed paper-lined 9-in. x 5-in. x 3-in. loaf pan. Bake at 300° for 1 hour and 45 minutes. Cool for 10 minutes; remove from pan to a wire rack. **Yield:** 24 servings.   —*Violet Cooper, Port Allegany, Pennsylvania*

Christmas Special Fruitcake

Strawberry Shortcake

This classic dessert can also be made with other seasonal fruits such as blueberries, raspberries or peaches. If desired, sprinkle 2 to 4 tablespoons sugar over the fruit 30 minutes before serving. The sugar will sweeten the fruit and make a tasty juice to spoon over each shortcake.

> 1/4 cup shortening
> 2/3 cup sugar
> 1 egg
> 1 teaspoon vanilla extract
> 1-1/2 cups all-purpose flour
> 2 teaspoons baking powder
> 1/4 teaspoon salt
> 1/2 cup milk
> Whipped cream
> 3 pints fresh strawberries, sliced

In a mixing bowl, cream shortening and sugar. Add egg and vanilla; beat well. Combine dry ingredients; add to the creamed mixture alternately with milk. Spread in a greased 9-in. square baking pan. Bake at 350° for 20-25 minutes. Cool on a wire rack. Cut into squares; split each piece in half horizontally. Spoon whipped cream and strawberries onto bottoms; replace tops. Garnish with more berries and whipped cream. Serve immediately. **Yield:** 9 servings.   —*Janet Becker Anacortes, Washington*

Buying and Storing Fresh Strawberries

- Purchase strawberries that are shiny, firm and very fragrant. A strawberry should be almost completely red, though some whiteness near the leafy cap is acceptable.

- Refrigerate unwashed strawberries with the caps on until ready to use. Just before using, wash and hull.

Tips for Making Homemade Ice Cream

- Before using your ice cream maker, it's important to read the manufacturer's instructions.

- Never use an ice cream recipe that does not cook the eggs thoroughly before the mixture is frozen.

- After freezing ice cream in your ice cream freezer, you will want to allow the mixture to "ripen" or harden before serving. Transfer the mixture from the ice cream freezer canister to chilled freezer containers and freeze for 3-4 hours.

- You may also leave the canister with the frozen ice cream in the machine. Remove the canister cover and dasher. Cover the canister opening with foil and replace the canister cover. Place a cork in the hole in the cover. Pack additional salt and ice into the machine to cover the lid of the canister. Let stand for 2-3 hours, adding more salt and ice as needed.

- When homemade ice cream has been in the freezer for more than 2-3 hours, you may need to let it stand at room temperature for 5-10 minutes for easier scooping.

Easy Chocolate Ice Cream

Use your blender to thoroughly combine the cocoa into the cream. Be sure to stir in the whipping cream by hand.

    2 cups half-and-half cream
1-1/2 cups sugar
    1/2 cup baking cocoa
      1 teaspoon vanilla extract
      2 cups whipping cream

Combine half-and-half, sugar, cocoa and vanilla in a blender; cover and process on low until smooth. Stir in whipping cream. Freeze in an ice cream freezer according to manufacturer's instructions. Allow to ripen in ice cream freezer or firm up in your refrigerator freezer 2-4 hours before serving. **Yield:** 1-1/2 quarts.

Cranberry Sherbet

After a big holiday meal, this is a welcome dessert to accompany your tray of Christmas cookies. Using gelatin and beating the frozen mixture keep this homemade sherbet smooth and creamy.

      1 package (12 ounces) fresh *or* frozen cranberries
2-3/4 cups water, *divided*
      2 cups sugar
      1 envelope unflavored gelatin
  1/2 cup orange juice

In a saucepan, combine cranberries and 2-1/2 cups of water. Bring to a boil; cook gently until all the berries have popped, about 10 minutes. Remove from the heat; cool slightly. Press mixture through a sieve or food mill (see Using a Sieve to Puree on page 297). Reserve juice; discard skins and seeds. In another saucepan, combine cranberry juice and sugar; cook over medium heat until the sugar dissolves. Remove from the heat and set aside. Combine gelatin and remaining water; stir until softened. Add to cranberry mixture with orange juice; mix well. Pour into a 2-qt. container; freeze for 4-5 hours or until mixture is slushy. Remove from the freezer; beat with an electric mixer until sherbet is a bright pink color. Freeze until firm. **Yield:** about 1-1/2 quarts.
      —*Heather Clement, Indian River, Ontario*

Cranberry Sherbet

Milky Way Ice Cream

(Also pictured on page 301)

It is important to chill the cooked egg mixture thoroughly before placing it in the ice cream maker to freeze. The colder the mixture, the faster it will freeze and the creamier the ice cream will be.

>   16 ounces Milky Way candy bars
>   1 quart whipping cream, *divided*
>   4 eggs
>   1-1/2 quarts milk
>   1 package (3.9 ounces) instant chocolate fudge
>   pudding mix
>   1 package (3.4 ounces) instant vanilla pudding
>   mix

In a double boiler, melt candy bars with half the cream. Beat eggs and remaining cream; whisk into melted chocolate. Cook and stir for 5 minutes. Cool. Beat milk and pudding mixes; fold into chocolate mixture. Chill several hours or overnight. Freeze in an ice cream freezer according to manufacturer's instructions. Allow to ripen in ice cream freezer or firm up in your refrigerator freezer 2-4 hours before serving. **Yield:** about 3 quarts. —*Jo Groth, Plainfield, Iowa*

Milky Way Ice Cream

Butter Pecan Ice Cream

The toasted nuts in this recipe are a little sweet and very crunchy because of the added sugar in the first step.

>   3/4 cup chopped pecans
>   3 tablespoons butter *or* margarine, melted
>   1 tablespoon sugar
>   1/8 teaspoon salt
>   **ICE CREAM:**
>   1/2 cup packed brown sugar
>   1/4 cup sugar
>   2 tablespoons cornstarch
>   2 eggs, beaten
>   1/3 cup maple-flavored syrup
>   2-1/2 cups milk
>   1 cup whipping cream
>   2 teaspoons vanilla extract

On a baking sheet, combine pecans, butter, sugar and salt; spread into a single layer. Bake at 350° for 15 minutes. Stir and bake 15 minutes longer. Cool. For ice cream, combine sugars, cornstarch, eggs and syrup in a double boiler. Gradually add milk. Cook over boiling water until mixture thickens. Remove from the heat; chill for several hours or overnight. Stir in nuts, cream and vanilla. Place in ice cream freezer and freeze according to manufacturer's instructions. Allow to ripen in ice cream freezer or firm up in your refrigerator freezer 2-4 hours before serving. **Yield:** about 2 quarts. —*Patricia Simms, Dallas, Texas*

Vanilla Ice Cream

For raspberry or strawberry ice cream, substitute 2 cups fresh or frozen berries for 1 cup half-and-half cream. Puree in a blender or food processor and add to the other ingredients before freezing.

>   2 cups whipping cream
>   2 cups half-and-half cream
>   1 cup sugar
>   2 teaspoons vanilla extract

In a bowl, combine all ingredients; stir until the sugar is dissolved. Freeze in an ice cream freezer according to manufacturer's instructions. Allow to ripen in ice cream freezer or firm up in your refrigerator freezer 2-4 hours before serving. **Yield:** 1-1/2 quarts.

*Frozen Ice Cream
Delight*

Berry Good Topping

Here's a topping that is wonderful served over angel food cake, shortcake or even pancakes.

1 pint fresh raspberries, *divided*
1/4 cup unsweetened apple juice
2 teaspoons cornstarch
**2 tablespoons unsweetened apple juice
  concentrate**
1/4 teaspoon vanilla extract

In a blender, cover and puree 1 cup of berries with apple juice. In a small saucepan, combine cornstarch and apple juice concentrate; stir until smooth. Add pureed berries. Cook over low heat, stirring constantly, until thickened. Cool. Add vanilla and remaining berries. Cover and store in the refrigerator. **Yield:** 1-1/2 cups. ⏱ 🍎   —*Martha Balser, Cincinnati, Ohio*

Peachy Dessert Sauce

Serve this pretty dessert sauce over ice cream, angel food cake or pound cake.

1 teaspoon cornstarch
1/4 cup water
2 tablespoons apricot jam *or* **preserves**
1-1/2 teaspoons sugar
1/2 teaspoon lemon juice
3/4 cup sliced fresh *or* **canned peaches**

In a small saucepan, combine cornstarch and water. Add jam, sugar and lemon juice; bring to a boil. Cook and stir for 1-2 minutes; reduce heat. Add peaches and heat through. Serve warm over ice cream, angel food cake or pound cake. Cover and store in the refrigerator. To reheat, microwave on medium for 1-2 minutes or until heated through. **Yield:** 3/4 cup.
                    —*Helene Belanger, Denver, Colorado*

Frozen Ice Cream Delight

You can prepare and freeze this dessert up to 1 week in advance. Before freezing, be sure to cover tightly with heavy-duty foil or use a pan with its own storage cover.

2 cups crushed cream-filled chocolate cookies
1/2 cup butter *or* **margarine, melted**
1/2 cup sugar
1/2 gallon chocolate, coffee *or* **vanilla ice cream,
  softened**
CHOCOLATE SAUCE:
2 cups confectioners' sugar
2/3 cup semisweet chocolate chips
1 can (12 ounces) evaporated milk
1/2 cup butter *or* **margarine**
1 teaspoon vanilla extract
TOPPING:
1-1/2 cups salted peanuts
**1 carton (8 ounces) frozen whipped topping,
  thawed**
1/2 cup crushed cream-filled chocolate cookies

Combine cookie crumbs, butter and sugar. Press onto the bottom of an ungreased 13-in. x 9-in. x 2-in. baking pan. Freeze for 15 minutes. Spread ice cream over crust; freeze until firm, about 3 hours. Meanwhile, combine the first four sauce ingredients in a saucepan; bring to a boil. Boil for 8 minutes. Remove from

Peachy Dessert Sauce

the heat and stir in vanilla; cool to room temperature. Spoon over ice cream; sprinkle with peanuts. Freeze until firm. Spread whipped topping over nuts and sprinkle with cookie crumbs. Freeze for at least 3 hours before serving. **Yield:** 12-16 servings.

—Sue Bracken, State College, Pennsylvania

Homemade Fudge Sauce

The addition of the cinnamon is a tasty touch that adds a little sparkle to this rich sauce. Serve it over ice cream or cake.

 1-1/4 cups sugar
  1 cup baking cocoa
 1/2 teaspoon ground cinnamon
  1 cup whipping cream
 1/2 cup milk
 1/2 cup butter (no substitutes), cut into 8 pieces
  2 teaspoons vanilla extract

In a heavy saucepan, combine sugar, cocoa and cinnamon. Add cream and milk; mix well. Bring to a boil over medium heat, stirring constantly. Cook for 2 minutes. Remove from the heat; cool for 15 minutes. Add butter and stir until melted. Stir in vanilla. Cool to room temperature. Cover and store in the refrigerator. Stir before serving. **Yield:** 3 cups.

—Trudy DeFelice, Columbia, South Carolina

Homemade Fudge Sauce

Peanut Butter Ice Cream Topping

Make a tasty sundae by topping chocolate ice cream with this creamy sauce and sprinkling with salted peanuts.

  1 cup packed brown sugar
 1/2 cup light corn syrup
  3 tablespoons butter *or* margarine
Pinch salt
  1 cup creamy peanut butter
 1/2 cup evaporated milk
Vanilla ice cream
Peanuts, optional

Combine brown sugar, corn syrup, butter and salt in a 1-1/2-qt. microwave-safe dish. Cover and microwave on high for 4 minutes or until mixture boils, stirring twice. Add peanut butter; stir until smooth. Stir in milk. Serve warm over ice cream. Sprinkle with peanuts if desired. Cover and store in the refrigerator. To reheat, microwave on medium for 1-2 minutes or until heated through. **Yield:** 2-3/4 cups.

—Karen Buhr, Gasport, New York

Praline Sundae Sauce

This dessert sauce really dresses up vanilla or coffee ice cream and makes a very special gift at holiday time.

 1/4 cup butter *or* margarine
 1-1/4 cups packed brown sugar
  16 large marshmallows
  2 tablespoons light corn syrup
Pinch salt
  1 cup evaporated milk
 1/2 cup chopped pecans, toasted
  1 teaspoon vanilla extract
Ice cream

Melt butter in a saucepan. Add brown sugar, marshmallows, corn syrup and salt. Cook and stir over low heat until marshmallows are melted and mixture comes to a boil. Boil for 1 minute. Remove from the heat; cool for 5 minutes. Stir in milk, pecans and vanilla; mix well. Serve warm or cold over ice cream. Cover and store in the refrigerator. **Yield:** 2-1/2 cups.

—Valerie Cook, Hubbard, Iowa

Cakes

This scrumptious assortment of savory classics and tasty new favorites just can't be topped when your family is calling for something sweet to eat. Chocolate Pound Cake (p. 321) and Apple Walnut Cake (p. 319) will take top honors at your next buffet or potluck.

Cakes can be divided into two different types—butter and foam cakes. Butter cakes—the kind covered here through page 324—contain fat (for example, butter, margarine, shortening, oil) and have a fine moist texture and a tender crumb. Foam cakes are covered beginning on page 325. No matter which variety of cake you make, your family and friends will be grateful that you took the time to make them a special treat.

Tips for Butter Cakes

- Measure all ingredients accurately and have them at room temperature before mixing. (See page 10 for proper measuring techniques.)

- Most butter cake recipes call for creaming the butter and sugar. Beat the butter, margarine or shortening and sugar with an electric mixer or wooden spoon to a light and fluffy consistency.

- Always use butter or regular margarine (containing no less than 80% vegetable oil) when making cakes. Do not use light or whipped butter, diet spreads or tub margarine.

- Use only the pan size recommended in the recipe.

- For a tender golden crust, use aluminum pans with a dull rather than a shiny or dark finish. If using glass baking dishes, lower the oven temperature 25°.

- Grease and flour baking pans for butter cakes that will be removed from the pans. Cakes that will be served from the pans should be greased but not floured. Some cake recipes call for the pan to be lined with waxed paper for easier removal of the cake from the pan. (Refer to Lining a Baking Pan with Waxed Paper on page 320.)

- Arrange the oven racks so that the cake will bake in the center of the oven.

- Preheat the oven 10-15 minutes before baking.

- Butter cakes are done when a toothpick inserted near the center of the cake comes out clean. Check for doneness at the minimum recommended baking time, then check every 2 minutes after that.

- Cool cakes for 10-15 minutes in the pan, unless recipe directs otherwise. Loosen the cake by running a knife around the edge of the pan. Turn out onto a wire rack and cool completely.

- If a cake sticks to the pan and will not come out when inverted, return to the oven for 1 minute; turn out again.

Preparing a Cake Pan

1 Grease the sides and bottom of the pan by spreading shortening with a paper towel over the interior of the pan.

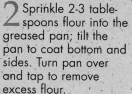

2 Sprinkle 2-3 tablespoons flour into the greased pan; tilt the pan to coat bottom and sides. Turn pan over and tap to remove excess flour.

Chocolate Layer Cake

This chocolate cake uses brown sugar to give extra flavor and sour cream to add moistness. If you like white frosting on your chocolate cake, try the Fluffy Seven-Minute Frosting on page 331.

    1 cup butter *or* margarine, softened
    3 cups packed brown sugar
    4 eggs
    2 teaspoons vanilla extract
2-2/3 cups all-purpose flour
  3/4 cup baking cocoa
    1 tablespoon baking soda
  1/2 teaspoon salt
1-1/3 cups sour cream
1-1/3 cups boiling water
Chocolate Sour Cream Frosting (page 331)

In a mixing bowl, cream butter and brown sugar. Add eggs, one at a time, beating well after each addition. Beat on high speed until light and fluffy. Blend in vanilla. Combine flour, cocoa, baking soda and salt; add to the creamed mixture alternately with sour cream. Beat on low just until combined. Stir in water until blended. Pour into three greased and floured 9-in. round baking pans. Bake at 350° for 35 minutes or until a toothpick inserted near the center comes out clean. Cool for 10 minutes; remove from pans to wire racks to cool completely. Spread Chocolate Sour Cream Frosting between layers and over top and sides of cake. Store in the refrigerator. **Yield:** 12-14 servings.

—Sandy Johnson, Tioga, Pennsylvania

Carrot Layer Cake

When shredding the carrots for this cake, use a very fine shredder so the carrots will almost disappear as the cake layers bake.

FILLING:
    1 cup sugar
    2 tablespoons all-purpose flour
    1/4 teaspoon salt
    1 cup whipping cream
    1/2 cup butter *or* margarine
    1 cup chopped pecans
    1 teaspoon vanilla extract
CAKE:
 1-1/4 cups vegetable oil
    2 cups sugar
    2 cups all-purpose flour
    2 teaspoons ground cinnamon
    2 teaspoons baking powder
    1 teaspoon baking soda
    1 teaspoon salt
    4 eggs
    4 cups finely shredded carrots
    1 cup raisins
    1 cup chopped pecans
Cream Cheese Frosting (page 331)

In a heavy saucepan, combine sugar, flour and salt. Stir in cream; add butter. Cook and stir over medium heat until the butter is melted; bring to a boil. Reduce heat. Simmer, uncovered, for 30 minutes, stirring occasionally. Stir in pecans and vanilla. Set aside to cool. In a mixing bowl, beat oil and sugar for 1 minute. Combine flour, cinnamon, baking powder, baking soda and salt; add to the creamed mixture alternately with eggs. Mix well. Stir in carrots, raisins and pecans. Pour into three greased and floured 9-in. round baking pans. Bake at 350° for 35-40 minutes or until a toothpick inserted near the center comes out clean. Cool for 10 minutes; remove from pans to wire racks to cool completely. Spread filling between cake layers; frost top and sides of cake with Cream Cheese Frosting. Store in the refrigerator. **Yield:** 12-14 servings.
—*Linda Van Holland, Innisfail, Alberta*

Apple Walnut Cake

(Pictured on page 317)

This cake actually tastes as good—or better—on the second day. If time is a factor, you can freeze this cake frosted for up to 1 week before serving.

        3 eggs
        2 cups sugar
    1/2 cup vegetable oil
        2 teaspoons vanilla extract
        2 cups all-purpose flour
        2 teaspoons baking soda
        2 teaspoons ground cinnamon
    1/2 teaspoon ground nutmeg
    1/4 teaspoon salt
        4 cups diced unpeeled apples
        1 cup coarsely chopped walnuts
Cream Cheese Frosting (page 331)

In a mixing bowl, beat eggs, sugar, oil and vanilla. Combine flour, baking soda, cinnamon, nutmeg and salt; mix into the batter. Fold in apples and nuts. Spread into a greased 13-in. x 9-in. x 2-in. baking pan. Bake at 325° for 50-60 minutes or until a toothpick inserted near the center comes out clean. Cool in pan on a wire rack. Frost with Cream Cheese Frosting. Store in the refrigerator. **Yield:** 12-16 servings.
—*Judy Dennis*
Brown City, Michigan

Carrot Layer Cake

German Chocolate Cake

German Chocolate Cake

This spectacular cake is not frosted. Each layer is spread with a coconut-pecan filling and drizzled with chocolate icing. To save time, the cake can be baked days before and frozen until you're ready to assemble and serve it.

CAKE:
- 1/2 cup water
- 1 package (4 ounces) German sweet chocolate
- 1 cup butter *or* margarine, softened
- 2 cups sugar
- 4 eggs, *separated*
- 1 teaspoon vanilla extract
- 2-1/2 cups cake flour
- 1 teaspoon baking soda
- 1/2 teaspoon salt
- 1 cup buttermilk

FILLING:
- 1 cup sugar
- 1 cup evaporated milk
- 1/2 cup butter *or* margarine
- 3 egg yolks, beaten
- 1-1/3 cups flaked coconut
- 1 cup chopped pecans
- 1 teaspoon vanilla extract

ICING:
- 1/2 teaspoon shortening
- 1 square (1 ounce) semisweet chocolate

In a saucepan, heat water and chocolate until melted; cool. In a mixing bowl, beat butter and sugar until light and fluffy. Beat in egg yolks, one at a time. Blend in melted chocolate and vanilla. Combine flour, baking soda and salt; add to creamed mixture alternately with buttermilk. Beat until smooth. In another bowl, beat egg whites until stiff peaks form; fold into batter. Pour into three greased 9-in. round baking pans lined with greased waxed paper. Bake at 350° for 30 minutes or until a toothpick inserted near the center comes out clean. Cool for 10 minutes; remove from pans to wire racks. Carefully remove paper. For filling, combine sugar, milk, butter and egg yolks in a saucepan. Cook over low heat, stirring constantly, until thickened. Remove from the heat. Stir in coconut, pecans and vanilla. Cool until thick enough to spread. Spread on top of each cake layer; stack on a serving plate. For icing, melt shortening and chocolate; drizzle down sides of cake. **Yield:** 12-14 servings. —*Joyce Platfoot*
Botkins, Ohio

Oatmeal Chocolate Chip Cake

This is considered a snack cake because it doesn't have any frosting and is easily eaten on the run. If you pack lunches for your family, treat them to generous slices of this cake.

1-3/4 cups boiling water
  1 cup uncooked oatmeal
  1 cup packed brown sugar
  1 cup sugar
  1/2 cup butter *or* margarine, softened
  3 eggs
1-3/4 cups all-purpose flour
  1 tablespoon baking cocoa
  1 teaspoon baking soda
  1/4 teaspoon salt
  2 cups (12 ounces) chocolate chips, *divided*
  3/4 cup chopped walnuts

In a mixing bowl, pour water over oatmeal. Let stand for 10 minutes. Add sugars and butter, stirring until butter is melted. Add eggs one at a time, beating well after each addition. Sift flour, cocoa, baking soda and salt together. Add to batter; mix well. Stir in half of the chocolate chips. Pour into a greased 13-in. x 9-in. x 2-in. baking pan. Sprinkle walnuts and remaining chips on top. Bake at 350° for 40 minutes or until a toothpick inserted near the center comes out clean. Cool in pan on a wire rack. **Yield:** 12-16 servings.
—*Luanne Thomson, Mannheim, Germany*

Oatmeal Chocolate Chip Cake

Dusting Cakes with Confectioners' Sugar

To decorate and sweeten a cake with confectioners' sugar instead of frosting, place confectioners' sugar in a metal sieve or sifter; shake or sift over the top of the baked and cooled cake. To make a pattern, lay a doily over the cake; sift an even layer of sugar over all. Lift the doily straight up, leaving the pattern on the cake.

Chocolate Pound Cake

(Pictured on page 316)

The secret to a perfect pound cake is to cream the butter and sugar until light and fluffy, and to beat well after adding each egg.

  2 cups (12 ounces) milk chocolate chips
  1/2 cup butter *or* margarine, softened
  2 cups sugar
  4 eggs
  2 teaspoons vanilla extract
  1 cup buttermilk
  2 tablespoons water
2-1/2 cups sifted cake flour
  1/2 teaspoon salt
  1/4 teaspoon baking soda
  1/2 cup chopped pecans, optional
Confectioners' sugar, optional

In a saucepan over low heat, melt chocolate. Remove from the heat. In a mixing bowl, cream butter and sugar until light and fluffy. Add eggs one at a time, beating well after each addition. Blend in melted chocolate and vanilla. Combine buttermilk and water. Combine flour, salt and baking soda; add to batter alternately with the buttermilk mixture. Fold in nuts if desired. Pour into a greased and floured 10-in. tube or fluted tube pan. Bake at 325° for 1-1/2 hours or until a toothpick inserted near the center comes out clean. Cool for 10 minutes; remove from pan to a wire rack. Dust with confectioners' sugar if desired. **Yield:** 12-16 servings.
—*Ann Perry, Sierra Vista, Arizona*

Lazy Daisy Cake

Lazy Daisy Cake

A broiled frosting is the trademark of this melt-in-your-mouth yellow cake. While the cake is under the broiler, watch the frosting closely since it takes only minutes to brown and will quickly burn.

          2 eggs
          1 cup sugar
          1 teaspoon vanilla extract
          1 cup cake flour
          1 teaspoon baking powder
      1/4 teaspoon salt
      1/2 cup milk
          2 tablespoons butter *or* margarine
FROSTING:
          1 cup shredded coconut
      3/4 cup packed brown sugar
      1/2 cup butter *or* margarine, melted
          2 tablespoons half-and-half cream

In a mixing bowl, beat eggs, sugar and vanilla on high until thick and lemon-colored, about 4 minutes. Combine flour, baking powder and salt; add to egg mixture. Beat on low just until combined. Heat milk and butter in a small saucepan until butter is melted. Add to batter; beat thoroughly (batter will be thin). Pour into a greased 9-in. square baking pan. Bake at 350° for 20-25 minutes or until a toothpick inserted near the center comes out clean. Cool slightly. Combine frosting ingredients; spread over warm cake. Broil about 4 in. from the heat for 3-4 minutes or until the top is lightly browned. Cool in pan on a wire rack. **Yield:** 9 servings.
          —*Carrie Bartlett, Gallatin, Tennessee*

Pumpkin Cake Squares

When you need a dessert to feed a crowd, a sheet cake like this is an excellent option. This cake keeps well and is a real hit at any gathering, especially one around Halloween.

          4 eggs
   1-2/3 cups sugar
          1 cup vegetable oil
          1 can (15 ounces) solid-pack pumpkin
          2 cups all-purpose flour
          2 teaspoons ground cinnamon
          2 teaspoons baking powder
          1 teaspoon baking soda
          1 teaspoon salt
Cream Cheese Frosting (page 331)

In a mixing bowl, beat eggs, sugar, oil and pumpkin. Combine flour, cinnamon, baking powder, baking soda and salt; gradually add to pumpkin mixture and mix well. Pour into an ungreased 15-in. x 10-in. x 1-in. baking pan. Bake at 350° for 25-30 minutes or until a toothpick inserted near the center comes out clean. Cool in pan on a wire rack. Frost with Cream Cheese Frosting. Store in the refrigerator. **Yield:** 20-24 servings.
          —*Brenda Keller, Andalusia, Alabama*

Gingerbread

Gingerbread is a cake that is traditionally served without a frosting. A simple dollop of whipped cream is all you'll need to garnish this old-fashioned treat.

          1 egg
      1/2 cup sugar
      1/2 cup molasses
          5 tablespoons butter *or* margarine, melted
      2/3 cup water
   1-1/2 cups all-purpose flour
          1 teaspoon baking soda
          1 teaspoon ground ginger
      1/2 teaspoon salt
Whipped cream

Tips for Whipping Cream

• Chill the bowl and beaters before whipping cream and keep the cream refrigerated until ready to use.

• Place cream in a deep chilled bowl; whip on high until soft peaks form if using as a garnish or until stiff peaks form if frosting a cake.

• If sweetened whipped cream is desired, add 2 tablespoons confectioners' sugar to each cup of cream before whipping.

In a bowl, beat the egg; add sugar, molasses, butter and water. Mix well. In a mixing bowl, combine flour, baking soda, ginger and salt; add molasses mixture. Beat until well mixed. Pour into a greased 8-in. square baking pan. Bake at 350° for 30 minutes or until a toothpick inserted near the center comes out clean. Serve warm with whipped cream. **Yield:** 9 servings.

—*Ellouise Halstead, Union Grove, Wisconsin*

Butter Pecan Cake

Toasting the nuts in butter before adding to this cake adds extra flavor and keeps the nuts in the cake and the frosting crunchy.

     2/3 cup butter *or* margarine, softened
1-1/3 cups sugar
     2 eggs
     2 cups all-purpose flour
1-1/2 teaspoons baking powder
     1/4 teaspoon salt
     2/3 cup milk
1-1/2 teaspoons vanilla extract
1-1/3 cups chopped pecans, toasted, *divided*
BUTTER PECAN FROSTING:
     3 tablespoons butter *or* margarine, softened
     3 cups confectioners' sugar
     3 tablespoons milk
     3/4 teaspoon vanilla extract

In a mixing bowl, cream butter and sugar until light and fluffy. Add eggs, one at a time, beating well after each addition. Combine flour, baking powder and salt; add to creamed mixture alternately with milk. Stir in vanilla and 1 cup toasted pecans. Pour batter into two greased and floured 8-in. round baking pans. Bake at 350° for 30-35 minutes or until a toothpick inserted near the center comes out clean. Cool for 10 minutes; remove from pans to wire racks to cool completely. For frosting, cream butter and sugar in a mixing bowl. Add milk and vanilla; beat until light and fluffy. Add additional milk if needed. Stir in remaining toasted pecans. Spread between the layers and over the top and sides of the cake. **Yield:** 12 servings.

—*Virginia Gentry, Sutherlin, Virginia*

Toasting Nuts

To toast 1-1/3 cups chopped nuts, pour 3 tablespoons melted butter or margarine into a baking pan. Stir in nuts. Bake at 350° for 10 minutes, stirring twice. Cool. Use as directed in recipes.

Butter Pecan Cake

Spiced Pineapple Upside-Down Cake

You can prepare this cake either in a skillet or in a 13- x 9-inch pan. Either way, the results are delicious. Be sure to carefully invert the cake onto a serving platter as soon as you remove it from the oven.

1-1/3 cups butter *or* margarine, softened, *divided*
   1 cup packed brown sugar
   1 can (20 ounces) sliced pineapple, drained
 10 to 12 maraschino cherries
 1/2 cup chopped pecans
1-1/2 cups sugar
   2 eggs
   1 teaspoon vanilla extract
   2 cups all-purpose flour
   2 teaspoons baking powder
 1/2 teaspoon baking soda
 1/2 teaspoon salt
 1/2 teaspoon ground cinnamon
 1/2 teaspoon ground nutmeg
   1 cup buttermilk

In a small saucepan, melt 2/3 cup of butter; stir in brown sugar. Spread onto the bottom of an ungreased heavy 12-in. skillet or a 13-in. x 9-in. x 2-in. baking pan. Arrange pineapple in a single layer over sugar mixture; place a cherry in the center of each slice. Sprinkle with pecans and set aside. In a mixing bowl, cream sugar and remaining butter. Beat in eggs and vanilla. Combine the dry ingredients; add to creamed mixture alternately with buttermilk, mixing well after each addition. Carefully pour over the pineapple. Bake at 350° for 40 minutes for skillet (50-60 minutes for baking pan) or until a toothpick inserted near the center comes out clean. Immediately invert onto a serving platter. Cool before serving. **Yield:** 12 servings.
—*Jennifer Sergesketter, Newburgh, Indiana*

Moist Chocolate Cupcakes

Cupcakes are fun individual desserts that can be decorated with several different frostings, including the Mocha Frosting suggested below.

   1 cup boiling water
   1 cup mayonnaise*
   1 teaspoon vanilla extract
   2 cups all-purpose flour
   1 cup sugar
 1/2 cup baking cocoa
   2 teaspoons baking soda
Mocha Frosting (page 330)

In a mixing bowl, combine water, mayonnaise and vanilla. Combine flour, sugar, cocoa and baking soda; add to the mayonnaise mixture and beat until well mixed. Fill greased or paper-lined muffin cups two-thirds full. Bake at 350° for 20 minutes or until a toothpick inserted near the center comes out clean. Cool for 10 minutes; remove from pans to wire racks to cool completely. Frost with Mocha Frosting. Store in the refrigerator. **Yield:** about 1-1/2 dozen. ***Editor's Note:** Do not substitute light or low-fat mayonnaise for regular mayonnaise. —*Lorna Smith New Hazelton, British Columbia*

Moist Chocolate Cupcakes

Cupcakes from a Layer Cake

Batter for a two-layer 9-inch cake can be used to make 2 to 2-1/2 dozen cupcakes. Fill greased or paper-lined muffin cups two-thirds full. Bake at 350° for 15-20 minutes or until a toothpick inserted near the center comes out clean. Remove cupcakes from pan and cool on a wire rack. Frost as desired.

Foam cakes rely on beaten eggs to give them their fluffy, airy texture. The most common varieties include angel food, sponge and chiffon.

Angel Food Cake

Angel Food Cake

Angel food cake has little fat, so even people on restricted diets can indulge in a slice without guilt. This cake is especially flavorful with the addition of almond extract. Serve slices with fresh fruit or drizzle with the Cinnamon Apple Glaze on page 330.

1-1/2 cups egg whites (about 1 dozen), room temperature
1-1/2 teaspoons cream of tartar
1-1/2 teaspoons vanilla extract
1/2 teaspoon almond extract
1/4 teaspoon salt
1 cup sugar
1 cup confectioners' sugar
1 cup all-purpose flour

In a mixing bowl, beat egg whites, cream of tartar, extracts and salt at high speed. Gradually add sugar, beating until sugar is dissolved and stiff peaks form. Combine confectioners' sugar and flour; gradually fold into the batter, 1/4 cup at a time. Gently spoon batter into an ungreased 10-in. tube pan. Cut through the batter with a knife to remove air pockets. Bake at 350° for 35 minutes or until cake springs back when lightly touched. Immediately invert pan; cool completely. Run a knife around sides of cake and remove. **Yield:** 12-16 servings. 🍎 —*Lucille Proctor, Panguitch, Utah*

Tips for Foam Cakes

- Measure all ingredients accurately and have them at room temperature before beginning to mix. (See page 10 for proper measuring techniques.)
- Before beating egg whites, make sure your mixing bowl and beaters are clean of all fat residue by washing them thoroughly in hot soapy water and drying with a clean cloth.
- Beat egg whites at room temperature, making sure they do not contain any specks of egg yolk.
- Use only the pan size recommended in the recipe.
- For a tender golden crust, use aluminum pans with a dull rather than a shiny or dark finish.
- Do not grease or flour tube pans when baking foam cakes. To rise properly, the batter needs to cling to the sides of the pan.
- To avoid large air pockets in the baked cake, cut through the batter with a knife to break air pockets or bubbles.
- Preheat the oven 10-15 minutes before baking.
- Foam cakes baked in tube pans should be placed on the bottom rack of the oven.
- Foam cakes are done when the top springs back when touched and the cracks at the top of the cake look and feel dry.
- Cool cakes completely in the pan before removing.
- To remove foam cakes from tube pans, use a sawing action to run a thin sharp knife around the edge of the pan. If the cake pan has a removable bottom, lift out the cake and run a knife along the bottom of the cake. If the pan is one piece, turn out the cake onto a plate; tap the side of the pan with the flat side of a knife and lift the pan away from the cake.
- Cut foam cakes with a serrated knife or an electric knife with a back-and-forth or sawing action.

Coffee Angel Food Cake

When time is short, an angel food cake mix can come to the rescue. This recipe takes the basic mix and makes it special for the coffee lover.

> 2 teaspoons instant coffee granules
> 1-1/4 cups water
> 1 package (16 ounces) one-step angel food cake mix
> FROSTING:
> 1/2 cup butter *or* margarine, softened
> 3-3/4 cups confectioners' sugar
> 1 to 2 tablespoons instant coffee granules
> 1/4 cup milk
> 1/2 cup sliced almonds, toasted

In a mixing bowl, dissolve coffee in water; add cake mix. Mix, bake and cool according to package directions. For frosting, cream butter and sugar in a mixing bowl. Dissolve coffee in milk; add to the creamed mixture and beat until smooth. Frost the top and sides of cake. Garnish with almonds. **Yield:** 12-16 servings.

—*Carol Brown, Clyde, Texas*

Cooling a Foam Cake

There are several different designs of 10-in. tube pans. To properly cool an angel food, sponge or chiffon cake, invert the pan onto its legs until the cake is completely cool.

If your tube pan does not have legs, place the pan over a funnel or the neck of a narrow bottle until completely cool.

Chocolate Angel Food Cake

Chocolate Angel Food Cake

Bake this cake early in the day so it cools completely before you frost it. Chill the frosted cake at least 2 hours before serving for easier slicing.

> 3/4 cup sifted cake flour
> 1-1/2 cups plus 2 tablespoons sugar, *divided*
> 1/4 cup baking cocoa
> 1-1/2 cups egg whites (about 1 dozen), room temperature
> 1-1/2 teaspoons cream of tartar
> 1-1/2 teaspoons vanilla extract
> 1/4 teaspoon salt
> **Chocolate Whipped Cream Frosting (page 331)**

Sift together flour, 3/4 cup plus 2 tablespoons sugar and cocoa three times; set aside. In a mixing bowl, beat egg whites, cream of tartar, vanilla and salt until foamy. Add remaining sugar, 2 tablespoons at a time, beating about 10 seconds after each addition. Continue beating until stiff peaks form. Gradually fold in dry ingredients, 3 tablespoons at a time (batter will be thick). Spread into an ungreased 10-in. tube pan. Cut through batter with a knife to remove air pockets. Bake at 350° for 40-45 minutes or until the cake springs back when lightly touched. Immediately invert pan; cool completely. Run a knife around sides of cake and remove. Frost the top and sides with Chocolate Whipped Cream Frosting. Store in the refrigerator. **Yield:** 12-16 servings.

—*Mary Ann Iverson*
Woodville, Wisconsin

Orange-Glazed Sponge Cake

Making a Sponge Cake

1 Beat egg yolks in a mixing bowl until they begin to thicken. Gradually add 3/4 cup sugar, beating until the mixture is lemon-colored (shown at left). Blend in flavorings. Sift together flour and salt; beat into egg yolk mixture.

2 In another mixing bowl, beat egg whites until soft peaks form. Gradually add sugar, 1 tablespoon at a time, beating until stiff peaks form (shown at left).

3 Spoon a fourth of the egg white mixture into the yolk mixture; carefully fold in with a rubber spatula. Fold in the remaining egg white mixture just until combined. Don't overmix. Proceed with the recipe as directed.

Orange-Glazed Sponge Cake

The light texture of the cake and the orange flavor is very refreshing after a holiday meal of roasted turkey or ham.

> **6 eggs,** *separated,* **room temperature**
> **1-1/4 cups sugar,** *divided*
> **1/3 cup orange juice**
> **2 tablespoons grated orange peel**
> **1-3/4 cups all-purpose flour**
> **1/2 teaspoon salt**
> **ORANGE GLAZE:**
> **1 cup water**
> **1/2 unpeeled orange, finely chopped**
> **1/4 cup sugar**
> **1 tablespoon butter** *or* **margarine**
> **1/2 cup confectioners' sugar**

In a mixing bowl, beat egg yolks until slightly thickened. Gradually add 3/4 cup sugar, beating until thick and lemon-colored. Blend in orange juice and peel. Sift together flour and salt; add to batter. Beat until smooth. In another mixing bowl, beat egg whites until soft peaks form. Add the remaining sugar, 1 tablespoon at a time. Beat until stiff peaks form. Fold a fourth of the egg whites into the batter; fold in remaining whites. Spoon into an ungreased 10-in. tube pan; smooth the top. Bake at 350° for 40 minutes or until cake springs back when lightly touched. Immediately invert pan; cool completely. Meanwhile, for glaze, combine water, orange and sugar in a small saucepan; bring to a boil. Cook until very thick and almost all the water has evaporated. Remove from the heat; blend in butter and confectioners' sugar. Run a knife around sides of cake and remove to a serving platter. Spread warm glaze over the top and sides of cake. **Yield:** 12-16 servings.

—*Dorothy Lacefield, Carrollton, Texas*

Making a Cake Roll

1 After the cake has cooled for 5 minutes, cover it with a sheet of waxed paper (18 in. long), then a kitchen towel and a baking sheet. Holding the baking sheet tight to the baking pan, invert the pan so the cake comes out and lies flat on the towel. Gently peel away the waxed paper used to line the baking pan. Beginning with the narrow side, roll up the cake with the towel and waxed paper. Place on a wire rack until completely cool.

2 Carefully unroll cake on a flat surface. Spread filling over cake to within 1/2 in. of edge.

3 Beginning at the narrow end, roll up the cake loosely, pulling away the towel and waxed paper. Place seam side down on a serving platter. Proceed with recipe as directed.

Raspberry Cake Roll

Raspberry Cake Roll

This cake roll can also be filled with 3 cups of softened ice cream, rolled and stored in the freezer for a variation.

> **6 egg whites, room temperature**
> **1 teaspoon lemon juice**
> **1/4 teaspoon salt**
> **1/4 cup sugar**
> **1/2 cup plus 1 tablespoon sifted cake flour**
> **1 tablespoon grated lemon peel**
> **1 package (8 ounces) cream cheese, softened**
> **1/2 teaspoon vanilla extract**
> **1 cup whipped topping,** *divided*
> **1 pint fresh raspberries,** *divided*

Additional lemon peel

In a mixing bowl, beat egg whites, lemon juice and salt on low speed until foamy. Gradually add sugar, beating on medium-high speed until soft peaks form. Combine flour and lemon peel; gradually fold into egg white mixture 1/4 cup at a time. Line a greased 15-in. x 10-in. x 1-in. baking pan with waxed paper; grease the paper. Spread batter evenly in pan. Bake at 350° for 12-15 minutes or until cake springs back when lightly touched in center. Cool cake in pan on a wire rack for 5 minutes. Cover with waxed paper, then a kitchen towel and baking sheet or bread board. Invert pan so cake lies flat on towel. Gently peel away greased waxed paper from the cake and discard. Beginning with narrow side, roll cake with towel, keeping towel and waxed paper pressed to underside of cake. Place rolled cake on rack to cool. For filling, combine cream cheese, vanilla and 2 tablespoons of whipped topping in a bowl. Gently fold in remaining whipped topping. Cover and refrigerate until ready to use. Carefully unroll cake on a flat surface. With a spatula, spread filling evenly over cake to within 1/2 in. of edges. Sprinkle with 1-1/2 cups raspberries. Using towel to lift edge of cake, gently roll as before, this time pulling away towel and waxed paper. Place cake roll with seam side down on serving platter. Chill. Garnish with remaining raspberries and lemon peel. Serve chilled. **Yield:** 12 servings.

—*Virginia Quelch*
Las Cruces, New Mexico

Chocolate Lover's Chiffon Cake

This recipe uses cake flour, which is sold in a 2-pound box and gives cake a very fine texture. Serious bakers will want to have a box on hand for the recipes that call for it. (To substitute all-purpose flour, see page 381.)

    3/4 cup boiling water
    1/2 cup baking cocoa
  1-3/4 cups sifted cake flour
  1-3/4 cups sugar
  1-1/2 teaspoons baking soda
      1 teaspoon salt
    1/2 cup vegetable oil
      7 eggs, *separated*, room temperature
      2 teaspoons vanilla extract
    1/2 teaspoon cream of tartar
Chocolate Whipped Cream Frosting (page 331)

Combine water and cocoa in a small bowl until smooth; cool. In a large bowl, sift together flour, sugar, baking soda and salt. Make a well in the center; add oil, egg yolks, vanilla and cocoa mixture. Beat with a wooden spoon until smooth; set aside. In a mixing bowl, sprinkle cream of tartar over egg whites; beat until stiff peaks form. Fold into batter with a wire whisk. Pour into an ungreased 10-in. tube pan. Bake at 325° for 60-65 minutes or until cake springs back when lightly touched. Immediately invert pan; cool completely. Run a knife around sides of cake and remove to a serving platter. Prepare Chocolate Whipped Cream Frosting. To fill cake, cut a 1-in. slice off the top of the cake; set aside. Using a sharp knife, carve a tunnel out of cake, leaving a 1-in. wall on all sides; carefully remove cake. Fill tunnel with some of the frosting; replace cake top. Frost top and sides of cake with remaining frosting. Chill for 2-8 hours before serving. **Yield:** 12 servings.
—*JoAnn Plate, Oskaloosa, Iowa*

1 Cut a 1-in. slice off the top of the cake. Carefully set the slice aside. Using a very sharp knife, carve a tunnel in the cake, leaving a 1-in. wall on all sides. With a fork, carefully remove cake and save for another use.

2 Spoon some of the prepared frosting into the tunnel.

3 Carefully replace cake top. Frost top and sides of cake with remaining frosting. Chill for 2-8 hours before serving.

Tips for Dressing Up Plain Cakes

- For Black Forest Torte, prepare a chocolate or fudge cake mix in a 13-inch x 9-inch x 2-inch baking pan; cool. Spoon a 21-ounce can of cherry pie filling over the top of the cake. Spread 4 cups sweetened whipped cream over the pie filling and refrigerate at least 2 hours.

- To make an Angel Food Ice Cream Cake, slice a prepared angel food cake in thirds horizontally. Place bottom layer on a platter. Spread 1/2 quart of softened ice cream or frozen yogurt over cake; top with middle cake layer. Spread another 1/2 quart of ice cream or yogurt over cake; add top cake layer. Freeze at least 2-3 hours before serving. Serve with a dollop of whipped cream.

- For a quick fruit filling for a layer cake, spread 1/2 cup fruit preserves between the layers of a prepared white or yellow cake. Frost top and sides of cake with Buttercream Frosting (see page 330).

For weekday treats or special-occasion desserts, the frostings on these pages will add the perfect final touch to any homemade or store-bought cake.

Mocha Frosting

For the true chocolate lover, nothing goes with a chocolate cake like chocolate frosting. Coffee gives this frosting it's name.

  3/4 cup confectioners' sugar
  1/4 cup baking cocoa
  1/2 to 1 teaspoon instant coffee granules
Pinch salt
  1-1/2 cups whipping cream

Combine sugar, cocoa, coffee and salt in a mixing bowl. Stir in cream; cover and chill with beaters for 30 minutes. Beat frosting until stiff peaks form. Store frosted cake in the refrigerator. **Yield:** Frosts a two-layer cake or 1-1/2 dozen cupcakes.

Buttercream Frosting

For added fun, color this frosting with pastel liquid food coloring. Follow package directions for mixing colors and be careful to use only a drop or two at a time until the desired color is reached.

  1/2 cup shortening
  1/2 cup butter *or* margarine, softened
  1 teaspoon vanilla extract
  4 cups confectioners' sugar
  3 tablespoons milk

In a mixing bowl, cream shortening and butter. Add vanilla. Gradually beat in sugar. Add milk; beat until light and fluffy. **Yield:** Frosts a two-layer or 13-in. x 9-in. cake. ⊘

Cinnamon Apple Glaze

This cinnamon-flavored topping dresses up your basic angel food cake. For easier drizzling, prepare the glaze in a measuring cup with a spout.

  1/3 cup butter *or* margarine
  2 cups confectioners' sugar
  1/2 teaspoon ground cinnamon
  3 to 4 tablespoons apple juice *or* cider

Melt butter in a saucepan. Stir in the confectioners' sugar and cinnamon. Slowly add apple juice until the glaze is thin enough to drizzle. **Yield:** Glazes a 10-in. angel food cake. ⊘ —*Marlys Benning, Wellsburg, Iowa*

Filling and Frosting a Layer Cake

1 After the cake layers have completely cooled to room temperature, use a soft pastry or basting brush to carefully remove any loose crumbs on the top and sides of each layer. Trim off any crisp edges with a knife or kitchen shears.

2 To keep the serving plate clean, line it with strips of waxed paper around the edges. Center the first layer over the strips. Spread about 1/2 cup filling or frosting over the top to the edges. Repeat with the second layer if frosting a three-layer cake.

3 Top with the last layer. Frost the sides of the cake, building up the top edge of the cake slightly. Make large swirling strokes in a vertical pattern.

4 Spread remaining frosting over the top of the cake, smoothing right to the edges of the cake. Swirl top to match sides. Garnish or decorate if desired. Carefully remove waxed paper by pulling one piece at a time out from under the cake.

Fluffy Seven-Minute Frosting

This light-as-a-cloud frosting is much like a meringue. Try it over chocolate, white, yellow or angel food cake. For an added garnish, sprinkle the top and sides of the frosted cake with coconut.

1-3/4 cups sugar
1/2 cup water
4 egg whites, room temperature
1/2 teaspoon cream of tartar
1 teaspoon vanilla extract

In a saucepan, bring sugar and water to a boil. Boil for 3-4 minutes or until a candy thermometer reads 242° (firm-ball stage). Meanwhile, beat egg whites and cream of tartar in a mixing bowl until foamy. Slowly pour in hot sugar mixture; continue to beat on high for 7 minutes or until stiff peaks form. Add vanilla. Continue beating until frosting reaches desired consistency, about 2 minutes. **Yield:** Frosts a three-layer or tube cake.

Chocolate Sour Cream Frosting

Spread this rich creamy frosting over a chocolate, white or yellow cake. If desired, sprinkle the frosted cake with toasted chopped almonds or pecans.

1/2 cup butter *or* margarine
3 squares (1 ounce *each*) unsweetened chocolate
3 squares (1 ounce *each*) semisweet chocolate
5 cups confectioners' sugar
1 cup (8 ounces) sour cream
2 teaspoons vanilla extract

In a medium saucepan, melt butter and chocolate over low heat. Cool 5 minutes. In a mixing bowl, combine sugar, sour cream and vanilla. Add chocolate mixture and beat until smooth. Store frosted cake in the refrigerator. **Yield:** Frosts a three-layer cake. ○

Cream Cheese Frosting

This classic frosting is the perfect complement to carrot, apple-nut and spice cakes. To soften cream cheese in the microwave, place unwrapped packages on a microwave-safe plate; microwave on medium for 1 to 1-1/2 minutes or until softened.

3/4 cup butter *or* margarine, softened
2 packages (3 ounces *each*) cream cheese, softened
1 teaspoon vanilla extract
3 cups confectioners' sugar

Fluffy Seven-Minute Frosting

Frosting Tender Cakes

When a cake is very tender and the frosting is thick, crumbs may loosen from the cake while frosting. To prevent this, spread a very thin layer of frosting over the sides of the cake before frosting as described on page 330.

In a mixing bowl, beat butter, cream cheese and vanilla until smooth. Gradually beat in sugar. Store frosted cake in the refrigerator. **Yield:** Frosts a three-layer, 15-in. x 10-in. or 13-in. x 9-in. cake. ○

Chocolate Whipped Cream Frosting

This frosting is best served the same day it's made. For a quick dessert, purchase a prepared angel food cake and frost it.

3 cups whipping cream
1-1/2 cups confectioners' sugar
3/4 cup baking cocoa
2 teaspoons vanilla extract
1/4 teaspoon salt

Combine all ingredients in a mixing bowl; cover and refrigerate with beaters for 1 hour. Beat until stiff peaks form. Store frosted cake in the refrigerator. **Yield:** Frosts a two-layer or 10-in. tube cake. ○

Pies

Besides the fruity Fresh Raspberry Pie (p. 347) and Peach Pie (p. 336) shown here, this chapter provides many innovative ideas for mouthwatering meringues, custard-filled creations, chocolaty delights and refreshing ice cream treats.

Mastering the art of baking pies is simply a matter of a little know-how and a lot of practice. In this chapter, you'll learn how to make flaky pie pastry, tasty fillings and pretty toppings for blue-ribbon pies in short order!

Pastry for Single-Crust Pie

When rolling out the pastry, mend any cracks by wetting your fingers and pressing the dough together.

1-1/4 cups all-purpose flour
1/2 teaspoon salt
1/3 cup shortening
4 to 5 tablespoons cold water

In a bowl, combine flour and salt; cut in the shortening until crumbly. Gradually add water, tossing with a fork until a ball forms. Roll out pastry to fit a 9-in. or 10-in. pie plate. Transfer pastry to pie plate. Trim pastry to 1/2 in. beyond edge of pie plate; flute edges. Fill or bake shell according to recipe directions. **Yield:** 1 pastry shell (9 or 10 inches).

Baking a Pastry Shell

After placing pastry in the pie plate and fluting edges, prick the bottom and sides of the pastry with a fork to prevent the pastry from bubbling as it bakes. Line shell with a double thickness of heavy-duty foil. Bake at 450° for 8 minutes. Remove foil; bake 5-6 minutes longer or until light golden brown. Cool on a wire rack.

Freezing Pie Pastry

You can easily prepare a homemade pie anytime if you keep pastry dough or shells in the freezer. Shape dough into a flattened ball; wrap in plastic wrap and heavy-duty foil, then freeze. To freeze a single crust, roll the dough, place in pie plate and flute edges; wrap with heavy-duty foil. Freeze for several months. Allow dough or shells to thaw before using.

Preparing Perfect Pie Pastry

- Classic pie pastry recipes are prepared with solid shortening. Lard or butter-flavored shortening can be substituted for plain shortening if desired.

- Measure all ingredients carefully for best results.

- Combine flour and salt thoroughly before adding the shortening and water.

- Be sure to use ice-cold water. Add an ice cube to water; measure before adding to the flour mixture.

- The key to producing a flaky crust is to avoid overmixing once you start adding the water to the flour and shortening mixture.

- A floured surface is essential to prevent sticking when rolling out pastry. A pastry cloth and a rolling pin cover are good investments—they will keep the pastry from sticking and minimize the amount of flour used. The less flour you add while rolling, the flakier and lighter the pastry will be.

- Chill pie pastry dough 30 minutes before rolling to make it easier to handle.

- Choose dull-finished aluminum or glass pie plates for crisp golden crusts. Shiny pans can produce a soggy crust.

- Because of the high fat content in a pastry, do not grease the pie plate unless the recipe directs.

- Never prick the bottom of a pastry crust when the filling and crust are to be baked together.

Pastry for Double-Crust Pie

This recipe is also used when preparing a lattice-topped pie. See Making a Lattice-Topped Pie on page 338.

2 cups all-purpose flour
3/4 teaspoon salt
2/3 cup shortening
6 to 7 tablespoons cold water

In a bowl, combine flour and salt; cut in the shortening until crumbly. Gradually add water, tossing with a fork until dough forms a ball. Divide dough in half so that one ball is slightly larger than the other. Roll out larger ball to fit a 9-in. or 10-in. pie plate. Transfer pastry to pie plate. Trim pastry even with edge. Pour desired filling into crust. Roll out second ball; cut slits in pastry. Position over filling. Trim pastry to 1 in. beyond edge of pie plate. Fold top crust over bottom crust. Flute edges. Bake according to recipe directions. **Yield:** pastry for double-crust pie (9 or 10 inches).

Making and Shaping Single- and Double-Crust Pie Pastry

1 Combine flour and salt in a bowl. With a pastry blender or two knives, cut in shortening until the mixture is the size of small peas.

2 Sprinkle a tablespoon of cold water at a time over the mixture and gently mix with a fork. Repeat until all the dough is moist, using only as much water as necessary to moisten the flour.

3 Shape into a ball. (For a double-crust pie, divide dough in half so that one ball is slightly larger than the other.) On a floured surface or floured pastry cloth, flatten the ball (the larger one, if making a double-crust pie) into a circle, pressing together any cracks or breaks.

4 Roll with a floured rolling pin from the center of the dough to the edges, forming a circle 2 in. larger than the pie plate. The dough should be about 1/8 in. thick.

5 To move pastry to the pie plate, roll up onto the rolling pin. Position over the edge of pie plate and unroll. Let the pastry ease into the plate. Do not stretch the pastry to fit. For a single-crust pie, trim pastry with a kitchen shears to 1/2 in. beyond plate edge; turn under and flute as in step 8. For a double-crust pie, trim pastry even with the edge. For a lattice-crust pie, trim pastry to 1 in. beyond plate edge. Either bake the shell or fill according to recipe directions.

6 For a double-crust pie, roll out second ball into a 12-in. circle about 1/8 in. thick. With a knife, cut several slits in dough to allow steam to escape while baking. Roll up onto the rolling pin; position over filling.

7 With kitchen shears, trim top crust to 1 in. beyond plate edge. Fold top crust over bottom crust.

8 To flute the edge as shown at left, place your thumb on the inside of the crust and your other thumb and index finger on the outside of the crust. Press the dough to seal.

Maple-Glazed Apple Pie

Maple-Glazed Apple Pie

This double-crust apple pie uses gingersnaps to thicken the pie filling rather than flour, and maple syrup to glaze the crust. Both flavors make for a terrific-tasting apple pie!

Pastry for Double-Crust Pie (page 334)
 6 cups thinly sliced peeled tart apples, *divided*
 1/2 cup sugar
 1/4 cup packed brown sugar
 1/2 cup crushed gingersnaps
 1/2 cup chopped walnuts *or* pecans
 1/4 cup butter *or* margarine, melted
 1/2 teaspoon ground cinnamon
 1/4 cup maple syrup

Line a 9-in. pie plate with bottom crust; trim pastry even with edge. Place half of the apples in the crust; set aside. In a bowl, combine sugars, gingersnaps, nuts, butter and cinnamon; sprinkle half over apples in crust. Top with remaining apples and sugar mixture. Roll out remaining pastry to fit top of pie; cut slits in pastry. Place over apples. Trim, seal and flute edges. Cover edges loosely with foil. Bake at 375° for 35 minutes. Meanwhile, bring syrup to a gentle boil in a small saucepan. Brush hot syrup over pie and into vents. Bake, uncovered, 20 minutes longer or until crust is golden brown and filling is bubbly. Cool on a wire rack. **Yield:** 6-8 servings. *—Patricia Putnam Lakeland, Florida*

Perfect Apple Pie

When a basic apple pie is just what you want, try this classic recipe. Serve with vanilla ice cream sprinkled with a little cinnamon for added flavor.

Pastry for Double-Crust Pie (page 334)
 7 to 8 cups thinly sliced peeled tart apples
 2 tablespoons lemon juice
 1 cup sugar
 1/4 cup all-purpose flour
 1 teaspoon ground cinnamon
 1/4 teaspoon salt
 1/8 teaspoon ground nutmeg
 2 tablespoons butter *or* margarine
 1 egg yolk
 1 tablespoon water

Line a 9-in. pie plate with bottom crust; trim pastry even with edge. Set aside. In a bowl, toss apples with lemon juice. Combine sugar, flour, cinnamon, salt and nutmeg; add to apples and toss. Pour into crust; dot with butter. Roll out remaining pastry to fit top of pie; cut slits in pastry. Place over filling. Trim, seal and flute edges. Beat egg yolk and water; brush over pastry. Cover edges loosely with foil. Bake at 425° for 15 minutes. Reduce heat to 350°; remove foil and bake 40-45 minutes longer or until crust is golden brown and filling is bubbly. Cool on a wire rack. **Yield:** 6-8 servings. *—Judy Oudekerk, St. Michael, Minnesota*

Peach Pie

(Pictured on cover and page 333)

Lemon juice adds a nice tang but also keeps the peaches from turning dark. Frozen peaches can be used if they are first thawed and well drained.

Pastry for Double-Crust Pie (page 334)
 5 cups sliced peeled fresh peaches
 1 tablespoon lemon juice

1/2 teaspoon almond extract
1 cup sugar
1/4 cup quick-cooking tapioca
1/4 teaspoon salt
2 tablespoons butter *or* margarine

Line a 9-in. pie plate with bottom crust. Trim pastry to 1 in. beyond edge of pie plate; set aside. In a bowl, combine peaches, lemon juice and extract. Add sugar, tapioca and salt; toss gently. Pour into crust; dot with butter. Roll out remaining pastry; make a lattice crust. Seal and flute edges. Cover edges loosely with foil. Bake at 425° for 20 minutes. Remove foil; bake 20-30 minutes longer or until crust is golden brown and filling is bubbly. Cool on a wire rack. **Yield:** 6-8 servings.

Four-Fruit Pie

If you only have a small amount of several kinds of fruit, consider this pie recipe. Allow fruit pies to cool to room temperature for easier cutting.

Pastry for Double-Crust Pie (page 334)
1 cup sliced fresh *or* frozen rhubarb (1-inch pieces), thawed and drained
1 cup chopped peeled tart apple
1 cup fresh *or* frozen blueberries
1 cup fresh *or* frozen raspberries
1 teaspoon lemon juice
3/4 cup sugar
1/4 cup all-purpose flour
2 tablespoons butter *or* margarine
Additional sugar, optional

Line a 9-in. pie plate with bottom crust; trim pastry even with edge. Set aside. In a large bowl, gently toss rhubarb, apple, berries and lemon juice. Combine sugar and flour; stir into the fruit and let stand for 30 minutes. Pour into crust; dot with butter. Roll out remaining pastry to fit top of pie; cut slits in pastry. Place over filling. Trim, seal and flute edges. Cover edges loosely with foil. Bake at 400° for 20 minutes. Remove foil; bake 30-40 minutes longer or until crust is golden brown and filling is bubbly. Sprinkle with sugar if desired. Cool on a wire rack. **Yield:** 6-8 servings. —*Joan Rose, Langley, British Columbia*

Testing Pies for Doneness

- A pastry shell is thoroughly baked when it is a light golden brown.
- Fruit pies are done when the filling bubbles and the crust is light golden brown.
- Meringues are properly baked when the top has turned to a golden glow and the tips of the meringue peaks are a light golden brown.
- Custard pies are done when a knife inserted near the center comes out clean.

Protecting Pastry Edges From Overbrowning

The edges of a pie pastry often brown before the rest of the pie is thoroughly baked. To protect the edges, fold a 12-in. piece of aluminum foil in quarters. At the center fold area, cut out a 6- to 7-in. circle. Unfold foil and place over unbaked pie; crimp edges lightly. Remove after the first 20 minutes of baking, unless otherwise directed.

Four-Fruit Pie

Making a Lattice-Topped Pie

1 Place the bottom crust of a double-crust pie pastry in pie plate. Add filling. Trim pastry to 1 in. beyond plate edge. Roll out remaining pastry into a 12-in. circle. Using a pastry wheel or knife, cut into strips about 1/2 in. thick. Lay strips in rows 3/4 in. apart going in one direction. (Use the longest strips for the center and the shortest strips on the sides.) Fold every other strip halfway back. Starting at the center, add strips at right angles, lifting every other strip as the cross strips are put down.

2 Continue to add strips, lifting and weaving until the entire pie top is covered with a woven top.

3 Trim strips even with the pastry shell edge. Fold the bottom crust up and flute edges. Or to make a rope edge as shown at left, pinch the dough at a slant between your thumb and index finger.

Cherry Berry Pie

Fall Pear Pie

Brushing the top crust of this pie with a beaten egg adds a golden glaze to the crust.

Pastry for Double-Crust Pie (page 334)
    8 cups thinly sliced peeled ripe pears
  3/4 cup sugar
  1/4 cup quick-cooking tapioca
  1/4 teaspoon ground nutmeg
    1 egg, lightly beaten
  1/4 cup whipping cream, optional

Line a 9-in. pie plate with bottom crust; trim pastry even with edge. In a large bowl, combine pears, sugar, tapioca and nutmeg; pour into crust. Roll out remaining pastry to fit top of pie; cut slits in pastry. Place over filling. Trim, seal and flute edges. Brush with egg. Cover edges loosely with foil. Bake at 375° for 20 minutes. Remove foil; bake 35-40 minutes longer or until the crust is golden brown and filling is bubbly. Pour cream through slits if desired. Cool on a wire rack for 2 hours; refrigerate. **Yield:** 6-8 servings.

—*Ken Churches, San Andreas, California*

Cherry Berry Pie

With this pie, you can enjoy the taste of a fresh fruit pie even when berries are out of season.

    1 can (15 ounces) pitted red cherries
    1 package (10 ounces) frozen sweetened raspberries
  3/4 cup sugar
    3 tablespoons cornstarch
    3 tablespoons butter *or* margarine
  1/4 teaspoon almond extract
  1/4 teaspoon red food coloring, optional
Pastry for Double-Crust Pie (page 334)

Drain cherries and raspberries, reserving 1-1/4 cups juice; set fruit aside. In a saucepan, combine sugar and cornstarch; gradually stir in reserved juice. Cook and stir over medium heat until the mixture begins to boil. Cook and stir 2 minutes longer. Remove from the heat; stir in butter, extract and food coloring if desired. Gently fold in fruit. Cool slightly. Line a 9-in. pie plate with bottom crust. Trim pastry to 1 in. beyond edge of pie plate. Pour filling into crust. Roll out remaining pastry; make a lattice crust. Seal and flute edges. Cover edges loosely with foil. Bake at 375° for 20 minutes. Remove foil; bake 25 minutes longer or until crust is golden brown and filling is bubbly. Cool on a wire rack. **Yield:** 6-8 servings. —*Mamie Palmer Sault Sainte Marie, Michigan*

Farm Apple Pan Pie

The unique egg yolk pastry is easy to work with and makes a very rich-tasting crust. Prepare this pie when you need to feed a crowd.

EGG YOLK PASTRY:
>   5 cups all-purpose flour
>   4 teaspoons sugar
>   1/2 teaspoon salt
>   1/2 teaspoon baking powder
> 1-1/2 cups shortening
>   2 egg yolks, lightly beaten
>   3/4 cup cold water

FILLING:
>   5 pounds tart apples, peeled and thinly sliced
>   4 teaspoons lemon juice
>   3/4 cup sugar
>   3/4 cup packed brown sugar
>   1 teaspoon ground cinnamon
>   1/2 teaspoon ground nutmeg
>   1/4 teaspoon salt

Milk

Additional sugar

In a bowl, combine flour, sugar, salt and baking powder; cut in the shortening until the mixture is the size of small peas. Combine yolks and cold water. Sprinkle over dry ingredients; toss with a fork. If needed, add additional water, 1 tablespoon at a time, until dough forms a ball. Divide in half. On a lightly floured surface, roll half of the pastry to fit a 15-in. x 10-in. x 1-in. baking pan. Sprinkle apples with lemon juice; arrange half over dough. Combine the sugars, cinnamon, nutmeg and salt; sprinkle half over apples. Top with remaining apples; sprinkle with remaining sugar mixture. Roll out remaining pastry to fit pan; cut slits in pastry. Place over filling and seal edges. Brush with milk and sprinkle with sugar. Bake at 400° for 50 minutes or until crust is golden brown and filling is bubbly. Cool on a wire rack. **Yield:** 18-24 servings.

—*Dolores Skrout, Summerhill, Pennsylvania*

Apple Cranberry Pie

(Pictured on page 340)

Apples can be teamed with cranberry and orange to make an autumn pie that's sure to please. For a quick lattice crust that doesn't involve weaving pastry strips, place pastry strips in one direction 3/4 inch apart. Top with strips in the other direction 3/4 inch apart (see photo).

>   2 cups fresh *or* frozen cranberries
> 1-3/4 cups sugar
>   1/3 cup quick-cooking tapioca
>   1/4 cup water
>   2 teaspoons grated orange peel
>   3 cups thinly sliced peeled tart apples

Pastry for Double-Crust Pie (page 334)
>   1 egg white, beaten
>   1 tablespoon water

Additional sugar

In a saucepan, combine the cranberries, sugar, tapioca, water and orange peel. Bring to a boil, stirring occasionally. Remove from the heat and stir in apples. Set saucepan in a pan of cold water for 10 minutes, stirring occasionally. Meanwhile, line a 9-in. pie plate with the bottom crust. Trim pastry to 1 in. beyond edge of pie plate. Pour filling into crust. Roll out remaining pastry; make a lattice crust. Seal and flute edges. Beat egg white and water until foamy; brush over lattice top. Sprinkle with sugar. Cover edges loosely with foil. Bake at 375° for 20 minutes. Remove foil; bake 25-35 minutes longer or until crust is golden brown and filling is bubbly. Cool on a wire rack. **Yield:** 6-8 servings.

—*Janet Morgan-Cavallaro, Pincourt, Quebec*

Farm Apple Pan Pie

Coconut Banana Cream Pie
German Chocolate Pie
Strawberry Lover's Pie
Apple Cranberry Pie

Combining Egg Yolks and Hot Mixtures

When making a cream pie with egg yolks, the hot liquid needs to be added carefully to the egg yolks. Remove about 1 cup of the hot mixture and stir into the yolks. Return mixture to pan. Proceed with recipe as directed.

Coconut Banana Cream Pie

The coconut crust is a wonderful complement to this banana cream pie. You will need to watch the crust as it bakes to make sure it doesn't brown too quickly.

CRUST:
    7 tablespoons butter *or* margarine
    3 cups flaked coconut
FILLING:
    3/4 cup sugar
    1/4 cup all-purpose flour
    3 tablespoons cornstarch
    1/4 teaspoon salt
    3 cups half-and-half cream
    4 egg yolks, lightly beaten
    2 teaspoons vanilla extract
    2 large firm bananas, sliced
Whipped cream and sliced bananas, optional

In a skillet, melt butter over medium heat. Saute coconut until golden. Set aside 2 tablespoons for topping. Press remaining coconut onto the bottom and up the sides of a greased 9-in. pie plate. Bake at 350° for 7 minutes. In a saucepan, combine the sugar, flour, cornstarch and salt. Gradually add cream and bring to a boil. Cook and stir for 2 minutes. Remove from the heat. Stir a small amount into egg yolks. Return all to pan; cook for 2 minutes. Remove from the heat; add vanilla. Cool to room temperature. Place bananas in the crust. Cover with cream mixture. Chill until set, about 2 hours. Sprinkle with reserved coconut. If desired, garnish with whipped cream and bananas. Store leftovers in the refrigerator.
Yield: 6-8 servings.
—*Tammy Olson*
Bruce, South Dakota

German Chocolate Pie

This pie uses a deep-dish pie plate because it has a very generous amount of filling. If you like German Chocolate Cake, you'll have to try this pie version of that recipe.

    1 package (4 ounces) German sweet chocolate
    1/4 cup butter *or* margarine
    1 can (12 ounces) evaporated milk
1-1/2 cups sugar
    3 tablespoons cornstarch
    1/8 teaspoon salt
    2 eggs, lightly beaten
    1 teaspoon vanilla extract
    1 unbaked deep-dish pastry shell (9 inches)
1-1/3 cups flaked coconut
    1/2 cup chopped pecans

In a saucepan, melt chocolate and butter over low heat, stirring to blend. Remove from the heat and gradually stir in milk; set aside. In a bowl, combine sugar, cornstarch and salt. Stir in eggs and vanilla. Gradually stir in chocolate mixture. Pour into crust. Combine coconut and pecans; sprinkle over filling. Cover edges loosely with foil. Bake at 375° for 20 minutes. Remove foil; bake 25-30 minutes longer or until puffed and browned. Cool on a wire rack for 2 hours. Refrigerate at least 3 hours before serving. Store leftovers in the refrigerator.
Yield: 6-8 servings.
—*Cheryl Jacobson*
Chino Valley, Arizona

Strawberry Lover's Pie

Even though this recipe has several steps, it is easy to prepare and is a spectacular ending to any meal during strawberry season. It's best to serve this pie on the same day it's prepared.

    3 squares (1 ounce *each*) semisweet chocolate, *divided*
    1 tablespoon butter *or* margarine
    1 pastry shell (9 inches), baked
    2 packages (3 ounces *each*) cream cheese, softened
    1/2 cup sour cream
    3 tablespoons sugar
    1/2 teaspoon vanilla extract
    3 to 4 cups fresh strawberries, hulled
    1/3 cup strawberry jam, melted

In a saucepan, melt 2 squares of chocolate and butter over low heat, stirring to blend; spread or brush over the bottom and up the sides of pastry shell. Chill. Meanwhile, in a mixing bowl, beat cream cheese, sour cream, sugar and vanilla until smooth. Spread over chocolate layer; cover and chill for 2 hours. Arrange strawberries, tip end up, over filling. Brush jam over strawberries. Melt remaining chocolate; drizzle over all. Store leftovers in the refrigerator. **Yield:** 6-8 servings.
—*Lauretha Rowe, Scranton, Kansas*

*World's Best
Lemon Pie*

flour and salt. Gradually stir in water. Cook and stir over medium heat until thickened and bubbly. Reduce heat; cook and stir 2 minutes longer. Remove from the heat. Gradually stir 1 cup hot filling into egg yolks; return all to pan. Bring to a boil; cook and stir for 2 minutes. Remove from the heat. Stir in the butter, lemon juice and peel until butter is melted. Pour hot filling into pastry shell. In a mixing bowl, beat egg whites and cream of tartar on medium until soft peaks form. Gradually beat in sugar, 1 tablespoon at a time, on high until stiff, glossy peaks form and sugar is dissolved. Spread evenly over hot filling, sealing edges to crust. Bake at 350° for 12-15 minutes or until the meringue is golden. Cool on a wire rack for 1 hour; refrigerate at least 3 hours before serving. Store leftovers in the refrigerator. **Yield:** 6-8 servings.

—*Phyllis Kirsling, Junction City, Wisconsin*

Spreading a Pie Meringue

Spoon beaten meringue onto the hot pie filling. Gently spread meringue to the edges of the crust to seal and prevent shrinkage.

Grandma's Chocolate Meringue Pie

To prevent soft meringues from sticking to your knife when serving, dip the knife in a tall glass of water before making each cut in the pie.

　　3/4 cup sugar
　　　5 tablespoons baking cocoa
　　　3 tablespoons cornstarch
　　1/4 teaspoon salt
　　　2 cups milk
　　　3 egg yolks, beaten
　　　1 teaspoon vanilla extract
　　　1 pastry shell (9 inches), baked
MERINGUE:
　　　3 egg whites, room temperature
　　1/4 teaspoon cream of tartar
　　　6 tablespoons sugar

In a saucepan, combine sugar, cocoa, cornstarch and salt; gradually add milk. Cook and stir over medium-high heat until thickened and bubbly. Reduce heat; cook and stir 2 minutes longer. Remove from the heat. Stir 1 cup of hot filling into egg yolks. Return all to pan and bring to a gentle boil. Cook for 2 minutes, stirring constantly. Remove from the heat; stir in vanilla. Pour hot filling into pastry shell. In a mixing bowl, beat egg whites and cream of tartar on medium until soft peaks form. Gradually beat in sugar, 1 tablespoon at a time, on high until stiff, glossy peaks form and sugar is dissolved. Spread evenly over hot filling, sealing edges to crust. Bake at 350° for 12-15 minutes or until the meringue is golden. Cool on a wire rack for 1 hour; refrigerate at least 3 hours before serving. Store leftovers in the refrigerator. **Yield:** 6-8 servings.

—*Donna Vest Tilley, Chesterfield, Virginia*

World's Best Lemon Pie

The secret to a great meringue is adding the sugar gradually, a tablespoon at a time, to the egg whites and beating the meringue enough to dissolve the sugar. Check to see if the sugar is dissolved by rubbing a little meringue between your thumb and index finger. If you can feel the sugar granules, the meringue needs to be beaten a little longer.

　　　1 cup sugar
　　1/4 cup cornstarch
　　　3 tablespoons all-purpose flour
　　1/4 teaspoon salt
　　　2 cups water
　　　3 egg yolks, beaten
　　　1 tablespoon butter *or* margarine
　　1/4 cup lemon juice
　　　1 teaspoon grated lemon peel
　　　1 pastry shell (9 inches), baked
MERINGUE:
　　　3 egg whites, room temperature
　　1/4 teaspoon cream of tartar
　　　6 tablespoons sugar

In a medium saucepan, combine sugar, cornstarch,

Pumpkin Pecan Pie

This recipe is a cross between a pecan and a pumpkin pie. It is very rich and simply needs a small dollop of whipped cream for a garnish.

2 eggs
1/4 cup sugar
1/4 cup packed brown sugar
1 teaspoon all-purpose flour
1 teaspoon pumpkin pie spice
1/4 teaspoon salt
2/3 cup canned *or* cooked pumpkin
2/3 cup milk
1 unbaked deep-dish pastry shell (9 inches)

PECAN TOPPING:
2 eggs
1/2 cup dark corn syrup
2 tablespoons brown sugar
2 tablespoons molasses
1 tablespoon all-purpose flour
1 teaspoon vanilla extract
1/2 teaspoon salt
1/2 cup chopped pecans
1 cup pecan halves

In a mixing bowl, beat eggs, sugars, flour, pie spice and salt until smooth. Mix in pumpkin. Gradually beat in milk. Pour into crust. Cover edges loosely with foil. Bake at 425° for 10 minutes. Reduce heat to 350° and bake 15 minutes longer. Remove foil. For topping, beat eggs in a mixing bowl until foamy. Add corn syrup, brown sugar, molasses, flour, vanilla and salt. Pour over filling. Sprinkle with chopped pecans; cover with pecan halves. Bake, uncovered, 30-35 minutes longer or until set. Cool on a wire rack for 2 hours. Refrigerate until ready to serve. Store leftovers in the refrigerator. **Yield:** 6-8 servings. —*Jean Lockwood Bayfield, Colorado*

Pumpkin Pecan Pie

Sweet Potato Pie

A close cousin to pumpkin pie, this Southern favorite uses cooked sweet potatoes that are mashed without milk or butter. Substitute one 15-ounce can of sweet potatoes or pumpkin for the freshly cooked sweet potato if you like.

Pastry for Single-Crust Pie (page 334)
2 eggs
1 can (12 ounces) evaporated milk
1 teaspoon vanilla extract
1-1/4 cups sugar
1/2 teaspoon ground cinnamon
1/2 teaspoon ground nutmeg
1-1/2 cups mashed cooked sweet potatoes

TOPPING:
1/3 cup butter *or* margarine
1/3 cup all-purpose flour
1/2 cup packed brown sugar
1/2 cup flaked coconut
1/2 cup chopped pecans
Whipped topping *or* ice cream

Line a 9-in. pie plate with crust. Trim pastry to 1/2 in. beyond edge of pie plate; flute edges. Set aside. In a mixing bowl, beat eggs; add milk and vanilla. Combine sugar, cinnamon and nutmeg; add to egg mixture. Stir in sweet potatoes; beat until smooth. Pour into crust. Cover edges loosely with foil. Bake at 425° for 15 minutes. Remove foil. Reduce heat to 350°; bake 30 minutes longer. Combine the first five topping ingredients; sprinkle over pie. Bake for 10-15 minutes or until topping is golden brown. Cool on a wire rack for 2 hours; refrigerate until ready to serve. Serve with whipped topping or ice cream. Store leftovers in the refrigerator. **Yield:** 6-8 servings. —*Shari Millican Smyrna, Georgia*

Homemade Pumpkin Pie Spice

Combine 4 teaspoons ground cinnamon, 2 teaspoons ground ginger, 1 teaspoon ground cloves and 1/2 teaspoon ground nutmeg. Store in an airtight container. Substitute for store-bought pumpkin pie spice in any recipe. **Yield:** 7-1/2 teaspoons.

Old-Fashioned Custard Pie

You will need to prepare a double-crust pastry if you wish to make a braided crust edge (see below right). Otherwise, simply prepare a single-crust pie and flute in the traditional manner.

Pastry for Single- or Double-Crust Pie (page 334)
- 4 eggs
- 2-1/2 cups milk
- 1/2 cup sugar
- 1 teaspoon salt
- 1 teaspoon ground nutmeg
- 1 teaspoon vanilla extract
- 1 teaspoon almond extract

Line a 9-in. pie plate with crust. Trim pastry to 1/2 in. beyond edge of pie plate; flute edges or prepare a braided crust. Bake at 400° for 10 minutes. Meanwhile, beat eggs in a large bowl. Add remaining ingredients; mix well. Pour into crust. Cover edges loosely with foil. Bake for 20-25 minutes or until a knife inserted near the center comes out clean. Cool on a wire rack for 2 hours; refrigerate until ready to serve. Store leftovers in the refrigerator. **Yield:** 6-8 servings.

—*Maxine Linkenauger, Montverde, Florida*

Old-Fashioned Custard Pie

Pumpkin Patch Pie

If you'd like to make pumpkin pie from a fresh pumpkin, here's an easy recipe that eliminates the guesswork. Use a pie pumpkin for maximum flavor.

- 1 medium pie pumpkin (about 3 pounds)
- 2/3 cup sugar, *divided*
- 1-1/2 teaspoons ground cinnamon, *divided*
- 1/8 teaspoon salt
- 1/2 teaspoon ground ginger
- 1/2 teaspoon ground nutmeg
- 3 eggs, beaten
- 1 can (5 ounces) evaporated milk
- 1/2 cup milk

Pastry for Single-Crust Pie (page 334)

Wash pumpkin; cut a 5-in. circle around top stem. Remove top and set aside; discard seeds and loose fibers from inside. Combine 1/3 cup of sugar, 1/2 teaspoon of cinnamon and salt; sprinkle around inside of pumpkin. Replace the top. Place in a greased 15-in. x 10-in. x 1-in. baking pan. Bake at 325° for 1-1/2 hours or until very tender. Cool. Scoop out pumpkin; puree in a blender until smooth. Place 2 cups pureed pumpkin in a bowl. Add ginger, nutmeg and the remaining sugar and cinnamon. Stir in eggs, evaporated milk and milk until well blended. Line a 9-in. pie plate with crust. Trim pastry to 1/2 in. beyond edge of pie plate; flute edges. Pour filling into crust. Cover the edges loosely with foil. Bake at 375° for 20 minutes. Remove foil; bake 55-60 minutes longer or until a knife inserted near the center comes out clean. Cool on a wire rack for 2 hours; refrigerate until ready to serve. Store leftovers in the refrigerator. **Yield:** 6-8 servings.

—*Jane Van Deusen, Oneonta, New York*

Braiding Crust Edges

Prepare a double-crust pastry. Roll out large ball of dough to fit a 9-in. or 10-in. pie plate. Trim pastry edges even with plate edge; brush edges with water. Roll out remaining dough into a square 1/8 in. thick. With a knife, cut into 12 strips (1/4 in. wide). Braid three strips together on the edge of crust, attaching additional strips until entire edge is covered with braid. Press lightly to secure on rim of pastry. Cover edges with foil.

Strawberry Rhubarb Crumb Pie

Strawberry Rhubarb Crumb Pie

To make the crumb topping, take the butter directly from the refrigerator so that it can be cut into the flour mixture much like you do when making pastry.

Pastry for Single-Crust Pie (page 334)
   1 egg
   1 cup sugar
   2 tablespoons all-purpose flour
   1 teaspoon vanilla extract
   3/4 pound fresh rhubarb, cut into 1/2-inch pieces
      (about 3 cups)
   1 pint fresh strawberries, halved
TOPPING:
   3/4 cup all-purpose flour
   1/2 cup packed brown sugar
   1/2 cup quick-cooking *or* rolled oats
   1/2 cup cold butter *or* margarine

Line a 9-in. pie plate with crust. Trim pastry to 1/2 in. beyond edge of pie plate; flute edges. Set aside. In a mixing bowl, beat egg. Add sugar, flour and vanilla; mix well. Gently fold in rhubarb and strawberries. Pour into crust. For topping, combine flour, brown sugar and oats in a small bowl; cut in butter until crumbly. Sprinkle over filling. Bake at 400° for 10 minutes. Reduce heat to 350°; bake 35 minutes longer or until crust is golden brown and filling is bubbly. Cool on a wire rack for 2 hours; refrigerate until ready to serve. Store leftovers in the refrigerator. **Yield:** 6-8 servings.
                    —*Paula Phillips, East Winthrop, Maine*

Fluffy Cranberry Cheese Pie

When planning your Thanksgiving or Christmas dinner, keep this refreshing cranberry pie at the top of the list. If two pies are needed, serve this and traditional pumpkin pie for variety in color, texture and flavor at your dessert table.

CRANBERRY TOPPING:
   1 package (3 ounces) raspberry gelatin
   1/3 cup sugar
   1-1/4 cups cranberry juice
   1 can (8 ounces) jellied cranberry sauce
FILLING:
   1 package (3 ounces) cream cheese, softened
   1/4 cup sugar
   1 tablespoon milk
   1 teaspoon vanilla extract
   1/2 cup whipped topping
   1 pastry shell (9 inches), baked

In a mixing bowl, combine gelatin and sugar; set aside. In a saucepan, bring cranberry juice to a boil. Remove from the heat and pour over gelatin mixture, stirring to dissolve. Stir in the cranberry sauce. Chill until slightly thickened. Meanwhile, in another mixing bowl, beat cream cheese, sugar, milk and vanilla until fluffy. Fold in the whipped topping. Spread evenly into pastry shell. Beat cranberry topping until frothy; pour over filling. Chill for at least 6 hours. Store leftovers in the refrigerator. **Yield:** 6-8 servings.   —*Mary Parkonen*
                    West Wareham, Massachusetts

Fluffy Cranberry Cheese Pie

Making Crumb Crusts

Why rely on store-bought crumb crusts when you can easily prepare a better-tasting version from scratch? In a mixing bowl, combine crumbs, sugar and melted butter or margarine; blend well. Press the mixture onto the bottom and up the sides of an ungreased 9-in. pie plate. Chill 30 minutes before filling or bake at 375° for 8-10 minutes or until crust is lightly browned. Cool before filling.

Type of Crust	Amount of Crumbs	Sugar	Butter *or* Margarine, melted
Graham Cracker	1-1/2 cups (24 squares)	1/4 cup	1/3 cup
Chocolate Wafer	1-1/4 cups (20 wafers)	1/4 cup	1/4 cup
Vanilla Wafer	1-1/2 cups (30 wafers)	none	1/4 cup
Cream-Filled Chocolate	1-1/2 cups (15 cookies)	none	1/4 cup
Gingersnap	1-1/2 cups (24 cookies)	none	1/4 cup

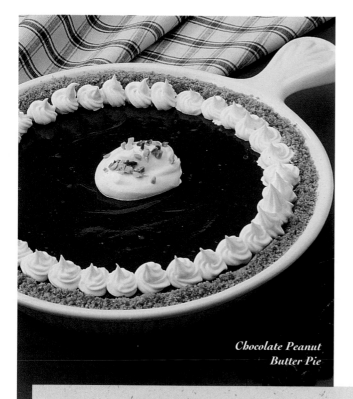

Chocolate Peanut Butter Pie

Chocolate Peanut Butter Pie

To enjoy a crisp crust, serve pies prepared with graham cracker crusts the same day they are prepared. Frozen ice cream pies are the exception.

        1 cup sugar
        6 tablespoons all-purpose flour
    1/2 teaspoon salt
        2 cups milk
        3 egg yolks, beaten
        1 teaspoon vanilla extract
        2 tablespoons peanut butter
        1 square (1 ounce) semisweet chocolate, melted
        1 graham cracker crust (9 inches), baked
Whipped cream
Chopped peanuts

In the top of a double boiler, over hot but not boiling water, combine sugar, flour and salt. Gradually add milk and cook for 10 minutes, stirring constantly. Pour a small amount of the hot milk mixture into the egg yolks; return all to double boiler. Cook for 4 minutes, stirring constantly. Remove from the heat; stir in vanilla. Cool for about 10 minutes. Divide mixture in half. To one portion, stir in peanut butter; mix well. To the remaining portion, stir in melted chocolate. Allow mixtures to cool completely. Fill pie crust with peanut butter mixture, then chocolate mixture. Chill for 2-3 hours. Just before serving, top with whipped cream and nuts. Store leftovers in the refrigerator. **Yield:** 6-8 servings. —*Kim Scott Byron, New York*

Making Crumbs

Place cookies or crackers in a heavy-duty resealable plastic bag. Seal bag, pushing out as much air as possible. Press a rolling pin over the bag, crushing the crackers to fine crumbs. Crumbs can also be made in a blender or food processor according to manufacturer's directions.

Boil for 2 minutes, stirring constantly. Remove from the heat; cool for 15 minutes. Gently stir in remaining berries; carefully spoon over filling. Chill 3 hours or until set. Store leftovers in the refrigerator. **Yield:** 6-8 servings.

—*Kim Erickson, Sturgis, Michigan*

Fresh Raspberry Pie

(Pictured on page 332)

When the raspberry patch is producing pints of precious raspberries, plan on preparing this seasonal treat. Because the raspberries are not cooked, they retain their garden-fresh flavor. A dollop of freshly whipped cream is a tasty topping.

　　1/4 cup sugar
　　1 tablespoon cornstarch
　　1 cup water
　　1 package (3 ounces) raspberry gelatin
　　4 cups fresh raspberries
　　1 graham cracker crust (9 inches), baked
Whipped cream, optional

In a saucepan, combine sugar and cornstarch. Stir in water until smooth; bring to a boil, stirring constantly. Cook and stir for 2 minutes. Remove from the heat; stir in gelatin until dissolved. Cool for 15 minutes. Place raspberries in the crust; slowly pour gelatin mixture over berries. Chill until set, about 3 hours. Garnish with whipped cream if desired. **Yield:** 6-8 servings.

—*Patricia Staudt, Marble Rock, Iowa*

Blueberry Cream Pie

Prepare a basic vanilla wafer crust (see page 346) or this recipe's sweeter version containing sugar and vanilla extract.

　1-1/3 cups vanilla wafer crumbs
　　2 tablespoons sugar
　　5 tablespoons butter *or* margarine, melted
　　1/2 teaspoon vanilla extract
FILLING:
　　1/4 cup sugar
　　3 tablespoons all-purpose flour
Pinch salt
　　1 cup half-and-half cream
　　3 egg yolks, beaten
　　3 tablespoons butter *or* margarine
　　1 teaspoon vanilla extract
　　1 tablespoon confectioners' sugar
TOPPING:
　　5 cups fresh blueberries, *divided*
　　2/3 cup sugar
　　1 tablespoon cornstarch

Combine the first four ingredients; press onto the bottom and up the sides of an ungreased 9-in. pie pan. Bake at 375° for 8-10 minutes or until crust just begins to brown. Cool. In a saucepan, combine sugar, flour and salt. Gradually whisk in cream; cook and stir over medium heat until thickened and bubbly. Cook and stir 2 minutes longer. Gradually whisk 1 cup hot filling into egg yolks; return all to pan. Bring to a gentle boil; cook for 2 minutes, stirring constantly. Remove from the heat; stir in butter and vanilla until butter is melted. Cool for 5 minutes, stirring occasionally. Pour into crust; sprinkle with confectioners' sugar. Chill for 30 minutes or until set. Meanwhile, crush 2 cups of blueberries in a medium saucepan; bring to a boil. Boil for 2 minutes, stirring constantly. Press berries through a sieve (see using a Sieve to Puree on page 297). Set aside 1 cup juice (add water if necessary). Discard pulp. In a saucepan, combine sugar and cornstarch. Gradually stir in blueberry juice; bring to a boil.

Blueberry Cream Pie

Tips for Serving Ice Cream Pies

- Crumb crusts that are going to be filled with ice cream do not need to be baked. Just refrigerate the crust for 30 minutes before adding the filling.
- Take ice cream pies out of the freezer 10-15 minutes before serving for easier slicing.
- Prepare ice cream pies a week or two ahead; cover well with heavy-duty foil to guard against freezer burn.

Strawberry Rhubarb Ice Cream Pie

Mud Pie

This pie is ready in no time at all. Simply assemble before dinner and freeze while enjoying the meal.

1 quart coffee ice cream, softened
1 chocolate crumb crust (9 inches)
1/2 cup chocolate syrup

Spread ice cream over crust; pour chocolate syrup on top and swirl with a knife. Cover and freeze for at least 1 hour. **Yield:** 6-8 servings.
—*Debbie Jones*
California, Maryland

Frozen Grasshopper Torte

Here's a no-bake dessert that serves many and can be prepared in advance. Preparing it in a springform pan makes for easy cutting and a pretty presentation.

4 cups crushed cream-filled chocolate cookies (about 40)
1/4 cup butter *or* margarine, melted
1 pint vanilla ice cream, softened
1 jar (7 ounces) marshmallow creme
1/4 cup milk
1/4 to 1/2 teaspoon peppermint extract
Few drops green food coloring, optional
2 cups whipping cream, whipped

Combine cookie crumbs and butter. Reserve 1/4 cup; press remaining crumbs onto the bottom of a 9-in. springform pan, two 9-in. pie plates or a 13-in. x 9-in. x 2-in. baking dish. Chill for 30 minutes. Spread ice cream over crust. Freeze. Meanwhile, in a bowl, combine marshmallow creme and milk; stir until well blended. Add extract and food coloring if desired. Fold in whipped cream. Spoon over ice cream and sprinkle with reserved crumbs. Cover and freeze until firm.
Yield: 12-16 servings.
—*Elma Penner*
Oak Bluff, Manitoba

Strawberry Rhubarb Ice Cream Pie

Use either your own homemade graham cracker crust or a purchased crust to make this easy springtime dessert.

1 quart vanilla ice cream, softened
1 graham cracker crust (9 inches)
1-1/2 cups sliced fresh *or* frozen rhubarb (1/2-inch pieces), thawed and drained
1/2 cup sugar
1 tablespoon cornstarch
1 tablespoon water
1 pint fresh strawberries, sliced

Spoon ice cream over crust; freeze. Meanwhile, in a saucepan over medium heat, cook rhubarb and sugar, stirring occasionally, until sugar dissolves and mixture boils. Combine cornstarch and water; stir into rhubarb mixture. Cook until thickened, stirring constantly. Cook 2 minutes longer. Cool. Fold in berries; chill. Spread over ice cream. Cover and freeze until firm.
Yield: 6-8 servings.
—*Connie Fleck*
Fort Atkinson, Wisconsin

Chocolate Malt Shoppe Pie

This is a refreshing pie that is welcomed during the hot summer months. To crush malted milk balls, place candy in a heavy-duty resealable plastic bag. On a hard surface, pound candy with the flat side of a meat tenderizing mallet or rolling pin until finely crushed.

   1 pint vanilla ice cream, softened
   1/2 cup crushed malted milk balls
   2 tablespoons milk, *divided*
   1 chocolate crumb crust (9 inches)
   3 tablespoons instant chocolate malted milk
     powder
   3 tablespoons marshmallow creme topping
   1 cup whipping cream
Additional whipped cream and malted milk balls

In a mixing bowl, blend the ice cream, crushed malted milk balls and 1 tablespoon milk. Spoon over crust. Freeze for 1 hour. Meanwhile, blend malted milk powder, marshmallow creme and remaining milk in a mixing bowl. Stir in whipping cream; whip until soft peaks form. Spread over ice cream layer. Cover and freeze several hours or overnight. Before serving, garnish with whipped cream and malted milk balls. **Yield:** 6-8 servings.
—Beth Wanek
Little Chute, Wisconsin

Sunshine Ice Cream Pie

Prepare this recipe all summer long because of its refreshing flavor. Substitute a vanilla wafer crust for the graham cracker crust if you like.

   1 pint vanilla ice cream, softened
   1 graham cracker crust (9 inches)
   1 pint orange sherbet, softened
   2 cups whipped topping
   1 can (11 ounces) mandarin oranges, drained
   2 tablespoons flaked coconut, toasted

Spread ice cream over crust; spread sherbert over ice cream. Freeze for at least 3 hours. Top with whipped topping. Cover and freeze. Just before serving, arrange oranges on top and sprinkle with coconut. **Yield:** 6-8 servings. *—Bonnie Polson, Moravia, Iowa*

Peppermint Stick Pie

If you like crunchy candy bars, you'll love this pie. If peppermint ice cream is not available, substitute mint-flavored ice cream.

   4-1/2 cups crisp rice cereal
     1 cup (6 ounces) semisweet chocolate chips,
       melted
     2 quarts peppermint stick ice cream, softened
Chocolate syrup *or* **chocolate fudge topping**
Crushed peppermint candies

Combine cereal and chocolate; mix well. Press onto the bottom and up the sides of an ungreased 10-in. pie plate. Freeze for 5 minutes. Spoon ice cream over crust. Cover and freeze at least 2 hours. Before serving, garnish with chocolate syrup and peppermint candies. **Yield:** 6-8 servings.   *—Mildred Peachey, Wooster, Ohio*

Peppermint Stick Pie

Cookies and Candies

As a treat for the eyes and taste buds, present folks with a dish adorned with homemade candies such as Pecan Delights (p. 368) and a cookie jar brimming with mouth-watering morsels like Ultimate Double Chocolate Brownies (p. 362) or Cranberry Nut Swirls (p. 357).

Whether you make easy bars, classic chocolate chip drop cookies, festive cutouts, sliced refrigerator cookies or fancy shapes with a cookie press, you'll enjoy baking and serving these tasty sweets.

Chocolate Chip Cookies
Grandma's Peanut Butter Cookies

Cookie Making Tips

- For best results, use regular shortening, butter or margarine (containing at least 80% oil) in cookie recipes. Whipped, tub, soft, liquid or reduced-fat products contain air and water and will produce flat, tough or underbrowned cookies.

- Measure all ingredients accurately using the measuring techniques and equipment suggested on page 10.

- Use shiny aluminum baking sheets without sides for golden brown cookies.

- Turn on your oven to the required temperature 10-15 minutes before baking.

- If a recipe directs you to grease the baking sheets, use shortening for best results.

- For even baking, make cookies the same size and thickness.

- Always place cookie dough 2 to 3 inches apart, unless otherwise directed, on cool baking sheets.

- Leave at least 2 inches around the baking sheet and the oven walls for good heat circulation. For best results, bake only one sheet of cookies at a time.

- Unless otherwise directed, let cookies cool for 1 minute on the baking sheet before removing to a wire rack. Cool completely before storing.

Shaping Drop Cookies

Fill a teaspoon or tablespoon with dough. Drop mounds of dough onto cool baking sheets using a second spoon or small rubber spatula to push the dough off the spoon. Place the dough 2 to 3 in. apart or as recipe directs.

Chocolate Chip Cookies

Try this recipe when you're looking for a basic chocolate chip cookie. If you like, leave out the nuts and double the chips.

    1 cup butter *or* margarine, softened
1/2 cup sugar
    1 cup packed brown sugar
    2 eggs
    1 teaspoon vanilla extract
2-1/3 cups all-purpose flour
    1 teaspoon baking soda
1/2 teaspoon salt
    1 cup (6 ounces) semisweet chocolate chips
3/4 cup chopped walnuts, pecans *or* hazelnuts

In a mixing bowl, cream butter and sugars on medium speed for 3 minutes. Add eggs one at a time, beating well after each addition. Add vanilla. Combine flour, baking soda and salt; gradually add to creamed mixture. Stir in chocolate chips and nuts. Drop by heaping tablespoonfuls 3 in. apart onto lightly greased baking sheets. Bake at 350° for 10-12 minutes or until light brown. Remove to wire racks to cool. **Yield:** 3 dozen.
—*Selmer Looney, Eugene, Oregon*

Grandma's Peanut Butter Cookies

Here's a classic recipe that is sure to please just about everyone. You can use either creamy or crunchy peanut butter and light or dark brown sugar.

  1 cup shortening
  1 cup peanut butter
  1 cup sugar
  1 cup packed brown sugar
  3 eggs
  3 cups all-purpose flour
  2 teaspoons baking soda
  1/4 teaspoon salt

In a mixing bowl, cream shortening, peanut butter and sugars. Add eggs one at a time, beating well after each addition. Combine flour, baking soda and salt; gradually add to creamed mixture. Roll into 1-1/2-in. balls and place 3 in. apart on ungreased baking sheets. Flatten with a fork. Bake at 375° for 10-15 minutes or until bottoms are lightly browned. Remove to wire racks to cool. **Yield:** about 4 dozen.   —*Janet Hall Clinton, Wisconsin*

Oatmeal Raisin Cookies

Be careful not to overbake these cookies; they won't be chewy if you do. The cookies should be light golden brown and slightly soft in the center before removing from the oven.

      1 cup shortening
      1 cup sugar
      1 cup packed brown sugar
      3 eggs
      1 teaspoon vanilla extract
  2-1/2 cups all-purpose flour
      2 teaspoons baking soda
      1 teaspoon salt
      1 teaspoon ground cinnamon
      2 cups old-fashioned *or* quick-cooking oats
      1 cup raisins
      1 cup coarsely chopped pecans, optional

In a mixing bowl, cream shortening and sugars. Add eggs one at a time, beating well after each addition.

Add vanilla. Combine flour, baking soda, salt and cinnamon; gradually add to creamed mixture. Stir in oats, raisins and pecans. Shape into 1-in. balls. Place 2 in. apart on ungreased baking sheets. Bake at 350° for 10-11 minutes or until golden brown. Do not overbake. Remove to wire racks to cool. **Yield:** about 3-1/2 dozen.
—*Wendy Coalwell, Abbeville, Georgia*

Old-Fashioned Gingersnaps

Prepare these spice cookies and store them in a cookie tin for several months. Leftover cookies could be used to make a gingersnap cookie pie crust (see page 346).

  3/4 cup butter *or* margarine
    1 cup sugar
    1 egg
  1/4 cup light *or* dark molasses
    2 cups all-purpose flour
    2 teaspoons baking soda
    1 teaspoon *each* ground cinnamon, cloves and ginger
  1/4 teaspoon salt
Additional sugar

In a mixing bowl, cream butter and sugar. Add egg and molasses; beat well. Combine flour, baking soda, cinnamon, cloves, ginger and salt; gradually add to the creamed mixture. Mix well. Chill dough until easy to handle. Roll into 1-1/4-in. balls and roll in sugar. Place 2 in. apart on ungreased baking sheets. Bake at 375° for about 10 minutes or until edges are firm and the surface cracks. Remove to wire racks to cool. **Yield:** about 4 dozen.   —*Francis Stoops, Stoneboro, Pennsylvania*

Old-Fashioned Gingersnaps

Molasses Spice Cutouts

This recipe is traditionally used to make gingerbread men, but use any shape you prefer. Serve the cookies plain or decorate with icing.

> 1 cup butter *or* margarine, softened
> 1-1/2 cups sugar
> 1 cup light *or* dark molasses
> 1/2 cup cold coffee
> 6 cups all-purpose flour
> 2 teaspoons baking soda
> 1 teaspoon salt
> 1/2 teaspoon ground nutmeg
> 1/4 teaspoon ground cloves
> ICING (optional):
>   1 envelope unflavored gelatin
> 3/4 cup cold water
> 3/4 cup sugar
> 3/4 cup confectioners' sugar
> 3/4 teaspoon baking powder
> 1/2 teaspoon vanilla extract

In a mixing bowl, cream butter and sugar; beat in molasses and coffee. Combine the flour, baking soda, salt and spices; gradually add to molasses mixture and mix well. Chill dough for 1-2 hours or until easy to handle. If needed, add additional flour before rolling. On a lightly floured surface, roll dough to 1/4-in. thickness. Cut with 2-1/2-in. cookie cutters dipped in flour. Place 1 in. apart on ungreased baking sheets. Bake at 350° for 12-15 minutes or until edges are firm and bottom is lightly browned. Remove to wire racks to cool. For traditional gingerbread men (as shown), use icing to add features as desired. To prepare icing, combine gelatin and water in a small saucepan; let stand for 5 minutes to soften. Add sugar. Heat and stir over very low heat until the gelatin and sugar dissolve. Transfer to a mixing bowl. Add confectioners' sugar; beat until foamy. Add baking powder and vanilla; beat until very thick, about 10 minutes. **Yield:** 7-8 dozen. —*Doris Heinen*
St. Cloud, Minnesota

Making Cutout Cookies

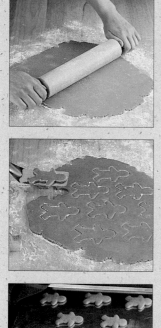

1 For easier handling, chill dough for 1 to 2 hours before rolling out. Lightly flour the surface and rolling pin. Roll out dough as evenly as possible to the recommended thickness.

2 Dip the cutter in flour, then press the cutter into the dough. Lift each cookie with a small metal spatula or pancake turner to support the cookie as it is moved to the baking sheet.

3 Bake according to recipe directions. With a metal spatula or pancake turner, remove cookies from the baking sheet to a wire rack, being careful to support the entire cookie. Cool completely before frosting or storing.

Molasses Spice Cutouts

Sugar Cookies

Try this recipe when you need a basic cutout sugar cookie anytime of the year. If you're in a hurry, simply sprinkle with granulated sugar or colored sugar before baking rather than frosting the baked cookies.

> 3/4 cup butter *or* margarine, softened
> 1 cup sugar
> 2 eggs
> 1 teaspoon vanilla extract
> 2-3/4 cups all-purpose flour
> 1 teaspoon baking powder
> 1/2 teaspoon salt
> Additional sugar, optional
> Confectioners' Sugar Cookie Frosting (at right)

In a mixing bowl, cream butter and sugar. Add eggs one at a time, beating well after each addition. Add vanilla. Combine flour, baking powder and salt; gradually add to creamed mixture. Chill dough for 1 hour or until easy to handle. On a lightly floured surface, roll the dough to 1/4-in. thickness. Cut with 2-1/2-in. cookie cutters dipped in flour. Using a floured spatula, place cookies 1 in. apart on greased baking sheets. Sprinkle with sugar if desired. Bake at 375° for 8-10 minutes or until lightly browned. Remove to wire racks to cool. Frost cookies if desired. **Yield:** 6-7 dozen.
—*Lynn Burgess, Rolla, Missouri*

Confectioners' Sugar Cookie Frosting

If you plan to frost the entire cookie, use 4 tablespoons of milk. If you want to outline or pipe designs on cookies, use 2 tablespoons of milk to make a thicker frosting.

> 3 cups confectioners' sugar
> 6 tablespoons butter *or* margarine, softened
> 1 teaspoon vanilla extract
> 2 to 4 tablespoons milk
> Food coloring*, optional

In a mixing bowl, beat sugar, butter, vanilla and milk until creamy. Add food coloring if desired. Frost cookies; decorate as desired. **Yield:** Frosts 6-7 dozen 2-1/2-in. cookies. ***Editor's Note:** For a richer color frosting, use paste food coloring, available at kitchen and cake decorating supply stores, instead of liquid food coloring.

Wishing Cookies
Cherry Christmas Slices

Wishing Cookies

There's an interesting story behind this cookie. Legend has it that if you break the cookie into three pieces and eat all three pieces without speaking, your wish will come true.

> 1 cup butter *or* margarine, softened
> 1-1/2 cups sugar
> 1 egg
> 2 tablespoons light *or* dark molasses
> 1 tablespoon water
> 1/2 to 1 teaspoon grated orange peel
> 3-1/4 cups all-purpose flour
> 1 teaspoon baking soda
> 1 teaspoon ground cinnamon
> 1/2 teaspoon ground ginger
> 1/4 teaspoon ground nutmeg
> ICING:
> 1 cup confectioners' sugar
> 1/2 teaspoon vanilla extract
> 1 to 2 tablespoons milk

In a mixing bowl, cream butter and sugar. Add egg, molasses, water and orange peel; mix well. Combine flour, baking soda, cinnamon, ginger and nutmeg;

Making an Icing Bag

1 To make a quick icing bag, take a small heavy-duty freezer bag and fill with icing; seal bag. Push icing into one corner of the bag. Cut a small tip from the corner.

2 Gather the bag just above the icing and gently squeeze the icing over cookies, making desired designs or outlining the edges.

gradually add to creamed mixture. Cover and chill for at least 2 hours. On a lightly floured surface, roll dough to 1/8-in. thickness. Cut into stars or desired shapes with a 2-1/2-in. cookie cutter dipped in flour. Place 1 in. apart on ungreased baking sheets. Bake at 375° for 6-8 minutes or until edges are lightly browned. Remove to wire racks to cool. For icing, combine sugar, vanilla and enough milk to achieve a drizzling consistency. Use icing to decorate cookies as desired. **Yield:** about 6 dozen. *—Katie Koziolek, Hartland, Minnesota*

Cherry Christmas Slices

You'll especially appreciate this recipe around the hurried holidays because the dough can be frozen for up to 2 months. So when planning your holiday cookie baking spree, be sure to include these.

1 cup butter *or* margarine, softened
1 cup confectioners' sugar
1 egg
1 teaspoon vanilla extract
2-1/4 cups all-purpose flour
2 cups red and green candied cherries, halved
1 cup pecan halves

In a mixing bowl, cream the butter and sugar. Add egg and vanilla; beat until fluffy. Add flour; mix well. Stir in cherries and pecans. Chill for 1 hour. Shape dough into three 10-in. rolls; wrap in plastic wrap and place in a freezer bag. Freeze for up to 2 months. To bake, cut frozen rolls into 1/8-in. slices. Place 1 in. apart on ungreased baking sheets. Bake at 325° for 10-12 minutes or until edges are golden brown. Remove to wire racks to cool. **Yield:** about 11 dozen. —*Katie Koziolek Hartland, Minnesota*

Cranberry Nut Swirls

(Pictured on page 351)

This is called a refrigerator cookie because the dough is formed into a roll and chilled in the refrigerator before slicing. The secret here is to chill the shaped dough for at least 4 hours. It's best if you can prepare the dough one day and slice it the next.

1/2 cup butter *or* margarine, softened
3/4 cup sugar
1 egg
1 teaspoon vanilla extract
1-1/2 cups all-purpose flour
1/4 teaspoon baking powder
1/4 teaspoon salt
1/2 cup finely ground fresh cranberries
1/2 cup finely chopped walnuts
1 tablespoon grated orange peel
3 tablespoons brown sugar
2 teaspoons milk

In a large mixing bowl, cream butter and sugar. Add the egg and vanilla; beat until light and fluffy. Combine flour, baking powder and salt; gradually add to the creamed mixture. Refrigerate for at least 1 hour. Combine cranberries, walnuts and orange peel; set aside. On a lightly floured surface, roll dough into a 10-in. square. Combine brown sugar and milk; spread over the dough. Sprinkle cranberry mixture to within 1/2

in. of edges; roll up tightly, jelly-roll style. Wrap in waxed paper; chill for at least 4 hours or overnight. Remove waxed paper. Cut into 1/4-in. slices and place 1 in. apart on well-greased baking sheets. Bake at 375° for 14-15 minutes or until edges are light brown. Remove to wire racks to cool. **Yield:** about 3-1/2 dozen.

—*Carla Hodenfield, Mandan, North Dakota*

Brown Sugar Icebox Cookies

A crisp buttery cookie, this is a perfect accompaniment to a cup of tea or coffee. If time is short, slice and bake as many as you need, then slice and bake the rest later.

1/2 cup butter (no substitutes), softened
1 cup packed brown sugar
1 egg
1 teaspoon vanilla extract
1-3/4 cups all-purpose flour
1/2 teaspoon baking soda
1/4 teaspoon salt
2/3 cup chopped pecans *or* flaked coconut

In a mixing bowl, cream butter and brown sugar. Add egg and vanilla; mix well. Combine flour, baking soda and salt; gradually add to creamed mixture. Fold in pecans or coconut (dough will be sticky). Shape into two rolls; wrap each roll in waxed paper. Chill 4 hours or overnight. Remove waxed paper. Cut into 1/4-in. slices and place 2 in. apart on ungreased baking sheets. Bake at 375° for 7-10 minutes or until edges begin to brown. Remove to wire racks to cool. **Yield:** about 3-1/2 dozen.

—*Eilene Bogar, Minier, Illinois*

Lemon Bars

Lemon bars are a melt-in-your-mouth sweet that every-one loves. To vary the shape on a cookie platter, you can also cut them into squares or even triangles.

CRUST:
- 1/3 cup butter *or* margarine, softened
- 1/4 cup confectioners' sugar
- 1 cup all-purpose flour

TOPPING:
- 2 eggs
- 1 cup sugar
- 2 tablespoons all-purpose flour
- 2 tablespoons lemon juice
- 1/2 teaspoon lemon extract
- 1/2 teaspoon baking powder
- 1/4 teaspoon salt

Confectioners' sugar

In a mixing bowl, cream butter and sugar. Add flour; beat until crumbly. Pat into an un-greased 8-in. square baking pan. Bake at 375° for 15 minutes. Meanwhile, for topping, combine eggs, sugar, flour, lemon juice, extract, baking powder and salt in a mixing bowl. Beat until frothy; pour over hot crust. Bake at 375° for 18-22 minutes or until light golden brown. Cool in pan on a wire rack. Dust with confectioners' sugar. Cut into squares. **Yield:** 1-1/2 dozen. —*Denise Baumert, Jameson, Missouri*

Lemon Bars

Toffee Squares

Here's a traditional holiday bar cookie that is a wonderful time-saver and a pretty complement to cutout cookies. In less than an hour, you can have 4-1/2 dozen cookies that are sure to please everyone!

- 1 cup butter *or* margarine, softened
- 1 cup packed brown sugar
- 1 egg yolk
- 1 teaspoon vanilla extract
- 2 cups all-purpose flour
- 1/4 teaspoon salt
- 2 packages (4 ounces *each*) German sweet chocolate
- 1/2 cup chopped nuts

In a mixing bowl, cream butter and sugar. Add egg yolk and vanilla. Combine the flour and salt; gradual-ly add to creamed mixture. Spread into a greased 13-in. x 9-in. x 2-in. baking pan. Bake at 350° for 20-25 min-utes or until golden brown. Melt chocolate in a heavy saucepan over low heat, stirring constantly. Spread over hot bars. Sprinkle immediately with nuts. Cool in pan on a wire rack. Cut into squares. **Yield:** 4-1/2 dozen.

Apricot Bars

This recipe is elegant enough to serve for dessert yet casual enough to take to a picnic. For a change of flavor, substitute hazelnuts for the walnuts.

- 3/4 cup butter *or* margarine
- 1 cup sugar
- 1 egg
- 2 cups all-purpose flour
- 1/4 teaspoon baking powder
- 1-1/3 cups shredded coconut
- 1/2 cup chopped walnuts
- 1/2 teaspoon vanilla extract
- 1 jar (12 ounces) apricot preserves

In a mixing bowl, cream butter and sugar. Add egg; mix well. Combine flour and baking powder. Gradually add to creamed mixture. Add coconut, walnuts and vanilla; mix well. Press two-thirds of dough into a greased 13-in. x 9-in. x 2-in. baking pan. Spread with preserves; crumble remaining dough over preserves (dough will be moist). Bake at 350° for 30-35 minutes or until gold-en brown. Cool in pan on a wire rack. Cut into squares. **Yield:** 3 dozen. —*Jill Moritz, Irvine, California*

Date Bars

These wholesome bar cookies freeze well. Simply cool in the pan, cut into squares and store in freezer containers or wrap in heavy-duty foil.

- 2-1/2 cups pitted dates, cut up
- 1-1/2 cups water
- 1/4 cup sugar
- 1/3 cup coarsely chopped walnuts, optional
- 1-1/2 cups quick-cooking oats
- 1-1/4 cups all-purpose flour
- 1 cup packed brown sugar
- 1 teaspoon salt
- 1/2 teaspoon baking soda
- 1/2 cup cold butter *or* margarine
- 1 tablespoon water

In a saucepan, combine dates, water and sugar. Cook over medium heat, stirring frequently, until very thick. Stir in walnuts if desired; cool. Combine oats, flour, brown sugar, salt and baking soda in a bowl. Cut in butter until crumbly. Sprinkle water over mixture; stir lightly. Pat half into a greased 13-in. x 9-in. x 2-in. baking pan. Spread with date mixture; sprinkle with remaining oat mixture and pat lightly. Bake at 350° for 35-40 minutes or until lightly browned. Cool in pan on a wire rack. Cut into squares. **Yield:** about 3-1/2 dozen.

—*Dorothy DeLeske, Scottsdale, Arizona*

Cutting Diamond-Shaped Bars

With a large knife, make cuts 1-1/2 in. apart diagonally in one direction. Then reverse and make cuts in the other direction to form diamonds.

Sugar Diamonds

Cutting these bar cookies into diamonds gives them a more festive look but with far less work than is required for cut-out cookies. Toasting the pecans will add even more flavor.

- 1 cup butter (no substitutes), softened
- 1 cup sugar
- 1 egg, *separated*
- 1/2 teaspoon vanilla extract
- 2 cups all-purpose flour
- 1/2 teaspoon ground cinnamon
- Pinch salt
- 1/2 cup chopped pecans

In a mixing bowl, cream butter and sugar. Add egg yolk and vanilla; mix well. Combine flour, cinnamon and salt; gradually add to creamed mixture. Spoon into a greased 15-in. x 10-in. x 1-in. baking pan. Cover dough with plastic wrap and press evenly into pan; remove wrap. In a small mixing bowl, beat egg white until foamy; brush over the dough. Sprinkle with pecans. Bake at 300° for 30 minutes or until light golden brown. Cool in pan on a wire rack 5 minutes. Cut into diamond shapes while warm. **Yield:** about 6 dozen.

—*Gladys De Boer, Castleford, Idaho*

Date Bars

Scottish Shortbread

Scottish Shortbread

Stored in an airtight container, these traditional cookies keep well for months. The secret to this recipe's success is to knead the dough for 5 minutes.

1 pound butter (no substitutes), softened
1 cup packed brown sugar
4 to 4-1/2 cups all-purpose flour

In a mixing bowl, cream butter and brown sugar. Add 3-3/4 cups flour; mix well. Sprinkle a pastry board or surface with some of the remaining flour. Knead for 5 minutes, adding enough remaining flour to make a soft, non-sticky dough. Roll to 1/2-in. thickness. Cut into 3-in. x 1-in. strips. Place 1 in. apart on ungreased baking sheets. Prick with a fork several times. Bake at 325° for 20-25 minutes or until cookies are lightly browned. Remove to a wire rack to cool. **Yield:** about 4 dozen. —*Rose Mabee, Selkirk, Manitoba*

Tassies

These tiny tarts make a pretty addition to any cookie tray or make a wonderful dessert by themselves. If you don't have miniature tart pans, use miniature muffin pans instead.

PASTRY:
    1/2 cup butter *or* margarine, softened
    1 package (3 ounces) cream cheese, softened
    1 cup all-purpose flour
FILLING:
    3/4 cup packed brown sugar
    1 tablespoon butter *or* margarine, softened
    1 egg
    1 teaspoon vanilla extract
Dash salt
    2/3 cup finely chopped pecans, *divided*

In a mixing bowl, beat butter and cream cheese until smooth; stir in flour. Chill for about 1 hour. Shape into

24 balls, 1 in. each. Place in ungreased small cookie tarts or miniature muffin tins; press dough onto the bottom and up the sides. Set aside. In another mixing bowl, beat brown sugar, butter and egg until combined. Add vanilla, salt and half of the pecans; spoon into shells. Top with remaining pecans. Bake at 375° for 20 minutes or until filling is puffed and pastry is light golden brown. Remove to a wire rack to cool. **Yield:** 2 dozen. —*Joy Corie, Ruston, Louisiana*

Pecan Meltaways

Sometimes called Mexican Wedding Cakes or Russian Tea Cakes, these are always a holiday favorite. When storing these tender cookies in a cookie tin or other container, place them in a single layer with waxed paper between each layer.

    1 cup butter *or* margarine, softened
    1/2 cup confectioners' sugar
    1 teaspoon vanilla extract
2-1/4 cups all-purpose flour
    1/4 teaspoon salt
    3/4 cup finely chopped pecans
Additional confectioners' sugar

In a mixing bowl, cream the butter, sugar and vanilla; mix well. Combine the flour and salt; gradually add to creamed mixture. Stir in pecans. Chill until easy to handle. Roll into 1-in. balls and place 1 in. apart on ungreased baking sheets. Bake at 350° for 10-12 minutes or until cookies are lightly browned. Roll in confectioners' sugar while warm. Remove to a wire rack to cool. Roll again in sugar before serving. **Yield:** about 4 dozen. —*Alberta McKay, Bartlesville, Oklahoma*

Tips for Mailing Cookies

- It's best to mail cookies or bars that are moist, chewy or soft. Cutout cookies are fragile and might break.
- Drop cookies travel better if you place two cookies bottom-to-bottom and wrap each pair with plastic wrap.
- Pack the cookies tightly so they don't shift in transit. Use crumpled waxed paper or bubble wrap to cushion the bottom, top and sides of a sturdy cardboard box or cookie tin and to fill any gaps between the cookies.
- Seal box tightly with tape; label the top and sides of the package "Fragile".

Tips for Making Pressed Cookies

- Be sure your butter, margarine or cream cheese is softened to room temperature before beginning.

- Always press cookies onto a cool baking sheet.

- If the dough is too soft and not making a sharp design, refrigerate briefly. If the dough is too stiff and won't move through the press, let the dough stand at room temperature briefly until it is the right consistency.

Holly Wreaths

This versatile spritz cookie dough can also be used to make any of the other shapes available with your cookie press. Decorator gel is available in a variety of colors in the grocery store. It adds instant fun and decoration to cookies.

 1 cup butter (no substitutes), softened
 1 package (3 ounces) cream cheese, softened
 1/2 cup sugar
 1 teaspoon vanilla extract
 2 cups all-purpose flour
Green candied cherries, cut into thin slices
Red-hot candies
Frosting and decorator gel

In a mixing bowl, cream butter and cream cheese. Add sugar; blend well. Stir in vanilla. Gradually add flour. Using a cookie press fitted with star tip, form dough into 2-1/2-in. wreaths on ungreased baking sheets. Bake at 375° for 10-12 minutes or until edges are firm but not brown. Remove to wire racks to cool. Decorate wreaths with green cherry "leaves" and cinnamon candy "berries" attached with a drop of icing (see Making an Icing Bag on page 356). Add bows with decorator gel. **Yield:** about 3 dozen. —*Dee Lien Longmont, Colorado*

Fruitcake Cookies

A no-bake cookie is always a welcomed addition to your list of holiday treats.

 6 cups chopped pecans (about 1-1/2 pounds)
 2 cups graham cracker crumbs (about 32 crackers)
 1-1/2 cups raisins
 1-1/4 cups chopped candied cherries (about 1/2 pound)
 1-1/4 cups chopped candied pineapple (about 1/2 pound)
 4-1/2 cups miniature marshmallows
 1/2 cup evaporated milk
 1/4 cup butter *or* margarine
 1-1/2 cups flaked coconut

In a large bowl, combine pecans, crumbs, raisins, cherries and pineapple. In a large saucepan, combine marshmallows, milk and butter; cook over low heat, stirring constantly, until melted. Pour over pecan mixture and mix well. Shape into 1-in. balls and roll in coconut, washing your hands frequently. Store in a covered container in the refrigerator. **Yield:** 7-8 dozen. —*Hazel Staley, Gaithersburg, Maryland*

Chocolate Crunch Brownies

Ultimate Double Chocolate Brownies

(Pictured on page 350)

These brownies keep well if stored in the refrigerator in an airtight container for 1 week. Or store them in the freezer for several months.

- 3/4 cup baking cocoa
- 1/2 teaspoon baking soda
- 2/3 cup butter *or* margarine, melted, *divided*
- 1/2 cup boiling water
- 2 eggs, beaten
- 2 cups sugar
- 1-1/3 cups all-purpose flour
- 1 teaspoon vanilla extract
- 1/4 teaspoon salt
- 2 cups semisweet chocolate chunks
- 1/2 cup coarsely chopped pecans

Confectioners' sugar

In a large bowl, combine cocoa and baking soda; blend in 1/3 cup melted butter. Add boiling water; stir until well blended. Stir in eggs, sugar and remaining butter. Add flour, vanilla and salt. Stir in the chocolate chunks and pecans. Pour into a greased 13-in. x 9-in. x 2-in. baking pan. Bake at 350° for 35-40 minutes or until brownies begin to pull away from sides of pan. Cool in pan on a wire rack. Dust with confectioners' sugar. Cut into squares. **Yield:** 3 dozen. —*Carol Prewett Cheyenne, Wyoming*

Chocolate Crunch Brownies

This specialty brownie makes a satisfying dessert when served with a scoop of mint ice cream.

- 1 cup butter *or* margarine, softened
- 2 cups sugar
- 4 eggs
- 1 cup all-purpose flour
- 6 tablespoons baking cocoa
- 2 teaspoons vanilla extract
- 1/2 teaspoon salt
- 1 jar (7 ounces) marshmallow creme
- 2 cups (12 ounces) semisweet chocolate chips
- 1 cup creamy peanut butter
- 3 cups crisp rice cereal

In a mixing bowl, cream butter and sugar; add eggs. Stir in flour, cocoa, vanilla and salt. Spread into a greased 13-in. x 9-in. x 2-in. baking pan. Bake at 350° for 25 minutes or until a toothpick inserted near the center comes out clean. Cool in pan on a wire rack. Spread marshmallow creme over cooled brownies. In a small saucepan over low heat, melt chocolate chips and peanut butter, stirring constantly. Remove from the heat; stir in the cereal. Spread over marshmallow layer. Chill 1 hour before cutting. Store in the refrigerator. **Yield:** 3 dozen. —*Pat Mueller Mitchell, South Dakota*

Dipped Peanut Butter Sandwich Cookies

When you need a quick-to-prepare sweet treat, try these. They even make great gifts. If desired, drizzle a contrasting melted chocolate over the top of the hardened dipped cookies.

- 1/2 cup creamy peanut butter
- 1 sleeve (4 ounces) butter-flavored crackers
- 1 cup (6 ounces) semisweet *or* milk chocolate chips *or* vanilla chips
- 1 tablespoon shortening

Spread peanut butter on half of the crackers; top with remaining crackers to make sandwiches. Refrigerate. In a small saucepan over low heat, melt chocolate chips and shortening, stirring until smooth. Dip sandwiches and place on waxed paper until chocolate hardens. **Yield:** 1-1/2 dozen. ① —*Jackie Howell Gordo, Alabama*

Chocolate Peanut Butter Brownies

Extremely rich, these brownies are best if they're cut into very small squares.

  1/2 cup butter *or* margarine
    2 squares (1 ounce *each*) unsweetened
      chocolate
    2 eggs
    1 cup sugar
  1/2 cup all-purpose flour
FILLING:
  1/2 cup creamy peanut butter
  1/4 cup butter *or* margarine, softened
 1-1/2 cups confectioners' sugar
    2 to 3 tablespoons half-and-half cream *or* milk
GLAZE:
    1 square (1 ounce) semisweet baking chocolate
    1 tablespoon butter *or* margarine

In a small saucepan over low heat, melt butter and chocolate; set aside. In a mixing bowl, beat eggs and sugar until light and lemon-colored. Add flour and melted chocolate; stir well. Pour into a greased 9-in. square baking pan. Bake at 350° for 25 minutes or until a toothpick inserted near the center comes out clean. Cool in pan on a wire rack. For filling, cream peanut butter and butter in a mixing bowl. Gradually add sugar. Stir in cream or milk until mixture reaches desired spreading consistency. Spread over cooled brownies;

Chocolate Peanut Butter Brownies

cover and chill for about 1 hour or until firm. For glaze, melt chocolate and butter in a saucepan over low heat, stirring until smooth. Drizzle over filling. Chill before cutting. Store in the refrigerator. **Yield:** about 5 dozen.
　　　　　　　　　　　—Patsy Burgin, Lebanon, Indiana

Maple Butterscotch Brownies

Brownies don't have to be made with chocolate in order to be delicious. These travel well in lunch boxes.

  1/2 cup butter *or* margarine, melted
1-1/2 cups packed brown sugar
1-1/2 teaspoons maple flavoring
    2 eggs
1-1/2 cups all-purpose flour
    1 teaspoon baking powder
    1 cup chopped walnuts
Confectioners' sugar, optional

In a mixing bowl, cream butter and brown sugar. Add maple flavoring. Add eggs one at a time, beating well after each addition. Combine flour and baking powder; add to creamed mixture. Stir in walnuts. Pour into a greased 9-in. square baking pan. Bake at 350° for 30 minutes or until a toothpick inserted near the center comes out clean. Cool in pan on a wire rack. Dust with confectioners' sugar if desired. **Yield:** 16 brownies.
　　　　　　　　　　—Grace Vonhold, Rochester, New York

Maple Butterscotch Brownies

Homemade candies are fun to make, serve and give as gifts. It is surprisingly easy to make candy in your kitchen using a minimum of ingredients and just a few pieces of special equipment. Use the tips and recipes that follow for delicious sweet treats every time.

Candy Making Tips

- Always measure and assemble all ingredients for a recipe before beginning. Do not substitute or alter the basic ingredients when making candy.

- Use heavy-gauge saucepans that are deep enough to allow candy mixtures to boil freely without boiling over.

- Use real butter or margarine containing at least 80% vegetable oil.

- Use wooden spoons with long handles for safe stirring when preparing recipes with hot boiling sugar.

- Humid weather affects results when preparing candies that are cooked to specific temperatures or that contain egg whites. For best results, make candy on days when the humidity is less than 60%.

- Store homemade candies in tightly covered containers unless otherwise directed. Don't store more than one kind of candy in a single container. Chewy candies like caramels, popcorn balls and taffy should be individually wrapped.

Cold-Water Test for Candy

When a candy thermometer is not available, candy mixtures can be tested by using the cold-water test. This test helps the cook determine the different stages of candy making to ensure foolproof results. All recipes in this book include both the cooking temperature and its corresponding stage for the cold-water test. For this test, you will need a small glass bowl or measuring cup filled with cold water.

Thread stage (230°-233°). Dip a metal spoon into the hot candy mixture. Hold the spoon over the cold water. The mixture should fall off the spoon in a fine thread.

Soft-ball stage (234°-240°). Drop a small amount of the hot candy mixture into the cold water. When cooled and removed from the water, the ball will flatten immediately and run over your finger.

Firm-ball stage (244°-248°). Drop a small amount of hot candy mixture into the cold water. When cooled and removed from the water, the ball will hold its shape and not flatten.

Hard-ball stage (250°-266°). Drop a small amount of the hot candy mixture into the cold water. When cooled and removed from the water, the candy will form a hard yet pliable ball.

Soft-crack stage (270°-290°). Drop a small amount of hot candy mixture into the cold water. When cooled and removed from the water, the candy will separate into threads that are hard but not brittle.

Hard-crack stage (300°-310°). Drop a small amount of hot candy mixture into the cold water. When cooled and removed from the water, the candy will separate into hard brittle threads.

For accurate temperature readings, it's important that you have the candy thermometer attached to the side of the saucepan and that you read the thermometer at eye level.

Christmas Hard Candy

Cinnamon and peppermint oils are available in cake decorating and candy supply stores and from mail-order sources.

3-1/2 cups sugar
1 cup light corn syrup
1 cup water
1/4 to 1/2 teaspoon cinnamon *or* peppermint oil
1 teaspoon red *or* green food coloring

In a large heavy saucepan, combine sugar, corn syrup and water. Cook over medium-high heat until a candy thermometer reads 300° (hard-crack stage), stirring occasionally. Remove from the heat; stir in oil and food coloring, keeping face away from mixture as odor is very strong. Immediately pour onto an oiled cookie sheet. Cool; break into pieces. Store in airtight containers. **Yield:** about 2 pounds. —*Jane Holman Moultrie, Georgia*

Christmas Hard Candy

Orange Taffy

The kids can help you make this recipe—allow them to wrap the taffy when it has cooled enough to handle. After you cut the foil or waxed paper into squares, they'll love wrapping and twisting the ends.

2 cups sugar
2 cups light corn syrup
1 can (6 ounces) frozen orange juice concentrate, undiluted
Pinch salt
1 cup half-and-half cream
1/2 cup butter *or* margarine

In a heavy saucepan, combine the first four ingredients. Cook and stir over medium heat until sugar is dissolved. Bring to a rapid boil and cook until a candy thermometer reads 245° (firm-ball stage). Add cream and butter; heat and stir until mixture reaches 245° again. Pour into a greased 15-in. x 10-in. x 1-in. pan; cool. When cool enough to handle, roll into 1-1/2-in. logs or 1-in. balls. Wrap individually in foil or waxed paper; twist ends. **Yield:** about 6 dozen.
—*Christine Olson, Horse Creek, California*

Using a Candy Thermometer

- The best and most reliable way to check the temperature of candy is to use a candy thermometer. If none is available, use the Cold-Water Test for Candy on page 364.

- Always use a thermometer designed for candy making. It must have a movable clip that's used to secure it to the side of the pan and to keep the end of the thermometer off the bottom of the pan.

- Check your candy thermometer for accuracy each time you make candy. Place the thermometer in a saucepan of boiling water for several minutes before reading. If the thermometer reads 212° in boiling water, it is accurate. If it rises above or does not reach 212°, add or subtract the difference to the temperature called for in the recipe.

- A candy mixture will cook very slowly when boiling until it reaches 220°, then it will cook quickly. It's important to closely watch the thermometer at this point.

- When finished using the thermometer, allow it to cool before washing to avoid breakage.

Dairy State Fudge

Add interest to your candy and cookie trays with a white fudge. For best results, don't use low-fat or fat-free cream cheese.

- **1 package (8 ounces) cream cheese, softened**
- **2 tablespoons butter (no substitutes)**
- **2 pounds white confectionery coating, broken into small pieces**
- **1 to 1-1/2 cups chopped pecans *or* walnuts**

Line a 9-in. square pan with foil and butter the foil; set aside. In a mixing bowl, beat cream cheese until fluffy; set aside. In the top of a double boiler, melt butter. Add confectionery coating; heat and stir until melted and smooth. Pour over cream cheese; beat until smooth and glossy, about 7-10 minutes. Stir in nuts. Pour into prepared pan. Cool. Remove from pan and cut into 1-in. squares. Store in the refrigerator. **Yield:** 64 pieces. —*Jan Vande Slunt, Waupun, Wisconsin*

Dairy State Fudge

Creamy Caramels

Once you make homemade caramels, you'll never want to buy packaged ones again. Wrapping each candy in waxed paper or plastic wrap will keep them fresh and chewy for weeks.

- **1 cup sugar**
- **1 cup dark corn syrup**
- **1 cup butter *or* margarine**
- **1 can (14 ounces) sweetened condensed milk**
- **1 teaspoon vanilla extract**

Line an 8-in. square pan with foil and butter the foil; set aside. Combine sugar, corn syrup and butter in a 3-qt. saucepan. Bring to a boil over medium heat, stirring constantly. Boil slowly for 4 minutes without stirring. Remove from the heat and stir in milk. Reduce heat to medium-low and cook until a candy thermometer reads 238° (soft-ball stage), stirring constantly. Remove from the heat and stir in vanilla. Pour into prepared pan. Cool. Remove from pan and cut into 1-in. squares. Wrap individually in waxed paper; twist ends. **Yield:** 64 pieces. —*Marcie Wolfe, Williamsburg, Virginia*

Avoiding Fudge Foils

The recipes here instruct you to butter the foil in your pan before pouring in the fudge mixture. That way, when the fudge is cooled, you can easily lift the foil and fudge out of the pan and cut the fudge into squares.

Candy Bar Fudge

This recipe is bound to be a hit because it's a cross between fudge and a candy bar. Using your microwave is an easy, foolproof method of preparation.

- **1/2 cup butter *or* margarine**
- **1/3 cup baking cocoa**
- **1/4 cup packed brown sugar**
- **1/4 cup milk**
- **3-1/2 cups confectioners' sugar**
- **1 teaspoon vanilla extract**
- **30 caramels**
- **1 tablespoon water**
- **2 cups salted peanuts**
- **1/2 cup semisweet chocolate chips**
- **1/2 cup milk chocolate chips**

Line an 8-in. square pan with foil and butter the foil; set aside. In a microwave-safe bowl, combine the butter, cocoa, brown sugar and milk. Microwave on high until mixture boils, about 3 minutes. Stir in confectioners' sugar and vanilla. Pour into prepared pan. In another microwave-safe bowl, heat caramels and water on high for 2 minutes or until melted. Stir in peanuts; spread over chocolate layer. Microwave chocolate chips on high for 1 minute or until melted; spread over caramel layer. Chill until firm. Remove from pan and cut into 1-in. squares. **Yield:** 64 pieces. **Editor's Note:** This recipe was tested in a 700-watt microwave.

—*Lois Zigarac, Rochester Hills, Michigan*

Sweetheart Fudge

Family and friends will be pleasantly surprised that you've turned a few basic kitchen ingredients into this delectable candy!

    3 cups sugar
    2/3 cup baking cocoa
    1/8 teaspoon salt
1-1/2 cups milk
    1/4 cup butter *or* margarine
    1 teaspoon vanilla extract

Line an 8-in. square pan with foil and butter the foil; set aside. In a heavy saucepan, combine sugar, cocoa and salt. Stir in milk; bring to a rapid boil over medium heat, stirring constantly. Cook without stirring until a candy thermometer reads 234° (soft-ball stage). Remove from the heat; add butter and vanilla (do not stir). Cool to 110° (about 5 minutes). Beat with a spoon until fudge thickens and just begins to lose its gloss. Immediately spread into prepared pan. Cool. Remove from pan and cut into 1-in. squares. **Yield:** about 64 pieces.   —*Dorothy Anderson, Ottawa, Kansas*

Stirring Fudge

As soon as the fudge cools to 110°, beat it with a wooden spoon until it thickens and just starts to lose its gloss. This step could take up to 10 minutes.

Three-Chocolate Fudge

If you're making fudge for the first time or in a hurry, this might be the recipe to prepare. And if you're looking for holiday gift ideas, this recipe yields about 150 pieces of candy!

3-1/3 cups sugar
    1 cup butter *or* margarine
    1 cup packed dark brown sugar
    1 can (12 ounces) evaporated milk
  32 large marshmallows, halved
    2 cups (12 ounces) semisweet chocolate chips
    2 milk chocolate candy bars (7 ounces *each*), broken
    2 squares (1 ounce *each*) semisweet chocolate, chopped
    1 teaspoon vanilla extract
    2 cups chopped pecans

Line a 15-in. x 10-in. x 1-in. baking pan with foil and butter the foil; set aside. In a large saucepan, combine the first four ingredients. Cook and stir over medium heat until sugar is dissolved. Bring to a rapid boil; boil for 5 minutes, stirring constantly. Remove from the heat; stir in marshmallows until melted. Stir in chocolate chips until melted. Add chocolate bars and baking chocolate; stir until melted. Fold in vanilla and pecans; mix well. Pour into prepared pan. Chill until firm. Remove from the pan and cut into 1-in. squares. **Yield:** about 12 dozen pieces.   —*Betty Grantham Hanceville, Alabama*

Three-Chocolate Fudge

Varieties of Chocolate

MANY RECIPES call for chocolate chips, baking chocolate or candy coating. But how do you know what type of chocolate to choose from your grocer's shelves? Here's some insight on common types of chocolate.

Chocolate chips are sold in a variety of flavors, such as semisweet, milk chocolate and mint chocolate. Chips also come in butterscotch, peanut butter and vanilla (white). They are available in a choice of sizes—regular and miniature chips—as well as chunks.

Chips are designed to hold their shape during baking. They are usually used in cookies and bars but also work well in many recipes that call for melted chocolate.

Baking chocolate is available in unsweetened, semisweet, milk and German sweet chocolate as well as vanilla (white) chocolate. It is commonly sold in 8-ounce packages that are divided into 1- or 2-ounce squares or bars.

Baking chocolate is designed for melting. For faster melting, chop baking bars into smaller pieces. Chips can be melted in place of semisweet, milk or white baking chocolate. Simply substitute 6 ounces of the appropriate flavored chips for 6 ounces of baking chocolate.

Candy coating is available in dark, milk or white chocolate varieties. Labels sometimes refer to it as confectionery coating or almond bark. It is commonly sold in bulk in large individual blocks, in bags of flat discs and in packages of individual 1-ounce squares.

Candy coating is often used for dipping candies or coating fruits because it becomes firm at room temperature. If coating is unavailable, melt together 6 ounces of chips or baking chocolate (except unsweetened) and 1 tablespoon of shortening in place of 6 ounces of candy coating.

A. Chips
B. Baking chocolate
C. Bulk candy coating
D. Candy coating discs

Coconut Yule Trees

This pretty candy will add color and a festive touch to your cookie and candy tray.

> 3 cups flaked coconut
> 2 cups confectioners' sugar
> 1/4 cup butter *or* margarine, softened
> 1/4 cup half-and-half cream
> 1 teaspoon almond extract
> 2 to 4 ounces dark chocolate confectionery coating

Green sugar and red-hot candies

In a large bowl, combine the first five ingredients; mix well. Drop by tablespoonfuls onto a waxed paper-lined baking sheet; cover and chill for 1 hour. Shape into trees; return to the baking sheet. In a double boiler or microwave-safe bowl, melt confectionery coating. Spoon over or dip trunks of trees and set on waxed paper to harden. Decorate tops of trees with green sugar and red-hots. **Yield:** about 2 dozen.
—*Michelle Retterer, Marysville, Ohio*

Mocha Truffles

Truffles can be frozen for several months before dipping in chocolate. Thaw in the refrigerator before dipping.

> 2 packages (12 ounces *each*) semisweet chocolate chips
> 1 package (8 ounces) cream cheese, softened
> 3 tablespoons instant coffee granules
> 2 teaspoons water
> 1 pound dark chocolate candy coating

White candy coating, optional

In a microwave-safe bowl or double boiler, melt chocolate chips. Add cream cheese, coffee and water; mix well. Chill until firm enough to shape. Shape into 1-in. balls and place on a waxed paper-lined baking sheet. Chill for 1-2 hours or until firm. Melt chocolate coating in microwave-safe bowl or double boiler. Dip balls and place on waxed paper to harden. If desired, melt white coating and drizzle over truffles. **Yield:** about 5-1/2 dozen.   —*Stacy Abell, Olathe, Kansas*

Pecan Delights

(Also pictured on page 350)

Everyone loves chocolate-covered turtles. This recipe is even tastier than the store-bought candies and well worth the time in the kitchen.

2-1/4 cups packed brown sugar
1 cup butter *or* margarine
1 cup light corn syrup
1/8 teaspoon salt
1 can (14 ounces) sweetened condensed milk
1 teaspoon vanilla extract
1-1/2 pounds whole pecans
1 cup (6 ounces) semisweet chocolate chips
1 cup (6 ounces) milk chocolate chips
2 tablespoons shortening

In a large saucepan, combine the first four ingredients. Cook over medium heat until all sugar is dissolved. Gradually add milk and mix well. Continue cooking until a candy thermometer reads 248° (firm-ball stage). Remove from the heat; stir in vanilla until blended. Fold in the pecans. Drop by tablespoonfuls onto a greased or parchment paper-lined baking sheet. Chill until firm. Loosen from paper. Melt chocolate chips and shortening in a microwave-safe bowl or double boiler. Drizzle over each cluster. Cool. **Yield:** about 4 dozen. —*Linda Jonsson, Marion, Ohio*

Dipping Candy into Chocolate

Place candy on a table fork or a special two-tined candy fork; dip into the melted chocolate to cover entirely. Remove from the chocolate; scrape off any excess chocolate on the side of the bowl. Place on waxed paper to cool and harden.

Pecan Delights
Mocha Truffles

Marshmallow Puffs

Peanut Brittle

To make this recipe even more special, substitute cashews for the peanuts.

    3 cups sugar
    1 cup water
    1/2 cup light corn syrup
    1/4 cup butter (no substitutes), cubed
    1 teaspoon salt
    1 jar (16 ounces) unsalted dry roasted peanuts
1-1/2 teaspoons baking soda
    1 teaspoon water
    1 teaspoon vanilla extract

Grease two baking sheets and keep warm in a 200° oven. In a large saucepan, combine sugar, 1 cup water and corn syrup. Cook over medium heat, stirring constantly, until a candy thermometer reads 240° (soft-ball stage). Stir in butter, salt and peanuts; heat and stir until the mixture reaches 300° (hard-crack stage). Meanwhile, combine baking soda, 1 teaspoon water and vanilla. Remove saucepan from the heat; stir in baking soda mixture. Quickly pour half the mixture over each cookie sheet. Spread with a buttered metal spatula to 1/4-in. thickness. Cool before breaking into pieces. **Yield:** about 2-1/2 pounds.
—*Karen Lou Grenzow, Sumas, Washington*

Marshmallow Puffs

With only four ingredients, this candy recipe is easy and quick to prepare. The kids could help by arranging the marshmallows in the pan.

    36 large marshmallows
1-1/2 cups (9 ounces) semisweet chocolate chips
    1/2 cup chunky peanut butter
    2 tablespoons butter (no substitutes)

Line a 9-in. square pan with foil and butter the foil. Arrange marshmallows in pan. In a double boiler or microwave-safe bowl, melt chocolate chips, peanut butter and butter. Pour and spread over the marshmallows. Chill completely. Cut between marshmallows. **Yield:** 3 dozen. **Editor's Note:** This recipe was tested in a 700-watt microwave. ○
—*Dody Cagenello, Simsbury, Connecticut*

Almond Butter Crunch

This recipe looks and tastes just like the expensive store-bought toffee candy. Make several batches and pack in pretty holiday tins for gift-giving.

    1 cup butter (no substitutes)
    1 cup sugar
    1 tablespoon light corn syrup
    3 tablespoons water
    1 cup slivered almonds
    1 cup (6 ounces) semisweet chocolate chips
    1/3 cup chopped almonds

In a heavy saucepan, combine butter, sugar, corn syrup and water. Cook over medium heat, stirring constantly, until a candy thermometer reads 300° (hard-crack stage). Remove from the heat; stir in slivered almonds. Quickly pour onto a greased baking sheet, forming a 12-in. square. Sprinkle with chocolate chips, spreading with a knife when melted. Top with chopped almonds. Cool. Break into 2-in. pieces. **Yield:** about 1 pound.
—*Alice Endreson, Alta, Iowa*

Peanut Brittle

Chocolate Clusters

When you get the taste for a piece of candy, why not make your own? In about 30 minutes, you can prepare dozens of crunchy chocolate candies.

2 pounds white confectionery coating
1 cup peanut butter
4 cups crisp rice cereal
3 cups pastel miniature marshmallows
2 cups salted dry roasted peanuts

Melt confectionery coating and peanut butter in microwave or double boiler, stirring often to mix well. Add remaining ingredients; stir until evenly coated. Drop by teaspoonfuls onto waxed paper. **Yield:** 11 dozen. ○ —*Sara Ann Fowler, Illinois City, Illinois*

Tuxedo Strawberries

Tuxedo Strawberries

For a special occasion, prepare these novel treats. If time is too short to make the fancy tuxedo on each berry, simply dip the whole berry in melted chocolate or confectionery coating.

18 medium fresh strawberries
1 cup (6 ounces) vanilla chips
3-1/2 teaspoons shortening, *divided*
1-1/3 cups semisweet chocolate chips
Pastry bag *or* small heavy-duty resealable plastic bag
#2 pastry tip, optional

Line a tray or baking sheet with waxed paper; set aside. Wash strawberries and pat until completely dry. In the top of a double boiler over simmering water or in a microwave-safe bowl, melt vanilla chips and 1-1/2 teaspoons shortening. Dip each strawberry until two-thirds is coated, forming the "shirt" (see Fig. 1), allowing excess to drip off. Place on prepared tray; chill 30 minutes or until set. Melt chocolate chips and remaining shortening. To form the "jacket", dip each side of berry into chocolate from the tip of the strawberry to the top of vanilla coating (see Fig. 2). Repeat on the other side, leaving a white "v" in the center (see Fig. 3). Set aside remaining chocolate. Chill berries for 30 minutes or until set. Remelt reserved chocolate if necessary. If using a plastic bag, cut a small hole in the bottom corner. Insert pastry tip if desired. (You may pipe directly from bag. See page 356.) Fill plastic or pastry bag with melted chocolate. Pipe a "bow tie" at the top of the white "v" and two or three buttons down the front of the "shirt" (see Fig. 4). Chill for 30 minutes or until set. Completed strawberries may be stored in the refrigerator in a covered plastic container for 1 day. **Yield:** 1-1/2 dozen. —*Gisella Sellers, Seminole, Florida*

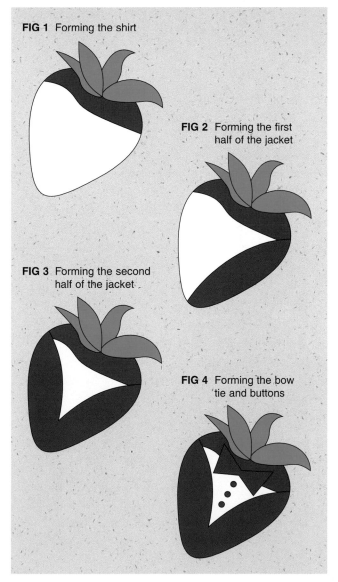

FIG 1 Forming the shirt

FIG 2 Forming the first half of the jacket

FIG 3 Forming the second half of the jacket

FIG 4 Forming the bow tie and buttons

Popcorn Caramel Crunch

White Christmas Candy

The kids will have fun crushing the candy canes for this recipe. Follow the same technique described for Making Crumbs on page 346.

2 pounds white confectionery coating
1-1/4 cups red *or* green crushed candy canes *or* peppermint candies (about 1/2 pound)

Melt confectionery coating in a microwave or double boiler, stirring until smooth. Remove from oven or heat; stir in crushed peppermint. Spread on waxed paper-lined cookie sheets; chill for 8-10 minutes. Break into small pieces; store in airtight containers. **Yield:** 2-1/2 pounds. ○ —*Carol Hammond, Helena, Alabama*

Caramel Apples

For even more fun and flavor, roll the bottom of each coated apple in chopped peanuts before setting on the waxed paper to cool.

1 cup butter (no substitutes)
2 cups packed brown sugar
1 cup light corn syrup
1 can (14 ounces) sweetened condensed milk
1 teaspoon vanilla extract
8 to 10 wooden sticks
8 to 10 medium tart apples

In a heavy 3-qt. saucepan, combine the butter, brown sugar, corn syrup and milk; bring to a boil over medium-high heat. Cook and stir until a candy thermometer reads 248° (firm-ball stage), about 30-40 minutes. Remove from the heat; stir in vanilla. Insert wooden sticks into apples. Dip each apple into hot caramel mixture; turn to coat. Set on waxed paper to cool. **Yield:** 8-10 apples.   —*Karen Ann Bland, Gove, Kansas*

Popcorn Caramel Crunch

For munching or gift-giving, this popcorn snack is chock-full of goodies. Store in airtight containers to keep the popcorn crisp.

4 cups popped popcorn
1 cup dry roasted peanuts
1 cup chow mein noodles
1/2 cup raisins
1 cup sugar
3/4 cup butter
1/2 cup light corn syrup
2 tablespoons water
1 teaspoon ground cinnamon

In a large greased bowl, combine the first four ingredients; set aside. In a large saucepan, combine sugar, butter, corn syrup and water. Cook over medium heat, stirring occasionally, until a candy thermometer reads 280°-290° (soft-crack stage). Remove from the heat; stir in cinnamon. Pour over popcorn mixture; stir until evenly coated. Immediately pour onto a greased 15-in. x 10-in. x 1-in. pan. When cool enough to handle, break into pieces. Store in airtight containers. **Yield:** about 8 cups.
—*Lucille Hermsmeyer, Scotia, Nebraska*

Chocolate Pizza

Old-Time Popcorn Balls

After shaping the popcorn balls, wrap with clear or colored plastic wrap. You can add a holiday touch by tying them with colored ribbons.

    2 quarts popped popcorn
1/2 cup molasses
1/2 cup sugar
1/3 cup water
   1 tablespoon vinegar
   1 tablespoon butter *or* margarine
1/4 teaspoon baking soda

Place popcorn in a large bowl and set aside. In a heavy saucepan, combine molasses, sugar, water, vinegar and butter. Cook over medium heat without stirring until a candy thermometer reads 235° (soft-ball stage). Add baking soda and stir well. Remove from the heat and immediately pour over popcorn, stirring gently with a wooden spoon until well coated. When cool enough to handle, quickly shape into 3-in. balls, dipping hands in cold water to prevent the syrup from sticking. **Yield:** 6-8 servings.   *—LaReine Stevens, Ypsilanti, Michigan*

Chocolate Pizza

When you need to take a dessert or treat to a potluck, here's a real showstopper that serves 16 to 20.

    8 ounces white confectionery coating, *divided*
    8 ounces semisweet chocolate chips
1/2 cup *each* salted peanuts, miniature
      marshmallows, crisp rice cereal, coconut and
      red and green candied cherries

In a heavy saucepan or double boiler, melt 6 oz. confectionery coating and all the chocolate chips. Stir in the peanuts, marshmallows and cereal. Pour onto a greased 10-in. pizza pan or a foil-covered 10-in. circle of cardboard. Spread to even out top. Sprinkle with coconut and top with cherries. Melt remaining confectionery coating; drizzle over pizza. Refrigerate. **Yield:** 16-20 servings. ◷   *—Norma Oosting*
Holland, Michigan

Menu Planning

From special Sunday suppers and home-style weekday meals to festive holiday buffets and casual outdoor gatherings, this chapter offers innovative ways to turn recipes in this book into complete menus all year. The Italian Supper pictured here features Mostaccioli Bake, Garlic Herb Bread and tossed salad with Herbed Salad Dressing.

Italian Supper

(Pictured at left)

Serves 6 to 8

This hearty meal is special enough to prepare for company yet easy enough to serve as a weekday meal.

Mostaccioli Bake (p. 249)
Garlic Herb Bread (p. 64)
Tossed salad with
Herbed Salad Dressing (p. 73)
Rainbow sherbet

Preparation Pointers

- Prepare the salad dressing a day in advance or several hours before serving.
- While the pasta is cooking, brown the sausage and prepare the sauce.
- Put the bread in the oven for the last 25 minutes of the mostaccioli's baking time.

Just the Two of Us

Serves 2

Here's a menu that's sized for just the two of you. This unique beef recipe delivers all the great taste of a traditional pot roast in just two hearty servings.

Midget Pot Roast (p. 106)
Tossed salad with
Blue Cheese Dressing (p. 73)
Dinner rolls
Gingerbread (p. 322)

Preparation Pointers

- Make and refrigerate the dressing up to 1 day ahead.
- Several hours before serving, prepare the gingerbread and clean and refrigerate the salad greens.
- During the last 10 minutes of the roast's baking time, warm the rolls in the oven.

Country-Style Special

Serves 6 to 8

Meat loaf and mashed potatoes are favorite fare in country kitchens, and now you can make your own tasty version of this classic meal.

Mom's Best Meat Loaf (p. 126)
Dilly Mashed Potatoes (p. 282)
Glazed Carrots (p. 271)
Cherry Berry Pie (p. 338)

Preparation Pointers

- Bake the pie several hours in advance.
- While the meat loaf bakes, peel and cook the potatoes and carrots. Keep the finished carrot dish warm over low heat.
- When the meat loaf is removed from the oven, drain and mash the potatoes.

Finger-Lickin'-Good Chicken

Serves 4 to 6

For Sunday dinner or anytime, crispy chicken hits the spot.

Oven-Fried Chicken (p. 131)
Peas and Potatoes (p. 278)
Creamy Sliced Tomatoes (p. 70)
Lazy Daisy Cake (p. 332)

Preparation Pointers

- Early in the day, bake the cake. Make the salad dressing and clean the salad greens; refrigerate.

- While the chicken bakes, prepare the peas and potatoes.
- Just before serving, slice the tomatoes, arrange the salad and the drizzle dressing over.

Easter Dinner

Serves 8

You'll have time to complete much of the meal preparation while the leg of lamb is roasting.

Herbed Leg of Lamb (p. 197)
Creamed Potatoes (p. 279)
Sesame Asparagus (p. 265)
Golden Glow Salad, doubled (p. 75)
Buttery Crescents (p. 46)
Lemon Custard in Meringue
Cups (p. 303)

Preparation Pointers

- Several days in advance, bake and freeze the crescent rolls.
- The day before, prepare the salad in an 8-cup mold or a 9-in. square baking dish, make the meringue cups, and prepare and refrigerate the lemon custard.
- Early the next day, defrost the rolls at room temperature.
- While the lamb roasts, peel the potatoes, place in a saucepan and cover with cold water.
- During the last 30 minutes of roasting time, cook, drain and mash the potatoes. Prepare the asparagus; cover and keep warm.
- While carving the lamb and making gravy, warm the rolls in the oven.
- Assemble the dessert just before serving.

Pretty Spring Brunch

Serves 6 to 8

Once family and friends taste these flavorful foods, this easy brunch may become an annual tradition at your house!

Orange Refresher, doubled (p. 34)
Asparagus Strata (p. 228)
Warmed ham slices
Hot Cross Buns (p. 50)

Preparation Pointers

- Prepare and refrigerate the strata the day before.
- Early the next morning, make the buns.
- During the last 15 minutes of the strata's baking time, warm the ham slices in a skillet over low heat and blend the orange drink.

Speedy Seafood Supper

Serves 2

Substitute orange roughy, sole or flounder if you like for the catfish.

Lime Broiled Catfish (p. 186)
Parmesan Noodles (p. 245)
Dilled Carrots (p. 270)
Ultimate Double Chocolate Brownies (p. 362)

Preparation Pointers

- Earlier in the day, bake the brownies and prepare and refrigerate the butter sauce for the fish.
- While water for the noodles comes to a boil and the broiler preheats, cook the carrots; add the dill sauce.
- While the noodles and fish cook, keep the carrots warm over low heat.

Easy, Elegant Entertaining

Serves 4

Most of this meal requires last-minute preparation, but you can make and refrigerate the pie up to 4 hours in advance.

Pork Tenderloin Diane (p. 166)
Baked Mushroom Rice (p. 236)
Herbed Broccoli (p. 269)
Strawberry Lover's Pie (p. 341)

Preparation Pointers

- One hour before serving, bake the rice casserole.
- Saute the pork 10 minutes before serving. Cook the broccoli 5-8 minutes before serving.

Fourth of July Celebration

Serves 8

Enjoy all the festivities this special day has to offer by using the suggested preparation tips below.

Dill Dip (p. 18)
Peppered Rib Eye Steaks (p. 121)
Grilled Mushrooms, doubled (p. 276)
Marinated Zucchini Salad (p. 80)
Patriotic Gelatin Salad (p. 74)
Patriotic Dessert (p. 309)

Preparation Pointers

- One day in advance, prepare the dip and cut up the vegetable dippers. Also make the zucchini salad, gelatin salad and dessert (up to the step of adding the fresh berries). Refrigerate all.

- Early the next day, top the dessert with the fresh berries and unmold the gelatin salad; refrigerate.
- Add the mushrooms to the grill 15 minutes before the steaks are done.

Festive Family Reunion

Serves 12 to 16

Entertaining for a crowd is easy when you select menu items that can be prepared days ahead of the big event.

Spiced Lemonade, doubled (p. 35)
Vegetable Appetizer Pizza (p. 27)
Honey-Glazed Snack Mix (p. 31)
Barbecued Pork Sandwiches (p. 101)
Red, White and Green Salad, doubled (p. 78)
Rosy Rhubarb Salad, doubled (p. 75)
Assorted relish platter
Fresh fruit salad
Chocolate Pound Cake (p. 321)

Preparation Pointers

- Up to 2 days in advance, prepare the lemonade and snack mix, and the pork for the sandwiches.
- The day before serving, make the cake and salads.
- The day of your party, prepare the vegetable pizza, cut up the fresh fruit, assemble the relish platter and heat the pork for the sandwiches in a Dutch oven or slow cooker.

Summertime and the Eating Is Easy!

Serves 4

Cooking on the outdoor grill is a fun, flavorful and fool-proof way to entertain during the summer months.

Grilled Tarragon Chicken (p. 148)
**Roasted corn on the cob with
Spicy Corn Spread (p. 272)**
Norwegian Coleslaw (p. 82)
Watermelon wedges

Preparation Pointers

- Make and refrigerate the coleslaw at least 1 week ahead of time.
- Prepare the corn spread a day or 2 before serving.
- Place the corn on the grill 15 minutes before starting the chicken.

A Harvest of Fall Flavors

Serves 4 to 6

You'll love the wonderful aromas that will fill your kitchen as these oven-prepared foods bake.

Honey Mustard Baked Chicken (p. 134)
Cheddar Parmesan Potatoes (p. 280)
Two large baked acorn squash
Apple Crisp (p. 310)
Hot chocolate or coffee

Preparation Pointers

- Prepare the apple crisp early in the day.
- Bake the chicken about 1-1/4 hours before serving.
- Place the squash in the oven during the last 45 min-

utes of the chicken's baking time; add the potatoes during the last 35 minutes.
- Warm the crisp in the oven while enjoying dinner.

Traditional Thanksgiving Dinner

Serves 10 to 12

A large holiday meal is easier to prepare if many of the dishes can be prepared in advance. This menu really gives the cook something to be thankful for!

Turkey with Country Ham Stuffing (p. 144)
Apricot-Glazed Sweet Potatoes (p. 282)
Fancy Brussels Sprouts, doubled (p. 269)
Easy Berry Relish (p. 292)
Golden Knots (p. 47)
Fluffy Cranberry Cheese Pie, doubled (p. 345)

Preparation Pointers

- Prepare, partially bake and freeze the rolls up to 2 weeks in advance.
- Make the relish 1 or 2 days ahead. Refrigerate.
- The day before serving, prepare the pies. Cook and peel the sweet potatoes; cover and refrigerate.
- Early Thanksgiving Day, prepare and refrigerate the stuffing until ready to place in the turkey.
- Place the sweet potatoes in the oven during the last 20 minutes of the turkey's roasting time.
- While making gravy and carving the turkey, bake the rolls and cook the brussels sprouts.

Holiday Brunch

Serves 10 to 12

Here's a holiday menu that gives you plenty of time in the morning to go to church, straighten up the house or just relax before your company arrives.

Holiday Wassail (p. 35)
Layered Fresh Fruit Salad (p. 83)
Scrambled Egg Casserole, doubled (p. 219)
Breakfast Sausage, doubled (p. 170)
Christmas Stollen (p. 49)

Preparation Pointers

- Prepare and freeze the stollen several weeks in advance.
- The day before, prepare the egg casseroles (one at a time), citrus sauce for the fruit salad and wassail. Refrigerate all.
- Early the next morning, defrost the stollen, assemble the fruit salad and reheat the wassail in a slow cooker. While the casseroles bake, fry the sausages.

A Christmas to Remember

Serves 12 to 16

If guests ask what they can bring, suggest that they prepare a recipe from your menu.

Homemade Eggnog (p. 35)
Festive Cheese Spread, doubled (p. 21)
Stuffed Crown Roast of Pork (p. 163)
Tangy Green Bean Casserole, doubled (p. 266)
Frozen Cranberry Salad (p. 83)
Icebox Cloverleaf Rolls (p. 47)
Christmas Special Fruitcake (p. 311)
Assorted Christmas cookies

Preparation Pointers

• Prepare and freeze the cranberry salad, fruitcake and cookies 1 to 2 weeks in advance.

• The day before, prepare and refrigerate the eggnog, cheese spread, dough for the rolls and green bean casseroles.

• Early the next morning, defrost the cookies and fruitcake. Bake the rolls (cool and store in an airtight container).

• One hour before dinner, whisk the eggnog and serve with the cheese spread. Remove the green bean casseroles from the refrigerator.

• Place the green bean casseroles in the oven during the last 30 minutes of the pork's roasting time.

New Year's Day Buffet

Serves 10 to 12

To kick off the New Year, prepare this easy buffet as a late brunch or early dinner.

Baked Ham with Cumberland Sauce (p. 173)
Black-Eyed Peas with Bacon, doubled (p. 241)
Sweet Potato Salad (p. 78)
Corn Muffins with Honey Butter (p. 56)
Cherry Cheesecake Tarts, doubled (p. 307)

Preparation Pointers

• The day before, prepare the black-eyed peas in a large Dutch oven, cook and peel the sweet potatoes, and make the sauce for the ham. Refrigerate all.

• Early New Year's Day, make the tarts, assemble the sweet potato salad and bake the corn muffins.

• Add the black-eyed peas to the oven during the last 30 minutes of the ham's baking time.

• While carving the ham, warm the muffins in the oven and reheat the sauce.

Super-Easy Super Bowl Party

Serves 12 to 16

Advanced planning is the key to this party so that you can enjoy your company and the game along with everyone else.

Three-in-One Cheese Ball (p. 20)
Tortilla Pinwheels (p. 21)
Sweet Gingered Chicken Wings, doubled (p. 27)
Santa Fe Chicken Chili (p. 95)
Big Sandwich, doubled (p. 97)
Apple Walnut Cake (p. 319)

Preparation Pointers

• Prepare and freeze the cheese balls and cake 1 week in advance.

• The day before, prepare and refrigerate the pinwheels, chicken wings and chili. Defrost cheese balls and cake in the refrigerator.

• Early the next day, assemble sandwiches; wrap and refrigerate.

• Reheat chicken wings, uncovered, at 325° for 20 minutes. Roll cheese balls in pepper, parsley and nuts; let stand at room temperature for 15 minutes.

• While serving appetizers, allow sandwiches to stand at room temperature for 15 minutes before baking. Heat soup in a Dutch oven or soup kettle over low heat.

Handy References

The guides in this chapter can give you quick answers to many of your daily culinary dilemmas. They include food, fruit, weight and measure equivalents...ingredient substitutions...herb information...food storage guidelines...table setting tips...and common cooking terms.

Equivalents and Substitutions

You'll find these equivalency charts invaluable when planning menus and grocery lists. Or when you're in a pinch while preparing a recipe, use the suggested ingredient substitutions. See pages 252 through 263 for vegetable equivalents.

Miscellaneous Food Equivalents

Bread	1 loaf = 16 to 20 slices
Bread crumbs	1 slice = 1/2 cup soft crumbs; 1/4 cup dry crumbs
Butter or margarine	1 pound = 2 cups; 4 sticks
Cheese	
Cottage	1 pound = 2 cups
Shredded	4 ounces = 1 cup
Chocolate chips	6 ounces = 1 cup
Cocoa, baking	1 pound = 4 cups
Cream cheese	8 ounces = 16 tablespoons
Cream, whipping	1 cup = 2 cups whipped
Egg whites	1 cup = 8 to 10 whites
Flour	
All-purpose	1 pound = about 3-1/2 cups
Whole wheat	1 pound = about 3-3/4 cups
Frozen whipped topping	8 ounces = 3-1/2 cups
Gelatin, unflavored	1 envelope = 1 tablespoon
Nuts	
Almonds	1 pound = 3 cups halved; 4 cups slivered
Ground	3-3/4 ounces = 1 cup
Pecans	1 pound = 4-1/2 cups chopped
Popcorn	1/3 to 1/2 cup unpopped = 8 cups popped
Walnuts	1 pound = 3-3/4 cups chopped
Sugar	
Brown sugar	1 pound = 2-1/4 cups
Confectioners' sugar	1 pound = 4 cups
Granulated	1 pound = 2-1/4 to 2-1/2 cups

Fresh Fruit Equivalents

Apples	1 pound (3 medium) = 2-3/4 cups sliced
Apricots	1 pound (8 to 12 medium) = 2-1/2 cups sliced
Bananas	1 pound (3 medium) = 1-1/3 cups mashed; 2 cups sliced
Berries	1 pint = 1-1/2 to 2 cups
Cherries	1 pound = 3 cups whole; 3-1/2 cups halved
Cranberries	12 ounces = 3 cups whole; 2-1/2 cups finely chopped
Grapefruit	1 medium = 1 cup juice; 1-1/2 cups segments
Grapes	1 pound = 3 cups
Lemons	1 medium = 3 tablespoons juice; 2 teaspoons grated peel
Limes	1 medium = 2 tablespoons juice; 1-1/2 teaspoons grated peel
Nectarines	1 pound (3 medium) = 3 cups sliced
Oranges	1 medium = 1/3 to 1/2 cup juice; 4 teaspoons grated peel
Peaches	1 pound (4 medium) = 2-3/4 cups sliced
Pears	1 pound (3 medium) = 3 cups sliced
Pineapples	1 medium = 3 cups chunks
Rhubarb	1 pound = 3 cups chopped (raw); 2 cups (cooked)
Strawberries	1 pint = 2 cups hulled and sliced

Weight and Measure Equivalents

Dash or pinch = less than 1/8 teaspoon

3 teaspoons = 1 tablespoon; 1/2 fluid ounce

2 tablespoons = 1/8 cup; 1 fluid ounce

4 tablespoons = 1/4 cup; 2 fluid ounces

5-1/3 tablespoons = 1/3 cup

8 tablespoons = 1/2 cup

10-2/3 tablespoons = 2/3 cup

12 tablespoons = 3/4 cup

16 tablespoons = 1 cup; 8 fluid ounces; 1/2 pint

7/8 cup = 3/4 cup plus 2 tablespoons

2 cups = 1 pint; 16 fluid ounces

4 cups = 2 pints; 1 quart; 32 fluid ounces

4 quarts = 1 gallon

8 quarts = 1 peck

4 pecks = 1 bushel

16 ounces = 1 pound

Emergency Ingredient Substitutions

When You Need...	In This Amount...	Substitute...
Baking powder	1 teaspoon	1/2 teaspoon cream of tartar plus 1/4 teaspoon baking soda
Broth	1 cup	1 cup hot water plus 1 teaspoon bouillon granules *or* 1 bouillon cube
Buttermilk	1 cup	1 tablespoon lemon juice *or* vinegar plus enough milk to measure 1 cup; let stand 5 minutes. *Or* 1 cup plain yogurt
Cajun seasoning	1 teaspoon	1/2 to 1 teaspoon hot pepper sauce, 1/2 teaspoon dried thyme, 1/4 teaspoon dried basil and 1 minced garlic clove
Chocolate, semisweet	1 square (1 ounce)	1 square (1 ounce) unsweetened chocolate plus 1 tablespoon sugar *or* 3 tablespoons semisweet chocolate chips
Chocolate, unsweetened	1 square (1 ounce)	3 tablespoons baking cocoa plus 1 tablespoon shortening *or* vegetable oil
Cornstarch (for thickening)	1 tablespoon	2 tablespoons all-purpose flour
Corn syrup, dark	1 cup	3/4 cup light corn syrup plus 1/4 cup molasses
Corn syrup, light	1 cup	1 cup sugar plus 1/4 cup water
Cracker crumbs	1 cup	1 cup dry bread crumbs
Cream, half-and-half	1 cup	1 tablespoon melted butter plus enough whole milk to measure 1 cup
Egg	1 whole	2 egg whites *or* 2 egg yolks *or* 1/4 cup egg substitute
Flour, cake	1 cup	1 cup minus 2 tablespoons (7/8 cup) all-purpose flour
Flour, self-rising	1 cup	1-1/2 teaspoons baking powder and 1/2 teaspoon salt plus enough all-purpose flour to measure 1 cup
Garlic, fresh	1 clove	1/8 teaspoon garlic powder
Gingerroot, fresh	1 teaspoon	1/4 teaspoon ground ginger
Honey	1 cup	1-1/4 cups sugar plus 1/4 cup water
Lemon juice	1 teaspoon	1/4 teaspoon cider vinegar
Lemon peel	1 teaspoon	1/2 teaspoon lemon extract
Milk, whole	1 cup	1/2 cup evaporated milk plus 1/2 cup water *or* 1 cup water plus 1/3 cup nonfat dry milk powder
Molasses	1 cup	1 cup honey
Mustard, prepared	1 tablespoon	1/2 teaspoon ground mustard plus 2 teaspoons vinegar
Onion	1 small (1/3 cup chopped)	1 teaspoon onion powder *or* 1 tablespoon dried minced onion
Poultry seasoning	1 teaspoon	3/4 teaspoon rubbed sage plus 1/4 teaspoon dried thyme
Sour cream	1 cup	1 cup plain yogurt
Sugar	1 cup	1 cup packed brown sugar *or* 2 cups sifted confectioners' sugar
Tomato juice	1 cup	1/2 cup tomato sauce plus 1/2 cup water
Tomato sauce	2 cups	3/4 cup tomato paste plus 1 cup water
Yeast	1 package (1/4 ounce) active dry	1 cake (5/8-ounce) compressed yeast

Basil

Known for its licorice-like flavor, basil leaves are used fresh or dried. Probably most frequently used in tomato or pasta dishes, basil also adds flavor to dips, soups, marinated salads, vegetables, stews, fish, beef, salad dressings, poultry and cheese dishes.

Guide to Common Herbs

Dried herbs need to be stored in tightly closed containers in a cool, dark, dry place. Keep them away from the heat of the oven or stovetop. Dried herbs begin to lose flavor after a year of storage. When fresh herbs are available, substitute them by using three times the amount of the dried herb called for in the recipe. For example, if a recipe calls for 1 teaspoon dried basil, substitute 1 tablespoon minced fresh basil.

Bay Leaf

Bay leaf is most often found and used as a dried whole leaf, but it can be finely crushed. Bay leaf is most effective when allowed to simmer or marinate in the recipe for several hours. Try 1 to 2 bay leaves in soups, stews, pot roasts, poultry dishes, gravies, sauces and pickle brines. Whole leaves are always discarded before serving.

Chives

An easy-to-grow perennial, chives have long spiky leaves that are used fresh, frozen or freeze-dried to add a mild onion taste to egg dishes, poultry and fish or to garnish cream soups, salads and cooked vegetables. Preserve your own garden chives by snipping into 1/4-inch lengths and freezing in airtight storage containers.

Cilantro

Also known as coriander or Chinese parsley, the zesty-flavored green leaves of this herb are used fresh in Mexican-style dishes. Cilantro leaves add distinctive flavor to salsas, Southwestern-style appetizers, dips, sauces, chili, pesto and rice and bean dishes. Cilantro is best added to dishes just before serving to retain its fresh flavor.

Dill

Both the green tops (dill weed) and seeds (dill seed) have a distinctive caraway flavor. Dill weed is used fresh or dried to season pickle brines, salad dressings, sauces, dips, fish, shellfish and egg dishes. It also makes a pretty garnish. Dill seed is most often used in pickle brines and salad dressings.

Garlic

This strong-flavored, pungent herb is available fresh, dried and in powder form and adds life to a variety of foods, including dips, soups, salad dressings, flavored butters, casseroles, sauces, stews, grilled foods, marinades and meat, bean, rice or vegetable dishes.

Marjoram

Used fresh or dried, marjoram's green leaves have a strong sweet aroma much like oregano. Add to meat, poultry, fish, egg, home-made sausage and vegetable dishes. It's especially good with Italian-style foods.

Mint

Available fresh and dried, mint has a spicy flavor and aroma. Use it in stews, sauces, salads and mint jelly. Mint is often used as a garnish for fruits, desserts and beverages such as iced tea.

Oregano

The dark green leaves of oregano are used fresh or dried in Italian, Mexican and Greek dishes. Oregano flavors soups, stews, chili, poultry, ground beef, seafood, marinades, salad dressings, sauces, hot or cold pasta dishes and pizza.

Parsley

Available in curly and flat-leaf varieties, fresh parsley adds a refreshing flavor and spark of green garnish to soups, salads, salad dressings, sauces, fish, poultry, poultry stuffings and potato, grain, bean and pasta dishes. Flat-leaf or Italian parsley has a stronger flavor than the traditional curly variety. Dried parsley is mild in flavor and color.

Rosemary

Known for its needle-like leaves, rosemary has a distinctive fragrant evergreen scent and bold flavor. Fresh or dried rosemary complements lamb, pork, poultry, marinades, potato dishes, herb butters and homemade savory breads.

Sage

The pale green leaves of sage can be enjoyed fresh or dried and rubbed into a fluffy powder. Sage is well-known for adding a distinctive flavor to poultry stuffings, poultry, roasted red meats, meat pies, soups, stews and Italian dishes.

Tarragon

Tarragon's long slender leaves have a mild licorice-like flavor and are used fresh or dried. Tarragon flavors chicken, poultry marinades, pasta salads, potato salads, vegetables, sauces, salad dressings, fish and egg dishes.

Thyme

Thyme has a bold earthy taste and a strong aroma. There are many varieties of fresh thyme, including the popular lemon-flavored plant. Use fresh or dried thyme to season fish, potato dishes, soups, stuffings, stews, rice pilaf, wild rice dishes, poultry and meat marinades.

Food Storage Guidelines

Depending on the food, the proper length of time to store items in the pantry, freezer or refrigerator can vary widely. The information that follows gives you a guide to help you enjoy your food when it's at its best.

Cupboard Storage Times

When buying dry or canned goods, make sure any dates on the packages or cans haven't expired. Don't purchase cans that are bulged or swollen. Store unopened dry foods in their original packages and keep opened products in airtight containers.

Food	Storage Time	Special Handling
Baking powder or soda	18 months	Keep in an airtight container after opening.
Bouillon cubes, granules	1 year	
Cake mixes	1 year	
Canned foods, commercial	1 year	
Cereals	Check package date	Keep in an airtight container after opening.
Chocolate, baking	1 year	Keep in a cool place.
Coconut	1 year	Refrigerate opened packages.
Coffee, fresh ground	2 to 3 weeks	Refrigerate or freeze opened cans or packages.
Flour, all-purpose	15 months	
Flour, whole wheat	6 months	Refrigerate or freeze during warm weather.
Fruit, dried	6 months	Refrigerate opened packages.
Gelatin	18 months	Keep in a dry place.
Herbs, dried	1 year	Keep in a cool, dark place. Refrigerate red spices.
Honey	1 year	
Jams, jellies	1 year	Refrigerate after opening.
Macaroni, spaghetti, dried pasta	1 year	Keep in an airtight container after opening.
Molasses	2 years	
Nonfat dry milk powder	6 months	Keep in an airtight container after opening.
Olive oil	1 year	Keep in tightly capped bottle away from heat and light.
Peanut butter	6 months	Refrigerate during warm weather.
Pudding mixes	1 year	
Rice, white	Indefinite	Keep in an airtight container in a cool, dry place.
Salad dressings, commercial	6 months	Refrigerate opened bottles.
Shortening	8 months	Store in a cool dark place.
Sugar, brown	4 months	Keep in an airtight container after opening.
Sugar, granulated	2 years	Keep in an airtight container after opening.
Syrups—corn, maple-flavored, maple	1 year	Refrigerate maple syrup after opening.
Vegetable oil	1 year	Keep in tightly capped bottle away from heat and light.
Yeast, active dry	Check package date	Refrigerate during warm weather.

Refrigerator and Freezer Storage Times

Keep your refrigerator temperature between 34° and 40°. Keep foods wrapped or placed in airtight containers, unless otherwise noted, to keep food from drying out and odors from transferring to other foods. Meats should be kept in the coldest part of the refrigerator and vegetables stored in the crisper.

Keep your freezer set at 0° for storage that is longer than a week or 2. Always wrap foods in heavy-duty foil or freezer paper, or place in freezer containers to guard against freezer burn.

Label and date all foods that go into the freezer so it is easy to identify the packages and use within the recommended dates. For large freezers, make an inventory list that includes the date each item was placed in the freezer. Then post it on the freezer door for quick reference.

High-Altitude Cooking

If you live in a high-altitude area and are unsure of the adjustments you might need to make in your recipes, consult your local county Extension office for assistance.

Food	Refrigerator	Freezer
Fresh Meat		
Chops (lamb)	3 to 5 days	4 to 6 months
Chops (pork)	3 to 5 days	4 to 6 months
Ground, stew meats	1 to 2 days	3 to 4 months
Roasts (beef)	3 to 5 days	6 to 12 months
Roasts (lamb)	3 to 5 days	4 to 6 months
Roasts (pork, veal)	3 to 5 days	4 to 6 months
Sausage (fresh pork)	1 to 2 days	1 to 2 months
Steaks	3 to 5 days	6 to 12 months
Cooked Meats		
Cooked meat, meat dishes	3 to 4 days	2 to 3 months
Processed meats		
Bacon	1 week*	1 to 2 months
Frankfurters	1 week*	1 to 2 months
Ham (fully cooked half)	3 to 5 days	1 to 2 months
Luncheon meats	3 to 5 days*	1 to 2 months
Sausage (smoked)	1 week	1 to 2 months
Fresh Poultry		
Chicken and turkey (whole)	1 to 2 days	1 year
Chicken pieces	1 to 2 days	9 months
Duck and goose (whole)	1 to 2 days	1 year
Turkey pieces	1 to 2 days	9 months
Cooked Poultry		
Covered with broth or gravy	1 to 2 days	6 months
Pieces not in broth or gravy	3 to 4 days	4 months
Cooked casseroles	3 to 4 days	4 to 6 months
Fish	1 to 2 days	3 to 6 months
Eggs		
Whites	2 to 4 days	12 months
Whole eggs (fresh in shell)	3 weeks	Can't freeze
Yolks	2 to 4 days	12 months
Cheese		
Cottage	5 days	Can't freeze
Hard cheese	3 to 4 months	6 months
Soft cheese	2 weeks	4 months
Ice cream	Can't refrigerate	1 to 3 months
Butter, margarine	1 month	3 to 6 months

*Dates apply to opened vacuum-sealed packages. Unopened vacuum-sealed packages can be stored in the refrigerator for 2 weeks or until the "use by" or "sell by" date expires.

Basic Table Setting

Setting the table is often a hurried task that leaves family members wondering about the correct placement of the flat- *ware, plates, napkins and glassware. The basic table setting pictured below is appropriate for most every occasion.*

A. Salad plate
B. Napkin
C. Salad fork
D. Dinner fork
E. Dinner plate
F. Knife
G. Teaspoon
H. Soup spoon
I. Water glass
J. Cup and saucer

The flatware is arranged around the plate in the order in which it will be used. If a salad is to be served, the salad fork is placed to the left of the dinner fork. The salad fork can be eliminated if no salad is served or placed to the right of the dinner fork and used as a dessert fork if appropriate. (The dessert fork can also be brought to the table when dessert is served.) If desired, a wine glass can be added between the water glass and the coffee cup.

Napkin Folding

Folded napkins are a fun, easy way to dress up your table. Best of all, you can do the folding days in advance!

Perhaps you've admired a "standing fan" (at left) on your dinner plate at a fancy restaurant. What you may not know is that you needn't be an expert to do one! Here's how:

1. Fold an open square cloth or paper napkin in half like a book. (If necessary, starch cloth napkins for crisp folds.) Beginning at the bottom edge, form 1-in. accordion-pleats until 4 in. remain.
2. Turn the napkin over so the pleats you just made are under the bottom edge and the flat side without pleats faces you. See Fig. 1. Fold the napkin in half from right to left so half of the pleats are now on top.
3. Fold the top down to form a 1-1/2-in. hem. See Fig. 2. Fold the top left corner down diagonally and tuck it under the pleats.

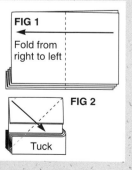

FIG 1
Fold from right to left

FIG 2
Tuck

Common Cooking Terms

Al dente—Italian term meaning "to the tooth" used to describe pasta that is cooked but still firm.

Au jus—Natural unthickened juices that collect while roasting meat.

Baste—To moisten foods while cooking by brushing with pan juices, butter, margarine, oil or a reserved marinade. See Stuffing and Roasting a Turkey on page 142.

Beat—To make a mixture smooth by rapidly mixing with a spoon, fork, wire whisk or electric mixer.

Bias cut—To cut foods diagonally into thick or thin slices. Most often used in stir-fries. See page 12.

Blanch—To partially cook fruits and vegetables by plunging into boiling water or placing over steam. Also used to loosen skins from tomatoes (see page 263), peaches and almonds.

Blend—To combine several ingredients with a spoon, electric mixer, blender or food processor, making a smooth mixture.

Boil—To heat liquids until bubbles form that cannot be stirred down. In the case of water, the temperature will reach 212° at sea level.

Bone—To remove raw or cooked meat from bones. See Boning Chicken Breasts on page 136.

Braise—To cook slowly in a small amount of liquid in a covered pan on the stovetop or in the oven. Generally used for less tender cuts of meat. See page 108.

Breading—A coating of fine bread crumbs or crackers used on meat, fish and vegetables. See page 187.

Broil—To cook foods 4 to 6 in. from a heat source.

Brown—To cook food in a small amount of fat over medium to high heat until the food becomes brown, sealing in the juices and developing rich pan drippings.

Caramelize—To heat sugar in a skillet or saucepan over low heat until melted and golden brown in color (see Making a Caramel Custard on page 308). Also refers to cooking onions in butter until soft, caramel-colored and rich in flavor.

Chop—To cut foods into 1/4-in. to 1/2-in. pieces. See page 12.

Coat—To dip or roll foods in flour, sugar or a sauce until covered. See page 109.

Combine—To place several ingredients in a single bowl or container and thoroughly mix.

Core—To remove the seed area of an apple or pear using a coring tool or a small knife.

Cream—To beat butter, margarine or shortening alone or with sugar using a spoon or mixer until light and fluffy.

Crisp-tender—Defines a stage of vegetable cookery where the vegetables are cooked until they are crunchy yet tender enough to be pierced with a fork. See page 255.

Cube—To cut foods into 1/2-in. to 1-in. pieces that are square in shape. See page 12.

Cut in—To break down and distribute butter, margarine or solid shortening into a flour mixture using a pastry blender or two knives. See Mixing and Cutting Biscuits on page 61.

Dash—A measurement less than 1/8 teaspoon that is used for herbs, spices or hot pepper sauce. Not an accurate measurement.

Deglaze—To add water, broth or wine to a pan in which food, usually meat, has been cooked to remove the browned drippings to make a rich gravy.

Dice—To cut foods into small cubes 1/8 in. to 1/4 in. in size. See page 12.

Dot—To break up small pieces of butter and distribute over the top of a dish or casserole.

Dredge—To lightly coat foods with flour or bread crumbs (see page 109).

Dress—To toss salads with salad dressing. Also, to remove the internal organs of fish, poultry or game.

Drizzle—To slowly spoon or pour a thin stream of an icing, melted butter or other liquid over food. See Shaping Cinnamon Rolls on page 51.

Dust—To sprinkle confectioners' sugar, baking cocoa or flour lightly over foods. See page 321.

Dutch oven—A multipurpose cooking vessel that can range in size from 5 to 8 qts. and is used to roast meats, cook soups and stews, boil pasta or steam vegetables. See Basic Pots and Pans on page 13.

Emulsify—To combine through a whisking action two liquids that traditionally separate, such as oil and vinegar, into a mixture that will not separate upon standing. See page 72.

Fillet—A boneless piece of fish, chicken or meat.

Fold—A method of mixing to combine light or delicate ingredients such as whipped cream or egg whites with other ingredients without beating. A rubber spatula is used to gently cut down through the ingredients, move across the bottom of the bowl and bring up part of the mixture. See Making a Sponge Cake on page 327.

Full rolling boil—To boil a liquid in which the bubbles created by the boil cannot be stirred down. See Making Berry Jam on page 296.

Fry—To cook food in a small amount of fat over medium to high heat.

Glaze—To coat the exterior of sweet or savory foods with a thin glossy mixture.

Grate—To rub foods, such as hard cheese, citrus peel and spices, over a grater to produce very fine particles.

Grease—To rub the inside of a baking dish or pan with fat to keep the contents from sticking. See Preparing a Cake Pan on page 318.

Grind—To transform a solid piece of food into smaller pieces using a meat grinder, food processor or mortar and pestle.

Headspace—An area left unfilled between the top of the food in a home canning jar or freezer container and the bottom of the lid. See Boiling-Water-Bath Basics on page 294.

Hull—To remove the green stem and leaves of strawberries.

Husk—To remove the outer leaves from an ear of corn.

Jelly roll—A dessert made by spreading a filling of jelly, cream or whipped cream over a sponge cake baked in a 15-in. x 10-in. x 1-in. pan. and rolling it into a log (see page 328). Jelly-roll style is used when any food is filled and rolled into a log shape.

Julienne—To cut foods into long thin matchstick

shapes about 2 in. long and 1/4 in. thick. See page 12.

Knead—To work foods, usually dough, by using a pressing and folding action to make it smooth and elastic. See Traditional Bread Mixing and Baking Method on page 40.

Line—To cover a baking sheet with a piece of waxed or parchment paper or foil to prevent sticking. See page 320.

Marinate—To tenderize and/or flavor foods, usually meat or raw vegetables, by placing in a liquid mixture of oil, vinegar, wine, lime or lemon juice, herbs and spices.

Mince—To cut foods into very fine pieces no larger than 1/8 in. Used most often for fresh herbs or garlic. See page 12.

Mix—To stir or beat two or more ingredients together with a spoon or a fork until well combined.

Moisten—To add enough liquid to dry ingredients while stirring gently to make a wet but not runny mixture. Often used in the preparation of muffins. See page 57.

Pan-Dressed—Fish or small game with the internal organs and head removed, making it ready for cooking.

Parboil—To boil foods, usually vegetables, until partially cooked. Most often used when vegetables are finished using another cooking method or chilled for marinated salads or appetizer dips.

Pare/Peel—To remove the skin from fruits and vegetables using a small knife or vegetable peeler. See page 12.

Partially set—A term that describes the consistency of chilled gelatin (resembles unbeaten egg whites) before fruits, vegetables and nuts can be added without floating.

Pinch—A small amount (less than 1/8 teaspoon) of a seasoning or spice that is easily held between the thumb and index finger. This is not an accurate measurement.

Pipe—To force a soft mixture such as whipped cream, frosting or mashed potatoes through a decorator's icing bag or pastry bag for a fancy garnish. See page 231.

Poach—To cook meat, fish, eggs or fruits in simmering liquid. See page 222.

Press—Often called a cookie press. Used to extract cookie dough in decorative shapes.

Prick—To pierce food or pastry with the tines of a fork to prevent them from bursting or rising during baking. See Baking a Pastry Shell on page 334. Also used when roasting ducks and geese to remove excess fat under the skin.

Punch down—To use a fist to deflate risen yeast dough after the first rising. See Traditional Bread Mixing and Baking Method on page 40.

Puree—To mash solid foods into a smooth mixture using a food processor, food mill, blender or sieve. See page 297.

Reduce—To thicken sauces and gravy by boiling down and evaporating a portion of the liquid in an uncovered pan. See page 105.

Roux—A French term for a mixture of flour and fat that is cooked together until golden brown and used to thicken gumbo soups and sauces. See page 213.

Saute—To cook or lightly brown foods in butter, margarine or oil until tender.

Scald—To heat milk or cream over low heat until just before it boils. Look for small bubbles around the edge of the liquid.

Score—To make thin slashes on the surface of meats to tenderize or decorate. See page 173.

Seed—To remove seeds from fruits and vegetables. See page 298.

Separate—To divide eggs into whites and yolks. See page 226.

Shred—To cut or tear foods into long thin strips (see page 100). In the case of soft cheese, carrots or potatoes, a metal shredder is used.

Shuck—To remove the meat of oysters, clams, etc. from their shells. Also refers to removing the husk from an ear of corn.

Sift—To pass dry ingredients, most often flour, through a fine-mesh strainer to remove lumps, add air and combine several dry ingredients.

Simmer—To cook liquids alone or a combination of ingredients with liquid just under the boiling point (180° to 200°).

Skim—To remove with a spoon a layer of fat or foam that rises to the top of cooking liquids. See Making Pan Gravy from Roasted Meats on page 145.

Snip—To cut herbs into small pieces using a kitchen shears. See page 12.

Soften—To bring butter, margarine, cream cheese or ice cream to a soft consistency by holding at room temperature for a short time.

Steam—To cook foods, covered, on a rack or in a steamer basket over a small amount of boiling water. Most often used for vegetables.

Steep—To place dry foods, such as tea leaves, in hot water to extract flavor and/or color.

Stir—To blend a combination of ingredients by hand using a spoon in a circular motion.

Stir-Fry—To quickly saute meats and vegetables while stirring constantly in a wok or a skillet. See page 116.

Stock—A long-simmered broth made from meat, poultry, fish and/or vegetables with herbs and spices. See Making Chicken Noodle Soup on page 87.

Strain—To separate solids from liquid by pouring through a colander or sieve. See page 86.

Stud—To insert seasonings like whole cloves in the surface of food, such as a ham. See page 173.

Stuff—To fill a cavity in fish, poultry or pork chops with a bread or rice, vegetable, fruit or nut mixture. See page 134.

Thread—To place pieces of meat and vegetable onto skewers…for instance, when making kabobs.

Toss—To quickly and gently mix ingredients with a spoon and fork. Often used in salads or pasta dishes.

Truss—To tie the legs and wings of poultry close to the body before roasting. If poultry is stuffed, the openings are closed with skewers that are tied or closed with string. See Stuffing and Roasting a Turkey on page 142.

Warm—To hold foods at a low temperature without further cooking, usually around 200°.

Whip—To beat rapidly by hand or with an electric mixer to add air and increase volume.

Whisk—A multi-looped wire mixing utensil with a handle used to whip sauces, eggs, cream, salad dressings, etc. to a smooth, airy consistency. See page 72.

Zest (Peel)—The outer portion of a citrus fruit. To remove zest or peel, use a small sharp knife, a grater, a vegetable peeler or a special gadget called a zester.

Recipe Index

This index lists every recipe by food category and/or major ingredient, so you can easily locate them.

APPETIZERS & SNACKS
Cold Appetizers
Best Deviled Eggs, 231
BLT Bites, 19
Tomato Bread Salad, 23
Tortilla Pinwheels, 21
Vegetable Appetizer Pizza, 27
Dips
Chili Cheese Dip, 25
Creamy Hot Beef Dip, 28
Dill Dip, 18
Fiesta Appetizer, 22
Guacamole, 22
Hot Crab Dip, 25
Mustard Egg Dip, 19
Hot Appetizers
Appetizer Stromboli, 29
Asparagus Appetizer Roll-Ups, 25
Bacon and Cheese Breakfast
    Pizza, 223
Baked Potato Skins, 27
Chickaritos, 24
Ham Buns, 98
Mini Hamburgers, 26
Moose Meatballs, 207
Sausage-Stuffed Mushrooms, 28
Sweet Gingered Chicken Wings, 27
Tangy Meatballs, 30
Tater-Dipped Veggies, 26
Snack Mixes
Buttery Onion Pretzels, 32
Honey-Glazed Snack Mix, 31
Spiced Pecans, 32
Three-Herb Popcorn, 31
White Chocolate Party Mix, 32
Spreads
Continental Cheese Spread, 18
Festive Cheese Spread, 21
Fireside Cheese Spread, 21
Roasted Garlic, 30
Three-in-One Cheese Ball, 20

APPLES
Apple Cranberry Pie, 339
Apple Crisp, 310

Apple-Stuffed Chicken, 141
Apple Walnut Cake, 319
Autumn Apple Salad, 74
Caramel Apples, 372
Cider Baked Squash, 283
Cinnamon Apple Glaze, 330
Cranberry Apple Punch, 33
Cranberry Apple Relish, 292
Crunchy Baked Apples, 309
Easy Applesauce, 291
Farm Apple Pan Pie, 339
Four-Fruit Pie, 337
Fruit and Nut Bread Pudding, 310
Goose with Apple-Prune Stuffing, 155
Maple-Glazed Apple Pie, 336
Oven Apple Butter, 296
Perfect Apple Pie, 336
Pork Chops with Apple Stuffing, 159
Puffy Apple Omelet, 231
Roasted Duck with Apple-Raisin
    Dressing, 154
Spiced Apple Pork Roast, 162
Sweet-and-Sour Red Cabbage, 270

APRICOTS
Apricot Bars, 358
Apricot-Glazed Sweet Potatoes, 282

ARTICHOKES
California Roast Lamb, 197
Artichoke Chicken, 137

ASPARAGUS
Asparagus Appetizer Roll-Ups, 25
Asparagus Strata, 228
Dill Butter for Asparagus, 264
Dilly Asparagus, 81
Oven-Baked Asparagus, 265
Pasta with Asparagus, 245
Sesame Asparagus, 265
Sugared Asparagus, 264

AVOCADOS
Fiesta Appetizer, 22
Guacamole, 22

BACON
Asparagus Appetizer Roll-Ups, 25
Bacon and Cheese Breakfast Pizza, 223
Bacon-Stuffed Burgers, 98
Baked Potato Skins, 27
Big Sandwich, 97
Black-Eyed Pea Chowder, 92
Black-Eyed Peas with Bacon, 241
BLT Bites, 19

Calico Beans, 243
Company Brussels Sprouts, 269
Country Cassoulet, 240
Maple Baked Beans, 241
Quick Baked Beans, 243
Sheepherder's Breakfast, 223

BANANAS
Banana Poppy Seed Dressing, 72
Best-Ever Banana Bread, 55
Coconut Banana Cream Pie, 341

BARLEY
Beef and Barley Soup, 89
Curried Lamb and Barley, 201
Wild Rice and Barley Pilaf, 237

BARS & BROWNIES
Apricot Bars, 358
Chocolate Crunch Brownies, 362
Chocolate Peanut Butter Brownies, 363
Date Bars, 359
Lemon Bars, 358
Maple Butterscotch Brownies, 363
Sugar Diamonds, 359
Toffee Squares, 358
Ultimate Double Chocolate
    Brownies, 362

BEANS
Baked Beans
Calico Beans, 243
Maple Baked Beans, 241
Quick Baked Beans, 243
Canned Beans
Black Beans and Sausage, 243
Chili Cheese Bake, 239
Fiesta Appetizer, 22
Ham, Red Beans and Rice, 242
Hearty Ribs and Beans, 169
Succotash, 242
Taco Soup, 94
Dried Beans
Chalupa, 165
Country Cassoulet, 240
Peasant Bean Soup, 92
Green Beans
Basil Buttered Beans, 266
Country Green Beans, 265
Red, White and Green Salad, 78
Tangy Green Bean Casserole, 266
Three-Bean Salad, 83

BEEF *(also see Ground Beef & Veal)*
Main Dishes
Baked Beef Stew, 113

Beef and Pepper Stir-Fry, 116
Beef Stew with Cheddar
    Dumplings, 113
Caraway Pot Roast, 108
Corned Beef and Cabbage, 112
Country-Fried Steaks, 117
Crisp Hash for Two, 119
Fantastic Beef Fajitas, 118
Grilled Beef Kabobs, 120
Hungarian Short Ribs, 110
Italian-Style Beef Liver, 117
Marinated Sirloin Steak, 121
Midget Pot Roast, 106
Mom's Roast Beef, 106
Old-Fashioned Swiss Steak, 109
Old-World Sauerbraten, 107
Peppered Rib Eye Steaks, 121
Peppery London Broil, 119
Perfect Pot Roast, 107
Round Steak Stroganoff, 110
Slow-Cooked Pepper Steak, 111
Southwestern Beef Brisket, 105
Standing Rib Roast, 115
Stuffed Beef Tenderloin, 115
Sandwiches
Big Sandwich, 97
Egg-Filled Buns, 227
French Dip Sandwiches, 100
Reuben Sandwiches, 99
Snacks
Creamy Hot Beef Dip, 28
Festive Cheese Spread, 21
Soups and Salad
Beef and Barley Soup, 89
Pronto Beef Vegetable Soup, 94
Spicy Beef Salad, 76
Steak Soup, 88

BEETS
Beet Relish, 292
Easy Pickled Beets, 266
Harvard Beets, 267
Spiced Baked Beets, 267

BEVERAGES
Buttermilk Shake, 34
Cranberry Apple Punch, 33
Holiday Wassail, 35
Homemade Eggnog, 35
Orange Refresher, 34
Orange Sherbet Party Punch, 33
Spiced Lemonade, 35
Strawberry Watermelon Slush, 34

BISCUITS & SCONES
Angel Biscuits, 62
Breakfast Scones, 63
Buttermilk Biscuit Sausage
    Pinwheels, 60
Cherry Cream Scones, 63

Mom's Buttermilk Biscuits, 60
Nutty Sweet Potato Biscuits, 61
Orange Biscuits, 62
Sour Cream 'n' Chive Biscuits, 61

BLUEBERRIES
Blueberry and Peach Cobbler, 310
Blueberry Buckle, 59
Blueberry Cream Pie, 347
Blueberry Sour Cream Pancakes, 66
Four-Fruit Pie, 337
Patriotic Dessert, 309
Tri-Berry Jam, 296

BREAD MACHINE RECIPES
Buttermilk Wheat Bread, 53
Onion Dill Bread, 53

BREADS (also see Biscuits & Scones; Bread Machine Recipes; Coffee Cakes; Corn Bread & Cornmeal; Doughnuts; French Toast, Pancakes & Waffles; Muffins; Rolls & Buns; Yeast Breads)
Best-Ever Banana Bread, 55
Cranberry Orange Bread, 54
Garlic Herb Bread, 64
Hush Puppies, 65
Irish Soda Bread, 54
Mom's Brown Bread, 54
Pumpkin Chocolate Chip Bread, 55
Southwestern Spoon Bread, 64

BROCCOLI
Broccoli Bake, 268
Broccoli-Ham Hot Dish, 176
Broccoli Mushroom Medley, 268
Broccoli Pie, 224
Chicken Broccoli Casserole, 153
Herbed Broccoli, 269

BRUSSELS SPROUTS
Company Brussels Sprouts, 269
Fancy Brussels Sprouts, 269

BUTTERS
Corn Muffins with Honey Butter, 56
Dill Butter for Asparagus, 264
Oven Apple Butter, 296
Sole in Herbed Butter, 183
Spicy Corn Spread, 272

CABBAGE & SAUERKRAUT
Cabbage Casserole, 270
Corned Beef and Cabbage, 112
Creamy Coleslaw, 82
Crunchy Pork and Rice Salad, 77
Easy Sauerkraut Salad, 81
Norwegian Coleslaw, 82
Reuben Sandwiches, 99
Sauerkraut Pork Chops, 160
Stuffed Cabbage Rolls, 125
Sunday Boiled Dinner, 174
Sweet-and-Sour Red Cabbage, 270

CAKES & CUPCAKES
Angel Food Cake, 325
Apple Walnut Cake, 319
Butter Pecan Cake, 323
Carrot Layer Cake, 319
Chocolate Angel Food Cake, 326
Chocolate Layer Cake, 318
Chocolate Lover's Chiffon Cake, 329
Chocolate Pound Cake, 321
Coffee Angel Food Cake, 326
German Chocolate Cake, 320
Gingerbread, 322
Lazy Daisy Cake, 322
Moist Chocolate Cupcakes, 324
Oatmeal Chocolate Chip Cake, 321
Orange-Glazed Sponge Cake, 327
Pumpkin Cake Squares, 322
Raspberry Cake Roll, 328
Spiced Pineapple Upside-Down
    Cake, 324

CANDIES
Almond Butter Crunch, 370
Candy Bar Fudge, 366
Caramel Apples, 372
Chocolate Clusters, 371
Chocolate Pizza, 373
Christmas Hard Candy, 365
Coconut Yule Trees, 368
Creamy Caramels, 366
Dairy State Fudge, 366
Marshmallow Puffs, 370
Mocha Truffles, 368
Old-Time Popcorn Balls, 373
Orange Taffy, 365
Peanut Brittle, 370
Pecan Delights, 368
Popcorn Caramel Crunch, 372
Sweetheart Fudge, 367
Three-Chocolate Fudge, 367
Tuxedo Strawberries, 371
White Christmas Candy, 372

CARAMEL
Caramel Apples, 372
Creamy Caramels, 366
Popcorn Caramel Crunch, 372

CARROTS
Baked Carrots, 271
Carrot Layer Cake, 319
Carrot Pilaf, 239
Dilled Carrots, 270
Glazed Carrots, 271
Peas and Carrots with Mint, 279

CASSEROLES (also see Lasagna and Meat Pies & Potpies)
Main Dishes
Artichoke Chicken, 137
Asparagus Strata, 228
Baked Stuffed Eggs, 231
Broccoli-Ham Hot Dish, 176
Chicken and Hash Brown Bake, 153
Chicken Broccoli Casserole, 153
Chicken Tetrazzini, 249
Chili Cheese Strata, 229
Chops and Chilies Casserole, 160
Country Cassoulet, 240
Curried Lamb and Barley, 201
Florida Seafood Casserole, 190
Hearty Ribs and Beans, 169
Herbed Macaroni and Cheese, 232
Hot Chicken Salad, 150
Italian-Stuffed Shells, 248
Lamb Noodle Stroganoff, 201
Mexican Turkey Roll-Ups, 152
Mostaccioli Bake, 249
New England Lamb Bake, 200
Pheasant and Wild Rice, 211
Scrambled Egg Casserole, 219
Tater Tot Bake, 124
Three-Cheese Enchiladas, 233
Tuna Mushroom Casserole, 187
Side Dishes
Apricot-Glazed Sweet
  Potatoes, 282
Baked Mushroom Rice, 236
Broccoli Bake, 268
Cabbage Casserole, 270
Cheesy Grits Casserole, 239
Cheesy Onion Casserole, 278
Chili Cheese Bake, 239
Corn Pudding Supreme, 274
Herbed Spinach Bake, 283
Hominy Casserole, 274
Sausage and Wild Rice
  Casserole, 171
Spaghetti Squash Casserole, 284
Spiced Baked Beets, 267
Sweet Potato Bake, 282
Tangy Green Bean Casserole, 266
Wild Rice and Barley Pilaf, 237

CAULIFLOWER
Cauliflower Au Gratin, 272
Cauliflower with Mushroom Almond
  Sauce, 272

CHEESE
Bacon and Cheese Breakfast Pizza, 223
Beef Stew with Cheddar
  Dumplings, 113
Blue Cheese Dressing, 73
Cauliflower Au Gratin, 272
Cheddar Chicken Potpie, 151
Cheddar Parmesan Potatoes, 280
Cheesy Grits Casserole, 239
Cheesy Onion Casserole, 278
Cheesy Vegetable Soup, 90
Cherry Cheesecake Tarts, 307
Chicken Cheese Lasagna, 247
Chili Cheese Bake, 239
Chili Cheese Dip, 25
Chili Cheese Strata, 229
Continental Cheese Spread, 18
Cream Cheese Frosting, 331
Dairy State Fudge, 366
Festive Cheese Spread, 21
Fireside Cheese Spread, 21
Fluffy Cranberry Cheese Pie, 345
Four-Cheese Lasagna, 246
Herbed Macaroni and Cheese, 232
Italian Parmesan Bread, 52
Lemon Cheese Braid, 50
Mini Blue Cheese Rolls, 64
Old-World Pizza, 233
Parmesan Noodles, 245
Stovetop Macaroni and Cheese, 232
Strawberry Cheesecake, 302
Three-Cheese Enchiladas, 233
Three-Cheese Souffles, 226
Three-in-One Cheese Ball, 20
Tortilla Pinwheels, 21
Wisconsin Potato Cheese Soup, 90

CHERRIES
Cherry Almond Glazed Ham, 172
Cherry Berry Pie, 338
Cherry Cheesecake Tarts, 307
Cherry Christmas Slices, 357
Cherry Cream Scones, 63
Northwest Cherry Salsa, 290

CHICKEN
Main Dishes
Apple-Stuffed Chicken, 141
Artichoke Chicken, 137
Barbecued Chicken, 148
Cheddar Chicken Potpie, 151
Chicken a la King, 153
Chicken and Dumplings, 135
Chicken and Hash Brown Bake, 153
Chicken Broccoli Casserole, 153
Chicken Cheese Lasagna, 247
Chicken Italiano, 137
Chicken Stir-Fry, 136
Chicken Tetrazzini, 249
Country Cassoulet, 240
Cranberry Chicken, 135
Greek Roasted Chicken and
  Potatoes, 140
Grilled Tarragon Chicken, 148
Honey-Mustard Baked
  Chicken, 134
Hot Chicken Salad, 150
Oven-Barbecued Chicken, 132
Oven-Fried Chicken, 131
Roasted Chicken and Potatoes, 138
Roasted Chicken with
  Rosemary, 140
Savory Roasted Chicken, 141
Skillet Chicken Stew, 136
Spicy Breaded Chicken, 133
Squash-Stuffed Chicken, 134
Sunday-Fried Chicken, 133
Sandwiches and Salad
Chicken Salad Sandwiches, 97
Grilled Chicken Salad, 76
Spicy Chicken Heroes, 99
Snacks
Chickaritos, 24
Sweet Gingered Chicken Wings, 27
Soup and Chili
Chicken Noodle Soup, 87
Santa Fe Chicken Chili, 95

CHILI
Buffalo Chili Con Carne, 208
Classic Chili, 95
Santa Fe Chicken Chili, 95

CHOCOLATE
Bars and Cookies
Chocolate Chip Cookies, 352
Chocolate Crunch Brownies, 362
Chocolate Peanut Butter
  Brownies, 363
Dipped Peanut Butter Sandwich
  Cookies, 362
Toffee Squares, 358
Ultimate Double Chocolate
  Brownies, 362
Cakes and Cupcakes
Chocolate Angel Food Cake, 326
Chocolate Layer Cake, 318
Chocolate Lover's Chiffon
  Cake, 329
Chocolate Pound Cake, 321
German Chocolate Cake, 320
Moist Chocolate Cupcakes, 324
Oatmeal Chocolate Chip Cake, 321
Candies
Almond Butter Crunch, 370

Candy Bar Fudge, 366
Chocolate Clusters, 371
Chocolate Pizza, 373
Coconut Yule Trees, 368
Dairy State Fudge, 366
Marshmallow Puffs, 370
Mocha Truffles, 368
Pecan Delights, 368
Sweetheart Fudge, 367
Three-Chocolate Fudge, 367
Tuxedo Strawberries, 371
White Christmas Candy, 372
Desserts
Chocolate Pudding, 306
Easy Chocolate Ice Cream, 312
Frozen Ice Cream Delight, 314
Homemade Fudge Sauce, 315
Milky Way Ice Cream, 313
Frosting
Chocolate Sour Cream Frosting, 331
Chocolate Whipped Cream
    Frosting, 331
Mocha Frosting, 330
Pies
Chocolate Malt Shoppe Pie, 349
Chocolate Peanut Butter Pie, 346
German Chocolate Pie, 341
Grandma's Chocolate Meringue
    Pie, 342
Mud Pie, 348
Peppermint Stick Pie, 349
Strawberry Lover's Pie, 341
Snacks
Pumpkin Chocolate Chip Bread, 55
White Chocolate Party Mix, 32

COCONUT
Brown Sugar Icebox Cookies, 357
Chocolate Pizza, 373
Coconut Banana Cream Pie, 341
Coconut Yule Trees, 368
Fruitcake Cookies, 361
German Chocolate Cake, 320
Lazy Daisy Cake, 322
Sunshine Ice Cream Pie, 349

COFFEE CAKES
Blueberry Buckle, 59
Cinnamon Swirl Kuchen, 59
Cream-Filled Coffee Cake, 48
Lemon Cheese Braid, 50
Strawberry Rhubarb Coffee Cake, 59

COOKIES (also see Bars & Brownies)
Brown Sugar Icebox Cookies, 357
Cherry Christmas Slices, 357
Chocolate Chip Cookies, 352
Cranberry Nut Swirls, 357
Dipped Peanut Butter Sandwich
    Cookies, 362

Fruitcake Cookies, 361
Grandma's Peanut Butter Cookies, 353
Holly Wreaths, 361
Molasses Spice Cutouts, 354
Oatmeal Raisin Cookies, 353
Old-Fashioned Gingersnaps, 353
Pecan Meltaways, 360
Scottish Shortbread, 360
Sugar Cookies, 355
Tassies, 360
Wishing Cookies, 356

COOKING FOR TWO
Basic Poached Eggs, 222
Basic Scrambled Eggs, 219
Basil Buttered Beans, 266
Braised Lamb Shanks, 198
Chops and Chilies Casserole, 160
Crisp Hash for Two, 119
Deluxe Ham Omelet, 220
Fried Eggs, 218
Hard-Cooked Eggs, 218
Herbed Baked Eggs, 229
Lime Broiled Catfish, 186
Linguini with Clam Sauce, 191
Midget Pot Roast, 106
Peppery London Broil, 119
Pheasant in Mustard Sauce, 211
Puffy Apple Omelet, 231
Sauerkraut Pork Chops, 160
Soft-Cooked Eggs, 218
Southwestern Grilled Lamb, 194
Spaghetti and Meatballs for Two, 127
Tater Tot Bake, 124
Tomato Basil Pasta, 248
Zesty Poached Eggs, 222

CORN
Corn Balls, 273
Corn Okra Creole, 276
Corn Pudding Supreme, 274
Cream-Style Corn, 274
Freezer Sweet Corn, 273
Fresh Corn Salad, 80
Red Corn Relish, 298
Roast Corn on the Cob, 273
Southwestern Spoon Bread, 64
Spicy Corn Spread, 272

CORN BREAD & CORNMEAL
Corn Bread Dressing with Oysters, 190

Corn Muffins with Honey Butter, 56
Corn Pudding Supreme, 274
Creole Stuffing, 144
Hush Puppies, 65
Sour Cream Corn Bread, 55
Southwestern Spoon Bread, 64
Turkey with Corn Bread Stuffing, 142
Wild Goose with Giblet Stuffing, 215

CRANBERRIES
Apple Cranberry Pie, 339
Cranberry Apple Punch, 33
Cranberry Apple Relish, 292
Cranberry Chicken, 135
Cranberry Doughnuts, 67
Cranberry Meatballs, 127
Cranberry Nut Swirls, 357
Cranberry Orange Bread, 54
Cranberry Salsa, 291
Cranberry Sherbet, 312
Cranberry Stuffing Balls, 171
Cranberry Sweet-and-Sour Pork, 167
Easy Berry Relish, 292
Fluffy Cranberry Cheese Pie, 345
Frozen Cranberry Salad, 83
Wild Rice and Barley Pilaf, 237

CUCUMBERS
Bread 'n' Butter Pickles, 299
Dill Pickle Spears, 299
Freezer Cucumber Pickles, 299
Sour Cream Cucumbers, 81

DESSERTS (also see specific kinds)
Apple Crisp, 310
Berry Rhubarb Fool, 306
Blueberry and Peach Cobbler, 310
Cherry Cheesecake Tarts, 307
Christmas Special Fruitcake, 311
Crunchy Baked Apples, 309
Lemon Custard in Meringue
    Cups, 303
Patriotic Dessert, 309
Raspberry Trifle, 305
Strawberry Cheesecake, 302
Strawberry Cream Puffs, 304
Strawberry Shortcake, 311

DIPS (also see Salsas)
Chili Cheese Dip, 25
Creamy Hot Beef Dip, 28
Dill Dip, 18
Fiesta Appetizer, 22
Guacamole, 22
Hot Crab Dip, 25
Mustard Egg Dip, 19

DOUGHNUTS
Cranberry Doughnuts, 67
Feather-Light Doughnuts, 49

DRESSING & STUFFING
Corn Balls, 273
Corn Bread Dressing with Oysters, 190
Country Ham Stuffing, 144
Cranberry Stuffing Balls, 171
Creole Stuffing, 144
Dutch Potato Poultry Stuffing, 144
Herbed Rice Stuffing, 143

DUMPLINGS
Beef Stew with Cheddar
    Dumplings, 113
Chicken and Dumplings, 135
Venison Pot Roast, 205

EGGS (*also see Quiche*)
Asparagus Strata, 228
Bacon and Cheese Breakfast Pizza, 223
Baked Stuffed Eggs, 231
Basic Poached Eggs, 222
Basic Scrambled Eggs, 219
Best Deviled Eggs, 231
Breakfast Burritos, 220
Breakfast Custard, 224
Chili Cheese Strata, 229
Curried Egg Salad Sandwiches, 100
Deluxe Ham Omelet, 220
Egg-Filled Buns, 227
Egg Pizzas, 229
Fried Eggs, 218
Grilled Ham and Egg Salad
    Sandwiches, 96
Ham and Potato Frittata, 221
Hard-Cooked Eggs, 218
Hearty Egg Scramble, 221
Herbed Baked Eggs, 229
Homemade Eggnog, 35
Mustard Egg Dip, 19
Old-World Puff Pancake, 227
Puffy Apple Omelet, 231
Scrambled Egg Casserole, 219
Sheepherder's Breakfast, 223
Soft-Cooked Eggs, 218
Three-Cheese Souffles, 226
Zesty Poached Eggs, 222

FRENCH TOAST, PANCAKES & WAFFLES
Blueberry Sour Cream Pancakes, 66
Buttermilk Waffles, 67
Freezer French Toast, 67
Old-World Puff Pancake, 227

FROSTING
Buttercream Frosting, 330

Chocolate Sour Cream Frosting, 331
Chocolate Whipped Cream
    Frosting, 331
Cinnamon Apple Glaze, 330
Confectioners' Sugar Cookie
    Frosting, 355
Cream Cheese Frosting, 331
Fluffy Seven-Minute Frosting, 331
Mocha Frosting, 330

FRUIT (*also see specific kinds*)
Christmas Special Fruitcake, 311
Empire State Muffins, 56
Fall Pear Pie, 338
Fruitcake Cookies, 361
Heavenly Jam, 295
Holiday Wassail, 35
Layered Fresh Fruit Salad, 83
Roast Lamb with Plum Sauce, 196
Spiced Pineapple Upside-Down
    Cake, 324
Strawberry Watermelon Slush, 34

GAME & FOWL
Buffalo Chili Con Carne, 208
Creamed Grouse on Toast, 212
Currant-Glazed Cornish Hens, 154
Goose with Apple-Prune Stuffing, 155
Grilled Venison and Vegetables, 204
Hasenpfeffer, 208
Moose Meatballs, 207
Pheasant and Wild Rice, 211
Pheasant in Mustard Sauce, 211
Pheasant Potpie, 210
Quail in Mushroom Gravy, 215
Rabbit Dijon, 209
Rabbit with Tarragon Sauce, 209
Roast Wild Duck, 215
Roasted Duck with Apple-Raisin
    Dressing, 154
Swiss Elk Steak, 206
Turtle Soup, 212
Venison Meat Loaf, 205
Venison Pot Roast, 205
Venison Tenderloin Sandwiches, 206
Wild Duck Gumbo, 213
Wild Goose with Giblet Stuffing, 215

GRAVY
Basic Pan Gravy from Roasted
    Meats, 145
Mushroom Gravy, 145

GRILLED & BROILED
Bacon-Stuffed Burgers, 98
Barbecued Chicken, 148
Barbecued Lamb Kabobs, 195
Barbecued Spareribs, 169
Barbecued Trout, 181
Dilly Grilled Turkey, 148

Greek Burgers, 195
Grilled Beef Kabobs, 120
Grilled Chicken Salad, 76
Grilled Ham Steak, 175
Grilled Lamb Chops, 194
Grilled Mushrooms, 276
Grilled Pork Tenderloin, 166
Grilled Salmon, 184
Grilled Tarragon Chicken, 148
Grilled Venison and Vegetables, 204
Herbed Orange Roughy, 183
Lime Broiled Catfish, 186
Marinated Sirloin Steak, 121
Marinated Thanksgiving Turkey, 149
Peppered Rib Eye Steaks, 121
Peppery London Broil, 119
Roast Corn on the Cob, 273
Southwestern Grilled Lamb, 194
Spicy Chicken Heroes, 99
Zesty Grilled Chops, 161

GROUND BEEF
Main Dishes
  All-Purpose Meat Sauce, 124
  Chili Skillet, 124
  Cranberry Meatballs, 127
  Four-Cheese Lasagna, 246
  Italian-Stuffed Shells, 248
  Mom's Best Meat Loaf, 126
  Old-World Pizza, 233
  Salisbury Steak Deluxe, 123
  Shepherd's Pie, 122
  Spaghetti and Meatballs for
      Two, 127
  Spaghetti Pie, 246
  Stuffed Cabbage Rolls, 125
  Summer Stuffed Peppers, 123
  Tater Tot Bake, 124
Side Dishes
  Beefy Spanish Rice, 238
  Calico Beans, 243
  Herbed Rice Stuffing, 143
Snacks
  Mini Hamburgers, 26
  Tangy Meatballs, 30
Soups and Sandwiches
  Bacon-Stuffed Burgers, 98
  Beef Lentil Soup, 93
  Classic Chili, 95
  Pronto Pizza Burgers, 99
  Sloppy Joes, 101
  Taco Soup, 94

HAM
Main Dishes
  Asparagus Strata, 228
  Baked Ham with Cumberland
      Sauce, 173
  Broccoli-Ham Hot Dish, 176
  Cherry Almond Glazed Ham, 172
  Church Supper Ham Loaf, 176

Deluxe Ham Omelet, 220
Dilly Ham Balls, 174
Grilled Ham Steak, 175
Ham a la King, 177
Ham and Potato Frittata, 221
Ham, Red Beans and Rice, 242
Hash Brown Quiche, 224
Hearty Egg Scramble, 221
Jambalaya, 188
Peachy Ham Slice, 175
Scrambled Egg Casserole, 219
Sunday Boiled Dinner, 174

Salads
Chef's Salad, 77
Ham Pasta Salad, 77

Sandwiches and Soup
Big Sandwich, 97
Grilled Ham and Egg Salad
    Sandwiches, 96
Ham Buns, 98
Split Pea Vegetable Soup, 93

Side Dishes
Cauliflower Au Gratin, 272
Country Green Beans, 265
Country Ham Stuffing, 144
Creole Stuffing, 144
Maple Baked Beans, 241
Succotash, 242

Snacks
Appetizer Stromboli, 29
Baked Potato Skins, 27

HOMINY
Cheesy Grits Casserole, 239
Hominy Casserole, 274

HONEY
Corn Muffins with Honey Butter, 56
Honey Bran Muffins, 57
Honey-Glazed Snack Mix, 31
Honey-Mustard Baked Chicken, 134
Honey Mustard Salad Dressing, 72
Honey Spareribs, 168

ICE CREAM
Butter Pecan Ice Cream, 313
Buttermilk Shake, 34
Chocolate Malt Shoppe Pie, 349
Cranberry Sherbet, 312
Easy Chocolate Ice Cream, 312
Frozen Grasshopper Torte, 348
Frozen Ice Cream Delight, 314

Milky Way Ice Cream, 313
Mud Pie, 348
Orange Sherbet Party Punch, 33
Peppermint Stick Pie, 349
Strawberry Rhubarb Ice Cream
    Pie, 348
Sunshine Ice Cream Pie, 349
Vanilla Ice Cream, 313

JAMS & JELLY
Heavenly Jam, 295
Rhubarb Jelly, 296
Strawberry Rhubarb Jam, 295
Tri-Berry Jam, 296

LAMB
Barbecued Lamb Kabobs, 195
Braised Lamb Shanks, 198
California Roast Lamb, 197
Creamy Lamb Stew, 198
Curried Lamb and Barley, 201
Greek Burgers, 195
Grilled Lamb Chops, 194
Herbed Leg of Lamb, 197
Lamb Chops with Mint Stuffing, 200
Lamb Noodle Stroganoff, 201
Mushroom Lamb Chops, 198
New England Lamb Bake, 200
Old-Fashioned Lamb Stew, 199
Roast Lamb with Plum Sauce, 196
Southwestern Grilled Lamb, 194

LASAGNA
Chicken Cheese Lasagna, 247
Four-Cheese Lasagna, 246

LEMON & LIME
Lemon Bars, 358
Lemon Cheese Braid, 50
Lemon Curd, 291
Lemon Custard in Meringue
    Cups, 303
Lemony Salmon Patties, 184
Lime Broiled Catfish, 186
Raspberry Lemon Muffins, 57
Spiced Lemonade, 35
Stirred Lemon Rice Custard, 307
World's Best Lemon Pie, 342

LENTILS
Beef Lentil Soup, 93

LIGHT RECIPES 🍎
Breads & Rolls
Caraway Rye Bread, 42
English Muffin Bread, 52
Golden Knots, 47
Italian Parmesan Bread, 52
Onion Dill Bread, 53
Sesame French Bread, 45
Soft Breadsticks, 47

Wholesome Wheat Bread, 45
Desserts
Angel Food Cake, 325
Old-Fashioned Rice Pudding, 305
Main Dishes
Baked Beef Stew, 113
Beef and Pepper Stir-Fry, 116
Chalupa, 165
Chicken Stir-Fry, 136
Dilly Grilled Chicken, 148
Foil-Steamed Salmon, 181
Golden Baked Whitefish, 183
Grilled Pork Tenderloin, 166
Grilled Salmon, 184
Grilled Tarragon Chicken, 148
Jambalaya, 188
Lime Broiled Catfish, 186
Pork and Winter Squash Stew, 165
Pork Tenderloin Diane, 166
Puffy Apple Omelet, 231
Sole in Herbed Butter, 183
Spicy Breaded Chicken, 133
Summer Stuffed Peppers, 123
Tomato Basil Pasta, 248
Relishes
Beet Relish, 292
Dilled Onions, 292
Pickled Mushrooms, 293
Salads and Salad Dressing
Buttermilk Salad Dressing, 72
Cherry Tomato Salad, 81
Dilly Asparagus, 81
Fresh Corn Salad, 80
Marinated Zucchini Salad, 80
Norwegian Coleslaw, 82
Sour Cream Cucumbers, 81
Spicy Beef Salad, 76
Three-Bean Salad, 83
Sandwiches
French Dip Sandwiches, 100
Venison Tenderloin
    Sandwiches, 206
Sauces and Toppings
Berry Good Topping, 314
Cranberry Salsa, 291
Fresh Tomato Salsa, 290
Herb Vinegar, 73
Mushroom Gravy, 145
Northwest Cherry Salsa, 290
Spicy Garden Salsa, 290
Side Dishes
Baked Carrots, 271
Baked Mushroom Rice, 236
Broccoli Mushroom Medley, 268
Carrot Pilaf, 239
Cider Baked Squash, 283
Dilled Carrots, 270
Fancy Brussels Sprouts, 269
Herbed Broccoli, 269
Parsnip Saute, 287
Peas and Carrots with Mint, 279
Pumpkin Vegetable Stew, 285

LIGHT RECIPES
Side Dishes (continued)
Root Vegetable Medley, 287
Southern Okra, 277
Spiced Baked Beets, 267
Texas-Style Spanish Rice, 237
Snacks and Beverages
Continental Cheese Spread, 18
Dill Dip, 18
Orange Refresher, 34
Strawberry Watermelon Slush, 34
Soups and Chili
Beef Lentil Soup, 93
Buffalo Chili Con Carne, 208
Chicken Noodle Soup, 87
Classic Chili, 95
Garden Vegetable Soup, 89
Gazpacho, 94
Peasant Bean Soup, 92
Pronto Beef Vegetable Soup, 94
Split Pea Vegetable Soup, 93
Steak Soup, 88
Turkey Vegetable Soup, 86

MEAT PIES & POTPIES
Cheddar Chicken Potpie, 151
Pheasant Potpie, 210
Shepherd's Pie, 122
Spaghetti Pie, 246
Turkey Dressing Pie, 151

MEATBALLS & MEAT LOAVES
Church Supper Ham Loaf, 176
Cranberry Meatballs, 127
Dilly Ham Balls, 174
Mom's Best Meat Loaf, 126
Moose Meatballs, 207
Spaghetti and Meatballs for Two, 127
Venison Meat Loaf, 205

MICROWAVE RECIPES
Candy Bar Fudge, 366
Marshmallow Puffs, 370
White Chocolate Party Mix, 32

MUFFINS
Corn Muffins with Honey Butter, 56
Empire State Muffins, 56
Honey Bran Muffins, 57
Raspberry Lemon Muffins, 57

MUSHROOMS
Baked Mushroom Rice, 236
Broccoli Mushroom Medley, 268
Cauliflower with Mushroom Almond Sauce, 272
Grilled Mushrooms, 276
Mushroom Gravy, 145
Mushroom Lamb Chops, 198
Pickled Mushrooms, 293
Quail in Mushroom Gravy, 215
Round Steak Stroganoff, 110
Sausage-Stuffed Mushrooms, 28
Tuna Mushroom Casserole, 187
Turkey with Mushroom Gravy, 147

MUSTARD
Honey-Mustard Baked Chicken, 134
Honey Mustard Salad Dressing, 72
Mustard Egg Dip, 19
Pheasant in Mustard Sauce, 211
Rabbit Dijon, 209
Sweet-and-Sour Mustard, 291

NUTS (also see Peanut Butter)
Almond Butter Crunch, 370
Apple Walnut Cake, 319
Butter Pecan Cake, 323
Butter Pecan Ice Cream, 313
Cauliflower with Mushroom Almond Sauce, 272
Cherry Almond Glazed Ham, 172
Chocolate Clusters, 371
Cranberry Nut Swirls, 357
Empire State Muffins, 56
Fruit and Nut Bread Pudding, 310
Honey-Glazed Snack Mix, 31
Nutty Sweet Potato Biscuits, 61
Peanut Brittle, 370
Pecan Delights, 368
Pecan Meltaways, 360
Popcorn Caramel Crunch, 372
Praline Sundae Sauce, 315
Pumpkin Pecan Pie, 343
Spiced Pecans, 32
Sugar Diamonds, 359
Tassies, 360
Three-Herb Popcorn, 31
Toffee Squares, 358
White Chocolate Party Mix, 32

OATS
Apple Crisp, 310
Date Bars, 359
Oatmeal Chocolate Chip Cake, 321
Oatmeal Raisin Cookies, 353

OKRA
Corn Okra Creole, 276
Southern Okra, 277

ONIONS
Buttery Onion Pretzels, 32
Cheesy Onion Casserole, 278
Dilled Onions, 292
Fried Onion Rings, 277
Onion Dill Bread, 53
Orange and Red Onion Salad, 71

ORANGE
Cranberry Orange Bread, 54
Golden Glow Salad, 75
Orange and Red Onion Salad, 71
Orange Biscuits, 62
Orange-Glazed Sponge Cake, 327
Orange Refresher, 34
Orange Sherbet Party Punch, 33
Orange Taffy, 365
Sunshine Ice Cream Pie, 349

PASTA & NOODLES (also see Lasagna)
Chicken Noodle Soup, 87
Chicken Tetrazzini, 249
Garden Vegetable Soup, 89
Ham Pasta Salad, 77
Herbed Macaroni and Cheese, 232
Homemade Noodles, 244
Italian-Stuffed Shells, 248
Lamb Noodle Stroganoff, 201
Linguini with Clam Sauce, 191
Meatless Spaghetti Sauce, 286
North Carolina Shrimp Saute, 189
Parmesan Noodles, 245
Pasta with Asparagus, 245
Round Steak Stroganoff, 110
Salmon Pasta Salad, 184
Spaghetti and Meatballs for Two, 127
Spaghetti Pie, 246
Spinach Noodles, 244
Stovetop Macaroni and Cheese, 232
Tomato Basil Pasta, 248
Tuna Mushroom Casserole, 187
Turkey Pasta Supreme, 249

PEACHES
Blueberry and Peach Cobbler, 310
Peach Pie, 337
Peachy Dessert Sauce, 314
Peachy Ham Slice, 175

PEANUT BUTTER
Chocolate Clusters, 371
Chocolate Crunch Brownies, 362
Chocolate Peanut Butter Brownies, 363
Chocolate Peanut Butter Pie, 346
Dipped Peanut Butter Sandwich Cookies, 362
Grandma's Peanut Butter Cookies, 353
Marshmallow Puffs, 370
Peanut Butter Ice Cream Topping, 315

PEAS
Black-Eyed Pea Chowder, 92
Black-Eyed Peas with Bacon, 241
Peas and Carrots with Mint, 279
Peas and Potatoes, 278
Split Pea Vegetable Soup, 93

PEPPERS
Beef and Pepper Stir-Fry, 116
Fantastic Beef Fajitas, 118
Slow-Cooked Pepper Steak, 111
Summer Stuffed Peppers, 123

PICKLES
Bread 'n' Butter Pickles, 299
Dill Pickle Spears, 299
Freezer Cucumber Pickles, 299

PIES
Chocolate Pies
    Chocolate Peanut Butter Pie, 346
    German Chocolate Pie, 341
Custard and Cream Pies
    Blueberry Cream Pie, 347
    Coconut Banana Cream Pie, 341
    Old-Fashioned Custard Pie, 344
Fruit Pies
    Apple Cranberry Pie, 339
    Cherry Berry Pie, 338
    Fall Pear Pie, 338
    Farm Apple Pan Pie, 339
    Fluffy Cranberry Cheese Pie, 345
    Four-Fruit Pie, 337
    Fresh Raspberry Pie, 347
    Maple-Glazed Apple Pie, 336
    Peach Pie, 336
    Perfect Apple Pie, 336
    Strawberry Lover's Pie, 341
    Strawberry Rhubarb Crumb
       Pie, 345
Ice Cream Pies
    Chocolate Malt Shoppe Pie, 349
    Frozen Grasshopper Torte, 348
    Mud Pie, 348
    Peppermint Stick Pie, 349
    Strawberry Rhubarb Ice Cream
       Pie, 348
    Sunshine Ice Cream Pie, 349
Meringue Pies
    Grandma's Chocolate Meringue
       Pie, 342
    World's Best Lemon Pie, 342
Pie Crusts
    Pastry for Double-Crust Pie, 334
    Pastry for Single-Crust Pie, 334
Pumpkin and Sweet Potato Pies
    Pumpkin Patch Pie, 344

Pumpkin Pecan Pie, 343
Sweet Potato Pie, 343

PIZZA
Bacon and Cheese Breakfast Pizza,
   223
Egg Pizzas, 229
Old-World Pizza, 233
Vegetable Appetizer Pizza, 27

POPCORN
Old-Time Popcorn Balls, 373
Popcorn Caramel Crunch, 372
Three-Herb Popcorn, 31

PORK *(also see Bacon, Ham and
Sausage)*
Barbecued Pork Sandwiches, 101
Barbecued Spareribs, 169
Breaded Pork Chops, 159
Breakfast Sausage, 170
Chalupa, 165
Chops and Chilies Casserole, 160
Cranberry Sweet-and-Sour Pork, 167
Creamy Pork Tenderloin, 167
Crunchy Pork and Rice Salad, 77
Grilled Pork Tenderloin, 166
Harvest Stew, 164
Hearty Ribs and Beans, 169
Herbed Pork Roast, 163
Honey Spareribs, 168
Mom's Best Meat Loaf, 126
Oven-Barbecued Pork Chops, 161
Pork and Winter Squash Stew, 165
Pork Chops with Apple Stuffing, 159
Pork Tenderloin Diane, 166
Sauerkraut Pork Chops, 160
Spiced Apple Pork Roast, 162
Stuffed Crown Roast of Pork, 163
Sunday Boiled Dinner, 174
Zesty Grilled Chops, 161

POTATOES *(also see Sweet Potatoes)*
Baked Potato Skins, 27
Cheddar Parmesan Potatoes, 280
Chicken and Hash Brown Bake, 153
Country Potato Pancakes, 280
Creamed Potatoes, 279
Crisp Hash for Two, 119
Dilly Mashed Potatoes, 282
Dutch Potato Poultry Stuffing, 144
German Potato Salad, 78
Greek Roasted Chicken and
   Potatoes, 140
Ham and Potato Frittata, 221
Hash Brown Quiche, 224
Oven-Roasted Potatoes, 279
Peas and Potatoes, 278
Red, White and Green Salad, 78
Roasted Chicken and Potatoes, 138

Sheepherder's Breakfast, 223
Shepherd's Pie, 122
Tater-Dipped Veggies, 26
Tater Tot Bake, 124
Twice-Baked Potatoes, 281
Wisconsin Potato Cheese Soup, 90

PUDDING & CUSTARD
Breakfast Custard, 224
Chocolate Pudding, 306
Corn Pudding Supreme, 274
Creamy Caramel Flan, 308
Fruit and Nut Bread Pudding, 310
Old-Fashioned Custard Pie, 344
Old-Fashioned Rice Pudding, 305
Stirred Lemon Rice Custard, 307

PUMPKIN
Pumpkin Cake Squares, 322
Pumpkin Chocolate Chip Bread, 55
Pumpkin Patch Pie, 344
Pumpkin Pecan Pie, 343
Pumpkin Vegetable Stew, 285

QUICHE
Broccoli Pie, 224
Crab Quiche, 189
Hash Brown Quiche, 224
Tomato Quiche, 225

QUICK RECIPES ○
Breads and Muffins
    Blueberry Sour Cream Pancakes, 66
    Breakfast Scones, 63
    Buttermilk Waffles, 67
    Cherry Cream Scones, 63
    Corn Muffins with Honey
       Butter, 56
    Freezer French Toast, 67
    Garlic Herb Bread, 64
    Mini Blue Cheese Rolls, 64
    Mom's Buttermilk Biscuits, 60
    Raspberry Lemon Muffins, 57
    Sour Cream 'n' Chive Biscuits, 61
Candies
    Chocolate Clusters, 371
    Chocolate Pizza, 373
    Marshmallow Puffs, 370
    White Christmas Candy, 372
Cookies
    Dipped Peanut Butter Sandwich
       Cookies, 362
    Fruitcake Cookies, 361
Desserts
    Berry Good Topping, 314
    Chocolate Pudding, 306
    Homemade Fudge Sauce, 315
    Peanut Butter Ice Cream
       Topping, 315
    Praline Sundae Sauce, 315

➡

QUICK RECIPES (continued)

Frosting
Buttercream Frosting, 330
Chocolate Sour Cream
Frosting, 331
Chocolate Whipped Cream
Frosting, 331
Cinnamon Apple Glaze, 330
Cream Cheese Frosting, 331

Main Dishes
Basic Poached Eggs, 222
Basic Scrambled Eggs, 219
Beef and Pepper Stir-Fry, 116
Chicken a la King, 153
Chicken Stir-Fry, 136
Country-Fried Steaks, 117
Cranberry Sweet-and-Sour
Pork, 167
Crisp Hash for Two, 119
Deluxe Ham Omelet, 220
Foil-Steamed Salmon, 181
Fried Eggs, 218
Golden Baked Whitefish, 183
Golden Catfish Fillets, 186
Grilled Ham Steak, 175
Grilled Salmon, 184
Hearty Egg Scramble, 221
Herbed Baked Eggs, 229
Herbed Orange Roughy, 183
Lime Broiled Catfish, 186
Linguini with Clam Sauce, 191
North Carolina Shrimp Saute, 189
Pan-Fried Trout, 187
Peachy Ham Slice, 175
Pork Tenderloin Diane, 166
Salisbury Steak Deluxe, 123
Skillet Chicken Stew, 136
Soft-Cooked Eggs, 218
Sole in Herbed Butter, 183
Stovetop Macaroni and Cheese, 232
Tomato Basil Pasta, 248
Turkey in a Hurry, 147
Turkey Minute Steaks, 147
Turkey Pasta Supreme, 249
Zesty Poached Eggs, 222

Salads and Salad Dressings
Banana Poppy Seed Dressing, 72
Blue Cheese Dressing, 73
Buttermilk Salad Dressing, 72
Easy Sauerkraut Salad, 81
Favorite French Dressing, 73
Herbed Salad Dressing, 73
Honey Mustard Salad Dressing, 72
Spicy Beef Salad, 76

Sandwiches
Chicken Salad Sandwiches, 97
Curried Egg Salad Sandwiches,
100
Pronto Pizza Burgers, 99
Reuben Sandwiches, 99

Venison Tenderloin
Sandwiches, 206

Sauces and Spreads
All-Purpose Meat Sauce, 124
Lemon Curd, 291
Mushroom Gravy, 145
Strawberry Rhubarb Jam, 295

Side Dishes
Basil Buttered Beans, 266
Beefy Spanish Rice, 238
Black Beans and Sausage, 243
Broccoli Mushroom Medley, 268
Carrot Pilaf, 239
Company Brussels Sprouts, 269
Corn Okra Creole, 276
Country Green Beans, 265
Creamed Potatoes, 279
Dilled Carrots, 270
Dilly Mashed Potatoes, 282
Fancy Brussels Sprouts, 269
Fried Green Tomatoes, 285
Glazed Carrots, 271
Grilled Mushrooms, 276
Harvard Beets, 267
Herbed Broccoli, 269
Oven-Baked Asparagus, 265
Oven-Roasted Potatoes, 279
Parmesan Noodles, 245
Parsnip Saute, 287
Pasta with Asparagus, 245
Peas and Carrots with Mint, 279
Quick Baked Beans, 243
Sesame Asparagus, 265
Southern Okra, 277
Sugared Asparagus, 264
Summer Squash Saute, 283
Texas-Style Spanish Rice, 237

Snacks and Beverages
Chili Cheese Dip, 25
Continental Cheese Spread, 18
Dill Dip, 18
Guacamole, 22
Honey-Glazed Snack Mix, 31
Hot Crab Dip, 25
Orange Refresher, 34
Strawberry Watermelon Slush, 34
Three-Herb Popcorn, 31

Soups
Black-Eyed Pea Chowder, 92
Garden Vegetable Soup, 89
Pronto Beef Vegetable Soup, 94
Taco Soup, 94

RAISINS & DATES
Date Bars, 359
Oatmeal Raisin Cookies, 353
Popcorn Caramel Crunch, 372
Roasted Duck with Apple-Raisin
Dressing, 154

RASPBERRIES
Berry Good Topping, 314
Cherry Berry Pie, 338
Four-Fruit Pie, 337
Fresh Raspberry Pie, 347
Raspberry Cake Roll, 328
Raspberry Lemon Muffins, 57
Raspberry Trifle, 305
Tri-Berry Jam, 296

RELISHES (also see Pickles)
Beet Relish, 292
Cranberry Apple Relish, 292
Dilled Onions, 292
Easy Berry Relish, 292
Pickled Mushrooms, 293
Red Corn Relish, 298
Tomato Chutney, 298

RHUBARB
Berry Rhubarb Fool, 306
Four-Fruit Pie, 337
Rhubarb Jelly, 296
Rosy Rhubarb Salad, 75
Strawberry Rhubarb Coffee Cake, 59
Strawberry Rhubarb Crumb Pie, 345
Strawberry Rhubarb Ice Cream
Pie, 348
Strawberry Rhubarb Jam, 295

RICE & WILD RICE
Baked Mushroom Rice, 236
Beefy Spanish Rice, 238
Black Beans and Sausage, 243
Broccoli-Ham Hot Dish, 176
Carrot Pilaf, 239
Chili Cheese Bake, 239
Chops and Chilies Casserole, 160
Crunchy Pork and Rice Salad, 77
Currant-Glazed Cornish Hens, 154
Florida Seafood Casserole, 190
Ham, Red Beans and Rice, 242
Herbed Rice Stuffing, 143
Herbed Spinach Bake, 283
Hot Chicken Salad, 150
Jambalaya, 188
Old-Fashioned Rice Pudding, 305
Pheasant and Wild Rice, 211
Sausage and Wild Rice Casserole, 171
Stirred Lemon Rice Custard, 307
Stuffed Cabbage Rolls, 125

Summer Stuffed Peppers, 123
Texas-Style Spanish Rice, 237
Three-Rice Pilaf, 238
Wild Rice and Barley Pilaf, 237

ROLLS & BUNS
Buttery Crescents, 46
Golden Knots, 47
Hot Cross Buns, 50
Icebox Cloverleaf Rolls, 47
Mini Blue Cheese Rolls, 64
Soft Breadsticks, 47
Special Cinnamon Rolls, 50

RUBS
Herbed Pork Roast, 163
Peppered Rib Eye Steaks, 121
Savory Beef Rub, 114

SALADS & SALAD DRESSINGS
Bean Salad
Three-Bean Salad, 83
Coleslaw
Creamy Coleslaw, 82
Norwegian Coleslaw, 82
Dressings
Banana Poppy Seed Dressing, 72
Blue Cheese Dressing, 73
Buttermilk Salad Dressing, 72
Favorite French Dressing, 73
Herbed Salad Dressing, 73
Honey Mustard Salad Dressing, 72
Fruit Salads
Autumn Apple Salad, 74
Frozen Cranberry Salad, 83
Golden Glow Salad, 75
Layered Fresh Fruit Salad, 83
Patriotic Gelatin Salad, 74
Rosy Rhubarb Salad, 75
Lettuce Salads
Orange and Red Onion Salad, 71
Strawberry Spinach Salad, 71
Wilted Lettuce, 71
Main-Dish Salads
Chef's Salad, 77
Crunchy Pork and Rice Salad, 77
Grilled Chicken Salad, 76
Ham Pasta Salad, 77
Salmon Pasta Salad, 184
Spicy Beef Salad, 76
Potato Salads
German Potato Salad, 78
Red, White and Green Salad, 78
Sweet Potato Salad, 78
Vegetable Salads
Cherry Tomato Salad, 81
Creamy Sliced Tomatoes, 70
Dilly Asparagus, 81
Easy Sauerkraut Salad, 81
Fresh Corn Salad, 80

Marinated Zucchini Salad, 80
Sour Cream Cucumbers, 81

SALSAS
Cranberry Salsa, 291
Fresh Tomato Salsa, 290
Northwest Cherry Salsa, 290
Spicy Garden Salsa, 290

SANDWICHES
Cold Sandwiches
Chicken Salad Sandwiches, 97
Curried Egg Salad
Sandwiches, 100
Hot Sandwiches
Appetizer Stromboli, 29
Bacon-Stuffed Burgers, 98
Barbecued Pork Sandwiches, 101
Big Sandwich, 97
Egg-Filled Buns, 227
French Dip Sandwiches, 100
Greek Burgers, 195
Grilled Ham and Egg Salad
Sandwiches, 96
Ham Buns, 98
Italian Sausage Sandwiches, 101
Mini Hamburgers, 26
Pronto Pizza Burgers, 99
Reuben Sandwiches, 99
Sloppy Joes, 101
Spicy Chicken Heroes, 99
Venison Tenderloin
Sandwiches, 206

SAUCES & TOPPINGS
All-Purpose Meat Sauce, 124
Berry Good Topping, 314
Easy Applesauce, 291
Herb Vinegar, 73
Homemade Fudge Sauce, 315
Homemade Steak Sauce, 293
Meatless Spaghetti Sauce, 286
Peachy Dessert Sauce, 314
Peanut Butter Ice Cream Topping, 315
Pesto, 293
Praline Sundae Sauce, 315
Sweet-and-Sour Mustard, 291

SAUSAGE
Appetizer Stromboli, 29
Bacon-Stuffed Burgers, 98
Black Beans and Sausage, 243
Breakfast Burritos, 220
Breakfast Sausage, 170
Buttermilk Biscuit Sausage
Pinwheels, 60
Cheesy Grits Casserole, 239
Church Supper Ham Loaf, 176
Country Cassoulet, 240
Cranberry Stuffing Balls, 171

Creole Stuffing, 144
Egg Pizzas, 229
Garden Vegetable Soup, 89
Herbed Rice Stuffing, 143
Italian Sausage Sandwiches, 101
Mostaccioli Bake, 249
Old-World Pizza, 233
Roasted Duck with Apple-Raisin
Dressing, 154
Sausage and Wild Rice Casserole, 171
Sausage-Stuffed Mushrooms, 28
Spaghetti and Meatballs for Two, 127
Stuffed Crown Roast of Pork, 163
Tomato Zucchini Stew, 170
Wild Duck Gumbo, 213

SEAFOOD & FISH
Baked Potato Skins, 27
Barbecued Trout, 181
Corn Bread Dressing with
Oysters, 190
Crab Quiche, 189
Crumb-Topped Salmon, 185
Florida Seafood Casserole, 190
Foil-Steamed Salmon, 181
Golden Baked Whitefish, 183
Golden Catfish Fillets, 186
Grilled Salmon, 184
Herbed Orange Roughy, 183
Hot Crab Dip, 25
Jambalaya, 188
Lemony Salmon Patties, 184
Lime Broiled Catfish, 186
Linguini with Clam Sauce, 191
New England Clam Chowder, 91
New Year's Oyster Stew, 191
North Carolina Shrimp Saute, 189
Pan-Fried Trout, 187
Salmon Pasta Salad, 184
Sole in Herbed Butter, 183
Stuffed Sole, 182
Tuna Mushroom Casserole, 187

SKILLETS & STIR-FRIES
Beef and Ground Beef
Beef and Pepper Stir-Fry, 116
Chili Skillet, 124
Crisp Hash for Two, 119
Fantastic Beef Fajitas, 118
Italian-Style Beef Liver, 117
Round Steak Stroganoff, 110
Salisbury Steak Deluxe, 123
Spicy Beef Salad, 76
Chicken
Chicken Italiano, 137
Chicken Stir-Fry, 136
Game and Fowl
Creamed Grouse on Toast, 212
Hasenpfeffer, 208
Pheasant in Mustard Sauce, 211

➧

SKILLETS & STIR-FRIES
Game and Fowl (continued)
    Rabbit with Tarragon Sauce, 209
Lamb
    Braised Lamb Shanks, 198
    Mushroom Lamb Chops, 198
Pork and Ham
    Cranberry Sweet-and-Sour
      Pork, 167
    Ham a la King, 177
    Pork Tenderloin Diane, 166
Seafood
    Golden Catfish Fillets, 186
    North Carolina Shrimp Saute, 189
    Pan-Fried Trout, 187
    Sole in Herbed Butter, 183

SLOW COOKER RECIPE
Slow-Cooked Pepper Steak, 111

SOUPS (also see Chili)
Basic Broth, 86
Beef and Barley Soup, 89
Beef Lentil Soup, 93
Black-Eyed Pea Chowder, 92
Cheesy Vegetable Soup, 90
Chicken Noodle Soup, 87
Garden-Fresh Tomato Soup, 91
Garden Vegetable Soup, 89
Gazpacho, 94
New England Clam Chowder, 91
Peasant Bean Soup, 92
Pronto Beef Vegetable Soup, 94
Split Pea Vegetable Soup, 93
Steak Soup, 88
Taco Soup, 94
Turkey Vegetable Soup, 86
Turtle Soup, 212
Wild Duck Gumbo, 213
Wisconsin Potato Cheese Soup, 90

SPINACH
Beef Lentil Soup, 93
Chicken Cheese Lasagna, 247
Herbed Spinach Bake, 283
Spinach Noodles, 244
Spinach-Topped Tomatoes, 286
Strawberry Spinach Salad, 71

SPREADS
Continental Cheese Spread, 18
Festive Cheese Spread, 21
Fireside Cheese Spread, 21
Lemon Curd, 291
Roasted Garlic, 30
Spicy Corn Spread, 272
Three-in-One Cheese Ball, 20

SQUASH
Cider Baked Squash, 283

Marinated Zucchini Salad, 80
Pork and Winter Squash Stew, 165
Spaghetti Squash Casserole, 284
Squash-Stuffed Chicken, 134
Summer Squash Saute, 283
Tomato Zucchini Stew, 170

STEWS
Baked Beef Stew, 113
Beef Stew with Cheddar
    Dumplings, 113
Chalupa, 165
Creamy Lamb Stew, 198
Harvest Stew, 164
New Year's Oyster Stew, 191
Old-Fashioned Lamb Stew, 199
Pork and Winter Squash Stew, 165
Pumpkin Vegetable Stew, 285
Skillet Chicken Stew, 136
Tomato Zucchini Stew, 170
Turkey Biscuit Stew, 150

STRAWBERRIES
Berry Rhubarb Fool, 306
Patriotic Dessert, 309
Strawberry Cheesecake, 302
Strawberry Cream Puffs, 304
Strawberry Lover's Pie, 341
Strawberry Rhubarb Coffee Cake, 59
Strawberry Rhubarb Crumb Pie, 345
Strawberry Rhubarb Ice Cream
    Pie, 348
Strawberry Rhubarb Jam, 295
Strawberry Shortcake, 311
Strawberry Spinach Salad, 71
Strawberry Watermelon Slush, 34
Tri-Berry Jam, 296
Tuxedo Strawberries, 371

SWEET POTATOES
Apricot-Glazed Sweet Potatoes, 282
Nutty Sweet Potato Biscuits, 61
Sweet Potato Bake, 282
Sweet Potato Pie, 343
Sweet Potato Salad, 78

TOMATOES
All-Purpose Meat Sauce, 124
BLT Bites, 19
Cherry Tomato Salad, 81
Creamy Sliced Tomatoes, 70
Eggplant with Tomato Sauce, 275
Fresh Tomato Salsa, 290
Fried Green Tomatoes, 285
Garden-Fresh Tomato Soup, 91
Meatless Spaghetti Sauce, 286
Red, White and Green Salad, 78
Spinach-Topped Tomatoes, 286
Tomato Basil Pasta, 248
Tomato Bread Salad, 23

Tomato Chutney, 298
Tomato Quiche, 225
Tomato Zucchini Stew, 170

TURKEY
Big Sandwich, 97
Dilly Grilled Turkey, 148
Marinated Thanksgiving Turkey, 149
Mexican Turkey Roll-Ups, 152
Teriyaki Turkey, 146
Turkey Biscuit Stew, 150
Turkey Dressing Pie, 151
Turkey Drumstick Dinner, 146
Turkey in a Hurry, 147
Turkey Minute Steaks, 147
Turkey Pasta Supreme, 249
Turkey Vegetable Soup, 86
Turkey with Corn Bread Stuffing, 142
Turkey with Mushroom Gravy, 147

VEAL
Mom's Best Meat Loaf, 126
Osso Buco, 109

VEGETABLES (also see specific kinds)
Chalupa, 165
Cheesy Vegetable Soup, 90
Creamed Kohlrabi, 276
Eggplant with Tomato Sauce, 275
Garden Vegetable Soup, 89
Gazpacho, 94
Grilled Venison and Vegetables, 204
Parsnip Saute, 287
Pronto Beef Vegetable Soup, 94
Pumpkin Vegetable Stew, 285
Roasted Chicken with Rosemary, 140
Root Vegetable Medley, 287
Shepherd's Pie, 122
Spicy Garden Salsa, 290
Steak Soup, 88
Succotash, 242
Summer Stuffed Peppers, 123
Sunday Boiled Dinner, 174
Tater-Dipped Veggies, 26
Turkey Vegetable Soup, 86
Vegetable Appetizer Pizza, 27

YEAST BREADS (also see Bread
Machine Recipes, Coffee Cakes and
Rolls & Buns)
Caraway Rye Bread, 42
Christmas Stollen, 49
Colonial Yeast Bread, 42
Country Swirl Bread, 44
Country White Bread, 40
English Muffin Bread, 52
Italian Parmesan Bread, 52
Sesame French Bread, 45
Sesame Wheat Braids, 43
Wholesome Wheat Bread, 45

Reference Index

Use this index as a guide to the many helpful hints and step-by-step instructions throughout the book.

APPETIZERS & SNACKS
Making roll-ups, 25
Making stromboli, 29
Making tortilla pinwheels, 21
Shaping chickaritos, 24
Storing popcorn, 31
Tips for making appetizers, 18

BEANS
Cooking dry beans, 240
Preparing dry beans for cooking, 92
Soaking methods for dry beans, 240
Substitutions for dry beans, 242

BEEF & GROUND BEEF
Basic cooking methods, 104
Braising beef, 108
Buying and cooking cuts of beef, 104
Buying and cooking ground beef, 122
Carving beef roasts, 107
Coating meat with flour, 109
Cooking beef in a slow cooker, 111
Roasting beef, 114
Slicing corned beef, 112
Slicing raw beef cuts, 118

BEVERAGES
Liquefying ice in a blender, 34
Making an ice ring, 33
Tips for making coffee and tea, 33

BISCUITS & SCONES
Mixing and cutting biscuits, 61
Removing biscuits from the pan, 62
Shaping scones, 63
Tips for making biscuits, 60

CABBAGE
Shaping cabbage rolls, 125
Shredding cabbage, 82

CAKES
Cooling a foam cake, 326
Cupcakes from a layer cake, 324
Dressing up plain cakes, 329
Dusting cakes with confectioners' sugar, 321
Making a cake roll, 328
Making a sponge cake, 327
Making butter cakes, 318
Making foam cakes, 325
Preparing a cake pan, 318

CANDIES
Avoiding fudge foils, 366
Cold-water test, 364
Confectionery coating varieties, 368
Dipping candy into chocolate, 369
Using and reading a candy thermometer, 365
Stirring fudge, 367
Tips for making candy, 364

CANNING
Boiling-water-bath basics, 294
Making berry jams, 296
Reprocessing unsealed jars, 295
Tips for canning, 294

CHEESE
Purchasing cheese, 20
Shaping a cheese ball, 20
Storing and cooking cheese, 232

CHICKEN *(see Poultry)*

COFFEE CAKES
Braiding a filled coffee cake, 50
Preparing a cooked filling, 48

COOKIES & BARS
Cutting diamond-shaped bars, 359
Mailing cookies, 360
Making an icing bag, 356
Making pressed cookies, 361
Preparing cutout cookies, 355
Shaping drop cookies, 352
Shaping peanut butter cookies, 353
Tips for making cookies, 352
Tips for making cutouts, 354

CRUMBS
Making crumbs, 346
Making fresh bread crumbs, 185

CUSTARD & PUDDING
Making a caramel custard, 308
Preventing film from forming on pudding, 305
Testing and cooling stirred custards, 307

DESSERTS *(also see specific kinds)*
Making cheesecake, 302
Making cream puffs, 304
Making homemade ice cream, 312
Making meringue cups, 303

EGGS
Beating egg whites, 226
Buying, storing and cooking eggs, 218
Combining egg yolks and hot mixtures, 341
Making an omelet, 220
Poaching eggs, 222
Scrambling eggs, 219
Separating eggs, 226
Stuffing eggs using a pastry bag, 231
Testing baked egg dishes for doneness, 225

FRIED FOODS
Deep-fat frying, 65
Keeping fried foods warm, 280

FROSTING
Filling and frosting a layer cake, 330
Filling and frosting a tube cake, 329
Frosting tender cakes, 331

FRUIT
Buying and storing strawberries, 311
Buying baking apples, 336
Mashing avocados, 22
Plumping raisins, 154
Sectioning citrus fruits, 83

GAME
Tips for cooking wild game, 204

GRAINS
Storing and cooking grains, 236

GRAVY
Pan gravy from roasted meats, 145
Reducing pan juices for gravy, 105
Thickening pan juices from braised beef, 106

GRILLING
Grilling beef, 120
Testing the temperature of outdoor grills, 121

HAM
Buying and cooking ham, 172
Carving a half ham with bone, 172
Roasting fully cooked ham, 172
Scoring and studding ham, 173

HERBS & SPICES
Homemade pumpkin pie spice, 343
Making a spice bag, 93
Preparing garlic for roasting, 30
Preparing herb butters, 264
Using an herb rub, 163

LAMB
Carving a leg of lamb, 196
Cooking and serving lamb, 194
Roasting lamb, 196

MEAT LOAF & MEATBALLS
Baking meatballs, 127
Making meatballs of equal size, 207
Tips for making meat loaf and meatballs, 126

MISCELLANEOUS
Browning a roux, 213
Lining a baking pan with waxed paper, 320
Stir-frying techniques, 116
Tips for whipping cream, 322
Toasting nuts, 323
Using a cooking bag, 211
Using a sieve to puree, 297

MUFFINS
Preparing muffins, 57
Tips for making muffins, 56

PASTA
Cooking spaghetti, 246
Making homemade noodles, 244
Making spaetzle, 205
Tips for cooking pasta, 245

PIE PASTRY & CRUSTS
Baking a pastry shell, 334
Braiding crust edges, 344
Decorating pastry crusts, 210
Freezing pie pastry, 334
Making a lattice-topped pie, 338
Making and shaping single- and double-crust pie pastry, 335
Making crumb crusts, 346
Preparing pie pastry, 334
Protecting pastry edges from overbrowning, 337

PIES (also see Pie Pastry & Crusts)
Spreading a pie meringue, 342
Testing pies for doneness, 337
Tips for serving ice cream pies, 348

PORK (also see Ham)
Basic cooking methods, 158
Buying and cooking pork, 158
Making ribs, 169
Pork tenderloin tips, 166
Roasting pork, 162
Sausage tips, 171
Tenderizing ribs, 168

POULTRY
Basic cooking methods, 130
Boning chicken breasts, 136
Carving basics, 140
Cutting up a whole chicken, 132
Disjointing chicken wings, 27
Freezing leftover poultry, 152
Handling raw poultry, 133
Making stuffing, 143
Pounding chicken breasts, 99
Preparing poultry for roasting, 139
Purchasing poultry, 130
Refrigerating cooked poultry, 141
Roasting poultry, 138
Stuffing and roasting a turkey, 142
Stuffing chicken breasts, 134
Testing for doneness, 131
Tips for roasting ducklings and geese, 155

QUICK BREADS
Freezing homemade waffles, 67
Preparing pancakes, 66
Tips for making quick breads, 54

SALADS & SALAD DRESSINGS
Making gelatin salads, 74
Making potato salads, 78
Tips for making salad dressings, 72
Tips for making salads, 70
Unmolding gelatin salads, 75
Whisking vinegar and oil dressings, 72

SANDWICHES
Preparing batter-dipped sandwiches, 96
Preparing stuffed burgers, 98
Shredding meat for sandwiches, 100
Tips for making sandwiches, 96

SEAFOOD
Basic cooking methods, 180
Breading fish, 187
Buying and cooking shrimp, 188
Buying and storing fish, 180
Peeling and deveining shrimp, 189
Stuffing fish fillets, 182
Testing fish for doneness, 181

SOUPS & STEWS
Making chicken noodle soup, 87
Making cream soups, 90
Straining broth, 86
Thickening stew, 199
Tips for making soup, 86

TURKEY (see Poultry)

VEGETABLES
Buying, storing, preparing and cooking vegetables, 252-263
Cleaning mushrooms, 257
Cooking spaghetti squash, 284
Cooking vegetables in salted water, 267
Cutting kernels from corncobs, 80
Handling chili peppers, 260
Making stuffed potatoes, 281
Making vegetable relishes, 298
Parboiling peppers, 123
Peeling tomatoes, 262
Preparing fresh artichokes, 197
Preparing mushrooms for stuffing, 28
Roasting corn in foil, 273
Salting eggplant, 275
Seeding cucumbers, 298
Steaming asparagus in foil, 265
Stuffing cherry tomatoes, 19

YEAST BREADS & ROLLS
Braiding breads, 43
Common problems and solutions, 39
Ingredients and utensils needed, 38
Making a swirl bread, 44
Making a twist-top bread, 45
Making batter breads, 52
Shaping and cutting cinnamon rolls, 51
Shaping caraway rye bread, 42
Shaping yeast rolls, 46
Traditional bread mixing and baking method, 40
Using bread machines, 53